Social Movement Studies in Europe

Protest, Culture and Society

General editors:
Kathrin Fahlenbrach, Institute for Media and Communication, University of Hamburg
Martin Klimke, New York University Abu Dhabi
Joachim Scharloth, Technische Universität Dresden, Germany

Protest movements have been recognized as significant contributors to processes of political participation and transformations of culture and value systems, as well as to the development of both a national and transnational civil society.

This series brings together the various innovative approaches to phenomena of social change, protest and dissent which have emerged in recent years, from an interdisciplinary perspective. It contextualizes social protest and cultures of dissent in larger political processes and socio-cultural transformations by examining the influence of historical trajectories and the response of various segments of society, political and legal institutions on a national and international level. In doing so, the series offers a more comprehensive and multi-dimensional view of historical and cultural change in the twentieth and twenty-first century.

Social Movement Studies in Europe

The State of the Art

Edited by

Olivier Fillieule and Guya Accornero

berghahn
NEW YORK · OXFORD
www.berghahnbooks.com

First published in 2016 by
Berghahn Books
www.berghahnbooks.com

© 2016 Olivier Fillieule and Guya Accornero

Library of Congress Cataloging-in-Publication Data

Social movement studies in Europe : the state of the art / edited by Guya
Accornero and Olivier Fillieule.
    pages cm. — (Protest, culture and society ; 16)
    ISBN 978-1-78533-097-1 (hardback : alk. paper) —
    ISBN 978-1-78533-098-8 (ebook)
  1. Social movements—Europe—History. 2. Europe—Social conditions.
I. Accornero, Guya, editor. II. Fillieule, Olivier, editor.
    HN373.5.S6265 2016
    303.4094—dc23

                                                              2015027718

British Library Cataloguing in Publication Data

A catalogue record for this book is available from the British Library

ISBN: 978-1-78533-097-1 hardback
ISBN: 978-1-78533-098-8 ebook

The text has been edited by Andrea Titterington Cravinho.
We are grateful to the Portuguese *Fundação para a Ciência e a Tecnologia*
and to the *Fonds des publications de l'Université de Lausanne* for supporting
the publication. We would also like to thank the two anonymous reviewers
whose comments helped us improve the quality of the manuscript.

Contents

Figures and Tables

Abbreviations

ACT UP: AIDS Coalition to Unleash Power
ADL: Anti-Defamation League
AFSP: Association Française de Science Politique
ANR: Agence Nationale de la Recherché
ANVUR: Agenzia Nazionale di Valutazione del Sistema Universitario
ATTAC: Action for a Tobin Tax to Assist the Citizen
CAPES: Coordenação de Aperfeiçoamento de Pessoal de Nível Superior
CEE: Central and Eastern Europe
CES: Centro de Estudos Sociais
CEVIPOF: Centre de Recherches Politiques de Sciences Po
CIES-IUL: Centro de Investigação e Estudos de Sociologia-Instituto Universitário de Lisboa
CND: Campaign for Nuclear Disarmament
CNT: Confederación Nacional del Trabajo
COSMOS: Centre on Social Movement Studies
CRAPUL: Centre de Recherche sur l'Action Politique de l'Université de Lausanne
CSM: Civil and Social Movement research
DEMOS: Democracy in Europe and Mobilization of Society
DFG: Deutsche Forschungsgemeinschaft
ECPR: European Consortium of Political Science Research
EIA: Environmental Impact Assessment
ERC: European Research Council
ESA: European Sociological Association
ESF: European Social Forum
ESMOs: Environmental Social Movement Organizations
ESRC: Economic and Social Research Council
ETA: Euskadi Ta Azkatasuna
FCT: Fudação para a Ciência e a Tecnologia

FIDESZ-MPSZ: Magyar Polgári Szövetség (Hungarian Civic Alliance)

FNS: Frontul Salvării Naţionale (Front of National Salvation)

FRG: Federal Republic of Germany

GDR: German Democratic Republic

GERMM: Study and Research Group on Transformations in Activism

GJM: Global Justice Movement

GLBTQ: Gay, Lesbian, Bisexual, Transgender, Queer

GMOs: Genetically Modified Organisms

HEFCE: Higher Education Funding Council

IBASE: Instituto Brasileiro de Análises Sociais e Econômicas

INSURA: Individual Surveys during Rallies

IRA: Irish Republican Army

JN: Junge Nationaldemokraten

KARAT: Coalition for Gender Equality

LULU: Locally Unwanted Land Use

MENA: Middle East and North Africa

MFA: Movimento das Forças Armadas

NDP: Nationaldemokratische Partei Deutschlands

NM: Nunca Más

NOW: National Organization for Women

NSM: New Social Movements

NWO: Nederlandse Organisatie voor Wetenschappelijk Onderzoek

PAH: Plataforma de Afectados por la Hipoteca

PCA: Political Claims Analysis

PEA: Protest Event Analysis

POS: Political Opportunity Structure

PP: Partido Popular

PPA: Political Process Approach

PREC: Processo Revolucionário em Curso

PRIN: Progetti di Rilevante Interesse Nazionale

RNGS: Research Network on Gender Politics and the State

SDS: Sozialistische Deutsche Studentenbund

SIMCA: Social Identity Model of Collective Action

SISP: Società Italiana di Scienze Politiche

SMM Send Mobilizing Messages

SMOs: Social Movement Organizations

SMU: Social Movement Unionism

SPA: Social-Psychological Approach

SPLC: American Southern Poverty Law Center

TEA: Transformation of Environmental Activism

TÜBİTAK: Scientific and Technical Research Council of Turkey

UEC: Union des Etudiants Communistes

UJC-ML: Union des Jeunesses Communistes Marxistes-Léninistes

UNED: Universidad Nacional de Educación a Distancia

UNIFEM: United Nations Development Fund for Women

USAID: United States Agency for International Development

UvA: Universiteit van Amsterdam

VU: Vrije Universiteit

WSF: World Social Forum

Foreword

James M. Jasper

When friends ask me for advice about editing volumes, my first recommendation is always, 'Don't do it.' They are treacherous, time-consuming challenges, with little payoff in recognition or institutional support. Plus the business model behind them has changed in recent years, with publishers no longer treating them like regular books that people will buy in stores, but instead as something akin to handbooks and encyclopaedias, which can be priced high because they are only sold to a handful of libraries.

Fortunately, Olivier Fillieule and Guya Accornero did not ask my advice, and they have created a brilliant volume that will teach us all—in Europe as well as outside it—about the vast scholarship on social movements that has appeared in Europe during the last several decades. It is always fun to be an intellectual tourist, finding out about other people's local customs and ideas, and this book is a delight in that way. It also provides conceptual souvenirs we can take home and use in our own research.

We used to hear a lot of comparisons between European and American theories and research methods, usually in the form of complaints about their mutual ignorance and as a prelude to some synthetic effort. This volume perhaps started in some such contrast, but the results should preclude this kind of talk in the future by showing how diverse scholarship is within Europe, making any discussion of a 'European approach' too simpleminded (the same could be said of any imagined 'American approach'). This reflects the movements themselves: some cross frontiers, but many are unique to one country and reflect its special history. And those that cross boundaries—such as environmentalism, labour or anti-globalization—take on local colours in each country. Even international arenas, such as those of the European Union, have their distinctive traditions, rules, alliances and decision-making spaces.

This is a book of distinctions and boundaries. The starting point may have been the United States versus Europe, but this is quickly displaced by a number of interesting contrasts between European nations themselves. In a fractal process, this too gives way to a diversity of movements and research programs within each country, some of which have counterparts in other countries and some of which do not. As Pierre Bourdieu suggested, academic life is a strategic arena, and we can push beyond his focus on national arenas to see a series of nested arenas at different levels, with individuals, universities and intellectual traditions jostling with each other.

The movements themselves show a similar pattern. Some movements view themselves as global, and have created or participated in arenas that transcend national boundaries, notably the European Parliament and Court, although they typically play in national arenas as well. Other movements are necessarily national, dealing with the arenas of the nation-state. But still others are quite local, although these remain overlooked in favour of the larger, more dramatic movements of broader scope. Individuals and organizations move among these arenas, whether formally or informally.

This book is itself necessarily a strategic intervention in several intellectual arenas, also ranging from international to local. It begins with the old US-European contrast primarily to demonstrate the diversity of approaches within Europe. Second, it should enable researchers to be sharper in their comparisons of movements themselves across national borders, as the diversity becomes a set of factors to include in our theories about mobilization. Third, the book establishes the energy, scope and productivity of the field of social movement studies in Europe, which has developed far beyond Alain Touraine's social movement theory of the 1970s and 1980s and continues to grow in complexity and sophistication thanks to the continuing vibrancy of protest throughout the world. Authors show understandable pride in all this activity, which may reflect some lingering sense of cross-Atlantic rivalry after all.

Around the world, research on protest has escaped the shadows cast by the grand theorists of the past. In the 1980s, Touraine and Charles Tilly were deployed as exemplars of European and American styles of research. Tilly bequeathed to us many down-to-earth concepts that are still in use, while for Touraine social movements were part of—and subordinate to—his theories of Society and History. One of the surprises of this volume is the relative absence of Touraine (although the term 'new social movements' appears), and the pervasive influence of Tilly's political process theory (although even here complexity lurks, as Kriesi's European version of political opportunity structure seems more influential but is not always carefully distinguished from Tilly's version). Marxist theories—which shaped Tilly and Touraine in such different ways—are largely absent (except in Ireland and the UK), perhaps because it is difficult to apply them to movements not based on social class. In the UK Marxism flourished as an intellectual tradition because the communist party was miniscule, whereas in many European nations (especially Eastern Europe) communists discredited it through Moscow-ordered party lines.

Like all strategic projects, an edited volume poses a number of dilemmas for those involved. Many of these are parallel to dilemmas that protestors also grapple with. The central trade-off (a version of the pyramid dilemma that protestors face over how much central control to have) is how much to discipline contributors to follow the editors' vision, fitting their chapters to the central theme and division of labour, versus allowing contributors to follow their own interests, perspectives and expertise. One offers a tighter book; the other is a platform for a series of (hopefully) interesting research summaries. This is also a scholars' version of what I call the extension dilemma that protestors face: the broader the movement or alliance that is built, the greater the risk that they will disagree about goals and tactics, and the more difficult it is to maintain a coherent player. Despite many well-established contributors, Accornero and Fillieule have produced a remarkably well-focused volume, with authors attentive to their assigned topics rather than riding their own hobby horses in new directions.

The pyramid/extension dilemma is only the start of the quandaries. Each author had to struggle with writing about the movements or about how the movements have been studied, differences between domestic and foreign scholars' views of the movements (which often amounted to insiders' and outsiders' perspectives), the rich depth of case studies versus the more abstracted summaries necessary for comparative research or even quantitative research. These are the trade-offs that all scholars of social movements continually face. One of the strengths of the volume is that authors have generally confronted these trade-offs explicitly rather than sweeping them under the proverbial rug. Most authors here are happy to encourage diverse methods as well as diverse theories. (They are dealing with the sorcerer's apprentice dilemma, where our own tools can take on a life of their own and dislodge our own goals.)

There is also a version of the Janus dilemma: how much attention should be given to internal audiences versus new, external audiences? This volume is not an introduction to the field for novices; it is solidly addressed to scholars of social movements and the students who aspire to become scholars. But for that reason, it is all the more useful to scholars, addressing advanced debates and subtle variations in theories and contexts that will inspire us all to think more clearly in our research and theory.

Another version of the Janus dilemma appears in the country descriptions: when scholars have extensive international connections (as in Italy) they do not necessarily create robust cultures of scholarship within their own countries. When they are more isolated (as Portugal used to be) they may develop unusual perspectives and vibrant domestic traditions. These days scholars who do not publish in English remain outside most international conversations.

Facing a trade-off between two principles for organizing the book, by country or by movement, the editors cleverly incorporated the tension into the organizing principle of the book by giving us a part of each.

Students of protest are inspired by the movements they study, revising their theories and methods with each new wave of activism. A long time ago, scholars reacted to movements they feared. The urban revolts of nineteenth-century Europe gave us crowd theory; the Nazis gave us mass-society theory. Today the dynamic is different; we are encouraged by protest movements that we admire. Each left-leaning movement stirs research among existing scholars, but also creates new scholars. A few activists from each movement go to graduate school and write dissertations about their seminal political experiences. As surely as major elections stimulate polling research, movements foster new protest research.

Scholars in different nations have had different raw materials to work with. In the 1980s and 1990s, ACT UP and other LGBTQ (lesbian, gay, bisexual, trans-sexual, queer) movements inspired a wave of new thinking about protest, especially concerning the dilemmas and dynamics of collective identities. These movements enabled scholars to see more clearly the cultural and emotional dimensions of protest, even as economic inequality was quietly growing in Western societies. My sense is that these movements gave a greater boost to North American research, although there were also European scholars who studied these movements, including Olivier Fillieule.

The opposite was true of the global justice movement, or the alter-globalization movement (a label that sounds better in Romance languages than in English). Partly because it was attacking the 'Washington consensus' and other efforts by US governments to liberalize world markets (under Clinton) and to bust unfriendly states (under Bush), the movement itself spread faster outside the US. So did scholarship about it, in part because of funding by the EU and its member states (see Sommier's excellent chapter). Like the LGBTQ movements, the social forums of the global justice movement were an intellectual's dream: experiments in how to talk, how to listen, how to overcome the distortions that power imposes on communication. But unlike LGBTQ, they have brought issues of economic inequality back to the forefront of movement research.

Do we see glimmers of the future in this volume, in a field reinventing itself, as Fillieule says in his chapter on France? Since Seattle in 1999 many scholars have rethought their commitment to nonviolence, forced to confront the Naughty or Nice dilemma: aggressive tactics such as breaking windows get attention, and often panic elites into concessions, although they most often bring down severe repression. Violence can work. Whatever our moral commitments, we must acknowledge these realities (see Kornetis and Kouki's chapter on Greece).

Second, self-consciously cultural theories do not seem to have gone as far in Europe as in the US, leaving considerable room for the rethinking of mechanisms of cultural construction, how meanings are packaged and conveyed, and emotional dynamics. This is a topic that fits well with the excitement, which we do see here, on the Internet and social media as means not only of mobilizing people but also of creating identities and goals of protest. Except for the Netherlands, few traditions have begun to bring social psychology into the mainstream of movement studies.

In all countries, there seem to be more contacts and engagement between activists and scholars than in past generations, partly because scholars of social movements are often former, and sometimes not-so-former, activists. Compared to the era of crowd or mass-society theories, when scholars had an Olympian distance from the 'mob' in the streets, we see fine-grained analyses from the point of view of activists, including their emotions, moral intuitions and the dilemmas they confront in making decisions.

In contrast to the event histories that structuralists embraced, when they added up protests across long periods, events are now being rethought for their internal dynamics, as various players react to one another, as new directions and goals emerge, as one decision leads to others. These interactions take unpredictable paths, since there are real, consequential choices to make, despite the undoubted influence of the political and economic structures that have been the focus of scholarly attention for so long. As Della Porta suggests, those structures are always changeable through action. Fluidity and contingency are back in fashion.

It is not always easy to mobilize people for a common purpose, and I applaud the editors and contributors for the massive effort behind this book. The result is an important milestone in how we think about protest and social movements.

James M. Jasper teaches in the PhD program in sociology at the Graduate Center of the City University of New York. His latest books include *Protest: A Cultural Introduction to Social Movements* and *Players and Arenas*. With Jan Willem Duyvendak he coedits the Amsterdam University Press book series, *Protest and Social Movements*. More information is available on his website, www.jamesmjasper.org.

Introduction

"So many as the stars of the sky in multitude, and as the sand which is by the sea shore innumerable": European Social Movement Research in Perspective

Guya Accornero and Olivier Fillieule

The emergence of social movements, 'the sustained, organised challenge to existing authorities in the name of a deprived, excluded or wronged population' (Tilly 1995: 144), is closely intertwined with the development of state building and nationalization, capitalism (i.e., industrialization and communication networks), urbanization and print capitalism (Anderson 1991; Gellner 1983; and Tilly 2004). This is why social movements initially appeared in Western Europe, around the mid-nineteenth century, apparently first in Great Britain (Tilly 1995: 144) and, subsequently, in the wake of the 1848 revolution, in continental Europe. Therefore, it is not surprising that all the founding fathers of the sociology of contentious politics were Europeans: German scholar yes Lorenz von Stein first introduced the term 'social movement' into scholarly discussion in his *History of the French Social Movement from 1789 to the Present* (1850); French thinkers Hypolyte Taine, Gustave Le Bon, Gabriel Tarde and particularly Emile Durkheim (with his *The Elementary Forms of Religious Life* published in 1912) can be considered the ancestors of the collective behaviour paradigm; and, above all, Karl Marx and Friedrich Engels were the first to develop a robust theory of working-class mobilization in *The Communist Manifesto* (1848) and inspired major political and theoretical contributions by thinkers such as Vladimir I. Lenin, Leon Trotsky, Rosa Luxemburg and later Antonio Gramsci. In the United States, it was only in the 1930s that the first Chicago School, building on Emile Durkheim, Karl Marx and Max Weber, started to develop a specific conception of collective behaviour and social movements that dominated research for more than twenty years.

Most reviews of the literature and textbooks on subsequent developments in the sociology of social movements have followed the same script. They neglect European research while describing how American theories of collective behaviour, characterised by a psycho-sociological and normative approach to the process of mobilization, largely ignoring macro-political and organizational factors, generally dominated the field, with prominent researchers such as Neil Smelser and Ted Gurr. The situation changed once again at the end of the 1960s, with an American paradigm shift in favour of the school of resource mobilization, and in Europe with renewed interest in social movements through the emergence of the 'new social movements' paradigm.

In the United States, the common theme uniting the various trends of the new model is the ideological legitimacy of social movement activity, perceived as the result of voluntary and intentional behaviour. Consequently, the central research focus shifts from the study of crowd movements to that of social movements, from analysis of deep-rooted causes of mobilization to a more complex study of the forms of action and goals that movements have in function of a given opportunity structure. Two major tendencies can be distinguished (Perrow 1979): one based on an entrepreneurial model (McCarthy and Zald 1973 and 1977) and another viewing collective action as nothing but the pursuit of politics by other means (Oberschall 1973; Gamson 1975; and Tilly 1978). This also extends to the field of social history, with the research of Michael Lipsky on tenants' movements (1968) and Samuel Popkin on small farmers (1979). Yet it is indeed the same theoretical substratum, that is, the utilitarian paradigm of individual rationality, and the same interest in resolving the paradox posed by Mancur Olson in 1965, which links all these works. This paradigm did not give way to a rival theory. It transformed itself from within, mostly spurred by Charles Tilly (1978) and later Doug McAdam (1982) who reintroduced the political dimension of mobilization, pushing the model to evolve towards what we currently tend to call the 'political process model'. This model emphasises the role of political opportunities, mobilizing structures and framing processes, along with protest cycles and contentious repertoires (Caren 2006).

In the European context, characterised by profound economic and social transformation (Inglehart 1977), the upheaval of May 1968 prompted renewed interest in research into social movements. These were considered 'new' movements, in view of the 'post-materialist' causes they defended, their values, forms of action and participants (Offe 1985; Cohen 1985). Most academics emphasised that this new research trend was first developed in Germany by researchers such as Claus Offe, Werner Brand and Herbert Kitschelt, owing to the development of citizen initiative groups (*Bürgeriniti-ativen* and *Bundesverband Bürgerinitiativen Umweltschutz*), and a strong ecological and antinuclear movement (Dalton and Kuechler 1990: 4). Yet this also happened in post-1968 France, with Alain Touraine (1971, 1978), and in Italy with one of his students, Alberto Melucci. This unified vision of a

'European identity paradigm', developing independently of the resource mo-bilization theory and uniformly inspired by a desire to explain the disappear-ance of the working class as a central actor in social movements, replaced by inter-classist movements concerned with post-materialist identity demands, certainly had some foundations in reality. Nonetheless, it is extremely sim-plistic, ignoring the diversity of social movement studies produced in the first half of the twentieth century in various social science disciplines in Eu-rope, and especially in its homogenization of political trajectories and intel-lectual traditions in European countries, as though, from Lisbon to Berlin and the Shetland Islands to Sicily, a single history unfolded, in the streets and in university lecture halls.

The main objective of this book is to offer the reader a more nuanced and comprehensive account of the complex and multifaceted ways that move-ment theory and research agendas have evolved in a selection of European countries. We will pay particular attention to variations between countries and show that many idiosyncratic routes have been followed, making it quite difficult to speak about a European model of social movement theory, just as it is misleading to refer to a unified American academia. However, since a strong dedifferentiation process has been at work in social science for more than twenty years, we will keep one puzzling question in mind: do the varie-ties of European intellectual traditions reflect increasingly convergent routes defined by an overly dominant American agenda or do national traditions remain strong and, if so, with what results?

Social Movement Studies and the 'Thrust of Real History'

The obvious link between larger socio-historical processes, the development of social movements and, subsequently, of a new area of research in social science[1] stresses that it is not 'internal logics but external concerns that are vital to understanding the sociological study of social movements' (Gusfield 1978: 122). Indeed, the first hypothesis that comes to mind when reflecting on the development of the sociology of social movements and the succession of paradigms which characterised it, is that of the 'thrust of real history', as Louis Althusser wrote in *Pour Marx* (1967: 80), social reality evolving outside the theories which consider it and theories finally being altered or bypassed by events, sometimes leading to very abrupt shifts in paradigms.[2] It was in reaction to the threat of social revolution, which appeared at the end of the nineteenth century, that the first works on mass movements ap-peared. Thus, the theory of the madding crowd owes much to the ghosts of thinkers frightened by the progress of liberal democracy. It was again in the name of ideological assumptions in favour of political pluralism and respect for institutional rules that social movements continued to be analysed in terms of irrational phenomena responding to frustrations right up until the middle of the 1960s. This was particularly the case in the United States, which was confronted immediately after the war with the emergence of the Civil Rights Movement and the development of political unrest in African American communities.

Subsequently, the abandonment of theories of collective behaviour for a rational vision of mobilization was in part due to the scale of collective action at the time and its dissemination among large segments of society, especially university students opposed to the Vietnam War. All this gave way to the progressive incorporation of the reflections of practitioners of mobilization, such as, for example Vladimir I. Lenin, Mao Tse Tung, Martin Luther King and Saul Alinsky, in academic analytical instruments. These leaders formulated general principles and lines of action, insisting on tactical choices and the social and organizational infrastructure required for success in their struggles. Thus, it is at least in part under the impetus of the thrust of this 'real history' that the field of the sociology of mobilization, with its own analytical instruments and theoretical issues, gradually emerged.

In addition to those exogenous factors of social movement theory development, two endogenous factors contributed to the creation of the field: first, 'the prevailing matrix of social science disciplines, their intellectual division of labour, and changes in both over time'; and second, 'shifts in the broader intellectual climate that transcends particular disciplines' (Buechler 2011: 2–3). Those two factors largely explain why social movement research in America developed the way it did, especially after the Second World War, through major paradigm shifts and smaller-scale permutations in an increasingly integrated and self-referencing way (McAdam and Shaffer Boudet 2012). In contrast, 'in Western Europe, the development of the study of social movements can hardly be described in terms of a major paradigmatic change. In line with its highly diverse cultural and scientific traditions, the study of social movements in various countries also followed very different courses and patterns' (Rucht 1991: 10).

In addition to these factors, it is important to note a further two dimensions which are characteristic of the rapid and profound transformations in the academic field at the end of the twentieth century, and that may have produced a more and more integrated theoretical perspective on social movements. First, what we could call 'the narrowing of academic spaces', to use Benedict Anderson's vocabulary, is associated with new practices. The development of the Internet, with increased interaction via e-mail, access to international literature through catalogues (including commercial services such as Amazon) and databases available online, has considerably reduced the cost of searching for information. Also, there has been an increase in study-abroad programs and research (via Erasmus programs in particular), all authorised by this other relatively recent transformation, in southern Europe, at least, which is the widespread adoption of English in academic work.

Furthermore, everywhere in Europe the criteria of academic excellence (and, thus, the paths for recruitment and, likewise, the chances of being published in quality journals) have gradually become aligned with international standards imported from the United States. To quote merely one example, this is the case of the *Revue française de science politique* or the *Revue française de sociologie,* which, in a recent editorial, announced that all articles published from now on will be translated into English and available online. From this, it follows that the journal's objective is to participate 'in the international chorus' of the discipline and, therefore, to publish works 'which by their nature will attract the attention' of professional sociologists outside of France (2012: 386). Even *Politix,* a journal of a school defending a critical approach to social sciences (that is, inspired by Pierre Bourdieu and Luc Boltanski), whose analytical framework had long been quintessentially French, finally became internationalised. In a recent article appearing on the occasion of the one hundredth edition of the journal and which reviewed its own history, Pierre Favre remarked that, when in 1991 a double edition was devoted to the 'construction of causes', the opening article could once again broach this foremost element of mobilization *without a single* English-language reference. This is no longer the case, and theme-based issues devoted to mobilization published since the year 2000 rely extensively on English references (Favre 2012). The same process is underway in most South European countries.

Globalization of Knowledge: Towards an Integrated European Community of Social Movement Scholars?

From the end of the Second World War to the late 1980s, the field of social movement research remained highly fragmented in Europe. During its incipient phase, research was strongly rooted in national traditions. It was only in the early 1990s that the scenario began to move towards one of progressive integration. As Diani and Císař stress in their study of the progressive construction of a European social movement community, in the early phase (1978–90) parallel developments in a number of European states took place, with quite a few significant collaborations across national borders; in the intermediate phase (1991–2001), a core of European researchers in close collaboration with non-European (mostly US-based) social scientists emerged; during the most recent phase (2003–12), a European community of social movement researchers consolidated but also differentiated along several lines of fragmentation (Diani and Císař, 2014).

More precisely, it was at the point when the sociology of social movements was playing an increasing role in American social science[3] that collaboration began with a small group of European and American researchers, following an initial conference held in Amsterdam in 1986 organised by Bert Klandermans. Two publications are crucial in this particular context: *From Structure to Action: Comparing Social Movement Research across Cultures,* edited by Bert Klandermans, Hanspeter Kriesi and Sidney Tarrow in 1988, and *Research on Social Movements: The State of the Art in Western Europe and the USA,* edited by Dieter Rucht in 1991. Both books sought to track the evolution of the field, notably in terms of the divergence between the European and American traditions.

The authors of *From Structure to Action* argue that after the intensification of contentious politics in the late 1960s and early 1970s, two new paradigms emerged: 'resource mobilization' in America and the 'new social movements' approach in Europe. In short, European scholars concentrated their analysis on major structural issues—the structural causes of social movements, their ideologies and relationship with the culture of advanced capitalist societies—whereas the focus of American research was predominantly on groups and individuals, their forms of action and motivations. Moreover, the authors stressed that, while there was some uniformity in studies conducted in the United States around the resource mobilization approach, the new social movement theory seemed to be more a convergence of different ideas than a uniform current.

Although dialogue was just starting at that time, as stressed by Bert Klandermans in his chapter, Dieter Rucht's work identified the continued separation and lack of communication between the American and European scholars of social movements. Moreover, this author speaks of the general difficulty of institutionalization in social movement studies: 'In comparison to sub-disciplines of, say, medicine or physics, which are well coordinated on the national and international levels and have their own established institutes, journals and congresses, the field of social movements is underdeveloped. … Moreover, language barriers come into play. To be sure, within a given country those people working on social movements for a longer period of time usually have knowledge of each other's work or even meet from time to time. But there may be fascinating studies written in Dutch or Italian unknown to a French or English scholar. And from the standpoint of an

American researcher, it may be still more difficult to have a close look at the debates in this broad range of Western European countries' (1990: 10–11).

Both these books rightly aimed to address this lack of communication and encourage international reflection on the various debates and approaches to social movements, above all by considering the different focuses of research in the United States and Europe. This 'transatlantic connection' continued over a number of years with the objective of bringing the political process paradigm and European approaches together. Anthologies were published encompassing contributions from both sides.[4] By the end of the first decade of the twenty-first century, one could thus confidently declare that the American sociology of social movements had definitely entered the sphere of reference of European researchers, and that American scholars are increasingly well-informed about what is going on in Europe. This is strikingly evident if one compares the *Blackwell Companion to Social Movements,* edited by Snow, Soule and Kriesi (2004), and the *Wiley-Blackwell Encyclopedia of Social and Political Movements,* edited by Snow and colleagues (2013), in which the proportion of European authors has increased dramatically.

While collaboration between European scholars was initially facilitated through dialogue with American researchers, the field in Europe has become relatively autonomous, mainly due to the role of the European Union's funding of international projects. This is the case, among others, for projects on the policing of protest (Della Porta and Reiter 1998; Fillieule and Della Porta 2006; Della Porta, Peterson and Reiter 2006), environmental movements (Kousis 1994; Rootes 2003), migration and citizenship (Koopmans et al. 2005), the politics of unemployment (Giugni 2009; Chabanet and Faniel 2012), no global movements (Della Porta 2007a; Sommier, Fillieule and Agrikoliansky 2008), the emergence of a European public sphere (Koopmans and Statham 2010; Della Porta and Caiani 2009), outcomes of social movements (Bosi and Uba 2009), and for a series of projects on participatory politics and democracy (Della Porta 2007 and 2009).

Social movement studies have now become an institutionalised 'sub-discipline' with sessions and standing groups in various scientific associations in different disciplinary areas, notably political science and sociology. At the international level, the European Sociological Association (ESA) and the European Consortium for Political Research (ECPR) hold workshops dedicated to social movements on a biannual or annual basis. A standing group specifically dedicated to social movement studies has been created along the lines of the ESA in 1999 and the ECPR, with first and foremost Participation and Mobilization (established in 2004), but also Extremism and Democracy (1999), Internet and Politics (2009), and Political Sociology (2010), which also show a strong interest in social movements. Furthermore, standing groups have been created at a national level. For instance the Study and Research Group on Transformations in Activism (GERMM) of the French Society for Political Science (AFSP) was launched in 1994 and operated until 2010; and the standing group on Social Movements and Political Participation of the Italian Society for Political Science (SISP) appeared following the annual congress in 2006, when there were three panels and sixteen papers presented in the section on these issues. In 2010 the section of the SISP annual conference organised by this standing group was responsible for six panels and thirty-seven papers, predominantly presented in English. In Italy too, there is COSMOS, under the wing of the European Institute (http://cosmos.eui.eu/Projects/cosmos/Home.aspx). The *Wissenschaft zentrum* in Berlin played a similar role in Germany, led by Dieter Rucht up to 2011 and now, along with younger colleagues, is part of the new *Institut für protest und Bewegungsforschung*, I.G. (http://protestinstitut.eu/). Moreover, reference should be made of the pioneer Centre for the Study of Social and Political Movements at the University of Kent (established in 1992); CRAPUL (http://www.unil.ch/iepi/page16548.html/) at the University of Lausanne (Switzerland), which started operating in 2002; the Forum for Civil and Social Movement Research (CSM) at the University of Göteborg (established in 2011); the Contentious Politics Circle at Panteion University and the newly created InCite research institute at the University of Geneva (https://www.unige.ch/sciences-societe/incite).

Social movement analysts have also been prominent in launching specific academic journals, such as *Environmental Politics,* a major publication site of research on environmental social movements; *Social Movement Studies* (2002); and, more recently, the online journal *Interface* (2012), all of which offer a valuable means of disseminating European research. Moreover, it should be highlighted that since 1997 the American journal *Mobilization* has had a European editor (Mario Diani until 2005 followed by Marco Giugni) managing European submissions. Similarly, some leading publishers have brought out series devoted to studies on social movements; for example, the Cambridge series on Contentious Politics and the Berghahn series on Protest, Culture and Society, which pay special attention to European studies.

To summarise the evolution of the last two decades of the field in Europe, it could be said that there has been an exponential intensification and expansion of social movement studies that has led to a rapid 'acceleration' in the growth of knowledge. There is no longer a sharp distinction between American and European approaches, in part due to the inception of a process of self-reflection on the theoretical and methodological assumptions of classic social movement studies and agenda—largely based on the 'contentious politics model'. European diversification in social movement research and the inclusion of new arenas and greater scope, which extend the range of classic instruments of analysis for social movements, contribute to this reflection. Furthermore, the adoption of new analytical approaches and theoretical and methodological innovations foster the diversification of the object of study. These two interdependent dynamics, one related to the object and the other to the approach, have helped to bring in innovations to this field of study and are produced concomitantly and sometimes collaboratively by both European and American scholars who are increasingly dissatisfied with the 'contentious politics model'.

Nowadays, the social movement community focuses not only on new aspects, such as different protest arenas or new geographical areas beyond a western focus, but also on institutional means of channelling protests, e.g. legal instruments. Moreover, following Jasper's innovative research agenda, renewed interest in activists' trajectories has been accompanied by particular focus on the emotional and affective aspects of the engagement and disengagement process. Additional research has also focused on the political and social effects of mobilization at the macro level of institutions. This has also highlighted the process of individual disengagement and the causes and factors which could lead to it. Furthermore, these issues are all related in some way to the debate on the effect of the repression of social movements, which could in turn be part of the wider discussion on the extent of political violence (Combes and Fillieule 2012; Bosi, Demetriou and Malthaner 2014). Finally, while the origin of social movement sociology was strictly linked, both in the United States and Europe, to the diffusion of progressive or left-wing movements, such as civil rights, student or feminist movements, more recently scholars have begun to employ these instruments to investigate conservative or right-wing mobilization. This diversification of the form of 'contentious politics' under analysis corresponds to a pluralization of approaches, both at a theoretical and methodological level. Social movement scholarship has also become increasingly diversified in recent years due to its openness to other disciplines, such as anthropology and the history of social psychology. The shifting of attention from the macrodimension of social movements and structural aspects of mobilization towards micro-level processes has also led to qualitative methods acquiring a more important role. For instance, ethnographic methods are useful to reconstruct individual trajectories or shed light on the effects of repression on groups and activists.

Moreover, some specific arenas, such as transnational movements, have spurred more cross-fertilization of approaches. Interdisciplinary and plural points of view, questions, theoretical frameworks and methodologies have converged into a harmonious, albeit 'hybrid', perspective rather than a restrictive school of thought. This is the case, for example, of the numerous studies published on the no-global movement (see Sommier's chapter in this volume), or works viewing the transnational dimension as an indisputable characteristic of the contemporary politics of protest (Teune 2010 on the transnationalization of contemporary protests; and Flesher Fominaya and Cox 2013 on anti-austerity movements); and likewise, books adopting a historical perspective (Kouki and Romanos 2011 on contentious politics since 1945 in Europe; Klimke, Pekelder and Scharloth 2011 on European movements in the wake of May 1968; and Gildea, Mark and Warring 2013 on '68ers).

In spite of everything written above, one should not hastily conclude that the sociology of social movements has become institutionalised in the European academic landscape. While in the United States a subfield has been constructed with defined boundaries, certification institutions and, therefore, gatekeepers, this is not true of Europe. Often, this is rather less due to lack of interest and more the result of the former centrality of the reflection on social change, on collective struggles and, thus, on social movements in European social science. Here we agree with Flesher Fominaya and Cox when they stress that 'because social movements are so central to European social theory, social movement theory in itself is not readily visible in Europe as a separate field of analysis' (2013: 20).

Furthermore, increased exchanges between the American and European academic worlds on one hand and between European academic worlds on the other do not mean that there is an integrated and unified community of social movement scholars. First, while Europeans have largely taken a path that enables them to appropriate the knowledge produced by American sociology, this is rarer amongst American researchers, even though the most prominent American scholars in the field systematically pay attention to the specifics of research affected by European theoretical and methodological traditions.[5] A glance at the table of contents of the journal *Mobilization* since it was first published is enough to observe that, while there are a number of European authors, almost all the published articles adopt a mainstream approach to contentious politics, both from the conceptual point of view and in terms of the investigative methods and modes of exposition employed. This certainly does not help the American public to become aware of the diversity and richness of European research. Instead it wrongly reinforces the notion that what is being done in Europe follows exactly the same lines as the work in the United States. Second, although today there definitely exists a group of researchers in different European countries who collaborate and engage in exchanges on the basis of a common foundation in the political process model, in each country their particular traditions endure, often resulting in research which slips under the radar of reviews of the literature.

These two observations have given rise to this book, which aims to offer a comprehensive and detailed overview of social movement studies in a wide selection of European countries.

The Book

This volume is divided into two sections. In the first, comparative chapters will provide reflections from experts on different kinds of social movements, on the state of the art of specific issues or movements, and on the way in which they have been analysed by increasingly transnational and comparative research. These are areas which have been the particular focus of research in recent years, and that international groups of researchers have repeatedly addressed, mainly thanks to European or other international research funds. The European Research Council has played a key role in fostering such international research projects and has made a significant contribution to the circulation of scholars and ideas and the development of transnational and comparative studies.

The first two chapters in the first section do not deal with a specific movement, but rather with cycles of protests involving different issues and claims. The section opens with Erik Neveu's chapter on the '68, which deconstructs the myth of this event—or series of events—as a Paris-centred cultural revolution. Neveu thus stresses the strong, and maybe stronger, relevance of the labour conflict and the broader range of types of mobilization. In the following chapter, Della Porta analyses the wave of mobilization in the context of the democratization process in Eastern and Central Europe around 1989. She stresses the lack of attention paid to grassroots politics by scholars of democratic transitions, more interested in elite-led processes. On the other hand, she points out that social movement scholars have overlooked democratizing processes, mostly concentrating their interest on democratic countries. Next, Karel Yon analyses the long and difficult process of integration of labour movements in the field of social movements theory. He stresses that, although the labour movement represents the social movement *par excellence*—around which most conflict theories have been developed— its study has long been the prerogative of other disciplines, such as industrial relations. As is the case of other movements, Caiani and Borri highlight the paucity of research on the movements discussed in their chapter. They claim that few have studied radical right-wing movements using a social movement approach. With the exception of studies on political violence and terrorism, most scholars dealing with the radical right focus on parties and elections, paying little attention to non-party organizations and subcultures.

In spite of the absence of powerful migrants' social movements, in his chapter Manlio Cinalli stresses that research in this field has been burgeoning. He depicts a landscape in which the discipline seems more 'contentious' than its object of study, and where controversies among different approaches—such as the structuralist or the cultural ones—characterised the academic debate until recent years. In the following chapter, Giugni and Lorenzini show that the situation of the movements of the unemployed and those whose employment is non-permanent is worthy of examination. Though mobilization in this field has been widespread and recurrent, according to the authors, it has been neglected by students of social movements. After emphasizing the relevance in the research of such elements as grievances, resources and opportunities, the authors underscore the lack of and need for more comparative studies. Following this, in her chapter on no global movements, Isabelle Sommier emphasises the dramatic differences between European and American research. Her words portray that European scholars saw this new and powerful movement as a chance for self-assertion and self-definition vis-à-vis American sociologists of social movements.

Kousis's chapter on research on the environmental movement stresses that, since the 1990s, this field has received major funding from the European Commission. This might explain a certain similar use of theoretical frameworks based on collective identity and political process paradigms. Bereni and Revillard deal with another 'historical' social movement, the women's movement. European research in this domain is distinguished from American research because it is less rooted in sociology. Instead it is firmly anchored in political science and focuses on the role of political institutions.

Finally, the more recent mobilizations against austerity politics are the object of the next chapter by Heloïse Nez. Here, the author describes a situation where the abundant literature produced on the wave of events is still quite uneven. At the same time, important questions still remain open, such as how can these movements be defined and why did they emerge now? Which is the relation between these and previous movements? Are there networks that connect these movements across space? A micro-sociological approach is suggested by the author in order to answer part of these questions.

The second section presents chapters dealing with national cases. In contrast to the selection made at the end of the 1980s by Dieter Rucht, our book does not concentrate exclusively on Northern European countries but includes the main southern countries (France, Spain, Portugal and Greece) and a selection of Eastern European countries (Russia, Hungary and Romania). To this we have added Turkey, which geographically belongs to Europe and whose political, economic and social history is increasingly intertwined with the rest of the continent. Of course, the selection of cases could always be criticised for omitting certain countries but we had to make choices in order to keep the book a reasonable size and find colleagues who would be both able and willing to deliver a chapter on the countries in which we were interested.

In this second section, four main patterns in the development of social movement studies can be detected. First, we can consider a group of countries where the influence of the American literature and its successful integration with local traditions was stronger and earlier. Italy, Germany, Switzerland and Sweden all seem to have followed such a path, although in a more or less decisive way and with significant variations. On the other hand, in some countries this influence and integration seem less developed, and very specific research paths were followed in an independent fashion. The reason for this tendency can be found in the strength of local traditions of studies in social movements which continue to be very influential in countries such as France, Great Britain and Ireland. In France, for instance, the influence of Pierre Bourdieu's thought in the social sciences also extended to the research on social movements. This can be seen in the special attention given to the process of political socialization and to cultural and social factors and the implications of political commitment. This focus on sociological aspects leads to a rediscovery of the micro dimension of political engagement and the sociological effects of activism. Besides the prominent relevance of specific movements, especially that of labour, studies on social movements in Britain is deeply rooted in Marxist historiography and ethnography. The early and incisive rupture of the new left in the late 1950s also had a great influence on the discipline's evolution. This contributed to shifting the attention 'from grand narratives of social transformation to local micro-histories of dissent and dissenters'. In Irish research on social movements, four main analytical paths have been particularly important: the history of pre-independence nationalism; postcolonial studies; peasant struggles; and working-class history. Radical left-wing-engaged scholarship had also been traditionally dominant in the country. In recent years, this perspective has been vigorously developed by scholars of the so-called 'Maynooth School', whose aims include that of developing 'a Marxist theory of movements starting from an Irish perspective'. The case of social movement studies in the Netherlands seems to be at the border of these two groups and this is due to a certain local 'bifurcation' in this research area. One can thus identify two main 'schools': social psychologists at the VU University in Amsterdam and political sociologists at the University of Amsterdam (UvA). The first school, which seems to be more linked to a national tradition, was created by Bert Klandermans and applies the social-psychological approach (SPA).

The second group, created by Hanspeter Kriesi, applies the political process approach (PPA), which has a clear North American origin.

A third group is comprised of countries which have undergone recent democratization processes. Here, two main patterns can be detected. In countries which experienced right-wing regimes, such as Spain, Portugal and Greece, radical left-wing movements emerged against the dictatorship, and continue to represent an essential legacy for actors still engaging in the struggle after the fall of the dictatorship. Consequently, research on social movements like the social movements themselves seems more focused on political than on social demands and issues. Thus, democratic transitions seem to constitute a genuine turning point, not only for the implementation of new political systems but also for social movement studies. In fact, only after democratic implementation was it possible to deal with issues related to social and political conflict at an academic level. A different pattern can be discerned in countries formerly subject to communist regimes. The cases examined here—Russia, Hungary and Romania—generally pay more attention to the concept of civil society than to that of social movements, perhaps because of the echoes of 'Marxism' the latter still evoke. Finally, Turkey does not fit into any of the patterns. Without entering into the debate on the kind of regime in force in this country—whether a hybrid or a securitarian one—we observe that history plays a forceful role in social movement studies there (Dorronsoro 2007). Moreover, as in countries which lived for a long period under authoritarian rule, such as Portugal, Turkey's case shows the influence of James Scott's approach. In paying more attention to hidden forms of resistance than to open struggles against authorities, such an approach seems particularly suitable to describe peoples' (re)actions in authoritarian contexts. In spite of these continuities among specific groups of countries, in this section we decided to adopt a geopolitical layout which seems to us more coherent and easy to read.

As usual a book such as this one could not be published without the collaboration and assistance of many people. First of all, we would like to thank the contributors for their participation and compliance with our remarks, suggestions and inflexibility of chapter length. We are also very grateful to James Jasper for writing the foreword to the volume. He is certainly one of the American scholars who has opened new tracks for research which are well in line with European sensibilities, and also Dieter Rucht, definitely one of the most rigorous European researchers and clearly among the most generous of the generation of our mentors. Finally we wish to thank the institutions with which we are affiliated: on one hand, in Switzerland, the University of Lausanne and especially CRAPUL which provided a favourable environment for working on the project, and hosted Guya Accornero for a postdoctoral stay in 2012; and on the other hand, in Portugal, CIES-IUL for the excellent working conditions, and FCT for providing the financial continuity necessary for such a project.

Guya Accornero is an advanced research fellow at the Centre for Research and Studies in Sociology of Lisbon University Institute (CIES-IUL), where she carries on a project funded by the Portuguese Foundation for Science and Technology (FCT). She has published articles in the journals *West European Politics, Democratization, Cultures and Conflits, Análise Social, Storia e Problemi Contemporanei*, and she is currently publishing a monograph entitled *The Revolution before the Revolution: Late Authoritarianism and Student Protest in Portugal* for Berghahn Books.

Olivier Fillieule is a research director at the CNRS (Sorbonne University, Paris), a professor of political sociology at Lausanne University (IEPI/Institute for Political and International Studies) and a member of CRAPUL (Research Centre on Political Action at Lausanne University). His latest books include *Demonstrations* (with D. Tartakowsky). A list of his research interests and publications is available at http://unil.academia.edu/OlivierFillieule.

Notes

The signatures of this paper appear in alphabetical order.
1. As Diani and Císař stress, the term 'social science' is more accurate here than 'sociology', because 'in this particular area of research it is virtually impossible, not to say misleading, to disentangle work conducted by sociologists from work conducted by other researchers, most notably, political scientists' (Diani and Císař, 2014: 172), but also historians, anthropologists and social psychologists.
2. Here we come up against the problem of boomerang effects, a thorny question in the history of science, and especially in political science, as Pierre Favre remarked: 'Can the transformations of the real objects which a science gives itself transform this science? Can an emerging social science be committed to other issues than those initially aimed at resulting from historical transformations of the social phenomena which it is studying? Are certain objects, due to the considerable visibility they acquire at particular moments, designed expressly for investigation?' (Favre 1989: 207–8).
3. According to a time-series of total and collective behaviour/social movement publications which appeared in the top four US sociology journals between 1960 and 2012, John McCarthy shows a dramatic increase starting in 1991–92, from a mean of less than 5 per cent to a mean of more than 15 per cent (unpublished graph shown at the CCC conference, Amsterdam, 2013).
4. For an up-to-date review of those publications, please see van Stekelenburg, Roggeband and Klandermans (2013).

5. See for example, and among others, collaborations between Daniel Cefai and Paul Lichterman (2006); Donatella Della Porta and Sidney Tarrow (2005); Mario Diani and Doug McAdam (2003); Myra Marx Ferree, William Anthony Gamson, Jürgen Gerhards and Dieter Rucht (2002).

References

Althusser, L. 1965. *Pour Marx*. Paris: François Maspero.

Anderson, B. 1991. *Imagined Communities*. London: Verso Books.

Bosi, L., and K. Uba. 2009. 'The Outcomes of Social Movements', *Mobilization* 14(4), no. 4: 405–411.

Bosi, L., C. Demetriou and S. Malthaner. 2014. *Dynamics of Political Violence. A Process-Oriented Perspective on Radicalization and the Escalation of Political Conflict*. Farnham: Ashgate.

Buechler, S. 2011. *Understanding Social Movements: Theories from the Classical Era to the Present*. Boulder: Paradigm.

Caren, N. 2006. 'Political Process Theory'. In *Blackwell Encyclopedia of Sociology*, ed. G. Ritzer. New York: Blackwell.

Cefai D., and P. Lichterman. 2006. 'The Idea of Political Culture'. In *Oxford Handbook of Contextual Political Studies*, ed. R. Goodin and C. Tilly, 392–414. Oxford and New York: Oxford University Press.

Cohen, J.L. 1985. 'Strategy or Identity: New Theoretical Paradigms and Contemporary Social Movements'. *Social Research* 52, no. 4: 663–716.

Combes, H. and O. Fillieule. 2011. 'Repression and protest structural models and strategic interactions'. *Revue francaise de science politique* 61, n. 6: 1–24.

Flesher Fominaya C. and L. Cox, eds. 2013. *Understanding European Movements: New Social Movements, Global Justice Struggles, Anti-austerity Protest*. London and New York: Routledge.

Dalton R. J., and M. Kuechler. 1990. *Challenging the Political Order: New Social and Political Movements in Western Democracies*. New York: Oxford University Press.

Della Porta, D. 2007a. 'La democrazia partecipativa e I movimenti sociali: Micro e macro-dinamiche'. In *Le nuove forme di partecipazione*, ed . B. Gelli, 73–86. Rome: Carocci.

Della Porta, D., ed. 2007b. *The Global Justice Movement: Cross-National and Transnational Perspectives*. Boulder: Paradigm.

———. 2009. *Democracy in Social Movements*. New York: Palgrave Macmillan.

Della Porta, D., and M. Caiani. 2009. *Social Movements and Europeanization*. Oxford: Oxford University Press.

Della Porta, D., A. Peterson and H. Reiter, eds. 2006. *The Policing of Transnational Protest*. Aldershot: Ashgate.

Della Porta, D., and H. Reiter. 1998. *Policing Protest: The Control of Mass Demonstration in Western Democracies*. Minneapolis: University of Minnesota Press.

Della Porta, D., and S. Tarrow, eds. 2005. *Transnational Protest and Global Activism*. Lanham: Rowman and Littlefield.

Diani, M., and D. McAdam, eds. 2003. *Social Movements and Networks*. Oxford and New York: Oxford University Press.

Diani, M., and O. Císař. 2014. 'The Emergence of a Social Movement Research Field'. In *Routledge Handbook of European Sociology,* ed. S. Kodornios and A. Kyrtsis. London: Routledge, 173–195.

Dorronsoro, G. 2007, ed. *La Turquie conteste : Mobilisations sociales et régime sécuritaire.* Paris: CNRS.

Durkheim, E. 2001 [1912]. *Elementary Forms of Religious Life.* Oxford: Oxford University Press.

Favre, P. 1989. *Naissances de la science politique en France, 1870–1914.* Paris: Librairie Arthème Fayard.

———. 2012. 'Politix. 1988–2012: Changement de générations, basculement de paradigme'. *Politix, Revue des sciences sociales du politique* (4) 100: 41–62.

Ferree, M. Marx, et al. 2002. *Shaping Abortion Discourse: Democracy and the Public Sphere in Germany and the United States.* Cambridge and New York: Cambridge University Press.

Fillieule, O., and D. Della Porta. 2006. *Police et manifestants.* Paris: Presses de SciencePo

Gamson, W. 1975. *The Strategy of Social Protest.* Belmont: Dorsey Press.

Gellner, E. 1993. *Nations and Nationalism.* Oxford: Blackwell.

Gildea, R., J. Mark and A. Warring. 2013. *Europe's 1968: Voices of Revolt,* Oxford: Oxford University Press.

Giugni, M., ed. 2009. *The Politics of Unemployment in Europe: Policy Responses and Collective Action.* Aldershot: Ashgate.

Gusfield, J. R. 1978. *Community: A Critical Response.* New York: Harper Colophon Books.

Inglehart, R. 1977. *The Silent Revolution: Changing Values and Political Styles among Western Publics.* Princeton: Princeton University Press.

Klandermans, B., H. Kriesi and S. Tarrow. 1988. *From Structure to Action: Comparing Social Movement Research across Cultures.* London: JAI.

Klimke, M., J. Pekelder and J. Scharloth. 2011. *Between Prague Spring and French May: Opposition and Revolt in Europe, 1960–1980.* New York and Oxford: Berghahn Books.

Koopmans, R., and P. Statham 2010. *The Making of a European Public Sphere: Media Discourse and Political Contention.* Cambridge: Cambridge University Press.

Koopmans, R., et al., eds. 2005. *Contested Citizenship: Immigration and Cultural Diversity in Europe.* Minneapolis: University of Minnesota Press.

Kouki, H., and E. Romanos. 2011. *Protest beyond Borders: Contentious Politics in Europe since 1945.* New York and Oxford: Berghahn Books.

Kousis, M. 1994. 'Environment and the State in the EU Periphery: The Case of Greece'. *Regional Politics and Policy* 4, n. 1: 118–135.

Lipsky, M. 1968. 'Protest as a Political Resource'. *The American Political Science Review* 62, no. 4: 1144–58.

Marx, K., and F. Engels. 1847. *The Communist Manifesto.* London: Merlin Press.

McAdam, D. 1982. *Political Process and the Development of Black Insurgency, 1930–1970.* Chicago: University of Chicago Press.

McAdam, D., and H. S. Boudet. 2012. *Putting Social Movements in Their Place: Explaining Opposition to Energy Projects in the United States, 2000–2005.* Cambridge: Cambridge University Press.

McCarthy, J. D., and M. N. Zald. 1973. *The Trend of Social Movements in America: Professionalization and Resource Mobilization.* Morristown: General Learning Press.

———. 1977. 'Resource Mobilization and Social Movements: A Partial Theory'. *American Journal of Sociology* 82, no. 6: 1212–41.

Oberschall, A. 1973. *Social Conflict and Social Movements.* Englewood Cliff: Prentice Hall.

Offe, C. 1985. 'New Social Movements: Challenging the Boundaries of Institutional Politics'. *Social Research* 52, no. 4: 817–68.

Olson, M. 1965. *The Logic of Collective Action: Public Goods and the Theory of Groups.* Cambridge: Harvard University Press.

Perrow, C. 1979. *Complex Organizations: A Critical Essay.* New York: Random House

Popkin, S. 1979. *The Rational Peasant.* Berkeley: University of California Press.

Rootes, C. 2003. *Environmental Protest in Western Europe.* Oxford: Oxford University Press.

Rucht, D. 1991. *Research on Social Movements: The State of the Art in Western Europe and the USA.* Frankfurt: Campus Verlag.

Snow, D.A., et al., eds. 2013. *The Wiley-Blackwell Encyclopedia of Social and Political Movements.* Oxford: Wiley-Blackwell.

Snow, D. A., S. A. Soule and H. Kriesi. 2004. *The Blackwell Companion to Social Movements.* Oxford: Blackwell.

Sommier, I., O. Fillieule and E. Agrikoliansky, eds. 2008. *Généalogie des mouvements alter-mondialistes en Europe: Une perspective comparée.* Paris: Karthala.

Teune, S., ed. 2010. *The Transnational Condition: Protest Dynamics in an Entangled Europe.* New York and Oxford: Berghahn Books.

Tilly, C. 1995. *Popular Contention in Great Britain, 1758–1834.* Cambridge: Harvard University Press.

———. 1978. *From Mobilization to Revolution.* Boston: Addison-Wesley.

———. 2004. *Social Movements, 1768–2004.* Boulder: Paradigm.

Touraine, A. 1971. *Production de la Société.* Paris: Seuil.

———. 1978. *La Voix et le Regard.* Paris: Seuil.

Van Stekelenburg, J., C. Roggeband and B. Klandermans. 2013. *The Future of Social Movement Research Dynamics, Mechanisms, and Processes.* Minneapolis: University of Minnesota Press.

Von Stein, L. 1964 [1850]. *History of the French Social Movement from 1789 to the Present.* New York: Bedminster Press.

PART I

European Social Movements in Comparative Perspective

Chapter 1

The European Movements of '68
Ambivalent Theories, Ideological Memories and Exciting Puzzles

Erik Neveu

> Those students who temporarily took over Paris … had no 'ratio-
> nal' reason to rebel, for they were for the most part pampered off-
> spring of one of the freest and most prosperous societies on earth.
> But it was precisely the absence of struggle and sacrifice in their
> middle class lives that led them to take the streets and confront
> the police. … [W]hat they rejected was life in a society in which
> ideals had somehow become impossible'. (Fukuyama 1992: 331)

For activists, researchers and citizens in many European countries, ''68'
would suggest a meaningful figure and a vintage year. That March, Polish
students were demonstrating for freedom of expression. The spring months
were those of the 'Prague Spring', the reforms developed by the Dubcek
government having been strongly supported by public opinion. German
students organised important protest movements. France faced the greatest social movement of its modern history with mobilizations by students,
industrial workers and an amazing variety of social groups. Italy opened its
contentious *bienni rossi* (Albanese 2006). Even in countries where the level
of mobilization was lower, activists and organised groups—mostly youth-
ful—challenged the established order and developed new lifestyles. Let us
just mention the Dutch 'Kabouters' and 'Provos', the Internationale Situ-
ationiste, the civil rights movement in Ulster, the first student strike in the
history of Yugoslavia in Belgrade, anti-Franco demonstrations in Madrid.
An enormous number of conferences and scholarly books, but also novels,
films and biographies, has documented these historical moments. The details
of the events, the causes and meanings of those months of mobilizations,
should thus be clear, even over-investigated, on the long shelves of this library. However, most social scientists would agree that writing about '68 is
a major challenge because of—rather than thanks to—the amazing mass of

interpretations that serve to shroud the 'events', compared to the relatively limited amount of precise, empirical investigations into the actors, events or social morphology data. Even the time frame of '68 is unclear. Should one focus on the core moment of mobilizations during the years 1968–69? Is it not methodologically sounder to make sense of these events over a longer time frame? But which one: 1962–81 for France, as in the landmark book edited by Artières and Zancarini (2008), or the time of the 'baby boomers' (1945–69) as another French historian suggests (Sirinelli 2003)? *Génération,* the best-selling nonfiction narrative of the French '68 covers the years 1963–75. Would it be better to think of '68 as the apex of the 1960s? Gitlin (1987) locates these events between 1958 and 1971, whereas Marwick (1998) extends them to 1974. The selection of a time frame would define which movements would be connected to '68, the outcome of these events being the emergence of organizations (especially terrorist ones) linked to their decay, as well as the birth of other entities (feminism, ecology) challenging their legacy.

But even if we imagine that scientific agreement could be reached on the *whos* and *whens* of events, as well as the *how* of methodological approach, a new challenge arises. How can access be gained to sources and research developed over the past forty years, in a great many countries? For the researcher, this would entail having command of many languages.[1] Moreover, some countries, such as Italy and France, have given birth to a cottage industry of research, whereas there is much less available about Eastern Europe.

And as Bracke (2012) has suggested, Southern and Northern Europe seem to belong to a study area so different that research results are poorly connected. It is thus not surprising that comparative studies are rare (Fraser et al. 1988). And even excellent books are more parallel case studies than springboards for global interpretive frameworks. This point is highlighted by Horn in his *The Spirit of '68* (2008), perhaps the book compiling the richest variety of sources in different languages. The recent work of Gildea, Mark and Warring (2013), which assembling the resources of oral history, pays more attention to the Eastern '68s (Poland, Czechoslovakia). The book takes the risky stance of having a truly comparative structure, questioning the different ways of becoming and being an activist, and comparing the importance of faith, the challenge of violence, the surprises of unforeseen social encounters which were both common experience, and major differences among European radicals.

Being aware of these challenges, this chapter is based on three methodological choices. The first of these will be to reason in a large time frame. Massive demonstrations, waves of strikes and violent unrest were indeed visible in most European countries, mostly between 1967 and 1973. If the 'events' of '68 can be located in short or mid-size time frames, the influence of this historical moment of mobilization, comparable only to 1848 in Europe, goes far beyond. The short '68 'events' have, for years, structured social movement repertoires, targets and legitimacy in European polities.

The second choice harks back to the hermeneutics versus empirical sides of the cottage industry publishing on '68. Social research needs theory to develop empirical fieldwork, and such reflexive fieldwork produces theoretical outputs. Our choice is thus to focus on the best of empirical studies. Should we go as far as completely ignoring the flow of interpretations based on the frail basis of personal remembrances or superficial investigations, or the production of fast thinkers using '68 as a peg for their soft concepts (individualism, post-industrialism, narcissistic society)? The answer is clearly no. In France and Italy, books and interpretive discourses which are sociologically hollow have had an enormous influence. They institutionalised explanations and memories of '68, making it something taken for granted, even among sociologists. It is thus a sociological imperative that is paying attention to their social effects and criticizing their fallacies.

The third option would be to consider '68 to be as much an unsolved puzzle as something having definitively received its explanations and obituaries. Making sociological sense of the range of the European '68s is a challenge only partially achieved, a puzzle whose solutions might be found in a solid and consensual body of research. And the issue of understanding '68 may also mean understanding part of the 1980s and beyond, since a generation of activists remained committed to a range of causes through their (unusually long) militant careers. Would it be excessive to suggest that the keys to understanding the present are also linked to the long '68? Among the casualties of these years of contention lies probably the master frame—the central ideological resource of most twentieth-century mobilizations: the Marxist toolkit—with its references to social class, and to economic exploitation as the origin of unjust societies—as the blueprint for a socialist future. The topicality of '68 could also originate in the question: why was there such a critical spirit among the privileged generations of baby-boomers, compared with the more difficult emergence of great mobilizations among populations and generations facing such discouraging experiences in contemporary Europe?

This short exploration of the '68 movements will be threefold. The first part briefly suggests that many of the initial empirical investigations of the May(s) developed—among European researchers reflecting on what they perceived as the radical 'newness' of these mobilizations—a framework that was at once stimulating and full of dead ends. The second part addresses the irresistible rise in the late 1970s and 1980s of a highly selective and politically biased memory-doxa on the '68 movements. The final pages will try to highlight current interpretive challenges as well as innovative research directions.

'68 as the Emergence of New Social Movements: What If Sociology Were Overbidding on Its Objects?

An extraordinary blossoming of mobilizations sprung from '68. The occupation (red flag at the balcony) of the building of the *Fédération Française de Football* by amateur players and sports journalists, criticizing the 'Mafia of coaches'—the 'hereditary system' of appointment at the head of the organization—is just one surprising expression of this diversity. When Melucci developed his mapping of the actors of '68 (1977: 150), he needed thirteen categories: feminism, sexual politics, consumerism, ecology, urban struggles, regional movements, ethnic groups, students, youth culture, anti-institutional protest, new working class, public service users and neo-religious movements. In the realm of European social sciences, '68 frequently triggered a renewal of reflection on social movements—which occasionally took off. What is striking here is the high level of agreement between academics from different countries (especially in Germany with K. Eder and C. Offe, Italy with A. Melucci and France with A. Touraine, later Reichmann and Fernandez Buey in Spain) around the idea that so-called new social movements (NSM) • that emerged in the wake of '68[2] were founded on new modes of action, new claims, in challenging classic conceptions of political participation, and ultimately in blurring the centrality of class conflict. Though NSM theory appears to be a European theory inspired by the European movements of '68, its impact extended to the whole academic community of social movement scholars thanks to the gradual convergence of American and European scholars that had taken place in the 1990s (see introduction to this volume).

Beyond its contribution to social movement studies, the '68 movement has left a legacy rich in social theory. Melluci's analysis of the growing importance of symbolic power and the role of science and information in power relationships remains illuminating, as are his reflections on the endless growth in social and institutional controls on lifestyles, bodies and cognitive tools. Many of Touraine's ambitious pages (1978) on what he describes as the *société programmée* and its new repertoires of social control triggering the resistance of modern social movements remain worthy of debate. But it is possible to admire the thought-provoking dimensions of this analysis and yet question the analytical system to which they belong.

Does that fact that 'newness' is a good fit for speaking of wine or fashion justify its use by academics to rate the value of theories? Were not many 'old' movements mobilised on qualitative issues such as, for example, the 1880s May Day demonstrations' demands for an eight-hour working day that would open up access to leisure and education? Using data from police recordings of demonstrations in France in the 1980s, Fillieule (1996) shows the vision of contemporary protest as mainly targeting post-materialist claims to be a myth. Did not the founding manifesto of French trade union-ism—the *Charte d'Amiens*—exclude any connection between trade unionism and political parties? Conversely, are long investigations needed to identify that in Germany, France or the Netherlands former NSM leaders have be-come national members of parliament, European members of parliament or politicians? Where are the green parties or the 'femocrats' (Hoskyns 1996) influencing EU gender policies coming from? The interactionist notion of 'career', in not subjecting its users to the pitfalls and teleology of 'natural his-tory', is probably more useful in understanding the trajectories of movement and leaders. We might also ask where those movements once depicted as the carriers of historical change are now, in many European countries. De-spite success stories in Scotland and Catalonia, how many regionalist move-ments have quickly vanished? Such has been the fate of organised feminism and consumer organizations in many countries. Melucci wisely noticed that, paradoxically, certain NSM, in denouncing the most disciplinarian and archaic dimensions of domination (the prison system, penalization of abortion), helped modernist factions of rulers get rid of these backward institutions. Combining the 'social' and the 'artistic' criticism of society (Boltanski and Chiapello 1999), the celebration of autonomy by NSM was not unambiguous. The desire for individual autonomy has sometimes been channelled into an over-commitment of individuals—body and soul—for the benefit of companies in participative management. It has been hijacked as a Trojan horse for the organised destruction of collective solidarity in the workplace. Demands for new rights have also given rise to new markets. Duyvendak (in Kriesi et al. 1995) shows, in the Dutch case, that once gay rights were established, the survival of a strong feeling of 'we-ness' is only one aspect—the rise of a market in gay meeting places, shops and social events is another.

Because it was in very close, sometimes over-friendly, relation with the movements it studied, Touraine's 'sociological intervention' was a resource for a rich, almost insider's knowledge of NSM. Combined with a kind of messianic quest for modernity's social historic movement, this closeness may have been ambiguous. Sociologists often paid more attention to in-depth interaction with activists and their discourse than to the objectification of actors and networks—as is only too clear when re-reading, for instance *La prophétie anti-nucléaire* (Touraine 1980). There is a scientific price to be paid for over-identification with the claims made by one's research objects. Here is another methodological legacy of '68.

'68 as the Cunning of Liberal Reason: When Repentant Activists and Media Intellectuals Beat Sociology in Memory Battles

Although '68 has sometimes spoken for itself in books and frameworks by the NSM analysts, it was soon spoken for by a small group of media intellectuals and event interpreters in countries such as France and Italy (and the United States). By the end of the 1970s a *doxa*—an official memory—which has served to straitjacket the events, was established internationally.

May '68 Revisited and Tamed: The French Conjuring Trick

In a book that was a stimulating revisitation of the French May, US historian Kristin Ross (2004) studied *May '68 and its afterlives*. Indeed, the May '68 at the core of media images, social memory and sometimes academic discussions is the result of fierce interpretive battles.

Two journalists, ex-participants in the movement, wrote *Génération*, which soon became the best-selling and quasi-official narrative of the French May. The book can be read as a sort of well-documented social movement thriller. It also provides an almost chemically pure sample of the official memory of the French '68. This memory—as history organised in a coherent and selective narrative—is based on six major interpretive operations.

The first of these defines '68 as a student-centred event mainly located in Paris, whose major actors are leaders of leftist organizations. Such framing implies that what happened in the provinces was of minor importance, that trade unions were second-ranking actors and that the working-class strike—the biggest ever in French history—was less significant than the upsurge of the *Quartier Latin*. This first reframing of events is combined with a vision of the strategic actors as belonging mostly to one of two Parisian networks: the older generation of the sixties dissenters inside the UEC (the Communist student organization) and the younger circles of Maoist intellectuals which was to give rise to the *Union des Jeunesses Communistes Marxistes-Léninistes* (UJC-ML), and later to the *Gauche Prolétarienne*—connected to the elite *Ecole Normale Supérieure*. Such a selection of the heroes worthy of being on the official picture of '68 pushes out of the frame thousands of middle-ranking activists, trade unionists, leaders of local strikes and mobilizations. A third dimension of the official narrative of May is its twin focus on ideology. Significant emphasis is given to the fascination of many leaders with the highbrow-modernist strand of Marxist ideology (Althusser), hybrid variants (Marx and Freud or Reich) or exotic blends (Mao, Castro). Activists were misperceiving society through the red-tinted spectacles of ideology. The narrative shows how threatening and dangerous these beliefs were. They had totalitarian potential. Revolutionary activists would have done terrible things to subject society to their dogmatic and out-dated vision of class struggle.

The official story does not ignore the need for a happy ending, which is supplied by three further interpretive frames. The first of these could be referred to as the 'Road to Damascus'. Here, the shock of the 'real' (Solzhenitsyn's *Gulag Archipelago,* the Vietnamese boat people) combined with the belated clear-sightedness of Maoist leaders discovering liberal thinkers or rediscovering Jewish spirituality was said to have refrained activists from going too far. One more framing operation would then suggest how the true and good '68 in fact had a festive dimension, how it was a libertarian insurrection against all institutional constraints, without any real violence. Soon developed by Regis Debray (1978), then in contributions from philosophers such as Lipovetski (1983) and Ferry and Renaud (1987), a final and strategic interpretive framing suggests that May '68 had been a Hegelian cunning of Reason and History. Whilst its actors believed they were playing the heroic remake of 1917, a mock revolution allowed modernization of the archaic structures of a *société bloquée.* It opened the door to the triumph of hedonist individualism—and to the slow death of ideological illusions. The true and final impact of '68 was the victory of a culture of permissive individualism, the dissolution of the uptight society through the new duties of pleasure, consumption and self-expression. Many movement leaders and actors, in tune with this new *zeitgeist,* even became the winners and successful social climbers of the new, cool and modernised capitalism.[3] The interpretive system suggested here was established as the grand narrative of '68 as early as the mid-1980s, constantly fed by a flow of books, films and novels. As Fukuyama's quote suggests, no book on high social theory could help making its own small comment on '68. The *doxa*'s strength also arises out of the hectic after-sale service of '68 by media-savvy ex-leaders and recycled *nouveaux philosophes.* Endlessly lecturing media audiences on May's dark sides and right interpretation represented, for them, a chance to both remain socially visible and invent a new style of 'media intellectual' (Pinto 1991). The weight of this *doxa* does not exclude minor re-interpretations. Modernization can go too far. This was a dimension of Sarkozy's 2006 attack on the terrible costs of '68's legacy of hedonism, paid for by the disappearance of respect for authority and hard work, the crisis in family ties and stability. The '68ers were also depicted as a selfish generation—overstaying their welcome in power and lecturing the young whilst having accumulated more than their fair share of the cake.

Variations on a French Tune

No doubt that the interpretations of '68 in Europe cannot be limited to the French case and the cottage industry of its explanations. It seems however possible to argue that, with significant national variations, the interpretive framework described in the French case is applicable to the construction of most memories and interpretations of '68. Any comparison with research on the US case (Collier and Horowitz 1989; Stephens 1998; Morgan 2010) and the building of a mainstream memory of the 'movement' years would, though, show that the arguments used to devaluate, or suggest a 'reassuring' reading of these events are very similar on both sides of the Atlantic (see also, for the UK, Salter 1973). One of the most shared schemes is the 'Perversity-Futility-Jeopardy' trilogy identified by Hirschman as the 'rhetoric of reaction'.

A different and partial convergence may be suggested between Germany and Italy. In both countries, terrorism (RAF, *Brigate Rossi*) and its management by state-policing (Della Porta 1995) weighed heavily on memory. The experiences of '68 in both countries had also comprised festive moments, the discovery of free speech and explosions of subjectivity (Passerini 1988). Italian activists had even created a level of connection with industrial workers which was unparalleled in Europe (Sommier 1998). However, violence, murder, bombing and years of imprisonment finally crushed competing memories of '68. The *nouveaux philosophes* scheme, which described any attempt at radical change as opening the doors to totalitarianism and the rule of 'man-eaters', could mobilise the reality of blood and death here. The crushing of '68 under the tombstone of terrorism was especially effective in Germany, with remembrance of Weimar opening the doors to Nazi rule, the strength of anti-communism and the low level of connection between the *Sozialistische Deutsche Studentenbund* (SDS) student movement and the unionised German working class. The Italian situation was more complex. As in France, former activists with strong media resources—*i pentiti* (the repentants)—had a significant influence (Capanna 2008), hammering the image of a *Sessantotto* made up of violence and dogmatic ideology. But the lasting presence of 'alternative' organizations, and the commitment of major academics and former activists, guaranteed the survival of and laid the groundwork for a new momentum towards better informed, more scientific approaches.

For the practical reasons mentioned above, and because memory battles are still in progress, presenting an overview of the current vision of '68 in Europe is more a task for collective research than something in which clear conclusions can yet be drawn. We would however suggest what might be coined a 'cultural hypothesis'. In a nutshell, the political legacy of '68—the connection of its actors with Marxist ideologies, the weight of working-class claims and mobilization, the criticism of capitalism—is something which receives limited and shrinking support, beyond the small world of leftist organizations and theorists.

Conversely, variations on the French 'modernist', 'cunning of liberal reason' frames are visible in many discourses of interpretation, in the press and media, both in academic research and during each commemoration. The core interpretive scheme here suggests that '68 had a lasting, and probably useful, influence in changes toward less formal, less frozen visions of culture and behaviours. This contentious year brought in more equality, less hypocrisy in gender relations, freer expression of sexual desires, lifestyles and identities. It shook up the most hierarchical, authoritarian and old-fashioned institutions and organizational habits. This can be seen in more informal clothing styles and growing first-name terms in direct interactions. More intimate, emotionally richer parent-child relationships resulted from '68. The great divide between the profane, everyday culture and Culture with a capital C, the transmission of which was the task of schools and cultural institutions—and serious media such as the Reithian BBC or the early French ORTF and Italian RAI—was transformed by '68 into a frontier blurring the hierarchies of Culture, entertainment and consumption. Strangely, this concept is almost never considered by the analysts of '68, yet the common denominator of these changes is precisely the Eliasian category of 'informalization' (Wouters 2007): a general reduction of differences in power between generations, classes, genders, a less disciplinarian and—paradoxically—more spontaneous and more reflexive way of managing everyday interdependencies.

Arthur Marwick's huge book on the 1960s is probably a significant academic sample of the analytical frame suggested here. Because it works for older readers as a mix of rediscovery of *temps perdu* and a *Lonely Planet* travel guide to the sixties, *The Sixties* is rich and pleasant. Its interpretation is clear: there was no such thing as the revolution promised by the programs of what he calls the 'Great Marxizant Fallacy'; although these years did give rise to a permissive 'cultural revolution', or 'if we prefer the route of semantic caution, then 'social and cultural transformation' would do very well' (1998: 801). But 'social' in Marwick's chapters is mostly identified with lifestyles and cultural consumption rather than any serious attention to social morphology, welfare policies or the changing patterns of class relationships. By focusing on cultural changes, Marwick could only discover the cultural legacy of '68. His unchallengeable affirmation that (political) revolution did not happen during the European 1960s substitutes one fallacy for another. The shadow of the 'great cultural reduction' covers up the fact that '68 was also—and more than once firstly—challenging power balance, including that of symbolic powers, and it fails to address the links and continuities between '68 activism and the mobilizations and counter-mobilizations of the 1980s and 1990s.

'68 as a Puzzle yet to Be Solved: Bringing Sociology Back In

Towards a Paradigmatic Shift?

The dominant orthodoxy, in its academic and journalistic versions, has been strongly challenged over the past ten years. Ross's 'Afterlives' of '68 posed some embarrassing questions, the most striking of which was her attack on teleological approaches, the neglect of serious fieldwork. She also highlighted the fallacy of deducing from the trends and events of the 1980s or 1990s the hidden meaning of '68. How was it possible to brush under the carpet—as a minor detail, or as the final spasm of a dying world—the participation of millions of industrial workers, beginning the greatest wave of strikes ever in France, Italy and other countries? Did not such a viewpoint underrate the importance of material claims—of struggles targeted on changes in the balance of power in politics, on the definition of an acceptable scale of fortune and income differences—beyond those demanding freer sexual expression or permissive attitudes to minority lifestyles? May '68 did have a festive and happy dimension, suddenly allowing access to expression and free speech to a great variety of persons and groups. Yet was it wise to forget that it was not always peaceful, and that a significant level of violence existed in the policing of protest, in the workplace?

The 2008 commemorations, with the usual tide of books by French, Italian and Anglophone publishers, gave a new momentum to this heterodox approach, easily discernible in France in the contributions of a large group of historians (Artières and Zancarini 2008) and sociologists and political scientists (Damamme, Gobille, Matonti and Pudal 2008). A choice shared by both books was to combine micro-studies and empirical investigations on the strikes, mobilizations in specific cities or among varied social groups, rather than to launch an umpteenth grand theory of '68. Activists were interviewed. Investigations were launched on forgotten issues such as the disappearance, post '68, of the population of *bonnes à tout faire* (housemaids) as a symbol of a crisis in forms of domination that were based on almost permanent physical proximity. The production of new data breaks with the endless game of interpreting existing data (more often of interpreting interpretations), sometimes indulged in by media-savvy former leaders of '68. Historians comb archives, meet retired trade unionists, investigate the particularities of the young rural workers who discovered factory work in the sixties. Sociologists collect activists' life stories, map their abandonment of commitments and re-investments in new kinds of movements. Political scientists (Pagis 2014) investigate 'alternative' innovations such as in the organization of schools, promoting a different definition of knowledge transmission.

In its best contributions, this flow of research combines macro- and micro-sociological approaches. The issues of social mobility and class structures are called into question. What exactly were the opportunities for upward mobility—the likelihood of reaching an occupation quite different from that of one's parents—for students whose first defining characteristic in many European countries (Bourdieu and Passeron 1964) was precisely that they belonged to an 'uppity' middle- and working-class generation, rather than being 'pampered offspring' imagined by Fukuyama, with no experience of 'sacrifice'? Strangely such questions, though perhaps lacking in intellectual grandeur, mobilised little attention in much of the previous avalanche of books and research. Current research—Von der Goltz (2013) on the DDR dissenters of '68, or Serenelli (2013) on Italian communards—also value the micro, face-to-face contact with yesterday's actors. If one can object that its interview-gathering is, once more, focused on the leaders and pays limited attention to the experience of rank-and-file activists, Gildea, Mark and Warring's (2013, see especially chapter 1) collective research clearly takes part in this refreshing brainstorm among scholars of the '68 years. Such approaches allow for a better understanding of the subjective experience of becoming an activist, of the emotional aspects of commitment, of the reflexive return on one's past. They give flesh, speech and more complexity to those often obscured by labels (leftists, feminists). They reveal the surprising differences, from one city to another, between local networks of activists. Such a change in research strategies is visible in France, where a multi-site team (SOMBRERO) collects life stories and maps the changing networks and organizational structures of leftists, trade unionists and feminists in five cities. Accornero leads a comparable project on the 'Long term effects of political engagement in Portugal and Spain'. In Italy, recent years have seen more books, more empirical research, and more attention to the variety of trajectories and experiences of the *Sessantontini* (Rossi 2008). This multifaceted work in progress raises new questions.

Rediscovering May '68 in All Its Versions

Sociology does not claim to be able to make sense of the 'true' and ultimate meaning of the various '68s, yet it can provide the data and interpretive tools for the development of one's own reflexive practice on these years.

A first critical re-reading of the '68s would challenge the opposition between materialist claims—which have been buried with the 'old', working-class,
part of '68—and the blossoming post-materialist claims on lifestyles, culture
and identities. Both dimensions have existed in every European country.
When the official narrative only highlights the claims that it considers as
qualitative or linked to new lifestyles, it simply betrays the very content and
meaning of the claims and mottos of most of the millions of Belgian, Italian
or French workers whose strikes almost always had goals concerning wages
or working conditions. The key argument here is that all empirical investigations reveal that—beyond the opposition between materialist and post-materialist issues—most of the claims developed by the actors of '68 were about
power and its distribution. For the most radical and politicised groups, this
claim was expressed in the promise of a different society, expressed in visions
of communism *autogestion, potere operaio.* Such goals were certainly those
of a small minority, even among the mobilised actors. But such an empirical objection does not close the debate on power. Whatever the mobilised
groups or however materialist the demands, mobilizations were firstly targeting power disparities between men and women, experts and laypeople,
academics and students, physicians and patients. Many industrial strikes had
a qualitative dimension, expressing revolt against the lack of respect (Vigna
2007; see also Maravall 1978 about Spain), the reduction of the workforce to
a mechanical 'means of production', incapable of bringing about a reflexive
contribution to the organization of production. A significant proportion of
farmer mobilizations can also be linked to their feeling of being trapped in
a new system of business relations, transforming them into powerless sub-
contractors of food-processing companies. Beyond the reality of its 'cultural'
dimensions, challenging the established distribution of wealth and division
of labour in society and debating about what could be a just polity was part
and parcel of most of '68's mobilizations. This point invites thinking long-
term continuities both in the central role gained by contentious politics and
in the lasting struggle against imbalances in power-knowledge relationships.
When they question the abuse of symbolic authority by science, technology
or economics, when they put on the political agenda issues concerning the
regulation of financial flows or the organization of fair international trade,
many among the most significant social movements of the 2000s suggest
continuities with the sixties.

Looking back at the various '68s also invites us to make sense of what
Gobille (in Dammame et al. 2008) terms the 'heterodoxic vocation'. Why
did a generation whose career opportunities and 'affluent' economic background seemed more promising than those of today's twentysomethings produce so many long-distance activists? May '68 was also an amazing moment

of collapse of what Berger and Luckmann call the 'conceptual and social ma-chineries of Universe Maintenance'. Explanations for this social earthquake have rarely been convincing. The 'frustration' approach—which seeks to ex-plain activist motivation as a result of intuitive knowledge of the diminished value of their academic qualifications—is a better fit for the next generation, born in the 1980s or 1990s. It cannot make sense of the working-class mo-bilization. The 'cunning of reason' approach says nothing about the tim-ing of mobilizations. Reducing analytical choices in order to make sense of the anti-institutional upsurge as an unconscious anticipation of the needs of modern capitalism or the expression of repressed upward social mobility ambitions suggests a weak and Machiavellian vision of social action. Com-bining the macro of social morphology, the micro of trajectories and the meso of local histories and configurations would open the doors to a more sociological understanding. It would reconsider the importance of Catholic youth movements in the production of activist dispositions. It would re-think leftist movements as also being 'machineries' producing services such as the taming of an academia that is often opaque to newcomers, the supply of political positioning allowing a kind of loyalty to the parental social group for upwardly mobile youth, an elegant way of being Marxist and radical for those educated in a deep anti-communist tradition. A sociologically revisited '68 would combine the impact of social mobility and the changing profiles of young industrial workers. It would perceive '68 as being a rare moment of anomy due to massive social mobility. It would pay attention to the inven-tion of a teenage culture, the crisis of symbolic order and how these things are reflected in the critical perception of all established forms of the division of work in society. It should also question—as Southern Europe remains like a white area on the map of our understanding—what was the specific con-tribution of the youth reactions to interminable or ferocious dictatorships in Greece, Spain and Portugal.

Looking for an articulation between the short '68 'events' and the long '68 years would also mean exploring the activists' life stories and trajectories. One of the results of '68 was that it produced a generation of activists du-rably disposed to investing its energies in social problems and new mobili-zations. Collecting life stories from '68 activists often means travelling with them through decades of the history of the mobilizations in their city or country. Such activist longevity has been shown in France (Neveu, in Dam-mame et al. 2008), for example. It is also visible in the history of the young protesters of the Greek 'long sixties' (Kornetis 2013) or in the sixties' roots of the activists who would later take part in the Portuguese 'Eyelets' revolution' of 1974 (Accornero 2013). Networks of ex-activists enabled the survival of abeyance structures. Former '68ers re-invested skills and energies in the global justice movement or environmental mobilizations, with ATTAC (Action for a Tobin Tax to Assist the Citizen), for example, in France and other countries. Collecting life stories also means understanding how ex-activists have behaved in their jobs (mainly in the public sector) or in voluntary associations, as social change entrepreneurs, reforming institutions, redefining roles, challenging authoritarian routines. Such facts have fed the nostalgic celebration of a stainless and generous generation of veterans—as well as, conversely, the criticism of a cumbersome old guard reluctant to leave leadership positions. It may be more illuminating to question how such facts challenge the official memory. Did all the activists become happy consumers and individualist social climbers? Were their renewed commitments purely cultural, disconnected from the question of power? Do changes in European societies over the past forty years result only from the great juggernaut of the neo-liberal market and its heralds of individualism?

Is investigating events that took place almost fifty years ago worthy of more research, or would this be no more than rummaging through cold ashes? We hope to have shown that sociological exploration of this past could have at least three useful impacts. The first of these could be a critical re-reading of the innovations and—more often—dead ends of NSM theory. The second arises out of on-going scientific challenges which further understanding of this major historical event—its continuities as well as its irreducible singularity. The last could be getting rid of the mixture of crass ignorance and scornful arrogance that is condensed in Fukuyama's opening quote, and so visible in the *doxa* on '68.

These years are here to stay and to inspire social science and civic commitments.

Erik Neveu (born 1952) is professor of political science at the University of Rennes. He has been head of Sciences-Po Rennes and vice chair of the ECPR. His books and publications are especially dedicated to social movements, media and journalism, and cultural studies. Among his recent books: *Bourdieu and the Journalistic Field* (Polity Press, 2004 with Rod Benson, eds.), *Boys Don't Cry: Les coûts de la masculinité* (PUR, 2012, with C. Guionnet and D. Dulong, eds.) and *La construction des problémes publics* (Armand Colin, 2015).

Notes

1. This contribution does not claim to escape this limitation, since it is too dependent on research concerning Italy and France.

2. For a more complete discussion of these theories see Cohen (1985), Cox and Flesher Fominaya (2013) and Neveu (2015).
3. The story of this memory-building, or memory-mummification, is fully developed in my contribution to Baumgarten, Daphi and Ullrich (2014).

References

Accornero, G. 2013. 'Contentious Politics and Student Dissent in the Twilight of the Portuguese Dictatorship: Analysis of a Protest Cycle'. *Democratization* 1, no. 1: 1–20.

Albanese, G. 2006. *I due bienni rossi del Novecento: 1919–20 e 1968–69*. Roma: Ediesse.

Artières P. and M. Zancarini, eds. 2008. *68 Une histoire collective*. Paris: La Découverte.

Baumgarten, B., P. Daphi and P. Ullrich, eds. 2014. *Conceptualizing Culture in Social Movement Research*. London: Palgrave Macmillan.

Boltanski, L., and E. Chiappello. 1999. *Le nouvel esprit du capitalisme*. Paris: Gallimard.

Bourdieu, P. 1979. *La Distinction*. Paris: Minuit.

Bourdieu, P., and J. C. Passeron. 1964. *Les héritiers*. Paris: Minuit.

Bracke, M. A. 2012. 'One Dimensional Conflict? Recent Scholarship on 1968 and the Limitation of the Generation Concept'. *Journal of Contemporary History* 77, no. 3: 638–46.

Capanna, M. 2008. *Il Sessantotto al futuro*. Milano: Garzanti.

Cohen, J. 1985. 'Strategy or Identity: New Theoretical Paradigms and Contemporary Social Movements'. *Social Research* 52 no. 4: 663–716.

Collier, P., and D. Horowitz. 1989. *Destructive Generation: Second Thoughts about the 60s*. New York: Summit Books.

Damamme, D., B. Gobille, F. Matonti and B. Pudal, eds. 2008. *Mai–Juin 68*. Paris: éd. de l'Atelier.

Debray, R. 1978. *Modeste contribution aux discours et cérémonies du dixième anniversaire*. Paris: Maspero.

Della Porta, D. 1995. *Social Movements, Political Violence and the State*. Cambridge: Cambridge University Press.

Eder, K. 1982. 'A New Social Movement?' *Telos* 20: 5–21.

Ferry, L., and A. Renaud. 1987. *68–86 Itinéraires de l'Individu*. Paris: Gallimard.

Fillieule, O. 1997. *Stratégies de la rue*. Paris: Presses de Sciences Po.

Flesher Fominaya, C., and L. Cox. 2013, *Understanding European Social Movements: New Social Movements, Global Justice Struggles, Anti-Austerity Protest*. London: Routledge.

Fraser, R, ed. 1988. *1968: A Student Generation in Revolt. An International Oral History*. New York: Pantheon Books.

Fukuyama, F. 1992. *The End of History and the Last Man*. New York: Avon Books.

Gildea, R., J. Marks and A. Warring, eds. 2013. *Europe's 1968: Voices of Revolt*. Oxford: Oxford University Press.

Gitlin, T. 1987. *The Sixties, Years of Hope, Days of Rage*. New York: Bantam.

Goltz, von der, A. 2013. 'Making Sense of East Germany's 1968: Multiple Trajectories and Contrasting Memories'. *Memory Studies* 6, no. 1: 53–69.

Horn, G. R. 2008. *The Spirit of '68. Rebellion in Western Europe and North America (1956–1976)*. Oxford: Oxford University Press.

Hoskyns, C., ed. 1996. *Integrating Gender: Women, Law and Politics in the E.U.* London: Verso.

Kornetis, K. 2013. *Children of the Dictatorship: Student Resistance, Cultural Politics and the 'Long 1960s' in Greece.* London: Berghahn Books.

Kriesi, H., R. Koopmans, J. W. Duyvendak and M. G. Giugni 1995. *New Social Movements in Western Europe: A Comparative Analysis.* Minneapolis: University of Minnesota Press.

Lipovetski, G. 1983. *L'ère du vide: Essai sur l'individualisme contemporain.* Gallimard: Paris.

Maravall, J. L. 1978. *Dictadura y Disentimiento Político: Obreros y Estudiantes bajo el Franquismo.* Madrid: Alfaguara.

Marwick, A. 1998. *The Sixties.* Oxford: Oxford University Press.

Melucci, A. 1977. *Sistema Politico, partiti e movimenti sociali.* Milano: Feltrinelli.

Morgan, E. 2010. *What Really Happened to the 1960s: How Mass Media Culture Failed American Democracy.* St. Lawrence: University Press of Kansas.

Neveu, E. 2015. *Sociologie des mouvements sociaux.* Paris: La Découverte.

Pagis, J. 2014. *Mai 68/ Un pavé dans leur histoire.* Paris: Presses de Sciences Po.

Passerini, L. 1988. *Autorittrato di Gruppo.* Firenze: Giunti.

Pinto, L. 1991. 'La Doxa Intellectuelle'. *Actes de la recherche en Sciences Sociales* 90: 95–103.

Riechmann, J., and F. Fernandez Buey. 1995. *Redes que dan libertad: Introduccion a los nuevos movimientos sociales.* Barcelona: Paidos.

Ross, K. *May '68 and Its Afterlives.* Chicago: University of Chicago Press.

Rossi, A. 2008. *A colpi di cuore: Storie del Sessantotto.* Roma: Laterza.

Serenelli, S. 2013. 'Private 1968 and the Margins: The Vicolo Cassini's Community in Macerata, Italy'. *Memory Studies* 6, no. 1: 91–104.

Sirinelli, J. F. 2003. *Les baby-Boomers—Une génération 1945–1969.* Paris: Fayard.

Sommier, I. 1998. *La violence politique et son deuil.* Rennes: PUR.

Stephens, J. 1998. *Anti-disciplinary Protest: Sixties Radicalism and Post-modernism.* Cambridge: Cambridge University Press.

Touraine, A., Z. Hegedus and F. Dubet and M. Wievorka. 1980. *La prophétie anti-nucléaire.* Paris: Seuil.

Vigna, X. 2007. *L'insubordination ouvrière dans les années 68.* Rennes: PUR.

Wouters, C. 2007. *Informalization: Manners and emotions since 1890.* London: Sage.

Chapter 2

Mobilizing for Democracy

The 1989 Protests in Central Eastern Europe[1]

Donatella Della Porta

Even though social movement organizations (SMOs) are increasingly recognised, in political as well as scientific debates, as important actors in
democratic processes, their performance during the different steps of the
democratization process has rarely been addressed in a systematic and comparative way. On the one hand, in fact, social movements have been far from
prominent in the literature on democratization, which has mainly focused
on either socioeconomic pre-conditions or elite behaviour (Bermeo 1997).
On the other, social movement scholars, until recently, have paid little attention to democratization processes, mostly concentrating their interest on
democratic countries (especially on the Western European and North American experiences) where conditions for mobilization are more favourable. In
some ways, this is related with the tendency of those scholars to focus on
movements they sympathise with, in part with a theoretical interest for new
social movements, considered as typical of democratic and modernised societies, as well as to some provincialism common to political science and sociology, in which macro-discipline social movement studies are more rooted.

This is true also for the cycle of democratization in Eastern Europe
which has been studied more by transitologists than by contentious politics
scholars. In general, eastern European countries had in fact been analysed
within area studies, characterised by specific visions of one-party states as
most hostile to democratization. Sovietology developed as an area especially
in the United States, and its focus of research on Eastern Europe continues
to remain visible after the democratization process. In fact, with few exceptions, Eastern European scholars, when at all, tended to collaborate more
with US partners than with European ones (Diani and Císař, 2014). A partial exception is Germany, where West German scholars contributed to the
debate on the reunification of the two Germanys, with some emphasis on
the traditional theme of German exceptionalism.

Notwithstanding this paucity, however, the existing research points have fuelled some interesting theoretical debates that I shall summarise in what follows, looking in turns at mobilizing resources in the democratization process and the main framing, as well as the political opportunities and constraints for those struggling for democracy. I will point to the eventfulness of protests during transition, looking at relational, cognitive and affective mechanisms.

Mobilizing Resources for Democracy

First accounts of revolutions—and even of waves of protest—are often influenced by the so-called 'immaculate conception syndrome' (Rupp and Taylor 1987): they seem to come from nowhere, and develop suddenly and 'spontaneously'. However, research has found that, rather than coming from the Virgin Mary, new movements develop upon previous movements, which help in structuring the mobilization. This was also the case in the shifting of authoritarian regimes of Eastern Europe as, while the Western types of SMOs were certainly difficult to find, the hybrid forms that have replaced totalitarianism tended to practice a modicum of tolerance towards various forms of nongovernmental organizations. Notwithstanding repression, various groupings often survived (or emerged), taking forms different from those of the so-called advanced democracies. Some (though very limited) free spaces, outside of state control, tended to be used as 'locales that lie outside the scrutiny of the regime and its agents' (Johnston 2011: 113). Social gatherings, neighbourhood associations, unions, study groups, and recreational, intellectual or religious organizations sometimes assumed a duplicitous character, allowing for the development of sites of opposition. Usually (at least partially) secretive, these spaces do grant some freedom to express one's own mind, representing 'small islands of free thought and speech' (Johnston 2011: 103). Within research on authoritarian regimes in Eastern Europe the concept of civil society has been used to refer to groups that have little possibility to protest, but nevertheless form a sort of oppositional infrastructure. In particular, in-depth research on Poland has stressed the networking capacity of civil society as an important resource for mobilization (Osa 2003).

Research on Eastern Europe paid particular attention to the ways in which some characteristics of the authoritarian regimes allowed, repression notwithstanding, for the development of free spaces and gradual development of social movements. According to some authors, repression thwarted civil society altogether. For instance, Killingsworth (2012) criticised the very idea of the existence of a civil society in communist Eastern Europe; given repression, the dissident groups there were not autonomous, constituting, at best, a 'totalitarian public sphere' that was dominated by the party. Other scholars countered, however, that in 1989, 'Civil society has turned out to be the surprising protagonist of the East European transitions' (Di Palma 1991: 49).

Even if the Leninist state offered very reduced spaces for free expression to non-political organizations—with no access to policy-makers, media or courts—networks acting as mobilizing structures did indeed exist. Areas of opposition emerged in working-class politics, as associations were often allowed in the workplace and the failure of official unions brought about demands for free unions (Lovenduski and Woodall 1987). Intellectuals—from students to artists—also publicly advocated freedom of expression. Churches mostly compromised with the regime, but also mobilised in independent peace movements. New social movements emerged, as in the West, on peace, environmental protection and women's rights. The term 'civil society' has often been used to describe these forms of opposition. As Giuseppe Di Palma observed, 'A civil society of sorts survived in Eastern Europe, not just as a conventional clandestine adversary but as a visible cultural and existential counterimage of communism's unique hegemonic project' (Di Palma 1991: 49).

The organizational structure was very horizontal: it concentrated in urban areas, was composed by highly educated people which were politicised by communism. Citizens needed little organization to mobilize (Goodwin 2001: 277), often staging their own contentious events in the spatial symbols of the mobilised regime. Coordination was then made possible through oppositional umbrella organizations, which were rather light and internally heterogeneous, as reflected in the self-definition as 'forums': the Civic Forum in Czechoslovakia, New Forum in the German Democratic Republic (GDR), or Democratic Forum in Hungary. The homogenizing characteristics of the regime have been said to be reflected in a homogeneous civil society, thus explaining why the demise of the Eastern European regimes was so sudden.

To what extent this rather thin civil society was able to drive the mass mobilization of the velvet revolutions is however a question; the two cases of so-called mobilization from below are particularly debated: the GDR and Czechoslovakia. Research on the GDR such as that of Opp, Voss and Gern (1989) downplayed the role of civil society organizations, emphasizing instead the rationality of individual 'exiters'. Other scholars countered that those who stress the individual mechanisms of changing preferences 'may overestimate the spontaneity of the protest of October 9 by overlooking the role of the dissidents in providing elementary means of coordination' (Pfaff

2006: 126). Moreover, as Pfaff noted, 'the evidence suggests that ordinary citizens did not join the mass demonstration in a disorderly fashion. It appears that informal groups provided vehicles for mobilization. A citizen's willingness to protest may be based less on formal organizational ties than on the support of family, friends and acquaintances' (ibid.: 129).

The capacity of the civil society organizations to lead the protest varied, however, over time and space. In the GDR, dissident groups and protest seemed to move together in only one specific moment of the transition period: the one that started in October and ended with the opening of the Wall on 9 November 1989. After that date, the main civil rights organizations lost ground. If on 25 September demonstrators carried 'We Stay Here' banners and on 9 October they stated 'We Are the People', on 9 November the slogan of the mass protests shifted to 'Wir sind ein Volk' ('We Are One People'), indicating support for reunification, a position that the civil society organizations tended to oppose (Jessen 2009).

Transnational Contacts and 1989

Transnational contacts among social movement organizations were very relevant in 1989. As Kuran noted, in the days following the fall of Czechoslovakia's communist regime, a banner in Prague read: 'Poland-10 years, Hungary-10 months, East Germany-10 weeks, Czechoslovakia-10 days' (1991: 42). During the 1989 events, decisions taken by neighbouring countries were clearly influential. In June, the elections in Poland, with Solidarity entering parliament, raised hope for peaceful change in the Eastern bloc. During the 1989 wave, 'the success of antigovernment demonstrations in one country inspired demonstrations elsewhere. In early November, Sofia was shaken by its first demonstration in four decades as several thousand Bulgarians marched on the National Assembly. Within a week, on the very day throngs broke through the Berlin Wall, Todor Zhivkov's thirty-five-year leadership came to an end, and his successor began talking of radical reforms' (ibid.: 39). As Saxonberg (2001) observed, while it took five weeks in the GDR for the size of protests to get beyond one hundred thousand, in Czechoslovakia it took just a few days for the marches to involve over five hundred thousand people.

Beyond imitation, there were also transnational contacts from below. In the 1980s, transnational cooperation had developed across Eastern Europe. There were, for instance, meetings between Hungarian and Polish opponents on the mountain bordering the two countries. As sort of political picnics, they were filmed and sent to the Western media (Urban 1990). There were also contacts between the oppositional groups in the various Central and

Eastern European countries, and common initiatives that resonated with a shared history between the East German, Polish, Hungarian and Czechoslovakian opposition, such as protest action on the occasion of the various anniversaries of the Hungarian revolution or Charter 77. While hope in the support from Western parties and governments was followed by disillusionment (Poppe 1995: 256), peace activists in the GDR developed contacts with the peace movement. Women for peace in the GDR were in contact with other groups of women for peace; they wrote open letters in solidarity with the march against nuclear missiles from Berlin to Geneva (Kukutz 1995).

Work with Western pacifist organizations was pursued as 'détente from below'. Started by Charter 77, cooperation included in East and West Germany the Initiative for blocks-freedom in Europe. Relations developed especially with the Greens, via the peace movement. There were also close relations between the GDR opposition and Federal Republic of Germany (FRG) social movements, including solidarity against repression. Protest campaigns were carried out together by East and West German environmentalists against the export of West German garbage in the GDR, with blockades and police intervention on both sides at the end of 1988. Films about pollution in the GDR were exported and circulated in the West. Counterinformation included contacts with Western media, such as Radio Glasnost in West Berlin, collaboration with the newspaper *Taz*, and documentary films with the Berlin radio and television broadcasting service SFB.

Transnational social movement organizations were involved as well. In a comparative analysis of Latin America and Eastern Europe, Patricia Chilton (1995) suggested that peaceful and successful regime transformation is facilitated by civil society development and transnational exchanges. In particular, she pointed at the role of civil society development as détente from below.

These transnational linkages acted as additional resources in legitimating the opposition. In Czechoslovakia and the GDR, even if the national civil society was not particularly strong, it was embedded in very dense transnational networks. Hungarian activists contributed to this transnationalization, as they were more free to travel and host meetings (thus, for example, when the preparatory committee of the Helsinki Citizens' Assembly was arrested in Prague, they reconvened in Budapest).

Framing 1989

Talking about the eventful democratization in Eastern Europe, I mentioned cognitive mechanisms such as a growth of generality and politicization

(Della Porta 2014). These built upon diagnostic, prognostic and motivational frames that had developed in previous years and were subsequently transformed into action.

Within an initially moderate discourse, the corruption of those in power was contrasted with the honesty and commitment of civil society. References to corruption indeed allowed the protection of an 'original' idea of society as a positive point of reference, which had been betrayed by those in power. In fact, given the traditional Communist asceticism, even relatively small signs of enrichment of the elites produced indignation. This was all the more true when economic difficulties made the internal inequalities not only more visible but also more symbolically offensive. Especially for those who had believed in the reformability of real socialism, the frame of corruption allowed the maintenance of some loyalty to past beliefs. For others, corruption was proof of the inherent dysfunction of the communist system (ibid.).

The appeal to the nation against those who had betrayed this nation and its ideas was an important moment in the definition of a mobilizing discourse. The politicization of ethnicity was particularly relevant during and after some transitions in Eastern Europe, where democratization was accompanied by increasingly ethnic-based politics. This happened especially in countries that were ethnically heterogeneous and in which elites competed through the adoption of a nationalist discourse, in a search for alternative identities (Harris 2002). In all cases, however, there was a reference to a national history, reflected not only in the mobilization of the theatres in Czechoslovakia but also in the debate on German identities in the GDR, as well as, in general, in a frequent use of national celebrations. In all CEE countries, the opposition had initially taken mainly moderate tones, appealing not for a breakdown of the regime, but for reforms that would enable challenges to the corruption of its essence. Either instrumentally or because of a deeper belief, the calls were for a defence of various proclaimed principles against the lies of the regime. A combination of appeals to the nation and stigmatization of corruption helped to find a common denominator among disparate social groups and political ideas, at the same time allowing them to build upon legitimated ideas and widespread symbols.

Even if with different declinations, there was in the opposition a preference for dialogue rather than confrontation with the regime, as well as a tendency towards reforms (Fehr 1995). Still debatable is the degree to which this moderation was a strategic move to maintain some space for expression. Even though reformist framing enabled finding some interstices inside the regime, an instrumental justification is not fully satisfying given the articulation of the framing processes themselves. In fact, throughout the transition process, identities of participants were not fixed, but contested.

Movements for democracy in Eastern Europe have been accused of too easily having embraced Western capitalism. Jeff Goodwin thus summarised, 'The reason for this absence of ideological innovation is undoubtedly quite simple: "Bourgeois" liberalism and free market capitalism were appealing in Eastern Europe principally because—like Marxist-Leninism and the "Society model" in the Third World of the recent past—they seemed to represent the most visible alternative social order' (2001: 271). That no new ideas came from 1989 is, however, open to challenge.

While clearly no new ideology was created, the framing of the 'self' of the oppositional groups of 1989 was quite innovative. As Ulrich Preuss noted, these movements did not try to impose a common will of the people, but rather promoted the principle of self-government, citing 'the idea of an autonomous civil society and its ability to work on itself by means of logical reasoning processes and the creation of appropriate institutions' (1995: 97). In an original conception of civil society, informal 'micro-groups' allowed for the spread of 'horizontal and an oblique voice', with 'the development of semantically coded critical communication'. Horizontality was in symbolic contrast with the verticality of the regime, as dissidents built upon a moral opposition to the vanguard politics associated with communism (Goodwin 2001: 277).

A specific view of civil society was developed by intellectual dissidents, with cross-fertilization among different countries. Future president of the Czech Republic Havel took from philosopher Patocke the conception of living in truth as realization of human quality. For Havel, dissidents were not only the intellectuals in the opposition but all those 'who act as they believe they must' (Tucker 2000: 116), striving for a society in which they could live in truth and share that truth with the other members of the society. Living in truth was a moral act that allowed one to regain control over one's own sense of humanity: it corresponded to the building of authentic relations between the person and the universe. The essence of life was in 'plurality, diversity, independent self-constitution and self-organization' (ibid.: 142).

While this framing helped in mobilization against the regime, it also appeared problematic in sustaining mobilization after the transition to democracy. As Baker rightly noted, the radical view of the civil society that had developed in the opposition in Eastern Europe (as in Latin America) was 'tamed' after the transition, when a liberal conception of democracy prevailed. As he summarised, 'For the opposition theorists of the 1970s and 1980s, civil society was an explicitly normative concept which held up the ideal of societal space, autonomous from the state, wherein self-management and democracy could be worked out. That is, the idea of civil society was political and prescriptive' (Baker 1999: 2). Civil society theorists, such as

Michnik and Kuron in Poland, Havel and Benda in Czechoslovakia, and Konrad, Kis and Bence in Hungary, 'in addition to their calls for a more liberal politics of checks and balances, also saw civil society originally in the more positive, or socialist, terms of community and solidarity. Indeed, for many such theorists civil society indicated a movement towards post-statism; for control of power, while not unimportant, would be insufficient for the fundamental redistribution, or even negation, of power itself. If this was to be achieved, self-management in civil society was necessary' (ibid.: 15). The appeal to the construction of a community from below did not resonate with the delegated and majoritarian conceptions of democracy that dominated the institutions built after *die Wende*. The consolidation of a model of democracy based on a liberal conception, focusing on elected elites, in fact denied civil society a political role—a role that was instead monopolised by political parties. Procedural democracy thus obscured the substantive claims of the radical conception of civil society, contributing to reduce the participation of the citizens.

Repressing Protest in Eastern Europe

Throughout the history of the 'real socialist states', repression played a role in constraining protests, but also in increasing outrage toward the regime. Saxonberg (2012) noted that the repressive tactics in Eastern Europe catalysed rebellion, as they were perceived as outrageous acts. Thus, in Czechoslovakia, protest spread as rebellion against repression on 17 November; a similar process took place in the GDR after heavy repression in the beginning of October. In this reaction, one should consider the effect of the gradual, differentiated, and often reversed dynamics of liberalization. In the post–World War II period, repression had been so strong as to effectively thwart any open opposition. Although with some differences, repression changed in all Eastern European countries after Stalinism, generally becoming less tough.

Although repressive, the police state left more free spaces than usually recognised, moving from the mass arrests of the post-war era to heavy surveillance later on. Thus, the very forms of repression tended to create a division expressed in a public and conformist self, and a private, more rebellious one. This *Nischengesellshaft*, even though discouraging protest in the short term, also increased the chances in the long term, once an elite had mobilised, showing the potential for discontent and protest. So, given divided elites, 'islands of autonomy [began] to develop, particularly where a more liberalised political environment was joined with comparatively high levels of economic development and public resentment of communism' (Bunce 1999: 32).

In the 1980s, indeed, in the transition in Eastern European cases, the nonviolent development of the mobilization was explained by the constrained forms of repression: 'Had the civilian leadership or the top brass attempted to resist the opposition, the transfer of power would not have been so swift, and certainly not so peaceful. One of the most remarkable aspects of the East European Revolution is that, with the partial exception of Romania, the security forces and the bureaucracy just melted away in the face of growing public opposition' (Kuran 1991: 40).

In 1989, after some attempts at repression, even the less liberalised regimes mostly avoided violent tactics. Certainly repression strategies changed along with protest, as early attempts at repression during eventful democratization failed or backfired and mass demonstrations made old tactics ineffective. A careful analysis of the 'impossible repression' on 9 October 1989 in Leipzig, at the peak of the protest cycle, indicates that the police in the authoritarian regime had indeed no training and no strategy to deal with mass protest (Jobard 2006). So, as it became clear that the USSR had no intention to intercede, the masses of protestors proved too large for coercive interventions by police and security forces. Moreover, the party militia—often called upon to intervene—refused to charge against peaceful demonstrators: many of its members did not show up when called, or resigned. Considered as unreliable in its rank-and-file troops of conscripts, the military was not a practicable option for repression.

In sum, while repression had been particularly evil in the Stalinist years, both regimes became less brutal, if not more tolerant, following strategic turns in the Soviet Union. It was especially the loss of the support of the Soviet Army against potential opposition that represented a turning point, eventually leading away from brutal repression before and during the eventful democratization. This happened following diverse paths in different Eastern European countries. A *pacted* transition developed in Poland and Hungary where, in view of the economic difficulties and loss of consensus for the regime, a misalignment occurred within party elites, with a reformist wing allying with the moderate members of the opposition. In the GDR and Czechoslovakia, however, where party elites had been less permeable to new ideas of economic and political reform, we had a transition through rupture. In both countries the elites tried to use police, security and party militia to repress the protests, but the extent of the mobilization together with the lack of willingness of militia to follow orders convinced them of the need to leave without attempting strategies of brutal repression. Not only did the actual police reaction have constraining or liberating effects, but this is also true of the memory of repression during the development of the authoritarian movement.

Appropriating Opportunities in Eastern Europe

The Eastern European countries, as authoritarian one-party states, shared a specific ideology which combined with formal institutions to determine the context for the opposition. In particular, scholars have looked at the complex political culture and societal networks of 'really existing socialism' in order to explain the specific dynamics of contention during democratization. As Valerie Bunce pointed out, a main characteristic of Eastern European socialism that influenced the regime development was the ideological mission of the ruling elite: 'Unlike most dictatorships, which tend to be concerned with stability, if not a version of cultural and class nostalgia, and which operate within a capitalist economic framework, socialist regimes were future-oriented, avowedly anti-capitalist and premised on a commitment to rapid transformation of the economy, the society, and, following that, in theory at least, the polity as well' (1999: 21). These ideological concerns took the late developer and import substitution models to the extreme, creating autarkic economies and depressing agriculture and consumption, while increasing savings. In parallel, growth became a fetish, and production was concentrated on the markers of modernization. Linked to this was the Communist Party's construction of a compact economic and political monopoly (ibid.: 22). As party and state were fused, with the state relying on the party for its personnel as well as its resources, the result was an extraordinary penetration of the state by the party.

While this created a very powerful elite, its strength was temporary, as those characteristics fuelled a vicious circle: 'Over time and certainly by accident, the institutional framework of socialism functioned to deregulate the party's monopoly and to undermine economic growth. This set the stage for crisis and reform—and, ultimately, for the collapse of all of these regimes' (ibid.: 26). This happened especially through inter-elite conflicts along vertical and horizontal lines that developed especially during leadership succession. At the same time, conflicts among elites strengthened the role of society, as intra-party conflicts interacted with moments of protest (ibid.: 27), such as the one in the GDR in 1953, in Hungary in 1956, and in Poland in 1956, 1968, 1970–81, and 1980–81.

The fusion of the state and the party also tended to produce a broad potential base for the opposition through the creation of a large and homogeneous group of discontented, as 'the party's economic, political, and social monopoly, its commitment to rapid socioeconomic development, limited wage inequalities, and stable prices for consumer items, its preference for large enterprises and large collective forms, and its creation of consumer-deficit societies all worked together to give publics in the European socialist systems a remarkably uniform set of experiences' (ibid.: 28).

Faced with a potentially unified challenger, the all-powerful party functioned, in turn, as a unified target. A bias towards systemic uniformity also contributed to this target unification, as shared experiences produced uniform interests and a shared definition of the target. A similar argument is put forward by Jeff Goodwin (2001), who explains the 'refolutions' (mix of reform and revolution) in Central Eastern Europe as the product of a dependent and authoritarian state, characterised by unfulfilled promises of economic development. Neo-patrimonial in their fusion of political and economic power, the regimes in the 'second world' controlled important economic sectors; were economically and politically dependent upon support by foreign powers; and were disembedded from civil society. As in the Third World, repression, dependency and clientelism facilitated the development of a broad multiclass (and even multi-ethnic) coalition (of intellectuals and producers), targeting the party apparatus. In fact, the fusion of power induced politicization and nationalization of initially local struggles.

Linking the characteristics of civil society to those of the regime it was fighting, Di Palma noted that the very repressive connotation of the regime created, as a reaction, spaces for an opposition to emerge: 'Since the notion of a civil society is fundamentally antagonistic to communist doctrine, communism, unlike Western authoritarianism, should supposedly leave no space for civil society. Yet already for many years East European social scientists, most of them dissidents, have paid much attention to the fate of civil society during the period of normalization.' First of all, the stated aims were not achieved in reality—so the regime claims 'to a monopoly of public discourse, and related cognitive removal of increasingly degraded realities ... is also the spark that ignited both societal resistance and then cathartic rebounding when the crisis of communism exploded'. Civil society then emerged from this failure (1991: 63). In a similar vein, Christian Joppke (1995) pointed at the gap between promises and realizations, defining the Leninist regime as based on incorporation of the masses into the polity and mobilization of those masses towards an abstract and distant goal (ibid.: 5). This became a source of discontent especially in the post-mobilization phase, when the totalitarian intentions could not be implemented.

Even though civil society was weakened by the party's cognitive monopoly on public discourse and citizens' cooperation with the system, the monopoly of public discourse by the regime was however challenged by the dissidents. While Stalinism was successful in removing dissent through force, cognitive dissonance re-emerged during the normalization of the post-Stalinist period: 'Thus, the reassertion of reality and the recovery of community imbued dissent from communism with a moral justification and an impetus beyond that of most other movements against dictatorship. For the discrepancy between communist doctrine and reality showed that the responsibility for the degradation of reality stemmed from communism's refusal to learn' (Di Palma 1991: 67).

International opportunities and constraints played a particularly important role, as the spread of international norms (and treaties) helped first liberalization, and then democratization. Often mentioned, including in the very name of Charter 77, is the Helsinki Final Act that institutionalised the Conference on Security and Cooperation in Europe, creating an international framework for negotiations. In the Helsinki agreement, thirty-five European governments committed to respect 'civil, economic, social, cultural and other rights and freedoms, all of which derive from the inherent dignity of the human person' (Glenn 2001: 51; see also Bunce 1999: 61).

The removal of some international constraints on democratization clearly influenced the 1989 wave of mobilization for democracy. For the whole area, transformations in Soviet politics and policies were of most fundamental value; in particular, 'the sweeping political reforms introduced by Gorbachev in the late 1980s completely altered the Soviet government's response to civil resistance both in east-central Europe and in the Soviet Union itself' (Kramer 2011: 101). The wave of transitions in Eastern Europe was in fact strictly linked to the impact of the Soviet *glasnost*—especially after, in 1988, liberalization began to turn into opportunities for democratization (Whitehead 1996: 367), with Moscow's acknowledgment of the lack of realism in attempts oriented to avoid democratization through liberalization and reform.

So, as in the Third World where revolutions developed when colonialist powers started to feel that the costs of repressions were too high, in the Second World they occurred when the Soviet Union withdrew military help. As Goodwin concluded, 'What collapsed in Eastern Europe was not socialism but a type of dependent authoritarian socialist—just as what collapsed in the Third World had not been capitalism, or even 'backward' capitalism, but authoritarian models of 'colonial' and 'crony' capitalism' (2001: 274).

Eventful Protest in Transition from Below

Protest campaigns linked to episodes of democratization often appear as sudden and unexpected. Surprise clearly applied to 1989. Giuseppe Di Palma noted that 'before the demise of communism made the front pages around the world, few if any of the revisionist students of communism were betting on it' (1991: 52). Not only were Western scholars stunned but the sudden change also surprised East European dissidents as well: for instance, as late as the end of 1988, Czech dissident Vaclav Havel had expected the opposition to remain 'for the time being merely the seed of something that will bear fruit in the dim and distant future'. According to an opinion poll conducted a few months after the transition, only 5 per cent answered affirmatively to the question, 'A year ago did you expect such a peaceful revolution?' (cit. in Kuran 1991: 10–11).

Paradoxically, however, the surprise at extraordinary events is often accompanied by interpretations that stress their unavoidability. As Kuran noted, 'While the collapse of the post–World War II political order of Eastern Europe stunned the world, in retrospect it appears as the inevitable consequence of a multitude of factors. In each of the six countries the leadership was generally despised, lofty economic promises remained unfulfilled, and freedoms taken for granted elsewhere existed only on paper.' The question to address is therefore, 'If the revolution was indeed inevitable, why was it not foreseen? Why did people overlook signs that are clearly visible after the fact?' (Kuran 1991: 12–13). What is important, then, is that events suddenly start to fuel themselves, as action produces action. Protest events tend to cluster in time, as 'events and the contention over identity which they represent are not distributed randomly over time and space. Their appearance is structured both temporally and spatially' (Beissinger 2002: 16). In fact, protests come in chains, series, waves, cycles, and tides, 'forming a punctuated history of heightened challenges and relative stability' (ibid.: 16).

In research on democratization in Eastern Europe, explanations for this clustering have been offered at the micro, individual level, looking in particular, within game theoretical perspectives, at the demonstrative effects of protest. Within this type of approach, Kuran (1991) has interestingly suggested that—as 'mass discontent does not necessarily generate a popular uprising against the political status quo'—to explain conditions 'under which individuals will display antagonism toward the regime under which they live', one must consider the distinction between public and private preferences. In this approach, protest is expected to spread when particular conditions make less risky the public expression of oppositional preferences that have been held in private. Thus, a sort of revolutionary bandwagon derives from the contemporary fall in thresholds and rise in public opposition. As public opposition increases, it becomes easier to convince those with private preferences against the government to mobilise, but also to change the preference of the others.

Going beyond the individual level, my own analysis of eventful democratization in 1989 (Della Porta 2014) points at the power of action itself in creating and recreating environmental opportunities and organizational resources that influence the strategic interactions of various actors. If events fuel each other, it is because they are linked 'in the narrative of the struggles that accompany them, in the altered expectations that they generate about subsequent possibilities to contest; in the changes that they evoke in the behaviour of those forces that uphold a given order, and in the transformed landscape of meaning that events at times fashion' (Beissinger 2002: 17). If structural conditions are not (or do not seem) ripe, they might still mature during protest campaigns. That is, protest campaigns are eventful, as they produce structures and resources that favour mobilization rather than being a simple product of external and internal conditions. They produce fissions in the elites, as well as strengthen the opposition, by changing both the actual structures and the perceptions of costs and benefits. The analysis of structures must therefore be combined with procedural analysis (Parsa 2000, Wood 2000).

Stressing the transformative capacity of protest, I suggest that protest events in 1989 had cognitive, affective and relational impacts on the very actors that carry them out (for a similar approach, see Bennani Chraibi and Fillieule 2012). From the cognitive point of view, mechanisms of growth in generality and politicization developed into action. By *growth in generality* I mean the cognitive expansion of protest claims, from more specific to more general concerns, as a way to bridge different constituencies. Together with the growth in generality, there was a mechanism of *politicization of the protest discourse,* as the target of action is singled out in the government and the regime. While waves of protest started with specific complaints against economic decline or diffused corruption, protest gained momentum especially when a cognitive link was made between these grievances and government actions.

Cognitive mechanisms were paralleled by emotional ones, such as moral shocks, but also feelings of collective empowerment. *Moral shocks* developed as emotionally intense reactions of indignation against an action perceived as ethically unbearable. Episodes of brutal repression increased rather than quelled opposition, as they were perceived as outrageous by the population. They so facilitated mobilization in authoritarian regimes through the transformation of fear into rage. As negative emotions must be balanced by positive ones in order to fuel collective action, moral shocks were accompanied by a *feeling of collective empowerment,* as a set of positive emotions that produce an enhanced sense of agency through identity building and ties of solidarity. Emotional liberation was indeed important in explaining the development of protest, especially in risky forms of activism (Flam 2005).

Cognitive and affective mechanisms fuel relational processes, which take shape during eventful democratization. In various ways, coordination reduces the cost of participation as mobilization spreads. It has emerged, in fact, in *networked* and *aggregated* forms. As Osa (2003) noted, in Poland, waves of protest for democracy proceeded by bridging various groups, so that coordination was, at the same time, a precondition and an effect of mobilization.

Even if with limited resources, research on democratization in Eastern Europe has provided important contributions to social movement studies. First and foremost, it has shown that contentious politics exists and is important also in authoritarian regimes. This is true in the path of democratization through rupture, but also in *pacted* transition, when at times protests pushed uncertain elites towards liberalization. Research has also pointed at the importance of eventful protests. In regimes that had been depicted as the most difficult to democratise, as people started to mobilise for democracy they were able to produce resources for mobilization as well as political opportunities. Initially tiny minorities, isolated and repressed opponents conquered consensus as they took to the street, changing the relations among the various political and social actors. Finally, research on democratization in Eastern Europe highlighted also the role of international actors and transnational processes. While national context remained of fundamental importance, the changing international context, as well as cross-national diffusion of ideas allowed for a new wave of democratization to shake an entire region.

Donatella Della Porta is professor of political science and dean at the Scuola Normale Superiore in Florence, where she directs the Centre on Social Movement Studies (COSMOS). She also directs a major ERC project, *Mobilizing for Democracy*, on civil society participation in democratization processes in Europe, the Middle East, Asia and Latin America. Among her very recent publications are: *Methodological Practices in Social Movement Research* (Oxford University Press, 2014); *Spreading Protest* (ECPR Press 2014, with Alice Mattoni), *Participatory Democracy in Southern Europe* (Rowman and Littlefield, 2014, with Joan Font and Yves Sintomer); *Mobilizing for Democracy* (Oxford University Press, 2014); *Can Democracy Be Saved?* (Polity Press, 2013); *Clandestine Political Violence* (Cambridge University Press, 2013, with D. Snow, B. Klandermans and D. McAdam, eds.); *Blackwell Encyclopedia on Social and Political Movements* (Blackwell, 2013); *Mobilizing on the Extreme Right* (Oxford University Press, 2012, with M. Caiani and C. Wagemann); *Meeting Democracy* (Cambridge University Press, 2012, with D. Rucht, eds.); and *The Hidden Order of Corruption* (Ashgate, 2012, with A. Vannucci). In 2011, she was the recipient of the Mattei Dogan Prize for distinguished achievements in the field of political sociology.

Notes

1. The author is grateful to the European Research Council for supporting this work with an advanced scholar grant on 'Mobilising for Democracy'. The ideas presented are of course the responsibility only of the author.

References

Beissinger, M. R. 2002. *Nationalist Mobilization and the Collapse of the Soviet State*. Cambridge: Cambridge University Press.

Bennani-Chraibi, M., and O. Fillieule. 2012. 'Toward a Sociology of Revolutionary Situations: Reflections on the Arab Uprisings'. *Revue française de science politique in English* 62, no. 5: 1–29.

Bermeo, Nancy. 1997. 'Myths of Moderation: Confrontation and Conflict during Democratic Transition'. *Comparative Politics* 29, no. 2: 205–322.

Boudreau, V. 2004. *Resisting Dictatorship: Repression and Protest in Southeast Asia*. Cambridge: Cambridge University Press.

Bunce, V. 1999. *Subversive Institutions: The Design and the Destruction of Socialism and the State*. Cambridge: Cambridge University Press.

Della Porta, D. 2014. *Mobilizing for Democracy: Comparing 1989 and 2011*. Oxford: Oxford University Press.

Di Palma, G. 1991. 'Legitimation from the Top to Civil Society: Politico-Cultural Change in Eastern Europe'. *World Politics* 44, no. 1: 49–80.

Diani, M., and O. Císař. 2014. 'The Emergence of a Social Movement Research Field'. In *Routledge Handbook of European Sociology*, ed. S. Kodornios and A. Kyrtsis. London: Routledge.

Flam, H. 2005. 'Emotions' Map: A Research Agenda'. In *Emotions and Social Movements*, ed. H. Flam and D. King, 19–41. London: Routledge.

Glenn, J. K. III. 2001. *Framing Democracy: Civil Society and Civic Movements in Eastern Europe*. Stanford: Stanford University Press.

Goodwin, J. 2001. *No Other Way Out*. Cambridge: Cambridge University Press.

Jobard, F. 2006. 'L'impossible répression. Leipzig. RDA, 9 octobre 1989'. In *Police et manifestants: Maintien de l'ordre er gestion des conflits*, ed. O. Fillieule and D. Della Porta, 175–200. Paris: Presses de Sciences-Po.

Joppke, C. 1995. *East German Dissidents and the Revolution of 1989: Social Movement in a Leninist Regime*. New York: New York University Press.

Kramer, M. 2011. 'The Dialectic of Empire: Soviet Leaders and the Challenge of Civil Resistance in East-Central Europe, 1968–91'. In *Civil Resistance and Power Politics: The Experience of Non-Violent Action from Gandhi to the Present*, ed. A. Roberts and T. Garton Ash, 91–109. Oxford: Oxford University Press.

Kuran, T. 1991. 'Now Out of Never: The Element of Surprise in the East European Revolution of 1989'. *World Politics* 44, no. 1: 7–48.

Osa, M. 2003. *Solidarity and Contention: Networks of Polish Opposition*. Minneapolis: University of Minnesota Press.

Parsa, M. 2000. *States, Ideologies and Social Revolutions: A Comparative Analysis of Iran, Nicaragua and the Philippines.* Cambridge: Cambridge University Press.

Whitehead, L. 1996. *The International Dimensions of Democratization: Europe and the Americas.* Oxford: Oxford University Press.

Wood, E. 2000. *Forging Democracy from Below: Insurgent Transitions in South Africa and El Salvador.* Cambridge: Cambridge University Press.

Chapter 3

A Long-Awaited Homecoming
The Labour Movement in Social Movement Studies

Karel Yon

Social movement studies have an ambivalent relationship with the labour movement. Originally, the latter was considered the social movement *par excellence*. And Marxism was its official theory, in the sense that the labour movement—both in its institutional and contentious forms, namely trade unions and labour parties on the one hand, and mass demonstrations, strikes and other workplace unrest on the other—was considered to be the natural expression of the antagonistic interests of the proletariat toward the other fundamental social class in capitalism, the bourgeoisie. Several founding fathers of social movement studies, such as Charles Tilly and Doug McAdam, were strongly influenced by Marxism at the beginning of their academic careers. So were European scholars, too, deeply anchored in social history (Thompson 1963) and interested in the changing patterns of class conflict (Touraine 1969). Many of them studied trade unions and strikes through the lens of labour history or industrial sociology (Touraine 1965; Shorter and Tilly 1974; Melucci 1976; Pizzorno et al. 1978; Offe and Wiesenthal 1980; Tarrow 1989). However, they all contributed to the construction of what would become a specific field of enquiry through the critique of the common understanding of how class conflict, or industrial action, occurs. Rejecting the mechanistic explanation of social conflict as the result of structural contradictions between labour and capital, they developed a new area of knowledge in documenting and analysing the *political dimension* of collective mobilization. This provoked a dual shift, both theoretical and empirical. Theoretically, their critique of economism led to the development of a series of operational concepts for studying the symbolic dimensions of action and the uncertain process of mobilization in itself. Empirically, they broadened the study of protest beyond the boundaries of worker unrest and considered the plural expressions of protest in society. Since then, the status of social movement studies is ambiguous: did it signal the death of the labour movement, the latter being historically eclipsed by new forms of protest, or has it enriched and completed the analysis of industrial conflict? Such ambiguity was especially strong in Europe, the cradle of the theories of new social movements (NSM). For Touraine in particular, the quest for a new post-industrial social movement was closely linked to the death knell of both Marx and the historical agents of class struggle (Dubet et al. 1984).

Labour Movement and Social Movement Studies: Two Different Worlds

As a consequence, scholars who continued to pay attention to the labour movement followed a very different path from the one that social movement specialists chose. One particular project symbolises this trajectory very well: the two-volume work coordinated by Alessando Pizzorno and Colin Crouch (1978) on the resurgence of class conflict in Western Europe after 1968. The starting point of the research was an attempt to understand the renewal of strikes and other social movements throughout Europe in the late 1960s, which contradicted the predictions that social scientists had made at the beginning of this same decade that industrial conflict had reached its end. They gathered industrial and political sociologists from several European countries (Italy, France, Great Britain, Belgium, West Germany and the Netherlands) and built an ambitious comparative project based on hypotheses drawn from the theories of Serge Mallet and Alain Touraine on the 'new working class' and 'new social movements'. The questions they raised were the very ones that would later drive numerous social movement studies: why are such groups as immigrants, unskilled workers, students or women at the centre of contemporary social protest? How can one explain the transformation of protest, which tends to become more volatile, sometimes violent, and spills over workplace boundaries? Why is it that collective action develops in a cyclic way, notably through strike waves? When their research was conducted and completed in the late 1970s, they ended up answering a very different question. They had developed a reflection on how the political systems of Western European democracies, confronted with an unprecedented economic crisis, assimilated or neutralised new claims and regained control over their system of interest representation. The concluding chapter of the second volume offers a theory for this process with the well-known text by Alessandro Pizzorno on 'Political Exchange and Collective Identity in Industrial Conflict'. In this chapter, Pizzorno explains that the function of labour unions is not only to negotiate with employers ensuring the continuity of production for higher wages and better work conditions but also to guarantee social consensus in exchange for greater institutional power granted by the state. He calls the latter 'political exchange'. Periods of conflict, he argues, emerge notably when trade unions refuse, or become unable to assimilate new collective identities, therefore losing their function of intermediation. Thus, at the dawn of the 1980s, the main question for labour movement specialists was no longer 'How can one explain the resurgence of class conflict?' but rather 'What are the consequences of the enrolment of labour within political exchange?' In the meantime, social movement scholars would address a different, but complementary interrogation: 'How can one explain that social conflict escaped outside the industrial arena?' That second question was in part a reply to the first one.

In the wake of that paradigm shift, labour movement specialists, whether economists, historians, sociologists or industrial relations scholars, focused increasingly in the 1980s on what they interpreted as the main effect of the incorporation of the labour movement in the state: its retreat. The crisis of the labour movement was depicted as a consequence of neo-corporatist arrangements (Lehmbruch and Schmitter 1982; Goldthorpe 1984), as the latter seemed to demobilise workers while at the same time labour representatives were associated with the dismantling of their own industrial strongholds (Mania and Sateriale 2003). This was especially the case throughout continental Europe, where social pacts became a common trend in most countries, and social dialogue a prevailing rhetoric at the level of the European community (Regini 1993; Gobin 1997; Martin and Ross 1999; Wagner 2005). In southern Europe (Spain, Portugal and Italy) and France, these studies were sometimes connected to the wider crisis of the communist movement (Accornero 1992; Bilbao 1995; Beaud and Pialoux 1999). In Germany, despite attempts made by Claus Offe to establish a theoretical framework that bridged the gap between the old labour and new social movements, empirical work on labour movements remained the area of industrial sociologists and political economists such as Wolfgang Streeck. While developing an interesting reflection about the persistent relevance of the category of class in the analysis of social movements,[1] the work by Klaus Eder focused on the phenomenon of 'middle-class radicalism'. The effects of trade union institutionalization in terms of the demobilization of workers became especially important in France where union density dramatically declined to less than 10 per cent of the workforce in the late 1980s (Rosanvallon 1988; Croizat and Labbé 1992). Everywhere, emphasis seemed to be increasingly placed on the effects of rising unemployment, flexibility and the precariousness of the workforce in shifting the balance of power away from the trade unions (Montlibert 1989; Martin Artiles 1995; Boltanski and Chiapello 1999). Meanwhile, in the context of neoliberal restructuring, the British labour movement had to face a violent attack that also affected labour scholars, forcing many of them to take shelter in business schools or to see some of their research carried out by the emerging discipline of human resource management (Ackers and Wilkinson 2008). This led to a greater insistence on social partnership, discrediting the role of labour unions as social movement organizations. The idea was 'that any return to a more "adversarial" pattern of industrial relations is either improbable or, if it is thought possible, would be undesirable for all those involved. … A significant number of writers (both in Europe and the United States) came to the conclusion that union survival and recovery turned on the willingness of unions and their members to behave 'moderately' and to offer concessions to the employer' (Kelly 1998: 14). Several scholars, generally Marxist-oriented, tried to preserve a more contentious definition of unionism (Béroud et al. 1998) or at least show that the very definition of unionism was itself a contentious matter (Hyman 2001). Nevertheless, the prevailing trend was to consider the labour movement either as a declining social form or as a mere agent of negotiation. However, the study of strike activity has remained a significant subfield among labour and industrial relations specialists (Van der Velden et al. 2007; Brandl and Traxler 2010), the topic being of public interest and therefore fed with statistical data produced by state and international agencies. But the dominant trend has been for scholars to show a shift towards labour quiescence from the late 1970s, with an overall decrease of strike activity in Western Europe (Gall 2013). All these developments show that the analysis of the labour movement in Western Europe continued to be embedded in the theoretical framework of industrial relations: labour conflict has rarely been considered as a topic of interest *per se,* but rather to the extent that it helps to understand the regulation of employment relations. As a consequence, reflections by labour scholars on social conflict hardly ever break free from the etiological illusion (Dobry 1986)—in other words, explaining collective action by its causes instead of analysing its very processes.

Thus, the labour movement on one hand and social movements on the other have been treated very differently in different disciplinary settings. Exploring the scholarly journals that delimit academic boundaries easily shows this. Very few articles are dedicated to workers' collective action in the two main journals specialised in social movement studies—namely, *Mobilization* and *Social Movement Studies*. Besides, most of their articles were written by US scholars and deal with the US labour movement. In parallel, very few scholars in the much older and broader field of industrial relations study labour unions and labour conflicts with the conceptual tools of social movement studies, as illustrated by the articles published in the two main

European journals specialised in the discipline (*Economic and Industrial Democracy* and *The European Journal of Industrial Relations*). Yet, the situation has been slowly changing.

Uneven Crossbreeding Attempts

During the 1990s there was a notable appearance of several works trying to combine the understanding of the labour movement with the conceptual tools of social movement studies. However, it is not so much a homogeneous body of work but rather a diverse series of approaches that vary according to national contexts—especially sociological traditions and varieties of unionism (Frege and Kelly 2004)—as well as epistemological positions.

The most accomplished attempt in updating the understanding of the labour movement with social movement theory was more performative than analytical: this was manifest in the concept of 'social movement unionism' (SMU) that was forged in the early 1990s by Peter Waterman (Waterman 1993). Waterman perceived this notion as a *strategic* category aimed at guiding the action of labour and social movement activists towards a new internationalism. Formerly a labour educator for the World Federation of Trade Unions in English-speaking Africa, Waterman in the early 1970s became a scholar at the Institute of Social Studies in the Hague where he studied unions, social movements and internationalism. He conceived the idea of social movement unionism in discussions with other scholars working especially on the South African labour movement. Influenced by post-structuralism and post-Marxist political thought and relying on NSM and feminist theories, he designed SMU as a way of connecting the labour movement to other democratic social movements. The concept was inspired by the experience of trade unions in semi-industrialised countries such as Brazil or South Africa, where they generally went beyond their economic role of bargaining agents by playing a substantial role in the democratization process. Yet it was also intended to underline the renewal of phenomena in the Western labour movement that were supposedly contrary to traditional bureaucratic union practice, such as labour-community alliances, direct action and grassroots forms of international solidarity. Even though it has been criticised as too reliant on the NSM theory (some scholars advocated for an alternative concept of 'radical political unionism', see Upchurch and Mathers 2012), the concept of SMU was very successful among scholars who developed a body of literature on union revitalization (which I will return to later). Besides, the notion pointed out a trend towards new forms of local/global solidarity to which the global justice movement would later give great visibility.

Because of the specificity of its industrial relations system, the French case deserves particular attention. As employees' rights are not conditional on union membership but guaranteed by the state, trade unions are less able to discipline workers than to mobilise them, hence the importance of strikes in the regulation of industrial relations (Sirot 2002). And yet, during the late 1980s and early 1990s, several major strikes in France—notably among railway workers, nurses, teachers and lorry drivers—were led not by unions but by *coordinations*: these were ephemeral organizations, formed by the workers themselves, which relegated trade unions to the background. Such phenomena seemed to confirm the idea that organised labour had lost its centrality in contemporary protest, and that new forms of organization and repertoires of collective action were developing so as to adjust to emerging claims regarding recognition and grassroots democracy that were especially strong among professionals (Hassenteufel 1991; Kergoat et al. 1992; Denis 1996). Resource mobilization theory helped to show that the unfolding of *coordinations* was less a mechanical expression of the new class structure (characterised by the development of service work), as the NSM theory would argue, but rather more an offshoot of the political socialization of the 1970s' generation of activists (Leschi 1996). Thus, when labour conflict came back as a topic of inquiry, it looked like the old labour movement was no longer its medium and that some new actors were to take over. Similarly, it is worth noticing that among the few sociological studies dedicated to trade union activism at that time, most of them dealt with new organizations promoting the practice of social movement unionism, especially the '*Solidaires, unitaires, démocratiques*' (SUD) unions (Sainsaulieu 1999; or in English, see Connolly 2010).

While anchored in specific national contexts, two books deserve particular attention, as they offer general propositions on how to crossbreed labour movement and social movement studies in an innovative way. Following previous major studies on class struggle and social movements in post-war Italy, Italian sociologist Roberto Franzosi, who was trained and recruited in the United States, published a landmark book in 1995 on the sociology of strikes (Franzosi 1995). Reflecting on what he called 'the puzzle of strikes', he suggests that theories that are typically contrasted when we try to understand industrial action should be put together in order to fit the different pieces of the puzzle. As strategic interactions, strikes indeed involve multiple actors within multiple settings. Not only does his work convincingly combine economic, political, institutional and organizational explanations, it also develops a methodological reflection on the respective advantages of quantitative and qualitative, historical reasoning. His work confirms the importance of cyclicity in protest, which Pizzorno and Tarrow had previously underlined. But he also stresses the 'dialectic nature of conflict' (Franzosi 1995: 349);

strikes are not only caused by various phenomena (economic trends, organizational resources, political opportunities, and so on), they also in turn, *cause* those phenomena. From that perspective, a major contribution in Franzosi's research is the uncovering of counter-mobilization strategies. In the case of Italy, he shows how the high level of shop-floor unrest throughout the 1970s, in the wake of the hot autumn of 1969, convinced employers to reorganise production. Thus, 'By the end of the 1970s, the unskilled worker who had fought the struggles of the late 1960s and early 1970s was no longer 'central' to the new forms of organization of production. Through decentralization, robotization and other restructuring plans, in the span of a decade the Italian employers had virtually eliminated from the class structure the type of workers who had been one of the key actors in the previous cycle of struggle' (Franzosi 1995: 16). Such a process eventually enabled employers to regain control over production, discipline workers and redeploy the victimization of union activists.

Similar preoccupations can be found in another major contribution, John Kelly's *Rethinking Industrial Relations* (1998), for which Franzosi's book is among the main sources of inspiration. Yet, Kelly's purpose is slightly different. He does not intend to focus on strikes but demonstrate how mobilization theory (i.e. social movement studies, especially the work by Tilly, McAdam, Gamson and Snow and Benford) can usefully nurture and reorient industrial relations research. The ambition is actually to regenerate the Marxist approach to industrial relations, which has been significant in British academia (as the work of Richard Hyman, founder of the *European Journal of Industrial Relations* illustrates; see Hyman 1975). By starting from issues that differ from mainstream industrial relations theories—namely, 'how does injustice lead to collective action' rather than 'how to get workers to work'—mobilization theory is in line with Marxist interrogations about exploitation. But it has the advantage of providing researchers with a set of concepts that are analytically sophisticated, and thus more effective in studying the process of collective action, from joining a union to partaking in various forms of protest. Moreover, they allow us to shed light on crucial aspects of the employment relationships—that is, repression against workers' mobilization by employers and the state—which mainstream industrial relations theories ignore.

Reconsidering Labour as a Social Movement: Recent Developments

Another central reference in Kelly's book is the ethnographic work by Rick Fantasia on labour action in the United States (Fantasia 1988). Strongly influenced by the work of Edward P. Thompson, Raymond Williams and, later, Pierre Bourdieu, Fantasia contributed, with other fellow US sociologists and historians, to renewing the study of labour by considering it as a social movement (Fantasia and Stepan-Norris 2004). From the late 1990s, a dynamic array of research on US labour movements sprouted up, simultaneously with a considerable shift of the top leadership in American organised labour in terms of organizing immigrant and precarious workers, as well as favourably considering alliances with other social movements (Bronfenbrenner 1998; Milkman 2000; Turner et al. 2001; Milkman and Voss 2004). In the wake of the SMU model, this body of research appeared as a vital resource in the context of the de-institutionalization of industrial relations. While critical labour historians had already pointed out the limitations of 'business unionism', this literature offered alternative ways of action based on the remobilization of union members, the building of alliances with community organizations, or the use of direct action such as shaming or civil disobedience. Criticizing Roberto Michel's 'iron law of oligarchy,' studies demonstrated that trade union institutionalization was not inevitable, that activists matter, that different 'framing processes' induce various forms of collective action, and that labour movements shape the employers' counter-movements and vice versa. Contrary to the previous studies of the 1980s, which were mostly theory-oriented, what would become the 'new labour' (or 'union revitalization') literature made use of the conceptual tools of social movement studies for an operational purpose. The idea was to conduct action research in order to produce expertise in the field of trade union organizing and mobilizing, hence the considerable number of case studies. Circulating mainly through union channels, labour-oriented think tanks and foundations (via the British Trades Union Congress, or the *Hans Böckler Stiffung* in Germany), the approach crossed the Atlantic and rekindled labour research, first in the UK, then in other European countries (Kelly 2002; Brinkmann et al. 2008; Gall 2009a, 2009b; Simms et al. 2013). For that reason, while this body of literature has had a significant resonance in the European labour movement (notably through the journal of the European Trade Union Institute, *Transfer*), it has not been necessarily well recognised in academic circles. One underlying explanation may be that its strong prescriptive dimension sometimes led to the writing of mere recipes for union renewal, at the risk of obscuring the description of *real* union practices (Thomas 2011). Another critique has been that the logic of this literature (that is, expert knowledge produced for unions) frequently implies a narrow definition of the labour movement as a *trade union* movement and focuses on union density, therefore neglecting forms of workers' collective action that emerge outside of those organizations (Sullivan 2010).

Parallel to the rise of the 'new labour' literature in the United States, several studies have appeared in Europe since the early 2000s investigating the changing situation and lines of action of the labour movement. However, this trend remains fairly modest and does not enable describing it as a shift in labour studies. But it is now acknowledged, at least, that labour organizations and labour actions are a legitimate object in the field of social movement studies. One of the main reasons is that, even if economic strikes are still falling, there has been a significant increase in the amount of public-sector and general strikes all around Europe (Kelly et al. 2013; Gall 2013). Gall even considers that the political mass strike is now 'the mainstay in the repertoires of contention of union movements in France, Greece, Italy, Portugal and Spain since the late 1990s,' and maybe also in Britain and Germany since the late 2000s (Gall 2013: 685). Relying on the 'political exchange' thesis, he suggests that such a phenomenon is a result of the hegemony of neoliberalism in Europe: not only labour movements regularly face right-wing, hostile governments, they also now have to mobilise against once-allied political parties who carry out neoliberal reforms of the social wage, labour law and welfare state, under the guidance of European Union institutions that seem more than ever bound to austerity and pro-market policies.

Thus, in France, the 1995 strikes and mass demonstrations against the reform of the social security system sparked a number of studies. And contrary to earlier predictions, *coordinations* vanished and trade unions returned to the forefront of protest. As a consequence, a new wave of studies emerged around trade unions and workers' mobilizations. Several issues of *Politix,* a scholarly journal for the social science of politics, illustrate their variety particularly well.[2] Social movement scholars in France notably mix the sociology of Pierre Bourdieu and symbolic interactionism. On the one hand, the Bourdieusian concept of social field is used to describe the landscape of organised labour and give a sense to its pluralism and evolution. On the other hand, given the existence of a strong tradition of workplace and political activism among unionists, many scholars pursue the sociology of labour activism by analysing activist habitus and careers. They share a common opposition to the Tourainian NSM theory, which they analyse, through the lens of reflexive, critical sociology, as a performative discourse, a self-fulfilling prophecy. A closer, empirical look at the workplace and union conflictuality also led to an understanding of how unions make strikes (Giraud 2009) and to the contesting of the over-simplistic thesis of the death of industrial conflict, by underlining the plurality of workplace protests (Béroud et al. 2008), from individual to collective action, from absenteeism to strikes or even bossnapping.[3] Multi-site ethnography that has combined the sociology of work and social movement theory has documented the struggles of illegal immigrant workers (Barron et al. 2011), or conflicts in the service sector, for instance among women cashiers (Benquet 2011, 2013).

In Southern Europe, the influence of both NSM and neo-corporatist theories, as well as the upsurge of mobilization by young, precarious workers outside traditional union organizations, may explain why labour movement studies have adopted a different perspective. Apart from a few studies on trade union members (Alos et al. 2000; Serrano del Rosal 2000), scholars have largely analysed labour conflict under the hypothesis of a new historical collective actor—generally the precariat (Standing 2011). Consequently, studies focus on the outsourcing of protest from the workplace to the urban space, and on the tensions between the old labour movement and new generations of contingent workers (Diaz-Salazar 2003; Antentas Collderram 2007; Estanque and Costa 2011; Lòpez-Calle, 2008). However, new research on recent anti-austerity protests in Portugal demonstrates that labour unions, and left-wing political parties alongside, are still key actors in the production of contention; 'new new' movements of young and precarious workers emerged in the wake of union-driven protests and went on to rely increasingly on those 'old old' actors in order to sustain their mobilization (Accornero and Ramos Pinto 2014).

While this kind of research deals with national labour movements, other studies address the contribution of labour to the Europeanization of protest (Balme and Chabanet 2008; Della Porta and Caiani 2009), be they about the contentious politics of unemployment (Mathers 2007; Chabanet and Faniel 2012) or the global justice movement (Agrikoliansky and Sommier 2005; Della Porta 2007). What they have in common is that they gather scholars from various European countries and analyse labour epiphenomenally, through the study of a wider object.[4] They point out two specific tensions. First, the labour movement entertains an ambiguous relationship with these mobilizations, as it is both within and outside the very institutions that protesters target. Second, its commitment is made difficult by the fact that such movements frequently convey frames of collective action that challenge labour as a relevant collective identity. However, these studies also show that labour unions and activists provide movements with precious resources, and outline the dense network of social movements in which labour activists circulate and interact with other groups. Beyond the European scene, similar tensions have been stressed regarding the role of labour organizations in building international solidarity movements (Costa 2008; Peterson et al. 2012). It is worth noting that several works on this subject, in the wake of Waterman's earlier reflection on social movement unionism, developed an original framework combining socioeconomics with global labour history and radical geography (Waterman and Wills 2001; Santos 2004).

We can see that a specific characteristic of labour movement studies, compared to other social movement studies, is a frequent continuing dialogue with Marxism. While this certainly was a stigma in the past, it may become an advantage, in these present times of erupting popular protest all over the world (Barker et al. 2013). Following the economic and financial crisis of the late 2000s, mobilizations of *Indignados* in Europe, the Arab Spring in the Middle East and North Africa and the Occupy movement in the United States, the hypothesis was thus developed of a new global cycle of contention in which labour and social issues have regained centrality, as opposed to previous post-materialistic protests (Estanque et al. 2013). This idea was clearly also in the minds of several recognised scholars in the field of social movement studies who recently committed themselves to examining whether the classical opposition between old and new social movements was still relevant. For instance, a collective project called 'Caught in the Act of Protest: Contextualising Contestation' compared climate change and May Day street demonstrations throughout Europe (Klandermans et al. 2012). One of its conclusions is that 'the traditional distinction between the new social movements, focusing on post-material issues, and the old ones, linked to class politics … seems more and more misleading' (Della Porta and Reiter 2012: 350). This enables thinking that the original ambiguity of social movement studies vis-à-vis the labour movement may finally be dispelled.

Karel Yon is CNRS research fellow in sociology at Ceraps, the Lille Centre for European Research on Administration, Politics and Society, Université de Lille Nord de France. He was Fulbright Fellow at Cornell's ILR School in 2013 and invited professor in political science at Université de Montréal in 2014. Among his recent publications are *La Fabrique du sens syndical: La formation des représentants des salariés en France (1945–2010)* (co-edited with Nathalie Ethuin, Croquant, 2014); and a translation into French, with a critical introduction, of Offe and Wiesenthal's 'Two Logics of Collective Action' (*Participations*, 2014-1).

Notes

1. He assumes this, provided that 'class has effects on collective action through cultural constructions which are generated in historically specific life-forms' (Eder 1993: 10).
2. See the special issues on 'Unionisation in France' (2009/85), 'Conflicts at work' (2009/86), and 'Health and Work' (2010/91).
3. The term, built by mixing 'boss' and 'kidnapping', refers to a form of lock-in where employees detain management in the workplace (Hayes 2012).

4. Indeed, there has not been any European research project dedicated to the contentious politics of labour since that of the 1970s mentioned above. Specific research on the labour movement in Europe is either focused on collective bargaining or trade union organizational development.

References

Accornero, A. 1992. *La parabola del sindacato*. Bologna: Il Mulino.

Accornero, G., and P. Ramos Pinto. 2014. '"Mild Mannered"? Protest and Mobilisation in Portugal under Austerity, 2010–2013'. *West European Politics*. DOI: 10.1080/01402382.2014.937587.

Ackers, P., and A. Wilkinson. 2008. 'Industrial Relations and the Social Sciences'. In *The Sage Handbook of Industrial Relations*, ed. P. Blyton, N. Bacon, J. Fiorito and E. Heery, 53–68. Los Angeles: Sage.

Agrikoliansky, E., and I. Sommier, eds. 2005. *Radiographie du mouvement altermondialiste: le second forum social européen 2003*. Paris: La Dispute.

Antentas Collderram, J. M. 2007. 'Sindicalisme i moviment "antiglobalizacio", una aproximacio a partir dels casos del forum social mundial i del tancament de l'empresa miniwatt.' PhD dissertation. Barcelona: Autonomous University.

Alos, R., et al. 2000. *La transformación del sindicato: Estudio de la afiliación de CCOO de Catalunya*. Barcelona: Viena/CONC.

Balme, R., and D. Chabanet. 2008. *European Governance and Democracy: Power and Protest in the European Union*. London: Rowman and Littlefield.

Barker C., L. Cox, J. Krinsky and A. Gunvald Nilsen, eds. 2013. *Marxism and Social Movements*. Leiden and Boston: Brill.

Barron, P., et al. 2011. *On bosse ici, on reste ici! La grève des sans-papiers: une aventure inédite*. Paris: La Découverte.

Beaud, S., and M. Pialoux. 1999. *Retour sur la condition ouvrière: enquête aux usines Peugeot de Sochaux-Montbéliard*. Paris: Fayard.

Benquet, M. 2011. *Les damnées de la caisse : Enquête sur une grève dans un hypermarché*. Bellecombe-en-Bauges: Croquant.

———. 2013. *Encaisser! Enquête en immersion dans la grande distribution*. Paris: La Découverte.

Béroud, S., R. Mouriaux and M. Vakaloulis. 1998. *Le Mouvement social en France: essai de sociologie politique*. Paris: La Dispute.

Béroud, S., et al. 2008. *La lutte continue? Les conflits du travail dans la France contemporaine*. Bellecombe-en-Bauges: Éd. du Croquant.

Bilbao, A. 1995. *Obreros y ciudadanos*. Madrid: Trotta.

Boltanski, L., and E. Chiapello. 1999. *Le Nouvel esprit du capitalisme*. Paris: Gallimard.

Brandl, B., and F. Traxler. 2010. 'Labour Conflicts: A Cross-National Analysis of Economic and Institutional Determinants, 1971–2002'. *European Sociological Review* 26, no. 5: 519–40.

Brinkmann, U. H., et al. 2008. *Strategic Unionism: Aus der Krise zur Erneuerung? Umrisse eines Forschungsprogramms*. Wiesbaden: VS Verlag für Sozialwissenschaften.

Bronfenbrenner, K., ed. 1998. *Organizing to Win: New Research on Union Strategies*. Ithaca: ILR Press.

Chabanet, D., and J. Faniel, eds. 2012. *The Mobilization of the Unemployed in Europe: From Acquiescence to Protest?* Basingstoke and New York: Palgrave Macmillan.

Connolly, H. 2010. *Renewal in the French Trade Union Movement: A Grassroots Perspective.* Oxford and New York: Peter Lang.

Costa, H. A. 2008. *Sindicalismo global ou metáfora adiada? Discursos e práticas transnacionais da CGTP e da CUT.* Porto: Afrontamento.

Croizat, M., and D. Labbé. 1992. *La fin des syndicats?* Paris: L'Harmattan.

Della Porta, D., ed. 2007. *The Global Justice Movement: Cross-National and Transnational Perspectives.* Boulder: Paradigm.

Della Porta, D., and M. Caiani. 2009. *Social Movements and Europeanization.* Oxford and New York: Oxford University Press.

Della Porta, D., and H. Reiter. 2012. 'Desperately Seeking Politics: Political Attitudes of Participants in Three Demonstrations for Workers' Rights in Italy'. *Mobilization* 17, no. 3: 349–61.

Denis, J.-M. 1996. *Les coordinations: recherche désespérée d'une citoyenneté.* Paris: Syllepse.

Diaz-Salazar, R. 2003. *Trabajadores precarios, el proletariado del siglo XXI.* Madrid: HOAC.

Dobry, M. 1986. *Sociologie des crises politiques: la dynamique des mobilisations multisectorielles.* Paris: Presses de la FNSP.

Dubet, F., A. Touraine and M. Wieviorka. 1984. *Le mouvement ouvrier.* Paris: Fayard.

Eder, K. 1993. *The New Politics of Class: Social Movements and Cultural Dynamics in Advanced Societies.* London: Sage.

Estanque, E., and H. Costa, eds. 2011. *O Sindicalismo Português e a Nova Questão Social: crise ou renovação?* Coimbra: Almedina.

Estanque, E., H. A. Costa and J. Soeiro. 2013. 'The New Global Cycle of Protest and the Portuguese Case'. *Journal of Social Science Education* 12, no. 1: 31–40.

Fantasia, R. 1988. *Cultures of Solidarity: Consciousness, Action, and Contemporary American Workers.* Berkeley: University of California Press.

Fantasia, R., and J. Stepan-Norris. 2004 'The Labor Movement in Motion'. In *The Blackwell Companion to Social Movements,* ed. D. Snow, S. Soule and H. Kriesi, 555–75. Oxford: Blackwell Publishing.

Franzosi, R. 1995. *The Puzzle of Strikes: Classes and State Strategies in Postwar Italy.* Cambridge and New York: Cambridge University Press

Frege, C., and J. Kelly. 2004. *Varieties of Unionism: Strategies for Union Revitalization in a Globalizing Economy.* Oxford and New York: Oxford University Press.

Gall, G. 2013. 'Quiescence Continued? Recent Strike Activity in Nine Western European Countries'. *Economic and Industrial Democracy* 34, no. 4: 667–91.

Gall, G., ed. 2009a. *The Future of Union Organising: Building for Tomorrow.* Basingstoke and New York: Palgrave Macmillan.

———. 2009b. *Union Revitalisation in Advanced Economies: Assessing the Contribution of Union Organising.* Basingstoke and New York: Palgrave Macmillan.

Giraud, B. 2009. 'Faire la grève: Les conditions d'appropriation de la grève dans les conflits du travail en France.' PhD dissertation. Paris: University of Paris 1.

Gobin, C. 1997. *L'Europe syndicale: entre désir et réalité: essai sur le syndicalisme et la construction européenne.* Brussels: Labor.

Goldthorpe, J. 1984. *Order and Conflict in Contemporary Capitalism.* Oxford and New York: Oxford University Press.

Hassenteufel, P. 1991. 'Pratiques représentatives et construction identitaire: Une approche des coordinations'. *Revue française de science politique* 41, no. 1: 5–27.

Hayes, G. 2012. 'Bossnapping: Situating Repertoires of Industrial Action in National and Global Contexts'. *Modern and Contemporary France* 20, no. 2: 185–201.

Hyman, R. 1975. *Industrial Relations: A Marxist Introduction.* London: Macmillan.

———. 2001. *Understanding European Trade Unionism: Between Market, Class and Society.* London: Sage.

Kelly, J. 1998. *Rethinking Industrial Relations: Mobilization, Collectivism and Long Waves.* London and New York: Routledge.

———. 2002. *Union Revival: Organising around the World.* London: Trades Union Congress.

Kelly, J., K. Hamann and A. Johnston. 2013. 'Unions against Governments: General Strikes in Western Europe 1980–2006', *Comparative Political Studies* 46: 1030–57.

Kergoat, D., et al. 1992. *Les infirmières et leur coordination.* Boulogne: Lamarre.

Klandermans, B., ed. 2012. 'Between Rituals and Riots: The Dynamics of Street Demonstrations'. *Mobilization* 17, no. 3 (special issue).

Lehmbruch, G. and P. Schmitter, eds. 1982. *Patterns of Corporatist Policy-Making.* London and Beverly Hills: Sage.

Leschi, D. 1996. 'Les coordinations, filles des années 1968'. *Clio: Femmes, Genre, Histoire* 3: 163–81.

Lopez Calle, P. 2008. *La desmovilizacion general: Jovenes, sindicatos y reorganizacion productive.* Madrid: La Catarata.

Mania, R., and G. Sateriale. 2003. *Relazioni pericolose: sindacati e politica dopo la concertazione.* Bologna: Il Mulino.

Martin Artiles, A. 1995. *Flexibilidad y relaciones laborales: Estrategias empresariales y acción sindical.* Madrid: Consejo Económico y Social.

Martin, A., and G. Ross, eds. 1999. *The Brave New World of European Labor.* New York: Berghahn Books.

Mathers, A. 2007. *Struggling for a Social Europe: Neoliberal Globalization and the Birth of a European Social Movement.* Aldershot: Ashgate.

Melucci, A. 1976. *Movimenti di rivolta: Teorie e forme dell'azione collettiva.* Milano: Etas Libri.

Milkman, R. 2000. *Organizing Immigrants: The Challenge for Unions in Contemporary California.* Ithaca: ILR Press.

Milkman, R., and K. Voss, eds. 2004. *Rebuilding Labor: Organizing and Organizers in the New Union Movement.* Ithaca: Cornell University Press.

de Montlibert, C. 1989. *Crise économique et conflits sociaux dans la Lorraine sidérurgique.* Paris: L'Harmattan.

Offe, C., and H. Wiesenthal. 1980. 'Two Logics of Collective Action: Theoretical Notes on Social Class and Organizational Form'. In *Political Power and Social Theory,* ed. M. Zeitlin, 1: 67–115. Greenwich: JAI Press.

Peterson, A., M. Wahlström and M. Wennerhag. 2012. 'Swedish Trade Unionism: A Renewed Social Movement?' *Economic and Industrial Democracy* 33, no. 4: 621–47.

Pizzorno, A. et al. 1978. *Lotte operaie e sindacato: il ciclo 1968–1972 in Italia*. Bologna: Il Mulino.

Pizzorno, A., and C. Crouch, eds. 1978. *The Resurgence of Class Conflict in Western Europe since 1968*. 2 vols. New York: Holmes and Meier.

Regini, M., ed. 1993. *The Future of Labour Movements*. London: Sage.

Rosanvallon, P. 1988. *La question syndicale: histoire et avenir d'une forme sociale*. Paris: Calmann-Levy.

Sainsaulieu, I. 1999. *La contestation pragmatique dans le syndicalisme autonome: la question du modèle SUD-PTT*. Paris: L'Harmattan.

Santos, B., ed. 2004. *Trabalhar o Mundo: os caminhos do internacionalismo operário*. Porto: Afrontamento.

Serrano del Rosal, J. 2000. *Transformación y cambio del sindicalismo español contemporáneo*. Cordoue: CSIC.

Shorter, E., and C. Tilly. 1974. *Strikes in France, 1830–1968*. Cambridge: Cambridge University Press.

Simms, M., J. Holgate and E. Heery. 2013. *Union Voices: Tactics and Tensions in UK Organizing*. Ithaca: ILR Press.

Sirot, S. 2002. *La grève en France: une histoire sociale (XIXe-XXe siècle)*. Paris: Odile Jacob.

Sullivan, R. 2010. 'Labour Market or Labour Movement? The Union Density Bias as Barrier to Labour Renewal'. *Work, Employment and Society* 24, no. 1: 145–56.

Standing, G. 2011 *The Precariat: The New Dangerous Class*. London: Bloomsbury.

Tarrow, S. 1989. *Democracy and Disorder: Protest and Politics in Italy, 1965–1975*. Oxford: Clarendon Press.

Thomas, A. 2011. 'Universitaires engagés et nouveaux cadres syndicaux aux États-Unis: une alliance pour faire face au déclin des syndicats?' *Genèses* 84, no. 3: 127–42.

Thompson, E. P. 1963. *The Making of the English Working Class*. London: Victor Gollancz.

Touraine, A. 1965. *Sociologie de l'action*. Paris: Seuil.

———. 1969. *La société post-industrielle: naissance d'une société*. Paris: Denoël.

Turner, L., H. Katz and R. Hurd, eds. 2001. *Rekindling the Movement: Labor's Quest for Relevance in the Twenty-First Century*. Ithaca: ILR Press.

Upchurch, M., and A. Mathers. 2012. 'Neoliberal Globalization and Trade Unionism: Toward Radical Political Unionism?' *Critical Sociology* 38, no. 2: 265–80.

Van der Velden, S., H. Dribbusch, D. Lyddon and K. Vandaele, eds. 2007. *Strikes around the World: Case-Studies of 15 Countries*. Amsterdam: Aksant.

Wagner, A.-C. 2005. *Vers une Europe syndicale: une enquête sur la confédération européenne des syndicats*. Bellecombes-en-Bauges: Croquant.

Waterman, P. 1993. 'Social-Movement Unionism: A New Union Model for a New World Order?' *Review (Fernand Braudel Center)* 16, no. 3: 245–78.

Waterman, P., and J. Wills. 2001. *Place, Space and the New Labour Internationalisms*. London: Blackwell.

Chapter 4

Beyond Party Politics:
The Search for a Unified Approach
Research on Radical Right-Wing Movements in Europe

Manuela Caiani and Rossella Borri

Despite the increasing interest in the extreme right, empirical research on radical right-wing movements is still selective and fragmented (Minkenberg 2005; Goodwin 2012).[1] On the one hand, extreme right studies have mainly focused on political parties and elections (e.g. Ignazi 2003; Carter 2005; Norris 2005), and have neglected important developments within nonpartisan organizations and subcultures (Mudde 2007: 5). On the other hand, as noted by Della Porta (2008), right-wing extremist movements have been mainly examined within political violence and terrorism studies and associated with socioeconomic pathologies (e.g. 'breakdown' theories that explain the development of violent behaviour by the dissolution of community bonds in mass society, or relative deprivation in moments of economic crises), while social movement works, emphasizing actors' strategic choices and opportunities, have been more interested in analysing left-wing radicalism (for some exceptions, see Koopmans et al. 2005; Caiani, Della Porta, Wagemann 2012; Mudde 2007; Rydgren 2005). Moreover, although there are numerous empirical studies within the field of political violence and terrorism investigating the causes and conditions of the emergence of extremism, attention to extreme right-wing movements is rare compared to other types of (extremist) organizations (e.g. Islamic religious organizations, etc.). A further difficulty concerning right-wing movements is, as Mudde (2007: 11–12) highlights, the 'terminological chaos' linked to the lack of a widely shared definition. Terms such as *extreme right, radical right, right-wing populism, anti-immigration movements* and *far right* are employed on the basis of a range of different interpretations of the phenomenon. Indeed, no fewer than twenty-six different definitions of extreme/radical right can be found in the recent literature on the topic (Minkenberg 2000), and furthermore, 'experienced analysts still disagree on categorization, labels and boundaries between its different manifestations' (Merkl 2003: 4). Some scholars emphasise specific ideological traits (e.g. Mudde 2007), and others focus on judicial criteria emphasizing the opposition to democratic principles (e.g. Backes) or to immigration (Fennema 1997). As a result, we have to acknowledge that the term *extreme* (or *radical*) *right* has multiple facets, with the common ideological cores being law and order, a state-centred economy and the importance of authority (ibid.).[2] One problem is that the real meaning of 'right' is ultimately attributed by the public discourse, reflecting a general tendency to simplify the world (Ignazi 2006). In addition, recent academic attempts to define the (new) extreme right have tended to shift attention from 'old' fascism to 'new populism'. 'Old' extreme right referring to fascism has been identified with ultra-nationalism, the myth of decadence, the myth of rebirth (anti-democracy) and conspiracy theories (Ignazi 1997; Merkl 1997; Eatwell 2003). Today, populism is considered as one of the four main traits that characterise the common ideological core of the new extreme right (the other three being nationalism, xenophobia and socio-cultural authoritarianism, that is, law and order) (Mudde 2007: 21). This interpretation is, however, controversial, as according to some commentators (e.g. Mammone 2009), it 'may serve as an unintended form of "democratic legitimization" of modern xenophobia and neo-fascism'. In other instances the definition is based on theory-driven ideological characteristics, as in the case of Minkenberg, who, interpreting right-wing radicalism as a reaction to social change (the so-called modernization theory), defines it as a 'political ideology whose core element is a myth of homogeneous nation, a romantic and populist ultranationalism directed against the concept of liberal and pluralistic democracy and its underlying principles of individualism and universalism' (2002: 337). Despite the still open debate on conceptual definition and terminology (which is beyond the scope of this chapter to address in detail), when analysing the causes of the emergence and endurance of extremist (right-wing) movements, one is confronted with three main types of explanations and 'schools of thought'.

There are those which emphasise, at an individual level, the role of ex-activists' psychological characteristics and their values and motivations (e.g. Canetti and Pedahzur 2002; Henry et al. 2005); those which focus, at a systemic level, on the environmental conditions and the social and political contexts that influence actors' strategic choices (e.g. Koopmans 2005; Van der Brug, Fennema and Tillie 2005); and finally, explanations, at a meso level, insisting on organizations as dynamic entrepreneurs of violence (e.g. Bjorgo 2004; Art, 2011). With specific reference to right-wing extremist mobilization, economic and social crises are mentioned (Prowe 2004), as well as political instability, allies in power (Koopmans 2005), the legacy of an authoritarian past (Koopmans et al. 2005), youth subcultures and hooliganism (Bjorgo 1995) and the diffusion of xenophobic values within society (Rydgren 2005); whereas it is controversial whether social support for radical groups decreases or encourages violence (Sageman 2004). These factors are generally analysed in isolation.

In what follows, we illustrate and critically discuss the existing literature on right-wing movements in Europe, analysing this at macro, meso and micro levels, offering case studies of applied research as explanations of the phenomena which are most commonly mentioned at each level.

Individual Level Studies or Micro-Level Explanations

Individual-level analyses of (right-wing) violent radicalization draw mostly on *psychological* and *socio-psychological explanations*. Generally speaking, these theories explain violent radicalization in terms of personality types and disorders, and personal traits and experiences that predispose individuals to engage in radical violence.

For example, seeking to shed light on the individual motivations which could explain the choice to join extreme right-wing social movements, Klandermans and Mayer (2006) focused on 157 extreme right-wing activists, from both political parties and movements, in five European countries (specifically, Belgium, the Netherlands, Germany, Italy and France). By conducting in-depth life-history interviews, they identify the most important reasons of activism in their subjects' past: first of all, the exposure to traditional, nationalist or even authoritarian values (ibid.: 171) during the activists' childhood; and second, feelings of stigmatization, together with a sense of loyalty and inclusion offered by the group. Indeed, the authors argue that, in line with Ignazi's 'silent counterrevolution' hypothesis (Ignazi 1992), this type of early socialization produces a sharp contrast between activists' traditional values and the values of post-industrial society (such as permissiveness, multiculturalism etc.), which would in turn make them lean towards extremism (ibid.).

Research on *extreme right political parties* (prominent in the investigation of the extreme right at least during the 1990s; see e.g. Ignazi 1992; Kitschelt 1995; Betz 1994) stresses the importance of the specific personality traits of right-wing leaders and/or of value orientations of their supporters (e.g. level of trust in representative institutions, xenophobia, orientation towards immigration; see Norris 2005; Rydgren 2012) for the emergence and growth of European extreme right parties.

Similarly, within the specific field of studies on political violence, psychological approaches point to individual characteristics (e.g. authoritarian attitudes) as motivating factors behind the decision to join right-wing *terrorist* organizations. However, psychological approaches have now reached the consensus that serious psychopathology among (right-wing) extremists is relatively rare and certainly not a critical factor in understanding or predicting extremist behaviour. In fact, as Sprinzak argues in his study of the development of extremist right-wing terrorism (1995), very few terrorists are characterised by pathologically violent political tendencies. Rather, individual terrorists are almost always the product of a 'complex process of social and political embitterment that transforms a handful of political activists into terrorists' (ibid., 20).

The possibility of finding a terrorist personality and/or any accurate profile (*profiling*)—psychological or otherwise—of extremists is still an open debate. Henry and colleagues (2005), for instance, stress that an inclination to 'right-wing authoritarianism' is a potential contributing factor to terrorism.[3] Similar results are reported in the study by Canetti and Pedahzur (2002), who, upon interviewing 1,247 Israeli university students, discovered that right-wing extremism was mainly associated with authoritarian attitudes, xenophobia, and supernatural beliefs.[4]

Among the social psychological approaches to radical right extremism, the importance of *belonging and identity* is also stressed. The search for status and identity is considered a main motivating factor when youths join racist groups and gangs, as Bjorgo (1997),[5] for example, showed, focusing on right-wing groups in Scandinavia. Young people frequently joined militant racist groups in search of protection against various enemies or perceived threats—whether school bullies or immigrant youth gangs. Conversely, there are also 'negative sanctions' which were found to play an important role for individuals in the process of reconsidering their affiliation with racist groups (Bjorgo 1997). The threat of such sanctions are normally more effective against new recruits who have not yet established strong ties of loyalty to a particular group and have not yet severed their ties to the 'normal' community.[6] More commonly, feelings among some activists that 'things are going too far', especially in terms of violence along with all the negative aspects of being part of a stigmatised and socially isolated organization have been found to represent the most important factors against remaining part of a racist group (ibid.).

To summarise, these micro-level accounts, either emphasizing activists' primary socialization, the search for status and identity, or authoritarian or xenophobic attitudes, are all focused on the 'demand side' of far-right politics, namely on the individual factors that lead people to sympathise with, join or vote for extreme right organizations. This approach has been questioned by other scholars (e.g. Mudde 2010: 1172), who highlighted that all these explanations of right-wing extremism implicitly share one assumption: under normal circumstances, demand for far-right politics should be low.

Macro-Level Approaches: The Importance of the Context

Macro-level studies offer several types of explanations for (right-wing) extremism. Despite their variations, they all focus on socioeconomic contextual variables (in particular on economic disparities, ethnic or class cleavages, and structural factors such as technology and communication) and/or cultural and even technological variables (such as political culture, religion and historical experiences), which can account for (right-wing) extremism. For example, among studies focusing on economic aspects, there is the so-called *deprivation school* which relates right-wing extremism to anomie and poverty, bridging the macro-level socioeconomic features and individual factors (e.g. Heitmeier 2002, Perrineau 2002).[7] In this regard, the sense of insecurity arising from the breakdown of traditional social structures (e.g. social class, family or religion) and the grievances generated in economic, social or political critical conditions, brought about by processes of globalization and modernization, are considered 'precipitant' factors favouring right-wing extremism and the emergence of violent behaviour. Similarly, studies on current right-wing radicals (both from political parties and non-partisan extreme right organizations) stress that these people are usually young (often not even eighteen years old), with a lower-class background and lack of education and professional skills (Merkl 2003). In addition, difficulties in primary socialization, due to the weakening of the sense of family and entrenchment in the community (ibid.) are also factors favouring right-wing extremism. However, evidence also exists which places in question the positive correlation between right-wing extremism and (low) economic status. For example, the study by Canetti and Pedahzur (2002) showed that right-wing extremist sentiments were unrelated to socioeconomic variables. Similarly, and contrary to common wisdom, a comfortable individual situation is found to be more conducive to extreme-right party affinity than job insecurity and deprivation (De Weerdt et al. 2004: 81, quoted in Mudde 2007: 223). In fact, according to Mudde, 'populist radical right parties are supported by people who want to hold on to what they have in the face of the perceived threats of globalization (i.e. mass immigration and the post-industrial society)' (Mudde 2007: 223).

Among studies which focus on the political macro-level factors of right-wing extremism, many of them stress the effects of the institutional framework on the development of the extreme right. As observed, right-wing populist politics 'is defined not only by idiosyncratic issues orientation, but also by structural constraints, such as those of the electoral system and the partisan alternatives it affords' (Denemark and Bowler 2002, quoted in Mudde 2007: 233). These studies concentrate alternately on long-term institutional variables (e.g. the characteristics of the electoral systems—see Kitschelt 2007; Arzheimer and Carter 2006; Givens 2005), as well as medium-term party-system factors (e.g. models of party competition—see Van der Brug et al. 2005; Carter 2005; Kietschelt 1995) and short-term contextual variables (e.g. immigration levels—see Lubbers, Scheeper and Billiet 2000; Van der Brug, Fennema and Tillie 2005).

Alternatively, there are studies (a minority, as mentioned in the introduction) which adopt some concepts and hypotheses from social movement studies in order to understand extreme right movements, such as the idea of *political opportunity structure* (e.g. Arzheimer and Carter 2006; Mudde 2007). This concept, used in social movement studies to explain the mobilization of social movements, refers both to stable contextual features (such as the institutional framework of a country, the functional and territorial distribution of powers, the party system or form of government), and to dynamic and contingent factors (such as the shift in the configuration of allies and opposition, new laws, or changes in power relations) (Tarrow 1994: 85, quoted in Mudde 2007: 233). While open opportunities imply easy access for new challengers in the political system, the lack (or the closing) of these opportunities often culminate in escalation (Della Porta 1995). In these terms, for example, Koopmans (2005), in a cross-country study of racist and extreme right violence in Europe,[8] argues that this type of extremism seems to be motivated more by the lack of opportunities (e.g. through established political channels of expression) than by the presence of grievances in society (e.g. presence of immigrants, economic difficulties, etc.).[9] Similarly, Arzheimer and Carter (2006) examine the influence of political opportunity structure on *right-wing extremist party vote*. By adopting a 'three-pronged approach' (ibid.: 5) that focuses on long-term institutional features, medium-term factors related to the party system and short-term contextual factors, they find that the unemployment level, the position of the main right-wing party, the degree of disproportionality of the electoral system and the presence of a grand coalition in government are key factors for variation in the success of extreme right parties across Western Europe (ibid.: 20).

Other studies focus on the relationship between *societal support* (or non-support) and violent (right-wing) radicalization, stressing that it can move in several and unexpected directions. For example, it has been said that the German 'societal consensus' against right-wing extremism can also be exploited by activists to reinforce their collective identity, by presenting themselves as victims (e.g. since regulations are so strict, they can even claim that their human rights are violated) (Wagemann 2005). Indeed, the nation's sensitivity concerning its historical past and German guilt have greatly increased the provocative potential of racist and anti-Semitic symbolism (Kersten 2004: 180), something which can be easily abused by the extreme right.

Finally, in various other works, the presence of relatively well-rooted and supportive (moderate) right-wing parties (known as *potential allies*) and/or more unstable countercultural milieus is considered to have an impact on the organizational strategic choices of right-wing radical groups (see Kersten 2004 on Germany). For instance, there is evidence that the area of hooliganism can be a fertile recruiting ground for extreme-right activists (Wagemann 2005). Usually, (violent) skinheads and other right-wing activists are organised both in an extremist group and in a more moderated and institutionalised organization, such as, for example, the JN (*Junge Nationaldemokraten,* the youth organization of the *Nationaldemokratische Partei Deutschlands,* NPD) in Germany. In fact, after several electoral defeats, the NPD has developed close contacts with militant activists (Heitmeyer 2002; Wagemann 2005). Non-partisan organizations are seen to be suitable loci of recruitment for activists, since a formal party organization is less attractive than group life in non-partisan violent organizations (Speit 2004: 19).

Within *cultural variables approaches,* waves of right-wing violence have been linked to the spreading of values such as extreme nationalism, intolerance, xenophobia, authoritarianism, opposition to the Left, and anti-parliamentarism (Prowe 2004). Indeed, cross-national differences exist on the presence of these values. From a historical perspective, cultural racism is considered today's substitute for the biological racism of the past (Wieviorka 2004).

Finally, more recently (in the last ten years), several works concur in stressing the crucial role of the Internet for current extreme right movements in Europe (see, for example, Burris, Smith and Strahm 2000; Caiani and Parenti 2013; Tateo 2005; Roversi 2006). It is argued that extreme right groups, which sometimes walk a fine line between legal, political and associative activity and the diffusion of violent and illegal content, have found the Internet to be a useful tool for worldwide communication and recruiting activities (Burris, Smith and Strahm 2000; Karmasyn, Panczer and Fingerhut 2000). The role of the Internet in propagating the ideology of right-wing extremist hatred has also been underlined. Various authors claim that the traditional tools of political consensus-seeking are found by extreme right groups in technologies known as computer-mediated communication environments (Hoffman 1996; Karmasyn, Panczer and Fingerhut 2000; Mininni 2002). Finally, several studies stress that isolated individual consumers may find a common cause in right-wing web sites, adding to the feeling that they are not alone, and thus potentially moving along the pathway from thought to action—responding to the extremist ideology of the virtual community (De Koster and Houtman 2008).

In brief, the main conclusion that we can derive from this section is that macro-level studies shed light on the contextual (pre-)conditions that may favour the emergence and diffusion of right-wing extremism; however, they could still greatly benefit from more intense consideration of low-scale mechanisms and middle-range political variables capable of providing a link between these pre-conditions and the individuals.

Group-Level Explanations: Organizations, Leaders, Ideology and Propaganda

Group-level analyses are, to date, more neglected in the literature on extremism and political violence. They focus in particular on organizations and their dynamics, leaders, ideologies and propaganda. Among the works on extreme right political parties, for instance, there are some (few) studies that employ qualitative data sources (such as interviews with party activists) to give accounts of the internal dynamics of right-wing activism and groups. For example, drawing on 140 interviews with party activists in different countries, Art (2011) explains the cross-national variation in radical right electoral support using the dynamics of party building, and, in particular, the skill of radical right parties to recruit and maintain a moderate and educated membership and leadership. Other meso-level studies underline the important role of *frames and the framing activity* of groups for their maintenance and survival. Bjorgo (2004) for instance, stresses that as with any collective actor, violent extreme right organizations have to motivate individuals to action, providing followers with rationales (norms and values) for participating and supporting their organization. Among others, they achieve this goal mainly through discourse (ibid.: 2004). The superiority of one race (or religion, gender, sexual orientation, etc.) over others (O'Boyle 2002: 28), racism in terms of 'otherness' (Minkenberg 1998: 45), right-wing activists as 'executers of a general will' (Heitmeyer 2002: 525) and 'blood' and 'honour' have all been identified as main elements of extreme right rhetoric (Wagemann 2005).

However, the role of ideology and, in particular, *political ideology* in current right-wing movements continues to be somewhat controversial. Indeed, whereas extreme right ideology is clearly identifiable, its militants have a very diffuse idea of politics and are not always politically engaged. Many studies argue that only a minority of recruits join right-wing extremist groups because they agree with their ideology and politics, or because there is some form of political commitment. It is noted, for example, that in most cases, young people do not join racist groups because they are racists, but instead they gradually adopt racist views because they have become part of a racist group. New recruits are usually less concerned about politics or ideological content, but frequently have vague feelings of hostility against foreigners (Bjorgo 1997).[10] Enticements to join violent right-wing groups, such as access to alcohol, the martial physicality and—very importantly—right-wing hate music are far more centrally motivating than political ideology (Merkl 2003; Zimmermann 2003; Wagemann 2005).[11] The desire to belong to a group also plays an important role (the 'protection factor', see Bjorgo 2005).

Other studies underline the role played by *political entrepreneurs* (i.e. the leaders of the organizations), who exploit the violent attitudes of the activists and provide them with the necessary ideological justifications. Because right-wing extremists generally dehumanise their enemies, attacks on target groups, such as black people or enclaves of foreign workers (in Europe) are justified by their ideology (Post 2005a: 150). Griffin (2003) underlines the role of 'dream time' in extreme right-wing political violence and postulates three distinct forms of political fanaticism that can lead to suicidal behaviour: the fanaticism of politicised religions, the fanaticism of political religions and the fanaticism of 'the loner' (ibid.: 87).[12] The role played by the need to 'sacralise' life appears to be of crucial importance in all the three forms.

The activists can fall back on the ideological frames which the entrepreneurs provide and use these frames for the choice of their victims (Wagemann 2005; Heitmeyer 2002, 2005). Thus, a very dangerous mixture of radical ideology and violent attitudes emerges: 'there is an overlap between the ideological orientation of the [ideologues of political right-wing extremism] and the willingness of [intoxicated members of youth gangs] to select objects of attack that meet [the required] ideological distinction' (Zimmermann 2003: 231).

Studies which focus on extremist organizations (from an organizational point of view) also look at *organizational changes* to explain current right-wing extremism in Europe, underlining as characteristic their looser and more flexible structures. In Germany for example, it had been found that most non-partisan groups, going back to the aftermath of the electoral decline of the NPD, are organised in a very particular way. Since they live in constant danger of being banned by the law, they dissolved their previous rigid structures and became organised in rather flexible 'Kameradschaften' ('comradeships') (Verfassungsschutzbericht 2003: 48).

Koopmans et al. (2005), in a cross-national study of extreme right discourses, pointed out the importance of the organizational characteristics in the groups' strategic repertoire of action. In particular, they link different organizational forms that extreme right groups may take (more institutional versus more flexible) with different (more moderate versus more controversial) political action (ibid.: 187). Moreover, according to the authors' findings, the presence of a specific organizational form in the public domain is, in turn, related to specific factors, in particular, the political space made available by the position of 'mainstream' political parties on immigration, as well as the electoral strength of extreme right parties (ibid., 195).

Summing up, the meso- (and micro-)level studies, regardless of the field within which they are located (political violence and terrorism versus electoral and political parties studies), emphasise that structural effects are not sufficient (alone) to explain right-wing extremism. Instead structural effects, such as the background conditions (i.e. social, economic, demographic, political or cultural) considered by macro-level studies, are mediated by the militants' perception of reality and small-group dynamics through which their political involvement develops (Della Porta 1995).

In this review of the literature on extreme right movements and organizations in Europe, we have seen that several approaches attempt to explain the 'when' and 'why' (e.g. the emergence, survival, success, impact, etc.) of right-wing extremism, as well as various fields and disciplines focusing on these aspects. However, in spite of the increasing academic attention given to the subject over the last two decades, the causes (and often the definition) of the extreme right remain unclear and discussions about it are open and controversial. In addition, interdisciplinary unifying approaches linking the findings coming from different approaches, as illustrated in the chapter, are still lacking. Instrumental paradigms seem incompatible with those that view (right-wing) extremist movements as expressive or pathological.

Nevertheless, what is certain from this overview is that there is now a common agreement among scholars that there is no single explanation of right-wing extremism and that in order to shed light on the phenomenon, it is necessary to consider the context of both structural (macro-level) and group-level dynamics, as well as conditions concerning the individual (micro level).

Secondly, as seen, the existing literature on the extreme right has so far been selectively focused, either on political parties and electoral behaviour or, on the other hand, on right-wing movement organizations and violence—often with discipline boundaries at play. However, as also underlined by our review, the extreme right is able to use a variegated action repertoire beyond violence, with some groups performing traditional political actions, and others more oriented towards cultural (symbolic and expressive) initiatives involving 'cultural activities, music, publishing, ecology, events planning, cooperative work, that become ways to express and disseminate their own vision of the world' (Di Tullio 2006: 37). Indeed, as another aspect of the broadening action repertoire of the extreme right, recent studies, as mentioned above, have also noted the increasing use of new technologies by extreme right movements, and in particular the Internet (for details, see Caiani and Parenti 2013). This is a topic (i.e. the far right and Internet politics) that deserves more attention in future research in the field, along with the development of new methodological tools of analysis that are able to grasp these new developments relating to the current extreme right in Europe, such as the use of social media and the new opportunities offered by Web 2.0 (Bartlett, Birdwell and Littler 2011).

To recapitulate, psychological, behaviouralist and social science theories of right-wing extremism are not intrinsically incommensurable with each other and there is no reason why they cannot be combined in studies of extreme right movements. Future research adopting a 'multi-level' framework for the explanation of the phenomenon (considering actors and circumstances together), which also takes into account the multifaceted nature of the extreme right milieu (i.e. party and non-partisan actors) and its variegated repertoire of action, is desirable.

Manuela Caiani is associate professor at the Scuola Normale Superiore in Florence, department of political science. She has been assistant professor at the Institute for Advanced Studies of Wien. She has worked on several comparative projects on collective action and Europeanization and on right-wing extremism. She has received many research grants, including a Marie Curie and the Lazarsfeld Award for the co-authored (with Della Porta and Wagemann) volume *Mobilizing on the Extreme Right,* Oxford University Press (2012). She has written articles for several international journals, including *Mobilization, Acta Politica, European Union Politics, South European Society* and *Politics.* Among her recent publications are *European and American Extreme Right Groups and the Internet,* Ashgate (with L. Parenti, 2013).

Rossella Borri holds a PhD in comparative and European politics from the University of Siena, Centre for the Study of Political Change (CIRCaP). During 2011–12, she worked as a research assistant in a comparative project on online right-wing radicalism led by Manuela Caiani at the Institute for Advanced Studies (IHS) of Wien. Her publications include "The Extreme Right, Violence and Other Action Repertoires" in *Perspectives on European Politics and Society* 14, no. 4 (with Manuela Caiani, 2013).

Notes

1. See, for example, the increasing number of publications and scientific book series devoted to the topic, such as the book series Mapping the Far Right (e.g. http://www.radicalism-new-media.org/index.php/activities/book-series/mapping-the-far-right), the Springer edition *Rechstsextremismus* (right-wing extremism) (www.springer.com/series/12738), or the different publications on extreme right-wing politics in the Routledge book series Extremism and Democracy (www.routledge.com/books/series/ED/). In addition, a number of European projects are concerned with extreme right organizations in Europe along with policies and measures to counter them. In this regard, we can mention the Demos project Populism in Europe, which analyses right-wing populist organizations by focusing on their on-line behaviour (see for example the report by Bartlett, Birdwell and Littler issued in 2011), and the EU-financed project Preventing and Countering Far-Right Extremism and Radicalisation: European Cooperation, carried out by the Institute for Strategic Dialogue in cooperation with the Swedish Ministry of Justice (see, for example, Goodwin 2012). Finally, there are many watchdog organizations in Europe which monitor extreme right movements and provide information on the development of the phenomenon, such as the Spanish Movimiento Contra la Intolerancia (www.movimientocontrolaintolerancia.com), Antifa, active in various European countries such as Germany, Denmark and the Netherlands, as well as the American Southern Poverty Law Center (SPLC) (www.splcenter.org) and Anti-Defamation League (ADL) (www.adl.org).

2. The term *extreme right* is rejected by some scholars, because it can also include groups well beyond the legal boundaries of democratic politics. Therefore, some prefer to adopt the label radical right, to describe organizations that are located closest to one pole on the standard ideological left-right scale. This type of labelling is especially common in German literature (e.g. Backes 2007), which draws upon the distinction of the German Federal Authority for the Protection of the Constitution between extremism, as 'opposed to the constitution', and radicalism as 'hostile to the constitution' (Minkenberg 2002: 172).

3. In particular, in collecting data on attitudes towards terrorism and intergroup violence from two samples (one in the United Stated and one in Lebanon), they found that Lebanese individuals who scored high on a scale of right-wing authoritarianism were more supportive of terrorist aggression against the United States. Nevertheless, they show also that the very same personality inclination may foster support (or not) for terrorism under different circumstances. In fact, Americans who scored high on right-wing authoritarianism were more supportive of tough anti-terrorism policies.

4. Supernatural (or paranormal) beliefs would be, according to the authors, the result of the revival of occultism in many Western cultures.

5. His analysis is based on interviews with over seventy former and current far-right militants in Norway, Sweden and Denmark.

6. However, it has been observed that some of these negative sanctions, such as branding them as 'racists' and 'Nazis', may also have the unintended effect of reinforcing the participation of new recruits in these stigmatised groups (Bjorgo 1997; on the German case, see Wagemann 2005).

7. As an example of such types of studies, research, focusing on right-wing violence in Germany, associated its increase during 1991 and 1994 with the pressure for social modernization after the re-unification of Germany, and the large number of asylum seekers (Heitmeyer 2002).

8. In particular: Switzerland, Germany, the Netherlands, France and Britain.

9. He finds that contrary to contemporary wisdom, but in line with the expectations derived from the opportunity model, the level of violence tends to be low where extreme right and racist parties are strong, and vice versa (ibid.: 202–3).

10. His extensive study is based on interviews with over seventy former and present participants in the far-right scenes in Norway, Sweden and Denmark.

11. This tendency towards a non-political right-wing movement is reinforced by recently emerging contacts between right-wing extremists and football hooligans (Kersten 2004, Merkl 2003).

12. Identified as an individual 'ideologically programmed by an eclectic mixture of extremist diagnoses of the crisis of the modern world or of national decline' (ibid.: 87).

References

Art, D. 2011. *Inside the Radical Right: The Development of Anti-immigrant Parties in Western Europe.* Cambridge: Cambridge University Press.

Arzheimer, K. 2012. 'Electoral Sociology: Who Votes for the Extreme Right and Why—and When?' In *The Extreme Right in Europe: Current Trends and Perspectives,* ed. U. Backes and P. Moreau, 35–50. Göttingen: Vendenhoeck and Ruprecht.

Arzheimer, K., and E. Carter. 2006. 'Political Opportunity Structures and Right-Wing Extremist Party Success'. *European Journal of Political Research* 45: 419–43.

Backes, U. 2007. 'Meaning and Forms of Political Extremism in Past and Present'. *Central European Political Studies Review* IX, no. 4: 242–62.

Bartlett, J., J. Birdwell and M. Littler. 2011. *The New Face of Digital Populism.* London: Demos.

Betz, H. 1994. *Radical Right-Wing Populism in Western Europe.* Houndmills, London: Macmillan.

Bjørgo, T. 1997. *Racist and Right-Wing Violence in Scandinavia: Patterns, Perpetrators and Responses.* Oslo: Tano Aschehoug.

———. 2004. 'Justifying Violence: Extreme Nationalist and Racist Discourses in Scandinavia'. In *Fascism and Neofascism: Critical Writings on the Radical Right in Europe,* ed. A. Fenner and E. D. Weitz, 207–18. Houndmills, Basingstoke: Palgrave Macmillan.

———. 2005. 'Introduction'. In *Root Causes of Terrorism,* ed. T. Bjorgo, 7–46. London: Routledge.

Bjørgo, T., ed. 1995. *Terror from the Extreme Right.* London: Frank Cass.

Burris, V., E. Smith and A. Strahm. 2000. 'White Supremacist Networks on the Internet'. *Sociological Focus* 33, no. 2: 215–35.

Caiani M., and L. Parenti. 2013. *The Dark Side of the Web: European and American Extreme Right Groups and the Internet*. London: Ashgate.

Caiani M., D. Della Porta and C. Wagemann. 2012. *Mobilizing on the Extreme Right: Germany, Italy and the United States*. Oxford: Oxford University Press.

Canetti, D., and A. Pedahzur. 2002. 'The Effects of Contextual and Psychological Variables on Extreme Right-Wing Sentiments'. *Social Behavior and Personality* 30: 317–34.

Carter, E. 2005. *The Extreme Right in Western Europe: Success or Failure*. Manchester and New York: Manchester University Press and Palgrave.

De Koster, W., and D. Houtman. 2008. '"Stormfront is Like a Second Home to Me": On Virtual Community Formation by Right-wing Extremists'. *Information, Communication and Society* 11, no. 8: 1155–76.

Della Porta, D. 1995. *Social Movements, Political Violence and the State*. Cambridge: Cambridge University Press.

Della Porta, D. 2008. 'Research on Social Movements and Political Violence'. *Qualitative Sociology* 31, no. 3: 221–30.

Denemark, D., and S. Bowler. 2002. 'Minor Parties and Protest Votes in Australia and New Zealand: Locating Populist Politics'. *Electoral Studies* 21, no. 1: 47–67.

De Weerdt, Y., et al. 2004. *Turning Right? Socio-economic Change and the Receptiveness of European Workers to the Extreme Right: Report on the Survey Analysis and Results*. Leuven: HIVA.

Di Tullio, D. 2006. *Centri Sociali di Destra*. Castelvecchi, Rome.

Eatwell, R. 2003. 'Ten Theories of the Extreme Right'. In *Right-Wing Extremism in the Twenty-First Century*, ed. P. H. Merkl and L. Weinberg, 47–73. London and Portland, OR): Frank Cass.

Givens, T. 2005. *Voting Radical Right in Western Europe*. Cambridge: Cambridge University Press.

Goodwin, M. 2012. 'Right-Wing Extremist Violence: Causes and Consequences'. In *The Radical Right: Violent and Non-violent Movements in Europe*, ed. Goodwin M., V. Ramalingam and R. Briggs, 35–57. London: Institute for Strategic Dialogue.

Griffin, R. 2003. 'Shattering Crystals: The Role of "Dream Time" in Extreme Right-Wing Political Violence'. *Terrorism and Political Violence* 15, no. 1: 57–95.

Heitmeyer, W. 2002. 'Rechtsextremistische Gewalt'. In *Internationales Handbuch der Gewaltforschung*, ed. W. Heitmeyer and J. Hagan, 501–46. Wiesbaden: Westdeutscher Verlag.

Henry, P. J., et al. 2005. 'Social Dominance Orientation, Authoritarianism, and Support for Intergroup Violence between the Middle East and America'. *Political Psychology* 26, no. 4: 569–84.

Hoffman, S. 1996. *The Web of Hate: Extremists Exploit the Internet*. New York: Anti-Defamation League.

Husbands, C. T. 2009. 'Country Report Great Britain'. In *Strategies for Combating Right-Wing Extremism in Europe*, ed. Bertlesmann Stiftung, 179–248. Gütersloh: Bertelsmann Stiftung.

Ignazi, P. 1992. 'The Silent Counter-revolution: Hypotheses on the Emergence of Extreme Right-Wing Parties in Europe'. *European Journal of Political Research* 22: 3–34.

———. 1997. 'The Extreme Right in Europe: A Survey'. In *The Revival of Right-Wing Extremism in the Nineties,* ed. P. L. Merkl and L. Weinberg, 47–64. London and Portland, OR: Frank Cass.

———. 2003. *Extreme-Right Parties in Western Europe.* New York: Oxford University Press.

———. 2006. *Extreme-Right Parties in Western Europe.* Updated and expanded paperback edition. Oxford: Oxford University Press.

Karmasyn, G., G. Panczer, and M. Fingerhut. 2000. 'Le négationnisme sur Internet: Genèse, stratégies, antidotes'. *Revue d'histoire de la Shoah:* 170.

Kersten, J. 2004. 'The Right-Wing Network and the Role of Extremist Youth Grouping in Unified Germany'. In *Fascism and Neofascism: Critical Writings on the Radical Right in Europe,* ed. A. Fenner and E. D. Weitz, 175–88. Houndmills, Basingstoke: Palgrave Macmillan.

Kitschelt, H. 1995. *The Radical Right in Western Europe: A Comparative Analysis.* Ann Arbor: University of Michigan Press.

———. 2007. 'Growth and Persistence of the Radical Right in Postindustrial Democracies: Advances and Challenges in Comparative Research'. *West European Politics* 30, no. 5: 1176–206.

Klandermans B., and N. Mayer, eds. 2006. *Extreme Right Activists in Europe: Through the Magnifying Glass.* London and New York: Routledge.

Koopmans, R. 2005. 'The Extreme Right: Ethnic Competition or Political Space?'. In *Contested Citizenship: Immigration and Cultural Diversity in Europe,* ed. R. Koopmans et al., 180–204. Minneapolis: University of Minnesota Press.

Koopmans, R., et al. 2005. *Contested Citizenship: Immigration and Cultural Diversity in Europe.* Minneapolis: University of Minnesota Press.

Lubbers, M., P. Scheepers and J. Billiet. 2000. 'Individual and Contextual Characteristics of the Vlaams Blok Vote?' *Acta Politica* 35: 363–98.

Mammone, A. 2009. 'The Eternal Return? Faux Populism and Contemporarization of Neo-fascism across Britain, France and Italy'. *Journal of Contemporary European Studies* 17, no. 2: 171–92.

Merkl, P. H. 1997. 'Why Are They So Strong Now? Comparative Reflections on the Revival of the Radical Right in Europe'. In *The Revival of Right-Wing Extremism in the Nineties,* ed. P. H. Merkl and L. Weinberg, 17–46. London and Portland, OR: Frank Cass.

Merkl, P. H. 2003. 'Stronger than Ever'. In *Right-Wing Extremism in the Twenty-First Century,* ed. P. H. Merkl and L. Weinberg, 23–46. London and Portland, OR: Frank Cass.

Minkenberg M. 1998. *Die Neue Radikale Rechte im Vergleich: USA, Frankreich, Deutschland.* Opladen: Westdeutscher.

———. 2000. 'The Renewal of the Radical Right: Between Modernity and Anti-Modernity.' *Government and Opposition* 35, no. 2: 170–88.

———. 2002. 'The Radical Right in Postsocialist Central and Eastern Europe: Comparative Observations and Interpretations'. *East European Politics and Societies* 16, no. 2: 335–62

———. 2005. 'From Party to Movement? The German Radical Right in Transition'. In *Political Survival on the Extreme Right: European Movements between the Inherited*

Past and the Need to Adapt to the Future, ed. X. Casals, 53–70. Barcelona: Institut de Ciències Polítiques i Socials.

Mudde, C. 2007. *Populist Radical Right Parties in Europe.* Belgium: University of Antwerp.

———. 2010. 'The Populist Radical Right: A Pathological Normalcy'. *West European Politics* 33, no. 6: 1167–86.

Mininni, G. 2002. *Virtuale.com: La parola spiazzata.* Naples: Idelson-Gnocchi.

Norris, P. 2005. *Radical Right: Voters and Parties in the Electoral Market.* Cambridge: Cambridge University Press.

O'Boyle, G. 2002. 'Theories of Justification and Political Violence: Examples from Four Groups'. *Terrorism and Political Violence* 14, no. 2: 23–46.

Perrineau, P. 2002. 'Le vote d'extrême droite en France: adhésion ou protestation?' *Futuribles* 276: 5–20.

Prowe, D. 2004. 'The Fascist Phantom and Anti-immigrant Violence'. In *Fascism and Neofascism,* ed. E. Weitz and A. Fenner, 125–40. New York: Palgrave Macmillan.

Roversi, A. 2006. *L'odio in rete: Siti ultras, nazismo ondine, jihad elettronica.* Bologna: Il Mulino.

Rydgren, J. 2005. 'Is Extreme Right-Wing Populism Contagious? Explaining the Emergence of a New Party Family'. *European Journal of Political Research* 44: 413–37.

Rydgren, J., ed. 2012. *Class Politics and the Radical Right.* Oxon: Routledge.

Sageman, M. 2004. *Understanding Terror Networks.* Philadelphia: University of Pennsylvania Press.

Schellenberg, B. 2009. 'Country Report Germany'. In *Strategies for Combating Right-Wing Extremism in Europe,* ed. Bertlesmann Stiftung, 179–248. Gütersloh: Bertelsmann Stiftung.

Speit, A. 2004. 'Wir Marschieren bis zum Sieg'. In *Braune Kameradschaften: Die neuen Netzwerke der militanten Neonazis,* ed. A. Röpke and A. Speit, 13–39. Berlin: Ch. Links Verlag.

Sprinzak, E. 1995. 'Right-Wing Terrorism in a Comparative Perspective: The Case of Split Delegitimization'. In *Terror from the Extreme Right,* ed. T. Bjørgo, 17–43. London: Frank Cass.

Tarrow, S. 1994. *Power in Movement: Social Movements, Collective Action and Politics.* Cambridge: Cambridge University Press.

Tateo, L. 2005. 'The Italian Extreme Right On-Line Network: An Exploratory Study Using an Integrated Social Network Analysis and Content Analysis Approach'. *Journal of Computer-Mediated Communication* 10, no. 2: article 10.

Van der Brug, W., M. Fennema and J. Tillie. 2005. 'Why Some Anti-immigrant Parties Fail and Others Succeed: A Two-Step Model of Aggregate Electoral Support'. *Comparative Political Studies* 38, no. 5: 537–73.

Verfassungsschutzbericht. 2003. Retrieved 10 October 2013 from http://www.bmi .bund.de/SharedDocs/Downloads/DE/Broschueren/nichtinListe/2004/Verfassungs schutzbericht_2003_Druck_de.pdf?__blob=publicationFile.

Wagemann, C. 2005. 'Right-Wing Extremism in Germany'. In *Patterns of Radicalization in Political Activism: Research Design,* ed. D. Della Porta and C. Wagemann, 23–50. Florence: Veto Project Report.

Wetzel, J. 2009. 'Country Report Italy'. In *Strategies for Combating Right-Wing Extremism in Europe,* ed. Bertlesmann Stiftung, 327–74. Gütersloh: Bertelsmann Stiftung.

Wieviorka, M. 2004. 'Racism, the Extreme Right, and Ideology in Contemporary France: Continuum or Innovation'. In *Fascism and Neofascism: Critical Writings on the Radical Right in Europe,* ed. A. Fenner and E. D. Weitz, 219–28. Houndmills, Basingstoke: Palgrave Macmillan.

Zimmermann, E. 2003. 'Right-Wing Extremism and Xenophobia in Germany: Escalation, Exaggeration, or What ?' In *Right-Wing Extremism in the Twenty-First Century,* ed. P. L. Merkl and L. Weinberg, 220–50. London and Portland OR: Frank Cass.

Chapter 5

Fields of Contentious Politics
Migration and Ethnic Relations

Manlio Cinalli

Over the last two decades migration has stood out as a crucial field of contentious politics, intertwined with a number of key issues such as the enforcement of border control, asylum, threats to national security, radicalization of ethnic and religious minorities and the integration of migrants and their descendants. Migration has also been placed at the core of the on-going construction of a supra-national EU polity, with the production of a large volume of directives and regulations, and stronger co-decisional powers of the European Parliament. In general migrants have become conspicuous because of their status as outsiders vis-à-vis European citizens. Only sometimes have they had sufficient political force and legal entitlements (including voting rights) to challenge restraining policies, stigmatizing discourses and the abusive attacks of anti-migrant politics. Being often too weak to speak out with their own voice, in their own name and for their own self-defence, migrants have also been the object of claims of other actors, including political parties looking for votes, interest groups, policymakers, social movements, as well as a large volume of other allies and opponents within civil society. Migration has thus become a key focus for scholars of contentious politics even where movements of migrants themselves have hardly been present at all.

A first effort of this chapter is to engage with the extensive scholarship of contentious politics in the migration field. A second, more specific effort, however, considers migrants in their crucial role of protagonists at the crossroads between national and European borders. On the one hand, migration has stood out as an external challenge at EU frontiers, with growing numbers of migrants who claim a number of key rights that cannot be contained within the exclusive remit of national states (for example, asylum, family reunion and human rights). The increasing production of EU-wide schemes and programmes has also shown the potential erosion of traditional national powers vis-à-vis processes of supra-national and transnational governance.

On the other hand, migration has clearly emerged as an internal challenge within the specific borders of national states, particularly when migrants have mobilised as collective groups, for example, on the base of ethnicity, national origins, language, religion and so forth. At times these mobilizations have pursued the acknowledgment of differential rights at the group level (for example, for religious minorities such as Muslims, Jews or Sikhs), thus strongly challenging the liberal framework of neutral individual equality.

There is a third point that this contribution wants to make. Studies of migration by scholars of contentious politics have often been in opposition to each other. This opposition has reiterated old disputes (see Fillieule and Accornero in this volume). So, for example, scholars working on structures of exogenous opportunities have been criticised by scholars working under a constructionist paradigm, and vice versa. Contention has also been strong within a same scholarly camp. For example, scholars working under the institutional approach have predicted very different cross-national trends in terms of convergence and divergence of migration politics (Cinalli and Giugni 2013a; Koopmans et al. 2005; Joppke 2007). At the same time, divisions over methods and concepts have been growing into normative diatribes (Pareck 2008; Koopmans 2010), with a paradoxical matching between the contentious politics of migration on the one hand and the contentious scholarship of migration on the other. At least until the late 2000s, this scholarly contest has served the purpose of nurturing a strong competition to secure available funding for large-scale projects. In the last few years, however, the trend has been reversed with the opening up of new research frontiers and the strengthening of truly comparative and multidisciplinary European scholarship.

In what follows, this chapter engages, first of all, with the extant scholarship of contentious politics in the migration field. I argue that this scholarship can be arranged on the basis of the standard distinction between structuralist approaches focusing on exogenous variables on the one hand, and more actor-centric approaches focusing on endogenous resources (both material and immaterial) on the other. This distinction also allows for saying more about scholarly contentiousness in the migration field. Afterwards, I propose a bi-dimensional grid in order to show how scholarship can crisscross conceptual and empirical divisions between the public and the policy domain on the one hand, as well as between the national and the supranational level on the other. Yet this grid allows for identifying a further point of scholarly division, namely, the existence of very different scholarly developments in Europe and the United States, respectively. Lastly, I conclude the chapter by emphasizing new directions for research in terms of discursive opportunities, relational structures and macro-micro dynamics.

Looking at Migration from
a Contentious Politics Perspective

Scholars of contentious politics have approached the migration field by bringing into it, first of all, their own repertoire of tools of analysis and conceptual understandings. The migration field thus strikingly shows the same distinction that one finds at the core of social sciences, namely the opposition between a structuralist approach focusing on the exogenous context and a more endogenous approach dealing with the variety of material and immaterial resources that actors use. Drawing upon main accounts of 'political opportunities structure' (for a review, see Meyer 2004), some scholars have established the idea that the political context of migration sets the parameters within which political mobilization is possible (Bloemraad 2006; Cinalli and Giugni 2011; Ireland 1994 and 2000). Recent works have referred to the contextual elements that impact upon actors that mobilise in the migration field (Cinalli 2004; Cinalli and Giugni 2011 and 2013a). Attention has been focused on the institutionalised political system of the national state in terms of laws and policies referring to entry and border controls, deportation, legal status, permits and access to welfare. It has been argued that reforms which promote the political engagement of migrants have a beneficial role for democracy (Jones-Correa 1998). Drawing upon teachings of multiculturalism (Kymlicka 1995; Taylor 1994), scholars have also pursued new venues to account for variations of laws and policies in terms of cultural pluralism and group rights (Cinalli and Giugni 2011 and 2013a; Giugni and Passy 2004 and 2006; Koopmans and Statham 1999; Koopmans et al. 2005).

Although citizenship and migration policies are defined at the national level, scholars of contentious politics have extended their studies beyond the national structures of political opportunities. On the one hand, there has been a substantial growth of studies at the sub-national level. Attention has thus been focused on the urban level of cities, where policies have a direct impact on the life of a large number of migrants (Body-Gendrot and Martiniello 2000; Garbaye 2005; Penninx et al. 2004). In particular, it has been argued that different sub-national contexts provide different opportunities for migrants to organise, to forge links with civil society, to mobilise collectively and to shape common identities. Some studies have also focused on the articulation of migration politics across the national and the sub-national level (Cinalli and El Hariri 2010; Morales and Giugni 2011). On the other hand, scholars have assessed the extent to which the contentious politics of migration enters the supra-national dimension of European governance (Cinalli and Nasri 2009; Guiraudon 2001) as well as broader dynamics of world politics (Chebel D'Apollonia and Reich 2008; Wihtol De Wenden 2013).

By applying the concept of political opportunities across the sub-national, the national and the supra-national levels, scholars have advanced the operationalization of political opportunities (Cinalli and Giugni 2008; Carol et al. 2009; Koopmans et al. 2012) in a way that can hardly be rivalled in other policy fields of research (but see Giugni in this volume).

As regards the second endogenous approach, scholars of contentious politics have paid attention to a large variety of material and immaterial resources. The migration field has been taken in its material dimension, focusing on internal structures, types of memberships and capacities for mobilization. Drawing upon the notion of 'altruism' (Giugni and Passy 2001), some scholars have assessed the extent to which resources may travel from more resourceful to less resourceful actors. A number of studies have shed light on the role of pro-beneficiary actors—for example, NGOs, charities, and movements from host society—which mobilise altruistically on behalf of the weakest groups of migrants (Cinalli 2007 and 2008; Simeant 1998a and 1998b). Studies have also inquired more closely into the role of group-level resources for the (un)successful incorporation of migrants (Ramakrishnan and Bloemraad 2008). As regards immaterial resources, scholars have considered the broader role of culture through the extensive treatments of beliefs, values and identities in the field of migration. Attention has been focused on cognitive constructions and their dynamic developments, as they can variably combine with, or stand in opposition to, each other (Mathieu 2006; Roggerband and Vliegenthart 2007). Research has also dealt with the emotional and public dimensions of migration politics. It has been argued that migration has a high potential for amplification into political contention because it can foster emotions about ethnicity, religion and race, thereby fuelling heated debates about 'cultural swamping', moral panics and xenophobic mobilizations (Thraenhardt 1993; Husbands 1994; Kaye 1998).

Taken together, this rich pluralism of approaches has contributed to nurture strong scholarly rivalries. Old disciplinary disputes of contentious politics (see Fillieule and Accornero in this volume) have been brought back in these contemporary studies, transforming the contentious field of migration into a field of contentious scholarship. Scholarly contention has also had a normative dimension in the evaluation of merits and defaults of different policy approaches. Seminal works shedding light on different types of citizenships (Brubaker 1992), policy challenges (Ireland 1994) and national philosophies (Favell 1998) have opened space for animated debates over citizenship regimes and best models of integration (Joppke 1998; Rex 2000), pushing some scholars to take a clear stance in the dispute between those who favour multiculturalism and those who oppose it (Parekh 2008; Koopmans 2010). Only very recently have scholars started to lessen these contrasts. A stronger emphasis has been put on the potential complementarity of individual rights and group rights (Cinalli and Giugni 2013a). The normative underpinnings of research dealing with migration and ethnicity have been acknowledged and systematically dealt with (Cinalli and O'Flynn 2014a and 2014b). Moreover, a number of studies have focused at the same time on structures, agency and the cognitive construction of migration politics by means of all-encompassing multi-level frameworks (Cinalli and Giugni 2013b; Morales and Giugni 2011).

Strong scholarly rivalries can similarly be found when looking at the main research networks and large-scale research projects that have been delivered in the field of migration. Throughout the 1990s and 2000s scholars of contentious politics were guided by main disciplinary concerns. For example, the MERCI project (Mobilization on Ethnic Relations, Citizenship and Immigration) has especially focused on 'citizenship regimes' through its extensive work on contextual determinants such as policies, rights and opportunities. By contrast, the MDEC (Multicultural Democracy in European Cities) has promoted the study of migrants' political integration by means of a research design and methodology that has put endogenous factors such as ethnic networks at the core of research. Only very recently a number of projects have been delivered on the base of multi-disciplinary frameworks and multi-lateral collaborations of researchers with different backgrounds. For example, the last two main EU funding schemes (Framework Programmes 6 and 7) have financed a number of cross-national 'consortia', gathering at the same time scholars working on contextual analysis, resources, frames, discursive opportunities, inter-organizational networks, individual participation and survey analysis (see for example the LOCALMULTIDEM and the EURISLAM projects). Clearly, the EU funding is playing a crucial impact for the future foundation of a truly European scholarship on migration. Suffice it to mention the constitution of the Network of Excellence IMISCOE—which currently involves twenty-nine institutional partners and many scholars with different disciplinary backgrounds—as well as the EU promotion of an extensive dialogue between scholars, policy analysts and practitioners under the MIPEX framework. Yet, national agencies also have their role to play. For example, the cooperation between research funding bodies in France (*Agence nationale de la recherché,* ANR), Germany (*Deutsche forschungsgemeinschaft,* DFG), the Netherlands (*Nederlandse Organisatie voor Wetenschappelijk Onderzoek,* NWO) and the UK (Economic and Social Research Council, ESRC) has allowed for specific research delivered on the 'Pathways to Power: Political Representation of Citizens of Immigrant Origin in Seven European Democracies' project (Pathways); while the Swiss National Science Foundation has enabled a cross-national team of researchers from Britain, France and Switzerland to start work in October 2014 on an innovative three-year project, whose main aim is to fill in the deep gap between normative theory and empirical research in order to inquire into the political inclusion of European Muslims.

National and Supra-national Europe across the Public and the Policy Domain

Scholarly works in the field of migration have dealt with both public and policy action. Figure 5.1 brings together a large number of scholarly analyses across different domains (public versus policy) and different levels (national versus supra-national), thus shedding light on different paths that can be followed when tackling these two dimensions at once. Corner A refers to a first research path that is confined within the framework of the national state. Some scholars have argued that occurrences in the public domain can shape policy decisions (Faist 1994; Husbands 1994), whereas other scholars have

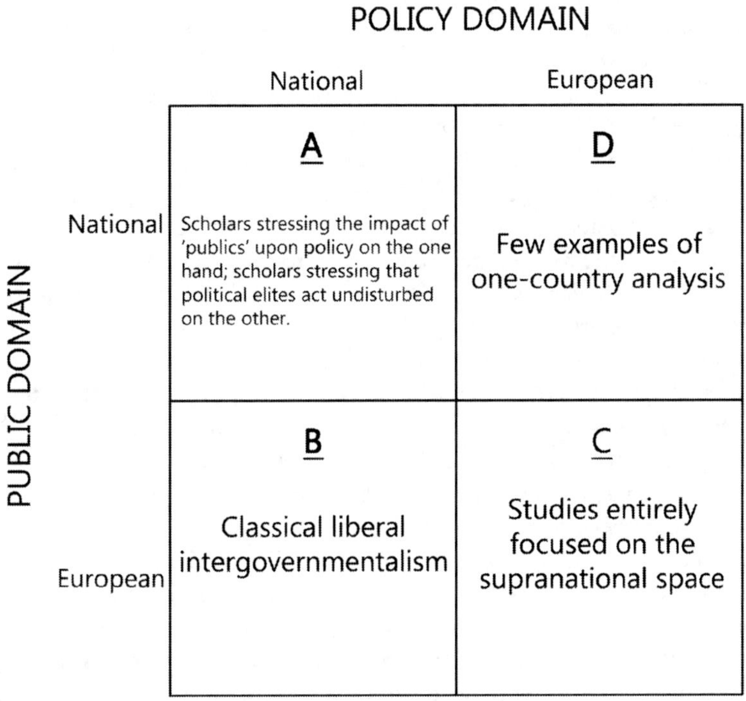

POLICY DOMAIN

	National	European
National	**A** Scholars stressing the impact of 'publics' upon policy on the one hand; scholars stressing that political elites act undisturbed on the other.	**D** Few examples of one-country analysis
European	**B** Classical liberal intergovernmentalism	**C** Studies entirely focused on the supranational space

PUBLIC DOMAIN

Figure 5.1. Scholarly debates across domains (public versus policy) and levels (nation-state versus EU)

suggested that political elites may act almost undisturbed from the noise of public discourse (Freeman 1998; Joppke 1997). Corner B refers to the two-way interaction between national institutions and policy-makers on the one hand and actors in the European public domain on the other. This space is currently the less animated in terms of migration research. While the hegemony of national institutions on the supra-national public sphere is a tenet of liberal inter-governmentalism (Moravsick 1993), the alternative notion of a European public domain prevailing over national decision-making is still unrealistic in the view of a number of scholars who have emphasised the poor evidence of a thriving European civil society (Hooghe 2008).

Corner C contains valuable studies of organizations and movements at the European level, dealing with supra-national sources of power and the increasing use of supra-national frames and discussions (Favell and Geddes 2000; Guiraudon 2001; Lefebure 2002). One should also emphasise that this type of research has been valuable in broadening the debate beyond the borders of the migration field, thus fostering the interest of normative and empirical students (Maloney and van Deth 2008; Smismans 2006). Scholars have evaluated the bottom-up role of European civil society (Della Porta and Caiani 2007; Ruzza 2006) alongside with the top-down power of European institutions (Smismans 2003). A number of works have dealt with the inclusion of European civil society within the new modes of European governance (Armstrong 2002; Della Porta 2008). Other works have placed under rigorous scrutiny the EU democratic dynamics across the public and the policy domain (Magnette 2003; Saurugger 2008), showing that European governance may stand against the weakest interests (Beyers 2004; Eising 2004).

Lastly, corner D focuses specifically on the relationship between national publics and EU policy-making and institutions. This focus follows in the footsteps of scholarly works that have dealt with mobilization dynamics across the national and the supra-national level (Balme et al. 2002; Giugni and Passy 2001). In particular, scholars have studied processes of adaptation of national publics. These processes may well enable the EU to obtain the full support of its own citizens, thereby providing an effective answer to the issue of democratic deficit (Gray and Statham 2005; Hooghe 2008). In addition, it has been stressed that the emergence of the EU (contrary to the emergence of the national state) happened only when national organizations and movements had already established themselves within national public domains. So the EU institutions and procedures may well open up new opportunities for existing organizations without prompting the rising of a pan-European civil society (Cinalli and Nasri 2009).

Overall, figure 1 identifies a multi-level framework that may help to bridge the different scholarly approaches of contentious politics in the migration field. Migration is today at the core of a multi-level process of governance, allowing for studies of actors and dynamics across the public and the policy domain at different levels. Hence, a main research challenge consists in the analysis of the complex readjustments taking place between the interventions of decision-makers and political elites on the one hand and the mobilization of various groups and organizations in the public domain on the other (Cinalli 2007 and 2008). This research has been useful to assess, for example, the extent to which policy-makers follow the preferences of organised publics, or rather intervene in line with anti-migration and xenophobic positions in the public domain (Faist 1994; Freeman 1998 and 2002; Thränhardt 1995). In the specific European context, however, there has been another main challenge. This latter refers to the multi-level dimension of migration under on-going processes of EU integration. Scholars of contentious politics have produced extensive analyses engaging with theories of post-nationalism, Europeanization and transnationalization (Della Porta and Caiani 2011; Imig and Tarrow 2001; Koopmans and Statham 2010; Sommier et al. 2008; Tarrow 2005). By applying a framework that pays attention to multi-level processes of mobilization and policy-making, space is thus opened to establish a strong tradition of studies on Europeanization and migration in single national states as well as in the broader European context (Cinalli and Nasri 2009; Gray and Statham 2005).

There are further specificities of the European scholarship, particularly when comparing with the US traditions in the migration field. Studies in the US context have mostly focused on economic and social integration (but see Jones-Correa 1998 for a noticeable exception), limiting the scope of migration politics to issues of representation and voting (Grofman et al. 1992; Leal et al. 2008; Tate 2003). Paradoxically, the studies of migration in the European context have paid much more attention to the foundational interest of US scholarship in the process of state formation (Tilly 1978; Tilly et al. 1975). It should be emphasised, however, that scholars across Europe and the United States have started to recompose these differences, both in substantial and formal terms, from the mid-2000s onward. While U.S. scholarship has increased its substantial interest in issues of citizenship and incorporation (Bloemraad 2006), research in Europe has focused on representation, voting and institutional effects (Bergh and Björklund 2011; Bird et al. 2011; Ruedin 2009). As mentioned, new networks of European researchers—such as Pathways—are emerging in order to bring forward these developments. Emphasis should also be put on the formalization of newly established consortia bringing together European and North American scholars (for example, the Network for Global Citizenship). Ultimately, the main ambition of this crucial cross-Atlantic re-composition consists of adopting a comparative, multilevel and diachronic approach allowing for a comprehensive framework that has space for many different cross-disciplinary concerns.

Crossing New Frontiers: Discourse, Networks, and the Macro-Micro Connection

In recent years scholars of contentious politics have started to work on novel aspects of migration politics. The migration field has thus enabled them to engage with an additional number of innovative research challenges. These challenges can be identified alongside the three main research frontiers that have just been crossed at the time of writing, namely, discursive opportunities, relational structures and macro-micro dynamics. First, scholars have argued that the political context cannot be approached as having only an institutional dimension. Their argument is that political opportunities stem also from symbolic practices and discourses which are prevailing in the field of migration (Blin 2008; Cinalli and Giugni 2011; Husbands 1994; Kaye 1998; Koopmans et al. 2005). Drawing upon teachings of 'framing' (for a review see Benford and Snow 2004), scholars have produced studies of 'discursive opportunities'. While analysing the (mis)match between institutions and discourse (Cinalli and Giugni 2011, 2013a and 2013b), these studies have engaged with a wide range of claims of migrants, ethnic groups and other minorities. A large variation of modes of political communication has thus been acknowledged (Bohman 1995; Cinalli and O'Flynn 2014a; Sanders 1997; Young 2000).

Second, some scholars have worked on the construction of a relational framework to advance the study of hidden factors and dynamics. Drawing upon network operationalization of multi-organizational fields of contention (Cinalli 2004 and 2008; Diani and McAdam 2003), some scholars have provided key accounts of ethnic capital in the field of migration (Fennema and Tillie 1999 and 2001; Jacobs et al. 2004). Scholars have strengthened research on actors, their position and their action in a way to foster key (invisible) interactions across the public and the policy domain. Attention has been focused on the role of cross-ethnic and non-ethnic networks, as well as on key distinctions between 'bonding', 'bridging', and 'linking' (Cinalli 2007; Phalet and Swyngedouw 2002; Jacobs and Tillie 2004). Contention over migration has been considered to be dependent upon network patterns, which vary across different national contexts. A number of works have also expanded research in a way linking individual participation to membership in associations and civil society organizations (Morales and Pilati 2011). Following all these research directions, it has been possible to provide key insights on relational dynamics for the inclusion of migrants' demands. These insights have also aimed to fill in the wide gulf between empirical research and normative theory (Cinalli and O'Flynn 2014a and 2014b).

This focus on relational dynamics has also contributed to advance studies of Europeanization. Research has dealt with actors' connections across the public-policy divide at the intersection of the national state and the EU. Actors in the migration field may use these ties to gain crucial access to supra-national policy-making, to pass preferences that may inform the elaboration of final EU decisions and to gain strength vis-à-vis rival actors. At the same time, the supra-national actors benefit from these ties, since national actors provide them with valuable information, access to national publics, as well as legitimization to compensate for 'democratic deficit'. Europeanization can thus be seized within specific network patterns allowing for information flowing, the sharing of mutual recognition, and the strengthening of public acknowledgment. This analysis is valuable to assess the extent to which actors from below seize key opportunities to engage in processes of decision-making alongside policy elites and institutions. Scholars of contentious politics have thus stood out in their way of evaluating the dynamic renegotiation of boundaries between migrants, national publics and the overall European polity (Cinalli and Nasri 2009). Different network patterns may thus be referred to key developments in terms of Europeanization, as they consist of the long-term structuring of invisible, yet fundamental interactions between organised publics and policy elites at different levels. This may also be a more likely path for Europeanization than the expectations that bottom-up European identities can follow spontaneously the setting up of EU institutions.

The last frontier that has just been crossed by scholars of contentious politics consists in the engagement with macro-micro dynamics. Drawing upon a number of pioneer studies that have used contextual factors to explain individual political participation (Anduiza 2002; Bühlmann and Freitag 2006; Franklin et al. 1996), scholars of contentious politics have taken political and discursive opportunities as additional explanatory factors—to be used side by side with other micro-level variables—to account for political participation of individual migrants (Cinalli and Giugni 2010 and 2011). In so doing, scholars of contentious politics have pushed the study of individual participation much closer to the analysis of institutions and policy-making. They have also opened space 1) for further research on the impact of specific policy interventions vis-à-vis the role of individual characteristics of migrants, and 2) for a systematic assessment of the predicting power of individual variables at the micro-level while controlling for cross-national differences in terms of institutional context and the dominant discourse.

This chapter has been developed on the base of three main points. The first point has placed emphasis on the rich production of scholars of contentious politics in the migration field. The second point has stressed that scholars of contentious politics have engaged with the complex space at the intersection across domains (public versus policy) and levels (national versus supranational). In so doing, scholars of contentious politics have provided innovative insights about processes of supra-nationalization. Their ambition has gone as far as assessing large-scale processes by which actor' interactions may fill in the public-policy divide across different levels, renegotiating borders between old polities and new ones. The final point has been that, at least until the late 2000s, scholars have used the contentious field of migration as a main field for engaging in scholarly contention. In particular, disciplinary concerns have deepened divisions between scholars focusing on exogenous opportunities and scholars dealing with cultural constructions; between post-national scholars and scholars working under a national perspective; between scholars of ethnic capital and scholars focusing on polarization and *communautarism*; as well as between European scholars on the one hand and scholars from the United States on the other. Yet, the most recent scholarly developments are quite encouraging. New research frontiers have been crossed in the 2010s, with a growing *entente*, both formally and substantially, among scholars with different disciplinary and geographical backgrounds.

Manlio Cinalli is Research Professor at CEVIPOF-Sciences Po (CNRS - UMR 7048). He has also worked at Columbia University, the EUI, the University of Oxford, the University of Geneva and the University of Leeds. Drawing upon comparative and multi-methods research, he has published widely on citizenship, exclusion, ethnic relations and migration. He has eight large grant awards in related research fields that have contributed more than £2.5 million of research funding to host institutions.

References

Armstrong, K. 2002. 'Rediscovering Civil Society: The European Union and the White Paper on Governance'. *European Law Journal* 8, no.1: 102–32.

Balme, R., D. Chabanet and V. Wright, eds. 2002. *L'action collective en Europe*. Paris: Presses de la Fondation Nationale des Sciences Politiques.

Benford, R. D., and D. A. Snow. 2000. 'Framing Processes and Social Movements: An Overview and Assessment'. *Annual Review of Sociology* 26: 611–40.

Bergh, J., and T. Björklund. 2011. 'Minority Representation in Norway: Success at the Local Level, Failure at the National Level'. In *The Political Representation of Immigrants and Minorities: Votes, Parties and Parliaments in Liberal Democracies*, ed. K. Bird, T. Saalfeld and A. M. Wüst. London: Routledge: 128–44.

Beyers, J. 2004. 'Voice and Access: Political Practices of European Interest Associations'. *European Union Politics* 5, no. 2: 211–40.

Bird, K., T. Saalfeld and A. M. Wüst, eds. 2011. *The Political Representation of Immigrants and Minorities: Votes, Parties and Parliaments in Liberal Democracies.* London: Routledge.

Blin, T. 2008. 'L'invention des sans-papiers: Récit d'une dramaturgie politique'. *Cahiers internationaux de sociologie* 2: 241–61.

Bloemraad, I. 2006. *Becoming a Citizen: Incorporating Immigrants and Refugees in the United States and Canada.* Berkeley: University of California Press.

Body-Gendrot, S., and M. Martiniello. 2000. *Minorities in European Cities: The Dynamics of Social Integration and Social Exclusion at the Neighbourhood Level.* Houndmills: Macmillan.

Bohman, J. 1995. 'Public Reason and Cultural Pluralism: Political Liberalism and the Problem of Moral Conflict'. *Political Theory* 23: 253–79.

Brubaker, R. 1992. *Citizenship and Nationhood in France and Germany.* Cambridge: Harvard University Press.

Carol, S., M. Cinalli, R. Koopmans and L. Maas. 2009. *Final Integrated Report Work Package 1.* EurIslam report.

Chebel d'Appollonia A., and S. Reich. 2008, eds. *Immigration, Integration and Security: America and Europe in Perspective.* Pittsburgh: University of Pittsburgh Press.

Cinalli, M. 2004. 'Horizontal Networks vs. Vertical Networks in Multi-Organisational Alliances: A Comparative Study of the Unemployment and Asylum Issue-Fields in Britain'. *EurPolCom* 8: 1–25. Leeds: University of Leeds.

———. 2007. 'Between Horizontal Bridging and Vertical Governance: Pro-Beneficiary Movements in New Labour Britain'. In *Civil Societies and Social Movements: Potentials and Problems,* ed. D. Purdue. Routledge: Houndmills: 177–92.

———. 2008. 'Weak Immigrants in Britain and Italy: Balancing Demands for Better Support versus Tougher Constraints'. In *Immigration, Integration and Security: America and Europe in Perspective,* ed. A. Chebel d'Appollonia and S. Reich. Pittsburgh: University of Pittsburgh Press: 300–20.

Cinalli, M., and M. Giugni. 2008. *WP1 Political Opportunity Structures Indicators: Guidelines for Data Collection.* LOCALMULTIDEM database, retrieved 1 September 2013.

———. 2011. 'Institutional Opportunities, Discursive Opportunities, and the Political Participation of Migrants'. In *Multicultural Democracy and Immigrants' Social Capital in Europe,* ed. L. Morales and M. Giugni. London: Palgrave: 43–62.

———. 2013a. 'Political Opportunities, Citizenship Models, and the Political Claims Making over Islam'. *Ethnicities* 13, no. 2: 147–64.

———. 2013b. 'Public Discourses about Muslims and Islam in Europe', *Ethnicities* 13, no. 2: 131–46.

Cinalli, M., and A. El Hariri. 2010. 'Contentious Opportunities in the Field of Immigration in France and Italy'. In *Migration and Welfare in the 'New' Europe: Social Protection and the Challenges of Integration,* ed. E. Carmel, A. Cerami and T. Papadopoulos. Bristol: Policy Press: 213–226.

Cinalli, M., and I. O'Flynn. 2014a. 'Public Deliberation, Network Analysis and the Political Integration of Muslims in Britain'. *British Journal of Politics and International Relations* 16, no. 3: 428–51.

———. 2014b. 'Pluralism and Deliberative Democracy'. In *Deliberative Democracy: Issue and Cases,* ed. S. Elstub and P. McLaverty. Edinburgh: Edinburgh University Press: 82–98.

Cinalli, M. and F. Nasri. 2009. 'L'immigration illégale en Europe: la mobilisation des acteurs de solidarité avec les chercheurs d'asile en Grande Bretagne et les sans-papiers en France'. *Sociologie et Société* 41, no. 2: 215–44.

Della Porta, D. 2008. 'The Emergence of European Movements? Civil Society and the EU'. *European Journal of Legal Studies* 1, no. 3: 1–37.

Della Porta, D., and M. Caiani. 2007. 'Europeanization from Below? Social Movements and Europe'. *Mobilization* 12, no. 2: 1–20.

———. 2011. *Social Movements and Europeanization.* Oxford: Oxford University Press.

Diani, M., and D. McAdam. 2003. *Social Movements and Networks: Relational Approaches to Collective Action.* Oxford: Oxford University Press.

Eising, R. 2004. 'Multilevel Governance and Business Interests in the European Union'. *Governance: An International Journal of Policy, Administration, and Institutions* 17, no. 2: 211–45.

Faist, T. 1994. 'How to Define a Foreigner? The Symbolic Politics of Immigration in German Partisan Discourse'. *Western European Politics* 17, no. 2: 50–71.

Favell, A. 1998. *Philosophies of Integration: Immigration and the Idea of Citizenship in France and Britain.* Basingstoke: Macmillan.

Favell A., and A. Geddes. 2000. 'Immigration and European Integration: New Opportunities for Transnational Political Mobilisation?' In *Challenging Immigration and Ethnic Relations Politics,* ed. R. Koopmans and P. Statham. Oxford: Oxford University Press.

Fennema, M. and J. Tillie. 2001. 'Civic Community, Political Participation and Political Trust of Ethnic Groups'. *Connections* 24: 26–41.

———. 1999. 'Political Participation and Political Trust in Amsterdam: Civic Communities and Ethnic Networks'. *Journal of Ethnic and Migration Studies* 25: 703–26.

Freeman, G. P. 1998. 'The Decline of Sovereignty? Politics and Immigration Restriction in Liberal States'. In *Challenge to the Nation-State: Immigration in Western Europe and the United States,* ed. C. Joppke. Oxford: Oxford University Press: 86–108.

———. 2002. 'Winners and Losers: Politics and the Costs and Benefits of Migration'. In *West European Immigration and Immigrant Policy in the New Century,* ed. A. M. Messina. Westport: Praeger: 77–98.

Garbaye, R. 2005. *Getting into Local Power: The Politics of Ethnic Minorities in British and French Cities.* Oxford: Blackwell.

Giugni, M., and F. Passy. 2004. 'Migrant Mobilization between Political Institutions and Citizenship Regimes: A Comparison of France and Switzerland'. *European Journal of Political Research* 43: 51–82.

———. 2006. *La citoyenneté en débat: Mobilisations politiques en France et en Suisse.* Paris: L'Harmattan.

Giugni, M., and F. Passy, eds. 2001. *Political Altruism? Solidarity Movements in International Perspective.* Lanham: Rowman and Littlefield.

Gray, E., and P. Statham. 2005. 'Becoming European? The Transformation of the British Pro-migrant NGO Sector in Response to Europeanization'. *Journal of Common Market Studies* 43, no. 4: 877–98.

Guiraudon, V. 2001. 'Weak Weapons of the Weak? Transnational Mobilisation around Migration in the European Union'. In *Contentious Europeans: Protest and Politics in an Emerging Polity,* ed. D. Imig and S. Tarrow. Lanham: Rowman and Littlefield: 163–84.

Hooghe, M. 2008. 'The Political Opportunity Structure for Civil Society Organizations in a Multilevel Context: Social Movement Organizations and the European Union'. In *Civil Society and Governance in Europe: From National to International Linkages,* ed. J. W. Van Deth and W. A. Maloney. Cheltenham: Edward Elgar: 71–90.

Husbands, C. T. 1994. 'Crises of National Identity as the New Moral Panics: Political Agenda-Setting about Definitions of Nationhood'. *New Community* 20, no. 2: 191–206.

Imig, D., and S. Tarrow, eds. 2001. *Contentious Europeans: Protest and Politics in an Emerging Polity.* Lanham: Rowman and Littlefield.

Ireland, P. 1994. *The Policy Challenge of Ethnic Diversity: Immigrant Politics in France and Switzerland.* Cambridge: Harvard University Press.

Jacobs, D., and J. Tillie 2004. 'Introduction: Social Capital and Political Integration of Migrants'. *Journal of Ethnic and Migration Studies* 30, no. 3: 419–27.

Jacobs, D., K. Phalet and M. Swyngedouw. 2004. 'Associational Membership and Political Involvement among Ethnic Minority Groups in Brussels'. *Journal of Ethnic and Migration Studies* 30: 543–59.

Jones-Correa, M. 1998. *Between Two Nations: The Political Predicament of Latinos in New York City.* Ithaca: Cornell University Press.

Joppke, C. 2007. 'Beyond National Models: Civic Integration Policies for Immigrants in Western Europe'. *West European Politics* 30, no. 1: 1–22.

Kaye, R. 1998. 'Redefining the Refugee: The UK Media Portrayal of Asylum Seekers'. In *The New Migration in Europe: Social Constructions and Social Realities,* ed. K. Koser and H. Lutz. London: Macmillan: 163–82.

Koopmans, R. 2010. 'Trade-Offs between Equality and Difference: Immigrant Integration, Multiculturalism and the Welfare State in Cross-National Perspective'. *Journal of Ethnic and Migration Studies* 36: 1–26.

Koopmans, R., and P. Statham, eds. 2010. *The Making of a European Public Sphere: Media Discourse and Political Contention.* Cambridge: Cambridge University Press.

Koopmans, R., I. Michalowski and S. Waibel. 2012. 'Citizenship Rights for Immigrants: National Political Processes and Cross-National Convergence in Western Europe, 1980–2008'. *American Journal of Sociology* 117: 1202–45.

Koopmans, R., et al. 2005. *Contested Citizenship.* Minneapolis: University of Minnesota Press.

Kymlicka, W. 1995. *Multicultural Citizenship: A Theory of Liberal Rights.* Oxford: Clarendon.

Leal, D. L., et al. 2008. 'Latinos, Immigration, and the 2006 Midterm Elections'. *Political Science and Politics* 41: 309–17.

Lefebure, P. 2002. 'Euro-manifs, contre-sommets et marches européennes: bilan de l'action protestataire transnationale dans la construction européenne depuis 30 ans'. In *L'Opinion européenne 2002,* ed. B. Cautres and D. Reynie. Paris: Presses de la Fondation nationale des sciences politiques : 108–30.

Magnette, P. 2003. 'European Governance and Civic Participation: Beyond Elitist Citizenship?' *Political Studies* 51, no. 1: 144–60.

Maloney, W., and J. Van Deth, eds. 2008. *Civil Society and Governance in Europe: From National to International Linkages.* Cheltenham: Edward Elgar.

Mathieu, L. 2006. *La double peine: Histoire d'une lutte inachevée.* Paris: La Dispute.

Meyer, D. S. 2004. 'Protest and Political Opportunities'. *Annual Review of Sociology* 30: 125–45.

Morales, L., and M. Giugni. 2011. *Social Capital, Political Participation and Migration in Europe: Migration, Minorities and Citizenship.* Basingstoke: Palgrave.

Morales, L., and K. Pilati. 2011. 'The Role of Social Capital in Migrants' Engagement in Local Politics in European Cities'. In *Multicultural Democracy and Immigrants' Social Capital in Europe,* ed. L. Morales and M. Giugni. London: Palgrave: 87–114.

Moravsick, A. 1993. 'Preferences and Power in the European Community: A Liberal Intergovernmentalism Approach'. *Journal of Common Market Studies* 31, no. 4: 473–519.

Parekh, B. 2008. *A New Politics of Identity: Political Principles for an Interdependent World.* Hampshire: Palgrave MacMillan.

Penninx, R., et al. 2004. *Citizenship in European Cities: Immigrants, Local Politics and Integration Policies.* Aldershot: Ashgate.

Phalet K., and M. Swyngedouw. 2002. 'National Identities and Representations of Citizenship: A Comparison of Turks, Moroccans and Working-Class Belgians in Brussels'. *Ethnicities* 2: 5–30.

Ramakrishnan, S., and I. Bloemraad. 2008. *Civic Hopes and Political Realities: Immigrants, Community Organizations and Political Engagement.* New York: Russel Sage Foundation.

Roggerband, C., and R. Vliegenthart. 2007. 'Divergent Framing: The Public Debate on Migration in the Dutch Parliament and Media, 1995–2004'. *West European Politics* 30, no. 3: 524–48.

Ruedin, D. 2009. 'Ethnic Group Representation in a Cross-National Comparison'. *Journal of Legislative Studies* 15, no. 4: 335–54.

Ruzza, C. 2006. 'European Institutions and the Policy Discourse of Organised Civil Society'. In *Civil Society and Legitimate European Governance,* ed. S. Smismans. Cheltenham: Edward Elgar: 169–95.

Sanders, L. 1997. 'Against Deliberation'. *Political Theory* 25: 347–76.

Sauregger, S. 2008. 'Interest Groups and Democracy in the EU'. *West European Politics* 31, no. 6: 1274–91.

Siméant, J. 1998a. *La cause des sans-papiers.* Paris: Presses de la Fondation nationale des sciences politiques.

———. 1998b. *Le travail humanitaire.* Paris: Presses de la Fondation nationale des sciences politiques.

Smismans, S. 2003. 'European Civil Society: Shaped by Discourses and Institutional Interests'. *European Law Journal* 9, no. 4: 482–504.

Smismans, S., ed. 2006. *Civil Society and Legitimate European Governance.* Cheltenham: Edward Elgar.

Sommier, I., O. Fillieule and E. Agrikoliansky, eds. 2008. *Généalogie des mouvements altermondialistes en Europe : Une perspective comparée.* Paris: Karthala.

Tarrow, S. 2005. *The New Transnational Activism.* Cambridge: Cambridge University Press.

Taylor, C. 1994. *Multiculturalism.* Princeton: Princeton University Press.

Thränhardt, D. 1995. 'The Political Uses of Xenophobia in England, France and Germany'. *Party Politics* 1: 321–43.

Tilly, C. 1978. *From Mobilization to Revolution.* New York: Random House.

Tilly, C., L. Tilly and R. Tilly. 1975. *The Rebellious Century: 1830–1930.* Cambridge: Harvard University Press.

Wihtol De Wenden, C. 2013. *La question migratoire au XXIe siècle: Migrants, réfugiés et relations internationales.* Paris: Presses de Sciences Po.

Chapter 6

Quiescent or Invisible?

Precarious and Unemployed Movements in Europe

Marco Giugni and Jasmine Lorenzini

On 1 May 1991 in Naples, Italy, a group of unemployed citizens, flanked by members of other associations, organised a symbolic march. The demonstration culminated in the occupation of an abandoned building (Baglioni 2012). which became a meeting place and headquarters of the movement, where protesters could coordinate common actions. This is only one among a number of similar actions carried out by unemployed people in Naples, including protest marches, occupations, and other activities aimed at fighting unemployment and its individual and social consequences. They occurred both before and after 1 May, and were mostly organised by local unemployment organizations.

In Magdeburg, Germany, about six hundred people attended a demonstration on 26 July 2004 to protest against a government reform program working towards establishing restrictions in social security, retirement, sickness and disability benefits, as well as rules regarding payment and job assignment for the unemployed (Lahusen 2009). This was just the burgeoning of what was to become a massive wave of protest—involving over a million people in 230 cities during that year—targeting the proposed labour market reform known as *Hartz IV* (Roth 2005). Unemployed people took an active part in the protest.

At least 50,000 people gathered in Amsterdam, Netherlands, on 14 June 1997 for a mass demonstration targeting the European Summit being held there, but more substantially to protest against unemployment, job insecurity and social exclusion (Chabanet 2008). Over the following couple of years, many other similar events took place across Europe, like the one in Cologne on 3–4 June 1999 specifically targeting the European Summit. These protests, which originated in France, have become known as European Marches against Unemployment, Job Insecurity and Social Exclusion, and a transnational coalition of actors gathered together at them. These later became part of what is referred to as the global justice movement.

These three examples suggest, firstly, that protest by unemployed people does occur and, secondly, that, in spite of a number of similarities, the manner of protest can take on different forms and be varied in scope: in each of these cases, respectively, a specific and localised protest sustained national opposition to a governmental measure and transnational mobilization targeting EU institutions and policies. To be sure, in the examples above, as in many other instances of mobilization, unemployed were not protesting alone, but were part of a broader coalition of discontented people mobilizing against unemployment and for job creation. This is especially true in the case of the European Marches against Unemployment, Job Insecurity and Social Exclusion. Yet often the unemployed are an important component of such protests, as they were during the 1930s, for example, when an unprecedented period of crisis and turmoil hit Europe and the United States in the wake of the financial crash and subsequent economic crises, arguably when an even more profound and long-lasting social crisis developed.

However, in spite of these prominent examples—and many others we could think of—the mobilization of the unemployed has received but scant attention by students of social movements, and the picture is even worse for collective action by precarious people. Part of the explanation rests on the fact that, as Chabanet and Faniel (2011) have pointed out, the mobilization of the unemployed is a recurrent but relatively invisible phenomenon. Part of the explanation, however, is also that scholars often argue that unemployed people face a number of important obstacles and problems preventing them to engage in collective action (Faniel 2004; Royall 1997, 2005). In the literature we find a number of explanatory factors for the mobilization of unemployed people or its absence, which we can broadly summarise in six aspects, that are likely to be interrelated and with a cumulative impact on the political mobilization of the unemployed (Berclaz et al. 2012). First, political interest and sophistication: an unemployed person might simply not be interested in politics and therefore not have any individual incentives to engage in collective action and protest activities. Second, 'objective' conditions: after all, in order to become mobilised as an unemployed person one first needs to be unemployed, and the more people in this condition giving rise to grievances about the situation of the labour market, the more likely it is that we would observe the emergence of a movement of the unemployed. Third, 'subjective' conditions: only partly related to the previous factor, for a social movement of unemployed to emerge there must be framing processes at work (see Benford and Snow 2000, Snow 2004 for reviews), that is, a social construction of the 'problem' of unemployment as well as the presence of discursive practices regarding actual collective action and its relation with societal issues. Fourth, identity: the emergence of a movement of unemployed also presupposes the formation of a collective identity and some degree of identification of individuals who are unemployed with the movement. Fifth, resources: internal resources are important for any social movement to emerge and perhaps all the more for movements of the unemployed, which often are very poorly equipped in terms of resources and organizational structures. Sixth, opportunities: as is the case of any other movement, the political opportunity structure—in terms of the openness or restrictiveness of the institutionalised political system, stability or instability of political alignments, presence or absence of political allies, and the state's capacity and propensity for repression (McAdam 1996)—must be favourable to the emergence of movements of the unemployed.

In what follows, we discuss the existing literature on the political mobilization of precarious and unemployed people, stressing in particular the role that scholars give to grievances, resources and opportunities in the explanation of mobilization or its absence. These explanatory factors are likely to be interrelated with a cumulative impact on the political mobilization of the unemployed. Furthermore, they all directly or indirectly relate to three core concepts used by social movement theory: grievances—including how they are framed—resources and opportunities. In the final section, we stress a number of weaknesses that we identify in this literature.

Grievances

Strain and breakdown theories of collective action have recently regained importance in social movement literature (Buechler 2004; Snow et al. 1998; Useem 1998). Research on strain and breakdown were often associated with the concept of 'malintegration', that is, weak networks and diffuse collective identity due to unemployment, family instability and disruptive migration (Useem 1998). Individuals taking part in collective behaviour were not only seen as frustrated but also as isolated or anomic (Kornhauser 1959). Following this research tradition, previous works on the unemployed 'had denied [them] the ability to organise and act collectively, or dismissed their movements as insignificant, ineffective, or dominated by outsider groups or agitators' (Reiss 2013: 1355).

In their seminal study on 'Poor People's Movements', Piven and Cloward (1979) stressed the role of grievances to explain the emergence of protest by the unemployed and unemployed collective action. The authors argue that inequalities are constant, but rebellion is rare. The masses remain quiescent in spite of inequalities of wealth and power because social structures exert control on individuals. Thus, the authors highlight the importance of perceptions in the emergence of protest: when individuals perceive their situations as 'unjust and mutable', then grievances have the potential to lead to protest. A change in the attribution of power is operating, as rulers lose legitimacy in the eyes of individuals who, at the same time, claim rights and believe in their chances of gaining them. A widespread loss of employment and the related income loss may lead to 'quotidian disruption' as explained by Snow et al. (1998). Their argument concurs with that of Piven and Cloward in that these authors consider framing important: the narratives associated with losses may help to push individuals into collective action. Additionally, 'it is this conjuncture of suddenly imposed deprivations and an uncertain future that gives rise to anger, indignation, and revolt' (Useem 1998: 227). In a recent study of the mobilization of young unemployed in Morocco, Emperador Badimon (2013) shows that both relative deprivation and framing play a role. The author shows that young post-graduates who mobilise on the issue of unemployment are often not unemployed—they are working in jobs that do not correspond to their aspiration as holders of university degrees—and, most importantly, they perceive employment in the public sector as a right for post-graduates. Hence, they mobilise in order to obtain access to employment in the public sector.

Recent protests in Southern Europe—most notably by the *Indignados* and Occupy movements—have spurred research on the links between the economic crisis, rising unemployment rates, austerity politics and social movements (Castañeda 2012; Della Porta and Andretta 2013). These studies entail a change in the definition of unemployed social movements. This modification in the definition of unemployed protest activities can be related to the transformation of the labour market. In post-industrial labour markets, concern among citizens and in particular among the younger generations involves not only unemployment but also entrance in the labour market, as well as precarious and flexible employment statuses.

Since the outset of the economic crisis, many social movements in Europe display citizens' mobilization against austerity politics. These movements involve broad coalitions of workers, students, trade union members and other citizens concerned with cuts in the welfare state and worsening of working conditions and workers' rights. These are not unemployed movements, but rather represent broad coalitions addressing changes in the labour market that reduce quality of work and life for citizens as well as a broader concern related to democracy and how citizens' voices and wishes are taken into account. The framing of these events involves a demand for change in the political management of the economy, the labour market and the welfare state. Thus, protesters call for more democracy to counter the effects of the crisis (Della Porta and Andretta 2013). As stressed by Piven and Cloward (1979), as the government's legitimacy diminishes, people demand changes and experience a new sense of efficacy.

Two lines of criticism have been addressed at the role of grievances as presented in 'Poor Peoples Movements'. First, a number of criticisms refer to the importance of resources and, in particular, organizational resources for the unemployed movements in the 1930s. Gamson and Schmeidler (1984) question the role that Piven and Cloward attribute to organizational resources. In their view, unemployed organizations do not only dampen but also spread and sustain insurgency by the unemployed (Gamson and Schmeidler 1984: 573). Moreover, the authors stress that unemployed organizations were able to use resources from their constituencies and hence maintain control over their actions and independence from elites. Thus, the authors criticise Piven and Cloward's rejection of the positive role of organizational resources. The second line of criticism builds not only on the role of resources but also on that of the political opportunities. Valocchi states that 'the early success of the unemployed workers movement was due not to spontaneity and disruptive potential but to a close articulation between the organizational context of protest and political environment' (Valocchi 1990: 198).

Resources

The political quiescence of the unemployed is often associated with their lack of resources (Bagguley 1991, 1992). Schlozman and Verba (1979), for example, focus on the individual resources derived from the socioeconomic status of individuals confronted with unemployment. In this perspective, a lack of voice, but also a lack of a collective identity, is seen as central in understanding the difficulties for unemployed people to unite towards collective action (Demazière and Pignoni 1998; Maurer 2001). Lack of voice is often related to the low socioeconomic status of the majority of the unemployed (Schlozman and Verba 1979). However, studying the lack of collective identity shows that the question is more complex since the lack of collective identity also results from the heterogeneity of the profiles of individuals confronted with unemployment in terms of education and profession, but also age, gender and nationality (Demazière and Pignoni 1998). The experience of unemployment varies across socioeconomic profiles (Schnapper 1999), and the common feature among unemployed persons is the lack of a paid job and the search for one (Demazière 2006). Hence, the feature that unites unemployed individuals is transitory by nature, since it is related to job search and motivation to leave their current situation.

Research conducted at the individual level of analysis reveals a focus on the lack of resources as an obstacle to participation in collective action by unemployed people. However, recent studies have countered the idea that unemployed persons intrinsically suffer from a lack of resources. Maurer and Pierru (2001) discuss the importance of what they call 'compensatory resources' of three types. The first type of resource is derived from political socialization, in particular, experiences of engagement in workers' social environments shaped by left-wing or communist thinking as can be found in certain trade unions in France. But this also includes prior involvement in other social movements or what the authors refer to as the 'multi-militants'. A second type of resource is the search for new social ties. Some unemployed individuals, who are more isolated or suffer more from a lack of structure and contacts associated to work, join organizations in order to regain a social affiliation. Lastly, the authors present anger as an expressive resource. Some unemployed individuals, who were not politicised before they joined the movements, knocked at the door to receive assistance and found a place that offered opportunities to express their anger. Additionally, time can be considered a resource for the unemployed. This can be related to the concept of biographical availability (Wiltfang and McAdam 1991). Nonetheless, a critical stand should be kept with regards to the idea of the biographical availability of unemployed persons. They may have time, but they may not have the mindset to engage in collective actions.

Certain works have examined how unemployed people may mobilise in spite of their poor internal resources. Thus, Reiss (2013) explains that the unemployed have overcome the limitations arising from their lack of resources not only by using a large repertoire of political action but also by developing cooperation with other social groups. In particular, a number of studies have analysed resources that can be drawn from civil society organizations and trade unions (Baglioni et al. 2008; Chabanet 2008; Cinalli and Füglister 2008; Faniel 2004; Linders and Kalander 2007; Richards 2009; Royall 2004). In a similar fashion, Bagguley (1992) points at the importance of organizational networks, in particular knowledge of how to organise and mobilise changing constituencies. The high turnover among unemployed persons is a challenge posed to their collective mobilization. However, it is important to note, with regard to this point, that alliances with trade unions depend on the specific issues at play since the unemployed are not the main constituency of trade unions and unemployment may be a more or less salient issue for other social groups (Faniel 2013).

Snow et al. (1998) have tried to reconcile research in breakdown theory and resource mobilization theory in their study of homeless people. They argue that 'quotidian disruption' leading to social movements does not imply that the individuals are isolated. Quite to the contrary, disrupting everyday routines may take place within groups of individuals who are embedded in interpersonal or organizational networks. Thus, in this view, breakdown and solidarity are not mutually exclusive and should not be opposed. Indeed, a study of the protest activities of young unemployed in Switzerland (Giugni and Lorenzini 2013) seems to confirm this idea, as the authors find that, while economic exclusion fosters protest activities among long-term unemployed youth, social exclusion hinders them.

Opportunities

Research and thinking on social movements and protest activities in the past decades have been heavily influenced by the political process model (McAdam 2011) and more specifically through the use of its main analytical tool, namely the concept of political opportunity structure. In spite of recent criticisms (Goodwin and Jasper 2004), the concept of political opportunities remains central, although not necessarily in its structural version nor with its original focus on formal political institutions. Work dealing with precarious and unemployed movements has also been conducted along these lines. An early example is provided in a study by Piven and Cloward (1979) which also considers the importance of opportunities, in particular electoral timing and citizens' support for the protesters. They 'distinguish between occasions when electoral instability favours those who protest and when it does not' (Lefkowitz 2003: 722).

In the 1930s, the unemployed engaged in repertoires of protest activities that included various forms of action such as demonstrations, rallies and sit-ins (Valocchi 1990: 195). Historical research on unemployed movements in the 1930s shows that these repertoires of contention included forms of protest used exclusively by the unemployed and which allowed unemployed movements to avoid state hostility in an attempt to transform contextual constraints into opportunities (Perry 2013). According to Piven and Cloward (1979), the success of the protests by the unemployed derived from their capacity to disrupt institutional routines. However, Valocchi (1990) contends that their success was related to the alliances and political relay that they were able to build. Contacts with authorities facilitated lobbying activities by the unemployed movements. This analysis lends support to the political opportunity argument, stressing in particular the role of a division among the elites, which is one of the main components of the political opportunity structure for the mobilization of social movements (McAdam 1996; Tarrow 2011). Similarly, Della Porta (2008) has looked at protest on unemployment (not strictly by the unemployed) in Europe and stressed, among other aspects, the importance of political opportunities for the emergence and development of protest in this field, including the role played by the alliances which the various actors establish among each other.

The political opportunity approach lends itself to comparative analyses, across space or time. To be sure, most existing analyses of the mobilization of the unemployed are focused on specific local or national situations. However, we also find some valuable cross-national comparisons. For example, Baglioni et al. (2008) have compared the mobilization of the unemployed in France, Germany and Italy. They show how their mobilization depends on the existence of favourable windows of opportunities and, more specifically, how the unemployed benefited from external developments that produced changes in potential mobilizing resources and created new allies and political entrepreneurs. The authors also stress that such opportunities were actively seized and produced by contentious actors, including the unemployed themselves. This is an important point, as criticisms of the political opportunity approach have often highlighted the structural bias inherent in this approach, leaving little room for agency (Goodwin and Jasper 2004). Similarly, Faniel (2004) compared the movement of the French unemployed of 1997–98 and the Belgian unemployed who mobilised against home visits. While not directly focusing on political opportunities, the author shows both the similarities between the two movements, but also their divergences arising from different institutional, social and political contexts. In particular, he shows the importance of the different implication of unions on the form of the mobilizations.

Comparisons can also be done across time. In this respect, Bagguley (1992) has compared the emergence of collective action by the unemployed in the 1930s and the quiescence of unemployed in the 1980s in Britain. The author emphasises the importance of the structure of the state (centralised or decentralised) and the provision of services to the unemployed through state-financed agencies. In the 1930s the local authorities had some power over unemployment benefits and could be influenced locally through protest activities, while in the 1980s the centralised welfare state would not waiver. Richards (2009) has made a similar cross-time comparison in his historical analysis of union behaviour towards the unemployed in Britain in the 1920s–30s and in the 1980s, two periods of high unemployment. His argument, however, focuses on internal resources rather than on the existence of political opportunities for mobilization. He links the emergence of a movement in the former period and the lack thereof in the latter period to the different levels of resources received by the unemployed. He also pin-points the ambiguous, if not hostile, behaviour that unions often display vis-à-vis the unemployed. Linders and Kalander (2010) also point out this ambiguous relationship between unions and the unemployed movements.

A recent strand of research adopts a revised political opportunity approach to inquire into the role of specific opportunities for social movement mobilization (Berclaz and Giugni 2005). In this perspective, political opportunities for mobilization do not stem primarily from the general features of the institutionalised system, but from more specific aspects related to the political field and the issues addressed by the movement, in this case the political field of unemployment. A six-country comparison following this approach has shown the importance of such specific opportunity structures for the mobilization of the unemployed (Giugni 2008). In this study, political opportunities are defined not only in terms of general institutional features such as the degree of openness or restrictiveness of the political system or the presence or absence of institutional allies, but above all as opportunities stemming from the ways in which the political field of unemployment is collectively defined. This approach has the advantage of bridging political opportunity theory and framing theory.

Other studies show that political opportunities—both general and specific—shape contention around unemployment and precariousness through both unemployment and labour market regulations. For example, historical research on unemployed mobilizations during the 1930s show the importance of the emergence of the concept of unemployed and the support of Communist parties (Pierru 2007). More recently, during the 2000s, situations of precarious employment have multiplied and reduced unemployment in particular among youth, women and migrants. In these contexts, the mobilization of precarious people has emerged at the regional and national levels, in particular in Italy (Choi and Mattoni 2010; Mattoni 2009) and France (Boumaza and Hamman 2007), where they are sometimes subsumed under the term *mouvements des sans* (Dunezat 2011; Mouchard 2002), but also at the transnational level, for example through the Euro Mayday Parade organised simultaneously in nineteen cities in 2006 (Mattoni 2009).

The Future of Research on Precarious and Unemployed Movements

In spite of the overall consensus on the perceived and existing limitations for the mobilization of the unemployed, the fact is that the unemployed do mobilise, as confirmed by a number of case studies and comparative research presented in this chapter. The rekindled interest in unemployed movements may be related to rising unemployment across the world. However, this interest was not initiated by political or social scientists, but rather by historians who revealed the importance of unemployed movements since the 1930s not only in Britain, the United States or Germany but also in France (Perry 2007; Reiss and Perry 2011; Richards 2009). In addition, the scholarly literature on precarious and unemployed movements is heavily biased in favour of the latter. Studies focusing on precarious people appear much less frequently (Abdelnour et al. 2009; Boumaza and Hamman 2007; Boumaza and Pierru 2007; Collovald and Mathieu 2009). Exceptions to those who focus primarily on unemployed movements include students of social movements and collective actions who, when they did examine the mobilization of precarious people, often looked in particular at precarious youth (Mattoni 2009; Okas 2007; Sinigaglia 2007). Indeed, work on the mobilization of unemployed people cannot be defined as a 'growth industry'. Nonetheless, there is a growing interest in this subject matter, as suggested by some recent collective endeavours (Chabanet and Faniel 2011, 2012; Giugni 2008; *Labour History Review* 2008; *Mobilization* 2008). And, in view of the current situation concerning unemployment levels across Europe and especially in Southern Europe, one may expect research in this field to grow in the near future. Also, works focusing on precarious people should be conducted more systematically.

The relatively sparse literature on the mobilization of unemployed, and even more so that of precarious, people is perhaps explained, at least in part, by the fact that these movements have sometimes tended to be subsumed under other movements, hence denying them autonomous status. For example, studies of the global justice movement (Della Porta 2007), the *Indignados* (*Current Sociology* 2013) or the Occupy movement (Gamson and Sifry 2013; *Social Movement Studies* 2012) are indeed also studies of when and how unemployed and precarious people engage in collective action, as much as they are studies of when and how youth engage in collective action. As a result, the mobilization of the precarious and unemployed is underestimated to the extent that they have been considered as part of other, broader movements. This is partly also due to the changing structure of the labour market, insofar as unemployment increasingly tends to be related to other statuses of outsiders with regard to the labour market rather than the more traditional status of unemployed. This underestimating also relates to the issue of how social movements are framed and more specifically to the difficulty of creating a collective identity around the social categories of the unemployed and the precarious. In this perspective, certain studies analyse and distinguish their struggle from that of people mobilizing on behalf of them (Dunezat 1998, 2009).

Notwithstanding the growth of the related literature, movements of the unemployed are a rare commodity. Yet, in some countries they are even rarer than in others. This calls for cross-national analyses of their mobilization. However, truly comparative studies are few and far between. The literature has developed mostly, if not entirely, as country-specific analyses—in particular in countries such as France, Germany and Italy, but in other contexts as well—hence overlooking the differences and commonalities among unemployed movements internationally. Indeed, here we find indirect comparisons aimed at singling out the peculiarities of specific national or local cases by comparing them with other cases, which sometimes take the form of collections of national case studies (Chabanet and Faniel 2012). However, only rarely have scholars engaged in genuine cross-national comparisons (Baglioni et al. 2008; Faniel 2004; Giugni 2008). The EU framework programmes of research funding can be of much help in this regard. Such a cross-national comparison occurred, for example, in an EU-funded project on the 'contentious politics of unemployment in Europe' (Giugni 2010), where an international team of researchers was able to study, among other things, the forms and levels of mobilization of the unemployed in six different European countries. Comparative analyses of this kind elucidate the role of contextual factors—in particular, those concerning the political-institutional context—as well as the interplay between internal and contextual factors in explaining the conditions under which unemployed people are effectively able to mobilise. In addition, they enable empirical generalizations beyond a specific case study. In our view, efforts at comparing precarious and unemployed movements in different contexts, not only national ones, should be multiplied in future research.

The lack of comparisons problem is exacerbated by the fact that the existing comparative studies almost entirely focus on the Western context (Europe and the United States). This holds for research on social movements in general and also more specifically for works on precarious and unemployed movements. In both cases, our knowledge would be enhanced by comparing the conditions, determinants and dynamics of the mobilization of precarious and unemployed movements in contexts which are relatively homogenous, such as Western countries, with contexts that are both culturally and institutionally very different, such as Eastern Europe or even more so the Middle East. In this regard, it could be greatly advantageous to study the recent protests occurring in the Arab world.

A related issue concerns the methods of analysis. While a wealth of different methodologies has been used to study precarious and unemployed movements, ranging from ethnographic studies and qualitative case studies to systematic quantitative analyses, most existing works focus on the unemployed once they are mobilised. This prevents the researcher from disentangling the factors enabling precarious and unemployed people to engage in collective action. Comparative analyses might help inasmuch as they provide variation in the degree of mobilization and different potential explanatory factors. However, a more systematic analysis of 'positive' and 'negative' cases might yield new insights into the conditions, determinants and dynamics leading to the political mobilization of precarious and unemployed people. Some have done so by comparing the unemployed who have participated with those who have not become involved (Maurer 2001). We think that this is a fruitful avenue for future research in this field.

Future research should also dig deeper into the motivations and reasons leading precarious and unemployed people to engage in collective action. This analysis would greatly benefit from systematically comparing precarious and unemployed people with people who have a regular job in order to ascertain whether the status of precarious and unemployed matters. In this way, studies conducted at the individual level complement well-researched studies on precarious and unemployed movements. Most importantly, the linkages between these two levels of analysis should be further investigated.

Marco Giugni is a professor at the Department of Political Science and International Relations and director of the Institute of Citizenship Studies (InCite) at the University of Geneva, Switzerland. His research interests include social movements and collective action, immigration and ethnic relations, unemployment and social exclusion.

Jasmine Lorenzini is a post-doctoral researcher at the EUI where she works on the POLCON project dealing with *Political Conflict in Europe in the Shadow of the Great Recession*. She holds a PhD from the University of Geneva, where she defended her thesis on *Unemployment and Citizenship: Social and Political Participation of Unemployed Youth in Geneva* in 2013.

References

Abdelnour, S., et al. 2009. 'Précarité et luttes collectives: renouvellement, refus de la délégation ou décalages d'expériences militantes?' *Sociétés contemporaines* 2, no. 74: 73–95.

Bagguley, P. 1991. *From Protest to Acquiescence? Political Movements of the Unemployed.* London: Macmillan.

———. 1992. 'Protest, Acquiescence and the Unemployed: A Comparative Analysis of the 1930s and 1980s'. *The British Journal of Sociology* 43, no. 3: 443–61.

Baglioni, S. 2012. 'The Mobilization of Unemployed in Italy: The Case of Naples' In *The Mobilization of the Unemployed in Europe: From Acquiescence to Protest?*, ed. D. Chabanet and J. Faniel, 131–54. New York: Palgrave Macmillan.

Baglioni, S., et al. 2008 'Transcending Marginalization: The Mobilization of the Unemployed in France, Germany, and Italy in a Comparative Perspective'. *Mobilization* 13, no. 3: 323–35.

Benford, R. D., and D. A. Snow. 2000. 'Framing Processes and Social Movements: An Overview and Assessment'. *Annual Review of Sociology* 26: 611–39.

Berclaz, J., and M. Giugni. 2005. 'Specifying the Concept of Political Opportunity Structures'. In *Economic and Political Contention in Comparative Perspective,* ed. M. Kousis and C. Tilly, 15–32. Boulder: Paradigm Publishers.

Berclaz, M., K. Füglister and M. Giugni. 2012. 'Political Opportunities and the Mobilization of the Unemployed in Switzerland'. In *The Mobilization of the Unemployed in Europe: From Acquiescence to Protest?*, ed. D. Chabanet and J. Faniel, 221–46. New York: Palgrave Macmillan.

Boumaza, M., and O. Hamman. 2007. *Sociologie des mouvements de précaires: espaces mobilisés et répertoires d'action.* Paris: L'Harmattan.

Boumaza, M., and E. Pierru. 2007. 'Des mouvements de précaires à l'unification d'une cause'. *Sociétés contemporaines* 65: 7–25.

Buechler, S. M. 2004. 'The Strange Career of Strain and Breakdown Theories of Collection Action'. In *The Wiley-Blackwell Encyclopedia of Social and Political Movements,* ed. D. A. Snow, D. Della Porta and B. Klandermans, 47–66. Malden: Wiley.

Castañeda, E. 2012. 'The Indignados of Spain: A Precedent to Occupy Wall Street'. *Social Movement Studies* 11, nos. 3–4: 309–19.

Chabanet, D. 2008. 'When the Unemployed Challenge the European Union: The European Marches as a Mode of Externalization of Protest'. *Mobilization* 13, no. 3: 311–22.

Chabanet, D., and J. Faniel. 2011. 'The Moblization of the Unemployed: A Recurrent but Relatively Invisible Phenomenon'. In *Unemployment and Protest: New Perspectives on Two Centuries of Contention,* ed. M. Reiss M. and Perry, 387–405. Oxford and New York: Oxford University Press.

Chabanet, D., and J. Faniel. 2012. *The Mobilization of the Unemployed in Europe: From Acquiescence to Protest?* New York: Palgrave Macmillan.

Choi, H.-L., and A. Mattoni. 2010. 'The Contentious Field of Precarious Work in Italy: Political Actors, Strategies and Coalitions'. *WorkingUSA* 13, no. 2: 213–43.

Cinalli, M., and K. Füglister. 2008. 'Networks and Political Contention over Unemployment: A Comparison of Britain, Germany, and Switzerland'. *Mobilization* 13, no. 3: 259–76.

Collovald, A., and L. Mathieu. 2009. 'Mobilisations improbables et apprentissage d'un répertoire syndical'. *Politix* 86: 119–43.

Cristancho, C. 2015. 'A Tale of Two Crises: Contentious Responses to Anti-austerity Policy in Spain'. In *Austerity and Protest: Popular Contention in Times of Economic Crisis,* ed. M. Giugni and M. Grasso, 189–210. Farnham: Ashgate.

Current Sociology. 2013. 'From Indignation to Occupation: A New Wave of Global Mobilization'. 61, no. 4.

Della Porta D. 2007. *The Global Justice Movement: Cross-National and Transnational Perspective.* Boulder: Paradigm.

———. 2008. 'Protest on Unemployment: Forms and Opportunities'. *Mobilization* 13, no. 3: 277–95.

Della Porta, D., and M. Andretta. 2013. 'Protesting for Justice and Democracy: Italian Indignados?' *Contemporary Italian Politics* 5, no. 1: 23–37.

Demazière, D. 2006. *Sociologie des chômeurs.* Paris: La Découverte.

Demazière, D. and M. T. Pignoni. 1998. *Chômeurs: du silence à la révolte. Sociologie d'une action collective.* Paris: Hachette littératures.

Dunezat, X. 1998. 'Des mouvements sociaux sexués'. *Nouvelles Questions Féministes* 19, nos. 2–4: 161–95.

———. 2009. 'Organisation du travail militant, luttes internes et dynamiques identitaires: le cas des "mouvements de chômeurs"'. In *Identifier - s'identifier: à propos des identités politiques,* ed. M. Surdez, M. Vögtli and B. Voutat, 155–76. Lausanne: Antipodes.

———. 2011. 'Mouvements des "sans", rapports sociaux et "exclusion sociale"'. In *Les mobilisations sociales à l'heure du précariat,* ed. D. Chabanet, P. Dufour and F. Royall, 203–26. Rennes: Presses de l'Ecole des hautes études en santé publique.

Emperador Badimon, M. 2013. 'Does Unemployment Spark Collective Contentious Action? Evidence from a Moroccan Social Movement'. *Journal of Contemporary African Studies* 31, no. 2: 194–212.

Faniel, J. 2004. 'Chômeurs en Belgique et en France: des mobilisations différentes'. *Revue internationale de politique comparée* 11, no. 4: 493–506.

———. 2013. 'Comparing Mobilizations against Three Social Reforms in the 2000s in Belgium'. In *Economic and Political Change in Asia and Europe: Social Movement Analyses,* ed. B. Andreosso-O'Callaghan and F. Royall, 163–77. New York: Springer.

Gamson, W. A., and E. Schmeidler. 1984. 'Organizing the Poor'. *Theory and Society* 13: 567–84.

Gamson, W. A., and M. L. Sifry. 2013 'The Occupy Movement: An Introduction'. *The Sociological Quarterly* 54, no. 2: 159–63.

Giugni, M. 2008. 'Welfare States, Political Opportunities, and the Mobilization of the Unemployed: A Cross-National Analysis'. *Mobilization* 13, no. 3: 297–310.

Giugni, M. 2010. *The Contentious Politics of Unemployment in Europe: Welfare States and Political Opportunities.* New York: Palgrave Macmillan.

Giugni, M., and J. Lorenzini. 2013. 'Employment Status and Political Participation: Does Exclusion Influence Protest Behavior of the Young Unemployed?' In *Economic and Political Change in Asia and Europe: Social Movement Analyses,* ed. B. Andréosso-O'Callaghan and F. Royall, 179–97. Dordrecht, New York: Springer.

Goodwin, J., and J. Jasper. 2004. 'Caught in a Winding, Snarling Vine: The Structural Bias of Political Process Theory'. In *Rethinking Social Movements: Structure, Meaning, and Emotion,* ed. J. Goodwin and J. Jasper, 3–30. Lanham: Rowman and Littlefield.

Kornhauser W. 1959 *The Politics of Mass Society.* Glencoe: Free Press.

Labour History Review. 2008. 'History of Unemployed Movements'. *Labour History Review* 73, no. 1 (special issue).

Lahusen C. 2009. 'The Hidden Hand of the European Union and the Silent Europeanization of Public Debates on Unemployment: The Case of the European Employment

Strategy'. In *The Politics of Unemployment in Europe: Policy Responses and Collective Action*, ed. M. Giugni, 151–72. Farnham: Ashgate.

Lefkowitz, J. 2003. 'The Success of Poor People's Movements: Empirical Tests and the More Elaborate Model'. *Perspectives on Politics* 1, no. 4: 721–26.

Linders, A., and M. Kalander. 2007. 'The Construction and Mobilization of Unemployed Interests: The Case of Sweden in the 1990s'. *Qualitative Sociology* 30, no. 4: 417–37.

Linders, A., and M. Kalander. 2010. 'A Precarious Balance of Interests: Unions and the Unemployed in Europe'. In *The Contentious Politics of Unemployment in Europe: Welfare States and Political Opportunities*, ed. M. Giugni, 97–126. New York: Palgrave Macmillan.

Mattoni, A. 2009 'Pratiques médiatiques multiples dans les mobilisations italiennes contre la précarité'. In *Identifier - s'identifier: à propos des identités politiques*, ed. M. Surdez, M. Vögtli and B. Voutat, 155–76. Lausanne: Antipodes.

Maurer, S. 2001. *Les chômeurs en action (décembre 1997–mars 1998): mobilisation collective et ressources compensatoires*. Paris: L'Harmattan.

Maurer, S., and E. Pierru. 2001. 'Le mouvement des chômeurs de l'hiver 1997–1998 Retour sur un "miracle social"'. *Revue française de science politique* 51, no. 3: 371–407.

McAdam, D., 1996. 'Conceptual Origins, Current Problems, Future Directions'. In *Comparative Perspectives on Social Movements: Political Opportunities, Mobilizing Structures, and Cultural Framings*, ed. D. McAdam, J. D. McCarthy and M. N. Zald, 23–40. Cambridge and New York: Cambridge University Press.

Mobilization. 2008. 'The Contentious Politics of European Unemployment'. 13, no. 3.

Mouchard, D., 2002. 'Les mobilisations des "sans" dans la France contemporaine: l'émergence d'un "radicalisme autolimité"?' *Revue française de science politique* 52, no. 4: 425–47.

Okas, L. 2007. 'Faire de nécessité vertu. Pratiques de la précarité des journalistes dans deux entreprises d'audiovisuel public'. *Sociétés contemporaines* 65, no. 1: 82–111.

Perry, M. 2007. *Prisoners of Want: The Experience and Protest of the Unemployed in France, 1921–45*. Hampshire: Ashgate.

Perry, M. 2013. 'The British and French Hunger Marches of the 1930s: An Exclusive Mode of Protest, a Cultural Transfer, and a Fulcrum of Success'. In *Economic and Political Change in Asia and Europe: Social Movement Analyses*, ed. B. Andreosso-O'Callaghan and F. Royall, 145–61. New York: Springer.

Pierru, E. 2007. 'Mobiliser "la vie fragile": Les communistes et les chômeurs dans les années'. *Sociétés contemporaines* 65, no. 1: 113–45.

Piven, F. F., and R. A. Cloward. 1979. *Poor People's Movements: Why They Succeed, How They Fail*. New York: Vintage Books.

Reiss, M. 2013. 'Unemployment Movements'. In *The Wiley-Blackwell Encyclopedia of Social and Political Movements*, ed. D. A. Snow, D. Della Porta and B. Klandermans, 1355–57. Malden: Wiley.

Reiss, M., and M. Perry. 2011. *Unemployment and Protest: New Perspectives on Two Centuries of Contention. Studies of the German Historical Institute London*. Oxford and New York: Oxford University Press.

Richards, A. 2009. 'Trade Unions and the Unemployed in the Interwar Period and the 1980s in Britain'. In *The Politics of Unemployment in Europe: Policy Responses and Collective Action*, ed. M. Giugni, 83–99. Farnham: Ashgate.

Roth, R. 2005. 'The Monday Demonstrations of 2004—Continuity, Break or New Horizons in Collective Action on Unemployment in Germany?' *Contentious Politics of Unemployment 2 April,* Geneva.

Royall, F. 1997. 'Problems of Collective Action for Associations of the Unemployed in France and in Ireland'. In *The Political Context of Collective Action: Power, Argumentation and Democracy,* ed. R. Edmonson, 146–62. London: Routledge.

———. 2004. 'Politics and Unemployment Organisations in France'. *Modern and Contemporary France* 12, no. 1: 49–62.

———. 2005. *Mobilisations de chômeurs en Irlande (1985–1995).* Paris: L'Harmattan.

Schlozman, K. L., and S. Verba. 1979. *Injury to Insult: Unemployment, Class, and Political Response.* Cambridge: Harvard University Press.

Schnapper, D. 1999. *L'épreuve du chômage.* Paris: Gallimard.

Sinigaglia, J. 2007. 'Le mouvement des intermittents du spectacle: entre précarité démobilisatrice et précaires mobilisateurs'. *Sociétés contemporaines* 65, no. 1: 27–53.

Snow, D. A. 2004. 'Framing Processes, Ideology, and Discursive Fields'. In *The Blackwell Companion to Social Movements,* ed. D. A. Snow, S. A. Soule and H. Kriesi, 380–412. Malden: Blackwell.

Snow, D. A., et al. 1998. 'Disrupting the "Quotidian": Reconceptualizing the Relationship between Breakdown and the Emergence of Collective Action'. *Mobilization* 3, no. 1: 1–22.

Social Movement Studies. 2012. 'Occupy!' 1, nos. 3–4.

Tarrow, S. 2011. *Power in Movement: Social Movements and Contentious Politics.* Cambridge and New York: Cambridge University Press.

Useem, B. 1998. 'Breakdown Theories of Collective Action'. *Annual Review of Sociology* 24: 215–38.

Valocchi, S. 1990. 'The Unemployed Workers Movement of the 1930s: A Reexamination of the Piven and Cloward Thesis'. *Social Problems* 37: 191–205.

Wiltfang, G. L., and D. McAdam. 1991. 'The Costs and Risks of Social Activism: A Study of Sanctuary Movement Activism'. *Social Forces* 69, no. 4: 987–1010.

Chapter 7

From Anti-globalization to Global Justice Movement
The Waterloo's European Battle

Isabelle Sommier

From the outset, research work has accompanied the alter-global movement, starting with its official birth at the WTO summit in Seattle in 1999. The first survey was conducted the following year for the Human Dike protest by a team from the United States on 13–24 November 2000 at the 2000 Conference of the United Nations Framework Convention on Climate Change in The Hague, Netherlands. From then on, the studies multiplied up to 2007 and decreased very significantly thereafter. In a previous article (Sommier 2015), I counted some twenty group surveys carried out at world or continental social forums: the Europeans kept pace with the North Americans,[1] there was one Australian team headed by Bramble which worked on the topic and one 'from the South' with periodic surveys conducted at World Social Forums (WSF) by IBASE.[2] No doubt there are several reasons why European research occupies a prominent place. First, the old continent was objectively the geographical area most concerned by the initial protests against neoliberal globalization. National and European Union authorities soon called for (and therefore funded) numerous reports and studies, which obviously had an impact on their orientation, as we shall see. Finally, following the new social movements (NSM), alter-globalization was to become the preferred field of investigation for European sociologists of social movements, who saw it as an opportunity to assert themselves in a sub-discipline hegemonised by their American colleagues.

As a result, the European research work has several specific features that are not found in studies carried out on the other side of the Atlantic. The first stems from the fact that it falls into this specialised research category within the discipline, whereas researchers in the United States came from broader backgrounds and in some cases made only brief incursions into the field of activism.[3] The Europeans have adopted a highly sociological approach and more varied empirical methods. Indeed, all of the group surveys made systematic use of the INSURA (INdividual SUrveys during Rallies) method formalised at the end of the 1990s by Favre et al. (Favre, Fillieule and Mayer 1997). The pioneering work of Della Porta et al. at the No-G8 mobilization in Genoa in the summer of 2001 (Andretta et al. 2002) and the first European Social Forum (ESF) (Della Porta et al. 2006a) provided the initial questionnaire model that was subsequently employed and amended for all the quantitative surveys, from those conducted at the ESFs in 2003 (Agrikoliansky and Sommier 2005) and 2006 (Andretta and Sommier 2009) to the 2011 World Social Forum (Siméant et al. 2015).

The circulation of the parent questionnaire obviously resulted in convergent questions: basic demographic date; membership in activist organizations; political orientation; degree of confidence in institutions and organizations.

At the same time—and this is the second specificity—all the European research combined statistical data with qualitative research material. For example, the surveys conducted in 2003 at the No-G8 in Evian and the second ESF included a great deal of qualitative research: participant observation of the alternative camps and counter-summit in Annemasse, and of the preparation of ESF organization (why and how such different and sometimes competing organizations decided to collaborate to organise the event and how they managed to do it, including the type of conflict resolution they used) as well as ethnographic observation at forty workshop sessions. The same approach was used the next year in the DEMOS (Democracy in Europe and the Mobilization of Society) Demos European survey led by Della Porta. The quantitative survey at the fourth ESF (Athens 2006) was only one tool; it was bolstered by the analysis of some thirty organizations involved in the alter-global cause in the six European countries surveyed[4] as well as interviews and observations of operating methods and activist use of the Internet. Clearly, studying the topic of alter-globalization gave European researchers a chance to work together more closely and it was facilitated notably by incentivizing state funding. For example, the survey on the No-G8 at Evian in 2003 was carried out jointly by teams from the universities of Lausanne, Geneva and Paris 1. It was extended via a European network set up the same year and coordinated by Paris 1, which brought together five European teams to work on the genealogy of the movement.[5] All the teams included young researchers or students, some of whom, through a spillover effect, undertook PhD dissertations on the topic, usually based on qualitative material. The influence of a few 'thesis producers' on the topics and approaches they chose is palpable. The third feature pertains to the specifically European nature of these studies. Contrary to their 'travelling' North American colleagues,[6] the Europeans remained focused on the national space of their home countries through monographs on mobilization events or domestic groups[7] or on European protests (counter-mobilizations at summit meetings held in Europe or ESFs). The surveys conducted by Siméant at the WSFs in 2007 (Nairobi) and 2011 (Dakar) were exceptions to the rule, which can be explained by the African Studies tradition in France.[8]

These specificities, particularly the methodological and disciplinary aspects, shed light on the particular orientations favoured by the European researchers. The first particular orientation arises from a broader reflection on the relationship between repression and recent social movements among which the alter-global cause; it raises thus the issue of a possible rupture in democratic law enforcement policy (1). It echoes the second specific feature, imposed directly by the multiplication of European research funding, concerning the relationship between these movements and democracy, which was seen as expressing a 'new' relationship to politics marked by dissatisfaction with representative democracy and learning how to engage in its deliberative, participatory forms (2). The third line of investigation aims to test the new, transnational character of alter-globalization, often taken for granted, by examining it from a long-term perspective view and within the national spaces from which it in fact derives. Combining qualitative and quantitative measurements and dialoguing mostly with extra-European research, it is therefore the most enlightening about what distinguishes the European approach from others (3).

Alter-globalization as a Laboratory to Work on Democracy within Social Movements

Researchers broke little new ground on the issue of state violence in democracy until the 2000s when it became an established field of scientific investigation, buoyed so to speak by the impact of anti-terrorism policies in the wake of 9/11 as well as by the repressive reaction to the alter-global movement developing during the same period (Fillieule and Della Porta 2006; Della Porta et al. 2006b). The images of Western metropolises in a state of siege, from Seattle to the death of Carlo Giuliani in Genoa in 2001, were indelibly linked to this protest. It raised the question of a possible break in the process of pacifying law enforcement operations, or even of an intrinsic transformation of democracies, associated with policy alignment, particularly in the area of security.

'Armoured' Democracies?

It is a widely accepted fact that the anti-terrorism policies adopted after 2001 considerably expanded the definition of terrorism and no less considerably contracted people's freedom. But perhaps the most original contribution of research on the 'ordinary' law enforcement practices henceforth used in Europe, particularly with regard to alter-globalization, involved tracing their origin back to innovations introduced in the European Union in the form of police cooperation to combat hooliganism.

Indeed, the police cooperation plan inaugurated the main components that were to be adopted against any cause viewed as a potential threat to law and order: increased militarization of the police, significantly strengthened preventive measures (recording data on individuals; exchanging information on demonstrators permitted by the Schengen Information System; preventing individuals from circulating or even closing borders to whole groups, which happened without any legal basis at the Nice Summit in December 2000; or in Germany refusing to allow nationals to leave the country), deploying security zones to prevent any contact between delegates and demonstrators by organizing the international meeting in a place that was difficult to access (WTO in Doha in November 2001, G8 in Kananaskis in June 2002) or by closing off part of the city where the summit was held through the famous no-entry 'red zone' (Fillieule and Della Porta 2006: 36; Ericson and Doyle 1999). In addition to these notable exceptions to the general principles that usually governed police action in democracies, practices were also employed in Göteborg and Genoa which deviated from the trend towards professionalised law enforcement that had been observed since World War II: a significant rise in the number of arrests, the use of real bullets, inconsistent orders oscillating between a laissez-faire attitude and gratuitous brutality.

The management of so-called alter-global demonstrations thus became tougher in the field, along with the legal and international regulatory procedures devised to prevent them from even taking place. The rise in the level of repression and the justifications given for it (alter-globalists were often assimilated to terrorist groups in various official documents) in turn fostered a unified perception of the situation within the ranks of protestors and the feeling of taking part in a single movement. These increasingly tough law enforcement policies concretely reflected philosophical writings on the state of emergency in democracy that permeated the most literate and radical part of the alter-global movement. And more prosaically, they seemed to vindicate the critical view shared by all the activists regarding how representative democracy works, as we shall see.

Policy Alignment and Europeanization

In addition to their observations, the researchers have proposed various interpretations of law enforcement standardization at alter-global events.

The law enforcement standardization stems from the standardization and transnationalization of the social movements themselves: the opposition to neoliberal globalization brought about a whole series of adaptations in law enforcement practices, which, in turn, unquestionably helped to crystallise opposition and unify the cause (Della Porta, Peterson and Reiter 2006). Fillieule prefers to see this phenomenon as the effect of increasingly professional police organizations and growing interdependence among governments in the area of police cooperation. Using a comparative survey, he demonstrates, together with Della Porta, the existence of a process to streamline and standardise the organization of law enforcement by national police in Western democracies. They argue that the field of police organization has been shaped by a series of isomorphic processes that have simultaneously tended to standardise modes of organization (e.g., the type of hierarchical links, differentiation between types of force and types of assignments, police training), doctrines regarding the use of force, professional expertise and routine practices (Fillieule and Della Porta 2006).

The hypothesis of police system alignment also reveals, from a neo-institutional perspective, the logic inherent to social movements, especially the alter-global movement, that tend towards transnationalization. This is the postulate of Giugni (2002) who argues that the convergence of types of government and the issues of political debate, linked to globalization and more specifically to the process of European Union integration, have led to a growing convergence in the forms of public debate, facilitating circulation of the issues and thereby the internationalization of protest.

The Democratic Issue at the Core of Alter-globalization

Whereas the first interpretation does not consider alter-globalization in itself or exclusively but merely as an illustration of a more general process, it is at the core of the second approach. Indeed, the question of how the alter-global movement is related to democracy has been a focal point of this line of research. These studies examine the movements' network structures, participatory democracy and horizontal relationships constantly claimed by activists though not always achieved, and the prefigurative experience of an alternative way of living and egalitarian social relationships in the counter-summit camps. Interest in this issue can also be explained by the profound mutations affecting European academic circles since the Bologna Process aimed at creating the European Higher Education Area, based on international cooperation and academic exchange. This reform led to standardised research contracts, particularly through bidding on EU funds for public policy-oriented research, at a time of budget cuts in national research bodies and white-paper programs.

A Space for Learning about Deliberative Democracy

The aspiration for 'radical democracy' did not arise from the alter-global movement, but instead dates back at least to the 1960s. Nevertheless it was sufficiently highlighted (starting with the choice of Porto Alegre and a 'Forum-space') to draw the attention of researchers, who had been aware of the issue of deliberative, participative democracy since the 1990s. Thus, for example, the survey conducted during the second ESF included ethnographic observation of forty workshop sessions to understand how people expressed themselves and what kind of speeches they made: did they tell a story of misery, a story of struggle, an individual or collective story..., who gave them their speeches and the practical details of speeches, etc. (Agrikoliansky and Sommier 2005)? Very early on, the study of local social forums also became a privileged place to observe participatory mobilization (Dufour 2013).

This analytic prism was to be considerably developed by calls for bids from institutions at the national, European[9] and international levels to undertake group projects or doctoral research[10] on the subject. The DEMOS project, funded by the European Union and directed by Della Porta, was the most ambitious prototype for such studies. It examined both the alter-global view of representative democracy and the internal practices of the organizations. The Global Justice Movement is presented as promoting democratization from below by encouraging grassroots participation and experiments with alternative modes of operation, against the backdrop of a power shift to institutions less subject to democratic control, the decline of voting and the current inability of parties to meet the varied demands of civil society (Della Porta 2005: 75). The study was based on four types of materials: participants' replies to questions on the degree of democracy in their membership group and the norms governing decision-making and conflict resolution; the quantitative analysis of 266 websites combined with in-depth interviews with the seven webmasters of the main organizations in each country; the internal documents of 244 social movement organizations pertaining to their operating methods, supplemented by interviews with the representatives of 210 of these organizations (which often diverge significantly from the official documents).

By combining these two aspects—participatory, based on the degree of delegated authority, and deliberative, based on the mode of decision-making (by vote or by consensus)—Della Porta reveals four operating methods. The most fully developed model—i.e., the most democratic because it is the farthest removed from representative democracy—is said to be 'deliberative participation' (decisions made in assembly by consensus), defined as 'decisional processes in which, under conditions of equality, inclusiveness, and transparency, a communicative process based on reason (the strength of the argument) may transform individual preferences, leading to decisions oriented to the public good' (Della Porta 2009a: 1). This choice was first correlated with the size of the organization (the larger the organization, the less likely it is to practice deliberative participation), followed by the cause it upholds (alter-global groups in the strict sense would be most favourable to this mode of functioning), when it was founded (after 1989) and how closely it identified with alter-globalization. In short, it claimed to participate in the originality of this open, inclusive and tolerant movement (ibid.: 43).

However, this enthusiasm can be attenuated. There have been some major exceptions to the democratic gains of alter-globalization, in particular in the French Association for the Taxation of Financial Transactions and Citizen's Action (ATTAC), which underwent an internal crisis in 2006 that exposed its strongly oligarchic, authoritarian mode of operation (Wintreberg 2007). It varies according to the two 'souls' of the movement distinguished by Pleyers (2010): it is of major importance in the 'way of subjectivity' that dominates in alternative camps, but less important or even non-existent in the 'way of reason' adopted by groups that give precedence to expertise, such as ATTAC once again. It also varies according to the level of education as shown by Doerr (2009): meetings at a transnational level are more deliberative than at national levels, in particular due to the use of multiple languages, which fosters respect for differences, and to the anti-hierarchical nature of the deliberation process. This democratic quality would need to be tested over time: openness and democratic functioning are often the rule in emerging groups, but grow weaker as they become institutionalised. Finally, as Freeman pointed out some time ago (1972), sometimes the worst tyranny is found in informal structures; and many activists denounced decision-making through consensus as a 'war of attrition' and 'cockfights.'

Middle-Class Radicalism

On the other hand, there could be no doubt about the activists' dissatisfaction with the functioning of institutions they denounced for abdicating to 'the dictates of the market' relayed by international organizations. Hence they have demanded a political surge (against economic domination) and a more profoundly democratic approach. All of the quantitative surveys conducted since 2002 paint a homogeneous portrait of participants at alter-global events, who situated their radicalism from a cultural and social point of view as 'middle-class radicalism' (now 'upper middle class'), which Cotgrove and Duff demonstrated as early as 1980. This already remarkable portrait stands out even more clearly in the only comparable survey conducted after ten years of experience at the WSF in Dakar in 2011, following several years of academic disinterest. By confirming (or even accentuating) already established trends, it countered criticism of the Western prism of research and therefore further highlighted the unusual character—to say the least—of commitment to the alter-global cause.

Alter-global activists possess a very high degree of cultural capital, which significantly distinguishes them from their non-activist compatriots. Their level of education is very high and it rose from one forum to the next: 69.5 per cent of the participants in the second ESF (2003) had college or university education, and 77.5 per cent at the WSF held in Dakar. They held high social positions: among attendees at the second ESF with an occupation, 42 per cent were executive managers or working in a high-level intellectual occupation, and 44.1 per cent worked in a mid-level occupation. Low-level occupations were dramatically under-represented: white-collar workers accounted for only 8.4 per cent of participants (40 per cent from the public sector) and blue-collar workers 2.2 per cent (Agrikoliansky and Sommier 2005). This breakdown, which is the reverse social stratification of the general population, was (remarkably) confirmed at the last WSF in Dakar. In that case, too, executives and high-level intellectual occupations (43.3 per cent) and mid-level professions (26.48 per cent) were predominant; among them, teachers (19.47 per cent) and healthcare and social workers (12.81 per cent) were the most numerous. Working-class categories were very underrepresented: 5.4 per cent white-collar workers, 3 per cent blue-collar workers, 1.45 per cent farmers and 5 per cent artisans, shopkeepers and small businessmen (15.37 per cent without a job). Of course one might reasonably conclude that the method actually discourages those with least cultural and social capital who are probably less inclined to fill out a questionnaire, but this bias is not enough to explain such a strong contrast nor does it invalidate the observation that the alter-global population is well integrated in the workplace (Sommier 2015).

The 'middle-class radicalism' of alter-global activists can be explained by their interest in politics and a feeling of political competence nurtured by their very high level of education and highly qualified jobs. They have a very critical attitude towards institutions: for instance, 82 per cent of the attendees at the second ESF did not trust national authorities, 76 per cent European authorities, 62 per cent the United Nations. The widespread distrust of institutions and their representatives did not, however, lead to a loss of interest in politics or a withdrawal from public life; on the contrary, 76 per cent of the participants at the second ESF declared they systematically voted in elections and 11 per cent often did so (respectively 65.11 per cent and 15.53 per cent of attendees in Dakar). The high degree of social integration and political participation of alter-global activists validates the theory produced by Tarrow (2005), who describes them as 'rooted cosmopolitans'. Indeed, the ability to project oneself into transnational issues and events presupposes solid resources and national roots.

A 'New' Cause for the Long Term

An alternative approach was introduced in 2003 to test and ultimately refute the three basic postulates regarding the alter-global cause put forward by militants and sometimes by the researchers studying the movement: first, that alter-globalism was 'radically new'; second, that it was 'unified', which meant it could be characterised as a single movement as if it were a homogeneous whole, equivalent from one country to the next; and third, that it was 'global', i.e., freed from 'weight' of national ties, or even the expression of an 'international civil society'. This approach reinserts the movement in its authentic history in two ways: first from a comparative, genealogical perspective, and second from a career perspective to examine how the cause affects the activists who embrace it and what it reveals about the activist space in which it is embedded in practice.

Comparison and Genealogy: The Influence of National and Organizational Contexts

The first perspective adopts a comparative approach and focuses mainly on the meso-sociological level of organizations, historicizing both upstream and downstream their tendency to become involved in the 'new' alter-global cause and subsequently, in some cases, to abandon it (Agrikoliansky et al. 2005; Sommier and Fillieule 2013 for France; Sommier et al. 2008 on five European countries; Lelandais 2011 on Turkey).

The comparative genealogy of alter-globalization in Europe reveals its diversity. This aspect has been repeatedly emphasised with regard to the structure of its component groups (trade unions, associations, observatories or intellectual clubs and NGOs) and the causes they espoused, which often significantly predated the alter-global movement. It developed in response to *national* opportunities and occasions arising from the specific dynamics of political fields, such as the effects of German reunification on the associative sector or the ferment of revolt in Great Britain that grew out of demonstrations against the poll tax, the motorway policy, laws against rave parties, etc. (Sommier et al. 2008). The enthusiasm for the new cause reflected in particular a change in the political balance and consequently in alliances among left-wing parties, trade unions and SMOs. One of the main factors behind the reconfiguration of the protest space was the disillusionment experienced by activists with left-wing governments in power and the political choices they made, neglecting or even overtly abandoning the labour movement pact between socialist or social-democratic parties and trade unions. In this context, aggravated by the social crisis and a sharp decline in labour conflicts, the trade unions were in a way forced to turn to new contentious groups. In this regard, it was indeed the competitive dynamics between national movements that underlay the fluctuating and reversible appeal of international issues and forms of action. This accounts for the variety of pioneers in each of the countries studied: the new social movements in Germany, the international solidarity organizations and the environmental movements in the United Kingdom, the new trade unions and Catholic Third World supporters in France and Italy, etc.

When the search for hypothetical structural causes is replaced by contextualised analysis of the conditions for the emergence and development of these mobilizations and their subsequent rapprochement, the movement is shown to be neither new nor unified. It was less the force of attraction of globalization than the dynamics at work within national spaces that led groups at the end of the 1990s to seek a new space for action at an international level. What accounts for the change in the scale of action that engendered internationalised protest? The comparison of the five countries in the study yields interesting parallels. In all of them, the appeal of international action appears to have corresponded to strategies of political positioning specific to actors eager to improve their own positions and increase their resources. It is therefore not surprising to observe that the international orientation was prompted less by the central actors in national protest fields than by marginal actors with limited resources, who saw the opening of European and international forums as a new avenue to express their demands, enhance their resources and acquire new ones.

Thus the very plasticity of the cause allowed for various forms of participation by the different movement families, depending on the mobilizing issue and the constraints within the country. If we look at how alter-globalization evolved from country to country, it is immediately obvious that the transnational orientation was by no means a constant. On the contrary, we observed, in Germany and France for example, that starting in 2003–4, the focus of the central actors and key topics turned away from international activism to domestic activism. The change in the scale of involvement was again linked or determined by national organizational strategies: in Germany, the mobilization against Schröder's 'Agenda 2010' reform, and in France against pension reform in 2003, followed by a suspension of any new activist front until the 2007 presidential elections.

This research work adopts a less idealistic view of the 'choice' of deliberative democracy. The studies bring out the organizational need to unify the multiple strands of the movement as well as the history and logic of action underlying the alter-global pioneers' desire for deliberation. Deliberation was considered essential partly for functional reasons to hold together and ensure the survival of weak, extremely diverse groups that were sometimes in competition or even opposed each other. It also provided a shared, positive identity at a time—let us remember—when autonomy and participation were the watchwords of activism.

Career and Long-Term Perspective

The second approach, this time at the micro-sociological level, concentrates on the two age groups shown by the quantitative surveys to be most involved in the alter-global cause: experienced activists who were the initial promoters of the movement and young, first-time activists. This approach adopts a career perspective to understand the inclination to support a cause whose appeal lies precisely in its claim to be 'new' and 'transnational' and test its continuity from a micro-sociological standpoint.

When we examine the social properties of the actors and the conditions governing the accumulation of international capital, there seem to be two sets of factors at work in the process of transnational involvement (Agrikoliansky and Sommier 2005). The first reflects the growing participation of European national elites and their children at the international level. Without a doubt, increased study-abroad programs, opportunities to live in foreign countries and learn other languages and greater professional mobility were crucial structural factors. They were necessary to generate the interest and involvement in the new cause of the group in the higher socio-professional categories that forms the social base of the alter-global movement. The second set of factors pertains to the role of seasoned activists, initiated to politics in the 1970s, who reoriented the know-how and resources acquired in the radical left or NSMs to the alter-global cause. It is important to understand their experience in militant international organizations (e.g. the Trotskyite International) or their activist commitments that drove them to train for new professions involving solidarity with the Third World and 'the damned of the earth'. All these factors help to explain how neoliberal globalization was able to crystallise an inter-generational protest movement at the beginning of the twenty-first century in which national and international dimensions are in practice closely interwoven.

Monitoring first-time activists requires a long-term perspective to assess their underlying motives and continued commitment to alter-globalization over time. By analysing alter-global activism from the moment of joining up to defection, Jossin (2013) has shown the extent to which the movement played a passing role in the trajectories of young French and German militants. At first, alter-globalization gave them the means to 'extract themselves from the field of national politics' and acquire experience and resources (especially 'transnational'), which were subsequently reinvested in the national field to the advantage of political parties such as the Ligue Communiste Révolutionnaire and Die Linke seen as 'new'. This is another observation that clearly diminishes the opposition between 'new' and 'old' social movements, which has also been made in the case of Lebanon (Abi Yaghi 2013).

Three conclusions can be drawn from this review of the literature pertaining to European research studies on alter-globalization. First, they hold a singular place, due to the fact that they have incubated in the sociology of social movements and combine quantitative and qualitative methods. Their uniqueness is partly due to the 'Latin' origins of the alter-global movement itself. It also stems from the challenge of doing research in a sub-field dominated by the United States. However, uniqueness does not mean isolation. Many transatlantic bridges have been created and European research on this topic is echoed by studies on Europe conducted by researchers in French-speaking Canada (Dupuis-Déri 2013; Dufour 2013). Second, the scientific and militant arguments are somewhat circular, which is quite common in the sociology of mobilizations. The degree of circularity is more or less pronounced depending on the author; and most evident in the position adopted by Pleyers (2010), which flows directly from his training in Touraine's sociology of intervention method. Third, in every instance, the attention of researchers was strong in the beginning and then dwindled rapidly starting in 2007 for several reasons: the evolution of the anti-global cause, which declined in Europe and entered a phase of organizational institutionalization; the decrease in funding for research projects on the topic; and specialists' loss of interest in movements that become institutionalised and/or routine. Some of them have since turned to the *Indignados* movement, where they have found stronger aspirations for other modes of democratic participation.

Isabelle Sommier is full professor of political sociology at Paris 1 Panthéon-Sorbonne University and researcher at the Centre européen de sociologie et de science politique. She has published on social movements theory (*Penser* *les mouvements sociaux,* with Olivier Fillieule and Eric Agrikoliansky, Paris, La Découverte, 2010), social movements (like *Généalogie du mouvement antiglobalisation en Europe: Une perspective comparée,* with Olivier Fillieule and Eric Agrikoliansky, Paris, Karthala, 2008; *Radiographie du mouvement altermondialiste,* with Eric Agrikoliansky, Paris, La Dispute, 2005; *Le renouveau des mouvements contestataires à l'heure de la mondialisation,* Paris, Flammarion, 2003), political violence, radicalization and terrorism (like *La violence révolutionnaire,* Paris, Presses de Sciences Po, 2008; *Officier et communiste dans les guerres coloniales,* Paris, Flammarion, 2005; *La violence politique et son deuil: L'après 68 en France et en Italie,* Presses Universitaires de Rennes, 1998).

Notes

1. In other words, three teams each, with the European teams directed by Della Porta, Sommier and Siméant, and the North American teams by Fisher, Reese and Chase-Dunn.
2. IBASE (*Instituto Brasileiro de Análises Sociais e Econômicas*) is a militant Brazilian research institute directly involved in the process of World Social Forums, where it carried out surveys in 2003, 2004, 2005, 2006 and 2007 based on participants' registration forms.
3. For example, Bramble is an economist and trade union leader, Reese is a specialist in the welfare state and women's issues, Fisher on the environment and Chase-Dunn a theoretician of world-systems, etc.
4. In addition to Italy (European Institute of Florence and the University of Urbino with Mario Pianta), the Universities of Kent (Chris Rootes), Geneva (Marco Giugni), Paris 1 (Isabelle Sommier) and the research centres of Berlin (Dieter Rucht) and Andalusia (Mario Jimenez).
5. The group included CRAPUL of the University of Lausanne (O. Fillieule), the University of Trento (M. Diani), European University Institute of Florence (D. Della Porta), the University of Berlin (D. Rucht) and the University of Madrid (M. Jimenez). Cf. Sommier et al. 2008.
6. For example, the studies directed by Reese at the World Social Forums in 2005 (Porto Alegre) and 2007 (Nairobi); those by Fisher in the Netherlands, the United States and Canada.
7. With the exception of young foreign PhD graduates, trained for example in France, but who did their dissertations on alter-globalization in their own countries, such as Gulçin Lelandais (2011) on Turkey, Marie-Noëlle Abi-Yaghi (2013) on Lebanon, and the thesis by Geoffrey Pleyers (2010) on the European and Latin American continents.
8. In Nairobi, the qualitative studies focused on how Africa was discussed and staged, how the idea of a capacity for action on the part of African inhabitants was mobilised and how references to Pan-Africanism and anti-imperialism were used. Cf. Pommerolle and Siméant 2008 and 2011. The qualitative and quantitative survey (poll of fifty-six questions applied to eleven hundred people in five languages: En-

glish, French, Spanish, Portuguese and Wolof, the national language of Senegal) conducted in 2011 in Dakar was at the intersection between African studies and alter-globalization.

9. First the DEMOS project ('Democracy in Europe and the Mobilisation of Society', 2004–8), continued in the project funded by the European Research Council (ERC) on 'Mobilising for Democracy: Democratisation Processes and the Mobilisation of Civil Society' (cf. Della Porta and Rucht 2013). But also—once again with D. Della Porta and her former doctoral student Nicole Doerr—research funded by the Ford Foundation on 'Global Democracy and Civic Education'.

10. With two main thesis producers on the issue, who happen to be associated: D. Della Porta (Doerr 2009) and D. Rucht (Haug 2010 on decision-making in the GJM, Teune 2012).

References

Abi-Yaghi, M. N. 2013. 'L'altermondialisme au Liban, un militantisme de passage: Logiques d'engagement et reconfiguration de l'espace militant (de gauche)'. PhD dissertation. Paris: University of Paris 1.

Agrikoliansky E., O. Fillieule and N. Mayer, eds. 2005. *L'altermondialisme en France: Genèse et dynamique d'un mouvement social.* Paris: Flammarion.

Agrikoliansky, E., and I. Sommier, eds. 2005. *Radiographie du mouvement altermondialiste français: le FSE de Paris Saint-Denis.* Paris: La Dispute.

Agrikoliansky, E., P. Blanchard, M. Bandler, O. Fillieule, F. Passy and I. Sommier. 2004. 'L'altermondialisme et les réseaux: Trajectoires militantes, multipositionnement et formes de l'engagement: les participants du contre-sommet du G8 d'Evian'. *Politix* 17, no. 67: 13–48.

Andretta M., D. Della Porta, L. Mosca, and H. Reiter. 2002. *Global, Noglobal, New Global: La protesta contro il G8 a Genova.* Bari-Rome: Laterza.

Andretta M., and I. Sommier. 2009. 'The Social Bases of the GJM Mobilization and Democratic Forms'. In *Another Europe: Conceptions and Practices of Democracy in the European Social Forums,* ed. D. Della Porta, 111–27. London and New York: Routledge.

Cotgrove, S., and A. Duff. 1980. 'Environmentalism, Middle-Class Radicalism and Politics'. *Sociological Review* 28: 333–51.

Della Porta, D. 2005a. 'Making the Polis: Social Forums and Democracy in the Global Justice Movement'. *Mobilization* 10, no. 1: 73–94.

Della Porta, D., ed. 2009a. *Democracy in Social Movements.* Basingstoke and New York: Palgrave Macmillan.

Della Porta, D., ed. 2009b. *Another Europe: Conceptions and Practices of Democracy in the European Social Forums.* London and New York: Routledge.

Della Porta, D., et al. 2006a. *Globalization from Below: Transnational Activists and Protest Networks.* Minneapolis: University of Minnesota Press.

Della Porta, D., A. Peterson and H. Reiter, eds. 2006b. *The Policing of Transnational Protest.* Aldershot: Ashgate.

Della Porta, D., and D. Rucht, eds. 2013. *Meeting Democracy.* Cambridge: Cambridge University Press.

Doerr, N. 2009. 'Listen Carefully: Democracy Brokers at the European Social Forums'. PhD dissertation. Florence: European University Institute.

Dufour, P. 2013. *Trois espaces de protestation*. Montréal: Presses de l'Université de Montréal.

Dupuis-Deri F., ed. 2013. *A qui la rue? Répression policière et mouvements sociaux*. Montréal: les éditions écosociété.

Ericson, R. V. and A. Doyle. 1999. 'Globalization and the Policing of Protest: The Case of APEC 1997'. *British Journal of Sociology* 50, no. 4, 589–608.

Favre, P., O. Fillieule and N. Mayer. 1997. 'La fin d'une étrange lacune de la sociologie des mobilisations: L'étude par sondage des manifestants: fondements théoriques et solutions techniques'. *Revue Française de Science Politique* 47: 3–28.

Fillieule, O., and D. Della Porta, eds. 2006. *Police et manifestants: Maintien de l'ordre et gestion des conflits*. Paris: Presses de Sciences Po.

Fillieule, O., and P. Blanchard. 2010. 'INdividual SUrveys in Rallies (INSURA): A New Tool for Exploring Transnational Activism?'. In *The Transnational Condition: Protest Dynamics in an Entangled Europe*, ed. S.Teune, 186–210. New York: Berghahn Books.

Freeman, J. 1972–73. 'The Tyranny of Structurelessness'. *Berkeley Journal of Sociology* 17: 151–64.

Giugni, M. 2002. 'Explaining Cross-National Similarities among Social Movements'. In *Globalization and Resistance*, ed. J. Smith and H. Johnston. Lanham: Rowman and Littlefield.

Haug, C. 2010. 'Discursive Decision-Making in Meetings of the Global Justice Movements: Cultures and Practices'. PhD dissertation. Berlin: Freie Universität.

Jossin, A. 2013. *Trajectoires de jeunes altermondialistes en France et en Allemagne*. Rennes: Presses universitaires de Rennes.

Lelandais, E. G. 2011. *Altermondialistes en Turquie: Entre cosmopolitisme politique et ancrage militant*. Paris: L'Harmattan.

Pleyers, G. 2010. *Alter-globalization: Becoming Actors in the Global Age*. Cambridge: Polity Press.

Pommerolle, M. E., and J. Siméant, eds. 2009. *Un autre monde à Nairobi*. Paris: Karthala.

Siméant, J., Pommerolle, M. E., and Sommier I. 2015. *Observing Protest from a Place: The World Social Forum in Dakar (2011)*. Amsterdam: Amsterdam University Press.

Sommier, I. 2015. 'What Can Quantitative Surveys Tell Us about GJM Activists?' In *Observing Protest from a Place: The World Social Forum in Dakar (2011)*, ed. J. Siméant, I. Sommier and M. E. Pommerolle, 21–40. Amsterdam: Amsterdam University Press.

Sommier, I., and O. Fillieule. 2013. 'The Emergence and Development of the No Global Movement in France: A Genealogical Approach'. In *Understanding European Movements: New Social Movements, Global Justice Struggles, Anti-austerity Protest*, ed. L. Cox and C. Flesher Fominaya, 47–60. London and New York: Routledge.

Sommier, I., O. Fillieule and E. Agrikoliansky, eds. 2008. *Généalogie des mouvements altermondialistes en Europe: Une perspective comparée*. Paris: Karthala.

Sommier, I., and M.-E. Pommerolle, eds, *Observing Protest from a Place: the World Social Forum in Dakar (2011)*, Amsterdam: Amsterdam University Press.

Teune, S. 2012. 'Corridors of Action Protest Rationalities and the Channeling of Anti-Summit Repertoires'. PhD dissertation. Berlin: Freie Universität.

Tarrow, S. 2005. *The New Transnational Activism*. Cambridge: Cambridge University Press.

Wintrebert, R. 2007. *Attac, la politique autrement ?* Paris: La Découverte.

Chapter 8

Theoretical Perspectives on European Environmental Movements
Transnational and Technological Challenges in the Twenty-First Century

Maria Kousis

Even though the roots of the environmental movement in Europe and North America go back to the early nineteenth and twentieth centuries (Diani 1995; Taylor 1997; Maher 2008), it has only been during the past four decades that the creation, establishment and transformation of a plethora of groups, organizations and networks with public claims for environmental protection have flourished. Since the 1970s, social scientists (mainly political scientists, sociologists and anthropologists) have produced an abundance of studies on the many and diverse facets of the environmental movement. Their analysis rests on a wide spectrum of theoretical approaches, mostly based on European and North American scholarly traditions. This chapter will place European studies of the environmental movement within this literature, and trace their theoretical and conceptual orientations.[1] It also aims to shed light on: (1) the ways in which European studies on the environmental movement, especially cross-national, developed under specific contexts—e.g., Europeanization; (2) the extent to which communication across the Atlantic has influenced either or both camps; and (3) the notable, durable divergence between the North American (US) and European theoretical traditions. Its ultimate aim is to highlight the new challenges which the movement faces in the twenty-first century.

Overall, the development of the environmental movement may be attributed to differences in political, economic and socio-historical contexts and/ or cultures. For example, the 'stark contrast between the American "winner-take-all" electoral system and West Germany's partially proportional system of representation probably accounts for the very different development histories of the American and West German environmental movements'

(McAdam et al. 1996: 12). In the case of the United States and West German anti-nuclear movements in the 1980s, key differences have also been attributed to the different national political contexts (McAdam et al. 1996: 18).

While different national contexts clearly matter (Kriesi et al. 1995; Kousis 2005; Kousis et al. 2008), economic globalization has led to the formation of transnational environmentalism since the 1980s (Kiefer and Benjamin 1993; Princen and Finger 1994). European integration also offered new economic and political opportunities which influenced environmental movements at the member-state level as well as the supra-national level (Eder 2009). This impact is even more prominent in the case of South European, Central and Eastern European countries (see Kousis and Eder 2001; Carmin and Fagan 2010; Císař 2010; Yanitsky 2013). Environmental activists in these countries have pursued their goals through European institutions, the European Court and the European Parliament, taking advantage of new opportunities in the form of emerging EU structures (Marks and McAdam 1996; Kousis 2004).

In the 1990s, transnational economic opportunities and constraints were on the increase in view of the rapid economic globalization, growing commercialization and privatization of research and development activities, and an entrepreneurial approach to science and technology, especially in the United States and the European Union, part of which addressed sustainable development and ecological modernization concerns (Jamison 2001; Kousis 2004). During this period, transnational mobilizing structures, including environmental social movement organizations (ESMOs), played an increasingly important role in the global political system (e.g. Della Porta and Tarrow 2006). Environmental associations and networks formed a strong force within the Global Justice Movement, mounting resistance to economic globalization and neoliberal policies and practices (Della Porta 2007). At this time, environmental transnational networks, cooperation and strategies emerged as a response to the growing need to face global environmental problems, such as climate change. Transnational environmental NGOs also supported local activists in the newer areas of production under a global political economy in Asia, such as China (e.g. Chen 2010).

By the mid-1990s, scholars also began to pay attention to the relationship between environmental movements and sustainable development or ecological modernization, especially in the context of genetically modified organisms (GMOs) and growing concern on climate change. They pointed to the competing frames of sustainable development (Baker et al. 1996), and the ways in which different types of environmental movements adhere to different sustainable development approaches and practices (Kousis 2004). Parallel concerns were expressed regarding the institutionalization, Europeanization and professionalization of the environmental movement (van der Heijden 1997; Jamison 2001[2]; Eder 1996[3]; Rucht 2001; Rootes 2007; Ruzza 2004[4]; Bluhdorn 2011; Kousis 2004). Professional environmental organizations not only adopt ecological modernization or sustainable development alternatives (van der Heijden 1999; Brand 1999) on the basis of cultural identity, but they also mobilise their expertise and often compete to seize the economic opportunities offered in the wider context of international and national economic policies targeting sustainability objectives. Following this opportunity spiral, new types of organizations are created, which are more exclusively oriented to professional consulting activities and advisory business firms (Kousis 2004).

In the past two decades, climate change has moved to a central position in debates on environmental politics (Price et al. 2014). By showing not only how climate change has shaped social movements but also how climate change contention shapes social change, Jamison (2010) offers a fresh critique on ecological modernization approaches.[5] Recent works point to the need for environmental action at the local, national and international levels to address climate change impacts (Rootes et al. 2012). Nevertheless, environmental activism has also surfaced against renewable energy projects aimed at addressing climate change impacts in the past decade, especially in the case of industrial wind farms. Communities against these renewable policies have demanded more sustainable projects which address the needs of local communities (e.g. Lekakis and Kousis 2013a).

As in the past, the recent economic crisis, which is tied to neoliberal and austerity policies (Moore et al. 2011), is likely to influence the intensity of resource exploitation and the easing of investments in unexploited areas, as seen in the struggles of local environmental protest against gold mining in Greece (Lekakis and Kousis 2013a). At the same time, while the crisis has relaxed compliance with EU environmental regulations, the environmental movement appears to be slow in responding to the environmental impacts of austerity policies across the EU. For professional environmental organizations, the different routes to exit the current crisis—i.e., sustainable development, ecological modernization, green growth or the green new deal (Lekakis and Kousis 2013b)—pose hard dilemmas and demanding choices.

The following sections first present dominant definitions of the environmental movement from different theoretical traditions. The theoretical approaches to the study of the environmental movement are offered in two sections, one on European and North American perspectives and the other on eclectic approaches. The concluding section proposes routes to future research while highlighting (1) the ways in which European studies on the environmental movement have developed; (2) the extent to which communication across the Atlantic has influenced studies on the environmental movement; and (3) the major milestones of the movement as well as the challenges it faces in the twenty-first century.

Defining Environmental Movements

In the late 1980s, Klandermans and Tarrow (1988: 19) agreed that the US and European environmental movements were embracing 'groups ranging from conservative or at least moderate conservation organizations to radical organizations that are not averse to direct confrontations with the government'. However, differences in the orientations and histories of the two continents, as well as increasing communication channels between European and US scholars, led to both diverging and converging perspectives on the environmental movement.

Convergence between European (Kriesi et al. 1995; Jamison 2001; Kousis 1999) and US (Gould et al. 1996; Schlosberg and Bomberg 2008) scholars is illustrated in their similar definitions of the environmental movement, which are comparable to Tilly's (1994: 7, 18) durable definition of social movements, as 'sustained challenges to power-holders in the name of interested populations, which appear in the form of professional movements, ad hoc community-based, or specialized movements, and communitarian, unspecialized movements, that give rise to a new community'. Their views converge on three basic forms of the environmental movement: formal environmental movement organizations; grassroots, community-linked groups; and radical, highly committed ecological groups.(e.g. Scarce, 1990) However, this definition is also linked to Political Process theories—originally produced in the United States.

Other, mostly European, scholars (e.g. Rootes and Brulle 2013), however, proposed alternative definitions of the environmental movement, adhering to European theoretical traditions following Diani's 'superior' definition of social movements (including environmental ones) as 'networks of informal interactions between a plurality of individuals, groups and organizations, engaged in a political or cultural conflict, on the basis of a shared identity' (Tilly 1994).

For Eder (2006, 2009), collective identities, or narrative constructions which enable controlling the boundaries of a network of actors, are also critical in the study of the environmental movement. He also views Europeanization as offering a space of boundary constructions and opportunities for national, sub-national and transnational stories competing with each other in the shaping of European identity projects. Similarly, rejecting resource mobilization theory and its utilitarian and individualistic assumptions and following Habermas and Touraine, Eyerman et al (1990) view social movements as late modernity's attempt to form new collective identities. This led them to define green movements as those embodying and driven by environmental consciousness.

A new European theoretical perspective has appeared since the late 1990s. Reflexive modernization studies on participatory governance in the 'politics of life' offer more encompassing definitions of activism, as public participation responding to this century's scientific challenges and limitations of the modernist and technocratic state (Larana 2001[6]; Beck 1995; Gottweis et al. 2008; PAGANINI[7] 2007: 28).

These aforementioned US-founded and EU-based conceptual approaches of understanding environmental movements ultimately led to different theoretical approaches, which are presented analytically in the sections below.

Theoretical Approaches to the Environmental Movement

Although their development is heavily shaped by their own actions, movements may largely be born of 'environmental[8] opportunities' (McAdam et al. 1996). Thus, even though the severity of ecological damage does not correlate highly with environmental mobilization, some critical environmental preconditions[9] are absolutely necessary for its existence (van der Heijden et al. 1992; Gould et al. 1996; Wolfson and Butenko 1992). Usually, 'environmental opportunities' have been overshadowed by the study of internal and anthropo-centred characteristics (e.g. political context) which are external to the movement.

McAdam et al. (1996) propose that three basic factors represent three well-tested theoretical approaches: the structure of political opportunities and constraints confronting the movement; the forms of organization (informal and formal) available to insurgents; and the collective processes of interpretation, attribution and social construction that mediate between opportunity and action. However, environmental movement studies not only reflect these approaches but they also have influenced the formation of new theoretical frameworks. Thus, seven theoretical approaches can be distinguished, sometimes in combinations: those of: Environmental Justice, the Treadmill of Production, Resource Mobilization, Political Process, State Interactions, Constructivist/Collective Identity/Reflexive Modernization and that of Networks.

Three dominant theoretical perspectives distinguish the works of North American scholars from their European colleagues: the Environmental Justice, the Treadmill of Production and the Resource Mobilization perspectives. These have not been embraced by European students of the environmental movement, as reflected in works on local/grassroots/community-based environmental movements. While Europeans tend to study local activism with the same theoretical, conceptual and methodological tools as those used to study national or transnational protests, North American scholars, mostly from the US but also from developing areas, analyse them through the lenses of Environmental Justice (e.g. Bullard 1990; Szasz 1994; Taylor 1999; Pellow 2000; Agyeman, Bullard and Evans 2003; Sze and London 2008; Carruthers 2008; Shiva 2005; Miranda et al. 2011). More recently, local protests related to climate justice (Goodman 2009) or Treadmill of Production perspectives (Gould, Schnaiberg and Weinberg 1996, 2004; Gould 2005) have occurred.

Founded in the 1980s and influenced by the socioeconomic and historical contexts, the Environmental Justice and Treadmill of Production schools devote special attention to the unequal exposure of minorities, workers and disempowered communities (environmental racism). Other social movement approaches include Resource Mobilization (Weinberg 1997; McLaughlin and Khawaja 2000) and cross-national political identities and values (Dalton 1994, 2005). Descriptive studies (e.g. Scarce 1990) are more characteristic of works by US scholars of the environmental movement, and less so by Europeans.

However, convergence is visible under the theoretical approaches of: (1) political process; (2) state interactions; (3) constructivist/collective identity/ reflexive modernization; and (4) networks. These have been adopted by both European and North American scholars, while a synthetic approach is followed by scholars within and beyond Europe.

European and North American Perspectives

The works by European and North American scholars of the environmental movement which are presented below reflect their mutual influences.

Political and Economic Opportunities and Threats/Organizational Approaches

The first cross-national studies of new social movements document changes in the structure of political opportunities and constraints which directly influence the emergence and rise of the environmental movement (van der Heijden, Koopmans and Giugni 1992; Kriesi et al. 1995). Environmental mobilizations are closely linked to conventional politics in the parliamentary and non-parliamentary national arenas. Kriesi and his collaborators study these interactions in the framework of the political opportunity structure which is comprised of national cleavage structures, prevailing strategies and alliance structures (Kriesi et al. 1995). A recent European cross-national study of cleavage politics, populist parties, electoral politics and protest, including environmental, offers a more comprehensive analysis aimed at raising understanding on the impacts of globalization (Hutter 2014). The political context influences the organizational structure, action repertoire, hegemonic discourse and the chances of success of environmental movements in First, Second, and Third World countries (van der Heijden, 1999).

The European Union has been viewed as a political opportunity for environmental collective action (Tarrow 2001), especially for Southern and Eastern EU member states (Kousis and Eder 2001). European integration has been considered as another political opportunity structure (Rootes 2007; Jiménez 2007; Eder and Kousis 2001) where EU agencies are often approached as legitimators of public demands. Environmental activists have pursued their goals through the European Court and the European Parliament, taking advantage of the new opportunities emerging from EU structures. Entry in the EU has often shifted power away from the nation-state regarding the strategies of environmental activists (Kousis 2004). What are the implications for environmental movements of EU member states? For some professional environmental movements, this means a shift towards their institutionalization as illustrated by lobbying in EU institutions (Mazey and Richardson 1993; Long and Lorinsci 2009).

According to Diani and Donati (1999), movement institutionalization offers an opportunity to differentiate between four types of organizations—public interest lobby, participatory protest organization, professional protest organization and participatory pressure group—based on diverse organization reactions to resource mobilization and political efficacy problems.

While the institutionalization of the environmental movement, especially its associational wing and the related neo-institutional discourse as a whole, has been widely recognised (e.g. Jamison 1996; Roose 2013), scholars do point to grassroots environmental activism, which persists and tends to engage in more radical actions (Kousis 1999; Rootes 1999, 2008; Voulvouli 2007; Seiffert 2008; Lekakis and Kousis 2013a). This is especially visible in peripheral European states, including Ireland (e.g. Kousis 1999; Tovey 2007).

At the protest coordination level, the relationship between Europeanization and the environmental movement may take different routes. Environmental movements could synchronise their collective actions across EU countries or build cross-national networks such as the European Environmental Bureau, which includes over one hundred organizations.

At the same time, EU policies have had different impacts on groups of member-states as reflected in European Commission (EC) projects[10] (Rootes 2007), labelled by some as leader (North European) and laggard (Southern European) nations (Kousis and Eder 2001; Kousis et al. 2008). In Southern European countries where democracies were consolidated in the 1980s, changes in the political context constitute an especially important factor as seen in the findings of other (EC-)funded research (Kousis, 1999[11]; Jiménez 2007). For these states, entry into the European Union was decisive in the establishment of the professional environmental organizations (Kousis and Eder 2001; Kousis, Della Porta and Jiménez 2008). In Spain, for example, the movement went through a process of organizational consolidation which led to its political leverage, but without forfeiting essential features of participatory organizational models (Jiménez 2007).

A similar experience is found in the effects of Europeanization on the Central and Eastern European countries that joined the EU in early 2004 (Hicks 2004; Císař 2010). This has fortified environmental activists who have shown a more assertive role in political contention (Císař 2010). In addition, the endogenously driven professionalization and institutionalization of civil society groups has been strengthened, as illustrated in the case of the implementation of the EU's Natura 2000 network in Hungary, Poland and Romania (Borzel and Buzogani 2010). Carmin and Fagan (2010) show how the limits of regime change combine with the opportunities of transnational linkage and public awareness to generate movements and campaigns that are genuinely agentic.

In addition to political opportunities and constraints, economic ones have become more important with economic globalization (Kousis and Tilly 2005). Economic opportunities and constraints may hinder or assist the formation of mobilizations, especially for local groups concerned with local problems. Economic opportunities include funding opportunities for ESMOs, as well as other structural economic conditions such as economic independence from polluting agents. For example, a movement is more likely to emerge when candidate mobilisers do not depend on the principal 'polluter' for their economic survival (Gould et al. 1996; Kousis 2004).

Another form of economic opportunities and constraints are ecological modernization and sustainable development projects and policies which are often adopted by large national or transnational environmental organizations (van der Heijden 1999; Brand 1999), especially under EU policies (Kousis 2004; Lekakis and Kousis 2013a). While promoting economic growth, these policies take into account ecosystem effects and use tools such as environmental impact assessment (EIA), cost-benefit analysis, resource accounting, eco-labelling, and risk assessment. The more conservative or professional wings of the ESMOs (e.g. those concerned with the preservation, for example, of specific wildlife areas or with the passing of a law requiring EIA) tend to support such schemes. Nevertheless, in the 1990s, belief in ecological modernization initiatives was questioned by some environmental organizations (Brand 1999). Strong sustainable development or biocentric approaches require institutional restructuring as well as environmental policy integration across sectors and, therefore, are neither easily adopted by states or supra-state bodies such as the European Union, nor by environmental organizations (Brand 1999).

Grassroots groups and deep- and political-ecology ESMOs are more likely to favour strong sustainable development, a more biocentric approach characterised by changes in patterns of production and consumption toward an environmentally regulated economy (Baker et al. 1997). It requires policies that maintain the productive capacity of all ecosystem resources—preserving or improving them as needed, while simultaneously addressing pressing social issues (Brand, 1999; Kousis 2013).

It was also during the late 1990s in the global North, that GMO opposition shifted away from social justice and towards environmental issues, due to (1) the impact of the 1992 Rio Earth Summit; (2) the 1999 'Seattle' protests against the WTO mostly carried out by environmental activists, which sparked the global justice movement; (3) heightened European concerns following the BSE scandal; (4) the establishment, transnationalization and environmental movement alliances with power; and (5) the vulnerability of the US and global regulatory systems to critique and their susceptibility to movement critique (Buttel 2005; Kousis 2010).

Illustrating the effects of both political and economic opportunities and constraints, Adair (2001) posits that the movement against nuclear power in the United States emerged due to the initial decline of the nuclear power industry, which was facing changes in financial and energy markets in the early 1970s. This led to its defence by nuclear proponents and political elites exposing power relations, but also to creating the conditions for a protest movement.

State Interactions

The responses of the state have also been acknowledged as an important factor in the movement's development, especially in European studies. Interactions between anti-nuclear movements and the state contributed to the mobilization and demobilization of these movements and to successive shifts in goals and strategies (Flam 1994; Rucht 1994). Political and economic opportunities and threats, resource mobilization and collective identities act selectively with state responses to assist or hinder environmental mobilizations, be they in Hungary, Russia and Estonia (Pickvance 1997) or Greece, Spain and Portugal (Eder and Kousis 2001).

Findings on Southern European grassroots environmental contention show: (1) a continuous pattern of tactical moves and countermoves between the state and its challengers and the related series of choices concerning actions, concessions, and non-concessions; (2) the dynamics of routes and cycles of contention driven mainly by actions regarding threat; and (3) the state's role as manipulator of both the value of success and the costs. Furthermore, the findings show how the state's choice whether to grant concessions or not depends on the issue, on surrounding political and economic events visible through a diachronic view of contention, and on protest intensity in terms of group size and actions (Kousis 2005).

The changing character of the interactions between the state and environmental movements, as supranational agencies in multi-level EU governance, is visible in a study of local environmental politics in France (Fillieule 2003).

Governmental responsiveness to public opinion and mobilizations has been the focus of recent cross-national EC funded research.[12] One of the related case studies concerns nuclear energy policy after the Fukushima disaster in a comparative perspective (Morales et al. 2013).

The need to move beyond state-movement interactions and also investigate other major stakeholders, including entrepreneurs, is noted in current research pointing to the environmental movement's role in the development of renewable energy as a way of confronting climate change (Vasi 2010). Such research would address Tilly's (2004) proposition about the strength of the links between professional environmental organizations and strong economic power holders.

Collective Identity/Constructivism/Reflexive Modernization

New social movements depend on the formation of a *collective identity* addressing issues related to autonomy and control, responsibility and omnipotence, irreversible information, reversible choices, as well as inclusion and exclusion (Melucci 1992). Collective processes of interpretation, attribution and social construction are mostly the focus of European scholars on the environmental movement, but have also been adopted by US scholars. Applying this approach to the nuclear issue, Welsh (1993) argues that the issues and content of public concern have not altered since the 1950s; however, what has changed is the dominant symbolic representation of technology, thus proving to be a determinant factor in the formation of local opposition.

Influenced by identity theorists such as Habermas and Touraine but valuing aspects of resource mobilization theories as well, Eyerman, et al (1990) stress new ways of seeing, on a cognitive plane, arguing that it is on the basis of 'guiding knowledge interests' that political strategies are chosen and collective identities are articulated in a comparative history of the environmental movement. Adopting Touraine and Eder's views on the creation of alternative discourses as a means to problematic structures, Brulle (1996) distinguishes between different types of environmental social movement organizations in the United States, from ecocentrism to ecofeminism.

Environmental discourse analysis through the study of framing and communicating environmental issues (Eder 1996; Brand 1999) combines elements from different theoretical approaches. Larana (2001) also adopts a constructivist approach to study the relationship between reflexivity, risk and collective action over waste management. He finds that in the Spanish cases, different frames played a significant role in the varying scale of contention over waste incineration.

During the 1990s, European works focused on ESMOs, green parties and anti-nuclear groups usually studying the movement at the regional, national or comparative level. Most of these studies were carried out by political scientists or political sociologists, centred on environmental social movement organizations, green parties or new collective cognitive identities. They were directly linked to the theoretical orientations of the social movement literature which is basically characterised by the collective identity/cognitive space (NSM) view, the political opportunity structure approach, structural orientations or more synthetic approaches.

Institutionalization of the movement has also been at the forefront in many works related to collective identity perspectives of the 1990s (Eder 1996; Rucht and Roose 2001; Bluhdorn 2011). As Eder (1996) argued, the movement which dominated the discourse on the environment, and succeeded in placing it on the environmental agenda in the 1980s, now witnesses the appropriation of environmentalism by the hands of the groups it had challenged.

Moving beyond the institutionalization of the environmental movement, reflexive modernization works of the past decade focus on public participation in the context of EU governance. For example, recent EC-funded cross-national research[13] offers a reflexive modernization approach to the study of local conflicts related to the implementation of the Habitats Directive. The concluding hypothesis is that such environmental EU multi-level governance controversies triggering new types of participatory practices can strengthen environmental consciousness as well as forms of promoting shared consciousness about conservation obligations within the European public sphere (Haila et al. 2007).

In this context of reflexive modernity, Mol (2000) points to the opportunities and challenges ecological modernization offers to ESMOs, while Toke (2011) argues that ESMOs have played a crucial role in the development of renewable technologies in EU countries, even though not similarly across the variety of national circumstances.

Under a similar reflexive modernity perspective, cross-national research by Reynolds et al. (2007) shows that the battle over GMOs eventually led to a transformation of the regulatory regime, resulting from an epistemological stalemate where neither side could establish with certainty the safety of GMO products. This shift occurred from nation-states to global markets, from discourses on safety to consumer choice and from risk calculation to the management of uncertainty (Reynolds et al. 2007).

Northern opposition to GMOs adopts discursive frames concerned with moral, cultural, material, health and environmental issues while engaging in actions such as lobbying, regulatory and policy disputes (related, for example, to food labelling), political consumption, public education and awareness-raising, or destruction of crops (Purdue 2000; Kettnaker 2001; Ansell et al. 2006; Schurman and Munro 2010). The anti-GMO movement is a new prototype of the environmental movement rather than an exception or a deviant case of a social movement, which is likely to incorporate nanotechnology concerns in its future claim-making repertoires (Kousis 2010). In the 2004 European Social Forum[14] sessions on science and genomics, concerns focused on justice as well as science-related issues (Welsh et al. 2007). Environmental organizations' campaigns against GMOs have spread to Russia, Ukraine, Belarus and Moldova (Ovcearenco 2006).

Environmental NGOs as well as industry, government and science agencies make variable efforts to apply lessons from the previous technology conflicts, especially those related to GMOs to address dilemmas raised by the application and use of nanotechnology (Balbus et al. 2007). According to Ackland and O'Neil (2008)[15] when it comes to the issue of nanotechnology, the environmental-bio/biotechnology online groups are more likely to focus on the new issue of nanotechnology than the more established environmental-global and environmental-toxic groups. A web analysis suggests that by taking up the nanotech issue, the environmental-bio group shows its ability to identify the new field—as reflected in the ETC Group's[16] (bio, Canada) sixth highest category.

Rejecting the resource mobilization approach, Ackland and O'Neil (2011) offer a new social movement theoretical explanation for the behaviour of 160 online environmental activist organizations, focusing on the relational or network aspect of collective identity formation at the organizational level.

They argue that the networking activities of online social movement organizations mainly relate to the formation of collective identity.

Resisting global waste and the impacts of the intensification of resource use, more recent movements such as freeganism, voluntary simplicity and dumpster diving have been the focus of later works (Barnard 2011), which apply new social movement theory to study issues of collective identity and strategy.

Networks

Combining different elements of the aforesaid interpretative perspectives, the green networks approach was established by Diani (1995) through his study of environmental movement networks in Italy as products of instrumental calculations reflecting the mobilisers' concerns for scarce resource allocation in a most rational manner. According to Rucht and Della Porta (2002), environmental conflicts have increasingly involved complex networks of actors at local, national and international levels, with activities involving all available channels, arenas and repertoires of action linked to environmental protest campaigns. Adopting Diani's theoretical framework, Di Gregorio (2012) recently showed that information and resource networks have a stronger role in coalition work among environmental social movement organizations (SMOs) than previously acknowledged. Networking is also viewed as an effective strategy in the global Environmental Justice movement against toxics (Pellow 2007).

Eclectic Approaches

A number of researchers have taken more eclectic routes. One such approach combines elements from resource mobilization, political opportunity structure and collective frame theories to describe and analyse environmental organizations in West Germany and France, as well as the French anti-nuclear movement (e.g. Rucht 1994, 2001; Rucht and Della Porta 2002).

The role of the media as well as opportunities for challengers, and the types of political discourse, are all considered important in analysing the nuclear issue for the United States, France and Germany, pointing to an issue culture transcending the national culture (Gamson and Modigliani 1989). Political communication through the media has been an important factor that has also been combined with risk perception, social problems and postmodernity theories to analyse the toxics movement. It is argued that periods of most intense media coverage are followed by social movement activities (see Szasz 1994). Ackland and O'Neil's (2008, 2011) study on 160 online environmental organizations also points out the critical role of digital communication.

The need to synthesise combinations of political opportunity, resource mobilization, networks and collective identity theories is reflected in a number of environmental movement works (see, for example, Rootes 2007; Barcena and Ibarra 2000; Rucht 1994, 1999; Della Porta and Piazza 2008; Rootes and Brulle 2013). Similarly eclectic are studies on climate change–related movements of the twenty-first century (Rootes et al. 2012; Price et al. 2014).

Finally a novel approach, the Epistemic Modernization of Science, centring on health, environmental, and other scientific and technical issues, expands the concept of the environmental movement to include concerns related to the impacts of new scientific achievements, in a new group of studies (e.g. Frickel 2004; Moore et al. 2011). Challenged groups include governments, international governance bodies, and international corporations involved in science based regulation and production.

Through an overview of the theoretical underpinnings of works on the environmental movement in European and North American settings this chapter offers three main findings. First, European and North American perspectives on the environmental movement show mutual influences. The most prominent theoretical frameworks by European and US scholars are those of collective identity and Political Process. Increasing communication between social movement scholars of the two continents as well as European Commission research funding have facilitated these epistemic exchanges, as reflected in the cross-national research and comparative works which have appeared since the 1990s mostly under the financial support of the European Commission.

Second, a strong transnational dimension characterises the environmental movement literature, as seen in many works on the dynamic relationship between EU institutions and professional environmental movement organizations, as well as grassroots environmental activists. This is particularly visible in works related mostly to sustainable development, ecological modernization and more recently to green growth or green new deal, EU policies aimed at responding to the pressures of economic globalization as well as the simultaneous mounting threats of climate change on a global scale.

Third, the challenges faced by the environmental movement are unprecedented, and the related studies in this direction are limited. In addition to the intensifying economic competitiveness on a global scale, new technological breakthroughs and new ways of engineering environments in the twenty-first century, such as biotechnology and nanotechnology, pose unparalleled risks which are deeper and more pervasive than those of the past. The European resistance against GMOs as well as more recent but very rare concerns on nanotechnology products mirror the increasing importance of science in environmental activism. Especially interesting is the growth of scientific activism and new science-oriented organizations (Frickel 2004) which are more able to articulate environmental concerns on these new issues of contention. Collaborations between environmental activists and scientists may influence alternative future strategies of technological innovation (Kousis 2010). As some of the works show, the new technological breakthroughs have also extended the environmental discourse to include ethical issues.

Future works by European and US scholars have much to gain if they take into account the challenges posed by the new milieu of a twenty-first century of rapid technological challenges in times of growing inequalities and accordingly extend their analytical conceptual and theoretical tools to study environmental contention in an age of crises.

Maria Kousis (PhD in sociology, the University of Michigan, 1984) is professor of sociology and director of the Center for Research and Studies in Humanities, Social Sciences and Pedagogics, at the University of Crete. She is/was partner in EC projects including TEA (Transformations in Environmental Activism), PAGANINI (Participatory Governance and Institutional Innovation), LIVEWHAT (Living with Hard Times) and TransSOL (European Paths to Transnational Solidarity). Publications include *Contested Mediterranean Spaces* (co-editors T. Selwyn and D. Clark, Berghahn Books, 2011), and *Environmental Politics in Southern Europe* (co-editor Klaus Eder, Kluwer, 2001). She is currently coordinator of the Greek team in the project GGCRISI (The Greeks, the Germans and the Crisis).

Notes

1. Parts of this chapter relate to Kousis 1998.
2. 1996–97: Public Participation and Environmental Science and Technology Policy Options (PESTO I and II) funded by the Nordic Environmental Research Program and the European Commission's research program on Targeted Socio-Economic Research (TSER) (1996–98); coordinated by A. Jamison, Aalborg University, partners: Sweden, Norway, Lithuania, Iceland, Netherlands, UK.
3. European Commission, DG XII, research project, Framing and Communicating Environmental Issues, coordinated by Klaus Eder, EV5V-CT92-0153.
4. European Commission, DG Research, ENV4-CT96-0198, EV5V-CT94-0389.

5. Sociology Lens and WIREs Debate: 'Climate Change Knowledge and Social Movement Theory', http://thesocietypages.org/sociologylens/2011/02/14/sociology-lens-wires-debate-climate-change-knowledge-and-social-movement-theory-2/.

6. 1996–99. European Commission FP4, Environment and Climate RTD program, coordinated by Enrique Larana (Universidad Complutense de Madrid SP) with Chris Rootes (UK). Policy-Making and Environmental Movements: The Case of Waste Management (ENV4-CT96-0239). http://www.kent.ac.uk/sspssr/polsoc/

7. 2004–7: European Commission, 6th Framework, STREP. Research Project "Participatory Governance and Institutional Innovation", PAGANINI. Coordinated by Herbert Gottweis, University of Vienna (A) [partners: K. Braun (D), Y. Haila(FIN), M. Hajer (NL), Szerszynski (UK), L. Rinkevicius (LIT), M. Kousis (GR)], http://www.univie.ac.at/LSG/paganini/.

8. I.e., contextual: socioeconomic and historical.

9. These preconditions are parts of an ecological marginalization process, which usually entails first the takeover of local natural resources by powerful private, state or supra-state interests. The result is a gradual or immediate disorganization of biological processes in ecosystems, the locals' loss of their resource base, and the generation of public health risks (Kousis 1998).

10. The European Commission (DG XII, Environment and Climate programme), 'Transformations in Environmental Activism' research project (1998–2001), applying protest-event analysis and other methods in Britain, France, Germany, Greece, Italy, Spain and Sweden over the years 1988–97. For a brief description of the TEA project (EC contract number ENV4-CT97-0514), see www.ukc.ac.uk/sociology/TEA.html.

11. 1994–96: European Commission, DG XII, Environment and Climate programme, 'Grassroots Environmental Action and Sustainable Development in the Southern European Union', contract No. EV5V-CT94-0393. Coordinated by Maria Kousis, University of Crete (GR) [partners: University of Salamanca (ESP); University of Aveiro (PT)].

12. 2012–17: Laura Morales, 'Democratic Responsiveness in Comparative Perspective', European Research Council, IDEAS (Sweden, Portugal, France, Norway, Greece) Grant http://www.responsivegov.eu/.

13. 'Participatory Governance and Institutional Innovation', PAGANINI.

14. Following the World Social Forum.

15. See also http://voson.anu.edu.au/papers.html. (last access June 30, 2014)

16. Former Action Group on Erosion, Technology and Concentration, and ETC since 2001.

References

Ackland, R., and M. O'Neil. 2008. 'Online Collective Identity: The Case of the Environmental Movement,' *Australian Demographic and Social Research Institute* working paper 4. The Australian National University.

———. 2011. 'Online Collective Identity: The Case of the Environmental Movement'. *Social Networks* 33, no. 3: 177–90.

Adair, S. 2001. 'The Origins of the Protest Movement against Nuclear Power'. *Political Opportunities, Social Movements, and Democratization* 23: 145–78.

Agyeman, J., R. D. Bullard and B. Evans, eds. 2003. *Just Sustainabilities: Development in an Unequal World*. Cambridge: MIT Press.

Ansell, C., R. Maxwell and D. Sicurelli. 2006. 'Protesting Food: NGOs and Political Mobilization in Europe'. In *What's the Beef? The Contested Governance of European Food Safety,* ed. C. Ansell and D. Vogel, 97–122. Cambridge, MA: The MIT Press.

Baker, S., et al., eds. 1997. *The Politics of Sustainable Development: Theory, Policy and Practice within the EU*. London: Routledge.

Balbus, J. M., et al. 2007. 'Protecting Workers and the Environment: An Environmental NGO's Perspective on Nanotechnology'. *Journal of Nanoparticle Research* 9: 11–22.

Barcena, I., and P. Ibarra 2001. 'The Ecologist Movement in the Basque Country'. In *Environmental Politics in Southern Europe,* ed. K. Eder and M. Kousis, 173–94. Dordercht: Kluwer Academic Publishers.

Barnard, A. V. 2011. '"Waving the Banana" at Capitalism: Political Theater and Social Movement Strategy among New York's "Freegan" Dumpster Divers'. *Ethnography* 12, no. 4: 419–44.

Beck, U. 1995. *Ecological Politics in an Age of Risk*. Cambridge: Polity Press.

Berny, N. 2013. 'Building the Capacity to Play on Multilevel Policy Processes: French Environmental Movement Organisations and the European Union'. *Social Movement Studies* 12, no. 3: 298–315.

Blühdorn, I. 2011. 'The Politics of Unsustainability: COP15, Post-ecologism, and the Ecological Paradox'. *Organization Environment March* 24, no. 1: 34–53.

Borzel, T., and A. Buzogani. 2010. 'Environmental Organisations and the Europeanisation of Public Policy in Central and Eastern Europe: The Case of Biodiversity Governance'. *Environmental Politics* 19, no. 5: 708–35.

Brand, K.-W. 1999. 'Dialectics of Institutionalization: The Transformation of the Environmental Movement in Germany'. *Environmental Politics* 8, no. 1: 35–58.

Brulle, R. 1996. 'Environmental Discourse and Social Movement Organizations: A Historical and Rhetorical Perspective on the Development of US Environmental Organizations'. *Sociological Inquiry* 66, no. 1: 58–83.

Bullard, R. D. 1990. *Dumping in Dixie: Race, Class, and Environmental Quality*. Boulder: Westview Press.

Buttel, F. H. 2005. 'The Environmental and Post-environmental Politics of Genetically Modified Crops and Foods'. *Environmental Politics* 14, no. 3: 309–23.

Carmin, J., and A. Fagan. 2010. 'Environmental Mobilization and Organisations in Post-socialist Europe and the Former Soviet Union'. *Environmental Politics* 19, no. 5: 689–707.

Carruthers, D. C., ed. 2008. *Environmental Justice in Latin America*. Cambridge: MIT Press.

Chen, J. 2010. 'Transnational Environmental Movement: Impacts on the Green Civil Society in China'. *Journal of Contemporary China* 19, no. 65: 503–23.

Císař, O. 2010. 'Externally Sponsored Contention: The Channelling of Environmental Movement Organisations in the Czech Republic after the Fall of Communism'. *Environmental Politics* 19, no. 5: 736–55.

Dalton, R. J. 1994. *The Green Rainbow: Environmental Groups in Western Europe.* London: Yale University Press.

———. 2005. 'The Greening of the Globe? Cross-National Levels of Environmental Group Membership'. *Environmental Politics* 14, no. 4: 441–59.

Della Porta, D. 2007. *The Global Justice Movement: Cross-National and Transnational Perspectives.* Boulder: Paradigm.

Della Porta, D., and S. Tarrow. 2005. *Transnational Protest and Global Activism.* Lanham: Rowman and Littlefield.

Della Porta, D., and G. Piazza. 2008. *Voices of the Valley, Voices of the Straits: How Protest Creates Communities.* New York: Berghahn Books.

Diani, M. 1995. *Green Networks: A Structural Analysis of the Italian Environmental Movement.* Edinburgh: Edinburgh University Press.

Diani, M., and P. Donati. 1999. 'Organisational Change in Western European Environmental Groups: A Framework for Analysis'. *Environmental Politics* 8, no. 1: 13–34.

Di Gregorio, M. 2012. 'Networking in Environmental Movement Organisation Coalitions: Interest, Values or Discourse?'. *Environmental Politics* 21, no. 1: 1–25.

Eder, K. 1996. 'The Institutionalisation of Environmentalism: Ecological Discourse and the Second Transformation of the Public Sphere'. In *Risk, Environment and Modernity: Towards a New Ecology,* ed. S. Lash, B. Szerszynski and B. Wynne, 203–23. London: Sage.

———. 2009. 'A Theory of Collective Identity: Making Sense of the Debate on a "European Identity"'. *European Journal of Social Theory* 12, no. 4: 427–47.

Eyerman, R., et al. 1990. *The Making of the New Environmental Consciousness: A Comparative Study of the Environmental Movements in Sweden, Denmark and the Netherlands.* Edinburgh: Edinburgh University Press.

Fillieule, O. 2003. 'Local Environmental Politics in France: Case of the Louron Valley, 1984–1996'. *French Politics* 1, no. 3: 305–30.

Flam, H. 1994. 'A Theoretical Framework for the Study of Encounters between States and Anti-nuclear Movements'. In *States and Anti-nuclear Movements,* ed. H. Flam, 8–26. Edinburgh: Edinburgh University Press.

Frickel, S. 2004. 'JUST SCIENCE? Organizing Scientist Activism in the US Environmental Justice Movement'. *Science as Culture* 13, no. 4: 449–69.

Gamson, W. A., and A. Modigliani. 1989. 'Media Discourse and Public Opinion on Nuclear Power: A Constructionist Approach'. *American Journal of Sociology* 95, no. 1: 1–37.

Goodman, J. 2009. 'From Global Justice to Climate Justice? Justice Ecologism in an Era of Global Warming'. *New Political Science* 31, no. 4: 499–514.

Gottweis, H., et al. 2008. 'Participation and the New Governance of Life'. *BioSocieties* 3, no. 3: 265–86.

Gould, K. A., D. Pellow, and A. Schnaiberg. 2004. 'Interrogating the Treadmill of Production'. *Organization and Environment* 17, no. 3: 296–316.

Gould, K. A., A. Schnaiberg and A. S. Weinberg. 1996. *Local Environmental Struggles: Citizen Activism in the Treadmill of Production.* Cambridge: Cambridge University Press.

Treadmill of ProductionHaila, Y., et al. 2007. 'Final Report, Work Package 4. Building Trust through Public Participation: Learning from Conflicts over the Implementation of the Habitats Directive'. Participatory Governance and Institutional Innovation [PAGANINI] Contract No. CIT2-CT-2004-505791. Retrieved 11 November 2013 from http://www.univie.ac.at/LSG/paganini/finals_pdf/WP4_FinalReport.pdf.

Hicks, B. 2004. 'Setting Agendas and Shaping Activism: EU Influence on Central and Eastern European Environmental Movements'. *Environmental Politics* 13, no. 1: 216–33.

Hutter, S. 2014. *Protesting Culture and Economy in Western Europe: New Cleavages in Left and Right Politics.* London: University of Minnesota Press.

Jamison, A. 2001. *The Making of Green Knowledge: Environmental Politics and Cultural Transformation.* Cambridge: Cambridge University Press.

———. 2010. 'Climate Change Knowledge and Social Movement Theory'. *Wiley Interdisciplinary Reviews: Climate Change* 4, no. 1: 811–23.

Jamison, A., and P. Ostby. 1997. *Public Participation and Sustainable Development (PESTO): Comparing European Experiences.* Aalborg: Aalborg Universitetsforlag.

Jiménez, M. 2007. 'The Environmental Movement in Spain: A Growing Force of Contention'. *South European Society and Politics* 12, no. 3: 359–78.

Kettnaker, V. 2001. 'The European Conflict over Genetically-Engineered Crops'. In *Contentious Europeans,* ed. D. Imig and S.Tarrow, 205–32. Lanham: Rowman and Littlefield.

Kiefer, C., and M. Benjamin. 1993. 'Solidarity with the Third World: Building an International Environmental-Justice Movement,' In *Toxic Struggles: The Theory and Practice of Environmental JusticeJustice,* ed. R. Hofrichter, 1226–36. Philadelphia: New Society Publishers.

Klandermans, B., and S. Tarrow. 1988. 'Mobilization into Social Movements: Synthesizing European and American Approaches'. In *From Structure to Action: Comparing Social Movement Research across Cultures,* ed. B. Klandermans, H. Kriesi and S. Tarrow, 1–38. London: JAI Press.

Kousis, M. 1998. 'A Theoretical Exposition of Environmental Movement Research Worldwide: The Challengers, the Challenged and "Sustainable Development"'. In *Sociological Theory and the Environment (RC24-ISA): Proceedings of the Second Woudschoten Conference,* Part II: Cultural and Social Constructivism. SISWO, University of Amsterdam.

———. 1999. 'Environmental Protest Cases: The City, the Countryside, and the Grassroots in Southern Europe'. *Mobilization* 4, no. 2: 223–38.

———. 2004. 'Economic Opportunities and Threats in Contentious Environmental Politics: A View from the European South'. *Theory and Society* 33, nos. 3–4: 393–415.

———. 2005. 'State Responses as Threats and Opportunities in Southern European Environmental Conflicts'. In *Economic and Political Contention in Comparative Perspective,* ed. M. Kousis and C. Tilly, 202–25. Boulder: Paradigm.

———. 2010. 'New Challenges for 21st Century Environmental Movements: Agricultural Biotechnology and Nanotechnology'. In *The International Handbook of Environmental Sociology,* ed. M. R. Redclift and G. Woodgate. 2nd edition. 226–244, Cheltenham: Edward Elgar.

———. 2014. 'Environment, Economic Crisis and Social Movements in Greece, under Troika Memoranda and Austerity Policies'. In *Social Aspects of the Crisis in Greece,* ed. S. Zambarloukou and M. Kousi. 199–230, Athens: Pedio Publisher. In Greek.

Kousis, M., D. Della Porta and M. Jiménez. 2008. 'Southern European Environmental Movements in Comparative Perspective'. *American Behavioral Scientist* 51, no. 11: 1627–47.

Kousis, M., and K. Eder. 2001. 'EU Policy-Making, Local Action, and the Emergence of Institutions of Collective Action'. In *Environmental Politics in Southern Europe: Actors, Institutions and Discourses in a Europeanizing Society*, ed. K. Eder and M. Kousis, 3–23. Dordrecht: Kluwer.

Kousis, M., and K. Psarikidou. 2011. 'Science and Community-Based Environmental Activism, Mediterranean Coastal Biodiversity and the EU: The Caretta Caretta Case in Greece'. In *Contested Mediterranean Spaces: Essays in Honor of Charles Tilly*, ed. M. Kousis, T. Selwyn and D. Clark. 122-154, New York: Berghahn Books.

Kousis, M., and C. Tilly, eds. 2005. *Economic and Political Contention in Comparative Perspective*. Boulder: Paradigm.

Kriesi, H., et al. 1995. *New Social Movements in Western Europe: A Comparative Analysis*. Minneapolis: University of Minnesota Press.

Larana, E. 2001. 'Reflexivity, Risk and Collective Action over Waste Management: A Constructive Proposal'. *Current Sociology* 49, no. 1: 23–48.

Lekakis, J. N., and M. Kousis. 2013a. 'Economic Crisis, Troika and the Environment in Greece'. *South European Society and Politics* 18, no. 3: 305–31.

———. 2013b. 'Economic Crisis and the Environment: European Challenges'. *Perspectives on Europe* 43, no. 1: 46–52.

Long, T., and L. Lorinsci. 2009. 'NGOs as Gatekeepers: A Green Vision'. In *Lobbying the European Union: Institutions, Actors, and Issues*, ed. D. Coen and J. Richardson. 169–185. Oxford: Oxford University Press.

Maher, N. M. 2008. *Nature's New Deal: The Civilian Conservation Corps and the Roots of the American Environmental Movement*. London: Oxford University Press.

Mazey, S., and J. J. Richardson. 1993. *Lobbying in the European Community*. Oxford: Oxford University Press.

McAdam, D., J. D. McCarthy and M. N. Zald, eds. 1996. *Comparative Perspectives on Social Movements: Political Opportunities, Mobilizing Structures and Cultural Framings*. Cambridge University Press.

McLaughlin, P., and M. Khawaja, 2000. 'The Organizational Dynamics of the US Environmental Movement: Legitimation, Resource Mobilization, and Political Opportunity'. *Rural Sociology* 65: 422–39.

Melucci, A. 1992. 'Liberation or Meaning? Social Movements, Culture and Democracy'. *Development and Change* 23, no. 3: 43–77.

Miranda, M. L., et al. 2011. 'The Environmental Justice Dimensions of Climate Change'. *Environmental Justice* 4, no. 1: 17–25.

Mol, A. 2000. 'The Environmental Movement in an Era of Ecological Modernization'. *Geoforum* 31: 45–56.

Moore, K., et al. 2011 'Science and Neoliberal Globalization: A Political Sociological Approach'. *Theory and Society* 40, no. 5: 505–32.

Morales, L., et al. 2013. 'External Shocks and Governmental Responsiveness to Public Opinion: A Case Study of Nuclear Energy Policy after the Fukushima Disaster'. *ECPR General Conference,* 5-7 September, Bordeaux.

Ovcearenco, A. 2006. 'La réglementation des organismes génétiquement modifiés dans les pays d'Europe de l'Est: Développement pendant la période transitoire de 1991–2001 et à l'heure actuelle'. *Journal International de Bioéthique* 17, no. 3: 65–93.

PAGANINI. 2007. Summary Report of the EC Project Participatory Governance and Institutional Innovation (PAGANINI): Department of Political Science, University of Vienna, Austria. http://www.univie.ac.at/LSG/paganini/.

Pellow, D. N. 2000. 'Environmental Inequality Formation: Toward a Theory of Environmental JusticeJustice'. *American Behavioral Scientist* 43, no. 4: 581–601.

———. 2007. *Resisting Global Toxics: Transnational Movements for Environmental Justice-Justice.* Cambridge: MIT Press.

Pickvance, K. 1997. 'Social Movements in Hungary and Russia: The Case of Environmental Movements'. *European Sociological Review* 13, no. 1: 35–54.

Price, S., C. Sauders and C. Olcese. 2014. 'Movements'. In *Critical Environmental Politics,* ed. C. Death., 165–174. London: Routledge.

Princen, T., and M. Finger. 1994. *Environmental NGOs in World Politics: Linking the Local and the Global.* London: Routledge.

Purdue, D. A. 2000. *Anti-GenetiX: The Emergence of the Anti-GM Movement.* Aldershot: Ashgate.

Reynolds, L., et al. 2007. Work Package 6: 'GM-Food: The Role of Participation in a Techno-Scientific Controversy', *Participatory Governance and Institutional Innovation,* European Commission, 6th Framework, STREP, http://www.univie.ac.at/LSG/paganini/

Roose, J. Forthcoming. 'The Institutionalization of Environmentalism in Germany'. In T. Doyle and S. MaGregor, eds. *Environmental Movements around the World: Shades of Green in Politics and Culture,* 1:23–44. Oxford: Praeger.

Rootes, C., ed. 1999. *Environmental Movements: Local, National and Global.* London: Frank Cass.

———. 2007. *Environmental Protest in Europe.* Oxford University Press, 109–34.

———. 2008. *Acting Locally: Local Environmental Mobilizations and Campaigns.* London: Routledge.

Rootes, C., A. Zito, J. Barry. 2012. 'Climate Change, National Politics and Grassroots Action: An Introduction'. *Environmental Politics* 21, no. 5: 677–90.

Rootes, C., and R. Brulle. 2013. 'Environmental Movements'. In *The Wiley-Blackwell Encyclopedia of Social and Political Movements,* ed. D. Snow et al. Oxford: Blackwell. DOI: 10.1002/9780470674871.wbespm464

Rucht, D. 1994. 'The Antinuclear Power Movement and the State in France'. In *States and Anti-Nuclear Movements,* ed. H. Flam,129–162. Edinburgh: Edinburgh University Press.

———. 1999. 'The Impact of Environmental Movements in Western Societies'. In *How Social Movements Matter,* ed. M. Giugni, D. McAdam and C. Tilly, 204–24. Minneapolis: University of Minnesota Press.

———. 2001. 'Lobbying or Protest? Strategies to Influence EU Environmental Policies'. In *Contentious Europeans: Protest and Politics in an Emerging Polity,* ed. D. R. Imig and S. G. Tarrow,125-142. Oxford: Rowman and Littlefield.

Rucht, D., and D. Della Porta. 2002. 'Environmental Campaigns in a Comparative Perspective'. *Mobilization* 7, no. 1 (special issue).

Ruzza, C. 2004. *Europe and Civil Society: Movement Coalitions and European Governance.* Manchester: Manchester University Press.

Scarce, R. 1990. *Eco-Warriors: Understanding the Radical Environmental Movement.* Chicago: The Noble Press.

Schlosberg, D. 2004. 'Reconceiving Environmental Justice: Global Movements and Political Theories', *Environmental Politics* 13, no. 3: 517–40.

Schlosberg, D., and E. Bomberg. 2008. 'Perspectives on American Environmentalism'. *Environmental Politics* 17, no. 2: 187–99.

Schurman, R. 2004. 'Fighting "Frankenfoods": Industry Opportunity Structures and the Efficacy of the Anti-biotech Movement in Western Europe'. *Social Problems* 52, no. 2: 243–68.

Schurman, R., and W. A. Munro. 2010. *Fighting for the Future of Food: Activists versus Agribusiness in the Struggle over Biotechnology.* Minneapolis and London: University of Minnesota Press.

Seiffert, F. 2008. 'Consensual NIMBYs, Contentious NIABYs: Explaining Contrasting Forms of Farmers GMO Opposition in Austria and France'. *Sociologia Ruralis* 49, no. 1: 20–40.

Shiva, V. 2005. *Earth Democracy: Justice, Sustainability, and Peace.* London: Zed Books.

Scarce, R. 1990. *Eco-Warriors: Understanding the Radical Environmental Movement.* Chicago: The Noble Press.

Szasz, A. 1994. *Ecopopulism: Toxic Waste and the Movement of Environmental Justice.* Minneapolis: University of Minnesota Press.

Sze, J., and J. K. London. 2008. 'Environmental Justice at the Crossroads'. *Sociology Compass* 2, no. 4: 1331–54.

Taylor, D. E. 1997. 'American Environmentalism: The Role of Race, Class and Gender in Shaping Activism 1820–1995'. *Race, Gender and Class* 5, no. 1: 16–62.

———. 1999. 'Mobilizing for Environmental JusticeJustice in Communities of Color: An Emerging Profile of People of Color Environmental Groups'. In *Ecosystem Management: Adaptive Strategies for Natural Resource Organizations in the Twenty-First Century,* ed. J. Aley et al., 33–68, Philadelphia: Taylor and Francis.

Tarrow, S. 2001. 'Contentious Politics in a Composite Polity'. In *Contentious Europeans,* ed. D. Imig and S. Tarrow, 233–51. Lanham: Rowman and Littlefield.

Tilly, C. 1994. 'Social Movements as Historically Specific Clusters of Political Performances'. *Berkeley Journal of Sociology* 38:1–30.

Toke, D. 2011. 'Ecological Modernisation, Social Movements and Renewable Energy'. *Environmental Politics* 20, no. 1: 60–77.

Tovey, H. 2007. *Environmentalism in Ireland: Movement and Activists.* Dublin: IPA Press.

Van Der Heijden, H. A. 1997. 'Political Opportunity Structure and the Institutionalisation of the Environmental Movement'. *Environmental Politics* 6, no. 4: 25–50.

———. 1999. 'Environmental Movements, Ecological Modernization, and Political Opportunity Structures'. *Environmental Politics* 8, no. 1: 199–221.

Van Der Heijden, H. A., R. Koopmans and M. Giugni. 1992. 'The West European Environmental Movement'. *Research in Social Movements, Conflicts and Change,* supplement 2: 1–40.

Vasi, I. B. 2010. *Winds of Change: The Environmental Movement and the Global Development of the Wind Energy Industry.* Oxford: Oxford University Press.

Voulvouli, A. 2007. 'Arnavutköy District Initiative from Environmentalism to Transenvironmentalism: Practicing Democracy in a Neighbourhood of Istanbul'. PhD dissertation. University College London.

Weinberg, A. 1997. 'Local Organizing for Environmental Conflict: Explaining Differences between Case of Participation and Nonparticipation'. *Organization and Environment* 10, no. 2: 194–216.

Welsh, I. 1993. 'The NIMBY Syndrome: Its Significance in the History of the Nuclear Debate'. *The British Journal for the History of Science* 26, no. 1: 15–32.

Welsh, I., A. Plows and R. Evans. 2007. 'Human Rights and Genomics: Science, Genomics and Social Movements at the 2004 London Social Forum'. *New Genetics and Society* 26, no. 2: 123–35.

Yanitsky, O. 2013. 'The Russian Environmental Movement between 1985 and 2010: Changing Trends, Shifting Values'. In *Environmental Movements around the World: Shades of Green in Politics and Culture,* ed. T. Doyle and S. MaGregor, 1: 139–64. Oxford: Praeger.

Chapter 9

From Grassroots to Institutions
Women's Movements Studies in Europe

Anne Revillard and Laure Bereni

The women's movement is commonly seen as one of the major 'new social movements' of the 1970s (Touraine 1982). Indeed, the revival of women's protest was an important component of the political landscape in which social movement scholarship developed in Western democracies. Yet while in the United States the study of women's movements and feminism has been key in building (and challenging) the main social movement paradigms (Freeman 1979; Katzenstein 1998; Taylor and Whittier 1998, 1999; Banaszak 2010), in many European countries women's movements have not received the same scholarly attention. Several factors account for this relative marginality. In France, for example, a late institutionalization of gender studies and the persistent dominance of class over other power relations in the definition of progressive politics contribute to explaining the late development of scholarship on contemporary women's movements (Bereni and Revillard 2012; Achin and Bereni 2013). A glance, however, at the major sociology and political science publishers and journals in English and French shows that European research on women's movements has witnessed a new dynamism in the last twenty years, particularly in the last decade, as a result of an increasing legitimization of gender studies, a renewal of feminist protest and a higher visibility of gender issues on government agendas.

Giving an overview of the major trends of European research on women's movements[1] is a very delicate task. Sociology and political science in Europe are still predominantly structured along national lines, therefore scattered in a variety of methodological perspectives, disciplinary fields and paradigms, and, last but not least, in a number of different languages.[2] As French-speaking sociologists reading scholarship in French and English, we have a limited view of the research actually done on women's movements in European countries. The state of the art offered in this chapter will thus necessarily overestimate the weight of research done in countries where English is the official language or the academic *lingua franca,* as well as research done in transnational European research arenas, which have grown in size in the last decade.[3] While this literature review does not account for the epistemological diversity of European social movement studies, it will reveal some interesting orientations of the most visible part of European scholarship on women's movements. It will also illustrate the ways in which the increasing Europeanization of research funding as well as academic standards and networks, particularly steady in the field of gender, have shaped the ways in which women's movements are being tackled (in terms of dominant research questions, disciplinary perspectives, and methodological tools).

This situated exploration of research on women's movements in Europe points to European peculiarities. While US literature on women's and other social movements has mainly developed in the field of sociology, European research has grown more steadily within the realm of political science. This disciplinary anchor has resulted in placing political institutions at the centre of the research agenda. Women's movements have often been studied as far as they relate to a diversity of political institutions, such as bureaucracies, parliaments, governments, policy-making, welfare states, parties and unions. Therefore, rather than appearing as an autonomous field of studies, European research on women's movements has often been embedded in a variety of political science subfields.

Other characteristics of the research on women's movements in Europe pertain to political and historical particularities of the European context, such as the weight of Marxist ideology both in the national political arenas and in academic circles; the historical experience of totalitarianism, dictatorships, and the two World Wars on European territory; the long-lasting divide of the continent around the Iron Curtain followed by 'democratic transitions' in post-socialist Central and Eastern European countries; the traditional strength of state institutions, yet challenged by the European Union integration process. All these political experiences have shaped the ways in which women's movements have unfolded and been studied in Europe.

Drawing on an exploration of English- and French-speaking literature on women's movements in Europe over the last three decades, this chapter is organised into four sections. The first maps out the founding studies on women's movements in Europe, which provided typologies based on country-specific case studies and cross-country comparisons. The second section examines studies of women's movements' interplay with the state and policy-making. The third section explores the body of literature addressing the relationship between women's movements and party/electoral politics. Finally, the fourth section focuses on recent trends of research which address the impact of European Union integration on women's advocacy.

Sorting Out the European Quilt of Feminist Protest

The 'New Women's Movement' under Scrutiny

Studies of women's movements first developed within each European country, often evolving from essays by movement intellectuals to more sociologically informed analyses relating to social movement theories. Complementing single-country case studies, cross-country comparisons were key in this first wave of research on European women's movements, and references to the United States were omnipresent. Comparison was sometime integrated in research designs (Jenson 1982; Bouchier 1984; Lovenduski 1986; Gelb 1989; Kaplan 1992) but more often emerged from scholarly exchanges between specialists of single-country cases (Dahlerup 1986; Katzenstein and Mueller 1987).

Like US works from the same period, these early works centred around the 'new women's movements' that had emerged in the 1960s and 1970s in Western European countries alongside many other 'new' protest movements to the detriment of non-feminist women's mobilization or the on-going transformations of 'old' women's organizations. These studies also did not engage in building operational categories for a broad-range comparison of women's movements in a variety of cultural contexts, a concern that would become central to subsequent comparative research (Beckwith 2000; Ferree and Mueller 2004). Rather, early research on European feminism focused on the distinctive features of the 'second wave', as opposed to the 'first wave' of feminism, which centred on political and civil rights. One of their concerns was to sort out the internal heterogeneity of unfolding European feminist movements.

Making Sense of the Diversity of Women's Movements: The Centrality of Ideology

The first studies of European second-wave feminisms mostly adopted the threefold distinction between liberal, socialist and radical (Bouchier 1984; Lovenduski 1986; Ferree 1987; Katzenstein and Mueller 1987; Kaplan 1992). While sharing the goal of improving the position of women in society, these three perspectives disagreed both on the roots of gender inequality and on the strategies that would lead to change. Liberal feminism was defined as advocating equal rights under the law as the means for women's emancipation. Socialist feminism referred to an 'attempt to combine feminist insights with socialist paradigms' (Ferree 1987: 173), pointing to the gender blindness of Marxist orthodoxy while sharing the belief that the oppression of women was structurally linked to the capitalist system. Radical feminism, finally, considered patriarchy as 'the oldest form of dominance' (Lovenduski 1986: 69) and called for a full politicization of so-called 'private' issues, identifying male violence and the control of women's bodies as the core of their oppression. Unlike socialist feminists, radical feminists put the emphasis on male-female contradiction rather than class unity, and unlike liberal feminists, they sought cultural transformation (through awareness-raising groups and grassroots campaigns for example) rather than legal reform. While liberal feminism dominated the US women's movement as early as the 1960s, it did not gain the same centrality in many European countries at the same time. Socialist feminism was a lively strand in countries where the Marxist tradition historically pervaded social and political movements, especially in Britain, but also in Italy and in France. Yet the most visible strand of the 'new' feminist movement in many European countries was radical feminism: in Germany, the Netherlands, France, Italy or Greece, radical feminism dominated women's movements in spite of contrasting political institutions and protest histories (Katzenstein and Mueller 1987). With a relative weakness of both radical and socialist wings in the women's movements, the Nordic countries stood out as an exception (Dahlerup 1986). In Sweden for example, gender equality advocates acted within mainstream, social democratic institutions (Gelb 1989), at a time when most other European women's movements were confronting the State and dominant political parties.

Partly deriving from ideological typologies, organizational classifications marked the first studies on Western second-wave women's movements. Influenced by the resource mobilization framework (McCarthy and Zald 1977), students of European women's movements first drew a distinction between 'women's rights' and 'women's liberation' (or 'autonomous') groups, a typology that was originally based on the US context (Ferree and Hess 1985) and echoed Freeman's distinction between an 'older' and a 'newer' branch of the US women's movement (Freeman 1979). At one end of the *continuum*, women's rights groups tended to be 'organised along traditional hierarchical lines with formal structures and clearly stated objectives' and to 'work hard to become respected and influential pressure groups'; at the other end, women's liberation groups 'have avoided formal organizational structures, political affiliation and hierarchy', and 'favoured more radical methods of direct action' (Lovenduski 1986: 62). While in the United States the strength of liberal feminism translated from the outset into large women's rights organizations, like the National Organization for Women (NOW), European women's movements of the 1970s tended to be mostly informal and decentralised, composed of small groups at the grassroots, which refused the principles of hierarchical organization and political representation. It is not until the 1980s that a growing part of European women's movements entered into a process of organizational formalization and dialogue with mainstream political institutions, as the latter became more and more open to feminist discourse (Banaszak, Beckwith and Rucht 2003).

Women's Movements, the State and Policy-Making

The Invention of State Feminism

European case studies were foundational in the reflections on feminist intervention within/from the state, or 'state feminism'. The term was first coined in 1983 by Ruth Nielsen in a comparative study of gender equality legislation in Europe (Nielsen 1983), and then applied in 1987 by Helga Hernes who argued that Scandinavian Welfare states could be analysed as 'women-friendly' (Hernes 1987). While the state was previously seen as inherently patriarchal, these works envisioned it as a possible site of feminist action. Dorothy McBride and Amy Mazur, who initially worked on the French case (McBride Stetson 1987; Mazur 1995), highly contributed to the diffusion of this idea of 'state feminism' in the 1990s by launching an international 'research network on gender politics and the state' (RNGS), which led to several publications in the wake of their 1995 landmark collection (McBride Stetson and Mazur 1995). This network focused on the state institutions formally created for the promotion of gender equality, analysing their role in the inclusion of both movement actors and ideas into the policy-making process. While 'institutionalization' had been commonly envisioned in terms of co-optation and de-radicalization, these studies called attention to the sustainable development of feminist ideas in some areas of the state. It should be noted that the broad comparative framework of the RNGS has tended to favour macro-level and positivist approaches[4] while other studies of feminist activism within the state, especially in Australia and in the US, have developed a more micro-sociological and constructivist perspective, notably focusing on the experience of individual 'femocrats' (Sawer 1990; Eisenstein 1996; Banaszak 2010).

Questioning the Divide between the State and 'Civil Society'

Reflections on feminism and policy-making led to new conceptualizations of women's movements interactions with institutional actors. Working on the Norwegian case in the early 1990s, Haalsa argued that women's achievements in Norwegian public policies could be partly accounted for by the emergence of 'strategic partnership' between women politicians, women bureaucrats and women activists (Haalsa 1998). Her conceptualizations were subsequently re-worked by other feminist political scholars, such as Vargas and Wieringa (1998) and Woodward (2003). For example, focusing on the network of women advocates at the level of European institutions, Woodward coined the expression 'velvet triangles' to refer to the strategic connections between women coming from political parties, the bureaucracy, civil society organizations and universities/consultancies.

Shedding light on the connections between feminist mobilization within civil society and institutional actors, these works have paved the way for re-thinking the definition of (feminist) protest politics, although they have been conducted within a public policy perspective rather than a social movement framework. Combining the insights of this body of feminist policy-making scholarship and social movement theory (Katzenstein 1998; Banaszak 2010), recent works on France, for example, have challenged the traditional definition on women's movements as being located *outside* mainstream institutions (Bereni and Revillard 2012; Bereni 2015; Revillard forthcoming).

It should be stressed that these conceptualizations have drawn on the experiences of European liberal democracies. Recent studies on Central and Eastern European countries under communist regimes have cast a different light on 'state feminism'. While autonomous civic organizations had often been quite active in the first half of the twentieth century (de Haan, Daskalova and Loutfi 2006), the state socialist regimes prohibited women's autonomous groups, restricting the public expression of women's advocacy to hierarchical, party-controlled mass organizations (Fuszara 2005).

Women's Movements Facing Party and Electoral Politics

Taking place within the rising field of studies on gender and politics, a great deal of research done on European women's movements in the last two decades has focused on their relationship to political parties and electoral politics. While a first set of research has addressed in broad terms the interplay between women's movements and political parties, more recent works have focused on the promotion of gender quotas.

Women's Movements and Party Politics

The first studies conducted on the relationships between women's movements and conventional politics have focused on their (complicated) relationship with political parties. These studies explored the influence of women's movements on political parties and, in turn, the ways in which political parties have shaped movement demands and tactics over time. Beyond their diversity, European political parties have been identified as particularly centralised and organised along ideological lines, compared to US parties. Although in most European countries emerging women's movements asserted their 'autonomy' *against* political institutions, including political parties, feminist and left-wing party activism frequently overlapped.[5] This was particularly the case in Italy (Della Porta 2003). After a few years of confrontation with autonomous feminist groups, the political organizations of the 'old left', notably the Italian Communist party, became increasingly open to feminist demands. Collaboration between autonomous groups and the women active in left-wing parties or trade unions was observable at the local level. Della Porta emphasises the influence of the left-wing organizations on the feminist movement: in ideological terms, this translated into a mix of 'post-materialist' claims for 'liberation' with traditional demands for socioeconomic equality. In organizational terms, the movement 'combined the decentralised structure typical of new social movements with resources for coordination provided by the parties of the Old and New Left and the trade unions' (Della Porta 2003: 61).

In France, the relationships between the new 'women's liberation movement' and major left-wing organizations appeared even more complicated and ambivalent. French political organizations of the Left had long been marked by an anti-feminist tradition, endorsing a 'universalist' conception of equality that left no room for representing women's specific interests (Jenson 1984). During its first years of development, the new feminist movement developed a confrontational relationship with the old left organizations. However, there was a strong 'class-struggle' component within the women's liberation movement from the beginning, engaging both in the autonomous women's movement and in left-wing organizations, and attempting to combine the insights of feminism and socialism. These discrete mobilizations within left-wing organizations, both unions and political parties, accounted for a gradual opening of the latter to feminist demands. By the early 1980s, the French Socialist party newly in office had endorsed feminism and pushed for new gender equality reforms, asserting a major 'symbolic' change in the party's history—yet with little impact on the position of women within the party (Appleton and Mazur 1993; Jenson and Sineau 1995; Bereni 2006).

As well as studies on State feminism, these works on women's mobilization within political parties (and trade unions) have participated in pointing to the continuity of the women's movement over time and provided an insightful critique of the dominant model of life cycles of social movement, in line with Verta Taylor's notion of 'abeyance structures' (Taylor 1989). Against the idea of the failure and disappearance of feminist protest, these analyses have showed how feminist activism has relocated within mainstream institutions (Katzenstein 1998).

Women's Movements and Gender Quotas

Another body of research has focused on women's organised efforts to increase women's political representation, both inside and outside political parties. In Nordic countries, access to formal political power appeared on the agenda of the women's movement as early as the 1970s. In the case of Norway, Bystydzienski showed that 'establishment women' (representing traditional women's organizations) and 'new feminists' joined their efforts to get more women into politics (Bystydzienski 1988). In other European women's movements of the time, the demand for a higher representation of women in political office remained very marginal. It is not until the 1980s, as 'autonomous' women's movements gradually shifted from a dominant anti-institutional stance to collaborating with mainstream institutions, that this demand became increasingly central in several countries. Comparing Great Britain and West Germany, Lovenduski explored the extent to which a 'strong' women's movement could account for the adoption of party strategies to promote women (Lovenduski 1997). She found that 'the strongest effects were in the parties in which women organised to pressure the parties from the inside' (1997: 202). By the turn of the 1990s in these two countries, mainstream progressive parties had set a gender quota system to bring more women among party candidates, resulting in a substantial rise in women MPs. By contrast, studies of the French case emphasised that the campaign for 'gender parity' took place in the 1990s mainly outside political parties, after the failure of organised women's pressures from the inside in the 1980s, partly because of the absence of strong internal women's organizations (Opello 2006; Lépinard 2007; Bereni 2015).

Over the last decade, the interplay between European women's movements and electoral politics has increasingly been studied within the rising field of comparative research on the adoption and implementation of gender quotas, following their dissemination across the globe (Caul Kittilson 2006; Dahlerup 2006; Lépinard 2007; Krook 2009). The dominant research question has been to account for quota adoption and make sense of a variety of quota systems. Women's organised mobilizations for quotas have been identified as one causal factor, along with strategic anticipations from political elites, alignment with dominant conceptions of equality in domestic settings and existing international norms supporting gender quotas (Krook 2006).

Women's Movements and European Union Integration

While early studies of women's movements in Europe mainly developed at the national level or in a cross-national perspective, scholarly attention was more recently drawn to the impact of the EU on women's mobilization, with questions such as: how do women's movements mobilise and lobby at the EU level, in interaction with EU gender equality policy-making? How do domestic movements make use of EU regulations in order to promote reforms at national level? How does European integration affect feminist mobilization within new member states?

Women's Movements and Multilevel Governance

In recent years, students of feminist activism within the EU have increasingly addressed the complexities of multilevel governance—political authority stemming from a growing number of instances, from the local to the supra-national levels. Drawing on Keck and Sikkink's insights (1998), a subfield of research has focused on the development of transnational advocacy at the EU level and on the strategies adopted by domestic movements to take advantage of these multiple levels of governance.

The growing popularity of the concept of 'transnational advocacy networks' partly reflected the rise of women's transnational organizing at the European level: the most prominent umbrella organization is the European Women's Lobby, created in 1990 in order to coordinate women's advocacy at the level of European institutions. Other networks focus on specific regions or issues, such as KARAT (Coalition for Gender Equality), a coalition of women's NGOs from Central and Eastern Europe created in 1997 (Fuszara 2005; Lang 2009). While these transnational organizations have contributed to the development of gender equality policy-making at the EU level, European institutions have reciprocally supported their development, as the involvement of 'civil society' has become a new cornerstone of EU governance (Montoya 2008; Jacquot 2010, 2015).

The institutionalization of gender mainstreaming in the EU provides a case in point of such interactions between transnational networks and gender equality policy-making. Defined as a strategy according to which gender equality concerns should be included at all stages of policy-making in all policy domains, gender mainstreaming had been promoted in the 1990s by transnational advocacy networks at the international level, in order to obtain its inclusion in the 1995 Beijing platform (True and Mintrom 2005). European NGOs then fought in favour of its adoption at the EU level, and the institutionalization of this policy tool later affected women's NGOs in several aspects, since they were asked to monitor programs, to serve as experts and sometimes to play a more active role in implementation, while the strategy was at the same time increasingly questioned by feminist advocates (Lang 2009; Jacquot 2010, 2015).

Analysing how women's movements navigate between these different levels of governance has been another important focus of recent studies, as well as a source of conceptual innovation (Banaszak, Beckwith and Rucht 2003). For example, studying mobilizations and policies against sexual harassment in the EU, Zippel expands on Keck and Sikkink's analysis of 'boomerang' patterns of mobilization by using the 'ping-pong' metaphor to refer to the fact that 'policy action often cycles back and forth between the EU and national levels, with each influencing the other' (Zippel 2004: 59). In the case of sexual harassment, while feminists faced hostility in many member states, the EU innovated in the turn of the 1990s with the enactment of soft-law measures in the absence of member-state legislations. In the 1990s, women's rights advocates used this soft law as a leverage to promote legislation at the domestic level, which in turn favoured the enactment of a more comprehensive and repressive piece of regulation at the EU level in the form of a directive passed in 2002.

Finally, this situation of multilevel governance provides a particularly stimulating context to explore women's movements' litigation strategies, which are still relatively understudied in Europe compared to the US (Bereni, Debauche et al. 2010; Anagnostou and Millns 2013; Cichowski 2013).

EU Integration and Its Effects on Feminist Advocacy in the New Member States

The study of the unfolding of women's mobilizing in Central and Eastern European (CEE) countries during the 'democratic transition', and later during the EU accession period, has provided significant contributions to scholarship on social mobilizations, notably regarding the influence of international/ supra-national dynamics on domestic activism (Cîrstocea 2006).

When freedom of association was again possible after years of authoritarian rule, the rebirth of women's activism within civil society took place in a context characterised by a general reluctance towards the concept of 'feminism' because of its association with communism (Einhorn 1993), as well as by an important role played by foreign funding. Indeed, soon after 1989, US and international aid flowed into Central and Eastern Europe countries, some of it—notably coming from the United States Agency for International Development (USAID), the Ford Foundation, the Soros Institute and the United Nations Development Fund for Women (UNIFEM)—being channelled to women's NGOs. External funding accelerated the 'NGOization' of feminism (Lang 1997): women's groups increasingly adopted formal organizational structures, professionalization increased and organizations tended to be more pragmatic and issue-specific. While some scholars criticised this influence of foreign funding as a form of pressure exerted on activists to adhere to a Western vision of feminism (Roth 2007), others saw in a more positive light the effect of this input of international funding, stressing how it contributed to the rebirth of a civil society (Sloat 2005).

Based on a study of activism in the Czech Republic, Hašková argues that it was only during the Czech Republic's preparation to access the EU that external funding really started to constrain activism, shaping activist agendas, accelerating professionalization and excluding organizations that did not fit in, be it organizationally or ideologically (Hašková 2005). She shows that the first wave of international funding that entered the Czech Republic in the first half of the 1990s broadly aimed at the 'development' of women's civic organizations, and was rather unconditional. It favoured the expansion of a broad range of organizations and the first steps of their professionalization. By contrast, in the EU accession period, this source of funding dried up and was replaced by EU and domestic funding, which were much more constraining and indeed had a significant effect on the shape of women's advocacy in the Czech Republic (Hašková 2005).

Current studies on women's movements in Europe make up a dynamic, albeit scattered, field of research. Its strong anchoring within political science, combined with the specificities and diversity of the European political context, has undoubtedly led to original questions and important conceptual innovations. The movements' relationship to the state, to political parties, as well as the interactions between women's advocacy and policy-making processes, have been major subjects of investigation.

Yet this increasing positioning of Anglophone women's movement research in Europe within political science, and within a certain form of political science (valuing positivist, macro-level studies) also raises several theoretical and methodological issues. The development of these studies within the framework of political science paradoxically led to a decentring of scholarly attention from women's movements as such. Indeed, the focus on the interactions between women's movements and various political institutions results in movements being taken into account only to the extent that they affect institutional dynamics, notably the shape and orientations of political parties, and the content of public policies. Indeed, our knowledge of movement impact has increased thanks to this body of research. But today this seems to be to the detriment of other aspects of activism which remain under-investigated, or whose analysis does not get the same visibility. These include the ideological and organizational diversity of women's movements, grassroots organizations with few connections to formal political institutions, non-mainstream women's movements (be they conservative or leftist), the dynamics of individual militancy in women's organizations, as well as historical perspectives on women's mobilizing. In other words, the classical anchoring of women's movement studies within social movement theory, with its foundational questions around resource mobilization, organizations, framing or repertoires of contention, seems to have been partly lost in the way.

This growing inscription of women's movements studies within the framework of mainstream political science, as well as the increasing influence of EU-level research funding on the ways in which research is conducted and published, also have potentially preoccupying methodological implications. The general evolution of mainstream Anglophone political science publications reveals a dominance of research frameworks operating at a predominantly macro level, with comparative devices that tend to sacrifice the depth of empirical investigation to the number of countries included in the project. The mobilization of quantitative data (which does not necessarily mean a rigorous use of quantitative methods leading to significant causal inferences), tends to be valued over ethnographic and historical methods (Bereni forthcoming). Yet the theoretical fruitfulness of in-depth qualitative investigation has been proven by many studies on women's movements, particularly in the United States (Staggenborg 1998). We can only hope that this perspective becomes more visible in the English-speaking field of 'European research' on women's movements.

Anne Revillard is an associate professor in sociology at Sciences Po, affiliated with the Observatoire sociologique du changement (OSC) and the Interdisciplinary Research Center for the Evaluation of Public Policies (*Laboratoire interdisciplinaire d'évaluation des politiques publiques,* LIEPP, ANR-11-LABX-0091, ANR-11-IDEX-0005-02). Her research focuses on policy and politics in the fields of gender and disability. Recent publications include 'Feminist Mobilization and Family Change: A Case Study of a Grassroots Women's Organization in Quebec', pages 86–98 in *The Golden Chain: Family, Civil Society and the State,* edited by Jürgen Nautz, Paul Ginsborg, and Ton Nijhuis (Oxford and New York, Berghahn Books, 2013) and *L'Etat des droits. Politique des droits et pratiques des institutions,* edited with Pierre-Yves Baudot (Paris, Presses de Sciences Po/Gouvernances).

Laure Bereni is a sociologist, permanent researcher at the National Centre for Scientific Research (CNRS) and affiliated with the Centre Maurice Halbwachs in Paris. Her primary research work focused on women's mobilizations for gender parity in political representation in France. Her book, *La bataille de la parité. Mobilisations pour la feminisation du pouvoir,* came out in 2015 with the French Press Economica (Paris). She is the author of several articles on the women's movement and feminism, including 'A Paradigmatic Social Movement? Women's Movements and the Definition of Contentious Politics' (*Sociétés contemporaines* 85, 2012), co-authored with Anne Revillard, and 'Women's Movements and Feminism: French Political Sociology Meets a Feminist Comparative Approach', in *The Oxford Handbook of French Politics: Toward a Comparative Politics of France,* edited by Andrew Appleton, Robert Elgie, Emiliano Grossman, and Amy Mazur (Oxford and New York, Oxford University Press, forthcoming).

Notes

1. This chapter focuses on the literature on women's movements, i.e., on mobilizing on behalf of and/or for the advancement of women. It does not address the large body of studies on gender and social movement, which tackles the ways in which gender structures a diversity of collective protests (Fillieule and Roux, 2009). The two fields have developed quite distinctly, particularly in Europe, where studies on women's movements have tended to take place in political science rather than in the field of social movements studies.

2. Although scholars are increasingly encouraged to read and write in English, a substantial part of European research in social science is written in languages other than English, and it is very rare that scholars mobilise research done in another language than their own or English.

3. These transnational research arenas are structured around European social sciences associations (like the European Consortium of Political Science Research, ECPR) and *ad hoc* scientific networks funded by European Research Institutions.

4. For example, evaluating—in order to eventually quantify—the impact of women's movements in the policy-making process, with women's policy agencies being considered as an 'intervening variable'.

5. In several European countries there was also an important overlap between feminist and union activism. The relationship between women's movements and unions—oscillating between confrontation and integration—has been particularly documented in the British case (Kirton 2006).

References

Achin, C., and Bereni, L., eds. 2013. *Dictionnaire genre et science politique: Concepts, objets, problèmes.* Paris: Presses de Sciences Po.

Anagnostou, D., and S. Millns. 2013. 'Gender Equality, Legal Mobilisation, and Feminism in a Multilevel European System'. *Canadian Journal of Law and Society* 28, no. 2: 115–31.

Appleton, A., and A. Mazur. 1993. 'Transformation or Modernisation: The Rhetoric of Gender and Party Politics in France'. In *Gender and Party Politics,* ed. J. Lovenduski and P. Norris, 86–112. London: Thousand Oaks.

Banaszak, L. A. 2010. *The Women's Movement Inside and Outside the State*. Cambridge and New York: Cambridge University Press.

Banaszak, L. A., K. Beckwith and D. Rucht, eds. 2003. *Women's Movements Facing the Reconfigured State*. New York: Cambridge University Press.

Beckwith, K. 2000. 'Beyond Compare? Women's Movements in Comparative Perspective'. *European Journal of Political Research* (37): 431–68.

Bereni, L. 2006. 'Lutter dans ou en dehors du parti? L'évolution des stratégies des féministes du Parti socialiste (1971–1997)'. *Politix* 73: 187–209.

———. 2015. *La bataille de la parité. Mobilisations pour la feminisation du pouvoir*. Paris: Economica.

———. Forthcoming. 'Women's Movements and Feminism: French Political Sociology Meets a Feminist Comparative Approach'. In *The Oxford Handbook of French Politics: Toward a Comparative Politics of France*, eds. A. Appleton, R. Elgie, E. Grossman and A. Mazur. Oxford and New York:Oxford University Press).

Bereni, L., et al. 2010. 'Quand les mouvements féministes font (avec) la loi: les lois du genre'. *Nouvelles Questions Féministes* 29, no. 1 (special issue).

Bereni, L., and A. Revillard. 2012. 'Un mouvement social paradigmatique? Ce que le mouvement des femmes fait à la sociologie des mouvements sociaux'. *Sociétés contemporaines* 85, 17–41.

Bouchier, D. 1984. *The Feminist Challenge: The Movement for Women's Liberation in Britain and the United States*. New York: Schocken Books.

Bystydzienski, J. M. 1988. 'Women in Politics in Norway'. *Women and Politics* 8: 73–95.

Caul Kittilson, M. 2006. *Women and Elected Office in Contemporary Western Europe*. Columbus: Ohio State University Press.

Cichowski, R. 2013. 'Legal Mobilisation, Transnational Activism, and Gender Equality in the EU'. *Canadian Journal of Law and Society* 28, no. 2: 209–27.

Cîrstocea, I. 2006. *Faire et Vivre Le Postcommunisme: Les Femmes Roumaines Face à La Transition*. Bruxelles: Editions de l'Université de Bruxelles.

Dahlerup, D., ed. 1986. *The New Women's Movement: Feminism and Political Power in Europe and the USA*. London: Sage.

———. 2006. *Women, Quotas and Politics*. London and New York: Routledge.

de Haan, F., K. Daskalova and A. Loutfi, eds. 2006. *A Biographical Dictionary of Women's Movements and Feminisms: Central, Eastern, and South Eastern Europe, 19th and 20th Centuries*. Budapest: Central European University Press.

Della Porta, D. 2003. 'The Women's Movement, the Left and the State: Continuities and Changes in the Italian Case'. In *Women's Movements Facing the Reconfigured State*, ed. L. A. Banaszak, K. Beckwith and D. Rucht, 48–68. New York: Cambridge University Press.

Einhorn, B. 1993. *Cinderella Goes to Market: Citizenship, Gender and Women's Movements in East Central Europe*. London: Verso.

Eisenstein, H. 1996. *Inside Agitators: Australian Femocrats and the State*. Philadelphia: Temple University Press.

Ferree, M. M. 1987. 'Equality and Autonomy: Feminist Politics in the United States and West Germany'. In *The Women's Movements of the United States and Western Europe*, ed. M. F. Katzenstein and C. M. Mueller. Philadelphia: Temple University Press.

Ferree, M. M., and B. B. Hess. 1985. *Controversy and Coalition: The New Feminist Movement in America.* Boston: G. K. Hall.

Ferree, M. M., and C. M. Mueller. 2004. 'Feminism and the Women's Movement: A Global Perspective'. In *The Blackwell Companion to Social Movements,* ed. D. A. Snow, S. A. Soule and H. Kriesi, 576–607. Oxford: Wiley-Blackwell.

Fillieule, O., and P. Roux, eds. 2009. *Le sexe du militantisme.* Paris: Presses de Sciences Po.

Freeman, J. 1979. 'A Model for Analyzing the Strategic Options of Social Movement Organisations'. In *The Dynamics of Social Movements,* ed. M. N. Zald and J. D. McCarthy, 167–89. Cambridge: Winthrop.

Fuszara, M. 2005. 'Between Feminism and the Catholic Church: The Women's Movement in Poland'. *Czech Sociological Review* 41, no. 6: 1057–75.

Gelb, J. 1989. *Feminism and Politics: A Comparative Perspective.* Berkeley: University of California Press.

Haalsa, B. 1998. 'A Strategic Partnership for Women's Policies in Norway'. In *Women's Movements and Public Policy in Europe, Latin America, and the Caribbean,* ed. G. Nijeholt, V. Vargas and S. Wieringa, 167–89. New York: Garland.

Hašková, H. 2005. 'Czech Women's Civic Organising under the State Socialist Regime, Socio-economic Transformation and the EU Accession Period'. *Czech Sociological Review* 41, no. 6: 1077–1110.

Hernes, H. 1987. *Welfare State and Woman Power: Essays in State Feminism.* Oslo: Norwegian University Press.

Jacquot, S. 2010. 'The Paradox of Gender Mainstreaming: Unanticipated Effects of New Modes of Governance in the Gender Equality Domain'. *West European Politics* 33, no. 1: 118–35.

———. 2015. *Transformations in EU Gender Equality Policy. From Emergence to Dismantling.* Basingstoke: Palgrave.

Jenson, J. 1982. 'The Modern Women's Movement in Italy, France and Great Britain: Differences in Life Cycles'. *Comparative Social Research* 5: 200–225.

———. 1984. 'The "Problem" of Women'. In *The French Worker's Movement,* ed. M. Kesselman, 159–76. London: George Allen and Unwin.

Jenson, J., and M. Sineau. 1995. *Mitterrand et les françaises: un rendez-vous manqué.* Paris: Presses de la FNSP.

Kaplan, G. 1992. *Contemporary Western European Feminism.* New York: Allen and Unwin.

Katzenstein, M. F. 1998. *Faithful and Fearless: Moving Feminist Protest inside the Church and Military.* Princeton: Princeton University Press.

Katzenstein, M. F., and C. M. Mueller. 1987. *The Women's Movements of the United States and Western Europe: Consciousness, Political Opportunity, and Public Policy.* Philadelphia: Temple University Press.

Keck, M. E., and K. Sikkink. 1998. *Activists beyond Borders: Advocacy Networks in International Politics.* Ithaca: Cornell University Press.

Krook, M. L. 2006. 'Reforming Representation: The Diffusion of Candidate Gender Quotas Worldwide'. *Politics and Gender* 2: 303–27.

———. 2009. *Quotas for Women in Politics: Gender and Candidate Selection Reform Worldwide.* Oxford and New York: Oxford University Press.

Lang, S. 1997. 'The NGOisation of Feminism'. In *Transitions, Environments, Translations:*

Feminisms in International Politics, ed. J. W. Scott, C. Kaplan and D. Keates. New York: Routledge, 101–20.

———. 2009. 'Assessing Advocacy: Transnational Women's Networks and Gender Mainstreaming in the European Union'. *Social Politics* 16, no. 3: 327–57.

Lépinard, É. 2007. *L'égalité introuvable: La parité, les féministes et la République.* Paris: Presses de Science Po.

Lovenduski, J. 1986. *Women and European Politics: Contemporary Feminism and Public Policy.* Amherst: University of Massachusetts Press.

———. 1997. 'Women and Party Politics in Western Europe'. *Political Science and Politics* 30, no. 2: 200–202.

Mazur, A. G. 1995. *Gender Bias and the State: Symbolic Reform at Work in Fifth Republic France.* Pittsburgh: University of Pittsburgh Press.

McBride Stetson, D. 1987. *Women's Rights in France.* New York: Greenwood Press.

McBride Stetson, D., and A. G. Mazur, eds. 1995. *Comparative State Feminism.* Thousand Oaks: Sage.

McCarthy, J. D., and M. N. Zald. 1977. 'Resource Mobilisation and Social Movements: A Partial Theory'. *American Journal of Sociology* 82, no. 6: 1212–41.

Montoya, C. 2008. 'The European Union, Capacity Building, and Transnational Networks: Combating Violence against Women through the Daphne Program'. *International Organisation* 62, no. 2: 359–72.

Nielsen, R. 1983. *Equality Legislation in a Comparative Perspective: Towards State Feminism.* Copenhagen: Women's Research Center in Social Science.

Opello, K. A. R. 2006. *Gender Quotas, Parity Reform and Political Parties in France.* Lanham: Lexington Books.

Revillard, A. Forthcoming. *La cause des femmes dans l'Etat.* Grenoble: Presses universitaires de Grenoble.

Roth, S. 2007. 'Sisterhood and Solidarity? Women's Organisations in the Expanded European Union'. *Social Politics* 14, no. 4: 460–87.

Sawer, M. 1990. *Sisters in Suits: Women and Public Policy in Australia.* Sydney: Allen and Unwin.

Sloat, A. 2005. 'The Rebirth of Civil Society: The Growth of Women's NGOs in Central and Eastern Europe'. *European Journal of Women's Studies* 12, no. 4: 437–52.

Staggenborg, S. 1998. 'Social Movement Communities and Cycles of Protest: The Emergence and Maintenance of a Local Women's Movement'. *Social Problems* 45, no. 2: 180–204.

Taylor, V. 1989. 'Social Movement Continuity: The Women's Movement in Abeyance'. *American Sociological Review* 54, no. 5: 761–75.

Taylor, V., and N. Whittier. 1998. 'Gender and Social Movements: Part 1'. *Gender and Society* 12, no. 6 (special issue).

———. 1999. 'Gender and Social Movements: Part 2'. *Gender and Society* 13, no. 1 (special issue).

Touraine, A., ed. 1982. *Mouvements sociaux d'aujourd'hui: acteurs et analystes.* Paris: Editions ouvrières.

True, J., and M. Mintrom. 2005. 'Transnational Networks and Policy Diffusion: The Case of Gender Mainstreaming'. *International Studies Quarterly* 45, no. 1: 27–57.

Vargas, V., and S. Wieringa. 1998. 'The Triangle of Empowerment: Processes and Actors in the Making of Public Policy for Women'. In *Women's Movements and Public Policy in Europe, Latin America, and the Caribbean,* ed. G. Nijeholt, V. Vargas and S. Wieringa, 3–23. New York: Garland.

Woodward, A. 2003. 'Building Velvet Triangles: Gender and Informal Governance'. In *Informal Governance in the European Union,* ed. T. Christiansen and S. Piattoni, 76–93. Cheltenham: Edward Elgar.

Zippel, K. 2004. 'Transnational Advocacy Networks and Policy Cycles in the European Union: The Case of Sexual Harassment'. *Social Politics* 11, no. 1: 57–85.

Chapter 10

Social Movements Facing the Crisis
Indignados and Occupiers in Europe

Héloïse Nez

The *Indignados* and Occupy movements, which emerged as of 2011 in Europe, have given rise to a rich and abundant literature.[1] These publications are nevertheless quite uneven in status and quality, not to mention in the cases studied. I have listed about one hundred references, the vast majority of which are on the '15M Movement' in Spain (named in reference to the date of the first demonstration on 15 May 2011). The others concern European countries such as Italy, Greece, Great Britain, Portugal, Ireland, France, the Netherlands and Slovenia, where movements of various magnitudes appeared, in the wake of the Spanish *Indignados* or the Occupy Wall Street (OWS) movement (launched on 17 September 2011). Some research also develops a European or international comparison. On drawing up this selection, I considered the books and the articles published in scientific journals, without pretending to be exhaustive. My selection does not include the books written by activists or journalists, scholars' interventions in demonstrations or assemblies, nor the press articles or blogs. It is important to note nevertheless that activists and participants in these movements have also supplied a significant written contribution with a high level of reflexivity.

This academic literature is itself plural. Numerous references are militant writings from researchers directly involved in these movements, who offer a personal interpretation, nourished by this double background (in Spain, for instance, see Taibo 2011). In these cases, authors do not use social science tools to analyse mobilizations as much as they develop positions from their own insider knowledge of movements. These publications represent an important contribution to the public debate and the reflections of the *Indignados* on their own practices, but they do not participate in academic debates concerning the nature and dynamics of social movements. However, numerous narrative testimonies describe democratic practices and suggest interpretations of the meaning of these mobilizations (in Spain, for example, see Botella 2011; Corsín and Estalella 2011; Nez 2011; Romanos 2011; Serrano 2012; Pestaña 2013). Other essays include the *Indignados* and Occupy movements to make general claims about, for example, the 'democracy of the common good' (Subirats 2011) or the 'principle of democracy' (Ogien and Laugier 2014). The main limitation of these works is their reliance on in-depth and contextualised empirical data. However, they offer a general reflection, often well documented on these movements and sometimes written 'amidst the heat of combat', constituting an important element for researchers to contribute to the debates, not only scientific but also political.

The works I consider here, by emphasizing their main inputs and limits, are closer to the sociology of social movements. The aim is to take stock of the acquired knowledge, to extricate the main debates running through the literature and offer research assessments, from four perspectives: (1) the socio-demographic profile and political behaviour of the *Indignados* and Occupiers; (2) the democratic practices implemented and their evolutions; (3) a temporal comparison with previous social movements; and (4) a spatial comparison between various *Indignados* and Occupy movements, which leads us to query the definition of the object.

Profile and Political Behaviours of the Participants

In Spain, several works develop a quantitative approach to identifying the social composition of the 15M, as well as the aims and motivations of its participants. They rest on the distribution of questionnaires during the camps in Salamanca (Calvo, Gómez-Pastrana and Mena 2011) and Bilbao (Arellano et al. 2012), or later by drawing on a sample of people who participated in the 15M in Madrid (Likki 2012) or by gathering data on major demonstrations in Spain between 2010 and 2011 (Anduiza, Cristancho and Sabucedo 2013). More classic public opinion studies have also been used to assess the degree of support for the 15M (CIS 2011; Metroscopia 2011). Among these quantitative works, some try to measure the influence of mobilizations on elections (Jiménez 2011; Anduiza, Mateos and Martin 2013).

In spite of the methodological issues they raise and that are sometimes acknowledged by their authors, these studies enable a better understanding of the participants' profile, quite different from the portrait put forward by the media: the *Indignados* are not only youths directly affected by the economic crisis, not do they consist mainly of marginal or 'anti-system' people. This is an intergenerational and highly educated movement, broadly supported by national public opinion. Although the students and the unemployed have been mobilizing, the majority of respondents claim to be in a rather good economic situation, but fear their future. However, in comparison with participants in previous demonstrations, 'they [are] more likely to be women and unemployed; they [are] younger and more educated' (Anduiza et al. 2013: 11). Only a few of them are involved in social or political organizations, but they vote more than the average and mostly hold left-wing views. They are concerned about economic and political issues, and their criticisms are directed to political leaders as well as bankers. The 15M supposedly had an influence on the increase of spoiled or blank ballots, and on the penalization of the overwhelmingly major parties in favour of smaller ones during the elections of 2011, but the causal links between both phenomena are not readily identifiable.

The comparative dimension is hardly developed to analyse the social composition of the *Indignados* and Occupy movements in Europe. Putting into perspective the investigations conducted in three Spanish cities emphasises variations at local scale and evolutions over time (Calvo 2013). For example, the prior degree of commitment of the *Indignados* and their left-wing orientation are more blatant in Madrid than in Bilbao or Salamanca, which is partly due to the time the investigation was administered (in November in the capital, in May in the other two cities) and hence informs that those less politically minded had left after the summer of 2011. Typologies of participants are also suggested, differentiating the *Indignados* from the alternative social movements, which develop anti-capitalist claims, and those without any prior experience, more prone to moderation (Taibo 2013).

To the best of my knowledge similar investigations have not been conducted in the camps of other countries, so the understanding of the profile of the *Indignados* and Occupiers in Europe remains limited. A European comparison could still enable us to know whether these are essentially downgraded members of the middle classes who mobilise their efforts or whether different social groups join forces; the situation probably varies according to the national contexts.

Ethnography of Democratic Practices

Ethnographic works question more the significance that activists give to their experiences, especially in terms of organizational practices and internal democracy (for instance, Cruells and Ibarra 2013). These studies highlight the specificities of the *Indignados* and Occupy movements in their different contexts. I note varieties of practices and forms of direct democracy: if deliberation and consensus are highly valued in general assemblies in Spain and the United States, groups appear more autonomous from the general assembly in Slovenia, and thus action and concrete activities (more than deliberation) are at the heart of activists' time (Razsa and Kurnik 2012).

These works also offer a genealogy of the democratic practices used in the assemblies of *Indignados* and Occupiers, which allows understanding the variations from one place to the other. In Spain, several sources of influence have inter-pollinated one other: the political culture of the self-managed occupied social centres, a generation of professionals educated in university courses specialised in participation, forms of discussion on the Internet and the social networks, as well as a political culture of the citizens open to dialogue (Nez and Ganuza 2012). In Slovenia, the democratic practices that were implemented stem instead from the struggles for migrants' rights; this explains why a slogan such as 'We are the 99 per cent' met with a mitigated echo, owing to its nationalist connotation (Razsa and Kurnik 2012).

Furthermore, following the practice of direct democracy over time in the assemblies of different Spanish towns shows that participants are able to limit the production of hierarchies and the emergence of leaders at the beginning of the process, by adopting particular rules with respect to the speaking and decision-making processes. However, the principles of horizontality and inclusion are challenged in the long-term, because the specialization of tasks leads to the emergence of leaders and the defection of participants (García 2012; Nez 2012; Rivero 2012; Estelella and Corsín 2013; Razquin 2014). Besides, even if women acquire more space and visibility compared with previous social movements and if some frames incorporate inter-sectionality of inequalities (Cruells and Ruiz 2014), interventions and political proposals continue to be mainly worn by men (Ezquerra and Cruells 2013). The combination of ethnographic observations with *a posteriori* viewing of videos seems here a promising methodological path to reconcile the practices with the principles put forward, such as rotation of functions or equality in addressing the assembly (Rivero 2012). The use of participant observation and photography also enables capturing a spatial analysis of the mobilization, for example by showing the effects of assemblies moving from public and open premises to private and closed spaces such as squats (Nez Forthcoming).

As defended by Razsa and Kurnik (2012), ethnography and comparison have a specific role to play in order to describe and discuss the variation in the forms of direct democracy practices which emerged with the *Indignados* and Occupy movements. Ethnography could also be used more extensively to finely query the interactions between *online* and *offline* protests, in order to test general assertions according to which an autonomous space of communication would emerge, at the crossroad of a virtual space and a physical public space (Castells 2012). This approach would thus complete the contributions focusing on the digital practices of the *Indignados* and Occupiers, stressing the role of the Internet in strengthening the mobilization (Arellano et al. 2012; Fuster and Subirats 2012; Gerbaudo 2012; Subirats 2012; Candón and Redondo 2013; Anduiza et al. 2013) and the emergence of informal political debates (Vicari 2013).

Continuities and Breakups with Previous Movements

Some of the ethnographic studies situate the recent protests vis-à-vis previous movements, in order to analyse the points of continuity and change. Juris (2012), for example, argues that the main difference between Occupy and the global justice movement (GJM) is the shift from already constituted groups' networks to the aggregation logic of individuals who do not always have previous activist experience. These changes are linked to the use of virtual social networks that enable convergence of a large number of participants in given locations. But this type of activism is more difficult to maintain over time and to structure around a formal program, and could be less socially and racially inclusive. Adell (2011), a Spanish sociologist who has followed Madrid demonstrations since the democratic transition in the 1970s, shows that direct filiations exist between the 15M demonstrations and previous ones, such as the 2003 Iraq anti-war protest or the 2004 mobilizations after the Atocha train station bomb attacks (see Aguilar and Romanos in this volume). Through a meticulous observation and description of the 15M demonstrations, he emphasises two novelties: the participatory practices, subject to stronger publicity and formalization with respect to the assemblies in the early days of the democratic transition, and Internet and Livestream uses, which increase the mobilization capacity and visibility of the movement.

Other authors develop this temporal comparison, by describing the previous movements mainly from secondary sources (Baumgarten 2013; Romanos 2013). When it does not rest on recent fieldwork, this type of research tends to transpose on the *Indignados* and Occupy movements analytical frameworks and theories produced to make sense of other cases (Della Porta 2012; Fougier 2012; Flesher 2014b). Nevertheless, these works have the merit of looking for continuity in collective action and escape the tendency to systematically see novelty in recent social movements. They show that the *Indignados* and Occupiers amplify or deepen previously existing practices in autonomous and global justice movements (Maeckelbergh 2012; Shihade, Flesher and Cox 2012; Della Porta 2014; Flesher 2014b). Similarities can be noted in the claims, repertoires of action and some actors. Several differences are, however, put forward with the global justice movement, like the superiority of the national level as the main target of protest (Della Porta and Mattoni 2014b; Flesher 2014a), the strength of territorial anchoring rather than the network form (Halvorsen 2012) or the decision-making procedures, with the shift from a consensus between organizations to consensus among individuals (Aguiton and Haeringer 2012). Some authors also argue that the global justice movement has been a spectator rather than an instigator of the *Indignados* mobilizations (Fougier 2012), which stand out by the number of participants and the opening of spaces for debate (Maeckelbergh 2012). In Spain, the comparison is done with the squatters' movement, which inspired the democratic practices of *Indignados* and provided them with logistic support, while the 15M in return changed the public perception of the squat (Abellán, Sequera and Janoschka 2012; Martínez and García 2012). Another comparison is developed with the free culture movement, which also inspired the 15M in terms of actors and claims (Fuster 2012; Fuster and Subirats 2012).

This time-related comparative perspective ought to be developed in order to pinpoint the break-ups and continuities of the *Indignados* and Occupy movements with previous mobilizations, and not limited only to the global justice movement. The risk of this approach is indeed that it might overlay pre-established interpretation grids on the *Indignados* and Occupiers, neglecting a careful analysis of the current movements, and freeze the terms of the comparison between two 'waves' of protest which would have succeeded each other. Finer genealogy of the *Indignados* and Occupy movements in each European country remains to be done, taking into account not only the influence of the global justice movement but also that of other national demonstrations and militant groups that emerged during the last decade. See, for instance, in Greece, Kousis (2014, 2016) replacing the *aganaktismenoi* (the Greek *Indignados*) in the anti-austerity campaign that began in 2010: while the *aganaktismenoi* movement initially started with such traditional protest groups as unions or political parties, new participants fortified the broad coalition against austerity measures. Similarly set apart are some stimulating reflections that question the international diffusion of social movements since the *Indignados* and Occupy cases (Romanos 2015, Forthcoming a; Roos and Oikonomakis 2014; Oikonomakis and Roos 2016); we lack studies to trace the links and networks that connect or fail to connect these movements across space. The comparison could thus be examined further from the perspectives of circulation and diffusion of experiences from one country to the other, but also from one mobilization to the other in the same country, including those which are developing at the same time as the *Indignados* and Occupy movements—just like the 'tides' which mobilise, in Spain, different sectors of public services against the cutbacks, by taking inspiration from the practices of the *Indignados* (Calle and Candón 2013).

International Comparisons and the Object Issue

The European and international comparative dimension remains small, whereas the vast majority of the contributions are monographs centred on a city or a country. The latter focus on the specificity of the mobilization in a unique national context, to understand, for example, in the Basque Country the difficult rooting of a movement 'from Spain' (Arellano et al. 2012) or the specifics of the 15M in Catalonia (Díaz and Ubasart 2012). Monographs seek to explain the failure of the movement in certain countries: in Italy, where political opportunities are not favourable and where anti-austerity protests compete with the *Indignados* identity (Zamponi 2012); in Portugal, where protests rely more on traditional organizations and focus on national stakes (Baumgarten 2013; Accornero and Ramos Pinto 2014); or also in Greece, where it is difficult to identify targets and prepare victorious actions in a police brutality context (Sotirakopoulos and Sotiropoulos 2013). Some works compare two cases: Occupy Slovenia and OWS, by investigating the differences in democratic practices from one site to the other (Razsa and Kurnik 2012); Occupy Amsterdam and Occupy Los Angeles, by showing the significance, for the continued movement, of the links that the Occupiers succeed in establishing with the local militant milieu (Uitermark and Nicholls 2012); or even the Spanish *Indignados* and the movement for social justice in Israel (Perugorría, Shalev and Tejerina 2016), by putting forward the role of the political and ideological cleavages in the success of these mobilizations.

Some special issues of journals, conference proceedings (Tejerina and Perugorría 2012) and books (Castells 2012; Flesher and Cox 2013; Della Porta and Mattoni 2014a; Ancelovici, Dufour and Nez 2016) develop an international comparative perspective, with various levels of in-depth consideration. *Social Movement Studies* (2012) has, for example, devoted two consecutive issues to the Occupy movements among a very wide diversity of local and national contexts, but this comparison is more a juxtaposition of short texts, with more or less data, than a real analytical and systematic comparison (Pickerill and Krinsky 2012). The project is similar in the special issue of *Interface* (2012), which tries to compare three contentious waves (the Arab revolutions, the 15M in Spain and Occupy in the United States) but is limited, for the movements of interest here, to a collection of contributions on the *Indignados*. *American Ethnologist* (2012) offers, from this viewpoint, a less ambitious special issue but much more coherent at the analytical level, composed of two very stimulating articles (Razsa and Kurnik 2012; Uitermark and Nicholls 2012), and one comment that places in dialogue both previous contributions on various themes, such as time and temporality, morals imaginary and conception of democracies (Nugent 2012). This article shows to what extent these mobilizations are rooted in a specific temporality of capitalism, where the political is no longer autonomous from the economic. Several authors (Benski et al. 2013; Langman 2013; Tejerina et al. 2013; Della Porta and Mattoni 2014b; Dufour, Nez and Ancelovici 2016) also emphasise the interest of re-integrating the economic policy in the study of social movements, given the central place of increasing social and economic inequalities in the protests emerging since 2011. The latter collective productions (*Current Sociology* 2013; Della Porta and Mattoni 2014a; Ancelovici et al. 2016) offer more integrated comparison of the *Indignados* and Occupy movements in different countries, by questioning the emergence of a 'new cycle of protest'. It is also the issue of the emergence of a new generation of activists and the properties common to the different post-2010 movements which is questioned in the *Development and Change* (2013) special issue, from a great diversity of mobilizations beyond the *Indignados* and Occupiers.

Several debates run through these comparative analyses. First of all, how can these movements be defined? Diverse terms are used: 'Occupy social movements', with reference to the protesting form aimed at occupying public spaces (Tejerina et al. 2013); 'Activisms 2010+', to take into account the current transformations of activism (Biekart and Fowler 2013); 'movements of the crisis', to address 'the economic and political protest from which these movements originated and at which they point' (Della Porta, Mattoni 2014b: 2); or still 'the movements of 2011', which would constitute a new global social movement (Glasius and Pleyers 2013). The terminology of social movement is also under debate in Spain: some authors prefer to speak about a 'space of mobilisation' (Calle 2013), while others defend the formation of a 'social movement' as the internal organization of the *Indignados* increased (Ibarra 2013). Behind the words, the stake is that of defining the object and the comparability of the cases (Dufour et al. 2016). Thus far, most comparative contributions seek to define characteristics common to these movements, such as the increased role of the Internet and social networks (Castells 2012; Biekart and Fowler 2013), while acknowledging that they fall within specific contexts. Some conclude on the emergence of a new generation of activists similar to that of 1968 (Gills and Gray 2012; Glasius and Pleyers 2013), others on the appearance of 'diverse manifestations of a new international cycle of contention' (Tejerina et al. 2013: 1) or a 'non-centralised and innovative momentum of multiple protest expressions' (Biekart and Fowler 2013: 532). Several authors look at the analysis framework of these mobilizations, stressing the interest of studying their emotional dimensions from a theoretical (Benski and Langman 2013) or empirical (Perugorría and Tejerina 2013) viewpoint, by focusing, for instance, on the strategic uses of humour (Romanos Forthcoming b).

But the answers to the question 'Why now?' asked in the introduction to the case in *Development and Change* (2013) remain incomplete. The factors underlying the involvement of the *Indignados* and Occupiers are mainly considered in analyses related to countries where such movement had a limited echo, in Italy (Zamponi 2012), Portugal (Baumgarten 2013), Great Britain (Sotirakopoulos and Rootes 2014), France (Chabanet and Lacheret 2016) and Ireland (Royall and Desbos 2016). The authors put forward several factors to explain the lower reception of *Indignados* and Occupy protests in these countries, such as political circumstances, the economic context or the specific characteristics of these movements (isolation, internal divisions, unclear narrative, etc.). A thorough and comparative analysis of these (and other) 'negative' European cases would probably enable us to go further in the analysis of the 'Why (not) now?'. This issue is also taking into account the transformations of capitalism and its variations in explaining the heterogeneity of the magnitude of the *Indignados* and Occupy movements in Europe.

Blind Spots and Avenues for Future Research

We have shown in this brief overview of the literature on the European *Indignados* and Occupiers that a remarkable amount of knowledge has been accumulated, over a few years, on the socio-demographic profile and political behaviour of the participants, on the democratic practices implemented in the assemblies and over the Internet, or on the elements of continuity with and change from previous social movements such as the global justice movement. Issues are still being debated, in particular regarding the definition and comparability of the cases. This recent research shows that the *Indignados* and Occupy movements are not so spontaneous or new as we could believe; instead, they maintain some affiliation and similarities with earlier social movements. The novelty lies mainly in the forms of commitment, the greater number of individuals and in the singular attention carried in the practices of internal democracy. While the interest for democratic practice is not new, it was at the heart of these movements and enabled a displacement of these practices from activist circles towards a much wider audience. These social movements are also singular because they are part of a period of huge economic crisis in Europe, which impacts both the origins and the main claims of the *Indignados* and Occupiers, prompting researchers to reconsider the effects of capitalism in the study of social movements.

This chapter also placed in evidence neglected angles that deserve greater attention: a European comparison of the social composition of the *Indignados* and Occupy movements; an ethnographic analysis of the *online* and *offline* protest, in order to better determine the role of the Internet and social networks in mobilizations; a finer genealogy analysis at a national scale, beyond an overall comparison with the global justice movement; a closer look at the factors of commitment, by exploring the case of European countries where the mobilization was smaller. Some of these avenues can be difficult to scrutinise *a posteriori*, since the *Indignados* and Occupy movements have declined or disappeared in several cities in Europe. But temporal setback would also enable the investigation of vantage points left relatively aside, such as the analysis of the activist trajectories before, during and after these moments of occupation. Only through this micro-sociological study can we reply precisely to the question of the continuities and changes with previous movements, while querying the impact of these mobilizations in terms of the political socialization of the participants—anticipated as 'one of the most important outcomes of this cycle of contention' (Tejerina et al. 2013: 7), although no study so demonstrates. Let us note finally that, in this very recent and rapidly evolving research field, several productions in progress or pending publication should provide answers, at least partially, to these blind spots in the literature.

Héloïse Nez is assistant professor of sociology at the Université de Tours and researcher in the UMR CITERES. The main topics of her research are social movements, participatory democracy, and citizen competence. She has coordinated a volume on *Streets Politics in the Age of Austerity: From the Indignados to Occupy* (with M. Ancelovici and P. Dufour), at the Amsterdam University Press, 2016. Among her last publications: 'The Struggle for a Voice: Associations versus Citizens in Participatory Budgeting' (with E. Ganuza and E. Morales), *International Journal of Urban and Regional Research* (2014); 'Délibérer au sein d'un mouvement social: Ethnographie des assemblées des Indignés à Madrid', *Participations* (2012).

Notes

1. This article was translated from the French by Patrice Cochet-Balmet with funding from CITERES. I wish to thank Marcos Ancelovici, Pascal Dufour and Eduardo Romanos for their comments.

References

Abellán, J., J. Sequera and M. Janoschka. 2012. 'Occupying the #HotelMadrid: A Laboratory for Urban Resistance'. *Social Movement Studies* 11, nos. 3–4: 320–26.

Accornero, G., and P. Ramos Pinto. 2014. '"Mild Mannered"? Protest and Mobilisation in Portugal under Austerity, 2010–2013'. *West European Politics* 10.1080/01402382 .2014.937587.

Adell, R. 2011. 'La movilización de los indignados del 15M: Aportaciones desde la sociología de la protesta'. *Sociedad y Utopía* 38: 141–70.

Aguiton, C., and N. Haeringer. 2012. '(S')occuper (de) la gauche, ou l'ignorer ?' *Mouvements* 69: 116–27.

American Ethnologist. 2012. 'Occupy Movements: AE Forum' 39, no. 2: 237–83.

Ancelovici, M., P. Dufour and H. Nez, eds. 2016. *Street Politics in the Age of Austerity: From the Indignados to Occupy.* Amsterdam: Amsterdam University Press.

Anduiza, E., C. Cristancho and J. M. Sabucedo. 2013. 'Mobilization through Online Social Networks: The Political Protest of the Indignados in Spain'. *Information, Communication and Society* 10.1080/1369118X.2013.808360.

Anduiza, E., I. Martín and A. Mateos. 2013. 'Las consecuencias electorales del 15M'. In *Las elecciones generales de 2011,* ed. E. Anduiza et al., 145–66. Madrid: CIS.

Arellano, J., et al. 2012. *15-M Bilbao: Estudio de dinámicas sociales en torno a las movilizaciones del 15-M en Bilbao.* Vitoria Gasteiz: Servicio Central de publicaciones del Gobierno Vasco.

Baumgarten, B. 2013. 'Geração à Rasca and beyond: Mobilizations in Portugal after 12 March 2011'. *Current Sociology* 61: 457–73.

Benski, T., and L. Langman. 2013. 'The Effects of Affects: The Place of Emotions in the Mobilizations of 2011'. *Current Sociology* 61: 525–40.

Benski, T., et al. 2013. 'From the Streets and Squares to Social Movement Studies: What Have We Learned?' *Current Sociology* 61: 541–61.

Biekart, K., and A. Fowler. 2013. 'Transforming Activisms 2010+: Exploring Ways and Waves'. *Development and Change* 44, no. 3: 527–46.

Botella, E. 2011. 'La démocratie directe de la *Puerta del Sol*', *La Vie des idées.* Retrieved 3 December 2014 from http://www.laviedesidees.fr/La-democratie-directe-de-la-Puerta.html.

Calle, Á. 2013. 'Democracias emergentes: Movilizaciones para el siglo XXI'. In *La democracia del futuro,* ed. M. Cruells and P. Ibarra, 169–77. Madrid: Icaria Editorial.

Calle, Á., and J. Candón. 2013. 'Sindicalismo y 15M'. In *La democracia del futuro,* ed. M. Cruells and P. Ibarra, 151–67. Madrid: Icaria Editorial.

Candón, J., and D. Redondo. 2013. 'Redes digitales y su papel en la movilización'. In *La democracia del futuro,* ed. M. Cruells and P. Ibarra, 103–29. Madrid: Icaria Editorial.

Calvo, K. 2013. 'Fighting for a Voice: The Spanish 15-M Movement'. In *Understanding European Movements,* ed. C. Flesher and L. Cox, 236–53. London: Routledge.

Calvo, K., T. Gómez-Pastrana and L. Mena. 2011. 'Movimiento 15M: ¿quiénes son y qué reivindican?' *Zoom Político,* Fundación Alternativas (4): 4–17.

Castells, M. 2012. *Redes de indignación y esperanza.* Madrid: Alianza Editorial.

Chabanet, D., and A. Lacheret. 2016. 'The Occupy Movement in France: Why Protests Have Not Taken Off'. In *Street Politics in the Age of Austerity,* ed. M. Ancelovici et al. Amsterdam, Amsterdam University Press.

CIS. 2011. *Barómetro de junio.* Estudio nº 2 905.

Corsín, J. A., and A. Estalella. 2011. '#Spanishrevolution'. *Anthropology Today* 27, no. 4: 19–23.

Cruells, M., and P. Ibarra, eds. 2013. *La democracia del futuro: Del 15M a la emergencia de una sociedad civil viva*. Madrid: Icaria Editorial.

Cruells, M., and S. Ruiz. 2014. 'Political Intersectionality within the Spanish Indignados Social Movement'. *Research in Social Movements, Conflicts and Change* 37: 3–25.

Current Sociology. 2013. 'From Indignation to Occupation: A New Wave of Global Mobilization'. 61, no. 4: 377–561.

Della Porta, D. 2012. 'Mobilizing against the Crisis, Mobilizing for "Another Democracy": Comparing Two Global Waves of Protest'. *Interface* 4, no. 1: 274–77.

———. 2014. 'Learning Democracy: Cross-Time Adaptation in Organisational Repertoires'. In *Spreading Protest*, ed. D. Della Porta and A. Mattoni, 43–69. Colchester: ECPR Press.

Della Porta, D., and A. Mattoni, eds. 2014a. *Spreading Protest: Social Movements in Times of Crisis*. Colchester: ECPR Press.

———. 2014b. 'Patterns of Diffusion and the Transnational Dimension of Protest in the Movements of the Crisis: An Introduction'. In *Spreading Protest*, ed. D. Della Porta and A. Mattoni, 1–18. Colchester: ECPR Press.

Development and Change. 2013. 'Debate: Transforming Activisms'. 44, no. 3: 527–704.

Díaz, F., and G. Ubasart. 2012. '15M: Trajectòries mobilitzadores i especificitats territorials. El cas català'. *Interface* 4, no. 1: 235–50.

Dufour, P., H. Nez and M. Ancelovici. 2016. 'From the Indignados to Occupy: Prospects for Comparison'. In *Street Politics in the Age of Austerity*, ed. M. Ancelovici et al. Amsterdam: Amsterdam University Press.

Estalella A., and A. Corsín. 2013. 'Asambleas populares: el ritmo urbano de una política de la experimentación'. In *La democracia del futuro*, ed. M. Cruells and P. Ibarra, 61–79. Madrid: Icaria Editorial.

Ezquerra S., and M. Cruells. 2013. 'Movilización, discursos y prácticas feministas del 15M'. In *La democracia del futuro*, ed. M. Cruells and P. Ibarra, 131–49. Madrid: Icaria Editorial.

Flesher, C. 2014a. *Social Movements and Globalization: How Protests, Occupations, and Uprisings Are Changing the World*. Basingstoke: Palgrave Macmillan.

———. 2014b. 'Debunking Spontaneity: Spain's 15-M/Indignados as Autonomous Movement'. *Social Movement Studies*, 10.1080/14742837.2014.945075.

Flesher, C., and L. Cox, eds. 2013. *Understanding European Movements: New Social Movements, Global Justice Struggles, Anti-Austerity Protest*. London: Routledge.

Fougier, E. 2012. 'De l'altermondialisme aux "Indignés": un nouveau souffle pour la contestation du capitalisme?' *Revue internationale et stratégique* 86: 26–36.

Fuster, M. 2012. 'The Free Culture and 15M Movements in Spain: Composition, Social Networks and Synergies'. *Social Movement Studies* 11, nos. 3–4: 386–92.

Fuster, M., and J. Subirats. 2012. 'Més enllà d'Internet com a eina "martell"—eina de la vella política: Cap un nou Policy Making? Els casos del Moviment de Cultura Lliure i pel Procomú Digital i el 15M a Catalunya'. Retrieved 10 May 2011 from http://bit.ly/HhGzcJ.

García, P. 2012. 'El 15M: de vuelta al barrio como espacio de lo político'. *Revista internacional de pensamiento político* 7: 291–310.

Gerbaudo, P. 2012. *Tweets and the Streets: Social Media and Contemporary Activism*. London: Pluto Press.

Gills B. K., and K. Gray. 2012. 'People Power in the Era of Global Crisis: Rebellion, Resistance, and Liberation'. *Third World Quarterly* 33, no. 2: 205–24.

Glasius, M., and G. Pleyers. 2013. 'The Global Moment of 2011: Democracy, Social Justice and Dignity'. *Development and Change* 44, no. 3: 547–67.

Halvorsen, S. 2012. 'Beyond the Network? Occupy London and the Global Movement'. *Social Movement Studies* 11, nos. 3–4: 427–33.

Ibarra, P. 2013. 'Introducción'. In *La democracia del futuro*, ed. M. Cruells and P. Ibarra, 5–15. Madrid: Icaria Editorial.

Interface. 2012. 'Special Section: A New Wave of European Mobilizations?' 4, no. 1: 183–286.

Jiménez, M. 2011. '¿Influyó el 15M en las elecciones municipales?' *Zoom Político* 4: 18–28.

Juris, J. S. 2012. 'Reflections on #Occupy Everywhere: Social Media, Public Space, and Emerging Logics of Aggregation'. *American Ethnologist* 39, no. 2: 259–79.

Kousis, M. 2014. 'The Transnational Dimension of the Greek Protest Campaign against Troika Memoranda and Austerity Policies, 2010–2012'. In *Spreading Protest*, ed. D. Della Porta and A. Mattoni, 137–69. Colchester: ECPR Press.

———. 2016. 'The Spatial Dimensions of the Greek Campaign against Troika's Memoranda and Austerity Measures, 2010–2013'. In *Street Politics in the Age of Austerity*, ed. M. Ancelovici, P. Dufour and H. Nez. Amsterdam: Amsterdam University Press.

Langman, L. 2013. 'Occupy: A New New Social Movement'. *Current Sociology* 61: 510–24.

Likki, T. 2012. '15M Revisited: A Diverse Movement United for Change'. *Zoom Político* 11: 1–16.

Maeckelbergh, M. 2012. 'Horizontal Democracy Now: From Alterglobalization to Occupation'. *Interface* 4, no. 1: 207–34.

Martínez, M. Á., and Á. García. 2012. 'Ocupar las plazas, liberar los edificios'. *ACME: An International E-Journal for Critical Geographies.*

Metroscopia. 2011. *Opinión de los españoles ante el 15M.*

Nez, H. 2011. 'No es un botellón, es la revolución! Le mouvement des indignés à Puerta del Sol, Madrid'. *Mouvements.* Retrieved 3 December 2014 from http://mouvements.info/no-es-un-botellon-es-la-revolucion/.

———. 2012. 'Délibérer au sein d'un mouvement social: ethnographie des assemblées des Indignés à Madrid'. *Participations* 3: 79–101.

———. Forthcoming. 'Les *Indignados* dans l'espace public urbain: Ethnographie visuelle des assemblées à Madrid'. In *Les lieux de la colère*, ed. H. Combes, D. Garibay and C. Goirand. Paris: Karthala.

Nez, H., and E. Ganuza. 2012. 'Entre los militantes y los laboratorios deliberativos: el 15M'. In *From Social to Political*, ed. B. Tejerina and I. Perugorría, 119–34. Bilbao: Universidad del País Vasco.

Nugent, D. 2012. 'Commentary: Democracy, Temporalities of Capitalism, and Dilemmas of Inclusion in Occupy Movements'. *American Ethnologist* 39, no. 2: 280–83.

Ogien, A., and S. Laugier. 2014. *Le principe démocratie: Enquête sur les nouvelles formes du politique.* Paris: La Découverte.

Oikonomakis, L., and J. Roos. 2016. 'A Global Movement for Real Democracy? The Resonance of Anti-austerity Protest from Spain and Greece to Occupy Wall Street'. In

Street Politics in the Age of Austerity, ed. M. Ancelovici et al. Amsterdam: Amsterdam University Press.

Perugorría, I., M. Shalev and B. Tejerina. 2016. 'The Spanish *Indignados* and Israel's Social Justice Movement: The Role of Political Cleavages in Two Large-Scale Protests'. In *Street Politics in the Age of Austerity,* ed. M. Ancelovici et al. Amsterdam: Amsterdam University Press.

Perugorría, I., and B. Tejerina. 2013. 'Politics of the Encounter: Cognition, Emotions, and Networks in the Spanish 15M'. *Current Sociology* 61: 524–42.

Pestaña, J. L. 2013. 'Vie et mort des assemblées', *La vie des idées.* Retrieved 3 December 2014 from http://www.laviedesidees.fr/Vie-et-mort-des-assemblees.html.

Pickerill, J. and J. Krinsky. 2012. 'Why Does Occupy Matter?' *Social Movement Studies* 11, nos. 3–4: 279–87.

Razquin, A. 2014. 'Tomar la palabra en el 15M: Condiciones sociales de acceso a la participación en la asamblea'. PhD dissertation. Cádiz: Universidad de Cádiz.

Razsa, M. and A. Kurnik. 2012. 'The Occupy Movement in Žižek's Hometown: Direct Democracy and a Politics of Becoming'. *American Ethnologist* 39, no. 2: 238–58.

Rivero, B. 2012. 'The Assemblies of 15th May Movement in Cáceres: An Example of Democracy School, a Road to Dialogic Society'. In *From Social to Political,* ed. B. Tejerina and I. Perugorría, 108–18. Bilbao: Universidad del País Vasco.

Romanos, E. 2011. 'Les Indignés et la démocratie des mouvements sociaux'. *La vie des idées.* Retrieved 3 December 2014 from http://www.laviedesidees.fr/Les-Indignes-et-la-democratie-des.html.

———. 2013. 'Collective Learning Processes within Social Movements: Some Insights into the Spanish 15M/Indignados Movement'. In *Understanding European Movements,* ed. C. Flesher and L. Cox, 203–19. London: Routledge.

———. 2015. 'Immigrants as Brokers: Dialogical Diffusion from Spanish *Indignados* to Occupy Wall Street'. *Social Movement Studies.*

———. Forthcoming a. 'De Tahrir a Wall Street por Puerta del Sol: La difusión transnacional de los movimientos sociales en perspectiva comparada'. *Revista Española de Investigaciones Sociológicas.*

———. Forthcoming b. '"No es una crisis, es que ya no te quiero": Humor y protesta en el movimiento 15M. *Revista International de Sociología.*

Roos, J., and L. Oikonomakis. 2014. 'They Don't Represent Us! The Global Resonance of the Real Democracy Movement from the Indignados to Occupy'. In *Spreading Protest,* ed. D. Della Porta and A. Mattoni, 117–36. Colchester: ECPR Press.

Royall, F., and C. Desbos. 2016. 'The Political Significance of Occupy in Ireland'. In *Street Politics in the Age of Austerity,* ed. M. Ancelovici et al. Amsterdam: Amsterdam University Press.

Serrano, J. E. 2012. 'Ethnographie de l'acampada. La politisation à marche forcée de la génération perdue'. *Multitudes* 50: 75–79.

Shihade, M., C. Flesher and L. Cox. 2012. 'The Season of Revolution: the Arab Spring and European Mobilizations'. *Interface* 4, no. 1: 1–16.

Social Movement Studies. 2012. 'Occupy!' 11, nos. 3–4: 1474–2837.

Sotirakopoulos, N., and C. Rootes. 2014. 'Occupy London in International and Local Context'. In *Spreading Protest,* ed. D. Della Porta and A. Mattoni, 171–92. Colchester: ECPR Press.

Sotirakopoulos, N., and G. Sotiropoulos. 2013. '"Direct Democracy Now!" The Greek *Indignados* and the Present Cycle of Struggles'. *Current Sociology* 61: 443–56.

Subirats, J. 2011. *Otra sociedad ¿Otra política? De 'no nos representan' a la democracia de lo común.* Barcelona: Icaria.

———. 2012. 'Algunas ideas sobre política y políticas en el cambio de época: Retos asociados a la nueva sociedad y a los movimientos sociales emergentes'. *Interface* 4, no. 1: 278–86.

Taibo, C. 2011. *Nada será como antes.* Madrid: La Catarata.

———. 2013. 'The Spanish *Indignados*: A Movement with Two Souls'. *European Urban and Regional Studies* 20: 155–58.

Tejerina, B., and I. Perugorría, eds. 2012. *From Social to Political: New Forms of Mobilization and Democratization.* Bilbao: Universidad del País Vasco.

Tejerina, B., et al. 2013. 'From Indignation to Occupation: A New Wave of Global Mobilization'. *Current Sociology* 61: 377–92.

Uitermark, J., and W. Nicholls. 2012. 'How Local Networks Shape a Global Movement: Comparing Occupy in Amsterdam and Los Angeles'. *Social Movement Studies* 11, nos. 3–4: 295–301.

Vicari, S. 2013. 'Public Reasoning around Social Contention: A Case Study of Twitter Use in the Italian Mobilization for Global Change'. *Current Sociology* 61: 474–90.

Zamponi, L. 2012. 'Why Don't Italians Occupy? Hypotheses on a Failed Mobilization'. *Social Movements Studies* 11, nos. 3–4: 416–26.

PART II

National Cases

Chapter 11

Social Movement Studies in Britain

No Longer the Poor Relation?

Brian Doherty, Graeme Hayes and Christopher Rootes

Tilly's famous claim that 'Britain created the social movement' (Tilly 1982) might lead readers to assume that scholarship on social movements would be firmly established as a central field of British social science. That is not the case. Or, rather, it is not the case in relation to the dominant approach to studying social movements as it has developed across North America and Europe in recent decades, anchored as it now is around the study of contentious politics, networks, framing and, latterly, emotions. Britain has, of course, produced some of this kind of social movement scholarship, as we will show, but British scholarship on social movements also has a distinctive texture and tradition, born out of the specific cultural, political and academic contexts in which the study of social movements emerged in Britain from the late 1950s, and of the subsequent development of relationships between British social movements and the study of social movements.

Therefore in this chapter we first survey the emergence of social movements and the varieties of scholarship that have developed since they became a focus of interest in the social and human sciences in the 1960s. An underlying theme within these various approaches is the question of national particularity. In parallel to the catalysing effects on the study of social movements of the US civil rights and anti–Vietnam War movements and the post-1968 movements in many other Western European countries, the development of social movement scholarship in Britain has been profoundly marked by the specific contours of British movement activism. Thus British writing on movements has been strongly influenced by the Labour movement, the Campaign for Nuclear Disarmament (CND), feminism, and most recently, the environmental and global justice movements.

These relationships have strongly influenced not just the subjects of and dominant approaches to social movements in Britain, but even the broad understanding of the objectives of such writing, and its disciplinary locations. Indeed, British sociology, despite the strength of its empirical drive and theoretical pre-occupations with structure and agency, has historically had remarkably little to say about social movements, a point well made by Bagguley, who over fifteen years ago asked why there was 'no sociology of social movements in Britain' (1997: 147). Even today, the contrast between the British Sociological Association and its European, American and international counterparts is stark; of the forty-four 'study groups' established within the BSA, not one is concerned primarily with social movements. Nor is any of the fifty-one 'specialist groups' within the UK Political Studies Association devoted to the study of political protest. Against this backdrop, the account of movement scholarship in Britain that we give here is undeniably partial—both because we cannot hope to be comprehensive, and because it inevitably reflects our own concerns and passions—but through it we attempt to explain the development of a 'British tradition' of movement analysis, which is pluri-disciplinary, overwhelmingly qualitative, and driven by concerns with context and movement agency. We discuss the challenges movement scholarship in Britain has faced and faces, and where future developments might lie.

History Matters

Tilly's claim about the invention of the social movement in Britain was based upon his analysis of the changing forms of contentious action between the mid-eighteenth and mid-nineteenth centuries, marking the emergence of the 'national social movement' (1995a). This happened in other countries too, notably the United States and France, but the British case was uncomplicated by the noise of a revolution, and so the causal elements of the context could be separated out from controversies about the influence of revolutionary events on popular consciousness. Tilly's study showed how by the 1830s new 'repertoires of action' had emerged, in which campaigners formed associations to engage with national political issues and pursue reforms in the political system. His was one of several important studies of nineteenth-century popular contention in Britain by American social scientists, including Steinberg's study of the discourses of Spitalfield Weavers (1995) and Calhoun's arguments that early industrial protest had more to do with defence of community than class consciousness (1982). Both were included along with Tilly in Traugott's important edited collection on *Repertoires and Cycles of Collective Action* (1995), a collection that included no contributions from British authors. Where then were the British researchers?

They were in fact writing about the same subjects, but in different ways. Tilly and others in the contentious politics school (perhaps most notably Tarrow) have been much more interested in historical analysis, and resistant to the search for social scientific laws, than most of North American sociology and political science; Tilly in particular is associated with a defence of the importance of context, and the impossibility of developing finite laws about human action (Tilly and Goodin 2006). Yet if the contentious politics approach to social movements is located in particularity and detail, it is equally concerned with an explanatory drive to scale up from this particularity to produce transferrable models of action. For Tilly and Tarrow, for example, the development of 'modular' repertoires is the result of large-scale structural changes across Western societies: if Britain was one of the most modern countries in these respects, it was only one of several, and finally hardly distinguishable from similar processes and transformations elsewhere (Tarrow 1995; Tilly 2004; Tilly and Tarrow 2007). If the school of contentious politics defined itself as seeking a middle ground between phenomenological interpretation and mono-causal structural and rational choice laws of social science, it has nonetheless produced an attempt to codify recurrent, de-contextualised mechanisms and processes, most notably in *Dynamics of Contention* (McAdam, Tarrow and Tilly 2001).

In contrast to this search for generalizable mechanisms and processes and causal explanations of action—apparent in the tools and vocabulary of resource mobilization, political opportunity, and repertoires of contention—British movement scholarship has been animated by rather different methodological concerns, and predominantly marked by a drive to scale *down* to the particular. Indeed, in Britain the sociology of social movements has been profoundly marked by its relation to historiography and ethnography. Particularly important is Edward (E. P.) Thompson's *The Making of the English Working Class* (1963), which remains a canonical text for British approaches to writing on social movements. The focus here is not on movements *per se*; rather, in this and other key writings by Thompson (such as *Whigs and Hunters,* 1975) and associated leftist historians, particularly within the Centre for the Study of Social History at the University of Warwick (Hay et al. 1975), the development of political movements of dissenters and radicals in the eighteenth and nineteenth centuries was linked to historiographic concerns with context, agency, culture, and class, explored through the lens of investigation into the forms of power in the new capitalist political economy and the resistant development of popular solidarities and collective consciousness amongst the 'common people'.

Thompson was one of the driving figures of what in Britain is known as the 'first New Left' (Kenny 1995). An informal group of Marxist academics and intellectuals with a wider grassroots base in New Left clubs and coffee houses, it developed strong ties with the newly formed CND in the late 1950s. Defined by its break with the Communist Party after the Soviet invasion of Hungary in 1956, the New Left's importance lies not only in its political analysis but also in the critical historiography that it produced. Most important here is Thompson's focus on English radicalism, and the claim that indigenous traditions of dissent were rooted in the lived experience of working-class communities, developed through popular struggles independently of the leadership of Marxist intellectuals, an approach reflected in the *History Workshop* journal and movement founded by another New Left historian, Raphael Samuel. Their reading of British radicalism and dissent was rejected by an important strand of the British intellectual left, perhaps most prominently by Tom Nairn and Perry Anderson, editors of the *New Left Review*. Whereas for Thompson pre-modern traditions were a resource for the creation of a sense of popular sovereignty, for his critics the key problem was that the British working class and the Labour Party were too conservative, resisting revolutionary ideas and seeking only incremental reforms rather than confronting capital through a fully developed critique of British state and society.

Movements and Academics

Why does this now rather archaic argument between Marxists, half a century old, matter for understanding the trajectory of scholarship on social movements in Britain? It matters because in the first New Left we find the first elaboration of many of the enduring (and inter-related) themes that evolved to become central concerns of British social movement scholarship. These include: a commitment to the importance of understanding the consciousness of activists as agents of social and political change, casting social movements as sites of the generation of critical discourse; a concern with the activist as much as with the movement as the basic unit of analysis; a concomitant primary commitment to highly contextualized qualitative enquiry over broad comparative frameworks, a scholarship 'from below' through archive or fieldwork, a location of contentious politics in 'everyday local practices' (Chatterton 2010); a focus on working-class organization and social history (though, as we will argue, more recent developments have broadened the disciplinary scope and movement focus of British scholarship); and, finally, an interest in scholarship as not simply interpreting the world but also effecting social change.

The exploration of grand narratives of social transformation through attention to local micro-histories of dissent and dissenters influenced a generation of historians after Thompson, and remains central to contemporary social historiographies of protest and class formation in the nineteenth century (see

Chase 2007 amongst others). As Navickas underlines in a recent overview of British social history, most such studies reject the 'quantifying approach … of "repertoires of protest" that first unsatisfactorily separated types of action that may have been connected, and second unfairly denigrated "pre-industrial" collective action as disorganized and unsophisticated' (2011: 197). Of course, protest historiography has inevitably expanded beyond a concern with class to other subjects, particularly as second-wave feminism developed in the 1970s. In keeping with qualitative, movement-centred methods, an important aspect of this drive has been the growth of oral history, whose initial push towards 'empowerment'—in the words of Paul Thompson, to 'give back to the people who made and experienced history, through their own words, a central place' (1978: 3)—has more recently been supplanted by a concern with advocacy, where practice, the act of recounting personal history, is in itself held to have a transformative potential (Abrams 2010: 169). Though far from uniquely, or even centrally, concerned with public forms of dissent—a key focus of oral history has been the study of the family, women's history, and ethnic minorities—the concern of oral historians with multiple, subaltern voices is nonetheless a significant element within the growing literature addressing the collective memory of struggle through the particular stories and experiences of individual activists (e.g. British Library 2012).

Though the 'new' social movements of feminism, gay and lesbian liberation, peace, environmentalism and anti-racism were central to the sense of a new politics in Britain from the 1970s to the 1990s, as they were in many countries, this did not necessarily entail a rejection of class politics. Indeed, Frank Parkin's seminal study of CND—*Middle Class Radicalism* (1968)—anticipated debates about the character of the 'new social movements' that were in the 1980s to become central to the field (see Taylor and Pritchard 1980), whilst Mattausch (1989) returned to the class character of the revived CND of the 1980s. As Cox and Flesher Fominaya (2013) maintain, the 'new' social movements are often misunderstood in the canonical accounts of the history of social movement thinking as necessarily 'post-Marxist', a position that underplays the enduring influence of the New Left. Vanguard models of party leadership, and hierarchical and patriarchal forms of organization as well as exclusively statist and top-down models of political agency were challenged variously by new green, feminist, autonomist, anarchistic and libertarian movements that committed themselves to experiments in developing less hierarchical modes of grassroots organization (known in Britain in the 1970s and 1980s as 'alternative politics'). Cox and Flesher Fominaya underline the new pluralism in strategic terms, identifying the 'slow emergence of a sense of *movements* rather than *movement*: not of the multiplicity of popular struggles as such, which was always a practical reality facing organizers, but of the growing impossibility of a single strategic organization' (2013: 23).

In Britain, as in many other European countries, these debates took place within a milieu in which socialist traditions remained a major influence. The question of how to understand the relationships between multiple forms of inequality, collective identities and movement strategies produced numerous debates, often fractious, as in the debates about class, race and sexuality which led to the dissolution of the annual Women's Movement Conference in the UK after 1978 and to important movement-based theorizing, notably the socialist feminist book *Beyond the Fragments* (Rowbotham, Segal and Wainwright 1979). Highly influential among activists and researchers alike in the 1980s, *Beyond the Fragments* offered a critique of the model of organization associated with the traditional Marxist left, which had relegated individuals' needs and personal lives as secondary to the discipline and commitment required of the professional revolutionary. Equally, social theory texts such as *Hegemony and Socialist Strategy* (1985), written by British-based scholars Laclau and Mouffe, sought to define this politics of multiple social movement subjects and were much debated by scholars and activists. Correspondingly, the dominant theme in British social movement scholarship concerned movements as the source of new political ideas and strategies (the 'why' of movements) rather than their mobilizing processes and structures (the 'how') (e.g. Blühdorn 2007).

Up to the late 1980s at least, the links between movements and university-based intellectuals on the British left were strong and theoretical analysis was an unquestioned part of movement culture; movement intellectuals regularly took part in conferences and contributed to debates at conferences of the non-Trotsykist left and in its magazines, such as *Marxism Today, Spare Rib* and *Peace News*. This sensibility—the imbrication of movement scholarship with movement objectives—remains hugely influential in British movement enquiry across different disciplines today, and is connected to a widespread sense of political and ethical responsibility to the movements under study. In some cases, this has meant engaging in campaigns as activists and drawing explicitly on personal experiences and commitments; scholars such as Paul Chatterton, Graeme Chesters, Jenny Pickerill, Alex Plows, Sasha Roseneil, Paul Routledge and Ian Welsh all write (at least to some extent) from this viewpoint, with reflection from feminist research and critical geography particularly prominent. In this vein, Marshall, Roseneil and Armstrong's work on the material cultural legacy of the Greenham Common Women's Peace Camp situates the relationship between scholarship and activism through 'polyvocal autoethnography' (2009), whilst for Routledge, the value-laden position of participant-activist research 'subverts the notion of observational distance', and has the potential to create a 'third space within and between academia and activism', whose negotiation opens up the possibility to 'live theory in the immediate' (1996: 401). Of course, as Routledge acknowledges, this position can be fraught; recent thoughtful contributions concerning these blurred, permeable and power-constituted boundaries emphasise the dilemmas inherent in negotiating these positions, and the need for collective strategic reflexive thinking over the ethics, objectives and processes of academic-activist praxis (see for example, Autonomous Geographies Collective 2010; Gillan and Pickerill 2011).

British Movement Scholarship Today

Bagguley's claim that there is 'no social movement research in Britain' (1997: 152) was thus an overstatement even at the time. From Parkin onward, British scholars engaged with American and, later, European theorizing on social movements. In the 1970s, Wilkinson (1971) and Banks (1972) authored popular texts, and Mann (1973) considered the bases of working-class mobilization. In the 1980s, the British comparative tradition included a compendium of work on social movements in France (Cerny 1982) and on feminism in the US and Britain (Bouchier 1983). Others studied environmentalism (Cotgrove 1982), CND in its original (Taylor 1988) and revived (Byrne 1988) iterations, and some published in US-based and European journals. Later Scott (1990) reviewed a broad range of American and European literature before examining the purported discontinuity between 'old' and 'new' social movements and rejecting it, and Foweraker (1995), who had previously studied social movements in Latin America, considered whether the allegedly ethnocentric American social movement theory provided tools for cross-nationally comparative analysis, and concluded that it did. Bagguley himself published on movements of the unemployed (1991) and the anti-poll tax movement (1995), while Rootes examined the new social movements and their social bases (1992, 1995).

Nevertheless, there were—and remain—fewer scholars of social movements in Britain than might be expected given the size of the country's social scientific community and the relative vibrancy of its social movements and movement traditions; there is still no national research group for movement scholars, and there is no nationally recognized 'Centre' for the study of social movements. The reasons lie in the failure of the relatively modest and moderate social movement mobilizations in Britain in the 1960s and 1970s to produce political crises or major innovations in the political landscape. In the 1980s, when continental European and American theorists were enthralled by the 'new' social movements and the emergence of new parties, British politics was dominated by the last-gasp struggle of the traditional trade union movement; the majoritarian electoral system gave little hope for new parties such as the Greens, and resistance cohered around the Labour Party, then in seemingly permanent opposition. By the 1990s, however, there were signs of change: the campaign against the poll tax was followed by widespread protests against road-building and around environmental issues more generally, and these stimulated renewed research and writing.

Several developments testify to the growing purchase of movement scholarship in academia. First, the Alternative Futures and Popular Protest Conference at Manchester Metropolitan University has run since 1996, covering a wide range of social movement scholarship, but mostly rooted in the British tradition of engagement within and political responsibility to the movements studied. *Alternative Futures* also shows the enduring influence of Marxism on parts of British social movement scholarship, particularly evident in studies of trade union militancy. Second, *Social Movement Studies* was founded (2002) as the second international specialist academic journal on social movements after the US-based *Mobilization*, and provides a distinctive forum for work on social movements. The research interests of the founding editors reflected the general characteristics of British social movement research: George McKay published influential studies of alternative and counter-cultural activism (1996, 1998) highlighting elements of a British tradition of 'do-it-yourself politics', from anti-roads protest camps and urban Reclaim the Streets parties to New Age travellers; Tim Jordan worked on the politics of Internet activists and 'hacktivism' and published on the culture of activism and its relationship to democracy (2004), which was more rooted in the tradition of interpreting the political meaning of activism than with the type of questions generally dealt with in *Mobilization*; Adam Lent published an important historical overview of post-war British social movements, tracing their ideological and organizational evolution over time (2002). Notably, none of the three founding editors was located in the mainstreams of the sociology of social movements or of contentious politics. This doubtless contributed to the journal's inclusive editorial policy. A third sign of the growth of social movement studies is the increasing number of courses on social movements, particularly in sociology departments. This has been aided in Britain, as elsewhere, by textbooks pitched for international readerships but citing some British cases (Tarrow 1994 [2011]; Diani and Della Porta 1996/8 [2005]). In addition, there have been textbooks or introductory works on social movements authored by British scholars (Byrne 1997; Crossley 2002; Chesters and Welsh 2011; Edwards 2014).

The assumptions underpinning scholarship on social movements are often differentiated by discipline. Much of the major work in critical geography looks beyond the UK to cases from the global South, developing conceptual analyses of solidarity (Featherstone 2008; Routledge and Cumbers 2009; Brown and Yaffe 2012) and global resistance (Amoore 2005), as well as making important contributions to studies of movement-based campaigns against development projects. International relations scholars have also contributed to research beyond the UK; notable examples include Eschle and Maiguashca's analysis of the varied forms of feminism and its frequent exclusion from accounts of the global justice movement (2005), and Death's use of 'counter-conducts' as a Foucauldian approach to explaining protests at global summits (2010). Meanwhile, because of the predominantly institutional focus of politics as a discipline, political scientists have most often written about movements rather than for them (normative analysis being reserved for political theorists) and addressed movements in relation to the state and government (national and sub-national). They have also most often written about movements as discrete actors, defined by their principal issue—thus feminism, peace, and environmentalism and global justice (Carter 1992; Byrne 1997; Lovenduski and Randall 1993; Welsh 2000, Rootes 2009; Rootes and Saunders 2007; Saunders and Rootes 2013). One reason for defining movements in this way is to facilitate cross-national comparative analysis—which remains the most influential approach to explanation in the discipline.

Environmental movements have been a particular focus of this kind of work (Doherty 2002a; Doyle and MacGregor 2013). Prominent examples include the Transformation of Environmental Activism (TEA) project, a cross-European study of eight countries, co-ordinated by Rootes, that gathered comprehensive data on environmental movements for the decade 1988–97, and pointed to the absence of a common European trajectory for environmental protest, and thus to largely domestic causes for the upsurge in direct-action environmental protest in Britain in the 1990s (Rootes 2003). British environmental direct-action groups have been the subject of numerous studies, placing them in national and local context (Doherty 1999; Doherty et al. 2007; Seel et al. 2000; Wall 1999); their legacy is also evident in the 'pink and silver' tendencies in European anti-capitalist protests (Chesters and Walsh 2004; Flesher Fominaya 2013) and the 'horizontalism' of the global justice movement. Writing from a position of engaged scholarship, Chesters and Walsh see this process as evidence for a de-territorialized global justice movement (2005; Welsh and Chesters 2006), an emphasis which stands in contrast to comparative political sociologists, who tend to stress national particularities and attenuated cross-national ties in studies of similar groups (Rüdig 1990; Doherty and Hayes 2012a, 2012b; Hayes 2013).

In the policy studies and public administration literature, writing on movements typically focuses on pluralism, (neo)corporatism, and the challenges posed by the arrival of new collective actors: 'new social movements' are primarily seen through the lens of what Grant identified as 'insider/outsider' actors in governance processes (2005). This approach casts the environmental movement in particular in terms of pressure and interest group politics, with a focus on established NGOs and their consequences for democratic participation. However, this school typically has tangential interest only in movements *qua* movements; Jordan and Maloney, for example, reject social movement perspectives as 'underdefined' (1997: 48–49). Rather, the concern is with the relationship between 'single-issue campaigns' and 'broad church parties', and the potential of citizens to gain a 'better return on their participatory investment by acting through specialist organizations' (Jordan 1998: 318; see also Jordan and Maloney 1997, 2007), with group status in policy development (Christiansen and Dowding 1994, Marsh et al. 2009), and with the effects of movement campaigns on governance regimes in general, and policy sub-system stability (in Westminster and Brussels) in particular (e.g. Marsh 1983; Richardson 2000; Toke and Marsh 2003; Baggott, Allsop and Jones 2004).

In sociology, social network analysis has become increasingly influential. It has been used to study: inter-organizational ties in Glasgow, showing that the city's enduring socialist politics produced a more cohesive network than Bristol, where cross-movement networks were much weaker (Diani et al. 2010); environmental groups and NGOs in London (Saunders 2007), showing that solidarity is better understood as a property of groups than of wider movements (Saunders 2008a; 2013); Friends of the Earth International, uncovering regional collaboration within a transnational social movement organization (Doherty and Doyle 2013); the adoption of militant tactics through inter-personal networks in the suffragette movement (Edwards 2014); and stability and turnover of personnel within the Provisional IRA (*Irish Republican Army*), (Crossley and Stevenson 2014). The approach in these studies remains essentially interpretive, using network mapping as a strategy of inquiry into movement cultures.

Over the past two decades, social movement scholarship in Britain has developed in new directions, informed by the burgeoning of social movement scholarship worldwide and by a decline in the salience of socialist identities. This development is perhaps bringing the study of social movements more clearly into the mainstream of sociology; one sign of this is the increasing integration of Bourdieu's concepts of field and habitus for reading movement positionality and cultural praxis. A key influence here is Crossley's work on psychiatric survivor movements (2006), complemented by subsequent work by Husu (2013), Ibrahim (2013) and Samuel (2013).

British scholarship on social movements is now also increasingly 'contentious', using the established tools of the transatlantic schools of social movement analysis: work in the 1990s by Roseneil on Greenham Common (1995), and Rootes (1997, 1999) on the environmental movement in particular, introduced a generation of social movement scholars to US and continental European movement analyses and political process approaches. In this vein, Hayes (2002) sought to explain divergent outcomes of environmental campaigns in France through the development of a meso-level, policy-network-focused approach to political opportunity, perspectives also employed in studies of environmental movements in Central and Eastern Europe (Lang-Pickvance et al. 1997, Lang-Pickvance 1998). Closer to home, Doherty examined the process of manufactured vulnerability in the development of protest camp tactics (1999a), and Doherty and Hayes compared anti-GMO crop trashing in Britain and France (2012, 2013). Others have provided analysis of landmark campaigns such as the opposition to the Conservative government's Poll Tax, which helped to bring down Margaret Thatcher (Bagguley 1995) and protests against fuel taxes in 2000 (part of a Europe-wide wave of protest), which caused short-term political paralysis but failed to develop into a social movement (Doherty et al. 2003). Surveys of protesters have increasingly been conducted as part of multi-national comparative studies (e.g. Rüdig), the 2003 anti-war protests (2010); the G8 Make Poverty History march in Edinburgh in 2005 (Saunders 2008a); and the 2009 climate change march in London (Wahlström, Wennerhag and Rootes 2013). Saunders et al. (2012) analysed survey data from protests in seven European countries as part of the Caught in the Act comparative project on contextualizing protest (www.protestsurvey.eu/), showing that participation in protest by novices, returners, repeaters, and stalwarts each required different explanations. Also significant is comparative work on environmental activism (Doherty and Doyle 2008, Rootes 2004); work on grassroots activism on environmental issues has chiefly been published in the journals *Local Environment* and *Environmental Politics* (Rootes 2008, 2013; Rootes and Leonard 2010). Other influential work focuses on cultural approaches to movements, including Saunders' reading of collective identity in environmental movements (2008b) and Flesher Fominaya's study of collective identity (2010) or on the diffusion of forms of protest, notably Biggs' analyses of sit-ins in the US civil rights movement (Andrews and Biggs 2006), the spread of suicide protests (Biggs 2013) and of ethnic violence in Gujarat (Biggs and Dhattiwala 2012).

There are, of course, social movements of the right as well as movements of the left in Britain, but as in many other countries they have most often been analysed from a distance by researchers, through survey data. In recent decades parties such as the National Front (in the 1970s and 1980s) and the British National Party (in the 2000s) have intermittently threatened electoral breakthroughs that have not been sustained, and their fractious internal politics has consistently undermined their ability to develop stable organization, outflanked by the Conservative Party in the late 1970s and 1980s (Gilroy 1987) and more recently by the populist UK Independence Party. Most work on far-right mobilization is focused on political parties (Husbands 1983; Carter 2005; Goodwin 2011; Biggs and Knauss 2012) and has concentrated more on elections and political opportunities, though there is clear scope for future work here on activism, mobilization and counter-mobilization.

Trends and Future Developments

Since the 1980s, scholarship on social movements has expanded considerably in Britain. There has also been a shift of focus, reflecting the decline of the influence of Marxism on political debates about and within social movements. It was never really accurate to speak of British exceptionalism, as if Britain did not have new social movements and its Left was only concerned with the Labour party (Eyerman and Jamison 1991: 37); Rootes (1992) showed that was a perception more reflective of the barriers to new parties in the British political system than of the social bases and politics of social movements. Yet an orientation towards the ideas of the Left remained important for most British researchers on social movements. Even if Marxism's star has declined, it has not disappeared altogether: for example Barker's study of solidarity, his co-edited collection on leadership within social movements (2001) and co-stewardship of the Alternative Futures Conference connects Marxist with other traditions of social movement research (Barker 2013).[1] Thus there are conversations rather than silences between Marxist and other traditions of research in Britain. Despite the diversification of movement research since the 1980s, there remains a predominant concern among British researchers with assessing the meaning of social movement action, whether through its ability to generate new ideas or what it tells us about current society. We have argued that this is a concern shared with the first New Left and the 'history from below' tradition, and that this leads in turn to a strong concern with political responsibility towards the movements being researched.

Given what we have argued to be a particular interest in Britain in movement-generated ideas, and judging the political significance of particular cases, this is one area where we might expect further developments that might contribute to theoretical development within Britain and beyond. There have already been important studies in this vein, which provide a platform for future work. Gillan has shown a route through the thorny issue of the relationship between framing and ideology (2006, 2008). Roseneil's two books on Greenham Common (1995, 2000) are revealing, in that whilst the first drew on standard social movement concepts such as political opportunities and repertoires of contention, the second drew on the same empirical material but placed it in relation to social theory, particularly queer theory, to draw out some features of Greenham Common that were novel—notably its lack of concern with (feminist) theory and its irreverence, both elements that were evident in the later 1990s and 2000s UK direct-action movements (see also Rucht 2013). British protest camps and related direct-action movements, from those against roads, GM crops, and climate change (Schlembach et al. 2012) to corporate malfeasance and inequality (UK Uncut and the British version of Occupy) can be read as defining a peculiarly British repertoire and tradition, albeit one that also has some international precursors, parallels and imitators (Feigenbaum, Frenzel and McCurdy 2013). There is scope for further work on the balance and direction of national and international influences in this field. Although generational differences within the women's movement have been the subject of recent projects by historians (British Library 2012) that may complement work on feminist generations in the United States (Whittier 1995), there is clear potential for more analysis of the generational continuities and differences between British activist generations in direct-action movements (Doherty 2002b).

The broadening of social movement research in Britain since the 1990s has meant that more researchers are working within European and comparative frameworks. Here we foresee two further areas for future work: the changing nature of movement organization and the effects of repression on social movements. The apparent increase in episodic protests and declining role of movement organizations in shaping activist identity, combined with the increased role of the Internet in mobilization and as a new public sphere of debate, has been already been the subject of research in Britain (Pickerill 2003; Gillan et al. 2008) and this is likely to be developed further in the coming years. British social psychologists have become increasingly interested in protest and contentious politics, following the examples of Reicher (1984) who effectively critiqued the 'irrationalist' interpretation of riots, and Drury and Reicher (2000, 2003) who explored identity formation and the dynamics of protest.

Research on repression of social movements in the UK has been minimal compared to the United States. There are notable exceptions (such as work by Waddington on protest policing 1998, and Waddington et al. on riots 2010); yet it is revealing that Poulson, Caswell and Grey (2014), comparing the content of *Mobilization* and *Social Movement Studies,* identify repression as a key area where the two journals attract submissions with different focuses. Recent developments may change this: police tactics such as 'kettling' (the isolation and containment of large numbers of demonstrators for long periods to prevent them from engaging in mobile protest) have been subjected to critical scrutiny in the media, in parliament and by the police Inspectorate. Similar tactics have been used by police in other Western countries and may signify a response to the uncertainty occasioned by the decline of formal organizations as guarantors of the expected negotiated rituals of the mass demonstration, but recent reviews of 'kettling' in Britain have recognised that its excessive use has been provocative and suggest instead a more strategic policing of demonstrations based on intelligence. Police intelligence gathering is itself controversial, however. Investigations by *Guardian* journalists, working with movement activists and whistleblowers from within the police, have shown that undercover officers were, going back to the 1960s, planted for many years in a wide range of social movement groups that the police deemed to be 'domestic extremists' or subversives even when they had no history of violence and posed no credible threat to state security (Lewis and Evans 2013). Social psychologists have previously examined how activists in roads protests were 'empowered' by their participation in protest (Drury and Reicher 2005). They may now examine the psychological effects on individuals and activist communities of the knowledge that those they considered fellow activists, and who became friends, lovers, and in some cases, fathered children with activists, were in fact undercover police.

If in the United States social movement research is definable as a sub-discipline of sociology centred on the contentious politics school, plus those who argue for more attention to activist culture and emotion, in Britain there is no analogous school of social movement research. Instead the phenomena of social movements are approached by a variety of social scientific methods across several disciplines. This, however, inhibits the institutionalization of social movement studies in Britain because the Higher Education Funding Council's (HEFCE) evaluation of departmental research 'outputs', conducted every five to seven years (now known as the Research Excellence Framework), is organized by disciplines, which increases institutional pressures to publish in high-ranking discipline-specific journals, and to address central disciplinary debates,[2] and acts as a disincentive to inter-disciplinary work. Research students, however, may be relatively insulated from such pressures. Not only is a great deal of the empirical research on social movements in Britain undertaken by research students but their collaboration across disciplines has also begun to bear fruit. The student-organised 2012 interdisciplinary conference, Theory, Action and Impact of Social Protest (TAISP), brought together at Kent over 160 delegates from a range of social science disciplines and spawned a new journal, *Contention: The Multidisciplinary Journal of Social Protest*. The second TAISP conference, in 2014, although it remained committed to interdisciplinary research, attracted official sponsorship from the British Psychological Society. It is conceivable that social movement research in Britain might, in future, be centred in social psychology rather than sociology or political science.

Most instances of contention that have given rise to significant mobilizations have been the subject of investigation. However, by comparison with the US, the study of social movements in Britain has been relatively uninstitutionalised and theoretically diverse; it has neither received formal recognition from learned societies, nor has it developed a dominant theoretical or methodological canon. Moreover, it has not enjoyed secure funding; it is noteworthy that much of the recent work on the environmental and global justice movements was EU-funded. Nevertheless, although the study of social movements has never been a central theme for any of the major professional associations nor a priority area for national research funding, the funding agencies have sometimes supported social movement research, the major British sociology journals and academic publishers have never been closed to social movement studies, and a considerable number of articles on social movements and social movement theory have made their way into print. Thus, although there is no distinctive British 'school' of social movement research, there is, as we hope we have demonstrated, a rich and varied tradition of social movement research. There is no reason to suppose that it will not continue.

Brian Doherty is professor of political sociology in the School of Politics, Philosophy, International Relations and Environment at Keele University (UK). His publications include books on *Environmentalism, Resistance and Solidarity* (2013, with Timothy Doyle) and *Ideas and Actions in the Green Movement* (2002); co-edited books on *Democracy and Green Political Thought* (1996), *Direct Action in British Environmentalism* (2000) and *Beyond Borders* (2008); and journal articles on these topics in *Comparative Political Studies,* the *European Journal of Political Research, Environmental Politics, Mobilization, Parliamentary Affairs* and *Political Studies.*

Graeme Hayes is reader in political sociology at Aston University (UK). He is author of *Environmental Protest and the State in France* (2002), co-author of *La Désobéissance civile* (2011, with Sylvie Ollitrault), co-editor of three books, *Occupy! A Global Movement: Hope, Tactics and Challenges* (2015);

Olympic Games, Mega-Events, and Civil Societies: Globalisation, Environment, and Resistance (2012); *Cinéma et engagement* (2005), and has published in journals including *Comparative Political Studies, Environmental Politics, European Journal of Political Research, Law and Policy,* and *Sociology.* He is an editor of *Social Movement Studies.*

Christopher Rootes is professor of environmental politics and political sociology, and director of the Centre for the Study of Social and Political Movements, at the University of Kent (UK). He has published extensively on environmental movements, Green parties and protest, and has edited six books: *A New Europe?* (1994); *The Green Challenge: The Development of Green Parties in Europe* (1995), *Environmental Movements: Local, National and Global* (1999), *Environmental Protest in Western Europe* (2003), *Acting Locally: Local Environmental Mobilizations and Campaigns* (2008) and *Environmental Movements and Waste Infrastructure* (2010). He is editor in chief of the journal *Environmental Politics.*

Notes

1. Scholar-activists of British origin such as John Holloway (2002) and Pete Waterman (2001) have also made influential contributions to debates about social movement strategy, but as this work has mostly been done away from Britain—in Mexico (Holloway) and the Netherlands (Waterman)—we have not claimed them as examples British social movement scholarship.
2. It had been hoped that new guidelines evaluating research 'impact' would facilitate engaged research with movements. However, this seems unlikely insofar as the terms in which 'impact' is constructed privilege measurable, auditable outcomes on the subjects of research—a near impossible task for researchers working on and with social movements.

References

Abrams, L. 2010. *Oral History Theory.* London: Routledge.

Amoore, L. 2005. *The Global Resistance Reader.* London: Routledge.

Andrews, K. T., and M. Biggs. 2006. 'The Dynamics of Protest Diffusion: Movement Organizations, Social Networks, and News Media in the 1960 Sit-Ins'. *American Sociological Review* 71, no. 5: 752–77.

Autonomous Geographies Collective. 2010. 'Beyond Scholar Activism: Making Strategic Interventions Inside and Outside the Neoliberal University'. *ACME* 9, no. 2: 245–75.

Baggott, R., J. Allsop and K. Jones. 2004. *Speaking for Patients and Carers: Health Consumer Groups and the Policy Process.* Basingstoke: Palgrave.

Bagguley, P. 1991. *From Protest to Acquiescence? Political Movements of the Unemployed.* London: Palgrave Macmillan.

———. 1995. 'Protest, Poverty and Power: A Case Study of the Anti–Poll Tax Movement'. *Sociological Review* 43, no. 4: 693–719.

———. 1997. 'Beyond Political Sociology? Developments in the Sociology of Social Movements'. *Sociological Review* 45, no. 1: 147–61.

Banks, J. A. 1972. *The Sociology of Social Movements.* London: Macmillan.

Barker, C. 1986. *Festival of the Oppressed: Solidarity, Reform and Revolution, Poland 1980–81.* London: Bookmarks.

———. 2013. 'Class Struggle and Social Movements'. In *Marxism and Social Movements,* ed. C. Barker, L. Cox, J. Krinsky and A. G. Nilsen, 41–62. Leiden: Brill.

Barker, C. Johnson, A. and M. Lavalette, eds. 2001. *Leadership and Social Movements.* Manchester: Manchester University Press.

Biggs, M. 2013. 'How Repertoires Evolve: The Diffusion of Suicide Protest in the Twentieth Century'. *Mobilization* 18, no. 4: 407–28.

Biggs, M., and R. Dhattiwala. 2012. 'The Political Logic of Ethnic Violence: The Anti-Muslim Pogrom in Gujarat, 2002'. *Politics and Society* 40, no. 4: 481–514.

Biggs, M., and S. Knauss. 2012. 'Explaining Membership in the British National Party: A Multilevel Analysis of Contact and Threat'. *European Sociological Review* 28, no. 5: 633–46.

Blühdorn, I. 2007. 'Self-Description, Self-Deception, Simulation: A Systems-Theoretical Perspective on Contemporary Discourses of Radical Change'. *Social Movement Studies* 6, no. 1: 1–19.

Bouchier, D. 1983. *The Feminist Challenge: The Movement for Women's Liberation in Britain and the USA.* Basingstoke: Palgrave.

British Library. Nd. 'Sisterhood and After: An Oral History of the Women's Liberation Movement'. Retrieved 4 November 2013 from www.bl.uk/learning/histcitizen/sisterhood.

Brown, G., and H. Yaffe. 2013. 'Non-Stop against Apartheid: Practicing Solidarity outside the South African Embassy'. *Social Movement Studies* 12, no. 2: 227–34.

Byrne, P. 1988. *The Campaign for Nuclear Disarmament.* London: Croom Helm.

———. 1997. *Social Movements in Britain.* London: Routledge.

Calhoun, C. 1982. *The Question of Class Struggle: Social Foundations of Popular Radicalism during the Industrial Revolution.* Oxford: Blackwell.

Carter, A. 1992. *Peace Movements.* London: Longman.

Carter, E. 2005. *The Extreme Right in Western Europe.* Manchester: Manchester University Press.

Cerny, P., ed. 1982. *Social Movements and Protest in France.* London: Frances Pinter.

Chase, M. 2007. *Chartism: A New History.* Manchester: Manchester University Press.

Chatterton, P. 2010. 'So What Does It Mean to Be Anti-capitalist? Conversations with Activists from Urban Social Centres'. *Urban Studies* 47, no. 6: 1205–24.

Chesters, G. 2012. 'Social Movements and the Ethics of Knowledge Production'. *Social Movement Studies* 11, no. 2: 145–60.

Chesters, G., and I. Welsh. 2004. 'Rebel Colours: Framing in Global Social Movements'. *Sociological Review* 52, no. 3: 314–35.

———. 2006. *Complexity and Social Movements: Multitudes at the Edge of Chaos*. London: Routledge.

———. 2011. *Social Movements: The Key Concepts*. London: Routledge.

Cotgrove, S. 1982. *Catastrophe or Cornucopia: The Environment, Politics, and the Future*. Chichester: Wiley.

Cox, L., and C. Flesher Fominaya. 2013. 'European Social Movements and Social Theory: A Richer Narrative?'. In *Understanding European Movements: New Social Movements, Global Justice Struggles, Anti-austerity Protests*, ed. L. Cox and C. Flesher Fominaya, 7–29. London: Routledge.

Crossley, N. 2002. *Making Sense of Social Movements*. Buckingham: Open University Press.

———. 2006. *Contesting Psychiatry: Social Movements in Mental Health*. London: Routledge.

Crossley, N., G. Edwards, E. Harries and R. Stevenson. 2012. 'Covert Social Movement Networks and the Secrecy-Efficiency Trade Off: The Case of the UK Suffragettes (1906–1914)'. *Social Networks* 34, no. 4: 634–44.

Crossley, N. and R. Stevenson. 2014. 'Change in Covert Social Movement Networks: The "Inner Circle" of the Provisional Irish Republican Army'. *Social Movement Studies* 13, no. 1: 70–91.

Death, C. 2010. 'Counter-Conducts: A Foucauldian Analytics of Protest'. *Social Movement Studies* 9, no. 3: 235–51.

Diani, M., I. Lindsay and D. Purdue. 2010. 'Sustained Interactions: Social Movements and Coalitions in Local Settings'. In *Strategic Alliances: Coalition Building and Social Movements*, ed. N. Van Dyke and H. J. McCammon, 219–38. Minneapolis: University of Minnesota Press.

Doherty, B. 1999a. 'Manufactured Vulnerability: Eco-Activist Tactics in Britain'. *Mobilization* 4, no. 1: 75–89.

———. 1999b. 'Paving the Way: The Rise of Direct Action against Road-Building and the Changing Character of British Environmentalism'. *Political Studies* 47, no. 2: 275–91.

———. 2002a. *Ideas and Actions in the Green Movement*. London: Routledge.

———. 2002b. 'The Revolution in High Lane: Direct Action Community Politics in Manchester in the 1970s'. *North-West Labour History Journal* 27: 60–64.

Doherty, B., and T. Doyle. 2013. *Environmentalism, Resistance and Solidarity: The Politics of Friends of the Earth International*. Basingstoke: Palgrave.

Doherty, B., and T. Doyle, eds. 2008. *Beyond Borders: Environmental Movements and Transnational Politics*. London: Routledge.

Doherty, B., and G. Hayes. 2012a. 'Tactics, Traditions and Opportunities: British and French Crop-Trashing Actions in Comparative Perspective'. *European Journal of Political Research* 51, no. 4: 540–62.

———. 2012b. 'Having Your Day in Court: Judicial Opportunity and Tactical Choice in Anti-GMO Campaigns in France and the United Kingdom'. *Comparative Political Studies* DOI 10.1177/0010414012439184.

Doherty, B., M. Paterson, A. Plows and D. Wall. 2003. 'Explaining the Fuel Protests'. *British Journal of Politics and International Relations* 5, no. 1: 1–23.

Doherty, B., A. Plows and D. Wall. 2003. '"The Preferred Way of Doing Things": The British Direct Action Movement'. *Parliamentary Affairs* 56, no. 4: 669–86.

Doyle, T. J., and S. MacGregor, eds. 2014. *Environmental Movements around the World: Shades of Green in Politics and Culture.* 2 vols. Santa Barbara, Denver and Oxford: ABC Clio / Praeger.

Drury, J., and S. Reicher. 2000. 'Collective Action and Psychological Change: The Emergence of New Social Identities'. *British Journal of Social Psychology* 39: 579–604.

———. 2005. 'Explaining Enduring Empowerment: A Comparative Study of Collective Action and Psychological Outcomes'. *European Journal of Social Psychology* 35: 35–38.

Drury, J., S. Reicher and C. Stott. 2003. 'Transforming the Boundaries of Collective Identity: From the "Local" Anti-road Campaign to "Global' Resistance?" *Social Movement Studies* 2: 191–212.

Edwards, G. 2014. 'Infectious Innovations? The Diffusion of Tactical Innovation in Social Movement Networks: The Case of Suffragette Militancy'. *Social Movement Studies* 13, no. 1: 48–69.

Edwards, G. 2014. *Social Movements and Protest.* Cambridge: Cambridge University Press.

Eschle, C., and B. Maiguashca. 2010. *Making Feminist Sense of the Global Justice Movement.* Oxford: Rowman and Littlefield.

Eyerman, R., and A. Jamison. 1991. *Social Movements: A Cognitive Approach.* Cambridge: Polity.

Featherstone, D. 2008. *Resistance, Space and Political Identities: The Making of Counterglobal Networks.* Oxford: Wiley-Blackwell.

Flesher Fominaya, C. 2010. 'Creating Cohesion from Diversity: The Challenge of Collective Identity Formation in the Global Justice Movement'. *Sociological Inquiry* 80, no. 3: 377–404.

Foweraker, J. 1995. *Theorizing Social Movements.* London: Pluto.

Gillan, K. 2008. 'Understanding Meaning in Movements: A Hermeneutic Approach to Frames and Ideologies'. *Social Movement Studies* 7, no. 3: 247–63.

Gillan, K., and J. Pickerill, eds. 2011. 'The Ethics of Research on Activism'. *Social Movement Studies* 11, no. 2 (special issue).

Gillan, K., J. Pickerill and F. Webster. 2008. *Anti-war Activism: New Media and Protest in the Information Age.* Basingstoke: Palgrave.

Gilroy, P. 1987. *There Ain't No Black in the Union Jack.* London: Unwin Hyman.

Goodwin, M. J. 2011. *New British Fascism: The Rise of the British National Party (BNP).* London: Routledge.

Hay, D., et al. 1975. *Albion's Fatal Tree: Crime and Society in Eighteenth-Century England.* Harmondsworth: Penguin.

Hayes, G. 2002. *Environmental Protest and the State in France.* Basingstoke: Palgrave.

———. 2013. 'Negotiating Proximity: Expert Testimony and Collective Memory in the Trials of Environmental Activists in France and the UK'. *Law and Policy* 35, no. 3: 208–35.

Holloway, J. 2002. *Change the World without Taking Power: The Meaning of Revolution Today.* London: Pluto.

Husbands, C. T. 1983. *Racial Exclusionism and the City: The Urban Bases of the National Front.* London: Routledge.

Husu, H. 2013. 'Bourdieu and Social Movements: Considering Identity Movements in Terms of Field, Capital and Habitus'. *Social Movement Studies* 12, no. 3: 264–79.

Ibrahim, J. 2013. 'The Struggle for Symbolic Dominance in the British Anti-capitalist Movement Field'. *Social Movement Studies* 12, no. 1: 63–80.

Jordan, G. 1998. 'Introduction. Politics without Parties: A Growing Trend?' *Parliamentary Affairs* 51, no. 3: 314–28.

Jordan, G., and W. A. Maloney. 1997. *The Protest Business? Mobilizing Campaign Groups.* Manchester: Manchester University Press.

———. 2007. *Democracy and Interest Groups: Enhancing Participation?* Basingstoke: Palgrave.

Jordan, T. 2004. *Activism! Direct Action, Hacktivism and the Future of Society.* Edinburgh: Reaktion.

Kenny, M. 1995. *The First New Left: British Intellectuals after Stalin.* London: Lawrence and Wishart.

Laclau, E., and C. Mouffe. 2001. *Hegemony and Socialist Strategy: Towards a Radical Democratic Politics.* London: Verso.

Lang-Pickvance, K. 1998. *Environmental Movements in Eastern Europe: A Comparative Study of Hungary and Russia.* Boulder: Westview.

Lang-Pickvance, K., N. Manning and C. Pickvance, eds. 1997. *Environmental and Housing Movements: Grassroots Experience in Hungary, Russia and Estonia.* London: Avebury.

Lent, A. 2001. *British Social Movements since 1945: Sex, Colour, Peace and Power.* Basingstoke: Palgrave.

Lovenduski, J., and V. Randall. 1993. *Contemporary Feminist Politics: Women and Power in Britain.* Oxford: Oxford University Press.

McKay, G. 1996. *Senseless Acts of Beauty: Cultures of Resistance since the Sixties.* London: Verso.

———. 1988. *DIY Culture: Party and Protest in Nineties Britain.* London: Verso.

Mann, M. 1973. *Consciousness and Action among the Western Working Class.* London: Macmillan.

Marsh, D., ed. 1983. *Pressure Politics: Interest Groups in Britain.* London: Junction Books.

Marshall, Y., S. Roseneil and K. Armstrong. 2009. 'Situating the Greenham Archaeology: An Autoethnography of a Feminist Project'. *Public Archaeology* 8, nos. 2–3: 225–45.

Mattausch, J. 1989. *A Commitment to Campaign: A Sociological Study of CND.* Manchester: Manchester University Press.

Nash, K. 2012. 'Human Rights, Movements and Law: On not Researching Legitimacy'. *Sociology* 46, no. 5: 797–812.

Navickas, K. 2011. 'What Happened to Class? New Histories of Labour and Collective Action in Britain'. *Social History* 36, no. 2: 192–204.

Parkin, F. 1968. *Middle-Class Radicalism: The Social Bases of the British Campaign for Nuclear Disarmament.* Manchester: Manchester University Press.

Perrigo, S. 1996. 'Women and Change in the Labour Party 1979–1995'. *Parliamentary Affairs* 49, no. 1: 116–29.

Pickerill, J. 2003. *Cyberprotest: Environmental Activism Online.* Manchester: Manchester University Press.

———. 2008. 'The Surprising Sense of Hope'. *Antipode* 40, no. 3: 482–87.

Plows, A., D. Wall and B. Doherty. 2004. 'Covert Repertoires: Ecotage in the UK'. *Social Movement Studies* 3, no. 2: 199–219.

Poulson, S., C. Caswell and T. Grey. 2014. 'Isomorphism, Institutional Parochialism, and the Study of Social Movements'. *Social Movement Studies* 13, no. 2: 222–42.

Reicher, S. D. 1984. 'The St. Pauls Riot: An Explanation of the Limits of Crowd Action in Terms of a Social Identity Model'. *European Journal of Social Psychology* 14: 1–21.

Richardson, J. 2000. 'Government, Interest Groups and Policy Change'. *Political Studies* 48, no. 5: 1006–25.

Rootes, C. 1992. 'The New Politics and the New Social Movements: Accounting for British Exceptionalism'. *European Journal of Political Research* 22, no. 2: 171–91.

———. 1995. 'A New Class? The Higher Educated and the New Politics'. In *Social Movements and Social Classes: The Future of Collective Action,* ed. L. Maheu, 220–35. London: Sage.

———. 1997. 'Shaping Collective Action: Structure, Contingency and Knowledge'. In *The Political Context of Collective Action,* ed. R. Edmondson, 81–104. London: Routledge.

———. 2003. 'The Transformation of Environmental Activism: An Introduction'. In *Environmental Protest in Western Europe,* ed. C. Rootes, 1–19. Oxford University Press.

———. 2004. 'Environmental Movements'. In *The Blackwell Companion to Social Movements,* ed. D. A. Snow, S. A. Soule and H. Kriesi, 608–40. Oxford: Blackwell.

———. 2009. 'Environmental NGOs and the Environmental Movement in England'. In *NGOs in Contemporary Britain: Non-state Actors in Society and Politics since 1945,* ed. N. Crowson, M. Hilton and J. McKay, 201–21. Basingstoke: Palgrave.

———. 2013. 'From Local Conflict to National Issue: When and How Environmental Campaigns Succeed in Transcending the Local'. *Environmental Politics* 22, no. 1: 95–114.

Rootes, C., ed. 1999. *Environmental Movements: Local, National and Global.* London: Frank Cass.

———. 2008. *Acting Locally: Local Environmental Mobilizations and Campaigns.* London: Routledge.

Rootes, C., and L. Leonard, eds. 2010. *Environmental Movements and Waste Infrastructure.* London: Routledge.

Rootes, C., and C. Saunders. 2007. 'The Global Justice Movement in Britain'. In *The Global Justice Movement: Cross-National and Transnational Perspectives,* ed. D. Della Porta, 128–56. Boulder: Paradigm.

Roseneil, S. 1995. *Disarming Patriarchy: Feminism and Political Action at Greenham.* Buckingham: Open University Press.

———. 2000. *Common Women: The Queer Feminisms of Greenham.* London: Cassell.

Routledge, P. 1996. 'The Third Space as Critical Engagement'. *Antipode* 28, no. 4: 399–419.

Routledge, P., and A. Cumbers. 2009. *Global Justice Networks: Geographies of Transnational Solidarity.* Manchester: Manchester University Press.

Rowbotham, S., Segal, L. and H. Wainwright. 1979. *Beyond the Fragments: Feminism and the Making of Socialism.* Nottingham: Merlin.

Rüdig, W. 1990. *Anti-nuclear Movements: A World Survey of Opposition to Nuclear Energy.* London: Longman.

Rüdig, W. and G. Karyotis. 2013. 'Beyond the Usual Suspects? New Participants in Anti-austerity Protests in Greece'. *Moblization* 18, no. 3: 313–30.

Samuel, C. 2013. 'Symbolic Violence and Collective Identity: Pierre Bourdieu and the Ethics of Resistance'. *Social Movement Studies* 12, no. 4: 397–413.

Saunders, C. 2007. 'Using Social Network Analysis to Explore Social Movements: A Relational Approach'. *Social Movement Studies* 6, no. 3: 227–43.

———. 2008a. 'The Stop Climate Chaos Coalition: Climate Change as a Development Issue'. *Third World Quarterly* 29, no. 8: 1509–26.

———. 2008b. 'Double-Edged Swords? Collective Identity and Solidarity in the Environment Movement'. *British Journal of Sociology* 59, no. 2: 227–53.

———. 2013. *Environmental Networks and Social Movement Theory.* London: Bloomsbury.

Saunders, C., et al. 2012. 'Explaining Differential Protest Participation: Novices, Returners, Repeaters and Stalwarts'. *Mobilization* 17, no. 2: 263–80.

Saunders, C. and C. Rootes. 2013. 'Patterns of Participation'. In *Meeting Democracy: Power and Deliberation in Global Justice Movements,* ed. D. Della Porta and D. Rucht, 72–96. Cambridge: Cambridge University Press.

Schlembach, R., B. Lear and A. Bowman. 2012. 'Science and Ethics in the Post-Political Era: Strategies within the Camp for Climate Action'. *Environmental Politics* 21, no. 5: 811–28.

Scott, A. 1990. *Ideology and the New Social Movements.* London: Unwin Hyman.

Seel, B., M. Paterson and B. Doherty, eds. 2000. *Direct Action in British Environmentalism.* London: Routledge.

Steinberg, M. W. 1995. 'The Roar of the Crowd: Repertoires of Discourse and Collective Action among the Spitalfields Silk Weavers in Nineteenth-Century London'. In *Repertoires and Cycles of Collective Action,* ed. M. Traugott, 57–87. Durham: Duke University Press.

Tarrow, S. 1998. *Power in Movement: Social Movements and Contentious Politics.* Cambridge: Cambridge University Press.

Taylor, R. 1988. *Against the Bomb.* Oxford: Oxford University Press.

Taylor, R., and C. Pritchard. 1980. *The Protest Makers: The British Nuclear Disarmament of 1958–1965, Twenty Years On.* Oxford: Pergamon.

Thompson, E. P. 1963/1991. *The Making of the English Working Class.* London: Victor Gollancz.

———. 1975. *Whigs and Hunters.* London: Penguin.

Thompson, P. R. 1978. *The Voice of the Past: Oral History.* Oxford: Oxford University Press.

Tilly, C. 1982. 'Britain Creates the Social Movement'. In *Social Conflict and Political Order in Modern Britain,* ed. J. Cronin and J. Schneer, 21–51. Brunswick: Rutgers University Press.

———. 1995. *Popular Contention in Great Britain, 1758–1834.* Harvard: Harvard University Press.

———. 2004. *Social Movements, 1768–2004.* Boulder: Paradigm.

Tilly, C., and S. Tarrow. 2007. *Contentious Politics.* Boulder: Paradigm.

Toke, D., and D. Marsh. 2003. 'Policy Networks and the GM Crops Issue'. *Public Administration* 81, no. 2: 229–51.

Waddington, D., F. Jobard and M. King, eds. 2009. *Rioting in the UK and France: A Comparative Analysis.* Cullompton: Willan.

Waddington, P. A. J. 1998. 'Controlling Protest in Contemporary, Historical and Comparative Perspective'. In *Policing Protest: The Control of Mass Demonstrations in Western Democracies,* ed. D. Della Porta and H. R. Reiter, 117–40. Minneapolis: University of Minnesota Press.

Wahlström, M., M. Wennerhag and C. Rootes. 2013. 'Framing "The Climate Issue": Patterns of Participation and Prognostic Frames among Climate Summit Protesters'. *Global Environmental Politics* 13, no. 4: 101–22.

Wall, D. 1999. *Earth First! and the Anti-roads Movement: Radical Environmentalism and Comparative Social Movements.* London: Routledge.

Waterman, P. 2001. *Globalization, Social Movements, and the New Internationalism.* London: Continuum.

Welsh, I. 2000. *Mobilising Modernity: The Nuclear Moment.* London: Routledge.

Wilkinson, P. 1971. *Social Movement.* London: Macmillan.

Chapter 12

Precarious Research in a Movement Society
Social Movement Studies in Germany

Sebastian Haunss

Research on social movements in Germany started late and has never really managed to establish a stable foothold within the German university system. Even today there are only two chairs with a formal denomination on social movements—both in the field of contemporary history, a discipline that has only recently started to connect its historical research to the larger body of social movement studies.[1] A lively social movement sector with frequent and large-scale protests on many issues has not changed the marginal position of social movement research in political science and sociology in Germany. However, despite its weak institutionalization, there is an active research community of mostly junior scholars which has produced a large corpus of theoretical and empirical research.

Earlier review articles (Rucht 1991a, 2011; Koopmans 1995; Hellmann 1999; Klein 2003, 2008; Rucht and Roth 2008a; Teune 2008) and edited volumes (Hellmann 1999; Klein, Legrand and Leif 1999) have mapped the terrain of social movement research in Germany and beyond. They largely agree on three aspects. First, from a tardy awakening, social movement researchers have since produced a broad body of research, although with strong focus on *new* social movements. Second, the field is dominated by merely a handful of researchers. And third, the initial focus on grand theories with weak empirical foundations has often been replaced by detailed empirical studies with weak theoretical underpinnings.

In this chapter I will not reiterate the findings of these review articles which provide very competent overviews of the field of social movement research in Germany. Instead I will highlight specific developments and works which are particularly important from this book's comparative perspective. The first part of this article briefly describes the institutional environment of social movement research in Germany, followed by a short section on early theoretical debates. The main part of the article discusses core contributions to the field, paying attention to important academic publications as well as publications by movement activists. Finally, I discuss some desiderata for future research on social movements in Germany.

Long Tradition and Limited Infrastructure

It is no coincidence that Vincenzo Ruggiero's and Nicola Montagna's social movement reader (Ruggiero and Montagna 2008) opens with excerpts from four classical German thinkers: Karl Marx and Friedrich Engels (1888), Georg Simmel (1950 [1908]) and Max Weber (1958 [1922]). From very different perspectives, the works of these authors addressed the structures and dynamics of social conflicts and highlighted the role of collective action of ordinary people in processes of social change. But this early focus on social movements (even though the now classical authors did not use this term) was lost in the post–World War II reconstitution of social sciences in Germany after twelve years of National Socialist rule.

Hubertus Buchstein (1992) has attributed the lack of research on social movements in the early years of the Federal Republic of Germany to two complementary trends: first, the dominance of an anti-pluralist perspective with a strong focus on the state and its institutions, and second, the self-identification with hierarchical forms of organization by protagonists of a pluralist perspective, who often had their political roots in the labour movement. Consequently, the concept of social movements was absent even in progressive introductory texts on political science (Kress and Senghaas 1972), and is still missing in most current introductions.[2]

In the 1970s, during the expansion of the university system, the political climate was marked by overt suspicion against leftist ideas. An administrative order (*Radikalenerlass*) prescribed a routine screening of all applicants in the public sector for suspected 'radical' opinions, and thus made sympathy or even a flagrantly strong interest in the leftist protests of the time a career risk (Zoll 2010). Under these conditions researchers who succeeded in getting a position at the universities often distanced themselves from their former political engagement in the social movements of the 1960s and generally refrained from choosing social movements as a topic of their research (Rucht 1991a: 176).

The numerous, large and sustained mobilizations of the peace, anti-nuclear and other movements of the 1980s and 1990s have not led to a re-examination of social movement research in social science departments in Germany. The increased attention that social movements received in the public sphere during 1988–89 did, however, create the opportunity for the establishment of a research unit on 'Public Sphere and Social Movements' at the Social Science Research Center Berlin (WZB), which became the focal point of social movement research in Germany until its dissolution in 2011.[3] Its long-time senior research fellow and co-director, Dieter Rucht, is certainly the most influential social movement scholar in Germany, as he has contributed like no other to the continuity and internationalization of social movement research in Germany.

Other institutional structures have been more short-lived. Notable examples of collaborative research on social movements in the recent past are Sigrid Baringhorst's research group on 'protest and media cultures in transition' (2005–10) (Baringhorst et al. 2010); Martin Klimke, Joachim Scharloth and Kathrin Fahlenbrach's EU-funded Marie Curie training network on European protest movements since the Cold War (2006–2010) (Fahlenbrach, Klimke, and Scharloth 2016); or a research network on 'new perspectives on social movements and protest', funded by the German Research Foundation (DFG) from 2012 to 2014 (Roose and Ullrich 2012).

Lacking sustained institutional support, social movement scholars in Germany have been more successful in establishing informal and communicative infrastructures. In an early overview of the state of social movement research in Germany, Dieter Rucht describes how a circle of thirty to forty social scientists interested in social movement research established a study group on (new) social movements in 1983 (Rucht 1991a: 189). The group was first loosely and later more formally affiliated with the German political science association (DVPW). In 1988 the group's newsletter developed into a quarterly journal, the *Forschungsjournal Neue Soziale Bewegungen* (FJNSB— *New Social Movements Research Journal*)[4] which publishes original research articles, policy papers, discursive political interventions and journalistic reports about movement- and research-related events (Rucht 1991a: 189; Klein 2008). Unlike the title suggests, the journal quickly broadened its focus to include a wide range of contributions on issues of civil society, civic engagement, associations, political parties and theory of democracy.

A closer look at the articles published in the research journal over the last twenty-five years reveals a picture that is strongly consistent with the low level of institutionalization of social movement research in Germany. Figure 12.1 plots the number of articles that individual authors have published in the research journal. It shows a very skewed distribution, typical of a large research community of mostly junior scholars who only sporadically publish on social movements.

Of the 1,018 authors who contributed to the journal with original articles or reports, 78 per cent (795 authors) have published only a single article

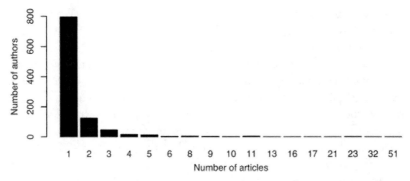

Figure 12.1. Number of articles per author in the *Forschungsjournal Soziale Bewegungen,* 1988–2013

in the journal; 994 authors (97.6 per cent) have written five or less articles in twenty-five years. Of the remaining twenty-four authors, nine have been part of the editorial team, leaving only a small group of fifteen authors with a continuous record of research on social movements and/or civil society who have published in the FJNSB. Not very surprisingly this short list of long-term social movement researchers is led by Dieter Rucht and Roland Roth, the editors of the two comprehensive volumes on social movements in Germany (Roth and Rucht 1991, 2008).

Grand Theories, Internationalization and Terminological Debates

In line with the fragmented nature of the research field, social movement research in Germany has not produced strong schools or paradigms. The low level of institutionalization leads to a pattern of publication where many authors publish only sporadically or merely for a short period as junior scholars on social movements and then move on to other issues.

When social scientists started to address the protests of the 1970s and early 1980s in Germany their research was influenced by widespread perception of fundamental social change. In a weaker version, social movements—or, to use the more common term at that time, citizens' initiatives (*Bürgerinitiativen*)—were interpreted in the context of a perceived crisis of parliamentary democracy as challengers of formal democratic majoritarian rule (Mayer-Tasch 1976; Guggenberger and Kempf 1978) or as countermovement to an authoritarian (*obrigkeitsstaatlichen*) mode of decision-making (Roth 1980). In a more far-reaching macro-sociological perspective, the 'new' social movements were interpreted as expressions of a crisis of modernity (Brand 1982; Brand, Büsser, and Rucht 1983: 13), drawing a sharp line between the 'old' (i.e. labour movement) and 'new' social movements. Authors who followed this second perspective conceded that the mobilizations of the 1980s had many organizational and ideological links to earlier protests in the 1950s and 1960s but insisted on the newness of current social movements in terms of constituency (working class versus middle class), orientation (modernist and materialist versus post-materialist and post-modernist), and organization (hierarchical versus decentralised) (Brand, Büsser and Rucht 1983: 242 ff.).

These early German social movement studies largely ignore the existing literature on social movements from other countries or merely refer to it very superficially. The translation and publication of major contributions of the US collective behaviour literature (Heinz and Schöber 1973) and Alain Touraine's influential book on the post-industrial society (Touraine 1972) in the early 1970s initially showed no influence on social movement research in Germany.

But this limited national perspective was quickly abandoned. The junior researchers who were driving the development of the research field in Germany at that time rapidly broadened their perspective, and social movement studies increasingly began to cite American, British and a few French and Italian authors. A number of publications explicitly introduced an international perspective—among them Dieter Rucht's discussion of the resource mobilization approach (Rucht 1984), and Karl-Werner Brand's edited volume with case studies on selected social movements in Germany, France, Great Britain, Sweden and the United States, as well as a brief comparative conclusion (Brand 1985). Furthermore, German researchers increasingly began to venture into the arena of the international scientific discourse (mainly derived from the United States) on social movements (Eder 1985; Kitschelt 1985; Offe 1985).

During the 1990s the field becomes thoroughly internationalised in terms of participation in international scientific networks and reception of the international literature, although still some idiosyncrasies persist. The often implicit normative assumption in much of the German literature that social movements would be inherently progressive actors becomes an issue of open debate in the context of the growing racist and radical right-wing mobilizations of the early 1990s (Leggewie 1994; Hellmann 1996a; Koopmans and Rucht 1996). As Koopmans has pointed out (Koopmans 1995: 95), this goes along with a usually too-narrow perspective of only the most recent 'new' social movements, as well as an insistence on categorical differences between the old and new movements.

Almost twenty years later these issues have only partially lost their relevance. The bulk of research still focuses on the 'good' and 'progressive' social movements of the left. Only occasionally have the tools of social movement research been applied to analyse radical right-wing (Virchow 2013) or religious fundamentalist (Reetz 2004) mobilizations. The predominant focus on *new* social movements has been attenuated by a new generation of historians who are increasingly starting to combine historical and social movement perspectives (Gilcher-Holtey 2001; Klimke and Scharloth 2008; Balz and Friedrichs 2012).

Important Contributions

An impressive body of research on social movements has accumulated since the late 1970s, but only a small number of publications have had a lasting impact on further research. According to Google Scholar, the most often cited German-language work on social movements is Joachim Raschke's encompassing historical study, in which he develops a taxonomy of historical specific forms of social movements, discusses the development of social movements in relation to large-scale social change, and analyses current social movements as *new* social movements of the post-industrial society based on a middle-class constituency, and with a focus on changes in the sociocultural sector (Raschke 1985: 411 ff.). Since Raschke's research has never been translated and because he never followed up on his initial work on social movements, his impact on social movement research outside the German-speaking scientific community remains negligible.

Among the conceptual contributions, Claus Offe's article on new social movements as challengers of the boundaries of institutional politics (Offe 1985), in which he claims that the *new* social movements politicise the institutions and standards of rationality and progress of advanced industrial societies, and thus challenge the boundaries between the private and the political, is the internationally most cited work of a German researcher on social movements. Raschke and Offe's contributions are usually cited in a summary fashion, but there is little research that explicitly builds on their works or engages with them in a more than superficial way.

A remarkable conceptual contribution from the same period is Friedhelm Neidhardt's short article, 'Some Ideas towards a General Theory of Social Movements' (Neidhardt 1985), in which he argues, against the mainstream American social movement literature of the time, that social movements should neither be understood as aggregations of individuals nor as a specific form of organization, but as 'mobilised networks of networks' (Neidhardt 1985: 197). Today this idea has gained currency with many scholars, although it is not associated with Neidhardt but rather with Mario Diani, who several years later introduced—independently and without knowledge of Neidhardt's German article—his network-centric definition of social movements as 'network[s] of informal interactions between a plurality of individuals, groups and/or organizations, engaged in a political or cultural conflict, on the basis of a shared collective identity' (Diani 1992: 13).

The standard work on social movements in Germany is Roland Roth's and Dieter Rucht's handbook on new social movements in Germany. The first edition was published in 1987 and updated and expanded after the German re-unification (Roth and Rucht 1991). This handbook contains several contributions on social movements in general (e.g. Brand 1991; Raschke 1991), various case studies on major social movements in Germany (gay movement: Holy 1991; women's movement: Knafla and Kulke 1991; antinuclear movement: Kretschmer and Rucht 1991; peace movement: Wasmuth 1991), articles on the organizational structure of social movements (Roth 1991; Rucht 1991b) and their embeddedness in macro social structures (Geiling and Vester 1991), and on the relationship between social movements and political parties (e.g. Pappi 1991; Wiesendahl 1991). These latter articles on organizational structures and democratic innovation address one recurring question that has preoccupied more than just social movement scholars: the impact of social movements on democratic procedures, institutions and norms (Hollstein 1979: Roth 1980; 1994; Rucht, Blattert and Rink 1997). The importance of this question in the German discourse on social movements reflects the assumption that social movements are often interpreted not just as means to attain specific political goals with unconventional forms of action, but as symptoms of democratic deficits and democratic innovators in the transformation of the authoritarian German post-war society towards a more open and tolerant 'movement society' (Neidhardt and Rucht 1993).

Roth and Rucht subsequently published a completely new edition of the handbook (Roth and Rucht 2008) with a strong focus on movement-specific case studies, now covering a much broader array of movements and mobilizations, and following a similar structure with sections on the respective movement's history, motives, structures, effects and forms of action. Apart from the two editors, Karl-Werner Brand is the only author who contributed both to the 1991 and 2008 version of the handbook—another sign of the discontinuity of the research field in Germany. Notable additions in the 2008 handbook are articles on urban social movements (Mayer 2008), the third world solidarity movement (Olejniczak 2008), citizens' movements in the GDR (Rink 2008), the autonomous and anti-imperialist movements (Haunss 2008), and the global justice movement (Rucht and Roth 2008b).

The handbook's focus on single movement case studies aptly reflects the larger landscape of German social movement research publications. Many monographs provide sometimes historical, often rather descriptive accounts of one single movement or a specific aspect or period of one movement. The particular importance of these works lies in their detailed and in-depth information about individual movements or whole policy fields, such as Arno Klönne's history of the German workers movement (Klönne 1980), Ute Gerhard's history of the first wave of the German women's movement (Gerhard 1990), Ilse Lenz's book on the new women's movement (Lenz 2009), Herbert Kitschelt's study on nuclear energy policy in Germany (Kitschelt 1980), and Werner Balsen and Karl Rössel's analysis of the third-world solidarity movement (Balsen and Rössel 1986). Sometimes these case studies offer unexpected insights, like Thomas Leif's book on the German peace movement in the 1980s, where the author analyses the movement as much less direct democratic and much more centralised than its public image would have it (Leif 1985). The downside of many of these individual case studies is that they only occasionally refer to each other and to more general research on social movements, and thus produce largely dispersed and unconnected knowledge about social movements.

Few studies follow an explicitly comparative approach. The most elaborated is certainly Felix Kolb's book on the political outcomes of social movements, in which he develops in a qualitative comparative analysis a set of causal mechanisms to explain success or failure of anti-nuclear movements in eighteen OECD countries (Kolb 2007). On a much smaller scale, Christian Lahusen and Britta Baumgarten compare protest of the unemployed in France, Germany and Sweden (Lahusen and Baumgarten 2006; Lahusen 2013). Sebastian Haunss compares processes of collective identity in the German autonomous movement and the second gay movement and points to surprising similarities between these otherwise rather different mobilizations (Haunss 2004). Thomas Balistier compares forms of street protest across time and between movements, diagnosing a differentiation of protest forms and a general trend towards less violent forms of protest (Balistier 1996).

Some studies provide methodological innovations. Dieter Rucht and his collaborators' ethnographic and comparative study on the five parallel and competing First of May demonstrations in Berlin 2002 provides a fascinating analysis of protest forms and rituals (Rucht 2003). Drawing on McPhail's earlier works (McPhail and Wohlstein 1983; McPhail 1994) this study has helped to (re-)establish the research practice of systematic observation of demonstrations which has more recently been employed in various other social movement studies (Andretta et al. 2003; Della Porta et al. 2006; Rucht and Teune 2008; Klandermans 2012). Jürgen Gerhards' frame analysis (although he does not use frame terminology in the original German article) of the protest mobilizations in Berlin against the 1988 IMF and World Bank meeting in Berlin is one of the most convincing empirical applications of the concept. It provides a clear-cut operationalization and strong explanatory power for the discursive cohesion of the broad protest coalition (Gerhards 1991; Gerhards and Rucht 1992).

Among the great diversity of research projects on social movements in terms of scale, one project merits special attention: Dieter Rucht, Friedhelm Neidhardt and Simon Teune's long-term project on protest event analysis (PEA) in Germany (Prodat).[5] Working from 1993 right up to 2011, the participating researchers compiled a dataset on protests between 1950 and 2002 based on the coding of articles in German quality newspapers (Rucht 1998, 2001; for a more general discussion of PEA, see: Koopmans and Rucht 2002). Building on this comprehensive dataset, Rucht and his collaborators demonstrate that participation in protest has fluctuated heavily with a trend of growing protest participation since the 1980s, to the extent that protest has indeed become commonplace in Germany today. The data shows the student movement's mobilizations of the late 1960s as a distinct peak in protest activity, but reveals that only a comparatively small number of activists participated in these student protests and that the protests had already reached their peak in terms of participation in 1967 (Rucht and Roth 2008a: 646). The Prodat project design was adopted by Doug McAdam, John McCarthy, Susan Olzak and Sarah Soule for a similar project in the United States (Dynamics of Collective Action), and inspired Ruud Koopman and Paul Statham's Merci and Europub projects in which they developed the political claims analysis (PCA) method, addressing several shortcomings of the protest event analysis approach (Koopmans and Statham 1999).

Beyond the strictly academic research literature, there is a large field of journalistic, popular science and movement literature which has so far been ignored in reviews of German social movement research. Yet, the dividing line between scientific and popular literature on social movements in Germany is often quite blurred and more a question of perspective and style than one of scientific rigour. The main research journal, the *Forschungsjournal Soziale Bewegungen,* is a case in point. It mixes contributions from engaged activists and politicians with scientific articles and reports about movement (research) related events. In the landscape of German social science publishing (e.g. Vorgänge, Berliner Debatte Initial, Prokla, Feministische Studien, Peripherie) this is not an uncommon combination.

The literature addressing international solidarity and the global justice movement is a typical example where academic and movement publications sometimes share the same authors and differ more in style and intended readership than in analytic depth (Walk and Boehme 2002; BUKO 2003). Research on the radical leftist, autonomous movement in Germany consists on the one hand of articles written from a limited theory-of-extremism perspective with the aim of discrediting and preventing the suspected political phenomenon (Pfahl-Traughber 1998, Jaschke 2006, Baron 2011), and on the other hand of analyses from (former) movement activists (Schultze and Gross 1997; Geronimo 2002; Haunss 2004), with only a few studies from critical observers (Busch 1989; Golova 2011). The women's movement is a prime example where scientific contributions and political interventions in movement debates have often been intrinsically interwoven (Linnhoff 1974; Krechel 1978; Dackweiler 1995), not just because of the duality of roles of activist and researcher but because they are explicitly meant to be inseparable as a result of the feminist critique of the 'abstract masculinity' (Hartsock 1983) of male normal science (Braun 1995).[6]

Other movements have been largely ignored in the social sciences, although activists have often written well-researched movement histories and analyses. The literature on the second gay movement in Germany has been documented—with very few exceptions—by (former) movement activists (Salmen and Eckert 1989; Holy 1991; Pretzel and Weiß 2012), and the same is true for the lesbian feminist movement (Dennert, Leidinger and Rauchut 2007), or migrants' mobilizations (Bojadžijev 2008).

Future Directions of Social Movement Research in Germany

The future development of social movement research is highly uncertain. One reason for this is the loss of the only pillar that has guaranteed some institutional stability, the research group on 'Public Sphere and Social Movements' at the Social Science Research Center Berlin, which has dissolved. An initiative to establish an institute for protest and movement research[7] hopes to compensate for this loss to some extent, but without solid and secured financial backing the prospects are uncertain (Haunss and Ullrich 2013).

As a result of the beneficial internationalization of social movement research, it makes little sense to formulate substantial desiderata at a national level. Maybe the biggest challenge for current social movement research—not just in Germany—is to understand the relationship between current profound social transformation processes associated with the catchwords post-Fordism, neoliberal governmentality, globalization, network society or post-democracy and the formation and decline of protest and social movements. Currently systematic social-theoretical reflection only takes place at the fringes of the research field. Apart from some early works, which were influenced by French neo- and post-Marxism debates and which understood social movements explicitly as expressions of macro-social processes of change (Touraine 1988; Melucci 1989), Charles Tilly's global historical perspective (Tilly 1984, 2004), and various not particularly fruitful system-theoretical approaches (Hellmann 1996b; Luhmann 1996), recent movement research usually remains limited to middle-range theories (Rucht 2011: 34). Currently a rationalist-strategic perspective with its 'instrumentalist-structuralist lens' (Johnston 2009: 3) is dominant—a result of the formative influence of US movement research and its perception of movements as specific groups of actors among others, in the pluralistic competition between interest groups (Eyerman and Jamison 1991: 27).

What are also needed are more systematic comparative studies across movements, time and polities. Existing comparative studies (Gelb 1977; Giugni 1995; Kriesi et al. 1995; Koopmans and Statham 2000; Kolb 2007) show how promising this approach is to gain deeper insights into the mechanisms and conditions that structure the chances of success and failure of social movements in achieving their policy goals. For social movement research in Germany this poses a specific problem, because meaningful comparative research usually has to be conducted in multi-national cooperative research projects; but without stable institutional structures, long-term cooperation is hard to establish.

Beyond research, a strong desideratum for social movement research in Germany would be the establishment of structured academic teaching and training programs to secure the transfer of knowledge about social movement research in a less coincidental manner.

Sebastian Haunss, PD Dr., is head of the research group on 'social conflicts' at the Research Center on Inequality and Social Policy (SOCIUM), University of Bremen. His research focuses on network analysis, empirical legitimation research, social movements, and intellectual property rights. Recent publications include *Conflicts in the Knowledge Society: The Contentious Politics of Intellectual Property* (Cambridge University Press 2013) and *Marktwirtschaft in der Legitimationskrise? Ein internationaler Vergleich* (with Frank Nullmeier et al., Campus 2014).

Notes

1. The two full and assistant professorships are at the Institut für soziale Bewegungen (Institute for Social Movements) at Ruhr-University Bochum. Only recently has the institute broadened its so far exclusive focus on the labour movement to include protest movements of the 1960s to 1980s.
2. The notable exception is the most recent edition of Bernauer et al.'s introduction to political science, which has a brief ten-page chapter on social movements (Bernauer et al. 2013: 357 ff.).
3. The original research unit was established 1988/89 and headed by Friedhelm Neidhardt. This was followed by two research groups with slightly different foci, on 'Political Communication and Mobilization' (headed by Dieter Rucht) and 'Civil Society, Citizenship and Political Mobilization in Europe' (headed by Dieter Rucht and Dieter Gosewinkel).
4. The journal changed its name to *Forschungsjournal Soziale Bewegungen* in 2011; the journal archive is available at: http://www.fjnsb.de/.
5. Further information about Prodat and the complete downloadable dataset is available at the project website (http://goo.gl/Tp5ntc). A more qualitative attempt to create a comprehensive chronology of protests in Germany and to provide background information on as many protests as possible so far only covers the period between 1949 and 1959 and shows no visible progress since 1996 (Kraushaar 1996).
6. A core journal of feminist research in Germany aptly reflects this dual character in its title 'contributions to feminist theory and practice' (*Beiträge zur feministischen Theorie und Praxis*).
7. Information on the initiatives and ongoing research projects of the institute are available at http://protestinstitut.eu/.

References

Andretta, M. et al. 2003. *No Global—New Global: Identität und Strategien der Antiglobalisierungsbewegung.* Frankfurt and New York: Campus.

Balistier, T. 1996. *Straßenprotest: Formen oppositioneller Politik in der Bundesrepublik Deutschland zwischen 1979 und 1989.* Münster: Westfälisches Dampfboot.

Balsen, W., and K. Rössel. 1986. *Hoch die internationale Solidarität: Zur Geschichte der Dritte-Welt-Bewegung in der Bundesrepublik.* Köln: Kölner Volksblatt-Verlag.

Balz, H., and J. H. Friedrichs, eds. 2012. *'All We Ever Wanted ...': Eine Kulturgeschichte europäischer Protestbewegungen der 1980er Jahre.* Berlin: Karl Dietz Verlag.

Baringhorst, S., et al. 2010. *Unternehmenskritische Kampagnen: Politischer Protest im Zeichen digitaler Kommunikation.* Wiesbaden: VS Verlag.

Baron, U. 2011. 'Die linksautonome Szene'. In *Linksextremismus in der Bundesrepublik Deutschland,* ed. U. Dovermann, 231–45. Bonn: Bundeszentrale für Politische Bildung.

Bernauer, T., et al. 2013. *Einführung in die Politikwissenschaft.* Baden-Baden: Nomos.

Bojadžijev, M. 2008. *Die windige Internationale: Rassismus und Kämpfe der Migration.* Münster: Westfälisches Dampfboot.

Brand, K. W. 1982. *Neue soziale Bewegungen: Entstehung, Funktion und Perspektive neuer Protestpotentiale; eine Zwischenbilanz.* Opladen: Westdeutscher Verlag.

―――. 1991. 'Kontinuität und Diskontinuität in den neuen sozialen Bewegungen'. In *Neue soziale Bewegungen in der Bundesrepublik Deutschland,* ed. R. Roth and D. Rucht, 54–70. Bonn: Bundeszentrale für politische Bildung.

Brand, K. W, ed. 1985. *Neue soziale Bewegungen in Westeuropa und den USA: Ein internationaler Vergleich.* Frankfurt and New York: Campus.

Brand, K. W., D. Büsser and D. Rucht, eds. 1983. *Aufbruch in eine andere Gesellschaft: Neue soziale Bewegungen in der Bundesrepublik.* Frankfurt and New York: Campus.

Braun, K. 1995. 'Frauenforschung, Geschlechterforschung und feministische Politik'. *Feministische Studien* 13, no. 2: 107–17.

Buchstein, H. 1992. 'Soziale Bewegungen als Thema der westdeutschen Nachkriegspolitologie'. *Forschungsjournal Neue Soziale Bewegungen* 5, no. 2: 77–85.

BUKO, ed. 2003. *Radikal global : Bausteine für eine internationalistische Linke.* Berlin: Assoziation A.

Busch, H. 1989. 'Die Bürgerinitiative in der Lederjacke: Anmerkungen zu den Autonomen'. *Vorgänge 101* 28, no. 5: 62–67.

Dackweiler, R. 1995. *Ausgegrenzt und eingemeindet: Die neue Frauenbewegung im Blick der Sozialwissenschaften.* Münster: Westfälisches Dampfboot.

Della Porta, D., et al., eds. 2006. *Globalization from Below: Transnational Activists and Protest Networks.* Minneapolis: University of Minnesota Press.

Dennert, G., C. Leidinger and F. Rauchut, eds. 2007. *Bewegung bleiben. 100 Jahre Politik, Kultur und Geschichte von Lesben.* Berlin: Querverlag.

Diani, M. 1992. 'The Concept of Social Movement'. *The Sociological Review* 40, no. 1: 1–25.

Eder, K. 1985. 'The "New Social Movements": Moral Crusades, Political Pressure or Social Movements?' *Social Research* 52, no. 4: 869–90.

Eyerman, R., and A. Jamison. 1991. *Social Movements: A Cognitive Approach.* Cambridge: Polity Press.

Fahlenbrach, K., M. Klimke and J. Scharloth, eds. 2016. *Protest Cultures: A Companion.* New York: Berghahn Books.

Geiling, H., and M. Vester. 1991. 'Die Spitze eines gesellschaftlichen Eisbergs: Sozialstrukturwandel und neue soziale Mileus'. In *Neue soziale Bewegungen in der Bundesrepublik Deutschland,* ed. R. Roth and D. Rucht, 237–60. Bonn: Bundeszentrale für politische Bildung.

Gelb, J. 1977. 'Social Movement "Success": A Comparative Analysis of Feminism in the United States and the United Kingdom'. In *The Women's Movements of the United States and Western Europe,* ed. M. Mueller, F. Katzenstein and C. McClurg, 267–89. Philadelphia: Temple University Press.

Gerhard, U. 1990. *Unerhört: die Geschichte der deutschen Frauenbewegung.* Reinbek bei Hamburg: Rowohlt.

Gerhards, J. 1991. 'Die Mobilisierung gegen die IWF- und Weltbanktagung 1988 in Berlin: Gruppen, Veranstaltungen, Diskurse'. In *Neue soziale Bewegungen in der Bundesrepublik Deutschland,* ed. R. Roth and D. Rucht, 213–34. Bonn: Bundeszentrale für politische Bildung.

Gerhards, J. and D. Rucht. 1992. 'Mesomobilization: Organizing and Framing in Two Protest Campaigns in West Germany'. *American Journal of Sociology* 98, no. 3: 555–96.

Geronimo. 2002. *Feuer und Flamme: zur Geschichte der Autonomen.* 2nd ed. Berlin: ID Verlag.

Gilcher-Holtey, I. 2001 *Die 68er Bewegung: Deutschland, Westeuropa, USA.* München: Beck.

Giugni, M. 1995. 'Outcomes of New Social Movements'. In *New Social Movement in Western Europe: A Comparative Analysis,* ed. H. Kriesi et al., 207–37. London: UCL.

Golova, T. 2011. *Räume kollektiver Identität: Raumproduktion in der 'linken Szene' in Berlin.* Bielefeld: Transcript.

Guggenberger, B., and U. Kempf, eds. 1978. *Bürgerinitiativen und repräsentatives System.* Opladen: Westdeutscher Verlag.

Hartsock, N. C. M. 1983. 'The Feminist Standpoint: Developing the Ground for a Specifically Feminist Historical Materialism'. In *Discovering Reality: Feminist Perspectives on Epistemology, Metaphysics, Methodology, and Philosophy of Science,* ed. S. G. Harding and M. B. Hintikka, 283–310. Dordrecht: Reidel.

Haunss, S. 2004. *Identität in Bewegung: Prozesse kollektiver Identität bei den Autonomen und in der Schwulenbewegung.* Wiesbaden: VS Verlag.

———. 2008. 'Antiimperialismus und Autonomie—Linksradikalismus seit der Studentenbewegung'. In *Die Sozialen Bewegungen in Deutschland seit 1945: Ein Handbuch,* ed. R. Roth and D. Rucht, 447–73. Frankfurt and New York: Campus.

Haunss, S., and P. Ullrich. 2013. 'Viel Bewegung—wenig Forschung. Zu- und Gegenstand von sozialwissenschaftlicher Protest- und Bewegungsforschung in der Bundesrepublik'. *Soziologie* 42, no. 3: 290–304.

Heinz, W. R., and P. Schöber, eds. 1973. *Theorien kollektiven Verhaltens: Beiträge zur Analyse sozialer Protestaktionen und Bewegungen.* Darmstadt/Neuwied: Luchterhand.

Hellmann, K. U. 1996a. 'Rechtsextremismus als soziale Bewegung? Bericht einer Tagung am 11. November 1995 im WZB.' *Forschungsjournal Neue Soziale Bewegungen* 9, no. 1: 89–91.

———. 1996b. *Systemtheorie und neue soziale Bewegungen: Identitaetsprobleme in der Risikogesellschaft.* Opladen: Westdeutscher Verlag.

———. 1999. 'Paradigmen der Bewegungsforschung: Eine Fachdisziplin auf dem Weg zur normalen Wissenschaft'. In *Neue Soziale Bewegungen,* ed. A. Klein, J. Legrand and T. Leif, 91–113. Opladen: Westdeutscher Verlag.

Hollstein, W. 1979. *Die Gegengesellschaft: Alternative Lebensformen.* Bonn: Neue Gesellschaft.

Holy, M. 1991. 'Historischer Abriß der zweiten deutschen Schwulenbewegung 1969–1989'. In *Neue soziale Bewegungen in der Bundesrepublik Deutschland,* ed. R. Roth and D. Rucht, 138–60. Bonn: Bundeszentrale für politische Bildung.

Jaschke, H. G. 2006. *Politischer Extremismus.* Wiesbaden: VS Verlag für Sozialwissenschaften

Johnston, H. 2009. 'Protest Cultures: Performance, Artifacts, and Ideations'. In *Culture, Social Movements, and Protest,* ed. H. Johnston, 3–29. Burlington: Ashgate.

Kitschelt, H. 1980. *Kernenergiepolitik: Arena eines gesellschaftlichen Konflikts.* Frankfurt and New York: Campus.

———. 1985. 'New Social Movements in West Germany and the United States'. *Political Power and Social Theory* 5: 273–324.

Klandermans, B. 2012. 'Between Rituals and Riots: The Dynamics of Street Demonstrations'. *Mobilization* 17, no. 3: 233–34.

Klein, A. 2003. 'Bewegungsforschung: Quo vadis? Ein Überblick zu Entstehung, Ausprägung und Forschungsstand'. *Vorgänge* (164): 12–21.

———. 2008.'20 Jahre Forschungsjournal Neue Soziale Bewegungen: Eine Zwischenbilanz'. *Forschungsjournal Neue Soziale Bewegungen* 21, no. 3: 239–55.

Klein, A., H. J. Legrand and T. Leif, eds. 1999. *Neue Soziale Bewegungen: Impulse, Bilanzen und Perspektiven.* Opladen: Westdeutscher Verlag.

Klimke, M., and J. Scharloth. 2008. *1968 in Europe: A History of Protest and Activism, 1956–1977.* New York: Palgrave Macmillan.

Klönne, A. 1980. *Die deutsche Arbeiterbewegung: Geschichte, Ziele, Wirkungen.* Düsseldorf: Diederichs.

Knafla, L., and C. Kulke. 1991. '20 Jahre neue Frauenbewegung: Und sie bewegt sich noch! Ein Rückblick nach vorn'. In *Neue soziale Bewegungen in der Bundesrepublik Deutschland,* ed. R. Roth and D. Rucht, 91–115. Bonn: Bundeszentrale für politische Bildung.

Kolb, F. 2007. *Protest and Opportunities: The Political Outcomes of Social Movements.* Frankfurt and New York: Campus.

Koopmans, R. 1995. 'Bewegung oder Erstarrung? Bestandsaufnahme der deutschen Bewegungsforschung in den letzten zehn Jahren'. *Forschungsjournal Neue Soziale Bewegungen* 8, no. 1: 90–96.

Koopmans, R., and D. Rucht. 1996. 'Rechtsradikalismus als soziale Bewegung', in *Rechtsextremismus. Ergebnisse und Perspektiven der Forschung,* eds J. W. Falter, H. G. Jaschke, and J. R. Winkler, *Politische Vierteljahresschrift Sonderheft* 27: 265–87.

———. 2002. 'Protest Event Analysis'. In *Methods of Social Movement Research,* ed. B. Klandermans and S. Staggenborg, 231–59. Minneapolis: University of Minnesota Press.

Koopmans, R., and P. Statham. 1999. 'Political Claims Analysis: Integrating Protest Event and Political Discourse Approaches'. *Mobilization* 4, no. 2: 203–21.

Koopmans, R., and P. Statham, eds. 2000. *Challenging Immigration and Ethnic Relations Politics: Comparative European Perspectives.* Oxford: Oxford University Press.

Kraushaar, W. 1996. *Die Protest-Chronik 1949–1959: Eine illustrierte Geschichte von Bewegung, Widerstand und Utopie.* Hamburg: Rogner and Bernhard.

Krechel, U. 1978. *Selbsterfahrung und Fremdbestimmung: Berichte aus der Neuen Frauenbewegung.* Neuwiedl: Luchterhand.

Kress, G., and D. Senghaas. 1972. *Politikwissenschaft: Eine Einführung in ihre Probleme.* Frankfurt: Fischer Taschenbuch Verlag.

Kretschmer, W., and D. Rucht. 1991. 'Beispiel Wackersdorf: Die Protestbewegung gegen die Wiederaufarbeitungsanlage. Gruppen, Organisationen, Netzwerke'. In *Neue soziale Bewegungen in der Bundesrepublik Deutschland,* ed. R. Roth and D. Rucht, 180–212. Bonn: Bundeszentrale für politische Bildung.

Kriesi, H., et al., eds. 1995. *New Social Movements in Western Europe: A Comparative Analysis.* Minneapolis: University of Minnesota Press.

Lahusen, C. 2013. 'The Protests of the Unemployed in France, Germany and Sweden (1994–2004): Protest Dynamics and Political Contexts'. *Social Movement Studies* 12, no. 1: 1–22.

Lahusen, C., and B. Baumgarten. 2006. 'Die Fragilität kollektiven Handelns: Arbeitslosenproteste in Deutschland und Frankreich'. *Zeitschrift für Soziologie* 35, no. 2: 102–19.

Leggewie, C. 1994. 'Rechtsextemismus—eine soziale Bewegung?'. In *Rechtsextremismus: Einführung und Forschungsbilanz*, ed. S. Kowalsky, 325–38. Opladen: Leske and Budrich.

Leif, T. 1985. *Die professionelle Bewegung: Friedensbewegung von innen*. Bonn: Forum Europa.

Lenz, I. 2009. *Die Neue Frauenbewegung in Deutschland: Abschied vom kleinen Unterschied. Ausgewählte Quellen*. Wiesbaden: VS Verlag.

Linnhoff, U. 1974. *Die Neue Frauenbewegung:n: USA—Europa seit 1968*. Köln: Kiepenheuer & Witsch.

Luhmann, N. 1996. *Protest: Systemtheorie und soziale Bewegungen. Herausgegeben und eingeleitet von Kai-Uwe Hellmann*. Frankfurt: Suhrkamp.

Marx, K., and F. Engels. 1888. *Manifesto of the Communist Party*. Retrieved 5 March 2011 from http://www.gutenberg.org/cache/epub/61/pg61.html.

Mayer, M. 2008. 'Städtische soziale Bewegungen'. In *Die Sozialen Bewegungen in Deutschland seit 1945: Ein Handbuch,* ed. R. Roth and D. Rucht, 293–318. Frankfurt and New York: Campus.

Mayer-Tasch, P. C. 1976. *Die Bürgerinitiativbewegung: Der aktive Bürger als rechts- und politikwissenschaftliches Problem*. Reinbek: Rowohlt.

McPhail, C. 1994. 'Social Behavior in Public Places: From Clusters to Arcs and Rings'. In *The Community of the Streets,* ed. S. Cahill and L. Lofland, 35–57. Greenwich: JAI Press.

McPhail, C., and R. T. Wohlstein. 1983. 'Individual and Collective Behaviors within Gatherings, Demonstrations, and Riots'. *Annual Review of Sociology* 9: 579–600.

Melucci, A. 1989. *Nomads of the Present: Social Movements and Individual Needs in Contemporary Society*. London: Hutchinson.

Neidhardt, F. 1985. 'Einige Ideen zu einer allgemeinen Theorie sozialer Bewegungen'. In *Sozialstruktur im Umbruch: Karl Martin Bolte zum 60,* ed. S. Hradil, 193–204. Opladen: Geburtstag.

Neidhardt, F., and D. Rucht. 1993. 'Auf dem Weg in die "Bewegungsgesellschaft"? Über die Stabilisierbarkeit sozialer Bewegungen'. *Soziale Welt* 44, no. 3: 305–26.

Offe, C. 1985. 'New Social Movements: Challenging the Boundaries of Institutional Politics'. *Social Research* 52, no. 4: 817–68.

Olejniczak, C. 2008. 'Dritte-Welt-Bewegung'. In *Die Sozialen Bewegungen in Deutschland seit 1945: Ein Handbuch,* ed. R. Roth and D. Rucht, 319–46. Frankfurt and New York: Campus.

Pappi, F. U. 1991. 'Die Anhänger der neuen sozialen Bewegungen im Parteiensystem der bundesrepublik Deutschland'. In *Neue soziale Bewegungen in der Bundesrepublik Deutschland,* ed. R. Roth and D. Rucht, 452–68. Bonn: Bundeszentrale für politische Bildung.

Pfahl-Traughber, A. 1998. 'Die Autonomen: Portrait einer linksextremistischen Subkultur'. *Aus Politik und Zeitgeschichte* B 9–10/98: 36–46.

Pretzel, A., and V. Weiß, eds. 2012. *Rosa Radikale: Die Schwulenbewegung der 1970er Jahre*. Hamburg: Männerschwarmverlag.

Raschke, J. 1985. *Soziale Bewegungen: Ein historisch-systematischer Grundriß*. Frankfurt and New York: Campus.

———. 1991. 'Zum Begriff der sozialen Bewegung'. In *Neue soziale Bewegungen in der*

Bundesrepublik Deutschland, ed. R. Roth and D. Rucht, 31–39. Bonn: Bundeszentrale für politische Bildung.

Reetz, D. 2004. 'Aktuelle Analysen islamistischer Bewegungen und ihre Kritik'. *Forschungsjournal Neue Soziale Bewegungen* 17, no. 4: 61–68.

Rink, D. 2008. 'Bürgerbewegungen in der DDR—Demokratische Sammlungsbewegungen am Ende des Sozialismus'. In *Die Sozialen Bewegungen in Deutschland seit 1945: Ein Handbuch,* ed. R. Roth and D. Rucht, 391–416. Frankfurt and New York: Campus.

Roose, J., and P. Ullrich. 2012. 'Neue Perspektiven auf soziale Bewegungen und Protest: Ein Nachwuchsnetzwerk stellt sich vor'. *Studentisches Soziologiemagazin* 5: 87–91.

Roth, R. 1991. 'Kommunikationsstrukturen und Vernetzung in neuen sozialen Bewegungen'. In *Neue soziale Bewegungen in der Bundesrepublik Deutschland,* ed. R. Roth and D. Rucht, 261–79. Bonn: Bundeszentrale für politische Bildung.

———. 1994. *Demokratie von unten: Neue soziale Bewegungen auf dem Wege zur politischen Institution.* Köln: Bund-Verlag.

Roth, R., ed. 1980. *Parlamentarisches Ritual und politische Alternativen.* Frankfurt and New York: Campus.

Roth, R., and D. Rucht, eds. 1991. *Neue soziale Bewegungen in der Bundesrepublik Deutschland.* Bonn: Bundeszentrale für politische Bildung.

———, eds. 2008. *Die Sozialen Bewegungen in Deutschland seit 1945: Ein Handbuch.* Frankfurt and New York: Campus.

Rucht, D. 1984. 'Zur Organisation der neuen sozialen Bewegungen'. In *Politische Willensbildung und Interessenvermittlung,* ed. J. Falter, C. Fenner and M. T. Greven, 609–20. Opladen: Westdeutscher Verlag.

———. 1991a. 'The Study of Social Movements in West Germany: Between Activism and Social Science'. In *Research on Social Movements: The State of the Art in Western Europe and the USA,* ed. D. Rucht, 175–202. Frankfurt and New York: Campus.

———. 1991b. 'Von der Bewegung zur Institution? Organisationsstrukturen der Ökologiebewegung'. In *Neue soziale Bewegungen in der Bundesrepublik Deutschland,* ed. R. Roth and D. Rucht, 334–58. Bonn: Bundeszentrale für politische Bildung.

———. 1998. 'The Structure and Culture of Collective Protest in West Germany since 1950'. In *The Social Movement Society: Contentious Politics for a New Century,* ed. D. S. Meyer and S. Tarrow, 29–57. Boulder: Rowman and Littlefield.

———. 2001. *Protest in der Bundesrepublik: Strukturen und Entwicklungen.* Frankfurt and New York: Campus.

———. 2011. 'Zum Stand der Forschung zu sozialen Bewegungen'. *Forschungsjournal Soziale Bewegungen* 24, no. 3: 20–47.

Rucht, D., ed. 2003. *Berlin, 1. Mai 2002. Politische Demonstrationsrituale.* Leverkusen: Leske and Budrich.

Rucht, D., B. Blattert and D. Rink. 1997. *Soziale Bewegungen auf dem Weg zur Instituionalisierung: Zum Strukturwandel 'alternativer' Gruppen in beiden Teilen Deutschlands.* Frankfurt and New York: Campus.

Rucht, D., and R. Roth. 2008a. 'Soziale Bewegungen und Protest eine theoretische und empirische Bilanz'. In *Die Sozialen Bewegungen in Deutschland seit 1945: Ein Handbuch,* ed. R. Roth and D. Rucht, 10–36. Frankfurt and New York: Campus.

———. 2008b. 'Globalisierungskritische Netzwerke, Kampagnen und Bewegungen'. In *Die Sozialen Bewegungen in Deutschland seit 1945: Ein Handbuch,* ed. R. Roth and D. Rucht, 493–512. Frankfurt and New York: Campus.

Rucht, D., and S. Teune, eds. 2008. *Nur Clowns und Chaoten? Die G8-Proteste in Heiligendamm im Spiegel der Massenmedien.* Frankfurt and New York: Campus.

Ruggiero, V., and N. Montagna, eds. 2008. *Social Movements: A Reader.* London and New York: Routledge.

Salmen, A., and A. Eckert. 1989. *20 Jahre bundesdeutsche Schwulenbewegung 1969–1989.* Köln: BVH Materialien.

Schultze, T., and A. Gross. 1997. *Die Autonomen: Ursprünge, Entwicklung und Profil der autonomen Bewegung.* Hamburg: Konkret Literatur Verlag.

Simmel, G. 1950. *The Sociology of Georg Simmel.* Glencoe: Free Press.

Teune, S. 2008. '"Gibt es so etwas überhaupt noch?" Forschung zu Protest und sozialen Bewegungen'. *Politische Vierteljahresschrift* 49, no. 3: 528–47.

Tilly, C. 1984. *Big Structures, Large Processes, Huge Comparisons.* New York: Russell Sage Foundation.

———. 2004. *Social Movements, 1768–2004.* Boulder: Paradigm.

Touraine, A. 1972. *Die postindustrielle Gesellschaft.* Frankfurt: Suhrkamp.

———. 1988. *Return of the Actor: Social Theory in Postindustrial Society.* Minneapolis: University of Minnesota Press.

Virchow, F. 2013. 'Creating a European (Neo-Nazi) Movement by Joint Political Action?'. In *Varieties of Right-Wing Extremism in Europe,* ed. A. Mammone, E. Godin, and B. Jenkins, 197–213. London and New York: Routledge.

Walk, H., and N. Boehme, eds. 2002. *Globaler Widerstand: Internationale Netzwerke auf der Suche nach Alternativen im globalen Kapitalismus.* Münster: Westfälisches Dampfboot.

Wasmuth, U. 1991. 'Von der Friedensbewegung der 80er Jahre zum Antikriegsprotest von 1991'. In *Neue soziale Bewegungen in der Bundesrepublik Deutschland,* ed. R. Roth and D.Rucht, 116–37. Bonn: Bundeszentrale für politische Bildung.

Weber, M. 1958. *From Max Weber: Essays in Sociology.* Ed. H. H. Gerth and C. W. Mills. Oxford: Oxford University Press.

Wiesendahl, E. 1991. 'Neue soziale Bewegungen und moderne Demokratietheorie: Demokratische Elitenherrschaft in der Krise'. In *Neue soziale Bewegungen in der Bundesrepublik Deutschland,* ed. R. Roth and D. Rucht, 561–78. Bonn: Bundeszentrale für politische Bildung.

Zoll, R, 2010. 'Der 'Radikalenerlass'. In *Friedens- und Konfliktforschung: Eine Einführung,* ed. P. Imbusch and R. Zoll, 485–509. Wiesbaden: VS Verlag, 485–509.

Chapter 13

Politics and People

Understanding Dutch Research on Social Movements

Jan Willem Duyvendak, Conny Roggeband
and Jacquelien van Stekelenburg

This chapter mostly focuses on social movement studies carried out in the Netherlands and dealing with the Netherlands. This rather 'national orientation' is not because Dutch scholars dealing with social movements are not working abroad (they are, e.g. Chabot in Cheney [US], and Koopmans in Berlin) or that foreign scholars do not write about the Netherlands (they do, e.g. Gladdish 1987). However, for a representative picture of social movement studies specifically addressing the Netherlands, it makes sense to look at clusters of scholars rather than individual contributions, and—at least for the time period considered herein—these clusters were working in the Netherlands itself.

We identify two groups of scholars—social psychologists at the VU University in Amsterdam and political sociologists at the University of Amsterdam (UvA)—who for many years represented the main local schools. For sure, many more scholars in the Netherlands at other universities carried out research on contentious performances, but they were either linked in one way or another to the two Amsterdam-based schools, or they worked in a somewhat isolated manner (Huberts 1988; Mamadouh 1992; Van Noort 1988; Valkenburg 1995), having little impact on the study of Dutch social movements at large. This case contrasts with that of the UvA and VU groups who applied international and comparative approaches from scratch. They applied and contributed to the most influential international paradigms of the past decades, such as the social-psychological approach (SPA), with strong emphasis on subjective processes in the creation of meaning (VU group) and the more 'objectivist' political process approach (PPA) (University of Amsterdam).

Conspicuously absent from the Dutch approaches to social movements is the so-called new social movement (NSM) approach. Although some have argued that the NSM approach was the 'European contribution' to the field of social movements *par excellence,* we have to conclude that most Dutch scholars contributed to Anglo-Saxon traditions, often being inspired and influenced by scholars such as McCarthy and Zald and, in particular, McAdam (1982). The sole exception is the work by Van der Loo, Snel and Van Steenbergen (1984), who understood the development of new social movements primarily in terms of autonomous cultural change, and not so much in relation to the political context.

One can speculate why certain approaches resonate so strongly in some countries and less in others. Here, we want to hypothesise that the Dutch political culture of openness towards protest and protestors has been mirrored in the popularity of scholarly approaches that emphasise the importance of political opportunities and resources, and the lack of popularity of the NSM approach. The latter is not because Dutch 'new' social movements have been weaker than their French and the Italian counterparts—to the contrary (Duyvendak 1995; Kriesi et al. 1995).

This is, however, not the full story: the development of a specific field of study is not only shaped by structural factors such as the social and political context but is also dependent on more contingent factors such as the role of individual social movement scholars. Two people have played a pivotal role in this respect: Hanspeter Kriesi, as the founder of the UvA-school and, even more so, Bert Klandermans, as the long-time leader of the social psychology of protest group at VU University.

Social Psychological Research into Social Movements

Bert Klandermans has studied the social-psychological approach at VU University since the 1970s. His 1983 dissertation already revealed the typical 'Klandermans' approach to social movements: a social psychological interpretation from an interdisciplinary comparative perspective. The SPA focuses on subjective variables and takes the individual as its unit of analysis (Klandermans 1997; Van Stekelenburg and Klandermans 2007, 2013). Social psychologists maintain that people live in a perceived world: they respond to the world as they perceive and interpret it. If we want to understand why people protest, we need to know how they perceive and interpret their world. Another characteristic of the VU group is what Klandermans (2013) describes as 'the virtue of comparison'. Only comparisons of place and time tells us how contextual variation works (see Klandermans 2012; Van Stekelenburg et al. 2012; Linden and Klandermans 2007; and Klandermans and Mayer 2006; Klandermans, de Weerd, Sabucedo and Rodriguez 2001).

In the last decade, the Dutch SPA of the VU group has been supplemented by social psychologists from Groningen University (around Postmes and Van Zomeren) and sociologists from Nijmegen (following Akkerman, who joined the VU group towards the end of 2013).

Demand, Supply and Mobilization

Successful mobilization brings together what Klandermans (2004) calls 'demand' and 'supply'. *Demand* refers to the will of (a segment) of the population to protest. *Supply* refers to social movement organizations and their appeals, and the opportunities staged by organisers to protest. Successful mobilization is a process that interconnects 'supply' and 'demand'. The dynamics of both supply and demand have fascinated the VU group over the past four decades: regarding the dynamics of supply, the process of mobilization and the role of organisers, and concerning the dynamics of demand, the question 'Why do people protest?' has been of central importance. This contrasts with Reicher's group, whose scholars tend to focus on emergent group phenomena and which departs regularly from social psychological identity theories, while the VU group tends to depart from social movement theory.

The Dynamics of Supply

Organisers need to pay attention to the following four aspects of mobilization: (1) formation of mobilization potentials, (2) formation and activation of recruitment networks, (3) arousal of motivation to participate, and (4) removal of barriers to participation. On the demand side, individuals go through four synchronous steps towards participation: (1) becoming part of the mobilization potential, (2) becoming a target of mobilization attempts, (3) becoming motivated to participate, and (4) overcoming barriers to participation.

Klandermans and Oegema's mobilization theory (1987) is based on a study that examined all four steps of the mobilization process from a mobilization campaign for the peace demonstration in The Hague in 1983. *Before* the demonstration, respondents were asked if they supported the campaign and intended to participate; *afterwards* they were asked if they had participated. Analytically distinguishing between the four steps revealed the *process* of mobilization. The net result of these different steps demonstrated that although three-quarters of the population felt sympathy for the movement's cause, only a small proportion of the general public actually participated (4 per cent).

Boekkooi studied the role of organisers. Protest does not emerge out of the blue, but it needs to be organised and mobilised. She examined how organisers 'weaved' their mobilizing structures, and the time it took protesters to make a firm decision to attend these protests (Boekkooi, Klandermans Van Stekelenburg 2011; see also Van Stekelenburg and Boekkooi 2013). In yet another study, Boekkooi shows how seemingly trivial quarrels in organisers' coalitions caused a relatively low turnout for the Dutch international anti-war demonstration in 2003.

The Dynamics of Demand

The dynamics of demand refer to the process of the formation of mobilization potential: grievances and identities are politicised, environments become supportive, and emotions are aroused (Klandermans 2013). This process of politicization (Simon and Klandermans 2001; Van Stekelenburg, Van Troost and Van Leeuwen 2012) is not a given fact, as Van Doorn et al. (2013) show in their study on why young Moroccans in the Netherlands do *not* become politicised.

Thirty years ago Dutch social psychologists began to investigate individual participation in protest. They began by demonstrating that instrumental reasoning controlled peoples' protest participation (e.g. Klandermans 1984). Gradually, they explored other motives that stimulate people to engage in protest. The first motive to be added was identification (e.g. Klandermans, Sabucedo and Rodriguez 2004; De Weerd and Klandermans 1999). Recently, group-based anger has been put forward as another motive (Van Zomeren et al. 2004). The social psychological answers to the question as to why people protest were provided in terms of grievances, efficacy, identity and emotions.

In practice all these concepts are interwoven, which is what the psychological branch to date focuses on. German social psychologists, Simon et al. (1998), proposed a *dual path model* in which they distinguished between the instrumental pathway proposed by Klandermans (1984) and an identity pathway. Van Zomeren et al. (2004) also propose a dual path model, comprising an instrumental and emotion pathway. The VU team integrated these elements into a single theoretical framework (Van Stekelenburg et al. 2007, 2009, 2011, 2012), developing a model that assigns a central, integrating role to identification. In order to develop shared grievances and shared emotions, a shared identity is needed. On the basis of a meta-analysis, Van Zomeren et al. (2008) came to the same conclusion.

More recently, the Groningen team zoomed in on the ideological motivation. They integrated moral conviction—strong and absolute stances on moral issues—with their social identity model of collective action (SIMCA, Van Zomeren, Postmes and Spears 2008). They found that moral convictions predicted protest through politicised identification, group-based anger and group efficacy (Van Zomeren, Postmes and Spears 2012), and that violations of moral convictions about social inequality can motivate advantaged group members to participate in protest against inequality (Van Zomeren et al. 2011).

Van Zomeren et al. (2011) also connect their model to normative and non-normative forms of protest: efficacious people experience anger and engage in normative protest, while non-efficacious people feel contempt and engage in non-normative protest. When physical threat produces fear, this leads to avoidance behaviour; however, when anger is created, this leads to confrontational behaviour: a 'nothing-to-lose-strategy' (Kamans et al. 2011).

More recently, the VU team proposed a new element to consider: social embeddedness (Klandermans et al. 2008).[1] Individual grievances and feelings are transformed into group-based grievances and feelings within social networks. Thus, migrants who felt efficacious were more likely to participate in protest provided that they were embedded in social networks, which offer an opportunity to discuss and learn about politics (e.g. Postmes, Haslam and Swaab 2005). Akkerman et al. examined how embeddedness in Dutch unions promotes strike participation: information and identification with the union (Born, Akkerman and Torenvlied 2013a), solidarity and punishment (Akkerman, Born and Torenvlied 2013b) all foster strike participation.

Political Opportunity Approach

When Hanspeter Kriesi arrived at Amsterdam in 1986 to become full professor in 'collective political behaviour', he was welcomed by many colleagues who had either been actively involved in recent protest waves or had been studying the new movements intensively (Outshoorn, Poldervaart, Van Praag, Van der Heijden and Wijmans). Kriesi introduced a coherent approach to the rather eclectic group of scholars in Amsterdam and published widely on social movements and protest in the Netherlands (1987a and 1987b, 1988, 1989a, 1989b and 1989c). Moreover, he launched an international comparative research project on 'new social movements' in Western Europe. This collective endeavour resulted in books and articles on Germany (Koopmans 1995), France (Duyvendak 1995), Switzerland (Giugni and Passy 1999) and the Netherlands (Wille 1994). Moreover, this group collectively produced the first comprehensive book on Dutch social movements (Duyvendak et al. 1992), and, perhaps most importantly, Kriesi and his collaborators wrote articles and a highly influential book on social movements in Western Europe in a comparative perspective (Kriesi et al. 1992, 1995).

In their work, the group showed the fertility of an approach focusing on differences in political opportunities for (new) social movements in Germany, France, Switzerland and the Netherlands. The relative strength and successes of the Dutch new social movements stand out in comparison with many other countries. These Dutch characteristics could be explained by the early pacification of 'old' political cleavages and the structural and cultural openness—chances of success and low levels of repression—to new forms of protest.

In its version of the political process approach, the Dutch team distanced itself in an early state of overly static and objectivist interpretations of political opportunities. Koopmans and Duyvendak (1995), in their work on the anti-nuclear energy movement developed an approach in which framing and opportunities both had their place. Their findings indicated that the construction of grievances and social problems, and the degree to which they give rise to social movement mobilization, are rooted not in aggrieving conditions but in political power relations. Koopmans and Duyvendak concluded that it was fruitful to combine the framing and political opportunity perspectives and to look at the political conditions under which specific discourses become imaginable.

It comes as no surprise then, that criticisms regarding the overly structuralist explanations of the PPA resonated strongly in the Netherlands. In more recent work, scholars of the University of Amsterdam (Broer and Duyvendak 2009, 2011; De Graaff and Broer 2012; Grootegoed, Broer and Duyvendak 2013) have challenged core assumptions of the structuralist PPA, inspired by American scholars who have emphasised the importance of emotions and culture in social movement research (Jasper 2011, 2012). In their work, these UvA researchers show how in the policy-making process itself, political subjectivities are formed that enable people to fight precisely those policies. Often, however, resonance rather than dissonance is the outcome of the political process: policymakers and people have the same definition of the situation and no mobilization occurs.

With the departure of Kriesi back to his homeland, Switzerland, in the late 1980s, and Koopmans' move to Berlin around 1994, the UvA group stopped functioning as a collective in the Netherlands. However, due to their work, a constructivist PPA was firmly established, as can be shown by the on-going research in this tradition in the Netherlands since then (Adam, Duyvendak and Krouwel 1999; Chabot and Duyvendak 2002; Duyvendak 1994, 1996a, 1996b, 1996c; Duyvendak and Nederland 2007; Duyvendak and Verplanke 2013; Hekma and Duyvendak 2011; Sunier 1998; Sunier et al. 2000; Van der Heijden 2000, 2005). Koopmans continued to work on the political process approach and incorporated the Netherlands in many of his comparative publications (e.g. Koopmans 1998, 2006; Koopmans and Statham 1999). Today, a new generation social movement scholars (Chabot, Heumann, Scholl, Rivat and Verhoeven), trained at the University of Amsterdam, use various approaches in their scholarly work.

Women's Movements and State-Feminism

A PPA-inspired line of social movement research in the Netherlands focuses specifically on the close relationship between the women's movement and the state. The work of Outshoorn, Oldersma, Roggeband and Verloo show that a favourable opportunity structure in the 1970s resulted in the rapid adoption of gender equality policies, strong state support for women's initiatives and the establishment of a women's policy machinery that held close ties to the women's movements. Generous state support led to the institutionalization and professionalization of many women's organizations, coined 'subsidised revolution' by Van Rossum (1992), and a decline in autonomous feminism.

While these developments confirm the basic PPA assumptions, the studies also voice criticisms and amendments to the PPA. One of the main criticisms is related to the central distinction between states/governments and social movements, where certain political configurations provide opportunities and constraints. Yet, studies of the Dutch women's movement point to large intersections between the state and movements and the implications of these intersections for theorizing political opportunity structures. Outshoorn (1994) initiated an important line of research that examines the interface between the Dutch women's movement and the state apparatus, also labelled state feminism. In 1995, Outshoorn, together with McBride and Mazur founded the *Research Network on Gender Politics and the State* (RNGS): a cross-national and longitudinal research project showing how partnerships between women's movement activists and the state, and in particular feminist insiders ('femocrats') open the possibility that states adopt feminist policies without 'outside' pressure or mobilization and thus create a different structure of opportunities within the state (Outshoorn 1997).

Another criticism involves the critical idea that protest occurs in cycles or waves. The mobilization of the women's movement does not coincide with the more general wave of protest in the Netherlands during the 1960s, and the mobilization pattern does not take on a typical parabolic shape, because there is no clear decline in movement participation and mobilization in the 1980s and 1990s (Outshoorn 2009).

One explication as to why the mobilization of the Dutch women's movement portrays a different shape compared to other Dutch social movements can be found precisely in the political context. Feminist scholars have drawn attention to the 'gendered-ness' of political opportunities. Roggeband's research on the women's movement against sexual violence (2002) shows how political opportunities varied between different branches of the women's movement depending on how the issue at stake related to the political domain. For instance, the problem of domestic violence was more difficult to politicise since it belonged to the realm of the private, compared to sexual harassment in the workplace. How problems are ideologically and strategically framed affects the political response and vice versa; and as Koopmans and Duyvendak have also emphasised in their work, framing may be adapted to certain discursive opportunities.

This relationship is explored in two international research projects (Mageeq and QUING) initiated in the Netherlands by Verloo. This research studies how feminist actors have been able to frame governmental policies and shows that the role of the women's movement and other relevant civil society organizations in gender equality policy-making has become problematic and limited (Verloo 2007; Lombardo, Meier and Verloo 2009).

Historical Perspectives on Social Movements in the Netherlands

A third important, but rather diffuse, line of research on social movements in the Netherlands has been historical research, not only on the extensive wave of new social movements in the 1960s and 1970s but also on older movements, in particular on labour and women's movements. An understanding in terms of 'decades' predominates in this historiography of recent protest waves. Several books have been published dealing with 'the 1960s' and 'the 1970s' (Kennedy 1995; Regtien 1988; Righart 1995). Most of the studies have a rather descriptive character, as is the case for the historical studies on the labour and women's movements as well.

Part of this work is related to the Amsterdam-based International Institute for Social History. This institute has generated a considerable body of research on labour movements, both in the Netherlands and elsewhere. While its initial concentration was mainly on the Dutch context, since the 1990s it has been working to globalise its focus and has initiated international and comparative research projects (Van der Linden 2002). Another point of emphasis within its considerable body of historic research centres on contemporary and historical women's movements (Meijer 1996; Mossink 1995; Poldervaart 1992, 2002, 2003, 2007; Ribberink 1998; Waaldijk 1998; Withuis 1990).

These historical studies do not represent a clear theoretical paradigm, nor do they articulate a social movement perspective or dialogue with dominant approaches in the field of social movement studies. Exceptions to this rule include the few studies that do not focus on specific movements but rather on trends across movements, for example, in action repertoires in the Netherlands since 1965 (Van der Klein and Wieringa 2006).

An Agenda for the Future Study of Social Movements in the Netherlands

When we look at the main trends in the study of protest in the Netherlands, there are some strong parallels with what has happened in other countries, particularly the United States. The 'classical approaches'—emphasizing grievances, anomie of alienated and frustrated marginal people, expressing themselves in irrational and expressive ways—were replaced by perspectives that highlighted the rationality of protest behaviour of well-organised and embedded people, with balanced costs and benefits of protest behaviour, depending on resources and political opportunities. However, the Dutch were not the most 'structuralist' among the researchers working within the political process approach. On the contrary, both the UvA and particularly the VU group were sensitive to the experiences and perceptions of potential participants: a favourable political opportunity does not have to be perceived as such.

Whereas the UvA group started from 'big structures', the VU group chose individuals as their starting point. Over time, however, their roads started to cross for three reasons: first, the UvA group was confronted with the fact that comparable opportunities 'impacted' potential protesters in different ways, depending not only on their divergent perceptions of these opportunities but also on their various motivations and emotions to participate in social movements. Moreover, a macro-analysis—based on the quasi-predictability of actors' behaviour in a given political opportunity structure—did not do justice to the particularities of every interaction between the different parties involved in protest behaviour. A far more precise focus on 'strategic interaction' (Jasper 2004, 2006, 2011; Duyvendak and Jasper 2015; Jasper and Duyvendak 2015) turned out to be necessary. Second, the VU group started to focus more on the contextual factors influencing quasi-individual decisions, summarised in the attention for individuals' informal, formal and virtual embeddedness. With regard to informal embeddedness, Van Stekelenburg et al. (2013) show, in their study on the emergence of collective action in neighbourhoods, that identification with a neighbour-hood rather than the amount of structural network nodes strengthens the experience of suddenly imposed grievances and efficacy and thereby spurs protest participation. Hence, sharedness emerges not so much in the *number* of contacts but rather in the experience of psychological connectedness. Regarding formal embeddedness, one recent study shows that 50 per cent of the sample (i.e. about 7,500 demonstrators) is unaffiliated, that is, they are *not* a member of the organizing social movement organization (Klandermans et al. under review). They show that organizing without organizations differs from traditional protest events in terms of mobilization and participation dynamics. In short, these studies empirically show how the traditional logic of collective action affects mobilization and participation and differs from the more recent mobilization and participation of so-called connective action (cf. Bennett and Segerberg 2012).

Third, and in addition to embeddedness, the VU team started to study 'cleavages' as another contextual factor shaping the social psychology of pro-test. Building on Kriesi's (1995) work, they argued that cleavages configure the dynamics of action both in conventional and unconventional politics. They show that social cleavages generate cleavage-specific protest demand and supply; socio-political conflicts are rooted in these cleavages—if con-flicts flare up, subsections of the cleavage's specific supply side come out of abeyance to stage protest events (Damen and Van Stekelenburg 2014).

When we look at the social cleavages of Dutch society today and the socio-political conflicts of the past decade, we see that huge shifts have oc-curred. Changes in the Dutch political landscape, with the rise of populist and right-wing political parties and reconfigurations of the state structure (due to uploading state responsibilities to the EU, and lateral loading to the market) have important implications for social movements in the Nether-lands. Not only is state responsiveness much lower but some social move-ments also face reversals or a backlash of earlier gains. For instance, equality policies are under threat due to state reforms (Roggeband 2014)Also, the shift to the right, with a focus on nationalism, a rejection of pluralism, and negative attitude towards internationalization, has not been conducive to mobilization of 'new social movements', for example, groups of women (Outshoorn and Oldersma 2007). The question thus emerges as to how so-cial movements deal with this backlash and, in some cases, even opposition to their demands (Roggeband, forthcoming). The relocation of formal pow-ers and policy-making responsibilities from the state to other policy-making levels and spaces forces social movements to seek alternative spaces to pro-mote their goals (Roggeband 2010). This requires further research and theo-rization of the dynamics at scales other than the national state; for example, of transnational actor constellations, their interactions and strategic alliances and how this affects national mobilization processes (Roggeband and Van Eerdwijk 2014).

Another important contextual factor is the global financial crisis. Do dynamics of participation in anti-austerity demonstrations differ from dynamics of participation in demonstrations focusing on immaterial goals? Are material motives (cf. Ronald Inglehart) back on the streets? Or are they combined with strong post-material motives? It is the last constellation that we find in a comparative study on sixty-nine street demonstrations dispersed over eight European countries. Hence, when a severe crisis hits citizens after times of prosperity, material motives may spur their protest, yet they are combined with post-material motives (Klandermans et al. under review b).

Apart from these recent changes in political and economic conditions, social movements have to deal with long-term macro-sociological trends such as *globalization, individualization* and *virtualization*. How this changing societal context influences the dynamics of contention is a question that movement scholars have to answer. This is, however, not a specific 'Dutch' task since these developments are global. Our future contribution is, therefore, not necessarily very 'Dutch' in nature. It might even be that thinking about the future of social movement studies in terms of *national* contributions will become rather outdated and obsolete. This is not only because research teams are increasingly more internationally composed and research is becoming more comparative, but it is also because the very idea that the Dutch context might engender a specific approach or contribution seems to make less sense than in the past. Methodological nationalism becomes increasingly problematic in a networked world.

Jan Willem Duyvendak is distinguished professor in sociology at the University of Amsterdam since 2003, after he had been director of the Verwey-Jonker Institute for social research (1999–2003) and professor of community development at the Erasmus University Rotterdam. His main fields of research currently are social movements, disadvantaged neighborhoods in large cities, community development, multiculturalism, urban renewal and 'feeling at home'. Some of his publications include *Policy, People, and the New Professional: De-professionalisation and Re-professionalisation in Care and Welfare* (2006, co-edited) and 'Citizen Participation in a Mediated Age: Neighbourhood Governance in the Netherlands' (2008) in *International Journal for Urban and Regional Research,* and 'Struggling to Belong: Social Movements and the Fight to Feel at Home' (2013) in *Contention in Context: Political Opportunities and the Emergence of Protest.* For more publications see: www.jwduyvendak.nl.

Conny Roggeband is assistant professor of gender and politics at the political science department of the UvA. Her research and teaching concentrates on the initiatives and responses that states take with regard to gender and ethnicity, and how social movements interact with the state. She has written on the politicization of gender-based violence, gender mainstreaming and equality policies, social movements and transnational feminist networking based on research conducted in the Netherlands, Spain and Latin America. Together with Bert Klandermans she edited *The Handbook of Social Movements across Disciplines* (Springer, 2007) and (with Van Stekelenburg and Klandermans) *The Future of Social Movement Research: Dynamics, Mechanisms and Processes* (2013). In 2014 she co-authored (with Anna van der Vleuten and Anouka van Eerdewijk) the book *Gender Equality Norms in Regional Governance: Transnational Dynamics in Europe, South America and Southern Africa* (Palgrave).

Jacquelien van Stekelenburg is associate professor of sociology (VU-University Amsterdam). She studies the social psychological dynamics of protest participation. She co-authored (with Klandermans) 'Individuals in Movements: A Social Psychology of Contention (*The Handbook of Social Movements across Disciplines,* Springer, 2007) and (with Klandermans and van der Toorn) 'Embeddedness and Grievances: Collective Action Participation Among Immigrants' (*American Sociological Review,* 2008). She edited (with Roggeband and Klandermans) *The Future of Social Movement Research: Dynamics, Mechanisms and Processes* (2013). Her current studies include a comparative study on street demonstrations (with Klandermans and Walgrave) and a study on emerging networks and feelings of belonging.

Notes

The signatures of this paper appear in alphabetical order.
1. For extensive overviews we refer to Klandermans 1997, Van Stekelenburg and Klandermans 2007, and Van Stekelenburg and Klandermans 2013.

References

Adam, B. D., J. W. Duyvendak and A. Krouwel, eds. 1999. *The Global Emergence of Gay and Lesbian Politics, National Imprints of a Worldwide Movement.* Philadelphia: Temple University Press.

Boekkooi, M. E., P. G. Klandermans and J. van Stekelenburg. 2011. 'Quarrelling and Protesting: How Organizers Shape a Demonstration'. *Mobilization* 16, no. 2: 498–508.

Bröer, C. and J. W. Duyvendak. 2009. 'Discursive Opportunities, Feeling Rules and the Rise of Protests against Aircraft Noise'. *Mobilization* 14, no. 3: 337–56.

———. 2011. 'Sensing and Seizing Opportunities: How Contentious Actors and Strategies Emerge'. In *Contention in Context: Political Opportunities and the Emergence of Protest,* ed. J. Goodwin and J. Jasper, 240–55. Stanford: Stanford California Press.

Brunsting, S., and T. Postmes. 2002. 'Social Movement Participation in the Digital Age: Predicting Offline and Online Collective Action'. *Small Group Research* 33, no. 5: 525–54.

Chabot, S., and J. W. Duyvendak. 2002. 'Globalization and Transnational Diffusion between Social Movements: Essentialist Diffusionism and Beyond'. *Theory and Society* 31: 697–740.

Damen, M. L., and J. Van Stekelenburg. Forthcoming. 'Crowd-Cleavage Alignment: Do Protest-Issues and Protesters' Cleavage Position Align?' In *Social Stratification and Social Movements: Digging in a Complex Relationship,* ed. J. Roose et al.

Doorn, M., J. Prins and S. Welschen. 2013. 'Protest Against Who? The Role of Collective Meaning Making in Politicization'. In *Dynamics, Mechanisms, and Processes: The Future of Social Movement Research,* ed. J. van Stekelenburg, C. Roggeband and P. G. Klandermans, 59–78. Minneapolis and London: University of Minnesota Press.

Duyvendak, J. W. 1994., ed. *De verzuiling van de homobeweging.* Amsterdam: SUA.

———. 1996. 'The Depoliticization of the Dutch Gay Identity, or Why Dutch Gays Aren't Queer'. In *Queer Theory/Sociology,* ed. S. Seidman, 421–38. Cambridge: Blackwell Publishers.

———. 1996a. 'Een beweging zonder natuurlijke vijand? Over de strategische dilemma's van de milieubeweging'. *Amsterdams Sociologisch Tijdschrift* 23: 144–69.

———. 1996b. 'De lotgevallen van een identiteitsbeweging onder een 'republikeins bewind'. *Sociale wetenschappen* 2: 47–67.

Duyvendak, J. W., et al., eds. 1992. *Tussen verbeelding en macht: 25 jaar nieuwe sociale bewegingen in Nederland.* Amsterdam: SUA.

Duyvendak, J.W. and J. Jasper, eds. 2015. *Breaking Down the State. Protestors Engaged,* Amsterdam: Amsterdam University Press.

Duyvendak, J. W., and T. Nederland. 2007. 'New Frontiers for Identity Politics? The Potential and Pitfalls of Patient and Civic Identity in the Dutch Patients' Health Movement'. *Research in Social Movements, Conflicts and Change* 27: 261–82.

Duyvendak, J. W., and L. Verplanke. 2013. 'Strategies for Sustainable Movements'. In *Space of Contention: Spatialities and Social Movements,* ed. W. Nicholls, J. Beaument and B. Meller, 69–83. London: Ashgate.

Giugni, M., and F. Passy. 1999. *Zwischen Konflikt und Kooperation: die Integration der Soziale Bewegingen in die Schweiz.* Chur: Ruegger.

Gladdish, K. 1987. 'Opposition in the Netherlands'. In *Opposition in Western Europe,* ed. E. Kolinsky. London and Sydney: Croom Helm.

Graaff, M. B., and C. Broer. 2012. '"We Are the Canary in a Coal Mine": Establishing a Disease Category and a New Health Risk'. *Health, Risk and Society* 14, no. 2: 129–47.

Grootegoed, G., C. Broer and J. W. Duyvendak. 2013. 'Too Ashamed to Complain: Cuts to Publicly Financed Care and Clients' Waving of Their Right to Appeal'. *Social Policy and Society* 12, no. 3: 1–12.

Hekma, G., and J. W. Duyvendak. 2011. 'The Netherlands: Depoliticization of Homosexuality and Homosexualization of Politics'. In *The Lesbian and Gay Movement and the State: Comparative Insights into a Transformed Relationship,* ed. M. Tremblay, D. Paternotte and C. Johnson, 103–17. Farnham: Ashgate.

Heijden, H. A. van der. 2000. *Tussen aanpassing en verzet: Milieubeweging en milieudiscours.* Amsterdam: AMBO.

———. 2005. 'Ecological Restoration, Environmentalism and the Dutch Politics of "New Nature"'. *Environmental Values* 14, no. 4: 427–46.

Huberts, W. 1988. *De politieke invloed van protest en pressie: Besluitvormingsprocessen over Rijkswegen.* Leiden: DSWO Press.

Jasper, J. 2004. 'A Strategic Approach to Collective Action: Looking for Agency in Social-Movement Choices'. *Mobilization* 9, no. 1: 1–16.

———. 2006. *Getting Your Way: Strategic Dilemmas in the Real World.* Chicago: Chicago University Press.

———. 2011. 'Emotions and Social Movements: Twenty Years of Theory and Research'. *Annual Review of Sociology* 37: 285–304.

———. 2012. 'Introduction'. In *Contention in Context: Political Opportunities and the Emergence of Protest,* ed. J. Goodwin and J. Jasper. Stanford: Stanford University Press.

Jasper. J. and J.W. Duyvendak. eds. 2015. *Players and Arenas. The Interactive Dynamics of Protest.* Amsterdam: Amsterdam University Press.

Kennedy, J. C. 1995. *Nieuw Babylon in aanbouw: Nederland in de jaren zestig.* Amsterdam: Boom.

Klandermans, B. 2013. 'The Dynamics of Demand'. In *Dynamics, Mechanisms, and Processes: The Future of Social Movement Research,* ed. J. van Stekelenburg, C. Roggeband and P. G. Klandermans, 3–16. Minnesota: University of Minnesota Press.

Klandermans, P. G. 1984. 'Mobilization and Participation: Social-Psychological Expansions of Resource Mobilization Theory'. *American Sociological Review* 49, no. 5: 583–600.

———. 2004. 'The Demand and Supply of Participation: Social-Psychological Correlates of Participation in Social Movements'. In *The Blackwell Companion to Social Movements,* ed. D. A. Snow, S. A. Soule and H. Kriesi. 360–379. Oxford: Blackwell Publishing.

———. 1997. *The Social Psychology of Protest.* Oxford: Blackwell.

———. 2012. 'Between Rituals and Riots: The Dynamics of Street Demonstrations'. *Mobilization* 17, no. 3: 233–35.

Klandermans, P. G., and N. Mayer. 2006. *Extreme Right Activists in Europe: Through the Magnifying Glass.* London: Routledge.

Klandermans, P. G., and D. Oegema. 1987. 'Potentials, Networks, Motivations, and Barriers: Steps toward Participation in Social Movements'. *American Sociological Review* 52: 519–531.

Klandermans, P. G., J. M. Sabucedo and M. Rodriguez. 2004. 'Inclusiveness of Identification among Farmers in The Netherlands and Galicia (Spain)'. *European Journal of Social Psychology* 34: 279–95.

Klandermans, P.G., and J. van Stekelenburg. 2013. 'Social Movements and Participation in Collective Action'. In *Oxford Handbook of Political Psychology,* ed. D. O. Sears, L. Huddy and R. Jervis, 774–812. Oxford: University Press.

Klandermans, P. G., J. van der Toorn and J. van Stekelenburg. 2008. 'Embeddedness and

Identity: Collective Action Participation among Immigrants'. *American Sociological Review* 73: 992–1012.

Klandermans, B., Van Stekelenburg, J. Damen, M.L., Van Leeuwen, A. and Van Troost, D. 2014 'Mobilization without Organization: The Case of Unaffiliated Demonstrators'. *European Sociological Review* 30(6), 702–716.

Klandermans, B., Van Stekelenburg, J. and Damen, M.L. 2016. 'Beneficiary and Conscience Constituencies: On Interests and Solidarity'. In *Austerity and Protest: Popular Contention in Times of Economic Crisis,* ed. M. Giugni and M. Grasso, 155–170. London: Ashgate.

Klein, M. van der, and S. Wieringa, eds. 2006. *Alles kon anders: Protestrepertoires in Nederland 1965–2005.* Amsterdam: Aksant.

Koopmans, R. 1995. *Democracy from Below: New Social Movements and the Political System in West Germany.* Boulder: Westview Press.

———. 1998. 'Globalization or Still National Politics? A Comparison of Protests against the Gulf War in Germany, France, and the Netherlands'. In *Social Movements in a Globalizing World,* ed. H. Kriesi, D. Della Porta and D. Rucht, 57–70. Houndmills-Basingstoke: Macmillan.

———. 2006. 'De politieke mobilisatie van allochtonen: Een vergelijking van Nederland, Duitsland, Frankrijk, Groot-Brittannië en Zwitserland'. In *Allochtonen in Nederland in internationaal perspectief,* ed. F. van Tubergen and I. Maas. Amsterdam: Amsterdam University Press, 111–36.

Koopmans, R., and J. W. Duyvendak. 1995. 'The Political Construction of the Nuclear Energy Issue and Its Impact on the Mobilization of Anti-nuclear Movements in Western Europe'. *Social Problems* 42: 235–51.

Koopmans, R., and P. Statham. 1999. 'How National Citizenship Shapes Transnationalism: A Comparative Analysis of Migrant Claims-Making in Germany, Great Britain and the Netherlands'. *Revue Européenne des Migrations Internationales* 17: 63–100.

Kriesi, H. 1987. 'De ontwikkeling van politiek protest in Nederland sinds de jaren zeventig'. *Acta Politica* 22, no. 1: 61–84.

———. 1987. 'Old and New Politics: The Dutch Peace Movement and the Traditional Political Organizations'. *European Journal of Political Science* 15: 319–46.

———. 1988. 'Local Mobilization Processes in the Dutch Peace Movement'. In *From Structure to Action: Social Movement Participation Across Cultures,* ed. P. G. Klandermans, H. Kriesi and S. Tarrow, 41–82. Greenwich: JAI-Press.

———. 1989. 'The Mobilization Potential of the New Social Movements in the Netherlands in 1986 and 1987: Its Structural and Cultural Basis'. In *New Social Movements and Value Change,* ed. H. B. G. Ganzeboom and H. Flap, 51–88. Amsterdam: Siswo Publications.

———. 1989. 'The Political Opportunity Structure of the Dutch Peace Movement'. *West European Politics* 12: 295–312.

———. 1989. 'New Social Movements and the New Class in the Netherlands'. *American Journal of Sociology* 94: 1078–116.

Kriesi, H., et al. 1992. 'New Social Movements and Political Opportunities in Western Europe'. *European Journal of Political Research* 22: 219–44.

———. 1995. *New Social Movements in Western Europe: A Comparative Analysis.* Minneapolis: University of Minnesota Press.

Linden, A., and P. G. Klandermans. 2007. 'Revolutionaries, Wanderers, Converts, and Compliants: Life Histories of Extreme Right Activists'. *Journal of Contemporary Ethnography* 36: 184–201.

Linden, M. van der. 2002. *Globalizing Labour Historiography: The IISH Approach.* Amsterdam: International Institute of Social History.

Loo, H. van der, E. Snel and B. van Steenbergen. 1984. *Een wenkend perspectief? Nieuwe sociale bewegingen en culturele veranderingen.* Amersfoort: De Horstink.

Lombardo, E., P. Meier and M. Verloo, eds. 2009. *The Discursive Politics of Gender Equality: Stretching, Bending and Policymaking.* London: Routledge.

Mamadouh, V. 1992. *De stad in eigen hand: Provo's, kabouters en krakers als stedelijke sociale beweging.* Amsterdam: UvA.

Meijer, I. C. 1996. *Het persoonlijke wordt politiek: Feministische bewustwording in Nederland 1965–1980.* Amsterdam: Het Spinhuis.

Mossink, M. 1995. *De levenbrengsters: Over vrouwen, vrede, feminisme en politiek in Nederland 1914–1940.* Amsterdam: IISG.

Noort, W. Van. 1988. *Bevlogen bewegingen: Een vergelijking van de anti-kernenergie, kraaken milieubeweging.* Amsterdam: SUA.

Oegema, D., and P.G. Klandermans. 1994. 'Why Social Movement Sympathizers Don't Participate: Erosion and Non-conversion of Support'. *American Sociological Review* 59, no. 5: 703–22.

Outshoorn, J. 1994. 'Between Movement and Government: "Femocrats" in the Netherlands'. *Schweizerisches Jahrbuch für Politische Wissenschaft* 34: 141–63.

———. 1997. 'Incorporating Feminism: The Women's Policy Network in the Netherlands'. In *Sex Equality Policy in Western Europe*, ed. F. Gardiner, 109–27. London and New York: Routledge.

———. 2000. 'Op zoek naar de vrouwenbeweging in de jaren negentig'. In *Emancipatie en subcultuur: Sociale bewegingen in Belgie en Nederland*, ed. T. Sunier, et al., 30–49. Amsterdam: Instituut voor Publiek en Politiek.

———. 2009. *Vrouwenbewegingen in internationaal perspectief.* Leiden: Universiteit Leiden

Poldervaart, S.1992. 'Het verdwijnen en weer opkomen van het vrouwenvraagstuk: De politieke vrouwenorganisaties en de vrouwenbeweging in de periode 1948–1973'. *Tijdschrift voor vrouwenstudies* 13, no. 2: 162–82.

———. 2003. 'Utopianism and Sexual Politics in Dutch Social Movements (1830–2003)'. *Conference Past and Present of Radical Sexual Politics, Amsterdam, 3–4 October.* Amsterdam: University of Amsterdam.

———. 2007. 'How Utopianism Disappeared from Dutch Socialist Feminism (1970–1989)'. *Spaces of Utopia* 6: 36.

Poldervaart, S., ed. 2002. *Leven volgens je idealen: De andere politieken van huidige sociale bewegingen in Nederland.* Amsterdam: Aksant.

Post, V., J. Oldersma and J. Outshoorn. 2006. 'Overwinteren of geruisloze mobilisatie? Ontwikkelingen in "de vrouwenbeweging" in Nederland sinds de jaren negentig'. *Tijdschrift voor Genderstudies* 9, no. 2: 12–25.

Postmes, T., S. A. Haslam and R. I. Swaab. 2005. 'Social Identity in Small Groups: An Interactive Model of Social Identity Formation'. *European Review of Social Psychology* 16: 1–42.

Regtien, T. 1988. *Springtij: Herinneringen aan de jaren zestig.* Zieken: Wereldvenster.

Ribberink, A. 1998. *Leidsvrouwen en zaakwaarneemsters: Een geschiedenis van de Aktiegroep Man Vrouw Maatschappij (MVM) 1968–1973.* Hilversum: Verloren.

Righart, H. 1995. *De eindeloze jaren zestig: Geschiedenis van een generatieconflict.* Amsterdam/Antwerpen: Uitgeverij De Arbeiderspers.

Roggeband, C. 2002. *Over de grenzen van de politiek: Een vergelijkende studie maar de opkomst en ontwikkeling van de vrouwenbeweging tegen seksueel geweld in Nederland en Spanje.* Assen: Van Gorcum.

———. 2004. 'Instantly I Thought We Should Do the Same Thing: International Inspiration and Exchange in Feminist Action against Sexual Violence'. *European Journal of Women's Studies* 11, no. 2: 159–75.

———. 2007. Translators and Transformers: International Inspiration and Exchange in Social Movements. *Social Movement Studies* 6, no. 3: 245–59.

———. 2010. 'Transnational Networks and Institutions: How Diffusion Shaped the Politicization of Sexual Harassment in Europe'. In *The Diffusion of Social Movements: Actors, Mechanisms, and Political Effects,* ed. K. Givan, et al. Cambridge: Cambridge University Press.

Roggeband, C. 2014. Gender mainstreaming in Dutch development cooperation: the dialectics of progress. *Journal of International Development,* 26, no. 3: 332–344.

Roggeband, C. forthcoming. Understanding the dynamics of opposition to gender equality: lessons from social movement theory. In *Opposition to Gender Equality.* Ed. M. Verloo. London: Routledge.

Roggeband, C., and A. van Eerdewijk. 2014. 'Reconceptualizing Gender Equality Norm Diffusion and Regional Governance: Logics and Geometries'. In *Gender Equality Norms in Regional Governance: Transnational Dynamics in Europe, South America and South Africa,* ed. J. M. Van der Vleuten, A. Van Eerdewijk and C. Roggeband. Houndmills: Palgrave.

Rossum, H. Van. 1992. 'De gesubsidiëerde revolutie? De geschiedenis van de vrouwenbeweging, 1968–1989'. In *Tussen Verbeelding en Macht. 25 jaar nieuwe sociale bewegingen in Nederland,* ed. J. W. Duyvendak, et al., 161–81. Amsterdam: SUA.

Simon, B., and P. G. Klandermans. 2001. 'Towards a Social Psychological Analysis of Politicized Collective Identity: Conceptualization, Antecedents, and Consequences'. *American Psychologist* 56, no. 4: 319–31.

Stekelenburg, J. van. 2012. 'The Occupy Movement, product of its time?' *Development,* 55, no. 2: 224–231.

Stekelenburg, J. van and M. Boekkooi. 2013. 'Mobilizing for Change in a Changing Society'. In *Dynamics, Mechanisms, and Processes: The Future of Social Movement Research,* ed. J. van Stekelenburg, C. Roggeband and P. G. Klandermans, 217–34. Minneapolis and London: University of Minnesota Press.

Stekelenburg, J. van, and P. G. Klandermans. 2007. 'Individuals in Movements: A Social Psychology of Contention'. In *The Handbook of Social Movements across Disciplines,* ed. P. G. Klandermans and C. Roggeband, 157–204. New York: Springer.

———. 2013. 'The Social Psychology of Protest'. *Current Sociology* 61: 886–905.

Stekelenburg, J. van, P. G. Klandermans, and W. W. van Dijk. 2009. 'Context Matters: Explaining Why and How Mobilizing Context Influences Motivational Dynamics'. *Journal of Social Issues* 65, no. 4: 815–38.

———. 2011. 'Combining Motivations and Emotion: The Motivational Dynamics of Collective Action Participation'. *Revista de Psicología Social* 26, no. 1: 91–104.

Stekelenburg, J. van, D. Van Troost and A. Van Leeuwen. 2012. 'Politicized Identity'. In *The Blackwell Encyclopedia of Social and Political Movements*, ed. D. A. Snow, D. Della Porta, B. Klandermans and D. McAdam, 974–977. Malden: Blackwell.

Stekelenburg, J. van, D. Oegema and P.G. Klandermans. 2010. 'No Radicalization without Identification: How Ethnic Dutch and Dutch Muslim Web Forums Radicalize over Time'. In *Identity and Participation in Culturally Diverse Societies: A Multidisciplinary Perspective*, ed. A. Azzi, et al., 256–74. Oxford: Blackwell Wiley.

Stekelenburg, J. van, et al. 2012. 'Contextualizing Contestation: Framework, Design, and Data'. *Mobilization* 17, no. 3: 249–62.

———. 2013. 'From Correlation to Causation: The Cruciality of a Collectivity in the Context of Collective Action'. Special issue on 'Societal Change' for the *Journal of Social and Political Psychology*.

Sunier, T. 1998. 'Islam and Interest Struggle: Religious Collective Action among Turkish Muslims in the Netherlands'. In *Muslim European Youth: Reproducing Ethnicity, Religion, Culture*, ed. S. Vertovec and A. Rogers, 39–59. Aldershot: Ashgate.

Sunier, T., et al., eds. 2000. *Emancipatie en subcultuur: sociale bewegingen in België en Nederland*. Amsterdam: Instituut voor Publiek en Politiek.

Valkenburg, B. 1995. *Participatie en sociale bewegingen. Een bijdrage aan de theorievorming over participatie, emancipatie en sociale bewegingen*. Utrecht: Arkel.

Verloo, M. 1992. *Macht en gender in sociale bewegingen. Over de participatie van vrouwen in bewonersorganisaties*. Amsterdam: SUA.

Verloo, M., ed. 2007. *Multiple Meanings of Gender Equality. A Critical Frame Analysis of Gender Policies in Europe*. Budapest: CPS Books.

Vliegenthart, R., D. van Oegema and P. G. Klandermans. 2005. 'Media Coverage and Organizational Support in the Dutch Environmental Movement'. *Mobilization* 10, no. 3: 365–81.

Waaldijk, B. 1998. *Feministische Openbaarheid: De nationale Tentoonstelling van Vrouwenarbeid*. Amsterdam: IISG/IIAV.

Weerd, M. de, and P.G. Klandermans. 1999. 'Group Identification and Social Protest: Farmers' Protest in the Netherlands'. *European Journal of Social Psychology* 29: 1073–95.

Wille, A. 1994. *The Accidental Activist Potential: Political Participation in the Netherlands*. Amsterdam: UvA.

Withuis, J. 1990. *Opoffering en heroïek: de mentale wereld van een communistische vrouwenorganisatie in naoorlogs Nederland, 1946–1976*. Amsterdam: Boom.

Zomeren, M. van, T. Postmes, and R. Spears. 2008. 'Toward an Integrative Social Identity Model of Collective Action: A Quantitative Research Synthesis of Three Sociopsychological Perspectives'. *Psychological Bulletin* 134: 504–35.

———. 2012. 'On Conviction's Collective Consequences: Integrating Moral Conviction with the Social Identity Model of Collective Action'. *British Journal of Social Psychology* 51: 52–71.

Zomeren, M. van, et al. 2004. 'Put Your Money Where Your Mouth Is! Explaining Collective Action Tendencies through Group-Based Anger and Group Efficacy'. *Journal of Personality and Social Psychology* 87, no. 5: 649–64.

Chapter 14

From Splendid Isolation to Joining the Concert of Nations
Social Movement Studies in France

Olivier Fillieule

In the eyes of foreign analysts, in political terms, France is characterised by three traits: its 'strong state', fairly impervious to pressure from a feebly organised civil society (Kriesi et al. 1995); a very low level of social capital, as measured by participation in associations (Vassallo 2010); and, nonetheless, displaying a driving propensity for political activism *via* unconventional political participation (Duyvendak 1994; Kriesi et al. 1995). This country, culturally springing from the Revolutions of 1789, 1830 and 1848, and marked by several great events, the Paris Commune of 1871, and the strikes of the Popular Front in 1936 and May 1968, could lay claim to being an archetype of 'demonstration democracy' (Etzioni 1970). However, although it was in France that the very first publications on mass movements appeared (by Henri Taine, Gustave Le Bon and Gabriel Tarde), the sociology of social movements continued marginally in this country right up to the early 1970s until the emergence of what is known as the 'new social movements paradigm' of which Alain Touraine was certainly one of the first representatives. However, while dominant in France in the 1970s and quite influential in Latin America, Tourainian sociology stood alone, isolated in international debates, and his star faded rapidly under the combined blows of the questioning of a so-called 'identity paradigm' and the desertion of some European researchers initially trained in the Tourainian tradition, at the forefront of which was Alberto Melucci and his increasingly controversial method of 'sociological intervention'. As a result, the study of social movements in France almost disappeared for over a decade, and collaboration between French and foreign researchers in this area became increasingly rare.

It was not until the 1990s that this academic field in France witnessed a revival, and indeed exponential growth, becoming the site of a significant accumulation of knowledge. While it would be impossible at this point to exhaustively enumerate all the relevant studies, they are summarised in three books: an encyclopaedia of social movements in France (Crettiez and Sommier 2006); a dictionary of social movements (Fillieule, Mathieu and Péchu 2009); and a handbook (Fillieule, Agrikoliansky and Sommier 2010). The specific aim of this chapter is to highlight the particular nature of French research and research on France. I will proceed in three steps. After I consider the stages of research development in this field of social science since the 1950s, I will offer several explanatory hypotheses of this evolution, culminating in the highlighting of certain aspects, which I believe distinguish the research produced in France from that of other European or North American research.

A History in Four Stages

First stage. In the 1950s and 1960s, the dominant academic paradigm in social history associated a macro-historical vision founded in part on the Labroussian paradigm (Revel 1996) and reified aggregates (social 'classes' as historical actors). In working-class social history, the social group serves as a collective hero, with activist groups as its most conscious expression. Characterised, implicitly and explicitly, by intellectual empathy, with the authors themselves being participants in the workers' movement, this research quickly gave great importance to the working-class activist, conferring on activist biographies a determining role from the very outset. In the postwar period, biographies of activists abounded. The *Biographical Dictionary of the French Workers' Movement* (Maitron 1964, 1997), a collective work of a community of historians united in their empathetic relationship with the 'workers' movement,' was its major achievement. In this context, the history of the French communist party and communist activists became a central concern. On one hand, there was an edifying history, supported by the quasi-official historians of the Party and, on the other, an eventful political history of communism, which challenged this instrumentalised history from the 1950s onwards. Annie Kriegel published a landmark essay on *Les Communistes français* in 1968, in which she developed the theme of the communist 'counter-society' and made the 'permanent' communist a dedicated, disciplined, nondescript and blind activist, hence opening doors for a sociology of communist activism, despite its intrinsic weaknesses (Pudal 1989).

Second stage. In the early 1970s, a fundamental shift in the issue, simultaneously academic, cognitive and political, gradually contributed to deflect the dominant paradigm into two main directions.

In the wake of the so-called new social movements, which appeared at the start of the decade, Alain Touraine and his team initiated a major trend in sociology. They undertook to construct a 'great theory' of social movements from a more comprehensive perspective, one that kept its distance from individual strategic rationality and questioned the processes by which collective actors would create solidarity and collective identities (Touraine 1973, 1978). Using Marxist analytical frameworks, the Tourainian school followed in the footsteps of the earlier analysts of the emerging inter-classist social movements, already published in Germany. They took into account (and perhaps for granted) the disappearance of the working class as a central actor in *the* social movement. Thus, a series of case studies was published on the anti-nuclear movement, the student movement, the mobilization of peripheral regions against the Jacobin state, and the Solidarity movement in Poland. However, Touraine's contribution remained at the fringes of academic debates, while the identity paradigm spread throughout much of Europe, via, among others, Alberto Melucci, his former student. Another research trend emerged during those years, focused on what was referred to as the 'urban social movements' and following Manuel Castells (1983; see Péchu 2006 for a review). However, these works have deliberately developed at a distance from social movement studies (Pickvance 1985) in spite of a number of common research questions and even field research.

In research on activism, less objectified and substantialist approaches than was formerly the case began to appear. Substantialism did not limit itself to the social group (the class), but also touched on other analytical categories that had to be deconstructed because they were still attached to the objectification of collective actors: 'the' activist, 'the believer/member', 'believing/membership', 'the' party or 'the organization', 'the' leadership of a particular group, etc. If we restrict ourselves to working-class history alone, we find that many works now studied the development of the workers' group from a socio-genetic perspective, following in the footsteps of E. P. Thompson and his seminal work, *The Making of the English Working Class* (1966), although this was only translated in 1988. We will not discuss this research in detail here. Gérard Noiriel has provided an outline of a synthesis of this work under a title deliberately at odds with substantialism, *Les ouvriers dans la société française, XIXe-XXe* (2007). The perspective he adopted profoundly altered earlier interpretive frameworks.

This shifting of the issue did not lead to a new unified historians' paradigm but rather to the multiplication of viewpoints or analytical scales. Nonetheless, certain key points may be discerned. First, increasing recourse to prosopography (or collective biography) allows us to study smaller activist groups and from various perspectives. This shift is especially true in the field of history. On the other hand, edifying biographies or autobiographies of activists were replaced by self-critical autobiographies by activists. In sociology and political science, research not only focused more specifically on questions raised by the Olsonian paradigm (Gaxie 1977) but also on Max Weber and Bourdieu's sociological reflection on the phenomena of political delegation and representation. This scientifically constructed doubt, combined with the resistance to substantialism, gave rise to the development of multiple analytical frameworks for activism. Introducing a break between activism and the motives claimed by activists, between activists and the groups they represent, this shifting of the issue helped to raise questions about the contradictions inherent in activism. Research gradually moved to a collection of analyses which are more critical of workers' activism, questioning their 'motivations', sometimes psychoanalysing their commitment, always insisting on the specific issues of representation, on social predispositions of the spokesperson, and on selective incentives or rewards for activism (symbolic, therapeutic, financial, promotional, social capital, cultural and other rewards).

Third stage. From the late 1970s onwards, French research in the field gradually slumped into a period of generalised sluggishness. On one hand, the pursuit by Tourainians of the 'true' social movement petered out and, on the other, there was little research on activism, in a political context (the 1980s) when the resurgence of the left to a position of power seemed to have permanently demobilised social movements (Duyvendak 1994). Now, this was precisely the time when, for reasons mentioned in the general introduction to this volume, there was a rapprochement between North American authors writing about the mobilization of resources and European researchers (Tarrow, Klandermans and Kriesi 1988). In spite of some rare but important efforts to disseminate the work of American writers and a few isolated publications of critical discussion of American literature (Birnbaum and Chazel 1971; Chazel 1975, 1993; Dobry 1986), the transplant did not succeed.[1] When Dieter Rucht was drawing up a description of the state of the art in the sociology of social movements in Europe and the United States, he could not find a single author to write a chapter on France (1991).

Fourth stage. At the start of the 1990s, the landscape was rapidly transformed, with a flourishing of initiatives in political sociology. At Sciences Po Paris, following Pierre Favre, there was renewed interest in protest activity (Favre 1990), and a series of PhD dissertations appeared in Sciences Po on the subject of demonstrations (Fillieule 1997), movements of illegal immigrants (Siméant 1998), the League for Human Rights (Agrikoliansky 2002) and the homeless movement (Péchu 2006). It was also at Sciences Po Paris that in 1994 Nonna Mayer and Olivier Fillieule created the Study and Research Group on Transformations in Activism (GERMM), a standing group of the Association Française de Science Politique that, for over twenty years, spearheaded a revival in research on political participation, then referred to as 'unconventional'.[2] At the same time, at the University Paris 1/Sorbonne, Philippe Braud launched a research program on political violence (Braud 1993) which gave rise to a series of doctoral studies (Bruneteaux 1996; Sommier 1998; Duclos 1998; Crettiez 1999), while Michel Offerlé supervised a number of projects on forms of collective action (Contamin, 2001 on the petition; Mariot 2006 on collective effervescence; Cossart 2013 on political meetings; Giraud 2009 on strikes).

This whole-scale recrudescence was enacted by a new generation of researchers who, encouraged by a few of their elders and supported by a number of European and North American Francophile (and often French-speaking) colleagues, started to investigate both hitherto neglected empirical topics and imported North American theories and concepts. Representative of this trend is the appearance, at the start of the decade, of two textbooks exploring the scope and range of the North American literature (Mann 1992; Fillieule and Péchu 1993) and an edited volume in which, for the first time, the principal references were in English (Fillieule 1993).

This new era was also characterised by three striking traits. One was the lack of comparative research and publications, apart from a few rare exceptions (e.g. Sommier 1998). Another was the preponderant role of research dedicated to repertories of action, in other words, to protest performances, signalling the triumph of Charles Tilly, who was still scorned by historians (e.g. Bourguinat 2002). For example, there were publications on demonstrations (Favre 1990; Fillieule 1997; Fillieule and Tartakowsky 2008), marches (*Le Mouvement social* 2003), hunger strikes (Siméant 1998; 2009), the barricades (Corbin and Mayeur 1997), petitions (Contamin 2001), squats (Péchu 2006, 2010), self-immolation (Grojean 2006), rent strikes (Hmed 2006), public meetings (Cossart 2013), strikes (Béroud et al. 2008; Giraud 2009; *Politix* 2009a and b); banquets (Robert 2009), ethical consumption (Dubuisson-Quellier 2009; ; 2010; 2014) and suburban riots (Waddington, Jobard and King 2009). Also, there was examination, beyond the forms of open, more immediate forms of protest, of the inclusion of modes of resistance to authority, starting with the research of James Scott, associated with the initiative to import social movement theory in research on the MENA (Middle East and North Africa) region (Bennani-Chraïbi and Fillieule 2003, 2012; Zaki 2005), on Latin America (e.g. Massal 2005) and on black Africa (Lafargue 1996; Pommerolle and Siméant 2009; Siméant, 2014) on the one hand. Furthermore, there was renewed interest in the modes of action deployed by those with the most resources (Pinçon and Pinçon-Charlot 2007; Offerlé 2009) who tend to adopt a phenomenological approach attentive both to performances as situated action composed of exchanges of blows and to the meaning that the actors give the situation.

On the other hand, while the period was characterised by a resurgence of research on labour movement, unions and strikes, the activism under examination was above all a 'novelty'. Research focused on the 'new struggles' of the day which were observable *in situ*. These included political associations (ATTAC; and SOS racism, Juhem 1998); solidarity movements (Lechien 2003; Duchesne 2003); humanitarian commitments (Dauvin and Siméant 2002; Collovald et al. 2002; Parizot 2003; Zunigo 2003); the struggles of the most deprived populations such as the homeless and unemployed for example (Fillieule 1993; Maurer 2001; Pierru 2003; Dunezat 2004; Péchu 2006; Mathieu 2006; Garcia 2005; Mouchard 2009; Chabanet and Faniel 2012); new union organizations (Bruneau 2006, on the Peasant Confederation of José Bové); battles on specific issues (Broqua 2005; Broqua and Fillieule 2001; Voegtli 2009, on AIDS and issues around homosexuality), or prostitution (Mathieu 2001); and associations connected with immigration (Siméant 1998; Hamidi 2006; Hmed 2006), the environment (Ollitrault 2008) and anti-globalization (Agrikoliansky, Fillieule and Mayer 2005; Agrikoliansky and Sommier 2005, Sommier, Fillieule and Agrikoliansky 2008). Other forms of political activism are studied from both a socio-genetic perspective and fresh analytical approaches: localised analysis and that of networks (Sawicki 1997; Mischi 2010 on left-wing political parties); as well as forms of activist reconversion (Fretel 2004). Political activism became quite diverse, from the National Front (Boumaza 2002; Bizeul 2003) to the Trotskyist party (LCR) (Johsua 2011) and right-wing parties (Bargel 2009; Haegel 2012). Finally, ''68' began to interest university researchers (Damamme et al. 2008; Pagis 2009), long after Isabelle Sommier published her ground-breaking thesis devoted to this issue from the perspective of a comparative analysis of France and Italy (Sommier 1996).

Today, the sociology of social movements is a structured sub-field, with its standing groups and distribution lists, its conferences and its seminars, a considerable number of publications, its dedicated series and, of course, its textbooks (Mann 1992; Fillieule and Péchu 1993; Neveu 1996; Mathieu 2004, 2012; Cefaï 2007; Fillieule, Mathieu and Péchu 2009; Fillieule, Agrikoliansky and Sommier 2010). French social movement scholars have increasingly attended international conferences and published more and more in English. North American references are no longer perceived as 'exotic', even if they are only rarely taken for granted.

The Factors Involved in the Turnaround

But how can we explain this upheaval in the 1990s outlined above? A thorough response to such a question requires us to draw upon epistemological instruments and the sociology of science. My remarks here are more modest in scope and I will simply mention some endogenous and exogenous factors allowing me to somewhat better explain the context of the last twenty-five years.

The first hypothesis that comes to mind when reflecting on the development of the sociology of social movements in France is that of the thrust of real history (see introduction to this volume). The generation in France which assumed control of this renewal of the sociology of social movements was socialised politically in the 1980s, the era of the socialist presidency of François Mitterrand who administered a blow to the social movements of the 1970s, fostered the increased power of the extreme right by introducing an electoral reform, and supported, even gave birth to, the anti-racist movements mobilizing youth against the traditional right (Duyvendak 1994; Juhem 1998). These years also saw the emergence of different public problems linked to the deteriorating economic situation, with the media beginning to speak about the 'new poverty' and the 'working poor', starting in 1984, at the time of the emergence of movements giving voice to the homeless, unemployed, etc. There were also many in this generation who were marked by the student movement of November–December 1986 against yet another university reform defended by the right, which had returned to power in March of that year. The serious difficulties surrounding the Parisian demonstrations of this movement, which gave rise to two parliamentary commissions of inquiry, played a key role in sparking the first research projects on street demonstrations (Favre 1990). This gradual renewal of social conflicts was further fuelled by the vast strike movement in the winter of 1995 and the spring of 2003, and gave rise to a new formulation of the social question which partially explains the emergence and success of the anti-globalization movement.

While this relative political effervescence generated an enkindling of research, this was also due to the formative role of its financing by public bodies. Thus, a number of state agencies financed or co-financed a good part of the research mentioned above, on the changes in participation in organizations, illegal immigrants, homeless, the battle against AIDS and environmental mobilization. A point which should be further stressed is that French researchers have long scantily benefited from research funding sources established by European bodies, depriving themselves of a major source of research financing on mainland Europe, exacerbated by the fact that, until the recent creation of the Agence Nationale de la Recherche (ANR), there was no equivalent in France to the National Science Foundation in the United States or the National Fund for Scientific Research in Belgium or Switzerland. This is added to the aforesaid endogenous elements related to the profound transformations in the academic field at the end of the twentieth century and which particularly affected the rather self-centred French Academy.

Finally, and I would like to stress this point, the renewal of the sociology of social movements is occurring at a crucial moment when the dominant contentious politics paradigm is still dominant but increasingly challenged. While the development, since the 1970s and 1980s, of a collection of works based on shared and consistent concepts and common methodological instruments was a necessary condition for the emergence of this sub-discipline, since the end of the 1990s the evolution of 'normal science' within this 'paradigm' seems to have gone as far as it could go. As with any paradigm, the model proposed by the adherents of the contentious politics approach has for the last two decades superficially responded to the critiques to which it has been subject without any deep-seated reform. It has become a sort of out-of-control monster, absorbing dissident works, the theoretical unity of which is more due to the strength of the institutions that structure it than to the consistency of the research program and theoretical tools it offers. In this context, the survival of key concepts (political opportunities, organizations and resources, contexts, and repertories of actions undertaken) is increasingly achieved at the cost of their lessening capacity to explain the protest phenomena and, especially, to give rise to new research questions. This means that we are moving towards a hybrid and multi-centred approach rather than to a new coherent paradigm (Smelser speaks about a *hybrid subfield* [2003] with respect to the sociology of social movements) based not only on a variety of disciplinary foundations but also on a diversity of intellectual and social contexts. This fragmentation of research agendas, methods and conceptual systems that main proponents of the contentious politics paradigm deplore, was particularly well received in France where, in a number of ways, this was anticipated. The fruitfulness of critical sociology, the suspicion towards positivist administration of proof and construction of argumentation, and the lack of success of stratospheric comparisons and of quantophrenia in favour of different forms of qualitative analyses can only reinforce the desire to further the dialogue with a sociology of social movements in the process of reinventing itself.

Across Borders: France within the Broader Academic Landscape

French publications in the field of social movements are increasingly anchored in the international literature. They are also distinguished both by their theoretical orientations, their refusal to be limited to a sub-discipline and, therefore, their fresh approach and, finally, by their choice of methods.

In terms of theoretical orientations, the intellectual influence of Marxist concepts, the socio-genetic and configurational thought of Norbert Elias and Bourdieusian critical sociology, and the expanding dominance of an inter-actionist paradigm in the domain of research on activism all give a relatively original coloration to current research, resulting in a series of alternatives to the dominant but contested paradigm of contentious politics (McAdam, Tarrow and Tilly 2001).[3]

Consideration of the emergence and development of a particular way of doing social science, inspired by contributions from socio-history (Bu-ton 2009b and the journal *Genèses*) and, thus, especially attentive to the genealogies of labels, causes and groups (Boltanski 1982), is essential to un-derstanding the French touch. This point brings us back to the promise of an approach referred to as constructivist, in tune with the work of Pierre Bourdieu, which leads to a questioning of the construction of groups by the state and by the groups themselves and thus to the struggles to form groups, such as the 'workers movement,' and 'the communist party' (Offerlé 1984; Pudal 1989), and generate collective identities. Along with the construction of groups comes the need to reflect on the construction of causes going be-yond the conundrum of interest versus altruism to focus on grasping the ways in which the processes affect the 'generalization of a cause' (Boltanski and Thévenot 1991) and the broadening of the causes in a less strategic way than suggested by framing analysis. Finally, while in the North American literature, the actors are often reduced to mere shadow puppet theatre, or disappear completely behind the holy trinity of political opportunity struc-tures, mobilizing structures and framing strategies. French researchers have explored the question of activism and the process of engagement much fur-ther, especially with reference to an interactionist model of careers (Fillieule 2001, 2010).

Doug McAdam and Hilary Shaffer Boudet recently launched a whole-hearted plea for an opening of the sociology of social movements, which in its academic structure is increasingly cut off from the rest of social science, withdrawn into its own world of reference and only working on 'mobili-zation, those who mobilise, and in general, internal movement dynamics. … Instead of situating movements in a fuller constellation of political and economic forces and actors, movements and movement groups increasingly came to be the central animating focus of the field' (2012: 21–22) This re-proach is much less meaningful for French research, which, since the outset, has operated in different sub-fields of social science and, thus, developed a constant dialogue with other disciplinary worlds.

This started with the activities of CEVIPOF (*Centre de recherches politiques de Sciences Po*) and, more particularly, GERMM, which contributed to not separating the research field on social movements from that focused on political participation, as has often been the case elsewhere. Therefore, the use of individual-level data has been integrated into the range of methodological approaches of social movement scholars since the beginning of the 1990s. Similarly, very early on, a dialogue was initiated with specialists in public policy (Muller and Surel 1998; Balme and Chabanet 2002; Lascoumes and Le Gallès 2007). This was particularly enriched by the connection established with the sociology of public scandals (Rayner 2005; Latté 2008), with the field of professional expertise (especially that of public health (Barbot 2002; Pinell 2002) and that of ecology (Ollitrault 2008), and finally with the literature on social problems, inspired by the work of Joseph Gusfield.[4] Consequently, much research has been produced at the boundaries of these different subfields, whether on the impact of alcohol and the consumption of tobacco on public health (Berlivet 2000), or the opposition to large-scale development projects (Valluy 1996; Lolive 1999; Fillieule 2003) or public policies for deaf and mutes (Buton 2009a) or retirees (Lambelet 2011) and the responses they elicited from the groups concerned. Finally, directly inspired by socio-legal studies developed by the law and society movement in the United States, a number of researchers have worked on the recourse to the legal system and legal action by protest groups, generating a now extensive body of work (see Israël 2009 and Agrikoliansky 2010 for a review). Furthermore, a number of media and cultural studies specialists, with Neveu in the forefront (1999), have established links between the sociology of media and the sociology of mobilization (Juhem 1999; Féron 2012). This represents an especially valuable contribution since the 1980s and 1990s were dominated internationally by protest event analysis, based on the written press as a source, without really questioning the logic of relying on media accounts of events. Also, the driving force of gender studies in the twenty-first century was partially to be found at the intersection of the sociology of activism and the sociology of work, thus, of the sociology of professions (Bereni 2007; Fillieule and Roux 2009; Leclercq and Pagis 2011).

Last but not least, we have witnessed the regeneration of the sociology of activism from an interactionist perspective, apparent in the last decade. This has had the effect of directly bringing together research in the slightly marginalised studies on socialization, understood as an assembly of conscious or unconscious processes by which, throughout their lives, individuals internalise the standards of authorities as diverse as the family, school, the professional milieu, their partners, etc. Consequently, contrary to the North American academic field where, as Virginia Sapiro (1989) remarked, researchers specializing in the sub-field of studies of socialization have kept their distance from the sociology of activism, French specialists in activism have considered questions about socialization studies as pivotal. This gives rise to reasoning in terms of 'careers' (Becker 1963), leading us to examine a number of essential dimensions of social identities and offering a powerful tool for thinking about relations between individuals and institutions, starting with forms of institutional socialization. These include (1) the acquisition of know-how and interpersonal skills, (2) a vision of the world (ideology) and (3) the restructuring of networks of sociability, in association with the construction of individual and collective identities (social networks and identities). In this area, ethnographic qualitative approaches prove best able to analyse activist work and its social division, starting with the observation that collectives are necessarily heterogeneous.

This last remark leads us to emphasise the particular nature of approaches developed in France in terms of methods. On the one hand, the French usually exercise caution with respect to undue simplifications of a stratospheric comparativism, which end up by losing sight of the weight of the historical, social, cultural, and economic contexts in which social movements are rooted. The numerous French studies referred to in this chapter readily demonstrate that we learn more about the dynamic of protests and collective action from in-depth case studies than in compiling vast databases that risk stripping the selected explanatory factors of all meaning. Faced with the 'heavy industry' of North American research, the still structurally hand-crafted dimension of French research, encouraging qualitative research over quantitative, is not a handicap, but rather an advantage. It offers a genuine means of investigating many paths outlined in theory but rather unexplored in practice, due to the lack of suitable methodological tools: the logic of activist trajectories; emotions and feelings (Traïni 2009, 2011); the dynamic of events; and the face-to-face interactions comprising the texture of protest.

The collection of work that in the United States or in Europe adopts this perspective (e.g. Snow and Anderson 1993; Lichterman 1996; Auyero 2003; Wood 2003; Mische 2008) demonstrates that this methodological renewal offers a fruitful avenue for future research, and an exciting opportunity for French researchers.

Finally, to conclude, one must acknowledge that, unlike in the United States where the success of social movement studies has produced an effect of closing off the field, its exponential development in France has, on the contrary, been reflected in the invasive spreading of its instruments and issues into a great number of academic domains. There is an important point of convergence with the increasingly voiced ambition across the Atlantic to reposition the study of protest activities in the context of the political, economic and social relations which surround them, taking into account the multiplicity of actors involved and their strategies. From this perspective, the recent propositions of James Jasper and Jan Willem Duyvendak (2015) or Neil Fligstein and Doug McAdam (2012) are very promising. It is in placing these social movements once again in their environment that we may hope to escape a disciplinary closing-in that too often leads to esoteric language and concepts, routinization and closing off the references employed. At the level of professionalization and autonomization to which the sociology of social movements has arrived, where it is no longer necessary for it to shut itself off in order to secure its very existence, in terms of methodological principles, it is time once again to most carefully heed this warning of Peter Berger (1963): 'That, in truth, a good part of what passes for sociology could be labelled barbarous, if by that we mean displaying an ignorance of history and philosophy, a narrow field of expertise, lacking broader horizons, a preoccupation with technical matters and a complete absence of literary sensitivity'.

Olivier Fillieule is a research director at the CNRS (Sorbonne University, Paris), a professor of political sociology at Lausanne University (IEPI/Institute for Political and International Studies) and a member of CRAPUL (Research centre on political action at Lausanne University). His latest books include *Demonstrations* (with D. Tartakowsky). A list of his research interests and publications is available on http://unil.academia.edu/OlivierFillieule.

Notes

1. It is only in the twenty-first century that many translated articles were contributing to popularizing the North American literature for a public which was largely not Anglophone via a number of edited volumes (Cefaï and Trom 2001; Bennani-Chraïbi and Fillieule 2003; Fillieule 2005; Fillieule and Della Porta 2006; Sommier, Fillieule and Agrikoliansky 2008). Finally, let us mention here the recent translation of *Contentious Politics* by Tilly and Tarrow (2008) and *Freedom Summer* by McAdam (2012).

2. On the transformation of activism, also see the research of Jacques Ion (1997), who prompted a lively debate in the French academic community.

3. To which must be added the emergence of a 'pragmatist' path of analysis initiated among others by Louis Quéré and Daniel Cefaï, but which for the moment is limited to a collection of normative prescriptions more than an empirical research program. Please see Cefaï and Trom (2001) and Cefaï (2007).

4. Including the book *The Culture of Public Problems*, which was translated in 2009 by Daniel Cefaï.

References

Agrikoliansky, E. 2002. *La Ligue Française des Droits de l'Homme et du Citoyen Depuis 1945 : Sociologie d'un Engagement Critique.* Paris: L'Harmattan.

———. 2010. 'Les Usages Protestataires du Droit'. In *Penser les Mouvements Sociaux,* ed. O. Fillieule, E. Agrikoliansky and I. Sommier, 225–44. Paris: La Découverte.

Agrikoliansky, E., O. Fillieule and N. Mayer, eds. 2005. *L'Altermondialisme en France. La Longue Histoire d'une Nouvelle Cause.* Paris: Flammarion.

Agrikoliansky, E., and I. Sommier., eds. 2005. *Radiographie du Mouvement Altermondialiste : Le Second Forum Social Européen.* La Dispute: Paris.

Althusser, L. 1967. 'Sur le Jeune Marx, Questions de Théorie'. In *Pour Marx.* Paris: Maspero.

Auyero, J. 2003. *Contentious Lives: Two Argentine Women, Two Protests, and the Quest for Recognition.* Durham: Duke University Press.

Balme, R., D. Chabanet and V. Wright, eds. 2002. *L'action collective en Europe : Collective Action in Europe.* Paris: Presses de Sciences Po.

Balsiger, P. 2014. *The Fight for Ethical Fashion: The Origins and Interactions of the Clean Clothes Campaign.* Aldershot: Ashgate.

———2010. 'Making Political Consumers: The Tactical Action Repertoire of a Campaign for Clean Clothes'. *Social Movement Studies* 9, no. 3: 311–29.

Barbot, J. 2002. *Les Malades en Mouvements : La Médecine et la Science à l'Epreuve du Sida.* Paris: Balland.

Bargel, L. 2009. *Jeunes socialistes/Jeunes UMP : Lieux et processus de socialisation politique.* Paris: Dalloz.

Becker, H. 1963. *Outsiders: Studies in the Sociology of Deviance.* New York. Free Press of Glencoe.

Bennani-Chraibi, M., and O. Fillieule. 2012. 'Towards a Sociology of Revolutionary Situations: Reflections on the Arab Uprisings'. *Revue Française de Science Politique* 62, no. 5: 1–29.

Bennani-Chraïbi, M., and O. Fillieule, eds. 2003. *Résistances et Protestations dans les Sociétés Musulmanes.* Paris: Presses de Sciences Po.

Bereni, L. 2007. 'Du "MLF" au Mouvement pour la Parité: La Genèse d'une Nouvelle Cause dans l'Espace de la Cause des Femmes'. *Politix* 2, no. 78: 107–32.

Berger, P. 1963. *Invitation to Sociology.* New York: Anchor Books.

Béroud, S., et al. 2008. *La Lutte Continue? Les Conflits du Travail dans la France Contemporaine.* Bellecombe-en-Bauges: Editions du Croquant.

Birnbaum, P., and F. Chazel. 1971. *Sociologie Politique.* Paris: Colin.

Bizeul, D. 2003. *Avec Ceux du FN: Un Sociologue au Front National.* Paris, La Découverte.

Boltanski, L. 1982. *Les Cadres. La Formation d'un Groupe Social.* Paris: Minuit.

Boltanski, L. and L. Thévenot. 1991. *De la Justification: Les Economies de la Grandeur.* Paris: Gallimard.

Boumaza, M. 2002. 'Le Front National et les Jeunes de 1972 à nos jours: Hétérodoxie d'un Engagement Partisan Juvénile'. PhD dissertation. Strasbourg: University Robert Schuman.

Bourguinat, N. 2002. *Les Grains du Désordre, L'État Face aux Violences Frumentaires dans la Première Moitié du XIXe siècle.* Paris: Editions de l'EHESS.

Braud, P., ed. 1993. *La Violence Politique dans les Démocraties Européennes Occidentales*. Paris: L'Harmattan.

Broqua, C. 2005. *Agir pour ne pas mourir*. Paris: Presses de Sciences Po.

Broqua, C., and O. Fillieule. 2001. *Trajectoires d'engagement: AIDES et Act Up*. Paris: Textuel.

Bruneau, I. 2006. 'La Confédération Paysanne: S'engager à Juste Distance'. PhD dissertation. Paris: Paris-X Nanterre.

Bruneteaux, P. 1996. *Maintenir l'Ordre*. Paris: Presses de Sciences Po.

Buton, F. 2009a. *L'Administration des Faveurs: L'Etat, les Sourds et les Aveugles (1789–1885)*. Rennes: Presses Universitaires de Rennes.

———. 2009b. 'Portrait du politiste en socio-historien: la socio-histoire dans les sciences politiques'. In *Pratiques et Méthodes de la Socio-Histoire*, ed. F. Buton and N. Mariot, 21–42. Amiens: PUF-CURAPP.

Castells, M. 1983. *The City and the Grassroots: A Cross-Cultural Theory of Urban Social Movements*. Berkeley and Los Angeles: University of California Press.

Cefaï D. 2007. *Pourquoi se Mobilise-t-on? Les Théories de l'Action Collective*. Paris: La Découverte.

Cefaï, D., and D. Trom, eds. 2001. *Les Formes de l'Action Collective: Mobilisations dans les Arènes Publiques*. Paris: Editions de l'EHESS.

Chabanet D., and J. Faniel, eds. 2012. *The Mobilization of the Unemployed in Europe*. Basingstoke and New York: Palgrave Macmillan.

Chazel, F. 1975. 'La Mobilisation Politique: Problèmes et Dimensions'. *Revue Française de Science Politique* 25: 502–16.

Chazel, F, eds. 1993. *Action Collective et Mouvements Sociaux*. Paris: Presses Universitaires de France.

Collovald, A., et al., eds. 2002. *L'Humanitaire ou le Management des Dévouements*. Rennes: Presses Universitaires de Rennes.

Combes, H., et al. 2011. 'Observer les Mobilisations'. *Politix* 93: 7–27.

Contamin, J-G. 2001. 'Contribution à une Sociologie des Usages Pluriels des Formes de Mobilisation: l'Exemple de la Pétition en France'. PhD dissertation. Paris: University of Paris 1.

Corbin, A., and J. M. Mayeur, eds. 1997. La Barricade. Paris: Publ. de la Sorbonne.

Cossart, P. 2010. *Le Meeting Politique: De la Délibération à la Manifestation (1868–1939)*. Rennes: PUR.

Crettiez, X. 1999. *La question corse*. Bruxelles: Complexe.

Crettiez, X. and I. Sommier, eds. 2006. *France Rebelle*. Paris: Michalon.

Dammame, D. et al., eds. 2008. *Mai–Juin 1968*. Paris: Editions de l'Atelier.

Darmon, M. 2006. *La Socialisation*. Paris: Colin.

Dauvin, P. and J. Siméant. 2002. *Le travail Humanitaire: Les Acteurs des ONG du Siège au Terrain*. Paris: Presses de Sciences Po.

Dobry, M. 1986. *Sociologie des Crises Politiques*. Paris: Presses de Sciences Po.

Dubuisson-Quellier, S. 2009. *La Consommation Engagée*. Paris: Presses de sciences Po.

Duchesne, S. 2003. 'Dons et Recherche de Soi, l'Altruisme en Question aux Restaurants du Coeur et à Amnesty International'. *Les Cahiers du Cevipof* 33.

Duclos, N. 1998. *Les Violences Paysannes sous la Vᵉ République*. Paris: Economica.

Dunezat, X. 2004. 'Chômage et Action Collective: Luttes dans la Lutte. Mouvements de

Chômeurs et Chômeuses de 1997–1998 en Bretagne et Rapports Sociaux de Sexe'. PhD dissertation. Paris: University of Versailles-Saint-Quentin-en-Yvelines.

Duyvendak, J. W. 1994. *Le Poids du Politique: Nouveaux Mouvements Sociaux en France.* Paris: L'Harmattan.

Duyvendak, J. W., and J. Jasper, eds. 2015. *Players and Arenas: The Interactive Dynamics of Protest.* Amsterdam: Amsterdam University Press.

Etzioni, A. 1970. *Demonstration Democracy.* New York, London, Paris: Gordon and Breach, Science Publishers.

Favre, P. 1989. *Naissances de la Science Politique.* Paris: Fayard.

Favre, P., ed. 1990. *La Manifestation.* Paris: Presses de Sciences Po.

Favre, P., O. Fillieule. and N. Mayer. 1997. 'La Fin d'une Etrange Lacune de la Sociologie des Mobilisations: L'Etude par Sondage des Manifestants. Fondements Théoriques et Solutions Techniques'. *Revue Française de Science Politique* 47, no. 1: 3–38.

Ferron, B. 2012. 'Les répertoires Médiatiques des Mobilisations Altermondialistes: Contribution à une Analyse de la Société Transnationale'. PhD dissertation. Rennes: University of Rennes 1.

Fillieule, O. 1997. *Stratégies de la Rue.* Paris: Presses de Sciences Po.

Fillieule, O. 2001. 'Post-scriptum: Propositions pour une Analyse Processuelle de l'Engagement Individuel'. *Revue Française de Science Politique* 51, nos. 1–2: 199–217.

Fillieule, O. 2003. 'Local Environmental Politics in France: The Case of the Louron Valley, 1984–1996'. *French Politics* 1, no. 3: 305–30.

Fillieule, O. 2010. 'Some Elements of an Interactionist Approach to Political Disengagement'. *Social Movement Studies* 9, no. 1: 1–15.

Fillieule, O., ed. 1993. *Sociologie de la Protestation: Les Formes de l'Action Collective dans la France Contemporaine.* Paris: L'Harmattan.

Fillieule, O., ed. 2005. *Le Désengagement Militant.* Paris: Belin.

Fillieule, O., E. Agrikoliansky and I. Sommier, eds. 2010. *Penser les Mouvements Sociaux.* Paris, La Découverte.

Fillieule, O., L. Mathieu and C. Péchu, eds. 2009. *Dictionnaire des Mouvements Sociaux.* Paris: Presses de Sciences Po.

Fillieule, O., and C. Péchu. 1993. *Lutter Ensemble: Les Théories de l'Action Collective.* Paris: L'Harmattan.

Fillieule, O., and D. Della Porta, eds. 2006. *Police et Manifestants, Maintien de l'Ordre et Gestion des Conflits.* Paris: Presses de Sciences Po.

Fillieule, O., and D. Tartakowsky. 2008. *La Manifestation.* Paris: Presses de Sciences Po. Trans. P. Aronoff and H. Scott. 2013. *Demonstrations.* Halifax and Winnipeg: Fernwood.

Fillieule, O., and P. Roux. 2009. *Le sexe du Militantisme.* Paris: Presses de Sciences Po.

Fligstein, N., and D. McAdam. 2012. *A Theory of Fields.* New York: Oxford University Press.

Fretel, J. 2004. 'Quand les Catholiques Vont au Parti'. *Actes de la Recherche en Sciences Sociales* 155: 77–89.

Garcia, G., 2005. 'Les Causes des "Sans" à l'Epreuve de la Médiatisation: La Construction Médiatique des mobilisations Sociales Emergentes'. PhD dissertation. Paris: University Paris IX.

Gaxie, D. 1977. 'Economie des Partis et Rétributions du Militantisme'. *Revue Française de Science Politique* 1, no. 27: 123–54.

———. 2005. 'Rétributions du Militantisme et Paradoxes de l'Action Collective'. *Revue Suisse de Science Politique* 11, no. 1: 157–88.

Giraud, B. 2009. 'Des Conflits du Travail à la Sociologie des Mobilisations: Apports d'un Décloisonnement Théorique et Empirique'. *Politix* 2, no. 86: 145–64.

Grojean, O. 2006. 'Investissement militant et violence contre soi au sein du Parti des travailleurs du Kurdistan'. *Cultures et conflits* 63: 101–12.

Haegel, F. 2012. *Les droites en fusion: Transformations de l'UMP.* Paris: Presses de Sciences Po.

Hamidi, C. 2006. 'Éléments pour une Approche Interactionniste de la Politisation: Engagement Associatif et Rapport au Politique dans des Associations Locales Issues de l'Immigration'. *Revue Française de Science Politique* 56, no. 1: 5–25.

Henry, E. 2007. *Amiante: Un Scandale Improbable. Sociologie d'un Problème Public.* Rennes: PUR.

Hmed, C. 2006. 'Loger les Etrangers "Isolés": Socio-Histoire d'une Institution d'Etat: la Sonacotra, 1956–2006'. PhD dissertation. Paris: University of Paris I.

Ion, J. 1997. *La Fin des Militants?* Paris: Editions de l'Atelier.

Israël, L. 2009. *L'Arme du Droit.* Paris: Presses de Sciences Po. Jobert, B., and P. Muller. 1986. *L'Etat en Action.* Paris: PUF.

Johsua, F. 2011. 'De la LCR au NPA (1966–2009): Sociologie Politique des Métamorphoses de l'Engagement Anticapitaliste'. PhD dissertation. Paris: Institut d'Etudes Politiques de Paris.

Juhem, P. 1998. 'SOS-Racisme, Histoire d'une Mobilisation "Apolitique": Contribution à une Analyse des Transformations des Représentations Politiques après 1981'. PhD dissertation. Paris: Université Paris X Nanterre.

———. 1999. 'La participation des journalistes à l'émergence des mouvements sociaux: Le cas de S.O.S. Racisme'. *Réseaux* 17(98): 119–52.

Kriegel, A. 1968. *Les Communistes Français: Essai d'Ethnographie Politique.* Paris: Seuil.

Kriesi, H., et al. 1995. *New Social Movements in Western Europe.* London: UCL.

Lafargue, J. 1996. *Contestations Démocratiques en Afrique: Sociologie de la Protestation au Kenya et en Zambie.* Paris: Karthala.

Lambelet, A. 2011. 'Agencement Militant ou Entre-Soi Générationnel? Militer dans des Organisations de Défense des Retraités'. *Politix* 96, no. 24: 81–95.

Lascoumes, P., and P. Le Gallès. 2007. *Sociologie de l'Action Publique.* Paris: Armand Colin.

Latté, S. 2008. 'Les "Victimes". La Formation d'une Catégorie Sociale Improbable et ses Usages dans l'Action Collective'. PhD dissertation. Paris: ENS.

———. 2012. 'La "force de l'événement" est-elle un artefact? Les mobilisations de victimes au prisme des théories événementielles de l'action collective'. *Revue française de science politique* 3, no. 62: 409–32.

Le Mouvement social. 2003. 'Les Marches', 202.

Lechien, M-H. 2003. 'Des militants de la "cause immigrée", Pratiques de solidarité et sens privé de l'engagement'. *Genèses* 1, no. 50: 91–110.

Leclercq, C., and J. Pagis. 2011. 'Les Incidences Biographiques de l'Engagement'. *Sociétés Contemporaines* 84: 5–23.

Lichterman, P. 1996. *The Search for Political Community: American Activists Reinventing Commitment.* New York: Cambridge University Press.

Lolive, J. 1999. *Les Contestations du TGV Méditerranée.* Paris: L'Harmattan.

Maitron, J., ed. 1997 [1964–]. *Dictionnaire Biographique du Mouvement Ouvrier Français.* Ivry-sur-Seine: Editions ouvrières puis Editions de l'Atelier.

Mann, P. 1992. *L'Action Collective: Mobilisation et Organisation des Minorités Actives.* Paris: Colin.

Mariot, N. 2006. *Bains de foule: Les Voyages Présidentiels en Province, 1888–2002.* Paris: Belin.

Massal, J. 2005. *Les Mouvements Indiens en Equateur: Mobilisations Protestataires et Démocratie.* Paris: Karthala.

Mathieu, L. 2001. *Mobilisations de Prostituées.* Paris: Belin.

———. 2004. *Comment Lutter? Sociologie et Mouvements Sociaux.* Paris: Textuel.

———. 2006. *La Double Peine: Histoire d'une Lutte Inachevée.* Paris: La Dispute.

———. 2012. *L'Espace des Mouvements Sociaux.* Paris: Le Croquant.

Maurer, S. 2001. *Les Chômeurs en Action.* Paris: L'Harmattan.

McAdam, D. 2012. *Freedom Summer.* Paris: Agone.

McAdam, D., and H. Schaffer Boudet. 2012. *Putting Social Movements in their Place.* Cambridge: Cambridge University Press.

McAdam, D., S. Tarrow and C. Tilly. 2001. *Dynamics of Contention.* Cambridge: Cambridge University Press.

Misch, A. 2008. *Partisan Publics: Communication and Contention across Brazilian Youth Activist Networks.* Princeton: Princeton University Press.

Mischi, J. 2010. *Servir la Classe Ouvrière: Sociabilités Militantes au PCF.* Rennes: Presses Universitaires de Rennes.

Mouchard, D. 2002. 'Les Mobilisations des "Sans" dans la France Contemporaine'. *Revue Française de Science Politique* 52: 425–48.

———. 2009. *Etre Représenté.* Paris: Economica.

Muller, P., and Y. Surel. 1998. *L'Analyse des Politiques Publiques.* Paris: Montchestien.

Neveu, E. 1996. *Sociologie des Mouvements Sociaux.* Paris: La Découverte.

———. 1999. 'Medias: Mouvements Sociaux, Espaces Publics'. *Réseaux* 17, no. 98: 17–85.

Noiriel, G. 2007. *Les Ouvriers dans la Société Française, XIXe–XXe.* Paris: Seuil.

Offerlé, M. 1984. 'Illégitimité et Légitimation du Personnel Ouvrier en France avant 1914'. *Annales ESC* 4: 681–713.

———. 2009. *Sociologie des Organisations Patronales.* Paris: La Découverte.

Ollitrault, S. 2008. *Militer pour la Planète: Sociologie des Ecologistes.* Rennes: PUR.

Pagis, J. 2009. 'Les Incidences Biographiques du Militantisme en Mai 68: Une Enquête sur Deux Générations Familiales'. PhD dissertation. Paris: ENS-EHESS.

Parizot, I. 2003. *Soigner les Exclus: Identités et Rapports Sociaux dans les Centres de Soins Gratuits.* Paris: PUF.

Péchu, C. 2010. *Les squats.* Paris: Presses de Sciences Po.

———. 2006. *Droit Au Logement, Genèse et Sociologie d'une Mobilisation.* Dalloz: Paris.

Pickvance, C. G. 1985. 'The Rise and Fall of Urban Movements and the Role of Comparative Analysis'. *Environment and Planning D: Society and Space* 3, no. 1: 31–53.

Pierru, E. 2003. 'L'Ombre des chômeurs—Chronique d'une indignité sociale et politique depuis les années 1930'. PhD dissertation. Amiens: Université of Picardie.

Pinçon, M., and M. Pinçon-Charlot. 2007. *Les Ghettos du Gotha: Comment la Bourgeoisie Défend ses Espaces*. Paris: Seuil.

Pinell, P. et al. 2002. *Une Epidémie Politique: La Lutte Contre le Sida en France (1981–1996)*. Seuil: Paris.

Politix. 2009a. 'Conflits au travail' 22, no. 86.

———. 2009b. 'La Syndicalisation en France' 22, no. 85.

Pommerolle, M-E., and J. Siméant. 2009. *Un Autre Monde à Nairobi, Le Forum Social Mondial 2007 entre Extraversions et Causes Africaines*. Paris: Karthala.

Pudal, B. 1989. *Prendre Parti: Pour une Sociologie Historique du PCF*. Paris: Presses de Sciences Po.

Rayner, H. 2005. *Les Scandales Politiques, l'Opération 'Mains Propres' en Italie*. Paris: Michel Houdiard Editeur.

Revel, J. 1996. *Jeux d'Echelles, de la Micro-Analyse à l'Expérience*. Paris: Hautes Etudes/Gallimard/Le seuil.

Robert, V. 2009. *Le temps des Banquets: Politique et Symbolique d'une Génération (1818–1848)*. Paris: Publications de la Sorbonne.

Rucht, D., ed. 1991. *Research on Social Movements: The State of the Art in Western Europe and the USA*. Frankfurt: Campus.

Sapiro, V. 1989. 'The Women's Movement and the Creation of Gender Consciousness: Social Movements as Socialization Agents'. In *Political Socialization for Democracy*, ed. O. Ichilov, 266–80. New York: Teachers College Press.

Sawicki, F. 1997. *Les Réseaux du Parti Socialiste: Sociologie d'un Milieu Partisan*. Paris: Belin.

Sawicki, F., and J. Siméant. 2009. 'Décloisonner la Sociologie de l'Engagement Militant'. *Sociologie du travail* 51: 97–125

Siméant, J. 1998. *La Cause des Sans Papiers*. Paris: Presses de Sciences Po.

———. 2009. *La Grève de la Faim*. Paris: Presses de Sciences Po.

———. 2014. *Contester au Mali: Formes de la Mobilisation et de la Critique à Bamako*. Paris : Karthala.

Smelser, N. 2003. 'On Comparative Analysis: Interdisciplinarity and Internationalization in Sociology'. *International Sociology* 18, no. 4: 643–57.

Snow, D. A., and L. Anderson. 1993. *Down Their Luck: A Study of Homeless Street People*. Berkeley: University of California Press.

Sommier, I. 1998. *La Violence Politique et son Deuil: L'Après 68 en France et en Italie*. Rennes: PUR.

———. 2003. *Le Renouveau des Mouvements Contestataires à l'Heure de la Mondialisation*. Paris: Flammarion.

Sommier, I. and O. Fillieule. 2013. 'The Emergence and Development of the "No Global" Movement in France: A Genealogical Approach'. In *Understanding European Movements: New Social Movements, Global Justice Struggles, Anti-Austerity Protest*, ed. C. Flesher Fominaya and L. Cox, 47–60. London and New York: Routledge.

Sommier, I., O. Fillieule, and E. Agrikoliansky, eds. 2008. *Généalogie des Mouvements Altermondialistes en Europe: Une Perspective Comparée*. Paris: Karthala.

Tarrow, S., Klandermans, B, Kriesi, H., eds. 1988. *From Structure to Action: Comparing Movement Participation across Cultures.* Greenwich: JAI-Press.

Thompson, E. P. 1996 *The Making of the English Working Class.* New York: Vintage Books.

Tilly, C. 1986. *The Contentious French.* Harvard: Harvard University Press. Trans. *La France conteste: De 1600 à nos Jours.* 1986. Paris: Fayard.

Tilly, C., and S. Tarrow. 2008. *Politique(s) du Conflit: De la Grève à la Révolution.* Paris: Presses de Sciences Po.

Touraine, A. 1973. *Pour la Sociologie.* Paris: Seuil.

———. 1978. *La voix et le Regard.* Paris: Seuil.

Traïni, C. 2011. *La Cause Animale, 1820–1980: Essai de Sociologie Historique.* Paris: PUF.

Traïni, C., ed. 2009. *Emotions … Mobilisation !.* Paris: Presses de Sciences Po.

Valluy, J. 1996. 'Coalition de Projet et Délibération Politique: le Cas du Projet d'Implantation de Décharges de Déchets Industriels dans la Région Rhône-Alpes (1979–1994)'. *Politiques et management public* 14, no. 4: 101–31.

Vassallo. F. 2010. *France, Social Capital and Political Activism.* Basingstoke: Palgrave Macmillan.

Voegtli, M. 2009. 'Luttes Contre le Sida, Luttes Homosexuelles: Histoires Croisées d'Engagements Militants en Suisse'. PhD dissertation. Lausanne-Paris: University of Lausanne and EHESS.

Waddington, D., F. Jobard and M. King, eds. 2009. *Rioting in the UK and France: A Comparative Analysis.* Oxford: Willan Publishing.

Wood, E. J. 2003. *Insurgent Collective Action and Civil War in El Salvador.* New York: Cambridge University Press.

Zaki, L. 2005. 'Pratiques Politiques au Bidonville, Casablanca (2000–2005)'. PhD dissertation. Paris: Institut d'Etudes Politiques.

Zunigo, X. 2003. *Volontaires chez Mère Teresa.* Paris: Belin.

Chapter 15

Internationalization with Limited Domestic Recognition

Research on Social Movements in Italy[1]

Lorenzo Bosi and Lorenzo Mosca

Italy has been described as a country with a weak state governed by frag-mented and clientelistic elites employing repressive and exclusionary strat-egies towards conflict. In the post-war period it has experienced different cycles of protest, including times of violent ruptures in terms of action rep-ertoires, and long dormant ones (Tarrow 1989; Della Porta 1996).

In the late 1960s and throughout the entire 1970s Italy underwent a long wave of protest that spread to the schools, the factories, the welfare services, the army, the entire political system, the church, the prisons and even within families (Tarrow 1989). One of its short-term legacies has been the renewed interest of the Italian scientific community in research on social movements, which started to challenge the dominant Marxist interpretation of collective action in which mobilization was usually understood as a unique outcome of socioeconomic structural changes and working-class agency. In an article mapping the field in Italy until the late 1980s, Mario Diani and Alberto Melucci argued that 'it was only in the 1960s … that research on collective action in Italy took its first uncertain steps toward autonomy' (1988: 334). In fact, such a 'revolutionary' path would have been unimaginable without the '68 cycle of protest and its legacy. Scholars working within an orthodox Marxist perspective were challenged in their interpretations by the social movements of the time, and likewise these same movements challenged the 'traditional' left and their intellectuals. Italian research on social move-ments in this sense, like in other European countries, 'has largely developed through engagement with movements' (Flesher Fominaya and Cox 2013: 3).

In this chapter we do not claim to offer a comprehensive treatment of the work published on social movements in Italy. We exclude works done by historians,[2] journalists, the social movement activists themselves, as well as publications produced by foreign scholars on the Italian case.[3] In the first section we present three Italian generations of social movement scholars. In the following section we introduce the principal areas of empirical research on social movements considering academic articles and books that have been published since the 1990s, thus updating the mapping exercise of Diani and Melucci (1988). In the concluding section we will briefly present a research agenda stressing some relevant issues that, we believe, still need to be answered by Italian social movement scholars.

Three Generations of Social Movement Scholars in Italy

Beside the efforts by Alberto Melucci (see below), Francesco Alberoni (1968) and Alessandro Pizzorno (1988) to develop a sociology of social movements—focusing on how social conflicts are politicised and transformed into collective action—many other scholars coming from 'neighbouring areas' have explored this field, devoting most of their interest to the contemporary Italian labour movement and 'new' social movements (Diani and Melucci 1988: 337). These researchers published a few works on the 'hot' topic of the time and then moved mostly on to the 'safety' issue of conventional forms of participation, where there is stronger recognition among the Italian academia and, most importantly, where greater resources are to be found.

Rather differently from his colleagues, Melucci is an Italian scholar who has devoted most of his career to the social movement field, investigating the socio-political project of collective action and its historical significance from a constructivist perspective. He offered a first mapping of the Italian social movements 'arising around youth, urban, women's, ecological and pacifist, ethnic and cultural issues' (Melucci 1996: 97) through 'participatory action research' (1996; 1998), based on ethnographic studies and focus-group techniques. Melucci introduced the Italian academia to the major contributions of US scholars and other works on post-industrial societies (1976; 1984), and established a cultural approach to the study of social movements with particular focus on the on-going process of collective identity ('we-ness') creation and survival in submerged/latent networks of individuals, groups and organizations (1977, 1982, 1996). Melucci interpreted the changing Italian socio-political context of the 1970s and 1980s with the decline of class struggle (post-industrial society) and the emergence of 'new' actors challenging the separation between public and private and uninterested in obtaining any institutional representation in favour of pure direct action. Compared with previous movements, these did not demand material goods and resources but rather challenged the dominant cultural codes of the elites (1996). Melucci argues that in their very existence in alternative lifestyles and local communities, social movements embody actors capable of producing cultural innovation, through the generation of information communicating alternative meanings, which are vital to promote democratization during everyday forms of contention. Well recognised as one of the leading thinkers behind new social movement (NSM) theory (jointly with Castells, Habermas, Offe and Touraine) and the founding 'grandfather' of social movements studies in Italy, Melucci can also be seen as representing an important *trait d'union* between the first and the second generation of social movement scholars in the country.

Because of their studies in foreign universities, with part of their careers having taken place outside their country of origin, and since most of their research has been published in English, what we could call the 'second generation' of social movement scholars in Italy (i.e. Donatella Della Porta [see below], Mario Diani [see below], Antimo Farro [2006], Roberto Franzosi [1995], and Carlo Ruzza [1990; 2009]) has been strongly embedded in the international community. By bringing insightful attempts to link rational, structural and cultural aspects of social movements they have been able to have a say in the epistemic community of social movement scholars. In part constrained by the lack of domestic academic recognition and lacklustre interest in social movement studies in the aftermath of the cycle of mobilization in the late 1960s and 1970s, this new generation searched for recognition of its scientific work within the international social movement field as a way to escape the parochialism and closeness of the Italian academia. The full recognition of Italian scholars in the field at the international level is testified by one of the most cited handbooks on the topic, co-authored by Donatella Della Porta and Mario Diani, which was first published in Italian and then translated into English (1999) and other languages. Only after having achieved strong international acknowledgment were these scholars able to then be considered in the Italian academia, obtaining prestigious positions and seating on the editorial boards of the leading peer-review journals of the country. The propensity of this second generation to international networking and collaboration has also been reflected in their participation in European and extra-European research projects, particularly within the European framework programs (e.g. Tea, Unempol, Europub.com, Demos, LocalMultiDem, etc.) (Diani and Císař 2014). At the same time this further internationalization has implied that no specific Italian tradition, method (quantitative or qualitative) or level of analysis (macro, meso or micro) concerning the study of social movements has developed further apart from the NSM paradigm mentioned above, in the 1970s and 1980s. This had consequences on the limited growth of the field domestically, since debates on social movements studies took place mostly at the international level. The tendency to confront, as well as the need to be recognised among their social movements colleagues in other countries, and their minor presence in national debates occurred alongside a partial legitimization of social movement studies inside the Italian academia.

An emblematic example is that of Donatella Della Porta, who has conducted in-depth empirical research not only in Italy but also in other Western European countries and more recently in Latin American, Eastern European and Middle Eastern countries. Besides methodological pluralism (Della Porta and Keating 2008; Della Porta 2014), this author has embraced the mainstream social movement approach in a non-dogmatic way, combining resource mobilization, political process and framing theories and, more recently, the contentious politics approach. She has refined and integrated these theories through the empirical study of other cases apart from the United States, where these theories have been developed, and applied them to a variety of issues such as political violence (Della Porta 1990, 1995, 2013), policing (Della Porta and Reiter 2004) and democratization (Della Porta 2009). As such, Della Porta has shown the capacity to merge analytical approaches originally built with reference to the US case, particularly through her long collaboration with Sidney Tarrow, with those emerging in Europe.

Another case is that of Mario Diani who has, in a similar manner, entered into dialogue with the international social movement community by combining the Italian tradition of research on collective action stemming from Alberto Melucci, Diani's mentor, with mainstream American approaches. His work, where relevance is ascribed to theory and concept formation in different modes of coordination of collective action (Diani 2012), has been always combined with close attention paid to empirical research, moving 'from metaphor to substance' (2003a). This has allowed him to identify, first of all, social movements 'as a distinctive type of social network' (Diani 2015: 11). Throughout his career Diani has built on a relational approach to study social movements using social networks methodological techniques (1988, 1995, 2015). This has not only distinguished his work among social movement scholars but also among those interested in civil society, as it becomes explicit in his latest research where the investigation focuses on the network of citizens' organizations that form the 'cement' of civil society in the cities of Bristol and Glasgow (Diani 2015).

Recalling the family metaphor, we can state that if Melucci has been the founding 'grandfather' of the field in Italy, Donatella Della Porta and Mario Diani, with their active role within PhD programs respectively in Florence (first at *Università di Firenze* and later at *Scuola Normale Superiore*) and Fiesole (European University Institute) and Trento, can be considered the 'parents' who have contributed, and are still contributing, to the formation of a new generation of young researchers. This 'third generation' of social movement scholars has started to play an important role within the international community, mostly at a European level, as some of its members have been active conveners of the mid-term conferences and standing groups on social movements and political violence in the European Sociological Association (ESA) and European Consortium for Political Research (ECPR). Furthermore they have brought the social movements literature to different fields of research in Italy and abroad: communication and digital media studies (Alice Mattoni, Stefania Milan, Lorenzo Mosca, Claudia Padovani and Lorenzo Zamponi); participatory and deliberative democracy (Massimiliano Andretta and Luca Raffini); public policies (Paolo Graziano and Gianni Piazza); political consumerism studies (Francesca Forno and Simone Tosi); European studies (Emanuela Bozzini and Manuela Caiani); labour studies (Loris Caruso, Anna Curcio and Gigi Roggero); research on weakly resourced groups (Simone Baglioni, Matteo Bassoli, Manlio Cinalli and Katia Pilati); political parties (Fabio De Nardis and Daniela Piccio); ethno-nationalist studies (Adriano Cirulli); political violence (Lorenzo Bosi); normative theory and international relations (Raffaele Marchetti); youth political culture (Luca Alteri); religious studies (Alberta Giorgi and Emanuele Polizzi); urban studies (Tommaso Vitale); gender studies (Elena Del Giorgio); social network analysis (Matteo Cernison and Elena Pavan), mathematical models and computer simulation (Delia Baldassarri).

While the first generation of Italian social movement scholars dealt with the mobilizations of the late 1960s and 1970s and the second one was politically socialised during this cycle of contention, the third generation is the first post-1968 generation in terms of political socialization and research interests. Most of them came of age in the early 1990s with Berlusconi's entrance into the political arena. The older ones among them were involved in the student's movement 'La Pantera' (1989–90) that gave rise to a long series of occupations (firstly in schools and universities and then in social centres) and most of them had witnessed the rise of the global justice movement, actively taking part in the anti-G8 protests in Genoa in 2001, in the first European social forum in Florence in 2002 and in the anti-war mobilizations in the following years.

Social movement research in Italy has certainly consolidated over the last decades (Della Porta and Biorcio 2013). Domestically, this has been reflected in: (1) the publication of two journals dedicated to the study of social movements, one from sociology and political science and the other from the field of history, respectively *Partecipazione e Conflitto* (2008) and *Zapruder* (2003); (2) the establishment of a social movement series within the publishing house FrancoAngeli; (3) the existence since 2006 of a standing group within the Italian political science association (SISP), called *Movimenti Sociali e Partecipazione*; (4) a specific focus on social movements as legitimate actors of the political system in introductory texts of political science (Pasquino 1986; Cotta et al. 2001) and political sociology handbooks (Biorcio 2003; Fantozzi and Turi 2006); (5) the achievement of three competitive national grants during the past decade (ministerial funding under PRIN—*Progetti di Rilevante Interesse Nazionale*) addressing, at least partially, non-conventional forms of action.[4]

Research on Social Movements in Italy

Before illustrating specific areas of research on social movements in Italy, we shall now present a brief analysis of the work that has been published over the past decade in what are generally regarded as the main journals in Italian political science and sociology of the top publishing house *Il Mulino* (also including *Carocci*).[5] As shown in figure 15.1, the number of articles focusing on social movements (broadly conceived[6]) that have been published on a yearly basis in Italian journals of politics and sociology is rather modest. Since the beginning of 2000 the average number per year is three, with this number ranging from a minimum of zero (2002 and 2009) to a maximum of five (2005, 2010 and 2011). Peaks can be explained by journals such as *Rassegna Italiana di Sociologia* and *Sociologica* that in the past dedicated special issues to social movements. Concerning a decade of publications, if we ignore the year 2009 (when *Partecipazione e Conflitto* started four-monthly regular publications)[7] the number of articles tends to be limited and rather

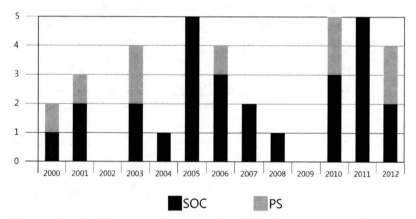

Figure 15.1. Articles on social movements published in Italian journals of politics and sociology since 2000

discontinuous, albeit of a higher volume at the end of the period under review. Overall, we found a higher presence of articles in sociological journals (twenty-seven versus nine in political science). This imbalance is confirmed when comparing the average number of articles published in the specified period in journals of sociology (around five) and politics (around three).

Interestingly, the profile of the authors of articles has changed over the decade; while in 2000 only senior scholars (including foreign ones) authored contributions in the analysed journals, in the following years the authorship became more diversified. However, until 2003 junior scholars (doing a PhD, with a completed PhD or working as assistant professors) only appeared as co-authors of senior scholars. The overall trend changed in 2005, although in the beginning junior scholars appeared mostly as single authors invited to contribute to a journal's special issue edited by a senior scholar. It is worth noticing that in 2012 junior scholars wrote all articles included in the analysis. Nonetheless, it should be stressed that the period of observation is limited and a wider time frame would be needed in order to assess the effective consolidation of these trends.

After providing a brief overview of publications on social movements in a selected sample of sociology and political science journals, we will now turn our attention to specific streams of research that we consider as those presenting more interesting results, methodological innovations or international resonance. In illustrating this research, we opted for a chronological order although this was not always possible, as some research fields tend to overlap over time.

Political Violence

In a recent review of the literature on political violence, Bosi et al. claimed that 'the most notable development in research [on the topic] is the increasing influence of theoretical approaches developed in the study of social movements' (2014: 3). This can be attributed to a large extent to the work of Della Porta (1990, 1995, 2013). She has been one of the first scholars coming from social movement studies to have shifted the attention from non-violent protest to the emergence of political violence. Her earlier work was based on resource mobilization theory and political process approach and relayed on an extensive use of official documents and life-history interviews with former armed activists (Della Porta 1990).

Starting from a focus on the Italian 'years of lead'—the cycle of political violence between 1969 and the early 1980s—Della Porta then moved on to a paired comparative study, which embraced the German case during the same period (Della Porta 1995), and has more recently compared left-wing clandestine groups with right-wing, ethno-national and religious ones through a most different systems comparative approach (Della Porta 2013). Her work has helped to situate political violence within the context of social, political and cultural conflicts, and to consider the switch to violence as being part of broader processes of political contention. Such 'de-exceptionalization' and 'de-essentialization' of political violence appears to have gained ground among the international scholarship. The richness of Della Porta's work lies in combining different levels of analysis (macro, meso and micro).

Partecipazione e Conflitto, the Italian journal of social movement studies, dedicated a special issue on the topic of political violence in 2012, publishing articles from foreign scholars in Italian, as a way of disseminating the most recent international research on the topic in Italy (Bosi and Della Porta 2012).

Policing Social Protest

While we have pointed out the importance of Della Porta (1995) for studies on political violence, through a social movement perspective, this work is also particularly helpful since it has enlarged the focus of the political process approach to the policing of social protest. In later works, often in collaboration with the historian Herbert Reiter, Della Porta has examined the methods and consequences of policing protest. These authors have produced rich empirical research on the policing of collective action in Italy between 1945 and the early 2000s through archival analysis and semi-structured interviews (Della Porta and Reiter 2004), which enabled them, in further studies, to draw up typologies about policing tactics, strategies and styles of control of collective action applicable to other cases.

Environmental Movements

The study of environmental movements has been particularly rich, both in terms of methodological innovation and theoretical developments as well as concerning its international resonance. Diani's book on the Italian environmental movement (1988; also see Biorcio and Lodi 1988; Farro 1991) translated into English (1995) has in fact introduced social network analysis within social movement studies (Diani 1995, 2015; Diani and McAdam 2003). Structural analysis of social movement networks shed light on internal cooperative and conflictual relations, also helping to explain mobilization dynamics and highlighting the role of different organizations in mobilization processes. This in turn has given rise to reflection on leadership and power dynamics within social movement networks (Diani 2003b).

However, probably the most important contribution of this research to the field concerns the definition of social movements as networks, a theoretical reflection drawn from the empirical evidence generated by network analysis (Diani 1992). More recently, Italian environmental activism has been studied through, among other methods, a protest event analysis of the last two decades (Della Porta and Diani 2004).

Anti-LULU Campaigns

Lately scholars' attention has moved from environmental movements to environmental conflicts and campaigns (Pellizzoni 2011). The main aim of the research on protest campaigns against Locally Unwanted Land Use (LULU) has been to criticise the scholars who dismiss such phenomena as 'NIMBYism' and to underline the major tendency in these conflicts to generalise the framing of protest and the territorial scope of action by creating networks connecting similar struggles around the country.

In a research mapping citizens' committees in six Italian cities, of the 107 groups recorded, only around a quarter (26 per cent) mobilised using a NIMBY discourse (i.e. single issues in a restricted territory), while the others tended to amplify the territorial and thematic range of their claims (Della Porta 2004: 28). As for other important anti-LULU campaigns,[8] the search for reciprocal support and visibility was reflected in a 'National Pact of Solidarity and Mutual Aid' (Caruso 2010) and convergence with mobilizations against war and for global justice. The research has highlighted the creative role of protest campaign in building a sense of community during the action. Local conflicts have also been studied in relations with public administration, inspecting mechanisms and processes that may push either political innovation or the conservation of the status quo (Podestà and Vitale 2010; Piazza et al. 2005).

The international resonance of some of these studies is testified by the translation of one of these books into English (Della Porta and Piazza 2008). Methods employed in the study of anti-LULU campaigns have mainly focused on case studies based on qualitative techniques such as participant observation, focus groups, in-depth interviews as well as newspapers and document analysis.

Global Justice Movement(s)

Research on the movement against neoliberal globalization has been rather prolific with different academic groups and scholars working on the anti-G8 protest in Genoa, on the European Social Forums (ESF) and on global and transnational movements (Andretta et al. 2002; Della Porta and Mosca 2003; Della Porta et al. 2006; Ceri 2002, 2003; Farro 2006; Montagna 2007; Farro and Rebughini 2008; Pianta 2001). The most interesting methodological innovation has been represented by surveys of participants in forums and counter-summits using self-administered questionnaires. For example, survey data have provided interesting information on Genoa's demonstrators, their profile, their organizational belonging and their perception of public authorities: the low trust in institutions as well as their repertoire of action (10 per cent declared to have used violence against things in the past), perception of violence and organizational membership (55 per cent did not belong to any organization present in Genoa to protest against the G8) in light of the crude repression by the police, help to explain the outcome of the demonstrations. The intertwinement between global justice mobilizations and anti-war movements has also received scholarly attention (Ceri 2009; Della Porta et al. 2003; Della Porta and Diani 2004b).

The capacity of this body of research to influence the international debate is clearly deducted by the German translation of one of these books (Andretta et al. 2002) and its subsequent rewriting and updating with new information from a survey of the participants in the first ESF held in Florence in 2002 (Della Porta et al. 2006). Although not new in social movement studies (Jasper and Poulsen 1995; Fillieule 1997), survey methodology appears to have experienced a revival of interest during the past decade as testified by its frequent adoption by transnational research teams (among others, Della Porta 2009; Walgrave and Rucht 2010).

Political Consumerism

This is a sub-field of research particularly new to social movements studies, although tactics such as boycotts have been widely used in the past, among other reasons, to 'reduce natural resources use, protect the environment, support fair working conditions and human rights, and meet essential, current human needs without compromising the ability of future generations' (Forno and Graziano 2012). Scholars have struggled to demonstrate the role of social movements in promoting political consumerism at the collective level instead of uniquely from an individual perspective.

In Italy, as in other Western countries, the diffusion of this form of action seems to be connected with the processes of globalization (Tosi 2006; Forno and Tosi 2009). Moreover, due to the high concentration of organised crime in Italy, this form of action has been studied in connection with social movement organizations, in contrast to the socioeconomic power of the Mafia (Andretta 1999; Forno 2012). Techniques employed by this stream of research include protest-event analysis, in-depth interviews and surveys as well as network analysis. Although political consumerism in Italy has been studied both theoretically and empirically, the relative lack of comparative research on this topic has limited the international diffusion of these works.

Weakly Resourced Groups: Students, Precarious Workers and Social Centres

Youth mobilizations have been often promoted by weakly resourced groups in the Italian context: from student movements, to precarious workers' rallies and contentious activities by social centres. Like its object of study—often very sparse and heterogeneous—the research on this topic has been very fragmented. However, an interesting feature of these mobilizations is that they often merged together, with overlapping membership being a defining characteristic of activists.

During the last few decades, student movements have activated against school and university reforms, being characterised by strong links at a local level and a general difficulty in generating a collective identity. The generational dimension of the phenomenon has, in fact, prevented continuity between this wave of mobilization and those preceding it, thus hindering the creation of a shared memory (Caruso et al. 2010). One of the forms of action typical of the student movement has been that of occupation. This action forms rapidly diffused from school and universities to abandoned buildings where social centres have flourished since the 1980s (De Sario 2009).

While there are numerous social centres in Italy today (over two hundreds), they are also very heterogeneous in cultural background, objectives and forms of action. In the last decade a sizable proportion has undergone an organizational evolution that could be interpreted as a process of commercialization and institutionalization (Della Porta and Diani 1999; Della Porta et al. 2006). Although social centres are highly fragmented around varying ideological orientations and different relationships with the institutions, they have actively taken part in some of the most important waves of Italian protest during the past twenty years: from anti-LULU mobilizations to student movements and summits and protests of the movement(s) against neoliberal globalization, thus contributing to the transformation of territorial conflicts into global movements (Piazza 2012; Mudu 2012).

Precarious workers have frequently mobilised with students and social centres (Roggero 2005), also creating their own very successful rallies and networks at a national and European level (i.e. May Day and EuroMayDay annual parades). The relevance of this stream of research is testified by the work of Alice Mattoni focused on the mobilization of precarious workers and their media practices, published in English (2012).[9]

Rescuing and innovating a research tradition stemming from the 1950s and 1960s, recent waves of youth mobilization have often been approached by engaged researchers who have in some cases developed forms of *auto-ricerca* (self-research) meaning that 'scholars were also activists, and the results were discussed among the participants in the protest. Research was methodologically rigorous employing the conceptual and analytical tools of empirical sciences, which have little or nothing to do with propaganda or ideology, in the belief that scientific empirically-based knowledge can offer social movements a solid interpretative framework for guiding informed political choices' (Giorgi and Piazza 2010: 59).

Possible Ways Forward

As discussed above, the study of social movements in Italy has been carried out by three generations of scholars that have personally experienced different cycles of protest. Although still missing widespread domestic recognition, Italian scholars appear to be quite integrated in the international community. While the first generation—and particularly Alberto Melucci, the founding 'grandfather' of the field—developed a cultural approach to the study of collective action distinctive from the American scholarship, the second generation (i.e. Della Porta and Diani) has instead employed, combined and refined all the classical concepts, approaches and tools of analysis developed by its American colleagues. The third generation portrays continuity with the second generation, embracing methodological pluralism, bridging different approaches and broadening the field to neighbouring areas. The field has gradually consolidated in terms of publications, research grants and institutional presence within professional associations.

A question that seems far to be answered by Italian social movement scholars concerns the reduced mobilization capacity during the current endless economic crisis. In the first place, Italy was at the forefront of mobilization on globalization at the dawn of the twenty-first century with massive demonstrations. Moreover, it had a role of leadership within European social movements by being the country chosen to host the first ESF (Della Porta et al. 2006) and by the important role played by the Italian organizational committee within the process of setting up the ESF (Haug et al. 2009). Secondly, although grievances do not automatically translate into mobilization, structural conditions such as the economic crisis should have favoured collective action as has occurred recently in other countries and in Italy during the 1970s and 2000s.

Scholars should reflect more on the reasons why recent protests against austerity did not have the same intensity and continuity in Italy as in other Mediterranean countries such as Spain and Greece (Della Porta et al. 2015). Some tentative answers have been given (Zamponi 2012). In Italy, student mobilizations against the economic crisis between 2008 and 2011 caused the emergence of groups with a well-defined political identity and radical forms of action that made the process of coalition-building more difficult. The negative outcome of the huge demonstration held in Rome on 15 October 2011 led to a loss of credibility of the new-born movement, following the street clashes and a series of divisions which could hardly be fixed in the short term. The political context was not favourable either: the presence of a technical government with bipartisan support and the sole opposition of the *Lega Nord* and *Italia dei Valori* until February 2013 minimised the movements' potential for mobilization, which usually reaches its peak when the left is in the opposition, as noted by several scholars (Della Porta and Diani 1999: 215).

Paradoxically, however, the on-going crisis of political parties and their failure to mediate between society and institutions generated great opportunities that have been successfully exploited by a collective actor that has rapidly transformed into a political party: the *Movimento 5 Stelle* (Mosca 2014a; 2014b; 2015). However, its unexpected success (25.5 per cent of votes in the low chamber in the political elections of February 2013), its refusal to collocate itself on the left-right axis and the opposition to any kind of political alliance require further reflection. To what extent can it be considered a genuine movement when its action tends to focus mainly on the electoral arena? What is its relationship with grassroots social movements in terms of claims, forms of action and activists' biographies? Has its entry into representative arenas opened up new channels of access to institutions for movements? Does its vision based on direct democracy mirror its real organizational practices? Social movement studies can offer useful insights and tools for the study of this new political phenomenon.

These last questions open up the opportunity to briefly reflect about the lack of interest in social movement outcomes within the Italian literature. We argue that this mostly stems from the fact that the responsiveness of the political system to social mobilizations has been rather weak in the history of the country. Since the literature on social movement effects has particularly focused on the political consequences of the action of social movements, this has probably hindered research on this specific sub-field. A possible way forward for studying social movement outcomes in Italy is to tackle this topic with different research agendas as Diani (1997) and more recently Bosi (2011) have stated, suggesting, respectively, focus on the capacity of social movements to produce social capital (as measured by social network analysis) and a shift from single-outcome analysis to processes of social change through 'path analysis' (Blee 2015) by looking at how different types of social movement outcomes mutually influence one another over time.

Lorenzo Bosi is a assistant professor at the Scuola Normale Superiore and member at the Centre on Social Movement Studies (COSMOS). He has published in several international academic journals and is co-editor of *Dynamics of Political Violence* (Ashgate, 2014), of *Political Violence in Context* (ECPR Press, 2015), of *The Dynamics of Radicalization: A Relational Comparative Perspective* (Oxford University Press, 2015) and of *The Consequences of Social Movements* (Cambridge University Press, 2015).

Lorenzo Mosca is associate professor at the Scuola Normale Superiore and an honorary member of the Centre on Social Movement Studies (COSMOS) at the European University Institute. His research concerns political participation, political communication, social movements and online politics and has been published in international journals such as *Journal of Public Policy, World Political Science Review, Information, Communication and Society, The International Journal of E-Politics, Global Networks, Journal of World-Systems Research* and *The International Spectator.*

Notes

1. We wish to thank Olivier Fillieule, Guya Accornero, Marco Giugni and the anonymous reviewers for their helpful comments on previous versions of this work. The chapter was collaborative, but each author contributed specifically to a section. Lorenzo Bosi wrote the section 'Three Generations of Social Movement Scholars in Italy' while Lorenzo Mosca wrote the section 'Research on Social Movements in Italy', including its sub-sections. Both authors contributed equally to the introductory and concluding sections.

2. However, particular mention should be made of the work of Luisa Passerini (1988) and Alessandro Portelli (1990). Working on the 1960s and 1970s Italian cycle of protest using oral history interviews, these authors have built an approach on collective memory research which is most specifically used in the study of memory of particular past issues or events. Scholars coming from different countries and working on topics not directly connected with collective action have used this approach in their research.

3. For an overview on the social movement scene in Italy, and how it has interacted with the changing political system of the country between the late 1960s and early 1990, see Della Porta (1996).

4. Political participation and representation: citizens' spontaneous committees and public policies of local governments (2000–2001—Florence and Bologna research units: http://cercauniversita.cineca.it/php5/prin/cerca.php?codice=MM14101481). Local social forums in Italy, France and Germany: three different models of mobilization (2002–3—only the Florence research unit: http://cercauniversita.cineca .it/php5/prin/cerca.php?codice=2002144527&testo=democrazia). Communication rights and movements (2006–7—Padua and Trento research units: http://cercauni versita.cineca.it/php5/prin/cerca.php?codice=2006148230).

5. This search includes journals that have been classified as belonging to political science (PS) and sociology (SOC) following the classification of the *National Agency* for assessment of the University System and Research (*Agenzia nazionale di valutazione del sistema universitario*, ANVUR), in 2012: *Rivista Italiana di Scienza Politica* (PS), *Rivista Italiana di Politiche Pubbliche* (PS), *Stato e Mercato* (PS), *Rassegna Italiana di Sociologia* (SOC), *Sociologica* (SOC), *Polis* (SOC), *Comunicazione Politica* (SOC), *Studi Culturali* (SOC).

6. The Italian words used for searching relevant articles in http://www.rivisteweb .it were the following: *azione collettiva, moviment*, protest*, attivist*, conflitt*, scioper*, mobilita*, campagn**. Since 2013 many Italian journals have started publishing partly or fully in English.

7. In 2008 only number zero was published featuring articles by prominent Italian scholars that have conducted research on political participation and social conflict.

8. Against the TAV (a high-speed railway in Val di Susa, close to the border with France), against the construction of a Bridge on the Messina Straits (between Sicily and Calabria), and to block the construction of a US military base in Vicenza.

9. Perhaps less systematic and continuous but still important has been research on other weakly resourced groups such as gays (Trappolin 2004), immigrants and women (Vitale 2012; Jacquot and Vitale 2014).

References

Alberoni, F. 1968. *Statu nascenti: studi sui processi collettivi.* Bologna: Il Mulino.

Andretta, M. 1999. 'Sistema Politico Locale e Protesta a Palermo'. *Quaderni Di Sociologia* 21: 68–89.

Andretta, M., et al. 2002. *Global, Noglobal, New Global: La protesta contro il G8 a Genova.* Roma: Laterza.

Biorcio, R. 2003. *Sociologia politica: Partiti, movimenti sociali e partecipazione.* Bologna: Il Mulino.

Biorcio, R., and G. Lodi, eds. 1988. *La sfida verde: Il movimento ecologista in Italia.* Padova: Liviana.

Blee, K. 2015. 'Personal Effects from Far-Right Activism'. In *The Consequences of Social Movements: Policies, People and Institutions,* ed. L. Bosi, M. Giugni and K. Uba, 66–84. Cambridge: Cambridge University Press.

Bosi, L. 2011. 'Movimenti e cambiamento sociale: l'interrelazione delle conseguenze'. *Società degli Individui* 42, no. 3: 69–78.

Bosi, L., and D. Della Porta. 2012. 'Violenza Politica: una introduzione'. *Partecipazione e Conflitto* 3: 5–17.

Bosi, L., C. Demetriou and S. Malthaner. 2014. *Dynamics of Political Violence*. Farnham: Ashgate.

Caruso, L. 2010. *Il territorio della politica: La nuova partecipazione di massa nei movimenti No Tav e Dal Molin*. Milano: FrancoAngeli.

Caruso, L. et al., eds. 2010. *Alla ricerca dell'Onda: I nuovi conflitti nell'istruzione superiore*. Milano: FrancoAngeli.

Ceri, P. 2002. *Movimenti globali: La protesta nel XXI secolo*. Roma: Laterza.

Ceri, P., ed. 2003. *La democrazia dei movimenti: Come decidono i noglobal*. Catanzaro: Rubbettino.

———. 2009. *Da no global a no war e ritorno: Metamorfosi del movimento globale*. Torino: Utet.

Cotta M., D. Della Porta and L. Morlino. 2001. *Scienza politica*. Bologna: Il Mulino.

De Sario, B. 2009. *Resistenze innaturali: attivismo radicale nell'Italia degli anni '80*. Milano: Agenzia X.

Della Porta, D. 1990. *Il terrorismo di sinistra*. Bologna: Il Mulino.

———. 1995. *Social Movements, Political Violence, and the State: A Comparative Analysis of Italy and Germany*. Cambridge: Cambridge University Press.

———. 1996. *Movimenti collettivi e sistema politico in Italia: 1960–1995*. Roma: Laterza.

———. 2013. *Clandestine Political Violence*. Cambridge: Cambridge University Press.

Della Porta, D., ed. 2004. *Comitati di cittadini e democrazia urbana*. Catanaro: Rubbettino.

———. 2009. *Another Europe: Conceptions and Practices of Democracy in the European Social Forums*. London and New York: Routledge.

———. 2014. *Methodological Practices in Social Movement Research*. Oxford: Oxford University Press.

Della Porta, D., M. Andretta and L. Mosca. 2003. 'Movimenti sociali e sfide globali: politica, antipolitica e nuova politica dopo l'11 settembre': *Rassegna Italiana di Sociologia* 1: 43–76.

Della Porta, D., et al. 2006. *Globalization from Below: Transnational Activists and Protest Networks*. Minneapolis and London: Minnesota Press.

Della Porta, D., and R. Biorcio. 2013. 'Partecipazione e movimenti sociali'. In *Quarant'anni di scienza politica in Italia*, ed. G. Pasquino, M. Regalia and M. Valbruzzi, 93–106. Bologna: Il Mulino.

Della Porta, D. and M. Diani. 1999. *Social Movements: An Introduction*. Oxford: Blackwell.

———. 2004a. *Movimenti senza protesta? L'ambientalismo in Italia*. Bologna: il Mulino. With the collaboration of M. Andretta.

———. 2004b. '"Contro la guerra senza se né ma": le proteste contro la guerra in Iraq'. In *Politica in Italia*, ed. V. della Sala and S. Fabbrini, 249–69. Bologna: Il Mulino.

Della Porta, D., and M. Keating, eds. 2008. *Approaches and Methodologies in the Social Sciences: A Pluralist Perspective*. Cambridge: Cambridge University Press.

Della Porta, D., and L. Mosca, eds. 2003. *Globalizzazione e movimenti sociali*. Roma: Manifestolibri.

Della Porta, D., L. Mosca and L. Parks. 2015. '2011: A Year of Protest on Social Justice in Italy'. In *Subterranean Politics in Europe*, ed. M. Kaldor and S. Selchow, 60–93. New York: Palgrave-McMillan.

Della Porta, D., and G. Piazza. 2008. *Voices of the Valley, Voices of the Straits: How Protest Creates Communities.* New York: Berghahn Books.

Della Porta, D., and H. Reiter. 2004. *Polizia e protesta: L'ordine pubblico dalla Liberazione ai 'no global'.* Bologna: Il Mulino.

Diani, M. 1988. *Isole nell'arcipelago: Il movimento ecologista in Italia.* Bologna: Il Mulino.

———. 1992. 'The Concept of Social Movement'. *Sociological Review* 40: 1–25.

———. 1995. *Green Networks: A Structural Analysis of the Italian Environmental Movement.* Edinburgh: Edinburgh University Press.

———. 1997. 'Social Movements and Social Capital: A Network Perspective on Movement Outcomes'. *Mobilization* 2, no. 2: 129–47.

———. 2003a. 'Social Movements, Contentious Actions, and Social Networks: "From Metaphor to Substance"?' In *Social Movements and Networks,* ed. M. Diani and D. McAdam, 1–20. Oxford: Oxford University Press.

———. 2003b. '"Leaders" or "Brokers"? Positions and Influence in Social Movement Networks'. In *Social Movements and Networks,* ed. M. Diani and D. McAdam, 105–22. Oxford: Oxford University Press.

———. 2012. 'Modes of Coordination of Collective Action: What Actors in Policy Making?'. In *Networks in Social Policy Problems,* ed. M. Scotti and B.s Vedres, 101–23. Cambridge: Cambridge University Press.

———. 2015. *The Cement of Civil Society: Studying Networks in Localities.* Cambridge: Cambridge University Press.

Diani M., and Císař O. 2014. 'The Emergence of a European Social Movement Research Field'. In *Routledge Handbook of European Sociology,* ed. S. Koniordos and A. Kyrtsis, 172–95. London and New York: Routledge.

Diani, M., and D. McAdam. 2003. *Social Movements and Networks.* Oxford: Oxford University Press.

Diani, M., and A. Melucci. 1988. 'Searching for Autonomy: The Sociology of Social Movements in Italy'. *Social Science Information* 27, no. 3: 333–53.

Fantozzi, P., and P. Turi. 2006. *Manuale di sociologia politica.* Roma: Carocci.

Farro, A. 1991. *La lente verde: Cultura, politica e azione collettiva ambientaliste.* Milano: FrancoAngeli.

Farro, A., ed. 2006. *Italia alterglobal: Movimento, culture e spazi di vita di altre globalizzazioni.* Milano: FrancoAngeli.

Farro, A., and P. Rebughini, eds. 2008. *Europa alterglobal: Componenti e culture del 'movimento dei movimenti' in Europa.* Milano: FrancoAngeli.

Fillieule, O. 1997. *Stratégies de la rue: Les manifestations en France.* Paris: Presses de Sciences Po.

Flesher Fominaya, C., and L. Cox, eds. 2013. *Understanding European Movements: New Social Movements, Global Justice Struggles, Anti-Austerity Protest.* London and New York: Routledge.

Forno, F. 2012. 'L'economia Solidale Come Forma Di Autorganizzazione Sociale Contro La Mafia'. *Il Ponte* 69, nos. 2–3: 85–92.

Forno, F., and P. R. Graziano. 2012. 'Political Consumerism and New Forms of Political Participation: The Gruppi di Acquisto Solidale in Italy'. *The ANNALS of the American Academy of Political and Social Science* 644: 121–33.

Forno, F., and S. Tosi. 2009. 'Partecipazione politica e denaro: una introduzione'. *Partecipazione e Conflitto* 3: 5–16.

Franzosi, R. 1995. *The Puzzle of Strikes: Class and State Strategies in Postwar Italy.* Cambridge: Cambridge University Press.

Giorgi, A. and G. Piazza. 2010. 'Scienze politiche e sociali, ricerche, auto-inchiesta'. In *Alla ricerca dell'Onda: I nuovi conflitti nell'istruzione superior,* ed. L. Caruso et al., 46–61. Milano: FrancoAngeli.

Haug, C., N. Haeringer and L. Mosca. 2009. 'The ESF Organizing Process in a Diachronic Perspective'. In *Another Europe: Conceptions and Practices of Democracy in the European Social Forums,* ed. D. Della Porta, 26–45. London and New York: Routledge.

Jacquot, S., and T. Vitale. 2014. 'Law as Weapon of the Weak? A Comparative Analysis of Legal Mobilization by Roma and Women's Groups at the European Level'. *Journal of European Public Policy* 21, no. 4: 587–604.

Jasper, J. M., and J. Poulsen. 1995. 'Recruiting Strangers and Friends: Moral Shocks and Social Networks in Animal Rights and Anti-Nuclear Protests'. *Social Problems* 42, no. 4: 493–512.

Mattoni, A. 2012. *Media Practices and Protest Politics: How Precarious Workers Mobilise.* Farnham: Ashgate.

Melucci, A. 1976. *Movimenti di rivolta: teorie e forme dell'azione collettiva.* Milan: Etas.

———. 1977. *Sistema politico, partiti e movimenti sociali.* Milan: Feltrinelli.

———. 1982. *L'invenzione del presente: Movimenti, identità, bisogni individuali.* Bologna: il Mulino.

———. 1996. *Challenging Codes: Collective Action in the Information Age.* Cambridge: Cambridge University Press.

———. 1998. *Verso una sociologia riflessiva: Ricerca qualitative e cultura.* Bologna: Il Mulino.

Melucci, A., ed. 1984. *Altri Codici: aree di movimento nella metropoli.* Bologna: Il Mulino.

Montagna, N., ed. 2007. *I movimenti sociali e le mobilitazioni globali: Temi, processi e strutture organizzative.* Milano: FrancoAngeli.

Mosca, L. 2014a. 'A Year of Social Movements in Italy: From the No-Tavs to the Five-Star Movement'. In *Italian Politics 2012,* ed. A. Di Virgilio and C. Radaelli, 267–85. New York: Berghahm.

———. 2014b. 'The Five Star Movement: Exception or Vanguard in Europe?' *The International Spectator* 1: 36–52.

———. 2015 'The Five Star Movement and Social Conflicts: Between Symbiosis and Co-optation'. In *Beppe Grillo's Five Star Movement: Organisation, Communication and Ideology,* ed. F. Tronconi, 153–177. Aldershot: Ashgate.

Mudu, P. 2012. 'I Centri Sociali italiani: verso tre decadi di occupazioni e di spazi auto-gestititi' *Partecipazione e Conflitto* 24: 69–92.

Pasquino, G., ed. 1986, *Manuale di scienza della politica.* Bologna: Il Mulino.

Passerini L. 1988. *Storia e soggettività: Le fonti orali, la memoria.* Firenze: La Nuova Italia.

Pellizzoni, L. 2011. *Conflitti ambientali: Esperti, politica, istituzioni nelle controversie ecologiche.* Bologna: Il Mulino.

Pianta, M. 2001. *Globalizzazione dal basso: Economia mondiale e movimenti sociali.* Roma: Manifestolibri.

Piazza, G. 2012. 'Il movimento delle occupazioni di squat e centri sociali in Europa: Una introduzione'. *Partecipazione e Conflitto* 1: 5–18.

Piazza, G., et al. 2005. 'Protest and Arguments: The Citizen's Committees' Campaigns against Traffic in Four Italian Cities'. *World Political Science Review* 1, no. 2.

Pizzorno, A. 1988. 'Considerazioni sulle teorie dei movimenti sociali'. *Problemi del Socialismo* 12: 11–27.

Podestà, N., and T. Vitale. 2010. *Dalla proposta alla protesta, e ritorno: Conflitti locali e innovazione politica.* Milano: Mondadori.

Portelli A. 1990. 'Intervistare il movimento: il '68 e la storia orale'. In *Il Sessantotto: l'evento e la storia,* ed. P. P. Poggio, 125–32. Brescia: Fondazione Luigi Micheletti.

Roggero, G. 2005. *Intelligenze fuggitive: Movimenti contro l'università azienda.* Roma: Manifestolibri.

Ruzza, C. 1990. 'Institutionalization in the Italian Peace Movement'. *Theory and Society* 26: 1–41.

———. 2009. *Re-inventing the Italian Right: Populism, Post-Fascism and Territorial Identity.* London and New York: Routledge.

Tarrow S. 1989. *Democracy and Disorder: Protest and Politics in Italy 1965–1975.* Oxford: Clarendon.

Tosi, S., ed. 2006. *Consumi e partecipazione politica: Tra azione individuale e mobilitazione collettiva.* Milano: FrancoAngeli.

Trappolin, L. 2004. *Identità in azione: Mobilitazione omosessuale e sfera pubblica.* Roma: Carocci.

Vitale, T. 2012. 'Conflitti urbani nei percorsi di cittadinanza degli immigrati: Una introduzione'. *Partecipazione e Conflitto* 3: 5–21.

Walgrave, S., and D. Rucht, eds. 2010. *The World Says No to War: Demonstrations against the War on Iraq.* Minneapolis and London: University of Minnesota Press.

Zamponi, L. 2012. '"Why Don't Italians Occupy?" Hypotheses on a Failed Mobilisation.' *Social Movement Studies* 11, nos. 3–4: 416–26.

Chapter 16

The Land of Opportunities?

Social Movement Studies in Switzerland

Philip Balsiger

A 'marginal field of research': this is how Hanspeter Kriesi (1990) characterised social movement studies in Switzerland in a review at the end of the
1980s. Little research had been done on social movements in Switzerland,
the review said, and even less so on the so-called new social movements
(203). Nonetheless, a few movements had attracted scholarly attention at
that time, if not always with the theoretical perspective of the sociology of
social movements: the right-wing anti-foreigner movement, the regional and
separatist movement in the Jura that had resulted in the creation of a new
canton in 1978 (e.g. Ganguillet 1985), the peace movement (Epple 1988),
the ecology movement (Lévy 1981) and the 'youth' movements of the late
sixties and the beginning of the eighties (Kriesi 1984). Kriesi himself played
a pioneering role in doing social movement research in Switzerland: in a
study using protest event data (Kriesi et al. 1981), and in case studies based
on interviews and surveys (Kriesi 1985) on 'political activation', he was the
first to look at these 'new' actors shaping the Swiss political process, and
offered an initial mapping of protest activity in Switzerland. The broader
field of political sociology and research on political participation, however,
was much more focused on institutionalised means of participation. The
scholarly neglect of protest and social movements certainly had something
to do with the availability and greater legitimacy of direct democratic means
of participation (Kriesi 1990).

More than twenty years separate us from Kriesi's assessment. Does it
still hold true? In terms of academic institutionalization, the situation has
notably improved: some tenured sociologists or political scientists are movement scholars, although this is only true for the French-speaking part of the
country. In German-language universities, movement studies barely exist.
It is mostly in terms of actual research that the situation has progressed.
Many studies have analysed Swiss social movements and protest from the
1990s onwards, often integrated into international research programs. In-

deed, some of the core contributions of 'European' social movement studies originated from Swiss research projects and scholars. I will start by briefly reviewing the most important of these studies, leaving aside work produced before 1990, already covered in Kriesi's exhaustive review. I shall then discuss the dominant theoretical perspectives on movements in Switzerland in the recent past and how they relate to international theoretical debates, teasing out the specificities of movement studies in Switzerland.

Main Research Projects and Findings

If one were to quickly characterise Swiss social movement studies over the past two decades, three major observations stand out. First, the study of social movements in Switzerland is more often than not comparative, frequently conducted within cross-country research projects. Second, movement studies in Switzerland have been very much influenced by the political process approach, and have also added some core insights to this perspective. Finally, a different strand present in Swiss social movements is more interested in activist trajectories and often takes a more critical stance to the political process model.

'New Social Movements in Western Europe' and Their Offspring

The 'new social movements' project directed by Kriesi (see Kriesi et al. 1995), based on a protest event analysis covering 1975–89, was certainly one of the major works in social movement studies at large, and movement studies in Switzerland in particular. Initially, Switzerland was not supposed to be part of the study covering France, Germany and the Netherlands; when Kriesi started the project, he had a position in Amsterdam, but then moved to the University of Geneva where he was offered a chair of comparative politics. Not only did this move lead to adding the Swiss case to the comparison, but according to Kriesi's recollection of the events, it also significantly influenced the theoretical framework of the study. The comparative politics perspective that came with his new position led Kriesi to increasingly focus on the concept of political opportunity structures. The new social movements study thus bridged two important theoretical traditions, an American one with the political process model, to which Kriesi's team added a strong focus on comparative state institutions, and a European one of the social origins of 'new' social movements, with cleavage structures as the key factor. In the study, Switzerland appears as a case with a particularly open opportunity structure, explaining the comparatively numerous protest events as well as their relatively moderate character in terms of action repertoires. Furthermore, the study establishes the importance of 'new' social movements in Switzerland (ecology, anti-nuclear, third world/solidarity, peace, squatter/urban) compared to the 'old' labour movement, and explains it through the pacification of the traditional class cleavage in Switzerland and the importance of a new cleavage in the middle class. Within the sector of 'new' social movements, the data shows that the anti-nuclear movement was the most active in the 1970s. By the 1980s, there was a sharp increase in protest events, due to the actions of the peace movement and urban movements. The ecology and solidarity movements, on the other hand, while strong in terms of membership numbers, use more institutionalised forms of action than protest (Giugni 1995).

In addition to the publications based on this dataset, a few studies from the 1990s focused on more specific aspects of social movements in Switzerland. Kriesi and Wisler (1995) were interested in the relationship between direct democracy and protest. Indeed, the wide availability of direct democratic instruments at local, regional and national levels in Switzerland raises the question of its effects on protest. Marginal political actors are expected to use direct democratic means rather than other repertoires such as demonstrations. Studying the peace movement, Epple (1988) argued that it had been weakened by direct democracy. The availability of direct democratic instruments drained movement resources, forced them to moderate demands and led to heightened bureaucratization and centralization. Other authors suggest that it can also be beneficial, for example, to allow a movement to re-mobilise for a particular referendum campaign (Kriesi 1990: 215) Using the important local institutional variation with regard to direct democratic instruments, Kriesi and Wisler (1995) analysed the role of direct democracy in shaping police tactics to respond to protestors. A comparison of Zurich's and Geneva's response to youth movements in the 1980s shows that in Zurich, where direct democracy is widely available, movements are expected to make use of it; 'unconventional' protest forms are less legitimate and repressive police tactics normal and widely accepted. In Geneva, where direct democratic instruments are less developed, the police followed a more appeasing strategy. In a recent book, Tackenberg and Wisler (2008) further develop this institutional-cultural argument by showing the contingent historical origins of police repertoires and their justifications in workers' protests of the 1910s and 1930s, again comparing Zurich and Geneva.

The second important development of this period is found in studies on extreme right-wing movements. Based on the structural analysis of the transformation of traditional cleavages and the rise of new ones, Kriesi argued that in addition to a new cleavage among middle classes triggered by increasing levels of education, the process of economic globalization led to the formation of another cleavage between 'losers' and 'winners' of this transformation. Contrary to the middle-class cleavage, globalization created a potential for right-wing movements fighting against the opening up of frontiers and defending national identities (Kriesi 1996). The analysis of the dataset from the new social movements project, which also included protest events from the right, showed that they were responsible for only 0.6 per cent of all protest events. However, the number of violent radical right-wing protests increased over this period (Gentile 1998). Perhaps more importantly, the radical right had mostly used party politics to express its demands, and with increasing success. For some Swiss movement scholars, this constituted a plea to bring the study of movements and political parties closer together, as both are highly intertwined. This would be done in the political claims analyses that came to characterise Swiss social movement studies in the following decade, at the price of relegating movements to a more marginal role in study designs.

Political Claims Analysis

The first of these political claims analysis projects was a study on immigration policies and citizenship (Giugni et al. 2005; Koopmans et al. 2005). Again, as part of an international research project, the study looked at political claims-making in the field of immigration policy in five countries, considering not only social movements but also all other actors that intervened in the public debate on this topic. Insisting on the importance of *discursive opportunity structures* characterizing immigration regimes, the research showed how the exclusive and assimilationist discourse dominating Swiss immigration policy handicapped immigrant claims-makers, and strongly favoured their right-wing opponents (Giugni and Passy 2002). A very similar study design was employed to investigate claims-making in the realm of unemployment, comparing countries with different welfare-state regimes (Giugni 2010). This analysis also tends to show how marginal social movement organizations were in shaping public discourses on unemployment compared to government actors, unions and political parties.

Political claims analysis was also applied to studying the debates around globalization and global justice that emerged on the Swiss movement agenda at the turn of the century. Beyeler and Kriesi (2005) analysed the international media coverage of protest against the World Economic Forum in Davos, Switzerland, and against the ministerial conferences of the World Trade Organization. Their analysis shows that the Swiss newspaper they studied— the *Neue Zürcher Zeitung*—mostly reported on the protests taking place in

Switzerland against the WEF, put security issues forward most of the time, and was generally very critical of protesters. Finally, in Kriesi et al.'s research on public debates and political transformations (2012), social movements had definitely moved to the background, since the project studied the re-shuffling of party politics and ignored the role of social movements in political transformations. One strand of it, however, attempts to bridge the analysis of party politics with movement politics. Building on the previous protest event database from the new social movements in Europe study, the project extends it up to 2006 and thus covers more recent developments in the movement arena (Hutter 2014). Comparing six countries, the study shows particular interest in examining how the rise of the cleavage linked to globalization affected movements, and therefore focuses on analysing the claims protesters raise. For Switzerland, this extension of protest-event data continues to stress the highly contentious 1980s—the mobilization of the global justice movement in the early 2000s did not lead to such high protest levels and was actually comparatively quite modest (Hutter and Giugni 2009). The cleavage opposing globalization winners and losers expressed itself more in the arena of party politics, through the rise of the right-wing party SVP, than in the street politics of the global justice movement (Hutter 2014).

Surveys in Rallies

The analysis of protest events and political claims strongly shaped Swiss social movement research. However, beyond such approaches, a number of studies on the global justice movement in Switzerland used survey techniques to yield insights into the participants of the movement. For the 2003 G8 summit in Evian, France, a bi-national research team conducted a survey among protesters in Geneva, Lausanne and Annemasse (France) (Sommier et al. 2004). Building on a research program developed earlier for the French case (Agrikoliansky et al. 2005), this research portrayed the organizational diversity of the movement, its different organizational components and their networks through declarations of organizational affiliations. In addition, it pointed at the co-presence of a group of 'overinvested' activists characterised by multiple organizational affiliations and a group of new protesters who tended to be non-affiliated. Another transnational research project with a Swiss branch on the global justice movements used similar methods—adding an organizational survey (Giugni and Nai 2013; Eggert and Giugni 2008). The latter study, based on surveys of demonstrations against the WEF, shows the relatively strong presence of organizations stemming from the previous 'new social movement' protest cycles, for example the environmental and solidarity movements, and the lesser importance of the new groups and organizations that have emerged in the protests against globalization.

Movement Outcomes

To be sure, not all movement research in Switzerland was done within transnational projects. A few important 'Swiss' contributions to movement studies in the past few decades did not follow this rule. This is true in particular of two fields of studies: movement outcomes and activism. Marco Giugni, the European editor of *Mobilization,* was a pioneer in studying movement outcomes (see the 1998 volume 'How Social Movements Matter', which he co-edited) (Giugni et al. 1998). In a comparative study on three movements in three countries (the anti-nuclear, ecology and peace movements in Switzerland, Italy and the United States) (Giugni 2004a), Giugni analysed the role of tactics, resources, political opportunities and public opinion in movement outcomes using time-series analysis based on protest event data and different outcome variables. He suggests that there is a joint-effect model of movement outcomes, where political opportunities (allies) and public opinion are crucial external resources for movements, strengthen the weight of protest and thus increase the chances that power holders meet movement demands (121). For Switzerland, Giugni's results show an impact of the ecology movement when combining the local, regional and national levels. His measures indicate no policy impact for the anti-nuclear and peace movements. However, Giugni looks at short-term effects: he relates outcome variables to movement activity preceding them by a year and thus does not grasp middle- and long-term outcomes. In addition, the degree of incorporation of movement demands in the political system and movement institutionalization is another form of movement outcomes (Giugni and Passy 1998). The weak Swiss state often 'delegates' tasks to integrated social movement organizations, for example in the sectors of environmental and development aid policies (Giugni and Passy 1998), in health policy (Voegtli and Fillieule 2012) or in the realm of pensioners (Lambelet 2012). Thus, the relationship between movements and the state in Switzerland goes far beyond confrontation.

Sociology of Activism

Another stronghold of movement studies in Switzerland is the sociology of activism. Florence Passy has been particularly interested in explaining why people join movement organizations and distinguishes between different types of activism—members, participants and activists, characterised by a growing intensity of commitment. Passy particularly focused on *altruist* forms of political participation (Passy 1998), and tried to understand the specificities of 'members of conscience' mobilizing for the sake of others (Passy and Giugni 2001). Through a survey of a Swiss SMO from the solidarity sector, Passy stressed the importance of socialization, interpersonal networks and decisions (agency) in the recruitment process (Passy 2001, 2003). Linking research on activists to the political claims analysis and the concept of discursive opportunities in the sphere of immigration, Passy and Giugni also studied the role of collective narrations in the formation of collective identities and choice of action repertoires (Passy and Giugni 2005).

Critical Perspectives on Activism and Social Movements

The researchers assembled in the *Centre de recherche de l'action politique* of the University of Lausanne (CRAPUL) also studied activism and activists, mostly focusing on the determinants and consequences of activist trajectories or 'careers', as Olivier Fillieule (2001) put it. Originally from France, Fillieule moved to the University of Lausanne in the early 2000s, and his work is thus part of both Swiss and French social movement studies. His move to Switzerland prompted the rise of a new group of researchers analysing movements, who have produced a number of studies on activism and activist careers. Using a Bourdieusian framework, Gottraux's study of the left-wing group *Socialisme ou Barbarie* was a precursor in analysing activist trajectories to understand the fate of movement organizations (Gottraux 1997).

Many studies applied the interactionist perspective, focusing on activist careers developed by Fillieule (2001, 2010a; Blanchard and Fillieule 2013) to different activist organizations and political parties. Gottraux and Péchu (2011) studied activists of the Swiss right-wing party SVP through interviews and participant observation. Their work aims to show that most of the activists in this radical right-wing party are not globalization 'losers'. A study by Bennani-Chraibi also focused on political parties, but in the Moroccan context (Bennani-Chraibi 2010). In addition to interviews and observation, this work is also based on surveys to reconstruct and quantitatively analyse activist careers, a technique that was also used in studies on the Swiss movement against AIDS, which showed the successive transformations of the Swiss gay movement and its reactions to this health crisis (Voegtli and Fillieule 2012; Delessert and Voegtli 2012). In research currently underway on gender and unionism, union activists are interviewed and surveys are made in three Swiss cantons; participant observation is used to shed light on gender dynamics in the daily routines of unions (Monney, Filleule and Avanza 2013). And Lambelet's study on seniors' association in Switzerland used qualitative methods including participant observation to understand the rarely addressed question of activism by retired people (Lambelet 2011a, 2011b, 2012). While some of these studies do not analyse social movements but rather parties, unions, or interest groups, their focus on activism and activist trajectories likens them to classic studies of movement activism, and constitutes a different form of how the study of movements, parties and interest groups came together in Switzerland. In this respect, reference should also be made to a number of conferences that were organised by the CRAPUL in Lausanne and gave rise to edited volumes on the topics of disengagement (Fillieule 2005), gender and activism (Fillieule and Roux 2009) and collective identity (Surdez, Voegtli and Voutat 2010).

Overall, the common point of the studies from the CRAPUL research group is their critical engagement with dominant theoretical approaches and a broad perspective on social movements and activism in general. They are influenced by French theoretical perspectives—Bourdieu's sociology, in particular—while still engaging the core social movements literature. In the Swiss context, they thus constitute a second pole next to the protest event and political claims studies firmly situated in the traditional political process framework. This is also true of my own work, which extends the traditional scope of movement studies focusing on the state to analysing interactions between movement actors and firms. Through a study of anti-sweatshop campaigns in Switzerland and France, this research emphasises the role of social movements in shaping consumer preferences (Balsiger 2010), and analyses the campaigns' interactions with firms and influence on the rise of new market niches (Balsiger 2012, 2014, 2015). Broadening the perspective in yet a different direction, scholars from the University of Lausanne have also researched police behaviour (Fillieule and Della Porta 2006), protest in authoritarian countries (Bennani-Chraibi and Fillieule 2004) and, recently, turned to investigate the upheavals of the Arab Spring. Fillieule and Bennani-Chraibi (2012) called for a sociology of revolutionary situations and a theoretical approach looking at micro-level interactions, and El Chazli (2012) analysed how 'depoliticised' Egyptians became revolutionaries in the course of the ousting of Mubarak.

Protest Cultures

A final research project that needs to be mentioned here can also be considered as developing a critical perspective, emphasizing the cultural aspects of social movements. Holding a professorship financed by the Swiss National Science Foundation, Oliver Marchart led a research group investigating media and protest. Closer to cultural studies and communication studies than the social movements framework, these studies looked at the use of different kinds of media and protest forms by precarious workers and their movements, such as the EuroMayDay protests. Contributions analysed the timing and coordination of online demonstrations (Marchart et al. 2007) or the use of images by protestors (Marchart and Hamm 2011).

A Swiss Perspective on Social Movements?

One aspect that characterises Swiss movement studies above all is the frequency with which Swiss movements are studied in comparative frameworks, most often when Switzerland is one of the cases in a cross-country study with researchers from different countries. Swiss movement research is therefore highly internationalised, although Switzerland's non-membership in the EU made financing sometimes troublesome, at least until the bilateral treaty of 2004 that allowed Swiss researchers to receive EU funding. Internationalization is also reflected in the languages of publications. The majority of research is published in English, especially in these comparative projects. Nonetheless, there is also a strong research tradition in French—the research by scholars from CRAPUL is often published in French, and addresses French scholars and approaches. Publications in German are much less common. This has to do with the fact that research on social movements in Switzerland, even when part of international projects, has been overwhelmingly done in universities from the French-speaking part.

Comparisons have proven useful to point out some distinguishing characteristics of social movements in Switzerland: their relatively high level of mobilization and use of moderate action forms, in particular petitions and direct democratic instruments. The Swiss case thus suggests the importance to analytically consider protest and more institutionalised forms of participation in an interlinked manner. Social movement organizations use direct democratic means of participation, and are often expected to do so, with other protest forms being perceived as less legitimate. Scholars have therefore pleaded against a clear-cut separation of the study of the spheres of institutionalised (party and interest group) politics and non-institutionalised movement politics. In the study of activism and mobilization processes, this was already the starting point of Switzerland's earliest studies on political activation or mobilization (Kriesi 1985), where new social movement actors such as the anti-nuclear movement were studied alongside interest groups, unions, and political parties. Hutter and Kriesi (2013) emphasised this point anew based on their work on political claims and protest: movement scholars, they say, neglect the existence of different channels of mobilization, in particular the electoral channel or channels of interest intermediation. Recent Swiss studies in the sociology of activism (Lambelet 2011; Péchu and Gottraux 2012) also study movements, interest groups and parties alike, analysing processes such as recruitment or socialization that can be found in all groups composed of activists mobilizing for a cause.

In the study of political processes and their contestation, the Swiss case therefore stands against a narrow understanding of social movements and protest, and begs in favour of studies of contentious political processes that look at all the actors attempting to shape them, some using movement tactics, some more institutionalised forms, some combining tactics from different arenas. Political claims analysis is one possible option for a more encompassing study of political processes: it does not focus on social movements alone, but takes as its analytical unity a policy field. However, social movements tend to fall out of the spotlight of this kind of approach, and we do not learn much about proper movement dynamics. Another way of studying political processes more broadly would be to analyse the interplay of movement actors with other players, see what kinds of tactics they use to challenge different kinds of social orders, and look at the transformations movements undergo in this course. Interesting questions arise when one addresses the articulation of different spheres—how collective actors usually defined as interest groups use movement tactics, or how movements lobby administrations, for instance, and how they combine tactical action repertoires (Fillieule 2010b).

Movement studies in Switzerland have also had considerable impact on theory. Kriesi and colleagues' work of the 1990s has been especially influential in shaping the conceptual toolkit of movement scholars. While there is no 'Swiss school' of movement studies, the research on new social movements (Kriesi et al. 1995) has managed to bridge theoretical traditions of the structural origins of movements with the political process model in an encompassing framework. Furthermore, through its comparative perspective, it has contributed to introducing institutional factors to the concept of political opportunity structures that had hitherto been neglected. State capacity or strength, the level of centralization, or the inclusiveness of the political system have become routine aspects for scholars to investigate when studying the interactions of movements with states.

Within Switzerland, this mostly structuralist approach has been very prominent. Textbook overviews of movements in Switzerland (Giugni 2004b) relate the standard view of movements reacting to political opportunities. Nonetheless, while theory-building by Swiss scholars has penetrated the international scholarly community, debates on existing movement theories in this community have not had much impact on Swiss movement studies in turn. The challenges to the political process model of the late 1990s (Goodwin and Jasper 1999, 2003; McAdam et al. 2001) have left few marks on Swiss movement studies. These issues were mostly taken up by the researchers from CRAPUL (Fillieule 2006; Fillieule et al. 2010), although domestic scientific debates on movements are rare. This is certainly also due to the small size of the specialised scientific community, and the lack of institutionalization thereof. Most Swiss scholars studying movements are political scientists, yet at the yearly conference of the Swiss political science association, panels on protest and movements are not common. Debates take place at the international level, not within the country.

The predominance of structuralist approaches and international research projects adopting macro-sociological methods (protest event or political claims analysis), and the relatively weak institutionalization of movement studies at Swiss universities, means that we know astonishingly little about many of the movements that have been active in Switzerland during the past forty years. While we do know, thanks to protest event analysis, how active the peace, solidarity or urban movements were over time, there is a lack of case studies that would allow us to place these movements in their historical context and to understand them also with the use of more qualitative methods. In other words, there is solid knowledge on the big panorama of movements in Switzerland, but historically rich sociological research on specific movements, organizations, or protest episodes is rare. Since Kriesi's case studies (1985), this kind of research has been neglected—with few exceptions such as Epple's (1988) study on the peace movement. In particular, we lack studies analysing the social movement field, focusing on the rise of new movements, interactions between different collective actors, the building of alliances and the games of distinction taking place. We do not know enough about which organizations compose(d) these movements and how internal fights shaped their outlook. Historical and qualitative studies would be required to complement—and maybe also challenge—some of the insights based on protest event or political claims data. Historians have very recently started to fill this gap for the movements of the 1970s (in particular (Kalt 2010; Schaufelbuehl 2009), but they rarely address questions of movement dynamics and do not engage with concepts and theories of social movement studies.

Many of the most interesting and influential movements that are active in Switzerland today or have shaped Swiss politics in the recent past have not (yet) been studied. This includes, notably, the movement for an independent and neutral Switzerland (AUNS), a sort of Swiss tea party from the 1990s that was very influential in shaping Swiss European policy and enabling the transformation and success of the radical right-wing party SVP; the ongoing struggle against flight routes at the Zurich airport, a NIMBY protest driven by citizens from some of Switzerland's most affluent communities with a cross-national dimension; the very influential movement against sexual delinquents, which has launched a series of successful popular initiatives; and the social media–coordinated youth protest taking the form of 'dance demonstrations' that recently unnerved the cities of Bern and Winterthur and were met with strong repression. These and similar contentious episodes and groups raise questions that are at the very heart of theoretical debates in current movement studies, regarding the interplay of different action forms, their interaction with authorities, the spread of protest in the social media age or the role of emotions.

Philip Balsiger is an assistant professor at the University of Neuchâtel, Switzerland, Institute of Sociology. He is a former Max Weber fellow at the European University Institute, and was a postdoctoral fellow at the Max Planck-Institute for the Study of Societies. His research focus is on the interactions of social movement organizations and corporations and on processes of market moralization. He is the author of *The Fight for Ethical Fashion: The Origins and Interactions of the Clean Clothes Campaign* (Ashgate), and has published in journals such as *Social Movement Studies, Journal of Consumer Culture,* and *Business & Society.*

References

Agrikoliansky, E., O. Fillieule, and N. Mayer, eds. 2005. *L'altermondialisme en France : La longue histoire d'une nouvelle cause.* Paris: Flammarion.

Balsiger, P. 2010. 'Making Political Consumers: The Tactical Action Repertoire of a Campaign for Clean Clothes'. *Social Movement Studies* 9, no. 3: 311–29.

———. 2012. 'Competing Tactics: How the Interplay of Tactical Approaches Shapes Movement Outcomes on the Market for Ethical Fashion'. *MPIfG Discussion Paper* 12/9.

———. 2014. *The Fight for Ethical Fashion: The Origins and Interactions of the Clean Clothes Campaign.* Aldershot, Burlington VT: Ashgate

———. 2015. 'Explaining Dynamic Strategies for Defending Company Legitimacy : The Changing Outcomes of Anti-Sweatshop Campaigns in France and Switzerland'. *Business & Society,* online berfore print, DOI: 10.1177/0007650315619471

Bennani-Chraibi, M. 2010. 'Quand négocier l'ouverture du terrain est déjà enquêter: Obtenir la passation de questionnaires aux congressistes de partis marocains'. *Revue internationale de politique comparée* 17, no. 4: 93–108.

Beyeler, M., and H. Kriesi. 2005. 'Transnational Protest and the Public Sphere'. *Mobilization* 10, no. 1: 95–109.

Blanchard P., and O. Fillieule. 2013. 'Fighting Together: Assessing Continuity and Change in Social Movement Organizations through the Study of Constituencies' Heterogeneity'. In *A Political Sociology of Transnational Europe*, ed. N. Kauppi, 79–108. London: Routledge.

Delessert, T., and M. Voegtli. 2012. *Homosexualités masculines en Suisse: De l'invisibilité aux mobilisations*. Lausanne: Presses polytechniques et universitaires romandes.

Eggert, N., and M. Giugni. 2008. 'Le mouvement altermondialiste en Suisse: L'héritage des nouveaux mouvements sociaux'. In *L'altermondialisme en Suisse*, ed. M. Bandler and M. Giugni, 79–114. Paris: L'Harmattan.

El Chazli, Y. 2012. 'On the Road to Revolution. How Did "Depoliticized" Egyptians Become Revolutionaries?' *Revue française de science politique* 62, no. 5: 79–101.

Epple, R. 1988. *Friedensbewegung und direkte Demokratie in der Schweiz*. Frankfurt: Haag + Herchen

Fillieule, O. 2001. 'Propositions pour une analyse processuelle de l'engagement individuel'. *Revue française de science politique* 51, no. 1: 199–215.

———. 2010a. 'Some Elements of an Interactionist Approach to Political Disengagement'. *Social Movement Studies* 9, no. 1: 1–15

———. 2010b. 'Tombeau pour Charles Tilly: Répertoires, performances et stratégies d'action'. In *Penser les mouvements sociaux: Conflits sociaux et contestations dans les sociétés contemporaines*, ed. O. Fillieule, E. Agrikoliansky and I. Sommier, 77–100. Paris: La Découverte.

Fillieule, O., ed. 2005. *Le désengagement militant*. Paris: Belin.

Fillieule, O., E. Agrikoliansky and I. Sommier, eds. 2010. *Penser les mouvements sociaux: Conflits sociaux et contestations dans les sociétés contemporaines*. Paris: La Découverte.

Fillieule, Olivier, and M. Bennani-Chraibi. 2012. 'Towards a Sociology of Revolutionary Situations: Reflections on the Arab Uprisings'. *Revue française de science politique* 62, no. 5: 1–29.

Fillieule, O., and M. Bennani-Chraibi, eds. 2003. *Résistances et protestations dans les sociétés musulmanes*. Paris: Presses de Sciences Po.

Fillieule, O., and D. Della Porta. 2006. *Police et manifestants*. Paris: Presses de Sciences Po.

Fillieule, O., and P. Roux. 2009. *Le sexe du militantisme*. Paris: Presses de Sciences Po.

Ganguillet, G. 1985. 'Le conflit jurassien: un cas de mobilisation ethno-régionale en Suisse'. *Rapport Nr. 2 du projet de recherche 'Le citoyen actif'*. Soziologisches Institut, Universität Zürich.

Gentile, P. 1998. 'Radical Right Protest in Switzerland'. In *Acts of Dissent: New Developments in the Study of Protest*, ed. D. Rucht, R. Koopmans, and F. Neidhard, 227–252. Berlin: Edition Sigma.

Giugni, M. 1995. *Entre stratégie et opportunité: Les nouveaux mouvements sociaux et Suisse*. Zürich: Seismo

———. 2004a. *Social Protest and Policy Change: Ecology, Antinuclear, and Peace Movements in Comparative Perspective*. Lanham: Rowman and Littlefield.

———. 2004b. 'Social Movements: Structures, Processes and Consequences'. In *Handbook of Swiss Politics*, ed. U. Klöti, et al. 2nd ed, 243–277. Zürich: Neue Zürcher Zeitung.

Giugni, M., ed. 2010. *The Politics of Unemployment in Europe: Welfare States and Political Opportunities*. Houndsmills: Palgrave.

Giugni, M., and A. Nai. 2013. 'Paths towards Consensus: Explaining Decision Making within the Swiss Global Justice Movement'. *Swiss Political Science Review* 19, no. 1: 26–40.

Giugni, M., et al. 2005. 'Institutional and Discursive Opportunities for Extreme-Right Mobilization in Five Countries'. *Mobilization* 10, no. 1: 145–62.

Giugni, M., and F. Passy. 1998. 'Contentious Politics in Complex Societies: New Social Movements between Conflict and Cooperation'. In *From Contention to Democracy*, ed. M. Giugni, D. McAdam and C. Tilly, 81–107. Lanham: Rowman and Littlefield.

———. 2002. 'Entre post-nationalisme et néo-institutionnalisme: la structuration des débats publics en Suisse dans le domaine de l'immigration et des relations ethniques'. *Swiss Political Science Review* 8, no. 2: 21–52.

Goodwin, J., and J. M. Jasper. 1999. 'Caught in a Winding, Snarling Vine: The Structural Bias of Political Process Theory'. *Sociological Forum* 14, no. 1: 27–54.

Gottraux, P. 1997. *Socialisme ou Barbarie: Un engagement politique et intellectuel dans la France de l'après-guerre*. Lausanne: Editions Payot.

Gottraux, P., and C. Péchu. 2011. *Militants de l'UDC: La diversité sociale et politique des engagés*. Lausanne: Editions Antipodes.

Hutter, S. 2014. *Protesting Culture and Economics in Western Europe: New Cleavages in Left and Right Politics*. Minneapolis: Minnesota University Press.

Hutter, S., and M. Giugni. 2009. 'Protest Politics in a Changing Political Context: Switzerland, 1975–2005'. *Swiss Political Science Review* 15, no. 3: 427–61.

Hutter, S., and H. Kriesi. 2013. 'Movements of the Left, Movements of the Right Reconsidered'. In *The Future of Social Movement Research*, ed. J. van Stekelenburg, C. M. Roggeband, and B. Klandermans. Minneapolis: University of Minnesota Press.

Kalt, M. 2010. *Tiersmondismus in der Schweiz der 1960er und 1970er Jahre: Von der Barmherzigkeit zur Solidarität*. Bern: Peter Lang.

Koopmans, R., et al. 2005. *Contested Citizenship: Immigration and Cultural Diversity in Europe*. Minneapolis: University of Minnesota Press.

Kriesi, H. 1984. *Die Zürcher Bewegung: Bilder, Interaktionen, Zusammenhänge*. Frankfurt: Campus.

———. 1990. 'Switzerland : A Marginal Field of Research in an Underdeveloped Social Science Community'. In *Research on Social Movements: The State of the Art in Western Europe and the USA*, ed. D. Rucht, 203–29. Frankfurt: Campus; Boulder: Westview Press.

———. 1995. 'Bewegungen auf der Linken, Bewegungen auf der Rechten: Die Mobilisierung von zwei neuen Typen von sozialen Bewegungen in ihrem politischen Kontext'. *Swiss Political Science Review* 1, no. 1: 1–46.

Kriesi, H., ed. 1985. *Bewegung in der Schweizer Politik: Fallstudien zu politischen Mobilisierungsprozessen in der Schweiz*. Frankfurt: Campus.

Kriesi, H., et al. 1995. *New Social Movements in Western Europe: A Comparative Analysis*. Minneapolis: University of Minnesota Press.

Kriesi, H., et al. 2012. *Political Conflict in Western Europe*. Cambridge and New York: Cambridge University Press.

Kriesi, H., et al., eds. 1981. *Politische Aktivierung in der Schweiz. 1945–1978*. Diessenhofen: Ruegger.

Kriesi, H., and D. Wisler. 1996. 'Social Movements and Direct Democracy in Switzerland'. *European Journal of Political Research* 30: 19–40.

Lambelet, A. 2011a. 'Âgencement militant ou entre-soi générationnel? Militer dans des organisations de défense des retraités'. *Politix* 96: 81–95.

———. 2011b. 'Understanding the Political Preferences of Seniors' Organizations: The Swiss Case'. *Swiss Political Science Review* 17, no. 4: 417–31.

———. 2012. 'L'implication des mouvements de retraités dans la décision politique'. *Gérontologie et société* 143: 51–61.

Lévy, R. 1981. 'Politische Basisaktivität im Bereich der Umweltproblematik'. *Schweizerisches Jahrbuch für politische Wissenschaft* 21: 9–37.

Marchart, O., S. Adolphs and M. Hamm. 2007. 'Taktik und Taktung. Eine Diskursanalyse politischer Online-Demonstrationen'. In *Dating.21 Liebesorganisation und Verabredungskulturen,* ed. M. Ries, H. Fraueneder, and K. Mairitsch, 207–24. Bielefeld: Transcript.8.

Marchart, O., and M. Hamm. 2011. 'Prekäre Bilder—Bilder des Prekären: Anmerkungen zur Bildproduktion post-identitärer sozialer Bewegungen'. In *Bilder und Gemeinschaft,* ed. B. Fricke, M. Klammer, S. Neuner. München: Fink, 377–99.

McAdam, D., S. Tarrow and C. Tilly. 2001. *Dynamics of Contention.* Cambridge and New York: Cambridge University Press.

Monney, V., O. Fillieule and M. Avanza. 2013. 'Les souffrances de la femme-quota: Le cas du syndicat suisse UNIA'. *Travail, genre et société* 30: 91–109.

Passy, F. 1998. *L'action altruiste.* Genève, Paris: Librairie Droz.

———. 2001. 'Socializing, Connecting, and the Structural Agency/Gap: A Specification of the Impact of Networks on Participation in Social Movements'. *Mobilization* 6, no. 2: 173–92.

———. 2003. 'Social Networks Matter: But How?' In *Social Movements and Networks,* ed. M. Diani and D. McAdam, 21–48. Oxford: Oxford University Press.

Passy, F., and M. Giugni. 2005. 'Récits, imaginaires collectifs, et formes d'action protestataire: Une approche constructiviste de la contestation antiraciste'. *Revue française de science politique* 55: 889–918.

Passy, F., and M. Giugni, eds. 2001. *Political Altruism: Solidarity Movements in International Perspective.* Lanham, Boulder, New York, Oxford: Rowman and Littlefield.

Schaufelbuehl, J. M., ed. *1968–1978. Ein bewegtes Jahrzehnt in der Schweiz.* Zürich: Chronos.

Sommier, I., et al. 2004. 'L'altermondialisme en réseaux'. *Politix* 68: 13–48.

Surdez, M., Voegtli, M., and B. Voutaz, eds. 2010. *Identifier, s'identifier: A propos des identités politiques.* Lausanne: Editions Antipode.

Voegtli, M. and O. Fillieule. 2012. 'Constitution, Diversification and Normalization of a Health Problem: Organizing the Fight against AIDS in Switzerland (1984–2005)'. *Contemporary Politics* 18, no. 2: 200–12.

Chapter 17

Studying Movements in a Movement-Become-State
Research and Practice in Postcolonial Ireland[1]

Laurence Cox

The site of some of Western Europe's most dramatic movement episodes, Ireland is a peculiar case for studying social movement research. The 1798 uprising was a significant element of the Atlantic Revolutions; the Land War (1879–82) initiated one of the world's most successful land reforms, with a near-complete transition from landlord-tenant relationships to peasant proprietorship; the period between 1916 and 1923 saw one of Western Europe's few successful independence movements; the Northern Irish 'troubles' from 1969 through to 1994 were Europe's longest-running episode of lethal internal violence; 1978–81 saw one of the few outright defeats of nuclear power worldwide; the women's and GLBTQ movements brought about a more dramatic change from institutionalised Catholic power than in most Northern contexts; and working-class community organizing has played a role in Ireland comparable to Latin American contexts. On the face of it, a strong social movements research agenda would seem natural.

However, most of these topics have been successfully colonised by other disciplines. In the independent state, history has emphasised questions of national legitimacy and the view from elites, often at the expense of researching popular organizing. Feminist and GLBTQ scholarship has similarly prioritised a celebratory or critical account of these struggles in which *movement* aspects are routinely secondary. Where Irish history is less unique, such as agrarian unrest, labour history and the left, strong tendencies to atheoretical empiricism have restricted wider dialogues.

As might be expected in a small postcolonial setting, movement-based theorizing and historiography have also made significant contributions, but as with academic work the key concerns have typically been to legitimate movements and explore their relationship to the state, particularly because movement intellectuals have often become (or started as) academics and state functionaries. The result, as in India, is a field dominated by discussions of the choices made by actors (often narrowed to leading figures or political parties) at well-known historical junctures, and their role in inflecting processes of state formation and restructuring. In parallel, Irish movements have also been a privileged ground for *literature* and debates over national identity.

Partly as a result, research on movements has often sought refuge in North American and British canonical orthodoxy and has minimised engagement with these literatures' movement-relevant aspects. A primary concern has been to convince others of the value of social movement studies for interpreting Ireland, rather than asking how the Irish experience might inform the development of social movement studies. Given the very particular course of Irish history, this is a missed opportunity.

Institutional Forms

Tovey and Share (2003: 23–41) note that Irish sociology moved from a largely uncritical, positivist approach to playful exploration for its own sake, marginalizing genuinely critical work in the process. This comment highlights the links between intellectuals and power characteristic of postcolonial settings. History and literature have moved from celebrating nationalism to hostility to popular action (or denying its existence other than as violence); political science, meanwhile, ignores anything independent of official politics. The prolific 'civil society' literature (with exceptions such as O'Donovan 2011) uncritically reproduces official perspectives and reduces popular activity to invited participation in officially created spaces. The state in its changing forms—from Protestant statelet to ethnic power balance in the north and from developmental nationalism to loyal Europeans in the south—is the elephant in the room of research on popular agency in Ireland, and it is unsurprising that in fields like history much of the best work on movements is done abroad.

In Ireland, leaders and intellectuals from popular organizations regularly become part of the political, media and literary establishment, whether due to movement success or state co-optation. There is a large public interest in some aspects of movement-state encounters, and it is not unusual for researchers to have close relationships with movement organizations. All this affects research on movements, as does research *outside* universities: some of the best-known writers in the field are journalists, independent historians, movement intellectuals, precarious academics, community activists, librarians, authors and the like. This is a healthy check on the state-centric role of credentialised researchers, although not immune to its own pressures.

Scale has other effects: fewer than a dozen academics on the island have social movement research as the leading element of their academic profile.[2] Thus most writing on social movements is situated within a broader, usually sociological, perspective. Hence, too, few researchers can have the luxury of focusing on a single movement or organization; good researchers also need to be aware of academic literatures which frame their topic differently; and many researchers are in dialogue both with movements and a wider public. All this enables a wider perspective than is possible in more specialised contexts—when researchers take advantage of it.

Overview of the Literature

Given the history and power of Irish social movements, much research in the area is largely descriptive, unconsciously assuming particular frameworks of analysis. Nevertheless there are often attempts to break out of this and engage with one form or another of explicit analysis of collective action. One such area is that of pre-independence nationalism, Northern Ireland (Smyth 2006; O'Keefe 2013), and postcolonial studies (O'Connor and Foley 2006; Cox 2013a). A second is in that of pre-independence peasant struggles (Donnelly 2009; Cronin 2012), labour and working-class history (Fagan 2000; O'Connor 2011; the journal *Saothar* is an important resource in this area) and the history of working-class politics in Ireland (Newsinger 2004; Ó Drisceoil and Lane 2005). Here the developing use of oral history, and the newly formed Centre for the Histories of Labour and Class in Galway, may play significant roles in the future. A third is in the area of feminism (Mahon 1995; Galligan 1998; Connolly 2002), gay rights (Ryan 2006) and, more broadly, equality (Baker et al. 2009). Nonetheless in all of these fields the wider discipline marginalises movement analysis.

US/Canonical Approaches

While one strand of Irish movement research has been keen to adopt international (read: US) approaches, this has been predominantly for local purposes, a fact underlined by the low levels of participation by Irish researchers in social movement events or publishing abroad. In thirty-six *issues* of the UK-based journal *Social Movement Studies,* for example, I identified a sum total of three Irish-related *articles:* one by an Irish-based author studying movements abroad, one by American academics using Northern Ireland as a comparator and one by an Irish-based author looking at movements in

Northern Ireland. Typically, 'canonical' social movement research in Ireland is a resource for local academic strategies: until recently Irish researchers have not been under the same pressure as their British counterparts to publish in the 'right' journals, and very few have had any regular commitment to social movement research networks of any kind.

There are a handful of honourable exceptions, notably Hilary Tovey (below) and Pauline Cullen, whose work (e.g. 2010) has focused particularly on NGOs, coalitions and the international arena; we can also note Frédéric Royall's work on various movements (e.g. Royall 2009). Writers abroad whose work has been primarily oriented towards Ireland should also be mentioned, notably Louise Ryan (e.g. Ryan and Ward 2007) on first-wave feminism and nationalism, and Lorenzo Bosi (e.g. Bosi and Alimi 2008), who has set Northern Irish political violence in its historical context.

Nonetheless there have been some attempts at defining the field in orthodox terms. In 1998 the social movements section of the ISA held its conference in Cork; a related volume was published eight years later (Connolly and Hourigan 2006). This offered a relatively conventional theoretical overview followed by a series of movement-specific chapters along similar lines (e.g. Mullally 2006) and excluding working-class struggles (labour, community activism). More recently, a special issue of the *Irish Journal of Sociology* (vol. 18, no. 2, 2010) took a rather more eclectic approach to social movements and civil society.

Macro Approaches

The best macro-theoretical approach, however, is Michel Peillon's (1982) *Contemporary Irish Society.* This uses Alain Touraine's model from *The Voice and the Eye* (1981) to analyse the class projects of different groups within Irish society, within the framework of an understanding of collective action as struggling over 'historicity', how society makes and remakes itself. Peillon shows convincingly how 'the project of the bourgeoisie, backed up by economic growth, has become the major aim of Irish society as a whole, backed up not only by the State but also by the farmers and the trade unions' (1982: 59). While this discussion of national-developmentalist hegemony calls out for an updating for neoliberal times, it remains the most substantial attempt to think through the relationship of social movements to Irish society, and deserves wider international attention as a model.

Three other macro-theoretical contributions can be noted here. Carol Coulter (1993) does for feminism what the best writers do for Irish environmentalism, distinguishing an official 'civil society'—drawing on international models and seeking inclusion within elites—from the 'incivil society' (Sen 2005) of working-class women's organizing, often framed within a nationalist approach (and hence subordinate to ethno-religious boundaries). Tomás Jones (2003) attempts a rethinking of canonical social movement accounts of the Irish experience, as does my own 'Gramsci in Mayo' (Cox 2011), part of a broader project to develop a Marxist theory of movements starting from an Irish perspective (Cox 2006; Barker et al. 2013). Much remains to be done in understanding the role of movements in a society so visibly shaped by them.

Rural Populism

The long history of Irish environmentalism raises many questions. One of the most robust findings is to undermine the image of such movements as predominantly urban and middle-class. Rural sociologist Hilary Tovey (1993) neatly distinguished between one aspect of Irish environmentalism which has had this character (and by now largely exists only in the form of NGOs) and attempts by rural communities, often disadvantaged, to struggle for forms of development in line with their own needs and interests rather than those of multinational corporations. This argument has been developed by Allen and Jones (1990, updated as Allen 2004) and by Liam Leonard (2007) who has used the term *rural populism* to describe this form of resistance. If the 'two environmentalisms' argument in some ways parallels US literature on environmental justice, in other respects the struggle for a different development has more of a postcolonial flavour.

Ireland has a particularly significant record here—one of the only states to defeat nuclear power entirely after a complex struggle (Dalby 1984), it saw battles over chemical plants in the southern province of Munster through the 1970s and 1980s, followed by local conflicts around incinerators, waste dumps and mobile phone masts. The struggles around the Shell/Statoil gas pipeline planned for Rossport, Co. Mayo (e.g. Garavan 2008; Slevin 2013), and the extension of fracking exploration across the western midlands have kept this issue alive.

One theme not fully addressed in this literature is how community-based rural environmentalism relates to newer forms of counter-cultural and direct-action ecology which draw from other European countries. Present in the Carnsore conflict, these approaches returned to public prominence with roads conflicts at Glen of the Downs (c. 1997–2000) and the archaeological site of Tara (c. 2003–10). Initial fears of internal struggles over 'movement imperialism' remained at the level of polemic attacks, while in Rossport, where state forces have alienated the local community, campaigners have shown their dedication to the conflict and a willingness to engage closely with community issues, leading to a much stronger alliance.

An unexpected dimension to Irish environmental research has been the particular attention given to organic farming, community gardening, farmers' markets and so on—the product in the long term of a generation of organic farmers (Tovey 1999) and attempts by the state to deploy the framework for conventionally oriented farmers: the agricultural research body Teagasc has been a reliable source of PhD scholarships. Some very interesting work has been done by, for example, Oliver Moore (2006) and Annette Jørgensen (2006). An attention to questions of knowledge and meaning-making has naturally bulked large here.

Tovey's recent (2007) *Environmentalism in Ireland,* finally, updates the picture and takes a much closer look at the individual and biographical level of environmental activism in Ireland, showing the extent of diversity and also to some extent the breakdown of some of these distinctions, facilitated by a greater informality in practical organization. She suggests that analysing Irish movements in terms similar to those used for Southern Europe by researchers like Maria Kousis.

Community Development

Working-class community organizing in Ireland, particularly the Republic, provides some particular challenges to research. Levels of participation since the 1960s have been extraordinarily high (Mullan and Cox 2000), bearing comparison more with ethnic minorities in the United States (Naples 1998) than with any European realities. Similar levels also appear in Northern Ireland, albeit subsumed under the framework of contending ethnic parties and paramilitary organizations (both of which were also present in the Republic but lost their grip on community organizing earlier).

However, as Geoghegan (2000) shows, characteristic of this movement in the past two decades has been a strategy of advancing class-based agendas *within* the language frameworks of top-down 'community development' (itself in turn arguably an attempt to co-opt the developing movement). This has undermined both activists' willingness to talk openly about their political strategies (with notable exceptions such as Lyder 2006 and Bissett 2009) and academics' ability to see community development as *movement* (Powell and Geoghegan 2004).

Nonetheless, a range of engaged researchers have carried out significant work on Irish community activism. The most impressive is Margaret Gillan

(2010), whose work explores the contested politics of technical knowledge in the production of community-based movement media within state-structured frameworks and adopts a participatory action research approach. Jean Bridgeman (2010) has similarly attempted to articulate the politics of working-class self-education. My own *Eppur si muove* (Cox 2013b) attempts a Marxist analysis of the history. Finally, Michael Punch (2009) has situated community activism within a specifically urban perspective.

For more externally located observers, we should mention Curtin and Varley's (1995) typology of community action, Niamh Hourigan's (2001) work on Irish-language organizing, Mark Boyle's (2005) attempt to use Sartre's dialectic to study the history of working-class community action in the Dublin suburb of Ballymun, and Alessandro Zagato's recent (2012) PhD thesis, which takes an autonomist line.

Engaged Scholarship

Along with the relative weakness of purely academic research on social movements has come a long history of engaged scholarship, shaped by movements' internal theoretical traditions and the political involvement of some academics. Such analyses were typically influenced by debates abroad. This is the case, for example, for the *Ripening of Time* journal (1976–82) associated with the Marxist-Leninist Revolutionary Struggle group; *Times Change* (1994–2000) linked to the Democratic Left party; John Goodwillie's *Colours in the Rainbow* (1988) and the journal *An Caorthann* (1994–98), both associated with the Green Party; or the extensive theoretical output linked to the anarchist Workers Solidarity Movement (1984–present). The Irish Left Online Document Archive (http://cedarlounge.wordpress.com/archive-index/) and the Struggle archive (http://struggle.ws/wsm/) are both useful sources for such material.

The 2007 symposium 'Everyday Creativity, Counter Cultures and Social Change' and the 2011 conference 'New Agendas in Social Movements Studies', by contrast, both represent research produced within the university but by engaged scholars, often starting from an activist background, and in dialogue with movements. My own work has largely taken place within this framework and has involved systematic collaboration with activist writers, particularly in community development (above) and the movement of movements (Curry and Cox 2010), with particular attention to methodology and the politics of knowledge (Barker and Cox 2002). Much of the work discussed above in terms of environmentalism and community activism adopts similar strategies, as does much writing on the alter-globalization movement (e.g. Finnegan 2005; Browne 2004; Meade 2008) and the 'Maynooth school' (below).

Maynooth school

This is largely shaped by the encounter between contemporary engaged social movements scholarship from the non-institutional left, and the impressive body of largely unwritten practice and theory developed within working-class Irish community activism. One meeting point for the two has been in radical forms of participatory action research as a methodological and political principle, and social movement practice as the field where such research can have most effect (in other words on participants' self-understanding, strategic action and reflection).

Early moments of this engagement were shaped by collaborations between myself and (respectively) youth worker Martin Geoghegan, Caitriona Mullan of Third System Approaches, Pat McBride and the Ballymun Oral History Project, care worker Shane Dunphy, and Margaret Gillan of Community Media Network. This developed into a postgraduate programme with activists carrying out participatory action research into movement practice at the National University of Ireland Maynooth, including the work of Chris Bermingham (2011) on birth activism; Jean Bridgeman on working-class cultures of resistance, Hilary Darcy on protest policing (ní Dhorchaigh and Cox 2011), Catherine Friedrich on movement knowledge, Asia Rutkowska (2007) on social centres, Anna Szolucha (2013) on activist decision-making.

This experience in turn made Maynooth a key node for the development of *Interface,* the academic/activist journal of social movement research, with its openness to a diversity of formats and sources of knowledge, its insistence on the importance of locally grounded understanding and its concern to develop dialogue across disciplinary boundaries and political traditions. Along with this came a push to rethink Marxism and feminism in particular as theories 'from and for' movements and to clarify the elements of a theory of movements present within each (Barker et al. 2013; Eschle et al. 2011).

A final (for now) stage has been the joint project between the departments of Sociology and Adult and Community Education of an MA course in Community Education, Equality and Social Activism which offers movement activists a year to reflect on their own experience, 'learn from each other's struggles' and build alliances, and develop their own movement's practice. This is perhaps the logical outcome of a trajectory focusing on the relationship between movement knowledge and academic research: an intensive engagement which is as yet mostly manifested in practice and activist debates rather than in journal articles or monographs. A developing archive of research on social movements in Ireland should disseminate this knowledge more widely.

An Agenda for the Future?

Social movements in Ireland present a range of challenges not only to Irish researchers but also to the wider field. Irish movement history is in important ways different from most Western European states. More use could be made of it as a counter-example or test case to avoid building local assumptions (for example, those relating to core Western European states) into theorizing. Such dialogues have a long history with majority world countries, going back to nineteenth-century Irish-Asian anti-nationalist connections and later solidarity movements with Latin America. The challenges faced in developing adequate theory for such comparisons highlight the rich potential of attempts to develop approaches which can work in the Irish context beyond the theoretically trivial level (e.g. 'applying' a particular form of organizational conceptualization to an Irish case).

In *Understanding European movements,* Cristina Flesher Fominaya and I (2013) proposed the concept of national or regional 'movement landscapes' to respond to this. The metaphor is intended to highlight four key features of movement realities:

(1) Landscapes have real, materially powerful features (movements are actors) but at the same time these cannot be understood in isolation from one another (movements are not units or atoms to be studied individually).

(2) Landscapes are shaped both by underlying structure (geology) and more surface features (vegetation, human activity etc.). Movements similarly operate in a layered reality similar to Bhaskar's critical realism: even when they are successful in affecting social structure their realities are structured differently to those of state power or public discourse. In this sense, Weber's 'class-status-party' distinctions or Lipset and Rokkan's cleavage theory are useful as highlighting different levels (social structure, group identity formation and internal institution-building, political parties and other forms of conflictual public representation).

(3) Landscapes are constructed historically, in processes which are still on-going and involve the gradual (sedimentation, erosion, uplift etc.)

and the cataclysmic (glaciation, vulcanism, submergence etc.) Similarly, movement actors operate both in moderately straightforward contexts of slow changes and in contexts shaped by past struggles, particularly the outcome of past waves of intense mobilization or revolutionary conflict.

(4) Landscapes are boundaried in various ways which cannot be easily thought away: plains versus hill country, major rivers and sea boundaries, forested and open areas, etc., can all be traversed, but such crossings require effort and different approaches. The boundaries between nationalist and unionist in Ireland, Christian and secular organizing, social democratic and Stalinist, institutional and non-institutional left, etc., remain fundamental structuring features even where alliances are constructed across these boundaries.

As yet this remains at the level of metaphor, but a serious comparison of European movement landscapes would be a major contribution from social movement studies. It is something which Irish activists have to consider when relating to 'Europe'—in ways similar to those faced by British, Scandinavian, or Southern European activists. This shared experience of difference highlights the need for a deeper and more structural conception of historical-comparative work in movement analysis at the level of national and regional movement landscapes; something which at present is often relegated to a descriptive introduction or anecdotal commentary.

A related question is how far local actors appropriate international movement identities and discourses and seek mutual recognition by international organizations. This process goes back at least as far as the French revolution and the links formed by radical democrats between states; the Irish, Polish and Italian nationalisms of the mid-nineteenth century and the crystallizing out of Marxist and anarchist identities slightly later had very long-term effects. The process continues through the struggles for recognition of different forces within the European Resistance, the movements of 1968, the construction of international feminist, environmental, peace, etc., networks in the 1980s; the processes leading to the European Federation of Green Parties and comparable, smaller processes on the far left; the construction of the European 'movement of movements' and now anti-austerity organizing. Naive comparative approaches can treat the presence of a national node as an unproblematic fact, rather than asking (as, for example, research on Green Parties has done) what local movement realities are represented by the choice to use a particular name and what the local impact of international affiliation is.

A particular feature of the Irish landscape is what I have described as 'movement-become-state' or (subsequently) 'movements from above'. The formation of the Irish state in the south was the result of a dramatic restructuring of hegemonic relations around a number of movements (peasants-become-farmers, nationalist, Catholic, elements of the workers' and women's movements, cultural-nationalist etc.) which then underwent significant processes of transformation as elements of each became loyal or dissident parts of the new power structure, while others were excluded or in some cases violently repressed in what has been called an Irish counter-revolution (Regan 1999).

The new state nonetheless relied on continuing processes of popular mobilization, increasingly now 'from above' (i.e. with the active support of state and capitalist power), for a range of institutionalised 'inside movements' (mainstream nationalism, Catholic organizations, conservative trade unions and women's groups, farming bodies etc.) structured around a national-developmentalist agenda but also an ethno-religious one. The effects of this process—in widespread popular collaboration with a 'carceral Catholicism' manifested in industrial schools, Magdalen asylums and widespread physical and sexual abuse—have left a politics of memory comparable to that of post-fascist states in Europe and Latin America.

'Movement-become-state' also highlights the complexities of these new forms of mobilization/organization/institutionalization; the challenge of theorizing co-optation in social movement activity (e.g. ritualised forms of direct action by 'insider' farmers' groups) and its effects on internal power relationships within movements (institutionalised leadership versus rank-and-file); the use of movement pasts to legitimate the official present (including in intellectual and academic work), etc. Tovey and Share (2003: 462–69) have attempted to use new social movement theory to analyse the development of lay Catholic fundamentalism, while Landy (2013) has explored the political constraints on migrant activism..

The ways in which these relationships shaped movement discourses (towards a focus on 'issues' and 'problems' and an often unquestioned reliance on policy mechanisms and state power, with the intervening steps of popular mobilization and mediation with the state largely left unspoken) are a heightened form of a situation familiar across Europe but which is often taken for granted rather than subjected to critical enquiry by scholars—whose interests and whose agency, within movements and outside them, are represented by this mode of discourse? In recent Irish history, processes of 'social partnership' (including trade unions in tripartite corporatist arrangements from 1987 until the late 2000s and the 'community and voluntary sector' for a rather shorter span) have had powerful effects on movement organizing which demand greater critical analysis—in particular as this process is now ending, with access to policy and funding increasingly barred, movement elites unable to return to strategies of mass mobilization and traditional movement supporters increasingly disaffiliated from institutional survival strategies.

At the origins of 'movement-become-state' in the south—and in the takeover of the northern state by conservative (unionist) movements relying on populist mobilization of the Protestant working class—lies the relationship between social movements and revolution, recently rediscovered in the 'Dynamics of Contention' literature but a central structuring fact of Irish history. Although Irish history post-1798 is not exceptionally violent by global standards, movement actors and opponents have adopted a particularly violence-oriented *rhetoric,* with strong religious and legitimating overtones (whether of martyrdom or of 'Peace') and Irish republicanism is one of the last long-term movements in Europe to maintain the Blanquist tradition of conspiratorial insurrectionalism.

More broadly, the relationship between movement, revolution and state has been as important in the case of nationalism in Ireland as for anti-fascist resistance in Western Europe and subsequent state legitimacy. These relationships are rarely considered as integral to social movement scholarship; but the very self-restrictions under which European movements typically operate (the awareness of the limits within which they can challenge state power without facing violent repression) are shaped by this wider history.

Two specific aspects of this are crucial at present, in Ireland and elsewhere in Europe. One is a more adequate theorization of movement waves (1789, 1848, 1916–24, anti-fascist resistance, 1968, 1989–90, movement of movements) and their relationship both to long-term processes of social change and to transformations in state structure and regimes of accumulation. In particular, if there is merit in Arrighi's (2004) analysis of relatively short-lived regimes of accumulation (e.g. as between Fordism and neoliberalism) and that of Wainwright (1994) and Lash and Urry (1987) of the relationship between the movements of 1968 and the crumbling of Fordism, what should be said of the long-term conflict between neoliberalism and European movements: going back into the mid-1990s, forcing a retreat from metropolitan summits by the mid-2000s, dealing substantial blows to the Bush project of permanent war in the same period and now intensifying as anti-austerity movements in many parts of Europe, with a consequent crisis of legitimacy in countries such as Greece, Italy and Ireland where Troika rules have in effect amounted to a soft coup against popular pressure? What needs to be theorised is not simply (as autonomists have it) the development of popular protest but equally the relative immunity of states to such protest at present. In other words, we need a movement-relevant analysis of the nature of power and struggle in the end years of neoliberalism—and one which indicates how movements might not simply contribute to dismantling it but also play a decisive role in shaping whatever comes next.

A final point which the Irish experience highlights is the role of culture, in various dimensions. One is that of movement milieux, alternative scenes and counter-cultures. Few movements (in Ireland or elsewhere) are entirely independent of one another, but the boundaries between them have not been adequately theorised. For example, what does it mean to treat the anti-nuclear power movement as part of the environmental movement or separate from it? Environmentalism and alternative lifestyles? Feminism and lesbian activism? Peace movements and the left? These are practical boundary and definition issues for movement strategists and organisers to whom research which starts with an axiomatic definition of its object has nothing to say.

In Ireland, where the relationship between radical movements and cultural change has been even more pronounced than elsewhere—moving rapidly from 'traditional', rhetorically rural, conservative Catholicism to a 'modern' Western European culture—the relationship between political and cultural movements requires more research. My own work on counter-cultures, new religious movements and Western Buddhism (Cox 2011; Cosgrove et al. 2011; Cox 2013a) has attempted one approach but far more remains to be done, not least in terms of understanding how such movements contribute to social change, often an explicit goal. Particular attention should be paid to movement media, the reception of cultural material from abroad, and the contexts within which both political and cultural movements organise (in Dublin, for example, they have routinely had to use the same rooms, the same noticeboards, and the same people).

As Hugh MacDiarmid noted, the universal *is* the particular. This is what each specific movement landscape contributes to our understanding of other landscapes.

Laurence Cox is lecturer in sociology at the National University of Ireland Maynooth. He is co-author of *We Make Our Own History: Marxism and Social Movements in the Twilight of Neoliberalism* and co-editor of *Understanding European Movements: New Social Movements, Global Justice Struggles and Anti-Austerity Protest; Marxism and Social Movements* and *Silence Would Be Treason: Last Writings of Ken Saro-Wiwa.* He is co-editor of the open-access social movements journal *Interface* (http://interfacejournal.net), co-chair of the Council for European Studies' social movements network and co-directs the NUIM MA in Community Education, Equality and Social Activism (http://ceesa-ma.blogspot.com).

Notes

1. Thanks to Terry Dunne for comments and suggestions on this chapter.
2. In writing this chapter I am conscious of being perhaps the only permanent academic on the island with the bulk of their *teaching* and doctoral supervision explicitly in this area.

References

Allen, R. 2004. *No Global.* London: Pluto.

Allen, R., and T. Jones. 1990. *Guests of the Nation.* London: Earthscan.

Arrighi, G. 2004. *The Long Twentieth Century.* London: Verso.

Baker, J., et al. 2009. *Equality.* 2nd ed. Basingstoke: Palgrave.

Barker, C., and L. Cox. 2002. 'What Have the Romans Ever Done for Us?' Helsinki: into-ebooks.

Barker, C., et al. 2013. *Marxism and Social Movements.* Leiden: Brill.

Bermingham, C. 2011. 'Association for Improvements in Maternity Services Ireland'. In *The 21ˢᵗ Century Motherhood Movement,* ed. A. O'Reilly, 147–57. Bradford: Demeter.

Bissett, J. 2009. *Regeneration.* Dublin: New Island.

Bosi, L., and E. Alimi. 2008. 'Un'analisi storica comparata dei processi di radicalizzazione'. *Ricerche di storia politica* 11, no. 3: 273–92.

Boyle, M. 2005. 'Sartre's Circular Dialectic and the Empires of Abstract Space'. *Annals of the Association of American Geographers* 95, no. 1: 181–201.

Bridgeman, J. 2010. 'A Matter of Trust'. *Interface* 2, no. 1: 154–67.

Browne, H. 2004. 'Consenting to Capital in the Irish Media'. *Irish journal of sociology* 13, no. 2: 129–41.

Connolly, L. 2002. *The Irish Women's Movement.* Basingstoke: Palgrave.

Connolly, L., and N. Hourigan. 2006. *Social Movements and Ireland.* Manchester: Manchester University press.

Cosgrove, O., et al. 2011. *Ireland's New Religious Movements.* Newcastle: Cambridge Scholars.

Coulter, C. 1993. *The Hidden Tradition.* Cork: Cork University Press.

Cox, L. 2006. 'News from Nowhere'. In *Social Movements and Ireland,* ed. L. Connolly and N. Hourigan, 210–29. Manchester: Manchester University Press.

———. 2011. *Building Counter Culture.* Helsinki: into-ebooks.

———. 2011. *Gramsci in Mayo.* Helsinki: into-ebooks.

———. 2013a. *Buddhism and Ireland.* Sheffield: Equinox.

———. 2013b. 'Eppur si muove'. In *Marxism and Social Movements,* ed. C. Barker et al, 125–46. Leiden: Brill.

Cronin, M. 2012. *Agrarian Protest in Ireland 1750–1960.* Dublin: Economic and Social History Society of Ireland.

Cullen, P. 2010. 'The Platform of European Social NGOs'. *Journal of Political Ideologies* 15, no. 3.

Curry, L., and L. Cox. 2010. 'Revolution in the Air'. *Irish Journal of Sociology* 18, no. 2: 86–105.

Curtin, C., and T. Varley. 1995. 'Community Action and the State'. In *Irish Society*, ed. P. Clancy et al., 379–409. Dublin: IPA.

Dalby, S. 1984. *The Nuclear Syndrome*. Belfast: INNATE. Retrieved 17 September 2014 from http://www.innatenonviolence.org/pamphlets/nuclearsyndrome.pdf.

ní Dhorchaigh, E., and L. Cox. 2011. 'When Is an Assembly Riotous, and Who Decides?'. In *Riotous Assemblies,* ed. W. Sheehan and M. Cronin, 241–61. Cork: Mercier.

Donnelly, J. 2009. *Captain Rock*. Madison: University of Wisconsin Press.

Doran, P., and J. Barry. 2009. 'The Environmental Movement in Ireland'. In *A Living Countryside?,* ed. J. McDonagh, T. Varley and S. Shorthall, 321–340. Farnham: Ashgate.

Eschle, C., et al. 2011. 'Feminism, Women's Movements and Women in Movement'. *Interface* 3, no. 2: 1–32.

Fagan, T. 2000. *Monto.* Dublin: North Inner City Folklore Project.

Finnegan, B. 2005. 'Social Forces Confront Neoliberalism'. MA dissertation. Dublin: Dublin City University.

Flesher Fominaya, C., and L. Cox. 2013. *Understanding European Movements.* Abingdon: Routledge.

Galligan, Y. 1998. *Women and Politics in Contemporary Ireland.* London: Continuum.

Garavan, M. 2008. 'Problems in Achieving Dialogue'. In *Environmental Argument and Cultural Difference,* ed. R. Edmondson and H. Rau, 65–94. Bern: Peter Lang.

Geoghegan, M. 2000. 'Meaning, Action and Activism'. MA dissertation. Waterford: Waterford Institute of Technology.

Gillan, M. 2010. 'Class, Voice and State'. PhD dissertation. Maynooth: National University of Ireland Maynooth.

Goodwillie, J. 1988. *Colours in the Rainbow.* Dublin: self-published.

Hourigan, N. 2001. *A Comparison of the Campaigns for Raidio na Gaeltachta and TnaG.* Irish Sociological Research Monographs 1. Maynooth: National University of Ireland.

Jones, T. 2003. 'New Social Movements'. Paper to Work Research Centre, Dublin.

Jørgensen, A. 2006. 'Negotiating Identity in the Networks of the Irish Organic Food Movement'. In *Alternative Futures and Popular Protest 2006—Conferences Papers,* ed. C. Barker and M. Tyldesley. Manchester: Manchester Metropolitan University.

Landy, D. 2013. 'Negotiating Power'. In L. Brennan (ed.). *Enacting Globalization.* Basingstoke: Palgrave.

Lash, S., and J. Urry. 1987. *The End of Organized Capitalism.* Cambridge: Polity.

Leonard, L. 2007. *The Environmental Movement in Ireland.* Berlin: Springer.

Lyder, A. 2006. *Pushers Out.* Bloomington: Trafford.

Mahon, E. 1995. 'From Democracy to Femocracy'. In *Irish Society,* ed. P. Clancy et al., 675–708. Dublin: IPA.

Meade, R. 2008. 'Mayday, Mayday!'. *Journalism* 9, no. 3: 330–52.

Moore, O. 2006. 'The Post-organic Consumer'. *International Journal of Consumer Studies* 30, no. 5: 416–27.

Mullally, G. 2006. 'Relocating Protest'. In *Social Movements and Ireland,* ed. L. Connolly and N. Hourigan, 144–67. Manchester: Manchester University Press.

Mullan, C., and L. Cox. 2000. 'Social Movements Never Died'. *ISA/BSA Social Movements Conference, November 2000.* Manchester: ISA/BSA.

Naples, N. 1998. *Grassroots Warriors*. London: Routledge.

Newsinger, J. 2004. *Rebel City*. London: Merlin.

O'Connor, E. 2011. *A Labour History of Ireland*. Dublin: UCD.

O'Connor, M., and T. Foley. 2006. *Ireland and India*. Dublin: Irish Academic Press.

O'Donovan, O. 2011. 'Irish Patients' Movements on the Move to Europe'. *New Agendas in Social Movement Studies 26 November*. Maynooth.

Ó Drisceoil, D. and F. Lane. 2005. *Politics and the Irish Working Class*. Basingstoke: Palgrave Macmillan.

O'Keefe, T. 2013. *Feminist Identity Development and Activism in Revolutionary Movements*. Basingstoke: Palgrave Macmillan.

Peillon, M. 1982. *Contemporary Irish Society*. Dublin: Gill and Macmillan.

Powell, F., and M. Geoghegan. 2004. *The Politics of Community Development*. Dublin: A&A Farmar.

Punch, M. 2009. 'Contested Urban Environments'. *Interface* 1, no. 2: 83–107.

Regan, J. 1999. *The Irish Counter-Revolution*. New York: St. Martin's.

Royall, F. 2009. 'Political Challengers, Service Providers or Service Recipients?' In *The Politics of Unemployment in Europe*, ed. M. Giugni, 117–32. Farnham: Ashgate.

Rutkowska, A. 2007. 'Counter Culture in Poland'. In *Everyday Creativity, Counter Cultures and Social Change*, ed. L. Cox, 47–55. Maynooth: action-research.

Ryan, L., and M. Ward. 2007. *Irish Women and the Vote*. Dublin: Irish Academic Press.

Ryan, P. 2006. 'Coming Out of the Dark'. In *Social Movements and Ireland*, ed. L. Connolly and N. Hourigan, 86–105. Manchester: Manchester University Press.

Sen, J. 2005. 'On Incivility and Transnationality'. Retrieved 23 June 2013 from http://cacim.net/twiki/tiki-read_article.php?articleId=58&page=9.

Slevin, A. 2013. 'Hegemony and Hydrocarbons'. PhD dissertation. Dublin: UCD.

Smyth, J. 2006. 'Moving the Immovable'. In *Social Movements and Ireland*, ed. L. Connolly and N. Hourigan, 106–22. Manchester: Manchester University Press.

Szolucha, A. 2013. 'Learning Consensus Decision-Making in Occupy'. *Research in Social Movements, Conflict and Change* 36: 205–33.

Touraine, A. 1981. *The Voice and the Eye*. Cambridge: Cambridge University Press.

Tovey, H. 1993. 'Environmentalism in Ireland'. *International Sociology* 8, no. 4: 413–30.

———. 1999. '"Messers, Visionaries and Organobureaucrats"'. *Irish Journal of Sociology* 9: 31–59.

———. 2007. *Environmentalism in Ireland*. Dublin: IPA.

Tovey, H., and P. Share. 2003. *A Sociology of Ireland*. Dublin: Gill and Macmillan.

Wainwright, H. 1994. *Arguments for a New Left*. Oxford: Blackwell.

Zagato, A. 2012. 'Community Development in Dublin'. PhD dissertation. Maynooth: National University of Ireland Maynooth.

Chapter 18

Successful Social Movement Outcomes without Social Movements?

Research on Swedish Social Movements and Swedish Social Movement Research

Abby Peterson

Within comparative social movement research during the 1980s the Swedish case posed an anomaly. In comparative studies of environmental and feminist movements, Sweden was grudgingly found to enjoy many of the policy outcomes that social movements struggled for in other countries, without the grassroots activism of either an environmental movement or a feminist movement. Paradoxically it seems, Sweden had auspicious social movement outcomes without social movements. This anomoly has stubbornly persisted in the comparative social movement literature. How could this situation evolve? In this chapter I will critically interrogate these studies and argue that the flawed construction of a Sweden without social movements is partly due to empirical shortcomings in their datasets and theoretical biases. But I will first briefly map social movement research in a country 'without social movements'.[1]

Swedish Social Movement Research

Social movement research on the so-called 'new' social movements in Sweden developed late, first emerging slowly in the 1980s. In part this was a result of the power of the Swedish labour movement, which was tantamount to Swedish academia's understanding of social movement. Industrial relations scholars and social historians conducted research on the labour movement, with little or no input from the emerging field of social movement research (for exceptions, see e.g. Olofsson 1988 and Hedström, Sandell, and Stern 2000). However, from its inauspicious beginnings new social movement research in Sweden has been solidly entrenched within the so-called identity paradigm gleaning inspiration from the work of Alain Touraine and above all Italian sociologist Alberto Melucci. From this common ground, three major theoretical strands of work have developed. The first body of work departs from a Gramscian notion of movement intellectuals. In *Social Movements: A Cognitive Approach*, Eyerman and Jamison (1990) introduced an approach where biographies of movement intellectuals are used to place social movements in political context and analyse the processes of articulation through which a social movement emerges. Eyerman (1994) further developed the notion of movement intellectuals and in Eyerman and Jamison (1998) the notion was broadened to include movement artists in their study of music and traditions (see also Peterson 2012 which further developed the idea to include 'artist painters'). Thörn (2006 and 2009) employed the same approach, but with a broader concept of key movement activists, to shed insight on the construction of the global anti-apartheid movement. Thörn has consistently argued that the political culture of post-war social movements must be understood as part of an increasing globalization of politics.

The second theoretical strand of research is based on a neo-Durkheimian stance. Using this approach, Peterson (1997 and 2001) distinguished between two major tendencies in contemporary protest: the ephemeral constructions of protest coalitions that bring divergent movement activists and organizations or networks into temporary political dialogues for a common cause *and* neo-sectarianism, the uncompromising militant politics of small action groups and networks. Drawing on Durkheim's sociology of morality, Jacobsson and Lindblom (2012 and 2013) conceptualise social movement activists as pursuers of moral ideals, which readily turns them into norm transgressors and has implications for the life-worlds of the activists as well as their social relationships. The third theoretical strand and the least influential in Sweden employs the notion of political opportunity structure (e.g. Jacobsson and Saxonberg 2013; Peterson et al. 2012). In a study of the animal rights movement in Sweden, Wahlström and Peterson (2006) introduced the concept of economic opportunity structure as a tool to grasp social movement protest aimed directly towards the market.

In the early 2000s new research areas opened with studies on the policing of protest in Sweden and Denmark (e.g. Della Porta; Peterson and Reiter 2006; Wahlström 2007, 2010, 2011a and 2011b). During the same period, research on the trade union movement was revitalised focusing on transnational union cooperation (Larsson 2013; Larson 2012; Larsson, Bengtsson and Seldén 2012) and May Day labour mobilizations (Peterson et al. 2012; Peterson, Wahlström and Wennerhag 2012). Urban movements and the politics of space were examined (Thörn, Wasshede and Nilson 2011; Thörn 2012). The global justice movement was analysed on the basis of a survey of participants at three Swedish Social Forum meetings (e.g. Sörbom and Wennerhag 2012; Wennerhag 2010) and theorised in Vinthagen (2008) and Haug (2013). The entry of resistance studies further extended the global perspective of Swedish social movement research (e.g. Chabot and Vinthagen 2007: Vinthagen 2006, 2008 and 2009).

While much of the social movement research in Sweden is empirically substantiated within the country with analyses of the feminist, environmental, peace, anti-racist, anti-apartheid, animal rights and labour union movements, a surprisingly large part of research has focused empirically on social movements outside Sweden. Much of Eyerman and Jamison's work has been based on social movements in the United States, particularly the civil rights movement. For example, Cassegård (2007 and 2011) has studied the precarity movement, homeless activism and the emergence of anarchist thought in Japan. Jacobsson and Saxonberg (2013) have analysed social movement activism in Central Eastern Europe and Wettergren (2005 and 2009) has studied the Adbusters movement.

So, despite the entrenched perception, even held dear by some Swedish researchers, that Sweden lacks a vital new social movement sector because the 'old' movements exert a stranglehold on the space for new political initiatives, where the political culture of consensus and 'the inclusive strategy of the government have undermined the possibilities of constructing a sharp border between movements and the state' (Thörn 2006: 87), Swedish social movement research has nevertheless thrived, as have Swedish new social movements. This is a fact, despite engrained notions of a Sweden lacking in dynamic social movements, which still prevail in international comparative analyses, as well as some Swedish case studies. This chapter focuses on two social movements—the environmental and feminist—both dynamic and relatively successful social movements in Sweden and which have figured most often in international comparative studies (see chapters 1 and 2 of this volume).

Environmentalism without Environmentalists

Jamison et al. (1990) produced a comparative study of environmentalism in Sweden, Denmark and the Netherlands which identifies the cognitive elements that characterise environmentalism as a specific form of political and social criticism and clarifies the international and nation-specific factors that shaped the development of environmentalism to a wider social movement in some countries and not in others. It is in this book that Eyerman and Jamison first fully employ their innovative notion of knowledge interests, which in this study is defined as the cognitive praxis of environmentalism, 'the core identity and deep structure through which environmentalism can be recognised by observers and which forms the basis of collective identity for activists themselves' (2). Knowledge interests provided the authors with a tool that could tease out the central components of environmentalism, which they then put to use in tracing differences in the development of environmentalism as a social movement in the three countries. These authors make a compelling case for the disappearance of environmentalism in Sweden as a social movement, while at the same time argue that the (non-)movement has been successful as a source for policy reform and professional knowledge production.

In this account by Jamison et al. (1990), the Swedish environmental movement had difficulty in finding its own identity. So while the authors acknowledge that environmentalism had emerged earlier in Sweden than in many countries as a significant political force, they argue that almost at its inception environmentalism in Sweden was subjected to incorporation pressures which made it difficult for an autonomous movement to develop. Unlike the situation for the emerging environmental movements in Denmark and the Netherlands, the authors maintain that the combined effects of parliamentary and administrative incorporation, together with a lack of a value-orientated 'alternativism' formulated by the budding and highly heterogeneous movement, were important demobilizing factors of the movement. By the 1960s, environmentalist issues had already begun to be incorporated in the administrative agencies of the Social Democratic government, but most importantly for their analysis, nowhere else in Europe was environmentalism brought so early into the parliamentary arena. The Swedish Green Party was formed in the wake of the narrow defeat in the 1980 nuclear power referendum and entered Parliament in 1988, which further cemented the parliamentary participation of Swedish environmentalism, which according to Jamison et al., diminishes the political space for a vital autonomous social movement.

This conclusion reflected the 'movement centrism' (McAdam and Tarrow 2010) of social movement research, which continues today and was well in line with the ubiquitous notion that the new social movements were by definition extra-parliamentary, posing their challenges exclusively from outside the established political system. In their analysis, social movements were necessarily autonomous, subsequently ignoring, in my opinion, the equally necessary relationships with parliamentary parties in order to achieve their goals (see Dalton, Recchia and Rohrschneider 2003: 744). Social movements rest on two legs: one firmly entrenched in civil society formulating challenges and alternatives outside the established political system, while the other leg negotiates within the terrain of the political system seeking concrete policy measures. For social movements seeking social, cultural *and* political change, *both* legs, or avenues of collective action, are necessary. While I agree that autonomous movement organizations and groups are vital for long-term social and cultural changes in environmental consciousness, attitudes and 'environmentally friendly' behaviour, as well as being instrumental for the formulation of alternatives, Jamison and his colleagues ignored the centrality of the movement's engagement with parliamentarism for long-term as well as short-term political change.

However, for Jamison and colleagues, even more insidious than the parliamentarism of Swedish environmentalism for the emergence and development of an autonomous environmental movement were the incorporation pressures from Social Democratic administrative bodies and the counter-attack imposed by the powerful unions. The former is a particularly strong element in Swedish political culture. Contemporary original issues formulated by new social movements are readily incorporated within the state administrative structure, but only selectively. Some organizations are consulted, some problems are recognised, and some problem-solving avenues may be pursued, while some are not. And these last are subsequently effectively marginalised. In addition to the parliamentarism of environmentalism, these processes of incorporation coupled with marginalization, led to a fragmentation and later a disintegration of knowledge interests, in other words the collective identity of the movement. At a cosmological level of knowledge interests, Jamison and colleagues contend that the gap between theory and practice was considerable, and while ideologues had emerged, they tended to be 'imported' publicists and academics and were not actively a part of the grassroots organizations to which they gave a voice. The activists themselves did not organically produce cosmological knowledge interests; rather, 'alternatives' were provided outside the movement. On the level of technological knowledge interest, they claim that it had been largely reduced to technicalities; the dominant pragmatic reformist political culture had pushed environmental organizations towards information-gathering on hazards and dissemination of information rather than social or theoretical analysis (62). Finally, in regards to the organizational level of knowledge interests, they make a case that the two dominant environmental organizations they studied in the late 1980s—Greenpeace and the Conservation Society—produced information rather than knowledge, and their organizational forms and strategies mirrored those in the established organizational cultures of industry and universities.

The processes of marginalization these authors describe are reflected in the empirical marginalization of the more radical value-oriented groups and organizations in their study. In particular they ignore the grassroots activities of women in the environmental movement; for example, the organization Women for Peace was actively involved in the anti-nuclear power issue even in the aftermath of the 1980 referendum, at that time engaged in the issue of nuclear-waste disposal. While there were women-only environmental groups and initiatives, many women chose to engage in mixed organizations gravitating towards protest campaigns, for example anti-road mobilizations and occupations of sites designated for nuclear-waste disposal, and value-oriented organizations such as Friends of the Earth and The Future in Our Hands where they constituted a majority among the membership (Merchant and Peterson 1986). Common to these women-dominated campaigns, groups and organizations were cosmological knowledge interests which rejected what they regarded as a male positivist view of nature and which was inspired by the feminist pioneer of Swedish environmentalism, Elin Wägner (1882–1949) (Peterson 1994). Two of her books first published in 1941 and 1949 were re-read within the context of the Swedish feminist movement in the 1970s and inspired a new generation of feminists in a radical environmentalism arguing that 'the proper way to treat nature is with caution, housekeeping and care' (Wagner 1978: 236; Tamm and Wagner 1949). These feminist-inspired groups and organizations, including the early Green Party programme, strove for ecological sustainability, which offered concrete alternatives in policies and practices that they argued were environmentally friendly. At the level of organizational knowledge interests the groups and organizations, including the Green Party, embraced innovative non-hierarchical organizational forms, which posed challenges to conventional modes of 'doing politics' (Merchant and Peterson 1996).

According to Jamison et al. (1990: 3), knowledge interests 'form that which a social movement holds in common; when the commonality splinters, for us the movement ceases to exist (and is transformed into an 'ideology')'. This, they asserted, was the fate of the Swedish environmental movement. The knowledge interests of Swedish environmentalism splintered and, for Jamison and his fellow researchers, the movement ceased to exist. This conclusion dovetails with, for example, Alain Touraine's understanding of social movements as having a unified collective identity, a common identity that constructs the movement as a movement. I argue that their empirical gender bias, together with their theoretical point of departure, skewed their understanding of the dynamics and inherent tensions within the Swedish environmental movement. As an important corrective to Jamison et al., Boström (2001 and 2010) has 'revisited' the Swedish environmental movement and Eyerman's and Jamison's notion of knowledge interests and cognitive praxis, arguing that the problem arose when these authors focused their analysis on the level of the movement. Boström, in contrast, acknowledges the diversity and concomitant tensions within the movement, and applies the notion of cognitive practices at the level of the organization. According to Boström (2010: 80), 'cognitive practice goes on in specific ways within each SMO, although each organization also relates its organization-specific cognitive practice to others'. Boström agrees that while Jamison et al. (1990) highlight an interesting tension between autonomy and incorporation, he found their analysis overly deterministic. Cognitive autonomy is always threatened, he argues, but it is the interaction of organizations in his study, with the state and with other organizations—the differentiation of the Swedish environmental movement—that provides the creativity that maintains and even develops the cognitive autonomy of the movement (Boström 2010: 83ff).

'Feminism without Feminists?'

Perhaps even more remarkable than environmentalism without environmentalists, during the 1980s researchers claimed that Sweden was a case of feminism without feminists (e.g. Gelb 1989 and 1990; Lovenduski 1986). Joyce Gelb (1989: 146) in a comparative study of feminism and politics in Britain, the United States and Sweden could not find, unlike the other two countries, a significant women's liberation movement. Likewise, British researcher Joni Lovenduski (1986: 98) claimed that 'one of the more surprising features of contemporary social and political life is the absence of a second-wave feminist movement of any size'. Gelb (1989: 146) argued that the relatively militant organization Group 8 was never able to develop into 'a strong and coherent feminist movement with major influence in Swedish politics'; rather, the struggle for women's liberation was conducted mainly within parties and other political institutions. 'Militant feminism was unacceptable in a consensus-orientated society' and there were neither significant alternative political structures nor awareness-raising groups.

The question arises as to how Gelb and Lovenduski could reach these conclusions. First, these scholars, eager to include a case with auspicious movement outcomes in an international comparison, came to a country at that time with poorly developed research on the women's movement and the few studies available on women's grassroots organizations and movement diversity were published in Swedish (a general point made in chapter 2 of this volume). Important ethnographic correctives are now available but they remain published in Swedish (e.g. Karlsson 1996; Eduards 2002; Schmitz 2007). Secondly, their research, in some respects like that of Jamison et al. (1990), was unsound because of their theoretical and empirical biases. Rather than studying a movement, both researchers focused on a single movement organization. Group 8 was just one among a number of autonomous women's liberation organizations that emerged throughout Sweden in the 1970s and the 1980s that saw an unprecedented decade of feminist institution-building: women's houses and women's house occupations; women's shelters; women's cafés; women's bookstores; feminist centres and women's studies at the universities and colleges; Kvinnohögskolan, a women's feminist summer school; women's summer camps and lesbian feminist summer camps; feminist rock bands and theatre productions, feminist poetry festivals; and perhaps most importantly, the Women's Folk High School in Gothenburg, a unique women-only school offering secondary and post-secondary education, which since its inception in 1980 has incorporated thousands of women, and a considerable number of immigrant women, with its feminist education philosophy. While the Swedish women's liberation movement during the 1970s and 1980s was not coherent, the grassroots movement was widespread, diversified and, like other feminist movements in Western democracies, composed of a dense network of groups, organizations and alternative feminist institutions and activities split along ideological divides (see Schmitz 2007).

How then was it possible to claim that Sweden lacked an autonomous women's liberation movement? Lovenduski (1986: 98ff) did not conduct empirical research in Sweden, which makes it difficult to identify any basis for her conclusions other than the then-entrenched mythical notion of Sweden's all pervasive 'statism'. With regards to Gelb, I argue that her observation that Sweden lacked a feminist movement was a consequence of an American researcher's summer vacation strategy of data collection confined to Stockholm, the capital of Sweden, and confined to interviews with thirty-one informants, who were for the most part non-activists. Gelb (1990: 138) claimed that the 'minute feminist movement is almost subterranean in character and visibility'. I argue that the feminist movement, while it was in part based on partisan political women's associations as Gelb points out, was neither subterranean nor minute but distributed across the country, and for the Swedish-speaking population far from invisible. The data was skewed which made it possible to ignore the wide diversity of feminist groups, institutions and activities which were spread across the country both within and well beyond the borders of the capital city. Gelb's conclusions were drawn in part from an empirical bias and in part from a theoretically skewed bias, which focused on a single organization, Group 8 in the 1970s, as a basis for a coherent autonomous feminist movement. The Swedish feminist movement was never a coherent or unified movement based on a single organization but was (and is) like social movements more generally, an action field or system constructed by a multitude of groups, organizations and networks with a diversity of collective identities. While a social movement may under specific situations appear as a unified and coherent collective, this is a tenuous and fragile unity, more an illusion (see Melucci 1989). A social movement *is* the dynamics of the contradictions and tensions among its constituent actors. And as Jacobsson and Saxonberg (2013) point out, social movement strategies are not a question of 'either-or'; they are not autonomous *or* co-opted and institutionalised; they are not claims-makers *or* service providers. Social movement strategies are not unilateral, but rather flexible given different situations. In other words, social movements embrace all of these strategies.

Gelb (1989: 139) contrasts the political opportunity structures in the three countries included in her study and characterises the Swedish system as consensual democracy where the centre of gravity in the polity lies in the cabinet and with a corporate state in which interest groups tend to be absorbed and in which alienated subgroups (such as autonomous feminist groups) that resort to violence, protest, or even dissent are uncommon. Gelb finds support for her contention in the work of fellow American movement scholars, Hilda Scott, and Sidney Verba and Gary Orren. Scott is cited in Gelb (1989) stating that 'Swedish unions and parties have literally pre-empted feminist demands' (210), and Verba and Orren are also quoted in the following words: 'In Sweden, the Social Democrats ... shaped feminist demands' (211). This leads Gelb to conclude that many of the demands that feminist movements in Britain and the United States were struggling for were won in Sweden due to the *largesse* of men in the Social Democratic Party and to a lesser degree of the unions. Gelb is ignoring the role played by the SDP women's association, as well as the women's associations in other parties. Women's associations, particularly the SDP women's association, has often found itself at odds with party leadership and they are not without political clout. For example, the SDP women's association led the struggle in the 1950s and early 1960s against Sweden acquiring a nuclear weapons arsenal forcing party leadership to reluctantly give in to their demands. The party political women's associations in general have been influential in family policy formulation, perhaps at least in part due to a political gender division of labour. Feminist-friendly equality and family policies did not appear without the impact of party political women. Even if the framework was laid in the late 1960s and early 1970s for progressive gender-equality and family policies, this was not achieved without the women's liberation movement's vanguard arm, the Social Democratic Women's Association, together with existing women's organizations (Karlsson 1996). These early favourable movement outcomes were not, I argue, the result of male politicians' munificence. However, the plurality of actors involved makes it nearly impossible to attribute these outcomes to a specific actor, whether movement, party, government agency or union; rather, the outcomes are a result of the complicated interactions between actors (Della Porta and Diani 2007: 227ff).

The Dynamic Processes of State and Social Movement Interactions

Della Porta and Diani (2007: 229) remind us that while we conventionally make a distinction between political and cultural movements, the former guided by a more instrumental logic and the latter a more symbolic logic, *all* movements make demands on the political system. The dynamic processes between state and social movement interactions must necessarily be untangled if we are to understand the outcomes (marking both successes, even partial, and potential backlashes or even demise) of the collective action of social movements. Furthermore, one can argue that the state tends to give with one hand and take with the other. Tilly (1978) pointed out that the state always pairs opportunities with threats. Social movements, if they do seek to have an impact on politics, must strategically navigate in this terrain of potential openings and closures (see also Goldstone and Tilly 2001). According to this line of thinking, what can be won in regards to concessions at the same time risks being met with repercussions for the movement.

Suh (2011: 443) defines movement institutionalization as a process of a social movement traversing the official terrain of formal politics and engaging with state institutions to enhance collective ability to achieve the movement's goals. However, a social movement does not traverse the official terrain of formal politics uniformly. Some movement organizations and groups will more readily engage with state institutions, while others are more reluctant. These are strategic choices taken by the various actors which constitute a movement. Conversely, state institutions will more readily engage with some movement organizations and groups, and will be more reluctant to engage with others. Interactions between social movements and the state are dynamic processes of give-and-take between both parties.

Both the Swedish environmental movement and women's liberation movement in the 1980s opted for what Suh (2011) labels a dual strategy of institutionalization. This dual strategy was most evident in Swedish environmentalism. Despite what Jamison et al. (1990) called the entrenched parliamentarism of Swedish environmentalism at that time with committed allies particularly within the Centre Party and the Left Party Communists, the movement actively chose to pursue politics in the electoral arena in order to enter policy-making bodies to effect political outcomes. This social movement strategy—forming a 'movement party' as the partisan arm of the movement—was surprising in that the movement was not without voice in the political system. After the nuclear power defeat in 1980, the movement nevertheless began the laborious task of mobilizing its supporters in the electoral arena, and in the 1988 election they broke the 4 per cent barrier and entered parliament with their direct challenges to the political system. The Swedish Green Party from its inception confronted traditional ways of 'doing politics'. During its early years in the 1980s, the party incorporated a variant of 'town hall' direct democracy with non-hierarchical organizational forms: for example, instead of a party leader they elected two rotating 'språkrör' (speakers), one woman and one man for a mandate period; party members who served more than two mandate periods were consigned to leave their posts. In general the principle of the rotation of political posts was to undermine political professionalism in order to retain proximity to its movement roots (Lundgren 1991). The movement constructed its partisan arm along the organizational principles of the 'alternative' environmental movement, bringing new challenges to how to do politics in Sweden.

Together with Greenpeace and the Conservation Society, both of which Jamison et al. (1990) argue epitomise professional 'result-oriented' environmental organizations, these researchers pointed out that during the 1980s a plethora of small organizations emerged and consolidated a new engagement with state bureaucracies, providing them with professional economic-technical environmental alternatives and committing to gathering and disseminating information. This collection of groups and organizations was joined by the newly formed Green Party to establish the state-oriented arm of the Swedish environmental movement and was most closely engaged with the political system. However, the Green Party retained a closer proximity to its value-oriented movement roots. The Green Party, I argue, afforded a bridge between this more institutionalised arm and the array of value-oriented direct-action campaigns, organizations and groups, which nevertheless persevered throughout the 1980s and provided the mobilization networks for the budding party. The Green Party relied upon these value-oriented groups to mobilise their voters. During the 1980s Swedish environmentalism was indisputably a cacophony of organizations, unquestionably fragmented, and split between the more technically leaning groups and organizations and the more value-oriented (women-dominated) campaigns, groups and organizations, and now with a movement party that succeeded in entering parliament at the end of the decade, I argue contrary to Jamison's and his colleagues' diagnosis, Swedish environmentalism had not expired. While during the 1980s the movement could not match the 1970s mass mobilization around the nuclear power issue, it rose to the challenge after the defeat in the 1980 referendum and took on new and more diversified organizational forms, which carried on the struggle of environmentalism.

Like the value-oriented environmental groups and organizations, at first glance it would appear that the more radical women's liberation groups had been marginalised, with the state seeming to rely more on their continued engagement with the more moderate organizations and party political women's associations. The Machiavellian notion of the state's 'divide and rule' response to social movements—incorporating some (more moderate) demands, co-opting various more moderate movement actors with organizational forms more like those in the state itself, while marginalizing more radical demands and actors—did converge with the Swedish state's strategy towards the women's liberation movement, but only at the central level of government and not entirely even at this level of the state. While the Social Democratic Women's Association was recognised for its role as vanguard for the party, the association has nevertheless often found itself at loggerheads with party leadership and has been met with a strategy of marginalization. The clash was most manifest during the latter 1970s and early 1980s when the association formulated demands for a six-hour workday, a stipulated father's month included in parental leave and gender quotas for political posts. These women's liberation issues made visible the power struggle between women and men in the party. The male party leadership accused the association of undermining party unity by bypassing the principle of loyalty, or in other words, standing loyally behind the 'official' party line. According to Karlsson (1996: 338), this conflict resulted in the women's association having a more isolated position in relation to the party during the 1980s. Karlsson argues that it was in response to these setbacks that during the 1980s the association began to profile itself more explicitly as part of the women's liberation movement emphasizing 'sisterhood' rather than party loyalty. In 1993 the association adopted a new feminist programme for 'Social Democratic feminists' (339).

During the 1980s the women's liberation movement diversified and above all dispersed geographically throughout the country—first in university cities and college towns and later to cities and towns across the country. The proliferation of 'women's culture' events across Sweden during this decade only partly heralded a retreat into counter-cultural activities, and this was also a decade of a 'politicization' of the movement around the issues of day-care, employment, violence towards women, pornography and prostitution. While the latter issues generated direct actions and protests at local levels, the demands were directed to central-level government, and the remaining issues were firmly entrenched at the local level of government (see Micheletti 1991: 149ff on the fragmentation of the Swedish state). Action groups for day-care, workplace groups, and particularly the shelter movement spread the messages and activities of the women's liberation movement countrywide. The dispersion of activities to support battered women brought feminist groups, both moderate and radical, in direct negotiations with municipal governments, as did efforts in many cities to establish women's houses. The former were often more or less co-opted as municipal service providers. The latter was not necessarily accomplished through traditional lobbying and petitioning. In 1983 women's liberation movement organizations in the small northern city of Umeå initiated a women's house occupation in a centrally located abandoned house. Over four hundred women took part in the three-month-long occupation, and the action engaged local media—TV, radio and press—almost daily with news about the occupation and reports on the women's liberation movement more generally and women's situation in society. Riot police evacuated the women and the house was demolished the same day; however less than three years later municipal authorities gave in to the women's demands and handed over the keys to a women's house which remains an active site for women's liberation activities today (Eduards 2002: 65ff). It is at the local level that the grassroots feminist movement has been most visible and where it has also most immediately impacted the lives of women in Sweden.

The Intrinsic 'Trade-Off'

In comparative studies, some states were seen as greater threats to social movements, while other, more closed and repressive Western democracies appeared to nurture more autonomous movements. Sweden was squarely placed among the former states. As we have seen, Jamison et al. (1990) traced the Swedish environmental movement's birth, erstwhile and short-lived period of movement vigour and, ultimately, if not its death, its fading away. Feminist researchers such as Gelb (1989 and 1990) and Lovenduski (1986) sketched the birth of an emasculated women's liberation movement with the formation of just one of its organizations, and quickly arrived in their studies to a proclamation of the fledgling movement's death. I have argued that these studies did not do justice to either the environmental or women's liberation movements in Sweden. They cannot adequately account for the political successes of either environmentalism or feminism, nor can they account for the long-term cultural impacts of these movements on the everyday practices of women and men in Sweden.

Katzenstein (1987: 3) reminded researchers that 'an assessment of the well-being of the women's movement must identify the multiple networks through which feminist consciousness is purveyed and activism is promoted.

Of particular importance here is the emergence of local and therefore less visible feminist organizations'. Good advice, well worth heeding. Nonetheless, later reflecting on the nonlinear relationship between social movements and state responsiveness, she contends that 'there [Sweden] the government has evinced a higher level of commitment to gender equality than most states in Western Europe or North America. Yet the feminist movement in Sweden is considerably less of a presence than in countries such as the United States or Italy where state policy lags well behind' (5).

Unable to grasp either the proliferation of feminist initiatives emerging during the 1980s, or the geographical dispersion of the women's liberation movement, foreign feminist researchers were quick to underestimate the achievements of the movement. Sweden, undeniably with auspicious movement outcomes—for example, in regards to gender equality legislation, the provision of childcare and a generous parental leave, the criminalization of the 'buyers' of sex—nevertheless had, according to these researchers, no women's liberation movement. The anomaly of Swedish exceptionalism was explained by the success of feminist demands. The responsiveness of the state to the new issues being raised by women left little or no space for an autonomous movement to thrive. Successful outcomes heralded the subsequent demise of the movement. Conversely, movements in countries which had little or no impact on state policies were found nevertheless to be dynamic and vital.

The same conclusion was drawn in regard to Swedish exceptionalism in environmentalism. Again auspicious movement outcomes in regards to public policies dealing with nuclear power, renewable energy development, conservation, sustainability, etc., foreshadowed the demise of the environmental movement in Sweden as a social movement (Jamison et al. 1990 and Jamison 2003). These studies focus on the interaction between social movements and the state, leading them to conclude that interactions that led to successful outcomes in turn led to negative consequences for the autonomy and vitality of the movement. Kitschelt (1986: 62) identified a 'curvilinear relationship between openness and movement mobilization, which shows that very closed regimes repress social movements, that very open and responsive ones assimilate them, and that moderately repressive ones allow for their broad articulation but do not accede readily to their demands'. This simplified interpretation led to the conclusion that Sweden had successfully assimilated both its environmental and women's liberation movements and in return the movements were munificently awarded with policy reforms. Moderately repressive states, in turn, enjoyed dynamic and broadly articulated movements but not the political impact these movements (or non-movements) enjoyed in Sweden.

There was an underlying trade-off in this comparative research—movement success in regards to procedural and substantive gains portended the death of the movement. The Swedish state in the various categorizations of political opportunity structures was portrayed as unique with an open political input structure highly responsive to movement demands *and* with a strong capacity to aggregate demands and implement new policies (e.g. Kitschelt 1986). With a state eager to assimilate movement demands and even movement actors, and with a state committed to defusing the challenges with progressive policy reforms, there was no space for a movement to exist much less thrive in Sweden. This over-simplification of the properties of the Swedish state (at a time when the classical model of Swedish corporatism was in decline, see Micheletti 1991), together with considerable empirical biases, perpetuated the stereotypical notion of Swedish exceptionalism.

In this chapter I have strived on the basis of the case of Swedish 'exceptionalism' to highlight what I argue has been a general limitation in comparative social movement research. In our search for viable explanations for the differences in (national) social movements and differences in their social movement outcomes there has been an over-riding tendency to seek simplified, often dichotomous, factors or variables.

In many of these studies Sweden provided the foil to which other movements and movement outcomes could be readily explained. Cogent generalizations regarding Swedish social movement politics provided crude but convincing explanations, which were, I argue, insensitive to the complicated processes of social movements' multi-levelled interactions with the state. I contend that a one-sided focus on differences in the comparative approach leads us to these unsophisticated explanations. If we were equally sensitive to potential similarities between movement politics in different national contexts we would be better equipped to grasp the complicated processes of social movement and state interactions. This new double focus might not yield fourfold tables, but we might acquire a more complete and systematic picture as to how social movements impact social, cultural and political life in different national contexts.

Abby Peterson is professor of sociology at the Department of Sociology and Work Science, University of Gothenburg. She has published widely in the fields of social movement studies, criminology and cultural studies. Peterson is former editor of *Acta Sociologica* (2005–11) and former president of the Swedish Sociological Association (2012–14).

Notes

1. I have chosen to focus the overview on research published in English, which is available to readers. This restriction unfortunately and necessarily omits a significant number of Swedish social movement studies.

References

Boström, M. 2001. *Miljörörelsens mångfald* [*The Diversity of the Environmental Movement*]. Lund: Arkiv Förlag.

———. 2010. 'Cognitive Practices and Collective Identities within a Heterogeneous Social Movement: The Swedish Environmental Movement'. *Social Movement Studies* 3, no. 1: 73–88.

Cassegård, C. 2007. 'Exteriority and Transcritique: Karatani Kojin and the Impact of the 90s'. *Japanese Studies* 27, no. 1: 1–18.

———. 2011. 'Public Spaces in Recent Japanese Political Thought and Activism: From the Rivers and Lakes to Miyashita Park'. *Japanese Studies* 31, no. 3: 405–22.

Chabot, S., and S. Vinthagen. 2007. 'Rethinking Nonviolent Action and Contentious Politics: Political Cultures of Nonviolent Opposition in the Indian Independence Movement and Brazil's Landless Workers Movement'. *Research in Social Movements, Conflicts and Change* 27: 91–122.

Della Porta, D., and M. Diani. 2007. *Social Movements: An Introduction.* 2nd ed. Maldon: Blackwell.

Della Porta, D., A. Peterson and H. Reiter, eds. 2006. *Policing Transnational Protest.* Aldershot-Brookfield: Ashgate.

Eduards, M. 2002. *Förbjuden handling: Om kvinnors organisering och feministisk teori* [*Forbidden Action: On Women's Organising and Feminist Theory*]. Malmö: Liber.

Eyerman, R. 1994. *Between Culture and Politics: Intellectuals in Modern Society.* Cambridge: Polity Press.

Eyerman, R., and A. Jamison. 1989. 'Environmental Knowledge as an Organisational Weapon: The Case of Greenpeace'. *Social Science Information* 28, no. 1: 99–119.

———. 1990. *Social Movements: A Cognitive Approach.* Cambridge: Polity Press.

———. 1998. *Music and Social Movements: Mobilizing Traditions in the Twentieth Century.* Cambridge: Cambridge University Press.

Gelb, J. 1989. *Feminism and Politics: A Comparative Perspective.* Berkeley, Los Angeles and London: University of California Press.

———. 1990. 'Feminism and Political Action'. In *Challenging the Political Order: New Social and Political Movements in Western Democracies,* ed. R. J. Dalton and M. Kuechler, 137–55. Cambridge: Polity Press.

Goldstone, J. and C. Tilly, C. 2001. 'Threat (and Opportunity): Popular Action and State Response in the Dynamics of Contentious Action'. In *Silence and Voice in the Study of Contentious Politics,* ed. R. R. Aminzade, et al., 179–94. New York: Cambridge University Press.

Haug, C. 2013. 'Organizing Spaces: Meeting Arenas as a Social Movement Infrastructure between Organisation, Network, and Institution'. *Organisation Studies* 34, nos. 5–6: 705–32.

Hedström, P., R. Sandell and C. Stern 2000. 'Mesolevel Networks and the Diffusion of Social Movements: The Case of the Swedish Social Democratic Party'. *American Journal of Sociology* 106, no. 1: 145–72.

Jacobsson, K., and J. Lindblom. 2012. 'Moral Reflexivity and Dramaturgical Action in Social Movement Activism: The Case of the Plowshares and Animal Rights Sweden'. *Social Movement Studies* 11, no. 1: 1–20.

———. 2013. 'Emotion Work in Animal Rights Activism: A Moral-Sociological Perspective'. *Acta Sociologica* 56, no. 1: 27–46.

Jacobsson, K., and S. Saxonberg, eds. 2013. *Beyond NGO-isation: The Development of Social Movements in Central and Eastern Europe*. Farnham-Burlington: Ashgate.

Jamison, A., et al. 1990. *The Making of the New Environmental Consciousness: A Comparative Study of the Environmental Movements in Sweden, Denmark and the Netherlands*. Edinburgh: Edinburgh University Press.

Johnston, H. 2011. *States and Social Movements*. Cambridge, UK: Polity Press.

Karlsson, G. 1996. *From broderskap till systerskap: Det socialdemokratiska kvinnoförbundets kamp för inflytande och makt i SAP [From Brotherhood to Sisterhood: The Social Democratic Women's Association's Struggle for Influence and Power in SAP]*. Lund: Arkiv.

Katzenstein, M. F. 1987. 'Comparing the Feminist Movements of the United States and Western Europe: An Overview'. In *The Women's Movements of the United States and Western Europe: Consciousness, Political Opportunity, and Public Policy*, ed. M. F. Katzenstein and C. M. Mueller, 3–22. Philadelphia: Temple University Press.

Kitschelt, H. 1986. 'Political Opportunity Structures and Political Protest: Anti-Nuclear Movements in Four Democracies'. *British Journal of Political Science* 16, no. 1: 57–85.

Larsson, B. 2012. 'Obstacles to Transnational Trade Union Cooperation in Europe: Results from a European Survey'. *Industrial Relations Journal* 43, no. 2: 152–70.

———. 2013. 'Transnational Trade Union Action in Europe'. *European Societies* DOI: 10.1080/14616696.2013.813958.

Larsson, B., M. Bengtsson, and L. Seldén, K. 2012. 'Transnational Trade Union Cooperation in the Nordic Countries'. *Management Revue* 23, no. 1: 32–48.

McAdam, D., and S. Tarrow. 2010. 'Ballots and Barricades: On the Reciprocal Relationship between Elections and Social Movements'. *Perspectives on Politics* 8, no. 2: 529–42.

Melucci, A. 1989. *Nomads in the Present: Social Movements and Individual Needs in Contemporary Society*. Philadelphia: Temple University Press.

Merchant, C., and A. Peterson. 1986. 'Peace with the Earth: Women and the Environmental Movement in Sweden'. *Women's Studies International Forum* 9, no. 4: 21–39.

———. 1996. 'Peace with the Earth: Women and the Environment in Sweden'. In *Earthcare: Women and the Environment*, ed. C. Merchant, 46–72. New York: Routledge.

Micheletti, M. 1991. 'Swedish Corporatism at a Crossroads: The Impact of New Politics and New Social Movements'. *West European Politics* 14, no. 3: 144–65.

Olofsson, G. 1988. 'After the Working-Class Movement? An Essay on What's "New" and What's "Social" in the New Social Movements'. *Acta Sociologica* 31, no. 1: 15–34.

Peterson, A. 1994. 'Elin Wägner and Radical Environmentalism in Sweden: The Good Earthworm'. *Environmental History* (2): 27–42.

———. 1997. *Rainbow Coalitions and Neo-Sectarianism: Youth and the Drama of Immigration in Contemporary Sweden*. Aldershot and Brookfield: Ashgate.

———. 2001. *Contemporary Political Protest: Essays on Political Militancy.* Aldershot and Brookfield: Ashgate.

———. 2012. 'Wounds That Never Heal: On Anselm Kiefer and the Moral Innocence of the West German Student Movements and the West German New Left'. *Cultural Sociology* 6, no. 3: 367–85.

Peterson, A., et al. 2012. 'May Day Demonstrations in Five European Countries'. *Mobilization* 17, no. 3: 281–300.

Peterson, A., M. Wahlström and M. Wennerhag. 2012. 'Swedish Trade Unionism: A Renewed Social Movement'. *Economic and Industrial Democracy* 33, no. 3: 621–47.

Schmitz, E. 2007. *Systerskap som politisk handling: Kvinnors organisering i Sverige 1968–1982* [*Sisterhood as Political Action: Women's Organizing in Sweden 1968 to 1982*]. Lund: Lund Dissertations in Sociology 76.

Suh, D. 2011. 'Institutionalizing Social Movements: The Dual Strategy of the Korean Women's Movement'. *The Sociological Quarterly* 52: 442–71.

Sörbom, A., and M. Wennerhag. 2012. 'Individualisation, Life Politics, and the Reformulation of Social Critique: An Analysis of the Global Justice Movement'. *Critical Sociology* 39, no. 3: 453–78.

Tamm, E., and E. Wagner. 1949. *Fred med jorden* [*Peace with the Earth*]. Stockholm: Bonniers.

Tarrow, Sidney. 1983. 'Struggling to Reform: Social Movements and Policy Change during Cycles of Protest'. *Western Societies Occasional Paper no. 15.* Ithaca: Center for International Studies, Cornell University.

Thörn, H. 2006. *Anti-Apartheid and the Emergence of a Global Civil Society.* Basingstoke and New York: Palgrave Macmillan.

———. 2007. 'Social Movements, the Media and the Emergence of a Global Public Sphere: From Anti-Apartheid to Global Justice'. *Current Sociology* 56, no. 3: 896–916.

———. 2009. 'The Meanings of Solidarity: Narratives of Anti-Apartheid Activism'. *Journal of Southern African Studies* 35, no. 2: 417–36.

———. 2012. 'In Between Social Engineering and Gentrification: Urban Restructuring, Social Movements, and the Place Politics of Open Space'. *Journal of Urban Affairs* 34, no. 2: 153–68.

Thörn, H., C. Wasshede and T. Nilson, eds. 2011. *Space for Urban Alternatives? Christiania 1971–2011.* Stockholm: Gidlunds.

Tilly, C. 1978. *From Mobilisation to Revolution.* Reading: Addison-Wesley.

Vinthagen, S. 2006. 'Power as Subordination and Resistance as Disobedience: Nonviolent Movements and the Management of Power'. *Asian Journal of Social Science* 34, no. 1: 1–21.

———. 2008. 'Is the World Social Forum a Democratic Global Civil Society?' In *The World and US Social Forums: A Better World Is Possible and Necessary,* ed. J. Blau and M. Karides, 131–48. Leiden: Brill.

———. 2009. 'Global Movements Facilitating Local Campaigns'. In *Unarmed Resistance: The Transnational Factor,* ed. H. Clark and A. Rigby, 184–90. London: Pluto Press.

Wagner, E. 1978 [1941]. *Väckarklockan* [*The Alarm Clock*]. Stockholm: Bonniers.

Wahlström, M. 2007. 'Forestalling Violence: Police Knowledge of Interaction with Political Activists'. *Mobilization* 12, no. 4: 389–402.

―――. 2010. 'Producing Spaces for Representation: Racist Marches, Counterdemonstrations, and Public-Order Policing'. *Environment and Planning D: Society and Space* 28, no. 5: 811–27.

―――. 2011a. 'Taking Control or Losing Control? Activist Narratives of Provocation and Collective Violence'. *Social Movement Studies* 10, no. 4: 367–85.

―――. 2011b. 'The Making of Protest and Protest Policing: Negotiation, Knowledge, Space, and Narrative'. *Göteborg Studies in Sociology* 47.

Wahlström, M. and A. Peterson. 2006. 'Between the State and the Market: Expanding the Concept of "Political Opportunity Structure"'. *Acta Sociologica* 49, no. 4: 363–77.

Wennerhag, M. 2010. 'Another Modernity Is Possible? The Global Justice Movement and the Transformations of Politics'. *Distinktion: Scandinavian Journal of Social Theory* 11, no. 2: 25–49.

Wettergren, Å. 2005. *Moving and Jamming: Implications for Social Movement Theory.* Akademisk avhandling, Karlstad: Karlstad University Studies.

―――. 2009. 'Fun and Laughter: Culture Jamming and the Emotional Regime of Late Capitalism'. *Social Movement Studies* 8, no. 1: 33–48.

Chapter 19

Is Spain Still Different?

Social Movements Research in
a Belated Western European Democracy[1]

Eduardo Romanos and Susana Aguilar

Following the idea embodied in the successful slogan invented during the
1960s to promote tourism in Franco's Spain, we want to analyse the state of
the art of the research on social movements and the movements themselves
to test if they have been at any point different in Spain as compared to other
Western countries. Factors underlying this difference (or lack thereof) will
be examined as well as the strong and weak points of the social movements'
agenda.

In a recent comparative study on the global justice movement in six
European countries and the United States (Della Porta 2007), the Spanish
case was found to be akin to the others, its contentious collective action
being part of a transnational protest cycle (Jiménez and Calle 2007). At
the turn of the century, Christian-oriented groups framed their grievances
similarly to like-minded groups in Europe: the anti-abortion movement has
abandoned religiously inspired and criminalizing slogans to embrace a more
nuanced and scientific-based approach to defend the 'rights of the foetus'
(Aguilar 2011). Converging with other neighbouring countries, students
and young people in Spain have led the protest against the European reform
of the university system (Bologna initiative), mobilised against unaffordable
prices in the housing market (Aguilar and Fernández 2010) and squatted
buildings (Adell and Martínez 2004; Martínez 2007, 2013), while demonstrators from all walks of life have crowded the streets against the Iraq war
(Morán 2006; cf. Jiménez 2007b). A number of studies, centred on gays,
women and environmentalists, have also shown remarkable resemblance to
their European counterparts (Jiménez 2005; Calvo 2007; Valiente 2007).
Even though some types of collective action are undoubtedly context related, such as the ethno-linguistic and nationalist movements in Catalonia
and the Basque Country (Tejerina 1999; Pérez-Agote 1987; Casquete 2006;

Johnston 1991); the solidarity movement, which has combined the demand to increase international aid (Ibarra 1999; Jerez and Romero 2002) with the occasional support to revolutionary Latin American groups (Gomá, Ibarra and Martí 2002); and the pro-peace movement (Tejerina et al. 1995; Funés 1998), which has mobilised against ETA terrorism, they are so in the same way as other movements which follow a path-dependence logic in their own countries. More recently, the potential distinctiveness of the particularly visible movement of *Indignados* has become blurred because the movement can be interpreted as belonging to a transnational contentious wave (Della Porta 2015; Flesher Fominaya 2014; Tejerina et al. 2013).

Unlike the first studies on popular mobilization, carried out by historians who focused on the labour movement and its *sui generis* features, the most recent research, mostly undertaken by sociologists and political scientists, has concluded that Spanish challengers are no longer different. Nor is there any difference in the main bulk of scholarly research that draws heavily on the political process model in order to explain how social movements have seized the opportunities created by electoral cycles and also been let down by particular governments. Cognitive and symbolic processes (Laraña 1999) as well as collective identities (Ibarra 2000) have also been analysed. However, both the research agenda and the social movements were not always so indistinctive in the past.

The Old and the New: Peculiarities of the Spanish Social Movements

Traditionally, two important peculiarities have characterised the Spanish social movements. First, the labour movement had been imbued with a strong anti-politics orientation that was particularly evident in the anarchists and also in other working-based groups (Álvarez Junco 1994; Juliá 1990). Second, the long-standing Francoist dictatorship (1939–75) left its footprint on collective action and contributed to the belated emergence of organised protest and new social movements.

Most historians have emphasised the non-inclusive character of the *Restauración* (1875–1923) as a way of explaining the anti-politics orientation of the labour movement.[2] However, Álvarez Junco (1994) has stressed that this orientation existed in France and Italy as well. Later on, obstacles to political participation were much more evident under the Francoist dictatorship, a regime that contributed nonetheless to politicizing the labour movement. Departing from exogenous political-oriented explanations, anti-politics has been interpreted as a product of the Spanish left-wing political culture that, 'following old millenarian patterns and pervaded by mid-nineteenth century romantic revolutionism, constructed its identity as an enemy of *all* "authorities" and the liberator from *all* oppressions' (Álvarez Junco 1994: 308, emphasis in original). Regardless of its origin, the continuity of the 'anti-politics frame' (Laraña 1999) that extended well into the first third of the twentieth century has differentiated the labour movement in Spain from its counterpart in Europe, where this feature had already vanished, or was in decline, at that time. All in all, anti-politics was not so much a well-entrenched trait of the Spanish labour movement on the whole but rather an element that pervaded the anarcho-syndicalist *Confederación Nacional del Trabajo* (CNT—National Labour Confederation). This organization, founded in 1910, played an extremely important political role during the troubled 1930s and had no parallel in any other like-minded political organization in the international context.

As to the second peculiarity, not only did Spanish new social movements arrive belatedly on the political scene but many that came to age after the Francoist regime were less radical, strong and centralised than their European counterparts (Jiménez 2005, 2007a). The collective experience of violence in the past might have contributed to the building of a non-violent political culture that has made radical repertoires of protest less frequent in Spain (Jiménez 2005). Violence was decisively used by the late Francoist regime whenever serious threats to its survival were perceived (Sánchez-Cuenca 2014). It was also an element of the Spanish transition (1975–82) that left an enduring influence on collective action. Following the first general elections in 1977, violence erupted more clearly than in Portugal and Greece. State repression was intense and many civilians lost their lives in demonstrations and road controls. Separatist, revolutionary, fascist and terrorist groups were among the main violent social actors (Sánchez-Cuenca and Aguilar 2009). The radical militancy of the urban ecological movement was another example: a spin-off of this movement was the campaign against the Lemoniz nuclear plant in which ETA was also involved (Tejerina 2001) and resulted in seven deaths.

Organizational weakness, as the second distinctive feature of the new social movements, might be partly explained due to the absence of a previous and shared counter-culture that could have bound different actors together. This would elucidate why movements have exhibited weaker ties of solidarity and mutual identification (Jiménez 2005). Politicization and *obrerismo* (workerism), as inherited features of the Francoist period, as well as the undisputable leadership of the parties during the transition, which helped eclipse the relevance of social movements, have also been identified as reasons for this weakness (Alonso 1991; Álvarez Junco 1994). Some authors have thus remarked that social movements' presence in the second half of the 1980s was practically irrelevant (Alonso 1991; Laraña 1993; Ibarra 2005).

An indisputable third difference has been the highly decentralised organizational model of the social movements. This has made state-level coordination difficult and hindered the creation of large organizations. Decentralization was the consequence of centrifugal forces such as the Catalan and Basque nationalism, the setting up of a quasi-federal state and the strength of the anarchist tradition in certain movements (Jiménez and Calle 2007). At the turn of the century, for instance, environmentalists embraced 'hundreds of groups scattered across Spain which were minority-based and contained feeble organizational structures' (Fernández 1999: 8).

Historical Studies on the Anarchist Movement

In view of the strength of the anarchist movement in Spain, it is not surprising that many historians have devoted significant resources to studying the issue. The troubled decade of the 1930s and the experiment of social revolution during the Spanish Civil War (1936–39), which adopted the shape of an industrial and agrarian collectivization in regions such as Catalonia, Eastern Aragon, and Valencia, have particularly been subject to scrutiny. Activists themselves have left important evidence on these events. Outside the movement, scholarly work on anarchism was initiated by Brenan (1943) and further pursued by Hobsbawm (1959), who transmitted the idea that the Spanish anarchism was a modern version of millenarism. This idea had a limited impact upon the young historians who, during the late Francoist and early transition years, had focused on the study of anarcho-syndicalism. Balcells, Izard, Termes and Cuadrat, in Barcelona, were all aware of Martí's work (1959) and paved the way for the emergence of 'a normalised and professional, and yet committed to the fight against Francoism, history of the workers movement' (Tavera 2002: 23). In Madrid, starting in 1976, different scholars gathered together in a workshop which, organised by Álvarez Junco at the Complutense University, set out to make progress on the history of the Spanish workers' movement. The workshop involved, among others, López Keller, Robles, Castro, de la Fuente and Martínez Dorado, all of whom were firstly influenced by *Le Mouvement Social* French school and, later on, by English Marxists such as E. P. Thompson, Eric J. Hobsbawm and George Rudé (Casanova 2013). Publications such as *Past and Present* opened up new perspectives that helped to (1) clarify that social movements were not the same as institutionalised *obrerismo* and (2) broaden topics of research and analytical approaches (e.g. peasant mobilizations, tax revolts, and republicans as agents of the popular protest at the turn of the twentieth century). Two highly influential studies at the time (1970s) dealt with the open clashes between the different ideological anarchist positions during the II Republic (Elorza 1971) and with the political ideology of the anarchism from the I International up to the setting up of the CNT (Álvarez Junco 1976).

The beginning of the democratic transition was accompanied by a growth of research centred on the history of the CNT, much of which shared an uncritical and laudatory position on its 'revolutionary achievements'. In the following years, new studies on the regional development of anarcho-syndicalism and its role in rural mobilizations, the international relations established by the anarchists, their cultural production and other topics related to the workers' movement as a whole (the violence and repression exerted upon it, the sociological profiles of the activists and their sociability patterns) (see Tavera 2002; Freán 2011), were also undertaken. More recently, the anarchists' exile and underground existence during the Francoist regime have attracted the attention not only of historians (Herrerín 2004) but also sociologists (Romanos 2011, 2014b, 2014c).

Impact of the Theories about the Democratic Transition on Social Movements' Research

Explanations concerning the transition to democracy in Spain have basically fallen into two different groups: those that have stressed the role played by political elites (reformist Francoists and the leaders of democratic parties) (Cotarelo 1992; Pastor 1992), and those that have also incorporated the protest of the masses in order to account for the demise of the dictatorship (Maravall 1978; Castells 1983; Laraña 1999). Bottom-up accounts have singled out working-class strikes and university students' turmoil as important factors that help democracy advance under uncertain circumstances (Maravall 1978; Laraña 1999). Other actors, such as rural movements (Herrera and Markoff 2011), neighbours (Castells 1983), nationalist groups (Johnston 1991; Pérez Agote 1987), some sectors of the Catholic Church, and women's networks, who set up housewives' associations (Radcliff 2002), have also been acknowledged as instrumental in the political change.

The choice between the elite versus the masses version of the transition has had important consequences for the research on social movements. 'Elitists' à la O'Donnell and Schmitter (1986) have emphasised how some enlightened authoritarian groups became aware of their progressive de-legitimacy and decided to reach an agreement with the leaders of the democratic parties in order to set new rules that could guarantee their political survival.

In Spain, these 'behind the curtains political pacts' were flanked by a commitment on the part of the opposition leaders to demobilise their rank and file. Many scholars have therefore interpreted that the Spanish democracy was flawed from its inception: betrayed by their leaders, social movements withered gradually away and relevant vindications were left aside or buried (disenchantment was the catchword), while the new democracy established restrictive participatory rules (del Águila 1988; Alonso 1991; Vidal-Beneyto 1977). However, other authors have pointed out that while the new regime did not break explicitly away with the old one, it was not because the democratic leadership dissipated the revolutionary enthusiasm of the masses: collective action during the late Francoist period and the first years of the transition did not offer a solid foundation for the building of a united political front (Sánchez-Cuenca and Aguilar 2009). 'Revolutionary-inspired' collective action was only present in massive urban unrest in three small cities: Getafe, Sabadell and Vitoria. Leaving aside the Basque Country, the rest of Spain did not experience any significant turmoil (Sánchez-Cuenca 2014).[3]

Going beyond these two perspectives, Fishman (1990) developed a meso-analysis which focused on the role of labor leaders at the workplace level during the political transition . According to him, the interest in mass demobilization by the elites of the labor movement only occurred because workplace leaders eventually internalized the legitimacy of democratic institutions. Their support to major national political agreements was not enthusiastic, but fueled by the moderation of the claims among their rank-and-file. In this sense, the political pacts 'from above' were consistent with the actual situation 'from below', in a context of economic crisis and shutting down of enterprises which facilitated workers' restraint (ibid.: 238–246).

Affirmation of the Social Movements in a Consolidated Democracy

The remarkable wave of protest identified just after Franco's death in 1975 begun to subside in 1978. After the failed *coup d'état* of 1981 and the electoral victory of the Socialists (PSOE) in 1982, democratic consolidation was characterised by a decrease of collective action. However, this was so only in relation to the previous unparalleled wave of protest. That is, Spanish society was not demobilized during the 1980s and 1990s: the European Social Survey unveils that, in a comparison with another 16 countries, Spain was, except for one occasion, the first country in terms of attendance to demonstrations over the last decade of the twentieth century (Jiménez 2011: 20).

The new period was also marked by the affirmation of the new social movements. As a result of the previous politicised context, some movements maintained a highly politicised profile: the cognitive frameworks of the gay (Calvo 2002) and environmental movements (Martín 2002), among others, were still heavily influenced by Marxism in the 1980s. The undisputable leadership of the pacifist movement in Europe was not replicated in Spain unless we consider the marches against the American military bases in the 1970s and the entry into NATO in the 1980s (Laraña 1999). A spin-off of this type of protest was the *insumisos* movement (Casquete 1996, 1998; Sampedro 2002), led by those youngsters who, by refusing to join the army and undertake the alternative service, helped to end conscription in 1996, when the Conservatives (*Partido Popular,* PP) won the elections.

The Socialist electoral victory was seen as a political opportunity by environmentalists' and women's groups, some of whose members became part of the new administration (Jiménez 2005; Valiente 2007). However, the PSOE did not prove to be minimally responsive to other challengers such as gays and lesbians (Calvo 2007), while its policies deceived many activists who eventually decided to leave the institutional realm. The government had to contend with the protest of Catholic groups, on the one hand, and students on the other (Laraña 1999), who took to the streets to protest against a number of educational reforms. Labour unrest, unleashed by the shutting down of inefficient public sector companies, and the organization of major rallies against terrorism, were also part of the collective action of the time.

The conservative PP government enjoyed rather peaceful street politics until it decided to join the war in Iraq in 2003. This war brought about one of the most important protests in recent history (Morán 2005; Jiménez 2007b). Coinciding in time, a new social movement called Nunca Máis (NM—Never Again), created after the *Prestige* oil spill in November 2002, also hit the headlines and joined the broad anti-war coalition. NM failed to achieve its goals because it neglected the construction of a cohesive identity and erroneously conceived the political opportunity window opened by the environmental catastrophe as a way to defeat the PP government in Galicia (Aguilar and Ballesteros 2004). On 13 May 2004, thousands of angry citizens, mostly youngsters who used their mobile phones to send mobilizing messages (SMS), gathered in front of the PP headquarters to protest against the fraudulent attempt of the government to blame ETA for the 11-M fundamentalist terrorist attack in Madrid (Sampedro 2005; Flesher Fominaya 2011).

Both the protest against the Iraq war and the flash-mob protest following the terrorist bombings were important lessons for a new generation of young activists who, shortly after the comeback to power of the socialist

PSOE (2004–11) and its immediate decision to withdraw the Spanish troops from Iraq soil, took to the streets again to protest against the Bologna initiative and the housing problem. The neglect of cognitive frameworks by the Movement for Decent Housing helps explain why it failed to sustain its mobilizing capacity over time. Education and housing were framed similarly as the selling out of two basic public services to greedy capitalist forces (Aguilar and Fernández 2010). A version of the political mediation theory has been used in order to explain how the gay movement's support to the new PSOE, under the leadership of Zapatero, was reciprocated by a more sympathetic attitude of the Socialists to their demands (Calvo 2010). Gays and women have been instrumental in the approval of various reforms and new legislation, such as same-sex marriage, the law against gender violence and the liberalization of abortion. The adversarial role played by the Catholic Church in the fight against these reforms has allied this institution with the more conservative churches but distanced itself from mainstream religious institutions in Europe (Aguilar 2012, 2011).

Institutionalization and Internationalization of Spanish Research

Academic institutionalization of social movement studies in Spain has followed different paths depending on the specific discipline under consideration. Historical analyses of the workers' movement have become part of an area called 'history of political thought and social movements', which is present in a number of university departments. The initial focus on workers' organizations and the intra-movement clashes has gradually shifted to other contenders, such as the political populist and the anti-clerical movements (Pérez Ledesma 1994; Cruz and Pérez Ledesma 1997; Castro 2005). One of the most productive centres in this field has been the department of history of the political thought and social movements at the Complutense University which, alongside the department of social history and political thought at the Open University (UNED), has been publishing the journal *Historia y Política* since 1999. Researchers from both departments have participated in the workshop on contemporary history organised by the Ortega y Gasset University Institute in Madrid. Another relevant publication in the field is *Historia Social*, created in 1988 by the Alzira-Valencia UNED Centre.

As has also happened elsewhere, historians in Spain were the forerunners in the study of social movements (Pérez Ledesma 1994). However, the belated development and consolidation of the sociology of social movements has differentiated Spain from countries such as France and Italy (cf. Adell,

Aguiar and Robles 2007). Belatedness can be explained by contextual reasons: in Europe, the sociological study of challengers was in tune with the evolution of the protests in the late 1960s and the subsequent emergence of new social movements (Della Porta and Diani 2006). Although comparatively tame, contentious action was also experienced in 1968 in Franco's Spain (Kornetis 2008) but new social movements, as aforementioned, took off later than their Western counterparts.

The most important sociological journal, *Revista Española de Investigaciones Sociológicas*, published its first article containing the 'social movements' keyword in 1986, eight years after its foundation. Sociological research on social movements has mushroomed ever since, but its institutionalization is still feeble. The working group on 'Collective Action, Social Movements and Social Change' is one of the oldest within the Spanish Federation of Sociology (Adell, Aguiar and Robles 2007), but its research members have complained about the lack of distribution lists, workshops and scientific journals in the field. Even though diverse research groups have promoted scholarly debates,[4] it is mostly confined to their members. Unlike other countries, no general dictionary on social movements exists in Spain while the only compilations on this topic have merely dealt with the different traditions in the workers' movement. Some exceptions are the Social Movement Yearbooks, published by the Betiko Foundation (fundacionbetiko.org) since 1999. Leaving aside a few translations, students can only count on a single textbook written by Spanish authors (Ibarra 2005).

Feeble institutionalization has been accompanied by the limited internationalization of the research. At times, this research has been influential (a good example is Castells' work on urban movements in 1983 during the early phase of the social movement research in Europe [Diani and Císař 2014]) but no extensive international collaborations have materialised. Remarkable 'joint-ventures' in the 1990s (e.g. Laraña, Johnston and Gusfield 1994) were peripheral to the transatlantic 'elite group' which steered the research agenda (Diani and Císař 2014). On the whole, Spanish scholars did not show up notably in international forums during the 1980s and 1990s. As a result, Spanish contribution to international debates has been scarce.

Nonetheless, this situation seems to be changing. Spanish teams are increasingly present in international projects. The impact of this growing internationalization can also be traced in the most influential journals and reference works. Recent contributions to *Mobilization* (Herrera and Markoff 2011; Morales and Ramiro 2011) have succeeded in bringing to an end the fourteen-year period of Spanish non-presence in the journal. Something similar has happened in *Social Movement Studies*, where different pieces of research on the new protest wave in Spain have been published. While no Spanish author was invited to the *Blackwell Companion to Social Movements* published in 2004, four have contributed essays to the *Wiley-Blackwell Encyclopedia of Social and Political Movements,* published in 2013.

The Public Side of the Social Movement Research

As has also happened elsewhere, the so-called 'public sociology of social movements' (Diani and Císař 2014) has been relatively important in Spain. During the late Francoist period and outset of the transition, new groups which were strongly permeated by left-wing parties set foot on the political stage. Unlike the old labour movement, these groups were far from being anti-political: in most cases, their political leaning derived from a strong relationship with the Communist Party (Álvarez Junco 1994). Thus, collective action was subordinated explicitly, as in the case of the university students' revolts (Maravall 1978), or implicitly, as with the neighbours' movement (Castells 1983), to the political fight against the dictatorship. Politicised social movements went hand in hand with politicised publications. However, the dearth of theoretically sound analyses and conclusive evidence were important drawbacks. Beginning in the 1970s, a few publications set out to narrate protest events, interpreting them from an unsophisticated Marxist standpoint. As Martín (2002), Fernández (1999) and Laraña (1999) have contended, no sound scholarly analysis was introduced in these works.

A more recent 'school' within public sociology has revolved around Rodríguez Villasante. His work is linked to the critical praxis of Ibáñez (1928–92), a sociologist who defended the need to go 'beyond sociology' in order to intervene in social change. Following this call, Villasante has promoted a research programme centred on the social movements' self-knowledge by means of a well-known methodology in Latin America: research-participatory action. Activist-researchers trained in this 'school' have participated in budgetary decisions in different cities (Ganuza and Francés 2012) and deliberative processes in the *Indignados* movement (Nez and Ganuza 2015).

Alter-Globalization and the *Indignados*

The heritage of the new social movements' organizational culture has been reflected in a fragmented global justice movement which, in Spain, has found less influential allies than elsewhere (Jiménez and Calle 2007). The more recent 15M movement (or *Indignados*) has, however, enjoyed broad media coverage and tried to develop into a functioning national-level network. The

Indignados would thus reinforce the trend towards the integration of Spanish social movements into the European scenario (Della Porta 2007). New activism in this and other types of protest is partly the result of a new generation of challengers who have shared a number of life experiences (multi-movement campaigns as well as voluntary work) that have facilitated the gradual building of cohesive identities and inter-organizational coordination (Jiménez 2006; Jerez, Sampedro and López 2008). Activist networks against neoliberal globalization worldwide have shared a radical democracy framework in addition to heterogeneous, horizontal and permeable organizations, and a repertoire based on civil disobedience and non-violent direct action (Flesher Fominaya 2007, 2010).

The *Indignados* movement has taken scholars and ordinary people aback due to its mobilizing capacity. This movement has managed to attract a substantial amount of people, many of whom lacked previous activist experience. Intense mobilization has also facilitated the recruitment of previously active social movements and social movement organizations (SMO), such as those involving squatters and the *Plataforma de Afectados por la Hipoteca* (PAH—Platform for People Affected by Mortgages). The *Indignados* movement has adopted the protest against eviction as its own and used its networks to give visibility to the calls for action over the housing problem. The movement against housing eviction is also important because the ability of the activists to combine conventional and non-conventional action and to diversify the range of actors involved (scale shift) seems to be breaking away from a deeply rooted pattern whereby interaction between protest movements and institutional actors was absent (Romanos 2014a; Fishman 2012).

Many researchers on social movements have logically begun to analyse the *Indignados* protest. Amongst other topics, the relationship of this movement to previous mobilizations, such as the global justice and the free culture movements; the activists' profile; the deliberative democracy put into practice; the identity-building process; the offline and online mobilization patterns; the mobilizing frames; and the transnational connection with other types of protest have been subject to scrutiny (see Nez in this volume). Many other research projects on the 15M are currently underway. Undoubtedly, this movement will concentrate much of the future effort of scholars interested in Spanish social movements. Questions open to further analysis are the activists' tactical repertoire and their contribution to the diffusion of a new transnational mobilizing wave, as well as the importance of emotions (on top of aggrieved feelings) related, for instance, to the humorous expressions of discontent. The 15M case can also advance our knowledge of the relationship between social movements and the electoral process, social protest and the economic crisis, online and offline mobilizations, and the different logics of connective/collective action. The new transnational wave of protest also offers an unbeatable scenario to compare social movements and will yield results that might support or refute theories about the origins, diffusion and outcomes of protest.

Spanish social movements are no longer different from their Western counterparts. The anti-politics orientation which was once prevalent in the anarchist and other workers' groups has faded away. The repressive political conditions during the late Francoist dictatorship as well as its success in generating a demobilised and apolitical society can explain the belated emergence of the new social movements (university students, neighbours' and housewives' associations, among others) and the restricted unrest of the old ones (workers'). The collective action undertaken by the new and old contenders, which was clearly anti-regime oriented and extensively permeated by the Communist Party, was mainly confined to the campus, the deprived quarters of the big cities and large factories, and did not reach society as a whole.

The onset of the transition to democracy was characterised by a substantial degree of social mobilization and political violence on the part of the state apparatus and the extremist groups on the right and left. This period was flanked by the blooming of publications written by the social activists themselves or by sympathetic authors. After 1981, the number of protests fell: a risk-averse society, indoctrinated with the values of 'peace and prosperity' for nearly forty years; the negotiated and consensual character of the transition; and the cautious political approach adopted by the left-wing political elites and workplace union leaders, which resulted in a concerted demobilizing effort of their rank and file, can all account for the more limited relevance and visibility of the social movements during the 1980s.

Decreasing collective action and the reluctance to employ radical repertoires (except for the Basque terrorist organization, ETA) were the consequences of the particular political scenario described above. The new quasi-federal state created by the 1978 Constitution alongside the political strength of nationalist forces help account for another peculiarity of the social movements in democracy: their decentralised structure and coordination problems at the state level.

So far, these are the *sui generis* features of the Spanish social movements. But what happened once democracy became consolidated after the left came to power in 1982? As in many other countries, the new electoral cycle (1982–96) was perceived as a political opportunity. Some sections of the women and environmentalist movements seized this opportunity to enter political institutions, whereas others continued their fight on the streets (the pacifists who resisted the country's accession to NATO, or the *insumisos* who refused to do the military service), or simply abstained from following either of the two strategies (the gay movement). The consequences of the 'long march through the institutions of power' were mixed: in some cases, public agencies were created to give voice to the movements (as happened with the Institute for Women) and activist-friendly pieces of legislation were passed, while in others, the reforms were seen as too modest or blatantly deceitful, with this ultimately leading to an abandonment of politics, if not to the eruption of clashes within particular movements (as was the case with the environmentalists). Not surprisingly, disenchantment was the catchword that described this phase. The Socialist government also encountered the street opposition of students and Catholic-inspired groups, who opposed their educational reforms for different reasons, and industrial workers, who fought against the shutting down of public enterprises. In the academic realm, the leadership of the historians in the study of the workers' movement gave way to new objects of analysis and approaches, adopted by sociologists and political scientists, who emphasised the importance of the constructive work undertaken by SMO and leaders as well as the structural changes that had paved the way for the emergence of new challengers and forms of mobilization. Even though most of this work lacked internationalization, the studies on social movements became institutionalised in the university realm.

Gradually, Spanish collective action became more attuned with Western protest: the massive manifestations against the Iraq war that took place under the new Conservative government (1996–2004) placed Spain at the forefront of a protest wave occurring in many European countries. Furthermore, the students who took to the streets to express their grievances about the selling out of goods such as education and housing, the groups which demanded a budgetary increase in third-world aid or those who protested against the liberalization of abortion and the approval of same-sex marriage, as products of the new Socialist government (2004–11), were on the same wavelength as like-minded contenders in the Western world. If anything, certain examples of collective action, such as the enormous demonstrations that followed some of the terrorist attacks of ETA, as well as those connected to ethno-linguistic cleavages, departed from regular protest elsewhere. But this can be explained by a path-dependence logic which also affected other countries. In a manner similar to the 'normalization' of the social movements, the research agenda of Spanish scholars has progressively become more internationalised and indistinguishable from mainstream literature.

Finally, the *Indignados* movement, which arose out of the widespread citizens' anger with the austerity measures implemented after the 2008 financial crisis and the succession of political scandals, can be easily connected with analogous protests such as Occupy in the United States. This movement and its numerous ramifications (the anti-eviction groups, the citizens' 'tides' against the privatization of the health system and limited resources for the public education system) are being thoroughly analysed at present, and international academic research cooperation in the study of similar phenomena elsewhere is mushrooming.

Eduardo Romanos is a Ramón y Cajal Fellow in the Department of Sociology I (Social Change) at the Universidad Complutense de Madrid. He received his PhD in political and social sciences from the European University Institute in Florence, and has worked as a postdoctoral fellow at the University of Trento. Among his most recent publications are articles in *Journal of Historical Sociology, Revista Española de Investigaciones Sociológicas, Contemporary European History,* and *Social Movement Studies.* His main research interests are in the areas of political sociology and historical sociology, with a particular focus on social movements and protest.

Susana Aguilar is a senior reader and accredited professor at the Universidad Complutense de Madrid, where she teaches social movements and political sociology. She is a doctor member of the Juan March Institute and has participated in many European Union research projects, dealing mostly with environmental issues, sustainable development and protest politics. She has published in *Administration and Society, The Journal of Public Policy, Environmental Politics, Politics and Religion, Regional Politics and Policies, Southern European Society and Politics,* and *Science and Public Policy.* In 2014, she was awarded for "best research" by the *Journal of Forestry.*

Notes

1. This work was supported by the Spanish Ministry of Economy and Competitiveness under Grant CSO2013-41035-P.
2. Anti-politicism is understood here as 'the disdain for parliamentary politics and reform' (Álvarez Junco 1994: 307).
3. The need to carefully measure collective action before reaching hasty political conclusions is badly needed. Different techniques have been discussed by authors such as Adell (2005), who has coined the term 'demonstra-meter' (*manifestómetro*). Jiménez (2011) has collected data on the number of demonstrations and demonstrators from 1980 to 2008.
4. Examples are Cibersomosaguas (Madrid), the Centre for the Study of the Social Movements (Barcelona), the Research Group on Society and Politics (Madrid) and the Centre for the Study of Collective Identity (Bilbao), among others.

References

Adell, R. 2005. 'Manifestómetro'. *Empiria* 9: 171–208.

Adell, R., F. Aguiar and J. M. Robles. 2007. 'Acción colectiva y movimientos sociales en la sociología española'. In *La sociología en España,* ed. M. Pérez Yruela, 481–502. Madrid: CIS.

Adell, R., and M. Martínez. 2004. *¿Dónde están las llaves? El movimiento okupa: prácticas y contextos sociales.* Madrid: La Catarata.

Aguilar, S. 2011. 'El Movimiento Antiabortista en la España del Siglo XXI: El Protagonismo de Grupos Sociales Laicos y la Alianza de Facto con la Iglesia Católica'. *Revista de Estudios Políticos* 154: 11–39.

———. 2012. 'Fighting against the Moral Agenda of Zapatero's Socialist Government (2004–2011): The Spanish Catholic Church as a Political Contender'. *Politics and Religion* 5, no. 3: 671–94.

Aguilar, S., and A. Fernández. 2010. 'El movimiento por la vivienda digna en España o el por qué del fracaso de una protesta con amplia base social'. *Revista Internacional de Sociología* 68, no. 3: 679–704.

Aguilar, S., and A. Ballesteros. 2004. 'Debating the Concept of Political Opportunities in Relation to the Galician Social Movement Nunca Más'. *Southern European Society and Politics* 9, no. 3: 28–53.

Alonso, L. E. 1991. 'Los nuevos movimientos sociales y el hecho diferencial español'. In *España a Debate. II. La Sociedad,* ed. M. Beltrán, 71–98. Madrid: Tecnos.

Álvarez Junco, J. 1976. *La ideología política del anarquismo español (1868–1910).* Madrid: Siglo XXI.

———. 1994. 'Social Movements in Modern Spain: From the Pre–Civil War Model to Contemporary NSMs'. In *New Social Movements: From Ideology to Identity,* ed. E. Laraña, H. Johnston and J.R. Gusfield, 304–39. Philadelphia: Temple University Press.

Brenan, G. 1943. *The Spanish Labyrinth: An Account of the Social and Political Background of the Spanish Civil War.* Cambridge: Cambridge University Press.

Calvo, K. 2002. 'Identidad, diferencia y disidencia sexual: el caso del movimiento de lesbianas y gays'. In *El reto de la participación: Movimientos sociales y organizaciones,* ed. J. M. Robles, 239–68. Madrid: Mínimo Tránsito.

———. 2007. 'Sacrifices That Pay: Polity Membership, Political Opportunities and the Recognition of Same-Sex Marriage in Spain'. *South European Society and Politics* 12, no. 3: 295–314.

Casanova, J. 2013. 'Lo que aprendí de Álvarez Junco'. In *Pueblo y Nación: Homenaje a José Álvarez Junco,* ed. J. Moreno Luzón and F. del Rey, 59–68. Madrid: Taurus.

Casquete, J. 1996. 'The Sociopolitical Context of Mobilization: The Case of the Anti-Military Movement in the Basque Country'. *Mobilization* 1, no. 2: 203–212.

———. 1998. *Política, cultura y movimientos sociales.* Bilbao, Bakeaz.

———. 2006. 'The Power of Demonstrations'. *Social Movements Studies* 5, no. 1: 45–60.

Castells, M. 1983. *The City and the Grassroots.* London: Edward Arnold.

Castro, D. 2005. 'Palabras de fuego: El anticlericalismo republicano'. *Journal of Spanish Cultural Studies* 6, no. 2: 205–25.

Cotarelo, R. 1992. 'La transición democrática española'. In *Transición política y consolidación democrática (1975–1986),* ed. R. Cotarelo, 10–16. Madrid: CIS.

Cruz, R. and M. Pérez Ledesma, eds. 1997. *Cultura y movilización en la España contemporánea*. Madrid: Alianza.

Del Aguila, R. 1988. 'El problema del diseño político de la transición en España'. *Documentación Social* 73.

Della Porta, D. 2015. *Social Movements in Times of Austerity: Bringing Capitalism Back In*. Cambridge: Polity Press.

Della Porta, D., ed. 2007. *The Global Justice Movement: Cross-National and Transnational Differences*. London: Paradigm.

Della Porta, D. and M. Diani. 2006. *Social Movement: An Introduction*. Malden: Blackwell.

Diani, M., and O. Císař. 2014. 'The Emergence of a Social Movement Research Field'. In *Routledge Handbook of European Sociology*, ed. S. Kodornios and A. Kyrtsis, 173–95. London: Routledge.

Elorza, Antonio. 1971. 'La utopía anarquista durante la Segunda República española'. *Revista de Trabajo* 36: 179–319.

Fernández, J. 1999. *El ecologismo español*. Madrid: Alianza.

Fishman, R. M. 1990. *Working-Class Organization and the Return to Democracy in Spain*. Ithaca: Cornell University Press.

———. 2012. 'On the Significance of Public Protest in Spanish Democracy'. In *Democràcia, Política i Societat: Homenatge a Rosa Virós*, ed. J. Jornada et al., 351–66. Barcelona: UPF.

Flesher Fominaya, C. 2007. 'Autonomous Movements and the Institutional Left: Two Approaches in Tension in Madrid's Anti-globalization Network'. *South European Society and Politics* 12, no. 3: 335–58.

———. 2010. 'Creating Cohesion from Diversity: The Challenge of Collective Identity Formation in the Global Justice Movement'. *Sociological Inquiry* 80, no. 3: 377–404.

———. 2011. 'The Madrid Bombings and Popular Protest: Misinformation, Counter-information, Mobilisation and Elections after "11-M"'. *Contemporary Social Science* 6, no. 3: 289–307.

———. 2014. *Social Movements and Globalization: How Protests, Occupations and Uprisings Are Changing the World*. New York: Palgrave Macmillan.

Freán, O. 2011. 'El anarquismo español: luces y sombras en la historiografía reciente sobre el movimiento libertario'. *Ayer* 84: 209–23.

Funés, M. J. 1998. *La salida del silencio: Movilizaciones por la paz en Euskadi, 1986–1998*. Madrid: Akal.

Ganuza, E., and F. Francés. 2012. *El círculo virtuoso de la democracia: los presupuestos participativos a debate*. Madrid: CIS.

Gomá, R., P. Ibarra and S. Martí. 2002. '¿Vale la pena moverse? Movimientos sociales como redes de acción colectiva crítica en la red de "governance" y su impacto en las políticas'. In *El reto de la participación*, ed. J. M. Robles, 111–46. Madrid: Mínimo Tránsito.

Herrera, A., and J. Markoff. 2011. 'Rural Movements and the Transition to Democracy in Spain'. *Mobilization* 16, no. 4: 455–74.

Herrerín, A. 2004. *La CNT durante el franquismo: clandestinidad y exilio (1939–1975)*. Madrid: Siglo XXI.

Hobsbawm, E. 1963. *Primitive Rebels*. Manchester: Manchester University Press.

Ibarra, P. 1999. 'Los movimientos por la solidaridad: ¿un nuevo modelo de acción colectiva?' *Revista Española de Investigaciones Sociológicas* 88: 233–60.

———. 2000. '¿Qué son los movimientos sociales?'. In *Anuario Movimientos Sociales: Una mirada sobre la red*, ed. E. Grau and P. Ibarra, 9–26. Barcelona: Icaria.

———. 2005. *Manual de sociedad civil y movimientos sociales*. Madrid: Síntesis.

Jerez, A., and A. J. Romero. 2002. 'Mirando al sur: una aproximación al movimiento por el desarrollo y la solidaridad en la España de los 90'. In *El reto de la participación*, ed. J. M. Robles, 269–300. Madrid, Mínimo Tránsito.

Jerez, A., V. Sampedro and J. A. López Rey. 2008. *Del 0'7% a la desobediencia civil: política e información del movimiento y las ONG de Desarrollo (1994–2000)*. Madrid: CIS.

Jiménez, M. 2005. *El impacto político de los movimientos sociales: un estudio de la protesta ambiental en España*. Madrid, CIS.

———. 2006. 'El movimiento de justicia global: una indagación sobre las aportaciones de una nueva generación contestataria'. *Revista de Estudios de Juventud*, 75: 29–41.

———. 2007a. 'The Environmental Movement in Spain: A Growing Force of Contention'. *South European Society and Politics* 12, no. 3: 359–78.

———. 2007b. 'Mobilizations against the Iraq War in Spain: Background, Participants and Electoral Implications'. *South European Society and Politics* 12, no. 3: 399–420.

———. 2011. *La normalización de la protesta (1980–2000): El caso de las manifestaciones en España*. Madrid, CIS.

Jiménez, M., and A. Calle. 2007. 'The Global Justice Movement in Spain'. In *The Global Justice Movement: Cross-National and Transnational Differences*, ed. D. Della Porta, 79–102. London: Paradigm.

Johnston, H. 1991. *Tales of Nationalism: Catalonia, 1939–1979*. New Brunswick: Rutgers University Press.

Juliá, S. 1990. 'Poder y Revolución en la Cultura Política del Militante Obrero Español'. In *Peuple, Mouvement Ouvrier, Culture dans l'Espagne Contemporaine*, ed. J. Maurice et al., 179–91. Paris: Presses Universitaires de Vincennes.

Kornetis, K. 2008. 'Spain and Greece'. In *1968 in Europe: A History of Protest and Activism, 1956–1977*, ed. M. Klimke and J. Scharloth, 253–66. New York: Palgrave McMillan.

Laraña, E. 1993. 'Movimientos sociales'. In *Tendencias sociales en España (1960–1990)*, ed. S. del Campo, vol. II, 381–424. Bilbao: Fundación BBV.

———. 1999. *La construcción de los movimientos sociales*. Madrid, Alianza.

Laraña, E., H. Johnston and J. R. Gusfield, eds. 1994. *New Social Movements: From Ideology to Identity*. Philadelphia: Temple University Press.

Maravall, J. M. 1978. *Dictadura y disentimiento político*. Madrid: Alfaguara.

Martí, C. 1959. *Orígenes del anarquismo en Barcelona*. Barcelona: Teide.

Martín, M. T. 2002. 'El desarrollo del movimiento ecologista en España'. In *El reto de la participación*, ed. J. M. Robles, 333–63. Madrid: Mínimo Tránsito.

Martínez, M. 2007. 'The Squatters' Movement: Urban Counter-Culture and Alter-Globalization Dynamics'. *South European Society and Politics* 12, no. 3: 379–98.

———. 2013. 'How Do Squatters Deal with the State? Legalization and Anomalous Institutionalization in Madrid'. *International Journal of Urban and Regional Research* (Early View).

Morales, L., and L. Ramiro. 2011. 'Gaining Political Capital through Social Capital: Policy-Making Inclusion and Network Embeddedness of Migrants' Associations in Spain'. *Mobilization* 16, no. 2: 147–64.

Morán, M. L. 2005. 'Viejos y nuevos espacios para la ciudadanía: La manifestación del 15 de febrero de 2003 en Madrid'. *Política y Sociedad* 42, no. 2: 95–113.

Nez, H., and E. Ganuza. 2012. 'Among Militants and Deliberative Laboratories: The Indignados'. In *From Social to Political: New Forms of Mobilization and Democratization (Conference Proceedings)*, ed. B. Tejerina and I. Perugorría, 119–36. Bilbao: UPV.

Pastor, M. 1992. 'Las postrimerías del franquismo'. In *Transición política y consolidación democrática (1975–1986)*, ed. R. Cotarelo, 31–46. Madrid: CIS.

Pérez Ledesma, M. 1994. '"Cuando lleguen los días de la cólera" (Movimientos sociales, teoría e historia)'. *Zona Abierta* 69: 51–120.

Pérez-Agote, A. 1987. *El nacionalismo vasco a la salida del franquismo*. Madrid, CIS.

Radcliff, P. 2002. 'Citizens and Housewives: The Problem of Female Citizenship in Spain's Transition to Democracy'. *Journal of Social History* 36, no. 1: 77–100.

Romanos, E. 2011. 'Factionalism in Transition: A Comparative Analysis of Ruptures in the Spanish Anarchist Movement'. *Journal of Historical Sociology* 24, no. 3: 355–80.

———. 2014a. 'Evictions, Petitions and *Escraches:* Contentious Housing in Austerity Spain'. *Social Movement Studies* 13, no. 2: 296–302.

———. 2014b. 'Emotions, Moral Batteries and High-Risk Activism: Understanding the Emotional Practices of the Spanish Anarchists under Franco's Dictatorship'. *Contemporary European History* 23, no. 4: 545–64.

———. 2014c. 'Radicalization from Outside: The Role of Anarchist Diaspora in Coordinating Armed Actions in Franco's Spain'. In *Dynamics of Political Violence,* ed. L. Bosi, C. Demetriou and S. Malthaner, 237–54. Farnham: Ashgate.

Sampedro, V. 1997. 'The Media Politics of Social Protest'. *Mobilization* 2, no. 2: 185–205.

———. 2002. 'Estrategias sociales de innovación política: el caso de la insumisión'. In *El reto de la participación,* ed. J. M. Robles, 211–38. Madrid: Mínimo Tránsito.

Sampedro, V., ed. 2005. *13-M: Multitudes Online*. Madrid: La Catarata.

Sánchez-Cuenca, I. 2014. *Atado y bien atado: El suicidio institucional del franquismo y el surgimiento de la democracia*. Madrid: Alianza.

Sánchez-Cuenca, I., and P. Aguilar. 2009. 'Terrorist Violence and Popular Mobilization: The Case of the Spanish Transition to Democracy'. *Politics and Society* 37, no. 3: 428–53.

Tavera, S. 2002. 'La historia del anarquismo español: una encrucijada interpretativa nueva'. *Ayer* 45: 13–37.

Tejerina, B. 1999. 'El poder de los símbolos: identidad colectiva y movimiento etnolingüístico en el País Vasco'. *Revista Española de Investigaciones Sociológicas* 88: 75–106.

———. 2001. 'Protest Cycle, Political Violence and Social Movements in the Basque Country'. *Nations and Nationalism* 7, no. 1: 39–57.

Tejerina, B., J. M. Fernández and X. Aierdi. 1995. *Sociedad civil, protesta y movimientos sociales en el País Vasco*. Vitoria: Servicio de Publicaciones del Gobierno Vasco.

Tejerina, B., et al. 2013. 'From Indignation to Occupation: A New Wave of Global Mobilization'. *Current Sociology* 61, no. 4: 377–92.

Valiente, C. 2007. 'Are Gender Equality Institutions the Policy Allies of the Feminist Movement? A Contingent Yes in the Spanish Central State'. *South European Society and Politics* 12, no. 3: 315–34.

Vidal-Beneyto, J. 1977. *Del franquismo a una democracia de clase*. Akal: Madrid.

Chapter 20

Revolutionary or Mild Mannered?

Social Movements and Social Movements Studies in Portugal

Guya Accornero

On 25 April 1974 the Portuguese New State, in force for forty years, was overthrown by a peaceful military coup led by the Armed Forces Movement (MFA).[1] The MFA presented a democratizing programme that included the establishment of a civilian government and free elections. After more than a decade of war on various fronts in Africa, the military also initiated a process of de-colonization that quickly culminated in the granting of independence to the former colonial peoples. This event not only represented a social and political rupture and a founding moment but it also flung open the gates to the development of various fields of studies in Portugal in the areas of sociology, political science and history, which had been censured and held back during the dictatorship.

Following well-founded studies in modern history and with a Marxian approach, the field of the social and economic history of Portugal was brought to light, after being set aside for many years in favour of a history aimed at glorifying Portugal's magnitude, especially the history of its discoveries. The generation of scholars exiled and trained in various countries, notably France, who returned to Portugal after the revolution, were of special relevance in this process. Ground-breaking work on the agrarian issue, the introduction of capitalism, the emergence of the proletariat and the class struggles in Portugal, among other events, began to appear in publications, and social conflict was for the first time at the centre of the official academic research agenda in Portugal.[2]

On the other hand, the Portuguese revolution not only opened up the possibility of studies on the role of social conflict and class struggle in the country's history, which had of course been completely absent during the dictatorship, but it also ended up becoming a new field of research in which social movements theory was applied for the first time. This chapter will begin with an overview of these studies, before turning to the research on patterns of conventional and unconventional political participation in Portugal. In the second section, we present a perspective that is close to the findings of James Scott although not always directly inspired by them; this is followed by the research on social movements by scholars of what I call the 'Coimbra School'. The final part of the chapter describes the potential of social movements research in Portugal as a result of the special historical, geographic and linguistic characteristics of the country.

When Power 'Fell to the Streets': Social Movements and the Portuguese Revolution

The coup of 25 April 1974 was immediately followed by broad political and popular mobilization. This turbulent period in contemporary Portuguese history, called the Processo Revolucionário em Curso (PREC—Revolutionary Process Underway), was characterised by intense conflict between opposing political forces; attempted coups and counter-coups; massive social mobilization; the occupation of houses, lands and factories; and, at the institutional level, the adoption of radical measures such as the nationalization of key private enterprises (banks, insurance companies, public transports and iron works, among others), the introduction of a minimum wage for civil servants and the institution of unemployment benefits.

These events are something of a 'laboratory' for scholars interested in social movements. A number of social scientists have stressed that the PREC was one of the most intense periods of mobilization in post-war Europe[3]; however, there are considerable variations, and it is intertwined with institutional dynamics. Most contemporaneous reports and subsequent academic analyses portray this popular mobilization as an exceptional phenomenon. In the words of the political scientist Manuel Braga da Cruz (1995), it was a mobilization with neither past nor future in the history of Portuguese politics. In his view, the high level of political and social engagement of the Portuguese population during the revolution was due to political and social decompression, which had the effect of liberating accumulated tensions; however, he adds that the ensuing demobilization shows that the underlying political culture had not changed.[4] Howard Wiarda shares this view: he believes Portuguese political culture is historically non-participatory, except during the democratic transition when the 'other Portugal' exploded into revolution (2006: 123). Similarly, Philippe Schmitter tries to explain the intense post-revolutionary mobilizations as an 'awakening' of civil society resulting from the institutional vacuum left after the *coup d'état* (Schmitter 1999).

Although dealing with the social mobilizations of the PREC, none of the abovementioned interpretations refer to social movements theory, but situate themselves more in the frame of 'transition studies'. The instruments of social movements sociology were first applied in Portugal precisely to analyse the Portuguese revolution. Durán Muñoz (1997a, 1997b and 2000) was the first scholar to use the concept of political opportunity structure (POS) to explain the diffusion of mobilization following the coup. Palacios Cerezales (2003b) then fruitfully used the concept in conjunction with Michel Dobry's theory of political crisis (Dobry 1986) to analyse the Portuguese transition. The latter studies make a fundamental contribution to the understanding of the Portuguese case, and have the merit of integrating social movement theory into the theoretical framework and methodology deployed by the literature on transitions and democratization in Portugal.

These studies, like those that came before, reproduce the vision of a country partially 'in slumber' until the day of the revolution and after the consolidation of democracy. Both Muñoz and Cerezales consider the opening of the political opportunities after the *coup d'état* to be the direct cause of the great mobilizations during the PREC. As a result, to some extent they underestimate the role of previous mobilizing networks, resources and earlier engaged militants. This is done in part to avoid deterministic interpretations, which were iterated by some historians' reconstructions (Dawn Raby 1990; Reis 1991; Rosas 1998 among others). The incorporation of Dobry's theory of political crisis by Cerezales is an important advance in this direction since there is no certainty as to the outcome of events in times of political crisis.

These studies have been absolutely innovative and constitute a fundamental step in both the evolution of the understanding of the Portuguese revolution and the introduction of social movements studies in Portugal. The work of Pedro Ramos Pinto is partially based on different premises. His doctoral thesis in history, published by Manchester University Press (Ramos Pinto 2013), is strongly rooted in social movements theory, as are related articles (Ramos Pinto 2008 and 2009); nevertheless, even though he considers the relevance of opening opportunities structures, he places the urban movement into a historical context and links its emergence to the social and political transformations that preceded it, namely the evolution of national and local policy, economic and social conditions and the emergence of urban communities with the required capacity for mobilization.

Accornero (2010, 2013b and 2016) makes a direct attempt to renew the interpretation of the origins and role of social movements during the Portuguese regime change through a dialogue with previous studies by Muñoz and Cerezales. Importance is given to pre-existing social conditions which might have given rise to political opportunities and the reciprocal influence of institutional politics and social movements as opposed to the unilateral effects of the former on the latter.

The Mild-Mannered Hypothesis

The POS theory been strongly called into question and reformulated in the last decades.[5] Nevertheless, it was generally applied, in his original formulation, in several studies on Portuguese transition. This contributed to consolidate the common vision of Portuguese civil society as one that was sleeping until awakened during the revolution thanks to the miracle of the opening of the political opportunity structure. This leads us to the second point of our analysis of the Portuguese social movements studies: the assumption of the mild-mannered Portuguese that is symmetrical and complementary to that of a 'revolution without a past'.

Paradoxically, the country in which there was perhaps the greatest social mobilization in post-war Europe is also one that most scholars consider to have a 'mild-mannered' tradition when called on to mobilise and make political and social demands. According to Ramos Pinto, many believe Portugal is living up to its reputation of being a country with a 'weak civil society' (Ramos Pinto 2012). As Ramos Pinto reminds us, it was the dictator Salazar (1928–68) who labelled the Portuguese a 'mild-mannered' people 'averse to political radicalization, violence and political mobilization.' This was a key aspect of the dictatorship's propaganda narrative, and this 'sound-byte' was part of its demobilization strategy.' Ramos Pinto adds that 'the infantilization of an entire population has always been the foundation of top-down "civilizing" projects.' (Ramos Pinto 2012: 3).

A number of studies on the political attitudes of Portuguese citizens since the democratic transition have underlined that Portugal is characterised by civil society's low level of involvement in political life (Villaverde Cabral 1997 and 2000; Freire 2000; Freire and Magalhães 2002; Freire 2003; Magalhães 2005; Pequito Teixeira and Almeida Pereira 2012).

In a 2005 study, Pedro Magalhães stresses the distance of Portuguese citizens from political institutions and underlines that 'the most prevalent and consequential attitudinal-behavioural syndrome in Portuguese politics remains one where strong political disaffection is associated to low levels of all kinds of political participation, including voting in elections, resorting to conventional forms of political action or engaging in unconventional civic activism' (Magalhães 2005: 988). However, not all authors agree with the image of Portugal as a country characterised by a low level of civic engagement. Robert Fishman, for example, states that democratization by revolution 'enables those representative systems that have such origins to approximate the goal of full political equality among citizens more than otherwise comparable polities' (Fishman 2012: 233). This author argues with respect to Portugal that 'institutional power holders in this post-revolutionary democracy think of demonstrations as a fundamental and normal component of the political system' (Fishman 2012: 238).

Alternatively, the Fernandes analysis of the Portuguese engagement in civic associations stresses that 'because of the legacies of prolonged authoritarian rule during most of the twentieth century, both Portugal and Spain show the weakest civil societies and organizations of representation of lower and middle groups in all the Western European democracies' (Fernandes 2012: 1), but 'Portugal, although having both a less developed economy and historically a weaker democratic tradition than Spain's, was a democracy that between the early 1970s and the mid-1990s offered more opportunities for the organised civic expression of popular interest' (Fernandes 2012: 1), and this would be a consequence of 'the mode of transition from authoritarian rule' (Fernandes 2012: 1).

While all these analyses deal with the issue of unconventional forms of participation and, with the exception of Fishman, consider that Portuguese people have as little interest in participating in strikes, demonstrations, petitions, etc., as in voting, no studies are specifically dedicated to weighing up the role of these forms of unconventional participation in Portugal.[6] A preliminary analysis (Accornero and Ramos Pinto 2014) only demonstrated that between 1980 and 1995, people's engagement in protest activities was much lower in Portugal than in Greece. Nevertheless, a better understanding of Portuguese mobilization in comparison with those of other European countries would require more systematic study of this aspect.

It is because specific research on social movements in Portugal during the democratic period is extremely rare that I have quoted all these studies even though they are not directly contextualised in social movements sociology. A project funded by the Calouste Gulbenkian and the McArthur Foundation on 'Reinventing Social Emancipation' was hosted by the Centro de Estudos Sociais (CES—Centre for Social Studies) of Coimbra and directed by sociologist Boaventura de Sousa Santos between 1999 and 2001, in order 'to identify and study in detail experiences taking shape through resistance to hegemonic, neoliberal globalization and to its consequences in different areas of social life' (De Sousa Santos and Nunes 2004: 2).

Some results of this investigation reflecting the project's engaged perspective have been published in a special issue of the journal *South European Society and Politics* (vol. 9, no. 2 [2004]). The introduction of this special issue states that 'studies of the recent historical experience of Portugal have brought to the fore features such as: the absence of a strong, organised civil society, of social movements and citizen organizations and associations' (De Sousa Santos and Nunes 2004: 11). Indeed, it seems that even in this case the 'mild-mannered' assumption is not critically reproduced. Most studies support this assumption by quoting other studies, which in turn often also quote other studies. It seems impossible to find the original empirical study demonstrating the 'mild-mannered hypothesis'.

Actually, research on specific movements is quite rare. Moreover, the different movements under analysis generally seem to be shooting stars, appearing only to quickly disappear, apparently unrelated or lacking continuity in their specific history. This is because these movements effectively seem unconnected and not contextualised in a history of contention. It is the case, for example, of the *Geração Rasca* (the desperate generation) movement (Seixas 2005)—a student movement that developed in 1994–95; or of the 'alterglobalization' in Portugal—considered by the (very few) authors who analysed it as a precarious network of civic organizations that 'still has not reached the status of a social movement' (Pires Lima and Nunes 2008); or the pro-abortion movements (Monteiro 2012). But while this image of sporadic movements is partially grounded in factual evidence, by looking at militants' trajectories—an approach almost unknown in Portugal—we could detect unexpected links among these movements and perhaps go beyond this syncopated vision.

Although based on different premises, more recent research on current anti-austerity movements also underlines that, unlike Spain, Greece and Turkey or, more recently, Brazil, Portugal has difficulty in transforming sporadic and sometimes huge demonstrations, for example the event of 2 March 2013 with around eight hundred thousand demonstrators in Lisbon alone, into sustained mobilization (Ramos Pinto 2012; Baumgarten 2013). Meanwhile, other studies have demonstrated that citizen mobilization actually intensified after 2010, both before and after the financial bailout of 2011 (Accornero and Ramos Pinto 2015; Estanque et al. 2013). In this period there was an increase in different kinds of protest activities in Portugal: from the most 'media-friendly' and in part ephemeral—like the big demonstrations called by new groups that emerged in the specific context of austerity—to more 'low-profile' but long-term and steady forms of protest—such as the dockworkers' months-long strikes.

'The Art of Not Being Governed' in Portugal

The studies quoted generally confirm that during the democratic period, Portuguese citizens seem to be less willing to engage in any kind of political or social activities, such as elections, civic associations, strikes, demonstrations, etc., than other European citizens. However, other important historical studies stress the role of civil society in the process constructing the modern Portuguese State. The pioneer study by Fátima Patriarca on *A Questão Social no Salazarismo*, for example, highlights the different ways in which Portuguese society resisted the Estado Novo's 'occupation'. The work of Dulce Freire also follows a similar line from the perspective of agrarian history and rural anthropology in underlining various forms of resistance to Estado Novo institutions at the rural level, for example through contraband (Freire 2012; Freire, Rovisco and Fonseca 2009).

An analogue position emerges from *The Making of State Power in Portugal 1890–1986*, a project financed by the Portuguese Foundation for Science and Technology (FCT)[7] and hosted by Universidade Nova (Lisbon), Instituto de Ciências Sociais (Lisbon), Universidad Complutense (Madrid) and Birkbeck College (London). The first congress organised under its wing, 'State Popular Protest and Social Movements in Contemporary Portugal', declared that its main aim was 're-opening the institutions to the upstream social and political tensions ... arguing that the historical body of the State does not depend only on its perpetuity, but also on a relation of constant transformation between institutions and society'.[8]

A congress entitled 'The Art of Not Being Governed: James C. Scott in Iberia' was held under this project with guest speakers such as Professor James Scott himself and Spanish and Portuguese scholars who adopt his approach, and aimed 'to discuss research focused mainly on Iberia and that closely deals with Scott's legacies'. I argue that, if scholars dealing with social movements in Portugal were to take this perspective into consideration, it would allow them to go beyond the two abovementioned perspectives: that of the Portuguese as a 'mild-mannered' people and that of 25 April as a 'revolution without a past'. Moreover, it would also allow researchers to recognise the actual role of the various and often hidden forms of resistance adopted by Portuguese society throughout its history. In this regard, mention should also be made of a series of articles by Diego Palacios Cerezales. They constitute a sort of history of the contentious performances in modern Portugal, from the institutionalization of the liberal state up to the end of the Estado Novo (mid-nineteenth century to 1974) (Palacios Cerezales 2007, 2009, 2010, 2011b, 2012).

Cerezales' interest in the social roots of political phenomena means that he also addresses the way in which political institutions have been trying to control and repress society's resistance (Palacios Cerezales 2003a, 2006, 2011c). He thus dedicated his doctoral thesis—published in the book *Portugal à Coronhada: Protesto Popular e Ordem Pública nos Séculos XIX e XX*

(2011d)—to the analysis of the strategies of public order and policing protests in Portugal from 1834 to 2000. Accornero (Accornero and Villaverde Cabral 2011; Accornero 2013a) adopts a more micro perspective but also faces the issue of political repression. She analysed the effects of authoritarian coercive measures, notably political prisons, on the trajectories of extreme-left militants—mainly Communist and Maoist—in the last decades of the Estado Novo and immediately after the transition. Yet again, this analysis stresses the way in which unpredictable forms of resistance can be developed even in situations of strong domination, for example in political prisons. This is the only study to date where the concepts of militant trajectories and career have been applied in the Portuguese case.

The Coimbra School and the 'Epistemology of the South'

This last section is dedicated to a brief introduction of what can be termed the 'Coimbra School', or the tradition of studies on social movements and citizens' participation begun by the sociologist Boaventura de Sousa Santos at Coimbra CES and further continued by other Portuguese and Brazilian researchers who trained there. The perspective is different to that of the 'classical' social movements sociology and represents in part a parallel tradition, strongly rooted in South America and mainly in Brazil.

Boaventura de Sousa Santos was one of the promoters and main ideologists of the Portalegre World Social Forum. This militant school of thought is closely associated to the alter-globalization perspective and sees social movements as a form of democracy from below, as the participatory budget or the deliberative democracy. These must be developed by global citizens—and mainly by the citizens of the 'South of the World'—in contrast to what is considered as the top-down process of globalization, imposed by the north of the world. Derived from the postmodern paradigm, the so-called 'epistemology of the south' is thus a theoretical construct by which De Sousa Santos and his followers aim to challenge what they consider the epistemology of the north, imposed by the richest countries. According to this view, colonialism would also have imposed 'an epistemological domination, an extremely unequal relation of knowledge-power' (De Sousa Santos and Menezes 2010: 19).

Trained in law, De Sousa Santos was an exponent of the critical legal studies. The deconstruction of the hidden aspects of domination and exclusion, which are intrinsic in the law as a product of the elites, can also be seen in De Sousa Santos' sociological work, and thus the epistemology of the South must be regarded from this perspective. The abovementioned project on 'Reinventing Social Emancipation' is in line with this commitment to challenge what is considered the mainstream and elitist dominant paradigm in social sciences. This is also the aim of the on-going project (2011–16) 'Strange Mirrors, Unsuspected Lessons: Leading Europe to a New Way of Sharing the World Experiences—ALICE', also directed by De Sousa Santos and awarded the biggest Advanced Grant ever allocated to a social science project by the European Research Council (ERC).[9] Although not directly focused on social movements, they have a strong presence in this project. In fact, this can be considered as a direct consequence of De Sousa Santos' engagement in the World Social Forum and the application of the claims and paradigms of the alter-globalization movement in social sciences. The project on 'Counter-Hegemonic Globalization and Participatory Democracy: Experiences at the North-South Meeting Point', financed by the Fudação para a Ciência e a Tecnologia (FCT—Portuguese Foundation for Science and Technology) and by the Brazilian Coordenação de Aperfeiçoamento de Pessoal de Nível Superior (CAPES—Federal Agency for the Support and Evaluation of Graduate Education) is directly linked to social movements dynamics.

Some of the main Portuguese studies on workers' movements, notably by the sociologist Elisio Estanque, have also come from the Coimbra School. A peculiarity of Estanque's analysis, which also has militant and normative features, is the attention given to globalization's hard consequences on labour relations, and the way that workers might face them: 'The intensification and expansion of precariousness, the fragmentation of productive processes, and the disregarding of rights and dignity associated to labour relations, are creating a new form of struggle which is based around work and the struggles for the recovery of its dignity will affirm a new state of politicization. This appears to be happening through new socio-occupational movements that are presently raging across societies on a global level' (Estanque and Costa 2012a: 268). In the most recent work by this author, these aspects are linked to the Portuguese situation following the 2011 bailout and the external monetary intervention (Estanque et al. 2013).

A Boundary or an Open Frontier?
The Potentialities of a Semi-Peripheral Country

As we have already seen, the Coimbra school of thought also covers divergent ground from that explored by parallel traditions developed in the United States and Europe on social movements. In fact, Portugal's geographic, historical and linguistic position could rightly make it a common ground for crossing different traditions of thought, like those of Brazil, Portuguese-speaking Africa and Asia, and Europe.

Instead, many studies are being conducted in Portuguese, both in Portugal and in Brazil, which are largely unknown by European scholars. It could also be argued that Portuguese-speaking researchers often disregard or do not confront other European researchers. This is clearly demonstrated by the fact that translations of American or European books on social movements into Portuguese are extremely rare. In the library catalogue of Campinas University, the largest university in Brazil, in the State of Sao Paulo, there are only two Portuguese translations of books of the first American generation of scholars on social movements: Charles Tilly, *As revoluções europeias,* and Sidney Tarrow, *Poder em movimento: movimentos sociais e confronto político.* And the book by Donatella Della Porta, *O movimento por uma nova globalização,* is the only translation of a work by the first generation of European scholars. This is not the case of authors such as Alberto Melucci or Alain Touraine, who have many translated works in Brazil and Portugal.[10] Moreover, almost all the aforesaid translations—except that of Tilly's book—are Brazilian publications and are not found in Portuguese bookstores or libraries. Thus, although many books on social movements are available in the original language in academic libraries in Portugal, Portuguese scholars have been seriously hindered by this lack of access to them in bookstores, particularly prior to the diffusion of platforms such as Amazon or e-books. This has limited the horizons of social movements research in Portugal and has hampered the debate. It has led to certain concepts of social movements theory being frozen, some of which have already been called into question outside the country. Therefore, although 'classics' of the social movements theory are assimilated, new findings do not circulate, such as those on the role of emotions, networks or militants' trajectories.

This is offset to some extent by the strength of other approaches, for example the 'Scott tradition'—a definition which also encompasses a series of studies not directly influenced by Scott's works—or the 'Coimbra School'. Nevertheless, I believe Portuguese research on social movements would benefit greatly from communication among the different paradigms. Finally, I consider that Portugal's specific geographic, historical and linguistic circumstances mean that it has the potential to be a key centre for cross-fertilization among the different approaches and traditions. This reflection is even more pertinent if we consider the diffusion of the Portuguese language which is spoken on four continents[11] by about 240 million people and is the sixth most spoken language in the world. This cross-fertilization process would give rise to new perspectives of analysis, and attention would be drawn to contexts that are often almost overlooked by social movements scholars, for example in African countries such as Angola and Mozambique where there has been a strong wave of protests in recent years.

Guya Accornero is an advanced researcher in political science at the Instituto Universitário de Lisboa (ISCTE-IUL), Centro de Investigação e Estudos de Sociologia (CIES-IUL), carrying on a project funded by the Fundação para a Ciência e a Tecnologia (FCT). She obtained her PhD from the Institute of Social Science of Lisbon University in 2010 following a period as a visiting student at the Centre for Advanced Studies in Social Sciences of the Juan March Foundation, Madrid. In 2011, she was invited researcher at the Lausanne University Research Centre on Political Action. She has published articles in English, French, Italian and Portuguese in the journals *West European Politics, Democratization, Cultures and Conflits, Análise Social, Storia e Problemi Contemporanei,* and she edited the special issue *Il Portogallo e la transizione alla democrazia* for the journal *Storia e Problemi Contemporanei.* She is currently publishing a monograph entitled *The Revolution before the Revolution: Late Authoritarianism and Student Protest in Portugal* for Berghahn Books.

Notes

1. The MFA was an organization of lower-ranked left-leaning officers in the Portuguese Armed Forces. It was created in 1973 mainly for professional reasons, but quickly it assumed also a clear political position against the dictatorship, and developed a plan to overthrow it and to establish a democratic regime in the country.
2. Among others: Villaverde Cabral 1974 and 1976.
3. Boaventura de Sousa Santos defines it as 'the broadest, deepest people's social movement in post-war European history' (Sousa Santos 1990: 27); Fernando Rosas as the 'last left-wing revolution in twentieth-century Europe' (Rosas 2004: 15) and Pedro Ramos Pinto as 'some of the widest popular mobilizations of post-war Europe' (Ramos Pinto 2008: iii).
4. For a critical analysis on this, see Palacios Cerezales (2003b: 106–7) and Varela (2006: 1231–40).
5. As Olivier Fillieule suggests, political opportunities are not structurally insensitive stocks that exist prior to action; rather, 'they are continuously updated through the relationship with the movements.' It is therefore important to look 'not only at the way in which the state players define the milieu in which individuals act but also the way protest groups help to modify the conditions in which individuals act' (Fillieule 2005: 214). On his hand, Doug McAdam underlines that 'changes in a system of institutionalized politics merely afford a potential challenger the opportunity for collective action. It is the organizational vehicles available to the group at the time the opportunity presents itself that condition its ability to exploit the new opening. In the absence of such vehicles, the group is apt to lack the capacity to act when afforded the opportunity to do so'. (McAdam : IX).
6. This does not mean that studies on contentious forms of politics do not exist; rather, it signifies that the assumption of Portugal as a country characterized by low levels of

social mobilization still does not seem empirically verified, above all in comparative terms.

7. http://www.fct.mctes.pt/projectos/pub/2006/Painel_Result/vglobal_projecto.asp?id Projecto=104166&idElemConcurso=2789 .

8. http://ihc.fcsh.unl.pt/pt/encontros-cientificos/congressos-e-coloquios/item/ 34640-col%C3%B3quio-internacional-%E2%80%9Cestado-protesto-popular-e-movimentos-sociais-no-portugal-contempor%C3%A2neo%E2%80%9D.

9. http://erc.europa.eu/succes-stories/new-vision-europe; http://alice.ces.uc.pt/en/ind ex.php/about/?lang=en. Actually, with the exception of this project, the main source of funds for projects directly or indirectly related to research on social movements in Portugal is the Portuguese Foundation for Science and Technology (FCT). As is the case in other similar institutions of other countries, the FCT, created in 1997 after the establishment of the department for science and technology, has represented an inestimable resource for the development of scientific research in Portugal, in the most diverse areas. Thanks to European Union structural funds, the FCT has consistently supported Portuguese academic investigation in different ways, with master's, doctoral and post-doctoral fellowships; funds for the organization of scientific meetings, academic publications and research projects. These funds for research, attributed after selection by an international committee, have enabled Portuguese researchers to consolidate international teams and carry on innovative investigation in various areas. The aforesaid project on *The Making of State Power in Portugal 1890-1986,* funded with €70,000 by the FCT, is such an example. Another case is the project *Participatory Budgeting as an Innovative Tool for Reinventing Local Institutions in Portugal and Cape Verde? A Critical Analysis of Performance and Transfers,* which received FCT funding of €163,449.

10. Both these authors, together with classic theorists like Antonio Gramsci, continue to be particularly influential in Portuguese and Brazilian traditions on social movements.

11. The Portuguese-speaking countries are Portugal, Brazil, Mozambique, Angola, Cape Verde, Guinea-Bissau, and São Tomé and Príncipe. Portuguese has co-official status in Macau in East Asia and East Timor in Southeast Asia.

References

Accornero, G. 2010. 'La rivoluzione prima della rivoluzione'. *Storia e Problemi Contemporanei* 54: 35–55.

———. 2012. 'Student Dissent and Contentious Politics in the Twilight of the Portuguese Dictatorship: Analysis of a Protest Cycle'. *Democratization* 20, no. 6: 1036–55.

———. 2013a. 'La répression politique sous l'Estado Novo au Portugal et ses effets sur l'opposition estudiantine: des années 1960 à la fin du régime'. *Cultures and Conflits* 89: 93–112.

———. 2013b. 'A mobilização estudantil no processo de radicalização política durante o Marcelismo'. *Análise Social* 48, no. 208: 572–91.

Accornero, G. 2016. *The Revolution before the Revolution: Student Protest and Political Process at the End of the Portuguese Dictatorship*. Oxford and New York: Berghahn Books.

Accornero, G., and M. Villaverde Cabral. 2011. 'Saldanha Sanches militante'. In *Estudos em Memória do Prof. Doutor J.L. Saldanha Sanches,* ed. P. Otero, F. Araújo and J. Gama, eds., 17–46. Coimbra: Coimbra Editora.

Accornero, G., and P. Ramos Pinto. 2015. '"Mild Mannered"? Protest and Mobilisation in Portugal under Austerity'. *West European Politics* 38, no. 3: 491–515.

Baumgarten, B. 2013. 'Geração à Rasca and Beyond: Mobilisations in Portugal after 12 March 2011'. *Current Sociology* 61, no. 4: 457–73.

Braga da Cruz, M. 1995. *Instituições políticas e processos sociais.* Venda Nova: Bertrand.

Dawn Raby, L. 1990. *Resistência antifascista in Portugal.* Lisbon: Salamandra.

De Sousa Santos, B. 1990. *O Estado e a sociedade em Portugal (1974–1988).* Porto: Afrontamento.

De Sousa Santos, B., and J. A. Nunes. 2004. 'Introduction: Democracy, Participation and Grassroots Movements in Contemporary Portugal'. *South European Society and Politics* 9, no. 2: 1–15.

De Sousa Santos, B., and M. P. Menezes. 2010. *Epistemologias do Sul.* São Paulo: Cortez (in English: De Sousa Santos, B. 2014. *Epistemologies of the South: Justice Against Epistemicide.* Boulder: Paradigm).

Della Porta, Donatella. 2007. *O movimento por uma nova globalização.* São Paulo: Edições Loyola.

Dobry, M. 1986. *Sociologie des crises politiques.* Paris: Presses de la FNSP.

Durán Muñoz, R. 1997a. 'Oportunidad para la transgresión: Portugal, 1974–1975'. *Ler História* 32: 83–116.

Durán Muñoz, R. 1997b. 'As crises económicas e as transições para a democracia: Espanha e Portugal numa perspectiva comparada'. *Análise Social* 32, no. 141: 369–401.

———. 2000. *Contención y transgresión: Las movilizaciones sociales y el Estado en las transiciones española y portuguesa.* Madrid: Centro de Estudios Políticos y Constitucionales.

Estanque, E., and H. A. Costa. 2012a. 'Labour Relations and Social Movements in the 21st Century'. In *Sociological Landscape: Theories, Realities and Trends,* ed. D. Erasga, retrieved 1 November 2013 from http://www.intechopen.com/books/sociological-landscape-theories-realities-and-trends/labour-relations-and-social-movements.

Estanque, E., H. A. Costa and J. Soeiro. 2013. 'The New Global Cycle of Protest and the Portuguese Case'. *Journal of Social Science Education* 12, no. 1: 31–40.

Fernandes, T. 2012. 'Civil Society after Dictatorship: A Comparison of Portugal and Spain, 1970s–1990s'. *Kellogg Institute Working Paper,* 384.

Fillieule, O. 2005. 'Requiem pour un concept: Vie et mort de la notion de structure des opportunités politiques'. In *La Turquie conteste. Mobilisations sociales et régime sécuritaire,* ed. Gilles Dorronsoro, 201-18. Paris: CNRS.

Fishman, R. 2012. 'Democratic Practice after the Revolution: The Case of Portugal and Beyond'. *Politics and Society* 39, no. 2: 233–67.

Freire, A. 2000. 'Participação e abstenção nas eleições legislativas portuguesas, 1975–1995'. *Analise Social* 35, nos. 154–55: 115–45.

———. 2003. 'Pós materialismo e comportamentos políticos: o caso português em perspectiva comparada'. In *Valores Sociais: Mudanças e Contrastes em Portugal e na Europa,* ed. J. Vala, M. Villaverde Cabral and Alice Ramos, 295–361. Lisbon: Imprensa de Ciências Sociais.

Freire, A., and P. Magalhães. 2002. *A Abstenção Eleitoral em Portugal.* Lisbon: Imprensa de Ciências Sociais.

Freire, D. 2012. 'Terra e liberdade: experiências de reforma agrária em Portugal no século XX'. In *Greves e conflitos sociais em Portugal no século XX,* ed. R. Varela, R. Noronha and J. Dias Pereira, 155–65. Lisbon: Colibri.

Freire, D., E. Rovisco and I. Fonseca, eds. 2009. *Contrabando na Fronteira Luso-Espanhola: Práticas, Memórias e Patrimónios.* Lisbon: Edições Nelson de Matos.

Magalhães, P. 2005. 'Disaffected Democrats: Political Attitudes and Political Action in Portugal'. *West European Politics* 28, no. 5: 973–91.

McAdam, D. 1999. *Political Process and the Development of Black Insurgency, 1930–1970.* Chicago: University of Chicago Press.

Monteiro, R. 2012. 'A descriminalização do aborto em Portugal: Estado, movimentos de mulheres e partidos políticos'. *Análise Social* 47, no. 204: 586–605.

Palacios Cerezales, D. 2003a. 'Um caso de violência política: o Verão quente de 1975'. *Análise Social,* 38, no. 165: 1127–57.

———. 2003b. *O poder caiu na rua: Crise de Estado e Acções colectivas na Revolução Portuguesa, 1975–1975.* Lisbon: Imprensa de Ciências Sociais.

———. 2006. 'Técnica, Política e o dilema da Ordem Pública No Portugal Contemporâneo (1851–1974)'. In *Lei e Ordem: Justiça Penal, Criminalidade E Polícia. Séculos XIX–XX,* ed. P. Tavares de Almeida and T. Pires Marques, 39–71. Lisbon: Livros Horizonte.

———. 2007. 'O princípio de autoridade e os motins antifiscais de 1862'. *Análise Social* 42(182): 35–53.

———. 2009. 'Ritual funerario y política en el Portugal contemporáneo'. In *Políticas de la muerte,* ed. J. Casquete and R. Cruz, 39–71. Madrid: La Catarata.

———. 2010. 'Extraños cuerpos políticos, el nacimiento del movimiento social en Portugal'. *Revista de Estudios Políticos* 147: 11–42.

———. 2011b. 'Embodying Public Opinion: From Petitions to Mass Meetings in Nineteenth-Century Portugal'. *E-Journal of Portuguese History* 9, no. 1: 1–19.

———. 2011c. 'Sin efusión de sangre: protesta, policía y costes de la represión'. In *A propósito de Tilly: conflicto, poder y acción colectiva,* ed. M. J. Funes, 247–64. Madrid: Centro de Investigaciones Sociológicas.

———. 2011d. *Portugal à coronhada: Protesto popular e ordem pública nos séculos XIX e XX.* Lisbon: Tinta da China.

———. 2012. 'Assinem assinem, que a alma não tem sexo! Petição colectiva e cidadania feminina no Portugal constitucional (1820–1910)'. *Analise Social* 47, no. 205: 740–65.

Palacios Cerezales, D., et al. 2013. 'Interview with James C. Scott: Egalitarianism, the Teachings of Fieldwork and Anarchist Calisthenics'. *Análise Social* 48, no. 207: 447–63.

Patriarca, M. F. 1995. *A questão social no salazarismo.* Lisbon: Instituto Nacional Casa da Moeda.

Pequito Teixeira, C., and de P. Pereira de Almeida. 2012. 'Is There Significant Erosion of Political System Support in Portugal? Longitudinal and Comparative Analysis (2000–10)'. *Portuguese Journal of Social Science* 11, no. 2: 135–60.

Pires Lima, M., and C. Nunes. 2008. 'Portogallo: il caso della creazione del Forum Sociale portoghese'. In *Europa alterglobal: Componenti e culture del 'movimento dei movimenti' in Europa,* ed. A. Farro and P. Rebughini, 176-186. Milan: Franco Angeli.

Ramos Pinto, P. 2008. 'Urban Social Movements and the Transition to Democracy in Portugal, 1974–1976'. *The Historical Journal* 51, no. 4: 1025–46.

———. 2009. 'Housing and Citizenship: Building Social Rights in Twentieth-Century Portugal'. *Contemporary European History* 18, no. 2: 199–215.

———. 2012. 'Protest and Civil Society in Austerity Portugal'. *Congress Political Consequences of the Economic Crisis: Voting and Protest in Europe since 2008, Georgetown, 17 April.* Georgetown: Georgetown University.

———. 2013. *Lisbon Rising: Urban Social Movements in the Portuguese Revolution, 1974–75.* Manchester: Manchester University Press.

Reis, A. 1991. 'A abertura falhada de Caetano: o impasse e a agonia do regime'. In A. Reis, ed., *Portugal Contemporâneo (1926–1974).* Mem Martins: Alfa.

Rosas, F. 1998. *O Estado Novo.* Lisbon: Estampa.

———. 2004. *Pensamento e acção política: Portugal século XX (1890–1976).* Lisbon: Noticias.

Schmitter, P. 1999. *Portugal: do autoritarismo à democracia.* Lisbon: Imprensa de Ciências Sociais.

Seixas, A. M. 2005. 'Aprender a democracia: Jovens e protesto no ensino secundário em Portugal'. *Revista Crítica de Ciências Sociais* 72: 187–209.

Tarrow, S. 2009. *O Poder em Movimento: Movimentos sociais e confronto político.* Petrópolis: Vozes.

Tilly, C. 1996. *As revoluções europeias 1492–1992.* Lisbon: Editorial Presença.

Varela, R. 2006. 'O 25 de Abril, a Espanha e a história'. *Análise Social* 42, no. 179: 1231–40.

Villaverde Cabral, M. 1974. *Materiais para a História da Questão Agrária em Portugal, séculos XIX e XX.* Porto: Inova.

———. 1976. *O Desenvolvimento do Capitalismo em Portugal no Século XIX.* Lisboa: A regra do jogo.

———. 1977. *O Operariado Português nas Vésperas da República, 1909–1910.* Lisboa: Presença.

———. 1997. *Cidadania política e equidade social em Portugal.* Oeiras: Celta.

———. 2000. 'O exercício da cidadania política em Portugal'. In *Trabalho e cidadania,* ed. M. Villaverde Cabral, J. Vala and J. Freire, 123-162. Lisbon: Imprensa de Ciências Sociais.

Wiarda, H. J., ed. 2006. *Development on the Periphery: Democratic Transitions in Southern and Eastern Europe.* Lanham: Rowman and Littlefield.

Chapter 21

From the Centre to the Periphery and Back to the Centre

Social Movements Affecting Social Movement Theory in the Case of Greece

Kostis Kornetis and Hara Kouki

Until recently Greece held a marginal position in social movement literature, both abroad and at home. It wasn't until the unprecedented urban riots of 2008 that the country came to the forefront, not only in terms of social activism—as it was positioned to become the prototype for contentious politics—but also for generating a paradigmatic shift in terms of theory. One of the primary objectives of this chapter is to identify the origins and features of this fundamental rift. Was this shift brought about by the so-called 'new December' events and the protests that followed the eruption of the economic crisis? Or was it facilitated by theoretical research on movements, and to what extent was this triggered by the greater contact of the Greek public with the existing theory?

The present chapter traces the state of the art of social movements in Greece in the post-1974 period, pointing in two directions. On the one hand it attempts to tackle the thorny issue of what social movement discipline can tell us about contemporary Greek society, in terms of its socio-political development and positioning within the global configuration of contentious politics over the past forty years. On the other, it aims to address the issue of what the Greek example can tell us about the research area of social movements as a whole. By adopting this holistic approach, we do not seek to present a comprehensive account of recent social movements in Greece, but rather to delineate the parallel progression of theory and action, and the extent to which each was fed and inseminated by the other over the years.

From the Centrality of the Democratic Transition to the Periphery of Social Movements

During the tumultuous decade of the 1960s, social movement action was on its rise and a parallel attempt was underway to theorise the 1968 events and their aftermath. Collective action, which was perceived up to this date as deviant and irrational, started to be considered as an object of study worthy of scientific analysis. Some Greek scholars working mainly on political philosophy in France, such as Cornelius Castoriadis or Kostas Axelos, had considerable influence both on the evolution of social movements and on the ways these were perceived in theory. Still, the impact of these thinkers on Greek theory was minimal until the 1980s, and Greece did not appear in protest-related research. However, the years of the Colonels' dictatorship (1967–74), and in particular the student uprising of November 1973 and the explosion in grassroots political activity in the first years of the democratic transition, led to considerable interest in the social dynamics and movements arising from below in the country (see Poulantzas 1976). At the same time, social movements had been transformed by the late 1970s and early 1980s into a separate field of research that would develop its own theoretical tools, schools of thought and sub-fields of study. During those years, the appearance—limited and slow, but persistent—of so-called new social movements in Greece showed the relative adherence of domestic contentious politics to the international paradigm of 'identity movements', including feminism and environmentalism. Nonetheless, until the 1990s studies on collective action within the country only rarely employed the theoretical tools and analysis of the sociology of social movements used in other countries, such as Italy and France, with the Greek case being relatively absent from social movement literature produced abroad. A practical reason for this was that the dialogue between Greek scholars and international bibliography and research was not regular, nor were the libraries of the country's universities endowed with peer-reviewed journals.

But the most important reason for this absence was that social change in the country has been read from the early 1980s onwards as a response to the wider Southern European environment in terms of its transition to democracy that catalogued the country under the peripheral or semi-peripheral paradigm (Diamandouros et al. 1995). Modernization in Spain, Portugal or Greece, understood in terms of economic and social reforms, was always lagging behind in relation to the Western metropolis. Based on this schema of belated industrialization and modernization, studies were mostly concerned with top-down party politics, the influence of 'foreign' agents on domestic politics and the country's incorporation within an international system of geopolitical power as influenced by dependency theories (Lyritzis 1991). Even if transition to democracy brought about significant changes, reforms were held back due to 'national' characteristics, such as state interventionism, corruption, a populist political system, a feeble civil society and above all the phenomenon of clientelism (see studies by Mavrogordatos 1993; Mouzelis 1986; Tsoukalas 1981; Dertilis 1977). This 'underdog' culture resisted the construction of a modern liberal state (Diamandouros 1994) and became the main interpretative framework to understand national political culture and explain the peripheral role of the country within the European Union (Triandafyllidou et al. 2013). Research on social change in the post-1974 period was thus primarily concerned with the causes of absence and divergence, searching not for what had happened but rather what ought to have happened (Liakos 2010).

This particularity had a direct impact on the social movements that emerged, or did not emerge for that matter (Mouzelis 1986). According to the aforesaid interpretative framework, it was due to the strong interference of partyism and state paternalism in the representation of social interests that social demands could not take shape as in other Western European countries or lead to the development of civil society structures. Due to this same narrative, Greek citizens were in many cases seen as slow in developing a Western type of citizenship ethos as a result of their traditionalist, corrupt and especially unruly tendencies. Domestic conflicts, disobedience or political violence have been most often attributed to the 'underdog' character of some segments of Greek society and to an 'endemic culture of violence', a result of the country's tardy modernization (Psimitis 2011). This strongly contentious political culture has been perceived as obstructing the imposition of meritocratic and efficient reforms in an 'underdeveloped' country (Xenakis 2010). Consequently, the role of collective mobilization in the search for social change has been largely downplayed and all the groups and individuals that engaged in social protest during the post-1974 period have remained invisible (Serdedakis 2015).

Hence, even if departing from different and in many cases conflictual theoretical schools and interpretations, scholars working on Greece both outside and within the country tended to downplay the role of collective mobilization in their investigation of social change. However, at the same time, important empirical work was done in terms of analysing, theorizing and historicizing different aspects of grassroots social action, mainly by historians. Some gave a scholarly form to the Marxist reading of Greek history made by earlier scholars (Kordatos 1932) combining Braudel with class analysis (Svoronos 1972; Asdrachas 1988). Within this tradition, the labour movement was a field that attracted much attention, both as a synchronic event and as a historical appearance (Moskof 1988; Koukoules 1983). Feminism continued to be seen in historical perspective and not through a framework of theory or gender studies (Avdela and Psarra 1989; Varikas 1995; Papageorgiou 1992). The student movement was similarly viewed either in terms of specific moments in time (Liakos 1988; Dafermos 2003) or as a linear progression by the people who had participated in it (Lazos 1987; Giannaris 1983). By privileging social movements as historical entities, these studies argued not only for the centrality of the former but at times even for their prophetic nature in relation to European experience (Vernardakis and Mavris 1991). While the importance of this body of work is undeniably crucial, the 'underdeveloped' and structurally 'dependent' condition of Greece remained dominant in the way literature perceived social change until the 1990s.

The Beginnings: What Can Social Movement Theory Tell Us about Greek Society?

This understanding of national political culture neither permitted social movements to emerge in the same frequency and quality as elsewhere, nor did it provide the imaginary or space necessary for them to be conceptualised or represented as such in the post-1974 years. However, it seems that reality challenged such theoretical assumptions: this longest period of democratic stability in the country's history has actually been shaped by a plurality of mass political movements and numbers of groups and individuals participating in contentious action. Workers' struggles, farmers' movements and student mobilizations took the form of subversive texts, street protests, strikes and massive demonstrations, school occupations or road blockades. This was especially the case after 1989, when global geopolitical changes were coupled with internal reconfigurations of party politics, the introduction of the neoliberal restructuring of national economy and a conservative unfolding of national identity. Throughout the transitional decade of the 1990s, mounting social discontent and protest culture challenged dominant discourses and new political subjectivities started to emerge. All this would contribute to the gradual unmaking of the so-called 'national consensus' of the post-1974 period.

It was precisely during those years that a handful of researchers embarked on the systematic study and teaching of social movements in an attempt to shape the field, both in theoretical terms and, most importantly, with a Greek twist. The new group was heterogeneous in its formation and influences. Serafeim Seferiades and Maria Kousis had a solid US background,

Nikos Serdedakis and Michalis Psimitis an Italian one, while Stelios Alexandropoulos produced his doctoral dissertation in Greece. But what all these scholars had in common was a concern for the way that social and political theory perceived and represented social change. Focusing on the state and the institutions of governance, research, both abroad and within the country, had presented a static and superficial picture of social dynamics, disregarding macro-historical understandings, while taking for granted the existing social structure (Seferiadis 2010). Through their individual research, workshops, publications and academic courses, these scholars sought instead to reincorporate the role of discontent and social movements into the study of the country's past, present and future.

A very eloquent example of this shift in academic interest was the special issue entitled 'Social Movements and Social Sciences' that appeared in a political science journal in 1996, co-written by social movement researchers from different backgrounds—the first of its kind in Greece. This volume included an activist trying to theorise her experience as a historian (Repousi), as well as a historian who was more connected to the macro perspective as an activist (Avdela) and social movement theorists who were attempting to distil theory to the Greek paradigm. On this occasion, all were quite critical towards their own conclusions (Psimitis). This introduction set the Greek case firmly within the wider context of social movement history and theory. In this opening text, social movements in both practice and their analysis were seen as challenging an exclusionary view of politics—in many cases adopted also by the left—by introducing into social and political conflicts new agents of change, such as women for instance. This new field of study would reveal alternative participatory patterns and democratic citizenship (Pantelidou). The issue included a bibliographical guide on social movements in general, and more specifically on feminism and ecology (Tsakiris).

The first scholar to introduce social movements as a separate field of research in Greek academia was Stelios Alexandropoulos, who in the mid-1990s started teaching related courses and seminars at the University of Crete. His body of research combines empirical work with theoretical thinking, as was already evident in his doctoral dissertation ('Collective Behaviour and Interest Representation in Greece before and after the Transition to Democracy', Panteion University, 1990) that explores new interpretative frameworks for the understanding of the Greek social and political reality after 1974. Apart from case studies, the scholar's seminal work was 'Theories of Collective Action and Social Movements' (vol. A, 2001), an intellectual history of the concept of social movements as well as a reflection on the way sociological thinking has evolved over time. For Alexandropoulos, the study of social movements was a way to pose questions on social change and human agency and combine theory with action. In this manner, the scholar critically set the tone for the path along which this field would be developed in the country.

After Alexandropoulos' death, the study of social movements continued to be central at the University of Crete mainly through the teaching and research of Nikos Serdedakis and Maria Kousis. Seminars, undergraduate and postgraduate courses and doctoral studies have been complemented by the 'Annual Graduate Meeting' on issues of sociological methodology, in which a separate strand of collective mobilization studies gathers interdisciplinary researchers from all over the country. While studying environmentalism, civil society or social agency in Greece (2000), Serdedakis adopts a historical approach to collective action (2007). In reflecting on issues of theory and methodology (1998), he is always concerned with building conceptual frameworks to bridge abstract theory with social transformations on the ground. Kousis has also focused on the environmental movement in Greece and has published extensively in academic journals both at home and abroad (1999, 2007, 2014) and co-authored a variety of books with academics from other countries (2005). By examining local contentious politics from a transnational perspective, she managed to place the Greek case firmly within comparative studies.

The same seems to apply to another important scholar in the field, Serapheim Seferiadis. In line with his doctoral dissertation 'Working-Class Movements (1780s–1930s): A European Macro-Historical Analytical Framework and a Greek Case Study' (Columbia University, 1998), Seferiadis has maintained a macro-historical vision in his studies on European and Greek labour history, syndicalism or anti-authoritarian mobilization (2005, 2008). He has published extensively in academic journals on issues involving theory and history of social movements (2007) and has co-edited volumes with international scholars, thus serving thus as a link with the global scholarly community. Seferiadis, along with other academics, has transformed Panteion University (Athens) into a major platform for the development of the social movement field in the country.[1] Apart from offering undergraduate and postgraduate courses and seminars in the field since the mid-1990s, Panteion also hosts the Contentious Politics Circle,[2] an interdisciplinary network of scholars researching collective action and organizing seminars and conferences. This activity has contributed to the assembly of a group of researchers from various disciplines, universities and research centres, who have transformed social movements into a critical field of study.[3] The conference 'Collective Mobilisations and Social Movements in the 21st Century', organised in 2006 in Athens, further testified to this by bringing together a number of important international researchers.

Social movement courses are also offered at the University of the Aegean (Botetzagias 2003). Apart from teaching, Michalis Psimitis in his seminal 'Introduction to Contemporary Social Movements' (2006) not only presents an encompassing synthesis and critique of existing theories but also reflects on the role social movements can acquire in a postmodern society against the realities of neoliberalism. Research is also being conducted at the University of Thessaloniki, while numerous other important scholars are studying social movements in other education establishments and research institutions (Simiti 2003, Afouksenidis 2006, Botetzagias and Boudourides 2007, Kavoulakos 2009). However, it is noteworthy that the link with the international academic community over the last few years has also been achieved via a growing number of young Greek scholars studying abroad who have produced work on collective action from a wide interdisciplinary approach (Kallianos 2012, Kornetis 2013, Vradis 2012). Historians, political scientists, geographers, economists and anthropologists have successfully complemented the research launched within the country and incorporated the case of Greece in mainstream intellectual currents. Ten years after the appearance of the first special issue on the matter, a new one entitled 'Contentious Politics, Social Movements' (2006) was published, reflecting the evolution and establishment of an articulate and important social movement field of study in the country.

As evident from above, what is distinctive about the group of scholars who launched social movement research in Greece is the fact that, apart from their specialised research interests, they have all engaged in a critique of social and political theory on social change. Through the formation of a new field of study, their concern and challenge has been to relate theory to the actual practice of collective action in order to grasp what 'in motion' in contemporary society. And something was moving indeed, as the work on protest culture spreading across the country—especially after the 1990s—was being done to a great extent outside academia. An avalanche of publications, documentaries and events was produced by groups and individuals who, active in mass movements across the country, sought to document their actual experience using theoretical tools. Notwithstanding the attempts referred to above, social movement studies still remained throughout those years a rather limited field within academia and in relation to the dominant perceptions of the way Greek society sought (or did not seek) for change.

2008 and After: How Greece Informs Theory

The December 2008 events in Greece, namely a series of nation-wide riots in the aftermath of the cold-blooded killing of fifteen-year-old student Alexandros Grigoropoulos in the centre of Athens by an armed policeman, could be considered a game changer in contentious politics, but also a veritable paradigmatic shift in terms of its theoretical analysis. These were three weeks of civil disobedience, violent demonstrations and destruction of public and private property, but also peaceful sit-ins outside Parliament. Impromptu demonstrations and extensive riots took place, several university and school buildings were occupied, protesters clashed daily with the police, and a general rage against state arbitrariness and police impunity was expressed all over the country. The death of Alexis (as he became known) triggered the most severe acts of civil unrest that the country had seen in its entire post-1974 era. Immediately afterwards, this wave of contention resounded beyond national politics in the form of solidarity protests, conflictual action and further unrest throughout Europe.

Something new was unfolding: lacking any clarity in terms of organization, membership, protest demands and goals, or cultural reference, those dramatic events were spontaneous, leaderless and collectively violent. The circumstances were unclear and the existing theory could not account for the reasons why the sum of all those groups of people that participated in the events—the unemployed graduates, schoolchildren and middle-class citizens—suddenly became more visible and inter-connected. Moreover, the very young age of most of the activists (previously thought to be apolitical), the active participation in the events by economic immigrants and the fact that there was an instantaneous transnational echo of those violent events were crucial elements that pegged this incident as hitherto unforeseen, not only in terms of the Greek context but also worldwide. Seen as a clear-cut rupture in public life, it provoked the puzzlement of the whole of society, while journalists and politicians rushed to condemn the outbreak of violence against the state as an 'isolated event.' The same also applied to some social scientists who labelled the events as 'irrational violence' and 'youth immorality', mostly related to the unruly 'underdog' culture reigning in the country ever since the restitution of democracy in 1974 (Kalyvas 2010). However, against such theoretical endeavours, the abrupt rejection of political and social certainties that was expressed in December soon proved to be a forerunner of things to come. The economic crisis was followed by an outbreak of contention in Greece, further contributing to bringing the country once again to the forefront of non-conventional social conflicts with international spillover. From the mass occupation of town squares to the alternative economy initiatives, new forms of social protest emerged in Greece that would soon be seen across the austerity-burdened South of Europe. Furthermore, in the years that followed, unprecedented protests and confrontations erupted in unrelated places, such as Bulgaria, Spain, France, Hungary, and beyond Europe, in Tunisia, Egypt and Algeria. At the same time, these 'newly found' protest events and movements had no traditional resources, organizational and mobilization structures or strategies. They were thus a far cry from axioms once posited by the social and political theory in general, and the social movement research area in particular, testifying that a radical change had taken place which widened the gap between theory and action.

Used to perceiving protest in clear-cut analytical categories, social scientists thus found themselves in an awkward position, especially protest scholars. In line with their critical stance since the 1990s, Greek social movement theorists were the first after the events of December 2008 to express the need for new analytical tools to connect the movements' past, present and future to the transformations that were taking place (Serdedakis 2009). Almost synchronically to the events, researchers started to reflect upon the lack of an available hermeneutical schema (Kouki 2009), the movement's rejection of past legacies and urge for a change of paradigm (Kornetis 2010) and to interpret protests in terms of their technological outlook (Memos 2009), precarious labour (Vogiatzoglou 2011), transnational ties (Bratsis 2010), mimesis of previous protest cycles (Karamichas), or emotional make-up (Kotronaki and Seferiades 2010), or as a meaningful course of action through which a new collective identity was constructed (Psimitis 2011). In 2009, a conference was organised at Panteion University entitled 'Rioting and Violent Protest in Comparative Perspective, Theoretical Considerations, Empirical Puzzles',[4] where, with the December events as a point of departure, young scholars and renowned academics together tested social movement theory.

After this intensification of contentious culture in Greece, a number of scholars—and in particular social theorists—started not only to attempt to predict and classify social movements but also, to a large extent, to move closer to collective action themselves. As in the 1960s' paradigm, academic symposia incorporated the movements' approach, workshops and colloquia on social movements and urban space multiplied focusing on activist perspectives, while some academics not only wrote academic papers but also became active interlocutors with the people in the streets.[5] All these phenomena renewed the interest of students and researchers at home but also abroad in social movement theory, progressively engendering further research on past and current movements.

Moreover, the 2008 events and what followed triggered all kinds of questions regarding the renewal of theory and the placement of the Greek paradigm within it. This was also reflected in a renewal in publishing and in the translation of standard texts regarding social movement theory. Della Porta and Diani's *Social Movements: An Introduction* and Erik Neveu's *Sociologie des mouvements sociaux* were both translated into Greek and published in 2010, each with lengthy introductions and explanatory footnotes; Charles Tilly's *Democracy* and Isabelle Sommier's *La violence révolutionnaire* were published in 2011, and so on. A special series was launched by the Savvalas publishing house edited by the political scientist Michalis Spourdalakis with a particular focus on the diffusion of social movement theory. At the same time, social movement theory grafted different disciplines, in particular urban studies and urban theory (Leontidou 2010, National Centre of Social Research 2012, Stavridis 2010), anthropology (Dalakoglou 2012), migration studies (Tsianos and Papadopoulos 2012), media studies (Triga 2011), contemporary art theory (Fotiadi 2011), philosophy (Sotiris), critical political theory (Stavrakakis and Sevastakis 2012, Kioupkioklis and Katsampekis 2013), gender studies (Athanasiou 2012), cultural studies (Papanikolaou 2011) and marketing research (Hatzidakis 2013). All these fields are undergoing constant transformation, as they are blended with novel questions and new tools that recognise conflict as an integral part of democracy.

Parallel to this, Greece's persistent presence in social action from 2008 up to the present day rendered it a central case study in international literature on social movements in times of crisis. It seemed as if there had been a parallel shift from a 'peripheral' paradigm of social action and self-perception but also of theory to a more central position, not only in direct dialogue with global developments in contentious politics but also to some extent at their forefront. 'Violent Protest, Contentious Politics, and the Neoliberal State' (2013), edited by Seferiadis and Johnston, departs from the assumption that reflection on the Greek case may provide the remedy for a lack of conceptual tools in social movement theory. As evident in a variety of publications (Arampatzi and Nicholls 2012; Kotronaki 2013; Butler and Athanasiou 2013; Sotirakopoulos and Sotiropoulos 2013; Vogiatzoglou and Sergi 2013; Kousis and Kanellopoulos 2014), the social movement reality itself brought along the need for a different discipline of social movements, and Greece reflected this change of paradigm.

The opposite effect of bringing theorists closer to the movements was to bring the movements themselves closer to theory. University and academia have never been the unique platform where methodological and conceptual battles were waged. However, it was after December 2008, when theory had proven to be insufficient and the 'limits to legitimate protest' were lifted that this became vociferously evident. Activists started theorizing their action and the movement's configuration, signalling a radical departure from a previous rejection of theory and its occasional academic mouthpiece.[6] Activists expressed the need to participate and influence the ways that discontent, protest, revolt and social change are perceived, narrated and framed. The collected volume *Revolt and Crisis* (2012), edited by Vradis and Dalakoglou, traces the country's transitional period from the revolt of 2008 to the ensuing economic crisis. Authors from around the world—including those on the ground in Greece—examine how "December" became possible, exploring its genealogy and legacies in the face of the impending economic crisis. *Democracy under Construction: From the Streets to the Squares—Experience, Analysis, Documents* (2012), edited by Giovanopoulos and Mitropoulos, provides an insight into the massive movement that has occupied central squares in Greece since May 2011. The chapters of the book were written by activists and academics that actually participated in the people's assemblies and thus offer both an empirical perspective and a theoretical reflection on social movements. Those two publications are indicative of a growing trend also evident in posters and leaflets in activist spaces that started to bear the imprint of theory. Discussions, festivals, workshops, projects and websites related to social movements[7] bring together activists and theorists in such a way that the distinction may be rendered obsolete in years to come. In the same vein, activists from abroad turned their attention towards the Greek protests, further contributing to theorizing, representing and diffusing these as integral parts of an international paradigm.

In 1974 Greece found itself at the centre of theoretical attention regarding its transition from an authoritarian regime to democracy. Soon afterwards, however, the country was attributed the position of a semi-peripheral society always lagging behind advanced Western democracies, including in its relationship to social protest. Departing from a problematization of such interpretative frameworks, social science researchers started to develop the field of social movement in the country during the 1990s. Their reflections were met with a social movement reality itself that after December 2008 triggered the need for a different conceptualization of collective action. This was further accentuated by the intensification of contention that followed the eruption of the Greek economic crisis in 2010. Over the last few years in Greece, theory began to merge with activist action, affecting the ways social change is perceived and represented. From a peripheral case, Greece came to reflect this change of paradigm.[8]

Back in peaceful 1990, Alexandropoulos was trying to figure out ways to bridge the chasm between the theories that emerge from *within* the movements and the scientific social theory that seeks to analyse them (Alexandropoulos 1990). The Greek experience itself, coupled with the *Indignados* movement in Spain, Occupy in the United States, and the Arab Spring in the Middle East and North Africa, provided the answer and was transformed into a metonym of a critique of social movement theory. Greece had been classified as a marginal case within this field of study because the theory itself had been crafted by putting normative limits to protest and conflict in many cases. The national experience may well act as a general critique of social and political theory that in the name of alleged neutrality is alienated from what is happening on the ground and how agents of change perceive themselves and the world around them. Confronted with the shattering of normality at every level of public life nowadays, what we need is a radical restructuring of the paradigm of social protest that will function as a contestatory depot for activists, theorists and citizens, worldwide.

Kostis Kornetis is assistant professor/faculty fellow at the Center for European and Mediterranean Studies, New York University. He received his PhD in history and civilization from the European University Institute, Florence. From 2007 to 2012 he taught in the history department at Brown University. His research focuses on the history and memory of the 1960s, the methodology of oral history, and the use of film as a source for social and cultural history. His book *Children of the Dictatorship: Student Resistance, Cultural Politics and the 'Long 1960s' in Greece* was published in 2013 by Berghahn Books.

Hara Kouki is a historian and has completed her PhD thesis at the law department at Birkbeck College, University of London (2015). She has worked as an affiliated researcher with ELIAMEP (Athens, Greece) and European University Institute, Robert Schuman Centre for Advanced Studies (Florence, Italy). Among other publications, Hara has co-edited *European Modernity and the Greek Crisis* (Palgrave, 2013) and *Protest beyond Borders: Contentious Politics in Europe since 1945* (Berghahn, 2011).

Notes

1. See the recently awarded PhD theses, Kanellopoulos (2009) and Papanikolopoulos (2013).
2. See http://contentiouspoliticscircle.blogspot.co.uk/
3. See Kanellopoulos, Kotronaki and Iakovidou (2011), and Kanellopoulos et al. (2013).
4. See http://englishsynedrio.blogspot.co.uk/
5. See law professor Costas Douzinas speaking in Syntagma Square on the right to resistance (June 2011), architecture scholar Stavros Stavridis in a local assembly on the right to the city (March 2012), or political science academic Karolos Kavoulakos at the People's University of Social Solidarity Economy (February 2013).
6. The protest at an academic conference on 1968 by student activists in June 2008, on the grounds that the history of contestation could not be theorised as it was 'written in the streets', is indicative (Kornetis 2009).

7. See 'Crisis Regimes and Emerging Social Movements in Cities of Southern Europe', http://urbanrise.net, organised by the urban collective Encounter Athens, or the research project http://www.crisis-scape.net/.
8. See the prominence of Greek protests in the alternative media collectives http://roarmag.org and http://www.globaluprisings.org/.

References

Afouksenidis, A. 2006. 'Urban Social Movements in Southern European Cities'. *City*, 10, no. 3: 287–93

Alexandropoulos, S. 1995. 'Issues of Social Movement Theory: Seeking Strategy or Identity'. *The Greek Review of Social Research* 86: 83–13. In Greek.

———. 2001. *Theories of Collective Action and Social Movements*. Athens: Kritiki. In Greek.

Arampatzi, A., and W. J. Nicholls. 2012. 'The Urban Roots of Anti-neoliberal Social Movements: The Case of Athens, Greece'. *Environment and Planning* 44, no. 11: 2591–610.

Asdrachas, S. 1988. *Greek Society and Economics*. Athens: Ermis.

Athanasiou, A. 2012. '"Who" Is That Name? Subjects of Gender and Queer Resistance, or the Desire to Contest'. *European Journal of English Studies* 16, no. 3: 199–213.

Avdela, E. 1996. 'Waged Labour as the Privileged Locus for the Construction of Social Movements in the Interwar Period'. *Greek Political Science Review* 8: 83–99.

Avdela, E., and A. Psarra, eds. 1989. *Feminism in Interwar Greece: An Anthology*. Athens: Gnosi. In Greek.

Bermeo, N. 1995. 'Classification and Consolidation: Some Lessons from the Greek Dictatorship'. *Political Science Quarterly* 110, no. 3: 435–52.

Botetzagias, I. 2003. 'The Re-emergence of the Greek Greens'. *Environmental Politics* 12, no. 4: 127–32.

Botetzagias, I., and M. Boudourides. 2007. 'Networks of Protest on Global Issues in Greece 2002–2003'. In *Civil Societies and Social Movements*, ed. D. Purdue, 109–23. Routledge: London.

Bratsis, P. 2010. 'Legitimation Crisis and the Greek Explosion'. *International Journal of Urban and Regional Research* 34, no. 1: 190–96.

Butler, J., and A. Athanasiou. 2013. *Dispossession: The Performative in the Political*. Berkeley: University of California Press.

Chliaoutakis, I. 1983. 'Le mouvement maoïste en Grèce: sociologie politique'. PhD dissertation: Université Lumière Lyon 2.

Dafermos, O. 2003. *Students and Dictatorship: The Antidictatorship Student Movement, 1972–73*. Athens: Gavriilides. In Greek.

Dalakoglou, D. 2012. 'The Crisis before "the Crisis": Violence and Urban Neoliberalization in Athens'. *Social Justice* 39, no. 1: 24–42.

Dertilis, G. 1977. *Social Transformation and Military Intervention*. Athens: Exantas. In Greek.

Diamandouros, N. 1994. 'Cultural Dualism and Political Change in Postauthoritarian Greece'. *Working Paper 1994/50*. Madrid: Centro de Estudios Avanzados en Ciencias Sociales.

Diamandouros, N., et al., eds. 1995. *The Politics of Democratic Consolidation: Southern Europe in Comparative Perspective*. Baltimore and London: The Johns Hopkins University Press.

Doxiadis, A. 1996. 'Utopia and Ethics: Social Movements in Contemporary Ideology'. *Greek Political Science Review* 8: 51–82.

Economides, S., and V. Monastiriotis, eds. 2009. *The Return of Street Politics? Essays on the December Riots in Greece*. London: The Hellenic Observatory.

Fotiadi, E. 2011. *The Game of Participation in Art and the Public Sphere*. Maastricht: Shaker Verlag.

Giannaris, G. 1993. *Student Movements and Greek Education: From Rigas Feraios to the Occupation Period*. Athens: Pontiki. In Greek.

Giovanopoulos, C., and D. Mitropoulos, eds. 2011. *Democracy under Construction: From Streets to Squares*. Athens: A Synecheia.

Greek Political Science Review. 2006. 'Contentious Politics and Social Movements' 27.

Hatzidakis, A. 2013. 'Commodity Fights in Post-2008 Athens: Zapatistas Coffee, Kropotkian Drinks and Fascist Rise'. *Ephemera*, no. 3: 459-468.

Iakovidou, J., K. Kanellopoulos and L. Kotronaki. 2011. 'The Greek Uprising of December 2008'. *Situations: Project of the Radical Imagination* 3, no. 2: 145–57.

Kallianos, Y. 2012. 'Politics of the Street: An Anthropological Study of Radical Politics during the December 2008 Revolt in Greece'. PhD dissertation. St. Andrews: University of St. Andrews.

Kalyvas, A. 2010. 'An Anomaly? Reflections on the Greek December 2008'. *Constellations* 17, no. 2: 351–65.

Kanellopoulos, K. 2009. 'Processes of Formation and Issues of Social Movement Theory: The Movement against Neoliberal Globalization'. PhD dissertation. Athens: Panteion University.

Kanellopoulos, K. et al. 2013. 'Movement Organizations in the Campaign against Memoranda and Austerity Politics: Movement Networks, Organizational Identities, Activists' Profiles', *4th Conference of Hellenic Sociological Society*, 12–14 December. Athens.

Karamichas, J. 2009. 'The December 2008 Riots in Greece'. *Social Movement Studies* 8, no. 3: 289–93.

Katsambekis, G., and A. Kioupkioklis, eds. 2014. *Radical Democracy and Collective Movements Today. The Biopolitics of the Multitude versus the Hegemony of the People*. Surrey and Burlington: Ashgate.

Kavoulakos, K. 2009. 'Security and Social Demands for Public Spaces: An Urban Movement of the 21st Century'. In *Trends of Social Transformation in Urban Space*, ed. Y. Maloutas et al, 387-426. Athens: (National Centre of Social Research (EKKE). In Greek.

Kordatos, G. 1972. *The History of Labour Movement*. Athens: Boukoumanis. First published in 1932.

Kornetis, K. 2009. 'Introduction: 1968–2008: The Inheritance of Utopia'. *Historein* 9: 7–20.

———. 2010. 'No More Heroes? Rejection and Reverberation of the Past in the 2008 Events in Greece'. *Journal of Modern Greek Studies* 28, no. 2: 173–97.

———. 2013. *Children of the Dictatorship. Student Resistance, Cultural Politics and the Long 1960s in Greece*. Oxford and New York: Berghahn Books.

Kotronaki L. 2013. 'Réapproprier la contestation dans la "démocratie de la crise": la forme Occupy'. In *La grande régression, la Grèce et l'avenir de l'Europe,* ed. N. Burgi, 175–190. Paris: le Bord de l'Eau.

Kotronaki L., and S. Seferiades. 2010. 'Sur les sentiers de la colère: L'espace-temps d'une révolte (Athènes, décembre 2008)'. *Actuel Marx* 48: 152–64.

Kouki, H. 2009. '"Where Do We Go from Here?" December 2008 Riots in Greece and Social Movement Analysis'. *Losquaderno* 14 (2009): 25–28. http://www.profession aldreamers.net/images/losquaderno/losquaderno14.pdf.

Koukoules, G. 1983. *For a History of the Greek Syndicalist Movement: Introduction to the Pedagogy of Historical Research.* Athens: Odisseas. In Greek.

Kousis, M. 1999. 'Environmental Protest Cases: The City, the Countryside, and the Grassroots in Southern Europe'. *Mobilization* 4, no. 2: 223–38.

———. 2007. 'Local Environmental Protest in Greece, 1974–1994: Exploring the Political Dimension'. *Environmental Politics,* 16, no. 5: 785–804.

———. 2014. 'Environment, Economic Crisis and Social Movements in Greece, under Troika Memoranda and Austerity Policies'. In *Social Aspects of the Crisis in Greece,* ed. S. Zambarloukou and M. Kousi, 199–229. Athens: Pedio. In Greek.

Kousis, M and Kanellopoulos, K. 2014. Impacts of the Greek Crisis on Contentious and Conventional Politics, 2010–2012, in *The Social Impacts of the Eurozone Debt Crisis,* ed. G. Tsobanoglou and N. Petropoulos, eds, 443–462, Athens: Gordios Books, in Greek.

Kousis, M., and C. Tilly, eds. 2005. *Economic and Political Contention in Comparative Perspective.* Boulder: Paradigm.

Lazos, C. D. 1987. *The Greek Student Movement 1821–1973.* Athens: Gnosi. In Greek.

Leontidou, L. 2010. 'Urban Social Movements in "Weak" Civil Societies: The Right to the City and Cosmopolitan Activism in Southern Europe'. *Urban Studies* 47, no. 6: 1179–203.

Liakos, A. 1988. *The Appearance of Youth Organizations: The Case of Thessaloniki.* Athens: Lotos. In Greek.

———. 2010. 'Modern Greek Historiography (1974–2000): The Era of Tradition from Dictatorship to Democracy'. In *(Re)Writing History: Historiography in Southeast Europe after Socialism,* ed. U.Brunbauer, 351–78. Münster: LIT, Verlag.

Lyritzis, C. 1991. *The End of 'Tzakia'.* Athens: Themelio. In Greek.

Maratzidis, N. 1996. 'The Political Party and Social Movements: Relationship between Communist Parties of the Mediterranean South and the New Social Movements'. *Greek Political Science Review* 8: 100–120.

Mavrogordatos, G. 1993. 'Civil Society under Populism'. In *Greece 1981–89: The Populist Decade,* ed. R. Clogg, 47–64. London: Macmillan/St. Martin's Press.

Memos, C. 2009. 'Dignified Rage, Insubordination and Militant Optimism'. *Ephemera* 9, no. 3: 219–33.

Mentinis, M. 2010. 'Remember Remember the 6th of December … A Rebellion or the Constituting Moment of a Radical Morphoma?' *Urban and Regional Studies* 34, no. 1: 197–202.

Moskof, K. 1988. *Introduction to the History of Labour Class and Labour Movement: The Formation of National and Social Consciousness in Greece.* Athens: Kastaniotis. In Greek.

Mouzelis, N. 1986. *Politics in the Semi-Periphery: Early Parliamentarism and Late Industrialization in the Balkans and Latin America.* London: Macmillan.

National Centre of Social Research (EKKE). 2012. *Greece: The Social Portrait.* Athens: EKKE. In Greek.

Pantelidou-Malouta, M. 1996a. 'Introduction: Social Movements and Social Sciences'. *Greek Political Science Review* 8: 1–16.

———. 1996b. 'The Feminist Movement, the Feminist Theory, and Citizenship'. *Greek Political Science Review* 8: 154–80.

Papageorgiou, Y. 1992. 'The Women's Movement and Greek Politics'. In *Women Transforming Politics,* ed. J. Bystydzienski, 67–79. Bloomingdale: Indiana University Press.

Papanikolaou, D. 2011. 'Archive Trouble: Cultural Responses to the Greek Crisis'. In *Beyond the Greek Crisis: Histories, Rhetorics, Politics,* ed. P. Papailias. Web Hotspot published by the journal *Cultural Anthropology.*

Papanikolopoulos. 2013. 'Protest and Democracy in Greece during the Pre-Dictatorship Era: The '60s Protest Cycle'. PhD dissertation. Athens: Panteion University.

Poulantzas, N. 1976. *The Crisis of Dictatorships: Portugal, Greece, Spain.* London: New Left Books and Humanities Press.

Psimitis, M. 1996. 'Alternative Social Movements: Seeking the Feasible among Subjective Needs and State Politics'. *Greek Political Science Review* 8: 17–50.

———. 2006. *Introduction to Contemporary Social Movements.* Athens: Diadrasi.

———. 2011. 'Collective Identities versus Social Exclusion: The December 2008 Greek Youth Movement'. *The Greek Review of Social Research* 136 (C).

Repousi, M. 1996. 'The Second Sex in the Left: Documents and Memories from the Feminist Intervention in the Rigas Ferraios Organization, 1974–1978'. *Greek Political Science Review* 8: 121–53.

Seferiadis, S. 1996. 'The Discreet Charm of Ideology: A Theoreticism and Eclecticism in the Study of the Greek Labour Movement'. *Greek Political Science Review* 8: 198–217.

———. 2007. 'Contentious Politics, Collective Action, Social Movements: An Overview'. *Greek Review of Political Science* 27: 7–42. In Greek.

———. 2010. 'The Latent Role of Collective Action in Greek Institutional Change (1974): Preliminary Thoughts on the Polytechneio Events'. *Greek Review of Political Science* 36: 119–33. In Greek.

Seferiadis, S., and H. Johnston, eds. 2012. *Violent Protest, Contentious Politics, and the Neoliberal State.* London: Ashgate.

Serdedakis, N. 1998. 'In the Heart of Social Movements: A Critical Reading of Contemporary Theory'. *Social Science Review* 24: 41–65. In Greek.

———. 2007. 'Collective Action and Students' Movement between 1959–1964: Structural Preconditions, Political Opportunities, and Collective Action Frames'. In *The Short 1960s,* ed. A. Rigos et al., 241–61. Athens: Castaniotis. In Greek.

———. 2009. 'The Crisis of Theory as an Opportunity'. *Ta Nea,* 11 January.

———. Forthcoming. 'Continuities and Non-continuities of Collective Action in the Transition from the "Stunted" Democracy to "metapolitefsi"'. In *From the Transition to Democracy to the Economic Crisis?* ed. E. Gazi, K. Kornetis and M. Avgeridis. Athens: Nefeli. In Greek.

Serdedakis, N., and S. Alexandropoulos. 2000. 'Greek Environmentalism: From the

Statu Nascendi of a Movement to Its Integration'. *ECPR Joint Sessions, Workshop on Environmental Organizations 14–19 April,* Copenhagen.

Sevastakis, N., and Y. Stavrakakis. 2012. *Populism, Anti-Populism, and the Crisis.* Athens: Nefeli. In Greek.

Simiti M. 2003. 'The Contemporary Feminist Movement: Ideological Confrontations and Political Dilemmas'. *Civil Society* 9: 50–53. In Greek.

Sotirakopoulos, N., and G. Sotiropoulos, 2013. '"Direct Democracy Now!": The Greek Indignados and the Present Cycle of Struggles'. *Current Sociology* 61: 443, DOI: 10.1177/0011392113479744.

Sotiris, P. 2010. 'Rebels with a Cause: The December 2008 Greek Youth Movement as the Condensation of Deeper Social and Political Contradictions'. *Urban and Regional Studies* 34, no. 1: 203–9.

Stavrides, S. 2010. 'The December 2008 Youth Uprising in Athens: Spatial Justice in an Emergent "City Of Thresholds"'. *Justice Spatiale/Spatial Justice.* www.jssj.org.

Svoronos, N. 1999. *Overview of Modern Greek History.* Athens: Themelio. First published in 1972.

Triandafyllidou, A., R. Gropas and H. Kouki, eds. 2013. *European Modernity and the Greek Crisis.* New York: Palgrave Macmillan.

Triga, V. 2011. 'Social Protest through Facebook in the Greek Context: The Case of the "I Don't Pay Movement". *Journal of Critical Studies in Business and Society* 2, nos. 1–2: 51–73.

Tsakiris, T. 1996. 'Bibliographical Guide for Social Movements Study'. *Greek Political Science Review* 8: 181–90.

Tsianos, V., and D. Papadopoulos. 2012. 'Crisis, Migration and the Death Drive of Capitalism'. *Afterall: A Journal of Art, Context and Enquiry* 31: 4–11.

Tsoukalas, C. 1981. *Social Development and State: The Construction of Public Space in Greece.* Athens: Themelio. In Greek.

Varikas, E. 1995. 'The Subject of Rights. The Gender of Politics. The Exclusion of Democracy'. *Synchrona Themata* 57: 42–58. In Greek.

Vernadakis, C., and G. Mavris. 1991. *Parties and Social Allies in Post-dictatorial Greece.* Athens: Exantas. In Greek.

Vogiatzoglou, M. 2011. 'A Precarious December: Flexible Workers' Unions in the Aftermath of a Youth Rebellion'. *6th ECPR General Conference 25–27 August,* Reykjavik.

Vogiatzoglou, M., and V. Sergi. 2013. 'Think Globally, Act Locally? Symbolic Memory and Global Repertoires in the Tunisian Uprising and the Greek Anti-austerity Mobilizations'. In *Understanding European Movements: New Social Movements, Global Justice Struggles, Anti-austerity Protest,* ed. C. Flesher Fominaya and L. Cox, 220–235. London: Routledge.

Vradis, A. 2012. 'Patterns of Contentious Politics Concentration as a "Spatial Contract": A Spatio-Temporal Study of Urban Riots and Violent Protests in the Neighborhood of Exarcheia, Athens, Greece (1974–2011)'. PhD dissertation. London: LSE.

Vradis, A., and D. Dalakoglou, eds. 2011. *Revolt and Crisis in Greece: Between a Present yet to Pass and a Future still to Come.* Oakland and Edinburgh: AK Press.

Xenakis, S. 2010. 'Balkanism in Greece as Dissidence against the West'. In *Roots, Rites and Sites of Resistance: The Banality of Good,* ed. L. Cheliotis, 178–95. New York: Palgrave Macmillan.

Chapter 22

A Militant Rather than Scientific Research Object

Social Movements Studies in Turkey[1]

Ayşen Uysal

Social movements have been a neglected subject in Turkey's national research agenda, nevertheless we can pinpoint two periods that saw an increase in the number of studies on social movements. The first period from 1960s to 1980 saw research focused on student and youth movements, while in the second period after 1980, studies have mostly discussed sectoral movements, such as the Kurdish, women's and environmental movements. Besides these two periods, labour or trade-union movements and youth movements (Uysal 2001) have always remained on the agenda.

For the author, the claim that social movements constitute a neglected area of research creates an immediate dilemma. While this evaluation is correct, it may give the impression of a hasty assessment because there are a significant number of studies on social movements. However, very few publications use social movement theories or refer to the research methods applied in this field.[2] These works are fairly recent and are mostly products of graduate studies. The major explanation for the recent increase in the number of studies using social movement literature and its methodologies can be found in master's and doctoral studies or academic visits for research purposes, particularly with European or American universities.

One of the main reasons for the lack of scientific research on social movements is the high risk of working on this subject. Factors such as the state tradition in Turkey, the security meta-ideology (Dorronsoro 2005), military coups and the meanings attributed to political participation all prevent the normalization of collective actions (Uysal 2005, 2010). This makes the field risky for academicians. With some exceptions, social movement studies have primarily focused on less risky issues since the 1980s with the new social movements (NSM) paradigm playing a facilitating role under the influence of N. Göle with Boğaziçi University becoming the centre for this kind of research. NSM theory has become particularly influential in Turkey because social movements have been associated with the left, and the left has shown an interest in this matter. Consequently, theoretical approaches within the post-Marxist paradigm have gained more attention. Through the impact of NSM theory, sectoral studies have gained greater prominence, such as on women's, environmental, Kurdish and labour movements. For instance, while there are numerous studies of women's movements, studies based on the social movement literature are limited.

Although there are only a very few studies using mobilization and social movement theories, concepts and methods, the literature is relatively rich in terms of translated publications aimed at mobilizing the masses or keeping a record of history. Some of these publications aim to spread the experiences of social movements in other countries, primarily in Latin America (Özbudun 2012; Yeğin 2003, 2006) to readers, especially to Turkish activists. Anti-globalization movements generally, and the Seattle experience in particular, occupy a privileged place (Uzun 2001; Cockburn and St. Clair 2003; Karakaş 2005), with translations and other articles on the '68 movement being prominent (Fraser 2008; Kurlansky 2008; Cogito 1998). More recently, information sharing on the Arab Spring and protest movements in Spain and Greece has become crucial (Benlisoy 2012), along with books about key social movements in Turkey. Most of these publications are journalistic in style, being mainly concerned with narrating events and ensuring that history is recorded (Karakaş 1992; Günçıkan 1996; Temelkuran 1997; Künar 2002; Reinart 2003; Sanlı 2003; Çınar and Üsterci 2008). For example, one book edited by two human rights activists, Ö. H. Çınar and C. Üsterci, focuses on reporting the experience of conscientious objection in Turkey and other countries, particularly Chile, Israel and Spain. The book also discusses the judicial repertoire of social movements through a variety of examples of lawsuits.

One of the major components of the literature in Turkey concerns studies conducted by police officers. The common feature of these works is their efforts to analyse social movements and street protests using G. Le Bon's theory. One of the most remarkable is I. Cerrah's thesis, written in the UK, on crowds and public order. This study keeps faith with G. Le Bon's ideas by applying ethnographic participant observation to classify crowds into three groups: spectator, dissenter and aggressive. Cerrah conducted thirty-three participant observations in Turkey, England and Wales between 1992 and 1995, sampling a wide range of meeting forms, from football matches, funerals and festivals to protest marches. The common element of studies conducted by police officers is that they focus on the crowds rather than groups or organizations, they emphasise the influences on crowds, and are predominantly concerned about how to keep demonstrations under control to prevent their 'contagious' effect.

The existing literature in Turkey can be classified under three titles: translated studies, original research and the contributions of foreign experts on Turkey. These three categories allow us to test several basic hypotheses. First, Turkey's national research agenda is shaped by social practices. Second, research agendas are transferable from one country to another, where the most important way of doing this is the translation of books and articles written in other languages. Third, none of these translations is innocent. Fourth, studies by Turkish researchers educated abroad play an important role in transferring theories and even practices (Bourdieu 2002; Dezalay and Bryant 2002). Finally, foreign researchers are social actors that transfer theories. These four hypotheses will be discussed in the following sections.

Translation Is Not Just Translation: Transfer of the Social Movements Literature

The selection of the publication to be translated is ultimately a matter of choice. Considering the specific books on social movements that have been translated into Turkish, we can see that NSM was the first imported approach. This theory facilitated its transfer for several reasons. One of the main factors is that Turkish researcher N. Göle, particularly known for her work on the Islamic movement, but who also focused on engineers and ideology (1998) in her early work, prepared her doctoral thesis under A. Touraine's supervision.[3] Subsequently, Göle's personal network in Turkey has become a major translator and publisher of Touraine's works. When she was at Boğaziçi University, her students also helped spread this theory. K. Çayır, who completed both his master's and doctoral degrees at Boğaziçi University under Göle's supervision, has carried out various studies with her, and his book *Yeni Toplumsal Hareketler: Teorik Açılımlar* [*New Social Movements: Theoretical Aspects*] is another example of the efforts to spread this theory. It includes chapters by seven authors who played key roles in constructing NSM theory, namely Touraine, Offe, Melucci, etc. This collection steers away from the classic paradigm of A. Touraine's new social movements to some extent, instead moving closer to J. Cohen and A. Arato's (1992: 505) line, which claims that identity and the personal sphere can be political (Çayır 1999: 26).

The approach of more recent studies has been imported from resource mobilization theory and its extension, political process/opportunity theory, rather than NSM theory, with Y. D. Çetinkaya (2008) being an important example. Çetinkaya emphasises the historical continuity of social movements, and highlights the problematic aspects of the NSM paradigm in his book on social movements. For him, the distinction between 'old' and 'new' social movements[4] is essentialist and overlooks many differences in order to force the theory to fit Turkey's case (Çetinkaya 2008: 50). To support his argument, Çetinkaya includes translations of articles by S. Tarrow[5] and C. Tilly in his compilation. Other chapters in this book include studies on social movements in various countries.

Along with this edited book, other books by several important authors in the social movement literature have been translated into Turkish to import their ideas. For example six books by A. Touraine have been translated into Turkish, as well as other writings published in compilations. Examples include *Critique de la modernité*, *Qu'est-ce que la démocratie* and *Le monde des femmes*. Six books by C. Tilly have also been translated into Turkish, including *Social Movements 1768–2004* in 2008 and *The Politics of Collective Violence* in 2009.

Regarded as one of the classic works in the field of social movements, J. C. Scott's book, *Domination and the Art of Resistance: Hidden Transcripts*, was translated and published by Ayrıntı Yayınları in 1995. This study of the daily practices of resistance, especially its definition of resistance, has become the main reference point for the studies conducted by the Iran specialist, A. Bayat, and has had more influence on poverty literature in Turkey than social movement studies. His Turkish doctoral students[6] and his conference presentations in Turkey have accelerated the process of translating his books into Turkish. Another reason for this interest in his work is his focus on resistance in a similar country, Iran, which is dominated by an authoritarian state structure. Bayat has gained popularity particularly from his definition of the 'quiet encroachment of the ordinary' (Bayat 1998: 7–8), which brings past discussions into the present by focusing on the movements of the poor and relations between the poor and revolution, rather than middle-class movements.

Another important contribution is Jasper's book, *The Art of Moral Protest: Culture, Biography and Creativity in Social Movements,* translated in 2002. In addition, social movements are mostly studied within the framework of class struggle so names such as Castells and Wallerstein are often referred to. As will be discussed in the following sections, social movements, especially after the 1980s, have generally been associated with urban studies in Turkey, so M. Castells has become the main reference point. The three volumes of *The Information Age: Economy, Society and Culture* were translated into Turkish in 2005. Another reference for the social movement literature based on the axis of urban studies is Harvey, almost all of whose most important works have been translated into Turkish. In particular, *Rebel Cities: From the Right to the City to the Urban Revolution* was translated into Turkish just before the recent Gezi protests and frequently referred to during them. Aside from urban studies, perspectives stemming from the Marxist tradition are the other essential reference, especially Arrighi and Wallerstein's *Antisystemic Movements*.

The influence of the Marxist tradition on the social movement literature is evident in other translated works. For instance, Thompson was one of the leading Marxist scholars and translations of his two classic works in the social movement literature, *The Making of the English Working Class* and *Custom in Common: Studies in Traditional Popular Culture*, were published by Birikim Yayınları. Through the impact of the leftist-Marxist tradition, the literature of translated works includes many books on revolution.[7]

Finally, Habermas' framework of deliberative democracy and Laclau and Mouffe's discussions of radical democracy have both been highly influential in Turkish academia. The Habermasian tradition can be seen in the field of communication, and in discussions about democracy and political participation (Köker 2007, Doğanay 2003). Regarding social movements, Arendt and Habermas are important references on civil disobedience.

The main common point of most of these works is that they have been translated into Turkish to contribute to the revolution debate. Just like the attribution of social movements to leftist organizations, translation of the literature of this field into Turkish is undertaken by leftist publishers. Publishing houses such as Ayrıntı, Metis, İletişim and Dipnot were all founded by earlier current activists. These publications have enabled their authors to continue to contribute or offer new contributions to these movements. That is, it becomes possible to continue to serve their cause, meaning that neither the selection of books to be translated is innocent nor are the publishers of these books neutral of political interests. Consequently, Turkish researchers interested in generating knowledge but unable to follow publications in other languages are constrained within the limits of this selection. This makes it essential to consider the original works on social movements.

Limited Sources: Case Studies on Social Movements

Each case study is a significant means for transferring ideas. Viewed in this manner, every scientific study on social movements simultaneously tests a paradigm in the field of Turkey.

In particular, Göle's studies have mobilised the paradigm of NSM in the analysis of social movements in Turkey. Göle has thought about the possible meaning of the dissident character and actions of engineers as a social category (Göle 1986: 119). She proposes three principles based on the founding factors of Touraine's (1965, 1978) definition of social movements in order to discuss the historical movement of engineers: 'identity principle (in whose name one acts), opposition principle (designation of the adversary), and totality principle (definition of public interest)' (Göle 1986: 120). The method implemented in her study is an adaptation of Touraine's method of 'sociological intervention' (Touraine 1980: 325) in the actions of engineers, where four focus group sessions were conducted with seven engineers working at the same factory (Göle 1986: 123–24).

Göle's research on the 1980s inspired and gave rise to a series of social movement studies collecting primary data by the middle of the 2000s. The first of these is a social history study of the 1908 Ottoman boycott by Çetinkaya (2004). Çetinkaya's work drew on the Ottoman archives of the Office of the Prime Minister and the Ottoman press of the time. The book discusses the significance of political opportunities in resorting to a boycott and how the boycott, acknowledged as the 'weapon of the weak' was used by different sections of society as a strategy. His book, which also investigates boycott organizations as the source of the social movement, is one of those rare works that discusses the effects of social movements, explaining the impacts of the boycott of 1908 both within and outside the empire.

Another scientific study drawing on the resource mobilization and political process approaches focuses on street protests in Turkey during the 1990s (Uysal 2005, 2010). In this study, Uysal analyses how repertoires of street protest, an interactive field between the state and protestors, and state control take shape. According to the study, the decision about which forms will become the strategies of protest is not independent of the state's perception of protests and protestors. Although the street is an important concept in the vocabulary of militants in Turkey, this subject has struggled to find a place on the agenda of scientific studies for various reasons. Therefore, Uysal's study is significant because it analyses the street as a militant field going beyond militant language. Uysal also demonstrates how, in the 1990s, streets in Turkey were still shaped by old forms of movements, organization and protest practices.[8]

After the 1980s, social movements found a place in urban studies. This literature, however, ignored the two fundamental paradigms in the field of social movements, with most studies so far relating social movements to the urban and urbanization fields, and focusing just on certain areas or quarters of the city. For example, they tend to study Istanbul's poor and/or ethnically and religiously diverse areas (Işık and Pınarcıoğlu 2001: 31–61). Among these are scientific studies of Gazi Quarter (Pérouse 2005: 127–45) and 1 Mayıs Quarter (Arslan 2004). The study on 1 Mayıs Quarter focuses on the forms of resistance and organization of the residents against the demolition of the quarter before 1980. Recently, the number of studies investigating the forms of resistance of social groups who have lost their homes because of urban transformation has also risen (Yücel and Aksümer 2012).

In summary, given the limited number of scientific studies, it would not be wrong to say that the literature of social movements in Turkey has remained at the stage of the transfer of theories for the last thirty years, without being fully able to move on to original production.

Contributions by Foreign Researchers

Leaving aside orientalist studies based on a myth of cultural and religious authenticity specific to Islamic societies, it is nevertheless clear that foreign scientists specializing on Turkey tend to focus on the issue of Islamic religious mobilizations. A large majority of studies, from the relatively old to the most recent, are concerned with the issue of religious mobilization (White 2002; Massicard 2005). For instance, Massicard (2005), analyses one religious minority, the Alevi movement, to explain how it came into being, how it is a polymorphic and divided movement, how it reflects a change of mode in the mobilization of the masses, the issue of conscripting militants from the leftist movement to Alevism, the Alevi movement as a field of alliance and conflict, the relationship of the movement with the surrounding universe and with other movements and actors, its repertoire of action and the issue of radicalization of the movement. One of the original aspects of the book is that it shows the articulation of local and international networks. It has proved to be an important contribution to literature and to transferring social movement theories to Turkey in that it applies methodologies of the literature of social movements to analyse a social movement in Turkey.

Another sectoral movement that has attracted as much attention as the Islamic movement in the scientific agenda of foreign researchers is the Kurdish movement, of which Bozarslan's work is among the most noteworthy. His book (1997) draws attention to two fundamental aspects. First, it consistently discusses the issue of repertoires of action in its analysis of the Kurdish movement. Second, it questions the relationships between state control and militant strategies in social movements. Another significant contribution to discussing the Kurdish movement from the perspective of repertoires of action is Grojean's work (2006), which focuses on self-immolation protests. His main contribution to the literature in Turkey is to add something to the almost empty field of political activism studies (Grojean 2013).[9]

Other studies focus on political participation as a more general issue rather than sectoral movement analyses. Such studies focus on women, minorities, the poor or other disadvantaged groups with regard to political participation. For example, Wedel (2001) investigates the relationship between politics and gender, focusing on the collective action of poor women living in Turkish slums and how this action empowers women within the framework of urban social movements. Wedel (2001: 120) defends the thesis that women resort to unconventional, informal modes of participation due to scarcity of resources for political participation. Specifically, women in poor slums resort to forms of collective action concerning infrastructure problems since these are the most immediate issues that need to be addressed in their daily lives (Wedel 2001: 120). The most significant performances of these women's repertoires of action in these urban spaces are protest forms like sit-ins and blockades (Wedel 2001: 123). One of the most important contributions of this work is that it draws attention to factors other than common interests that enable the collective to be a collective or not. Factors such as ethnicity or sect become important in defining the boundaries of the collective.

Another important publication that has contributed to the literature is *La Turquie Conteste. Mobilisations sociales et régime sécuritaire* (2005), edited by Dorronsoro, which includes chapters produced by scholars from France and Turkey. Besides presenting the results of various field studies, this work discusses how a security-centred state and government mentality affects social movements. Many of the scholars who contributed to this book have also led the publication of the online *European Journal of Turkish Studies*,[10] which has enriched the literature since 2004, with special issues on topics such as labour movements and the politics of coercion.

The studies in this group, of which just a few examples have been presented, constitute a significant component of the literature of social movements in Turkey regarding the operationalization of theoretical discussions in the field and the application of concepts. To a certain extent, these studies have been able to overcome earlier shortcomings in fieldwork.

What Kind of an Agenda for the Future?

Conducting fieldwork in the arena of social movements implies running the risk of facing various difficulties. The first difficulty is two-way, stemming from the nature of the subject. In countries like Turkey, where the risks and costs of political activism are high, access to the actors of social movements may not be easy. Even if access is gained, these actors may not be able to speak as openly and sincerely as they could in interviews. That is, many activists erect a barrier between themselves and the researcher from the beginning, even failing to respond to anonymous surveys in some cases, let alone participate in interviews. For example, many activists refused to contribute to a survey that we conducted in Ankara and Izmir on 1 September 2013 World Peace Day demonstrations out of mistrust. First, they are worried about the identity of the people conducting the survey. Are they state agents, undercover police officers or a real researcher? In many cases, activists assume the first possibility is true, and this is far from being paranoid since police infiltration of activist groups is a very common practice. Moreover, given this risk, activists do not want to divert their attention by responding to surveys. Such mistrust is higher with young militants. Illegal organizations, meanwhile, are just like closed books, and many political activists in Turkey identify being asked questions with police interrogations.

Alongside this difficulty presented by activists, researchers working on a social movement, specifically conducting fieldwork during street protests, risk harassment by the police, being blacklisted, being forced to become a secret agent, being exposed to police violence and being taken into custody.[11]

However, studies of social movements do not only cover risky fields. For instance, the studies focusing on the relationship between media and social movements, hence the theme of framing that constitutes an important and less risky axis for social movement studies, but these studies have also been virtually unexplored in Turkey. Based on its title, the book edited by Dağtaş, *Türkiye'de Sivil İtaatsizlik: Toplumsal Hareketler ve Basın* [*Civil Disobedience in Turkey: Social Movements and Press*] seems to offer some hope in this field. Unfortunately, however, this work does not go beyond discourse analysis of the content and form of news coverage by the media regarding movements like the protests of the *Cumartesi Anneleri* (Saturday Mothers), the environmental protests in Bergama and anti-NATO movements. It is very hard to establish how most articles relate to social movements and the media literature. One of the rare studies conducted in this field using the literature discussed here and its research techniques is that of Doğanay and Köker (2005). From three months of observation of a total of 480 prime-time news programmes for four national TV channels, they conclude that the visual media reproduce the state's rhetoric of the enemy when regarding the actors of social movements. The authors also draw the readers' attention to the media's tendency to render only individual or non-political protests as legitimate. Their study is a pathfinder for future scientific studies that will hopefully fill the current gaps in the field.

While the research object of street protests in social movement studies has been specifically disregarded.[12] It should be noted that the Taksim-Gezi protests, which left their mark in June 2013, have increased the level of interest in this field. Merely some of the articles written to analyse these recent events have referred to the literature of social movements (Uysal 2013a; Yıldırım 2013; Çetinkaya 2013). Street protests in Turkey are generally categorised within more comprehensive subjects, such as the history of the working class, history of May Day, history of unionism and strikes, or else discussed from a legal perspective within the framework of the Law on Assemblies and Demonstrations or in studies focusing on human rights (Tanör 1994). However, in many cases, the protests themselves are not the object of research, although this seems to have changed following the Gezi protests. There are already signs that the number of publications, panels and symposia will rise dramatically. While national or international symposia and conferences on social movements have only rarely been organised up to now, new steps are being taken to rectify this. One such project on social movements is supported by TÜBİTAK (Scientific and Technical Research Council of Turkey).[13]

Considering the current state of the literature, it is possible to draw several conclusions that could benefit future studies. Although Turkey has a rich history of social movements, there have been very few scientific studies based on primary data in this field, with current work relying on the importation of outside theories and practices. Although one should not ignore the significance of these studies, fieldwork conducted in Turkey is needed. Another argument concerns the relatively deprived and isolated condition of social movement studies. Social movements in Turkey, however, do not develop independently of the rest of the world because activists follow other countries' experiences, import repertoires of protest, and become part of social networks in other countries. Therefore, scientific studies on social movements should also avoid being imprisoned within national borders. Finally, studies in this field need to disassociate themselves both from the language of the media and the language of militancy. It is very hard for researchers to situate themselves in countries like Turkey, where state violence is evident and the polarization between the state and political activists is severe. This is one of the most pressing difficulties in this field.

In short, seen from these perspectives, the subject of social movements presents itself almost as a virgin research field in all its dimensions for social scientists in Turkey.

Ayşen Uysal is a professor at Dokuz Eylül University Department of Public Administration. She completed her undergraduate studies at Ankara University Faculty of Political Science Department of Public Administration and her master's at Paris 1 Panthéon-Sorbonne University. Uysal took her PhD degree in political science from the same university in 2005. She edited the books titled *Historical Sociology: Strategies, Problems and Paradigms* (with Ferdan Ergut, 2007) and *Political Islam and Liberalism* (2009). She published *Professional Politicians: Parties and Social Networks in Turkey* (with Oğuz Topak) in 2010. Uysal is currently conducting the research project titled "Politics in the Streets: Actors, Organizations, Demands and Repertoire of Action in Protest Events" funded by TÜBİTAK. She has published several articles on social movements, police, political activism and political parties in national and international journals and books.

Notes

1. This article is an outcome of the project titled 'Politics on the Street: Actors, Organizations, Issues and Repertoire of Protests' funded by TÜBİTAK (Project No. 112K542). I would like to thank S. Bengi Gümrükçü for her contributions.
2. The doctoral theses of Çetinkaya on the Ottoman boycott (İletişim, 2008), Uysal on protest repertoire and the effect of state violence on the determination of this repertoire and H. Ercan on the Kurdish movement within the framework of the concept of framing are rare examples which have used methodologies from the literature on social movements.
3. Göle completed her doctoral study at Ecole des Hautes Etudes en Sciences Sociales at the beginning of the 1980s before working as an assistant professor at Maison des Sciences de l'Homme, between 1983 and 1985.
4. The development of such movements with relatively fewer risks, such as the women's and environmental movements rather than the leftist movement, which received a heavy blow from the *coup d'état* of 12 September, and the rise of the Kurdish identity movement have created a perception that the hypotheses of NSM theory have been confirmed by Turkish research in the 1980s. This perception and these hypotheses are accepted as proving the validity of this theory without question. The NSM approach offers a simplified (Chabanet 2009: 376) dichotomous distinction between the 'new' and the 'old', which was easily adopted. Even the long-established women's movement, which remains the most studied subject in the context of new social movements, could not make people question the sharp distinction between the new and the old.
5. The third chapter of *The New Transnational Activism*.
6. For example, the editor of Bayat's first book in Turkish, Özgür Gökmen, was Bayat's doctoral student in the Netherlands (Bayat 2006).
7. Thus, it is no coincidence that Tilly's *European Revolutions 1492–1992* was his first book translated into Turkish. The other instances are Skocpol's *States and Social Revolutions: A Comparative Analysis of France, Russia and China*, E. J. Hobsbawm's *The Age of Revolution 1789–1848* and Misagh Parsa's *States, Ideologies and Social Revolutions: A Comparative Analysis of Iran, Nicaragua and the Philippines*.
8. Another study worth considering regarding collective street demonstrations is a book by Demirer called *Tören Simge Siyaset: Türkiye'de Newroz ve Nevruz Şenlikleri* [Cere-

mony Symbol Politics: Newroz and Nevruz Festivities in Turkey], which deals with the Newroz celebrations within the framework of the formation of collective identity. Although the work does not address the issue from the perspective of the social movement literature, it presents important anthropological and sociological field data on the use of forms of protest and the use of symbols, especially in open field protests. The book, which is a work of oral history, is based on the author's PhD dissertation submitted to Ohio State University.

9. On political activism, also see Uysal 2013b: 176–95 and 2013c: 109–128.

10. http://ejts.revues.org/

11. For the risks encountered by one researcher during such a study, see Uysal 2005.

12. Uysal's studies are the first of their kind in this field. For some examples, see Uysal, 2010 and 2006.

13. H. Özen, Ş. Özen, *Örgüt ve Toplumsal Hareket Kuramları Açısından Türkiye'de Altın Madenciliği Alanındaki Çatışmaların İncelenmesi* [*Analyzing Conflicts in the Field of Gold Mining in Turkey in the Framework of Organization and Social Movements Theories*], TÜBİTAK/SOBAG, 109K403, 2011, 136 pages. There is also an ongoing project. See Uysal, *Sokakta Siyaset: Protesto Eylemlerinde Aktörler, Örgütler, Talepler ve Eylem Repertuvarı* [*Politics on the Street: Actors, Organizations, Issues and Repertoire of Protests*], TÜBİTAK/SOBAG, 112K542. Since the resources of universities in Turkey are limited, scholars find funding for their research either from TÜBİTAK or within the framework of European Union Projects. However, the funding provided by TÜBİTAK to the field of social sciences has increased only recently. Meanwhile, several international foundations and associations also provide financial support for certain researchers.

References

Arrighi, G., T. K. Hopkins, and I. Wallerstein. 1991. *Sistem Karşıtı Hareketler* [*Antisystemic Movements*]. Istanbul: Metis.

Arslan, Ş. 2004. *1 Mayıs Mahallesi: 1980 Öncesi Toplumsal Mücadeleler ve Kent* [*1 Mayıs Quarter: Social Struggles and City Before 1980*]. Istanbul: İletişim Yayınları.

Bayat, A. 1998. *Street Politics: Poor People's Movements in Iran.* Egypt: Columbia University Press and the American University in Cairo Press.

———. 2006. *Ortadoğu'da Maduniyet: Toplumsal Hareketler ve Siyaset* [*Subaltern in the Middle East: Politics and Movements*]. Istanbul: İletişim.

Benlisoy, F. 2012. *Fransa ve Yunanistan'dan Arap Devrimi, 'The Occupy' Hareketleri ve Kürt İsyanına: 21. Yüzyılın İlk Devrimci Dalgası* [*From France and Greece to Arab Revolution, 'The Occupy' Movements and Kurdish Rebellion: First Revolutionary Wave of the 21st Century*]. Istanbul: Agora Kitaplığı.

Bilgen-Reinart, Ü. 2003. *Biz Toprağı Bilirik! Bergama Köylüleri Anlatıyor* [*We Know the Land! Peasants from Bergama Telling*]. Istanbul: Metis/Siyahbeyaz.

Bourdieu, P. 2002. 'Les Conditions Sociales de la Circulation Internationale des Idées'. *Actes de la Recherche en Sciences Sociales* 145: 3–8.

Bozarslan, H. 1997. *La Question Kurde: Etats et Minorités au Moyen-Orient.* Paris: Presses de Science Po.

Castells, M. 2013. *İnternet Çağında Toplumsal Hareketler* [*Networks of Outrage and Hope: Social Movements in the Age of Internet*]. Istanbul : Koç Üniversitesi Yayınları.

Chabanet, D. 2009. 'Nouveaux Mouvements Sociaux'. In *Dictionnaire des mouvements sociaux*, ed. O. Fillieule, L. Mathieu and C. Péchu, 371–378. Paris: Presses de Sciences Po.

Çayır, K. 1999. *Yeni Sosyal Hareketler* [*New Social Movements*]. Istanbul: Kaknüs.

Çetinkaya, Y. D. 2004. *1908 Osmanlı Boykotu: Bir toplumsal hareketin analizi* [*1908 Ottoman Boycott: Analysis of a Social Movement*]. Istanbul: Iletişim.

———. 2013. 'Tarih, Siyaset ve 2013 Bahar Ayaklanması' ['History, Politics and the 2013 Spring Uprising']. *Toplumsal Tarih*. 235: 30–37.

Çetinkaya, Y. D., ed. 2008. *Toplumsal Hareketler: Tarih, Teori ve Deneyim* [*Social Movements. History, Theory and Experience*]. Istanbul: Iletişim.

Çınar, H. Ö., and C. Üsterci. 2008. *Çarklardaki Kum: Vicdani Red. Düşünsel Kaynaklar ve Deneyimler* [*Sand in the Wheels: Conscientious Objection—Philosophical Sources and Experiences*]. Istanbul: Iletişim.

Cockburn, A., and J. St.Clair. 2003. *Seattle: Dünyayı Sarsan 5 Gün* [*Seattle: 5 Days That Shook the World*], trans. Y. Başkavak. Istanbul: Agora.

Cogito. 1998. 'Special Issue on May '68': 14.

Cohen, J., and A. Arato. 1992. *Civil Society and Political Theory*. Cambridge: MIT Press.

Dağtaş, E. 2008. *Türkiye'de Sivil İtaatsizlik, Toplumsal Hareketler ve Basın* [*Civil Disobedience, Social Movements and Press in Turkey*]. Ankara: Ütopya.

Demirer, Y. 2012. *Tören Simge Siyaset: Türkiye'de Newroz ve Nevruz Şenlikleri* [*Ceremony Symbol Politics: Newroz and Nevruz Festivities in Turkey*]. Ankara: Dipnot Yayınları.

Dezalay, Y., and B. G. Garth. 2002. *La Mondialisation des Guerres de Palais: La Restructuration du Pouvoir d'Etat en Amérique Latine, Entre Notables du Droit et Chicago Boys*, trans. L. Devillairs and S. Dezalay. Paris: Seuil.

Doğanay, Ü. 2003. *Demokratik Usüller Üzerine Yeniden Düşünmek* (Rethinking Democratic Procedures). Ankara: Imge.

Doğanay, Ü. and E. Köker. 2005. 'Le Cadrage des Protestations dans les Journaux Télévisés'. In *La Turquie Conteste: Mobilisations Sociales et Régime Sécuritaire*, ed. G. Dorronsoro, 51–68. Paris: CNRS éditions.

Dorronsoro, G., 2005. *La Turquie conteste: Mobilisations sociales et régime sécuritaire*. Paris: CNRS Editions.

Fillieule, O., L. Mathieu and C. Péchu, eds. 2009. *Dictionnaire des Mouvements Sociaux*. Paris: Presses de Sciences Po.

Fraser, R. 2008. *1968 İsyancı Bir Öğrenci Kuşağı* [*1968: A Student Generation in Revolt*], trans. K. Emiroğlu. 2nd ed. Istanbul: Belge Yayınları.

Göle, N. 1998. *Mühendisler ve İdeoloji: Öncü Devrimcilerden Yenilikçi Seçkinlere* [*Engineers and Ideology: From Pioneering Revolutionaries to Innovative Elites*]. 2nd ed. Istanbul: Metis.

Grojean, O. 2006. 'Mort Volontaire Combattante: Sacrifices et Stratégies'. *Cultures et Conflits* 63: 101–12.

Günçıkan, B. 1996. *Cumartesi Anneleri* [*Saturday Mothers*]. Istanbul: Iletişim.

Harvey, D. 2012. *Rebel Cities from the Right to the City to the Urban Revolution*. London and New York: Verso.

Işık, O., and M. Pınarcıoğlu. 2001. '1980 Sonrası Dönemde Kent Yoksulları Arasında Güce Dayalı Ağ İlişkileri: Sultanbeyli Örneği' ['The Power-Based Network Relations among the Urban Poor after 1980: The Case of Sultanbeyli']. *Toplum ve Bilim* 89: 31–61.

Jasper, M. J. 1997. *The Art of Moral Protest: Culture, Biography and Creativity in Social Movements.* Chicago: University of Chicago Press.

Karakaş, S. N. 1992. *Eylem Günlüğü: Zonguldak Maden Grevi ve Yürüyüşü Kasım 90– Ocak 91* [*Diary of Protest: Zonguldak Mine Strike and March, November 1990–January 1991*]. Istanbul: Metis/Siyahbeyaz.

Karakaş, Ş. 2005. *Biz bu Savaşı Durdurabiliriz* [*We Can Stop This War*]. Istanbul: Metis.

Köker, E. 2007. *Politikanın İletişimi İletişimin Politikası* [*Communication of Politics, Politics of Communication*]. Ankara: Imge Yayınları.

Kurlansky, M. 2008. *1968: Dünyayı Sarsan Yıl* [*1968: The Year That Rocked the World*], trans. Z. Savan. Istanbul: Everest.

Künar, A. 2002. *Don Kişot'larAkkuyu'ya Karşı: Anti Nükleer Hikayeler* (*Don Quixotes against Akkuyu: Anti-nuclear Stories*). Ankara: TMMOB—Elektrik Mühendisleri Odası Yayını.

Massicard, E. 2005. *L'Autre Turquie, Le mouvement Aléviste et Ses Territoires.* Paris: PUF.

Özbudun, S. 2012. *Latin Amerika'da Yerli Hareketleri* [*Indigenous Movements in Latin America*]. Ankara: Dipnot.

Pérouse, J. F. 2005. 'Les Compétences des Acteurs Dans les Micro-mobilisations Habitantes à Istanbul'. In *La Turquie Conteste: Mobilisations Sociales et Régime Sécuritaire*, ed. G. Dorronsoro, 127–45. Paris: CNRS éditions.

Sanlı, L., ed. 2003. *Toplumsal Hareketler Konuşuyor* [*Social Movements Speaking*]. Istanbul: Alan Yayıncılık.

Scott, J.C. 2008. *La domination et les arts de la résistance: Fragments du discours subalterne.* Paris: Editions Amsterdam.

Tanör, B. 1994. *Türkiye'nin İnsan Hakları Sorunu* [*Turkey's Human Rights Issues*]. 3rd ed. Istanbul: BDS Yayınları.

Temelkuran, E. 1997. *Oğlum Kızım Devletim: Evlerden Sokaklara Tutuklu Anneleri* [*My Son, My Daughter, My State: Mothers of Imprisoned from Houses to Streets*]. Istanbul: Metis/Siyahbeyaz.

Thompson, E. P. 2004. *İngiliz İşçi Sınıfının Oluşumu* [*The Making of the English Working Class*]. Istanbul: Birikim Yayınları.

———. 2006. *Avam ve Görenek* [*Custom in Common Studies in Traditional Popular Culture*]. Istanbul: Birikim Yayıncılık.

Tilly. C. 2008. *Toplumsal Hareketler 1768–2004* [*Social Movements 1768–2004*]. Istanbul: Babil Yayıncılık.

———. 2009. *Kolektif Şiddet Siyaseti* [*The Politics of Collective Violence*]. Istanbul: Phoenix.

Touraine, A. 1965. 'Mobilité Sociale, Rapport de Classes et Nationalisme en Amérique Latine'. *Sociologie du Travail* 1: 71–82.

———. 1978. *La Voix et le Regard.* Paris: Seuil.

———. 1980. 'La Méthode de la Sociologie de l'Action: l'Intervention Sociologique'. *Revue Suisse de Sociologie* 6(3): 321–35.

Uysal, A. 2001. 'Devletin Güvenliği ve Toplumsal Muhalefet Eylemleri: Kalemli Çete Örneği' ['State's Security and Social Opposition Protests: The Case of "Band With Pencils"']. *Birikim* 146: 64–84.

————. 2005. 'Faire de la Politique Dans la Rue: Actions Protestataires et Leurs Gestions Etatiques en Turquie Dans les Années 1990'. PhD dissertation. Paris: Université Paris 1 Panthéon-Sorbonne.

————. 2006. 'Organisation du Maintien de l'Ordre et Répression Policière en Turquie'. In *Police et Manifestants: Maintien de l'Ordre et Gestion des Conflits*, ed. D. Della Porta and O. Fillieule, 257–78. Paris: Presse de Sciences Po.

————. 2010. 'Riot Police, Street Politics and Repression Policies in Turkey'. In *Policing and Prisons in the Middle East: Formations of Coercion*, ed. L. Khalili and J. Schwedler, 191–206. London: Hurst and Company.

————. 2013a. 'Polis halkı isyana teşvik eder mi? Protesto eylemlerinin kaynağı olarak polis şiddeti' ['Do Police Incite Rebellion? Police Violence as a Source of Protest Events']. *Birikim* 291/292: 77–83.

————. 2013b. 'Devlet şiddetinin biyografik sonuçları: 1970'li yılların militanlarının siyasal yol haritaları' ['Biographical Consequences of State Violence: Political Trajectories of Militants of 1970s']. *Toplum ve Bilim* 127: 176–95.

————. 2013c. 'Comme des Pépins de Grenade Dispersés. Répression et Devenir des Militants de Devrimci–Yol en Turquie'. *Politix* 102: 109–128.

Uzun, T. 2001. *Cenova Günlüğü. Küresel Direniş: Antikapitalizm ve Savaş* [*Genoa Diary. Global Resistance: Anti-capitalism and War*]. Istanbul: Stüdyo Imge.

Wedel, H. 2001. *Siyaset ve Cinsiyet: Istanbul Gecekondularında Kadınların Siyasal Katılımı* [*Politics and Gender: Women's Political Participation in Istanbul's Squatter Settlements*], trans. C. Kurultay. Istanbul: Metis.

White, J. B. 2002. *Islamist Mobilization in Turkey: A Study in Vernacular Politics*. Seattle: University of Washington Press.

Yıldırım, Y. 2013. '68'in Üzerine 2000'ler Eklenince' ['2000s Added on the Heritage of '68']. *Birikim* 291/292: 141–45.

Yeğin, M. 2003. *Dünyanın Sokakları-1 Topraksızlar* [*Streets of the World-1, Landlesses*]. Istanbul: Versus.

————. 2006. *Dünyanın Sokakları-2 Patronsuzlar* [*Streets of the World-2, Piqueteros*]. Istanbul: Versus.

Yücel, H., and G. Aksümer. 2012. 'Kentsel Dönüşüme Karşı Kent Hakkı Mücadelesi: Kazım Karabekir Mahallesinde Mekansal ve Kimliksel Dayanışma Örüntüleri' ['Struggle for Right to the City against Urban Renewal: Patterns of Spatial and Identity-Based Solidarity in Kazım Karabekir Neighbourhood']. Retrieved 25 August 2013 from http://www.academia.edu/3219627/Kentsel_Donusume_Karsi_Kent_Hakki_Mucadelesi_Kazim_Karabekir_Mahallesinde_Mekansal_ve_Kimliksel_Dayanima_Oruntuleri.

Chapter 23

From Democratization to Internationalization

Studying Social Movements in Hungary

Aron Buzogány

Social movement research has always been on the backburner, so to speak, in Hungarian social science. Consequently, when one brings up the discipline in conversation, the first reaction is often that there is no such thing in Hungary. Some add that this is of little wonder in the absence of subjects to study. Indeed, for much of the 1990s and partly the 2000s, *társadalmi mozgalmak*—the Hungarian technical term for social movements, which strictly is translated as *societal* movements—have been, at first sight at least, hibernating, and so has social movement research.

However, a closer look provides for a more realistic perspective. The pessimist undertone usually stems from the implicit or explicit comparison with Western European societies and academic cultures. Together with other Central and Eastern European states, Hungary has undergone deep and overlapping political, economic and societal transformations during the last three decades. This triple transformation has left its imprints also on social science research, both regarding research interests and institutional background. Therefore, understanding social movements and social movement research in Hungary—or the lack of it—has to be seen in the unique transitional historical context of Central and Eastern Europe (CEE). This context is quite different to the situation of the initial setting faced by US and Western European movements, which triggered increased interest in studying social movements from the 1960s onwards. Parallels between CEE and Western social movements—women's activism, peace movements, environmentalism, later urban movements—are often more than obvious, even if they occurred with a significant time lag. However, being determined by different structural conditions, these movements might in fact have different goals and strategies as one would assume at first sight.

At the same time, Hungarian social movement research has also faced the well-known dilemma of this research tradition worldwide: that of being caught between the proverbial two stools of research oriented towards social structure and research interested in (institutionalised) political processes and dynamics (Szabó 2001). Seizing a middle ground by focusing on non-institutionalised actors operating in a loosely consolidated political environment was a promising perspective only during the early nineties. The subsequent consolidation of the political system has meant that non-institutionalised political activism has become politically channelled—or has become part of the third sector.

Adding to the amorphous characteristics of social movements, the academic disinterest in social movements was partly institutionally predetermined. The core disciplines where social movement research has found an academic shelter, political science and sociology, were undergoing sequences of hectic re-organization during the last two decades. After an initial upsurge in interest regarding societal mobilization in the founding years of both disciplines during the late 1980s and early 1990s, they have followed the development of Hungarian politics and societal life, which consolidated during the mid-nineties around a stable party system and was mainly concerned with the hiccups from a state-led economy towards market transition, including the rise in economic inequalities this has implied. Rather consequently, Hungarian political science developed a strong track record in party politics. Sociologists, at their turn, have mainly focused on survey-based research relating to questions of social transition and could also build on a strong tradition of elite research which predated the transition period (Konrád and Szelényi 1979). As a result, social movement research did not become a mainstream field of study in Hungary, but kept a quasi-underground existence at several elite research centres in Budapest, such as the Institute of Political Science of the Eötvös Lóránd (now Corvinus) University, the Central European University and the Institute for Political Science of the Hungarian Academy of Sciences. Academic journals which publish social movement–related research are the flagships of the Hungarian Political Science Association (*Politikatudományi Szemle*) and of the Hungarian Sociological Association (*Szociológiai Szemle*). More recently, a new graduate student journal, *Fordulat,* and a practitioner-oriented journal focusing on third-sector research, *Civil Szemle,* have been founded, and both show interest in these topics. To be sure, in all of these media outlets, studies relating to social movements are rather marginal.

By presenting an overview of the social movement research tradition in Hungary, this chapter provides a contextualization of the Hungarian social movement research, which is not only insular because of the limited reach of the Hungarian language but also because of its downright inward-looking tendency. The chapter will show that while rather peripheral in mainstream social science, this research is in fact richer than one might assume at first sight—even if it is often hidden behind main paradigms of established social movement research.

The chapter has the following structure. The next section will help to locate important historical traditions of Hungarian social movement research stemming from the transition period (late 1980s to early 1990s). The following sections follow more or less chronologically the main discussions related to social movement research in Hungary and give an overview of the consolidation period (1990s), as well as a time frame marked by external influences, partly related to Europeanization (2000s). Latest developments, summarised in the last chapter, include research on protest and participation in the emerging alternative scene and on the radical right wing. I will conclude by summarizing the contributions of Hungarian social movement's research in a wider perspective and suggest potential pathways it could follow.

Traditions of Transition: Civil Society and Democratization

Compared with many other countries of the Central and Eastern European region, from the 1960s until the collapse of the communist regime, state socialist Hungary was often characterised as the 'happiest barrack' in the Soviet camp. While still Marxist on the surface, the regime of János Kádár had slowly deviated from Stalinist principles and began experimenting with market reforms. Culture and research gradually became more open to contacts and influences from the West.

As a state socialist political system that at least theoretically drove its legitimacy from the workers' movement, historical research on Hungary's progressive and emancipative movements has been rather well established. But most of this research, for example that carried out at the Institute of Party History (*Párttörténeti Intézet*), has been dominated by ideological perspectives and prevented critical analysis (Szabó 2001). During the late seventies, Western social movement research arrived in Hungary and became translated and published in academic journals such as *Medvetánc* or *Ifjúsági Szemle*. As this scholarship mainly concerned the societal problems of Western capitalist societies, its reception was not problematic *per se* from the perspective of the ruling party. At the same time, by analysing examples of the civil rights movement in the United States or the rise of the ecological movement in Germany, a younger generation of researchers became influenced by this research tradition.

Much of the Hungarian underground opposition, which was formed by several Budapest-based intelligentsia subcultures in the early 1980s, had a background in humanities or social sciences and was directly or indirectly affected by societal developments in Western Europe. The imminent crisis of state socialism, which was unable to deliver its own formulated goals, had become more than obvious. During these years, Konrád and Szelényi's sociological study, *The Intellectuals on the Road to Class Power* (1979), showed the class bias of the socialist state and broached the issue of poverty in a theoretically classless society. Its two authors were forced into exile or quasi-exile. Alongside Adam Michnik from Poland and Václav Havel from Czechoslovakia, György Konrád became of one of the well-regarded dissident intellectuals from Eastern Europe during the late 1980s. His essayistic publications centred on utopian ideals of democracy and the role of civil society therein, which he regarded as being largely non-political (Konrad 1989). At the same time, this political philosophy was built on the idea of 'anti-politics' that defined civil society in terms of resistance against an oppressive state. The 'ideology of civil society' became an instrument of dissidents in the 1980s, propagating an alternative both to state socialism and Western capitalism. This tradition of opposition between the (oppressive) state and civil society remained as one of the major heritages of Hungarian civic activism also in the years of democratic consolidation.

During the early 1980s, a thriving underground opposition scene was active in Budapest (Szabó 2010). As highlighted by Falk's *The Dilemmas of Dissidence in East-Central Europe: Citizen Intellectuals and Philosopher Kings,* the intellectual debates taking place during this period also had important implications in shaping the future of Hungarian political development after the fall of communism (Falk 2003). One of the most important groups of the democratic opposition was the samizdat movement of the liberal intelligentsia that published the underground journal *Beszélő*. This samizdat journal brought together intellectuals of different political leanings, many of them still regarding themselves leftists, while others were in the process of re-defining themselves as liberals. The Beszélő Circle's activities continuously tested the limits of state oppression not only by publishing a journal without the consent and censorship of the ruling party but also by engaging in several initiatives that directly or indirectly called for more democracy (Szabó 2004b; Bozóki 2007; Szabó 2008).

However, 'more democracy' was only to be achieved indirectly. A pattern for mobilization by the Hungarian underground opposition was the involvement in activities which did not directly concur with the ruling party's line, but at the same time would highlight the limited reach of the system. Thus, in the early 1980s, the Dialógus group tried to establish an 'independent' peace movement in Hungary and organised unofficial peace demonstrations, which also echoed Western European developments and resulted in contacts with Western European activists (Haraszti 1982).

The largest blow to the Kádár regime was, however, the rise of environmental concerns and its associated mass mobilization. Effectively using the space provided for political mobilization by the legalization of associations and the rise of public concern about environmental damages, environmental groups became the main drivers of democratic transition in Hungary. The roots of these new groups were traditional conservation organizations, as well as church and university groups. Due to the restrictive nature of the one-party state, these groups were often forced to coexist with official state structures. These included the Hungarian Environmental Association which was set up by the National Patriotic Front, the quasi-civil societal arm of the ruling party. Other organizations developed within the structures of the Communist Youth League and its environmental organization, the Youth Environmental Council. But by the mid-eighties the ruling party was no longer able to control environmental groups. Mass demonstrations, triggered by plans for the Gabcikovo-Nagymaros Dam on the Danube by the Czechoslovak and Hungarian governments, became crystallizing points for the various opposition groups, with aims not restricted to environmental issues (Enyedi and Szirmai 1998; Pickvance 1998). In fact, environmental protection was the only area where initiatives from below did not automatically face immediate coercive reaction by the state (Gille 2002). While state administration initially regarded environmental protest partially even as a driver towards professional economic management and scientific progress, environmentalism soon became a 'Trojan horse' (cf. Gille 2002), not only for green activists and opposition groups but also for reformers within the state administration demanding market liberalism and democracy. Fighting simultaneously for environmental goals *and* human rights and democratic institutions (Hajba 1994), the 'Danube Circle', the organization representing the protestors, received both strong grassroots support and external help. Especially after the Circle received the Right Livelihood Award in 1985, Hungarian party leadership, which was increasingly reliant on Western loans, could not afford negative media effects derived from clamping down on green groups (Szirmai 1993; Vári and Tamás 1993; Enyedi and Szirmai 1998; Pickvance 1998; Szirmai 1999; Gille 2002).

Research on political mobilization during the late 1980s can be considered as the defining moment of modern Hungarian social movement research. Some studies, most eminently those of Máté Szabó, whose research on social movements and political protest spanning over three decades is the most relevant for the field analysed herein, investigate these developments by explicitly referring to mainstream theories of social movements, most often using the 'political process' perspective (Szabó 1994, 1996, 1998, 2001). Building on intimate knowledge mainly of West German social movement research, his research draws parallels between Hungarian developments and those occurring in other parts of Europe. However, this perspective has often overlapped with a parallel research agenda that is mostly unknown for Western European researchers on social movements: research on democratization and consolidation of formerly authoritarian states, termed 'transitology' (Schmitter 1995). Thus, while making references to social movement research, predominantly used to uncover the dynamics of mobilization, research on Hungarian social movement activism is more interested in systemic development from a semi-closed system towards a democracy and the roles 'movements' can play in this process. According to Szabó (1994), the societal sector carries distinct roles during the different phases of transition. During the crisis of the old regime, societal movements were the only available area where societal demands could be voiced. During the period of the regime change, their role was to mobilise mass support for agents of change or to influence modes or pace of managing systemic change. After the change of regime, the formerly oppositional social movements underwent institutionalization and differentiation.

Resulting from the focus on democratization and democratic consolidation, the dominant discourse on societal mobilization in Hungary was mainly framed as referring to 'civil society'. The theoretical underpinnings of this perspective were based on the aforementioned writings of dissident intelligentsia. In this context, *Civil Society and Political Theory* by Hungarian-born US political theorist Andrew Arato has offered an important theoretical interpretation of the re-emergence of Eastern European civil society from its ashes (Cohen and Arato 1992). Suspicion of close involvement of non-state actors in policy processes remained prevalent in the years of transformation, making the participation of non-state organizations in policy-making a critical issue.

Demobilization, Protest and Third-Sector Development

Compared to the expectations of the founding years, the following years of democratization cum economic hardship, the development of new cleavages and inequalities, and the shocks of transition to market capitalism have led to a rapid decline in political participation. While social mobilization played an important role in 'kick-starting' regime change, political change took place as an informal 'pact' decided at the roundtable talks between the old elites and the new opposition (Bozóki 1993). This already heralded the dawn of societal mobilization. After the regime change, the importance of mass mobilization declined rapidly and the establishment of new parties led to fragmentation of former movement activists when its members joined political parties on different sides of the political spectrum.

Two areas of research have been particularly prominent on social movement–related research on Hungary in the 1990s: the development of protest activities and the institutionalization of organised civil society as 'third sector'. During the early nineties many observers highlighted the inherent conflicts resulting from the 'double transition' towards capitalism and democracy (Offe 1991). Based on examples of Latin American transitions with extensive social mobilization, the main expectation was that of disruptive protests leading to destabilization of newly emerging democratic orders. For the newly established Hungarian democracy, the first shock came six months after the first democratic elections in October 1990. The 'taxi blockade', triggered by drastic increase of petrol prices, which found wide support within parts of the population and opposition parties was a central event for the emerging Hungarian democracy. The violent government response led to rapid disillusionment with democratically elected government and became a rare case where social scientists publicly debated theoretical concepts with immediate concern for political reality (Bozóki and Kovács 1991; Szabó 1993).

Following the taxi drivers' blockade, research interests on protest policing increased (Szabó 1999) and protest event analysis was employed to analyse dynamics of civic and social unrest. In this context, a Hungarian case study was part of large collaborative project focusing on protest mobilization in several Central and Eastern European countries, which was partly framed in terms of social movement research and employed protest event behaviour based on coding of newspaper articles (Szabó 1996; Ekiert and Kubik 1998; Kubik 1998). The main findings of the project were that high levels of protest do not automatically threaten democratic consolidation, but can in some cases even contribute to the robustness of a new democracy.

At the same time, researchers using more inter-regional comparative perspectives started questioning the pessimistic augury of the early 1990s regarding the upsurge of protest in Central and Eastern Europe, highlighting that in comparison to Latin America, most of the Central and Eastern European countries in fact experienced low levels of public protest that was unexpected taking into account the severe socioeconomic transition crises that the majority of the countries of the region went through after 1989. Greskovits' (1998) landmark study '*The Political Economy of Protest and Patience: East European and Latin American Transformations Compared*' pointed to the interplay of several structural, institutional and cultural factors preventing destabilizing collective actions in both regions (Greskovits 1998).

While potential protestors became pacified during the late 1990s, civil society organizations have increasingly become institutionalised and professionalised. Often, they became partners of the state in fulfilling social services. Research on institutionalised civil society organizations (*civil társadalom*) is among the best established fields in practically oriented Hungarian social science and mainly covers issues related to participation, volunteering and third-sector research, termed in Hungarian 'non-profit' (Kuti 1990). In statistical terms, the number of voluntary organizations exploded after the change of regime (Bocz 2009). This was also accompanied by a growing professionalization of non-profit organizations, which was partly triggered by legislation incentivizing donations to civil society organizations (Kuti 2010). Particularly in areas related to social services, outsourcing public competencies to (often publicly owned) non-profit organizations has become a development which is in line with reducing the size of the state.

At the same time, normative analyses highlight the exceptionally low political participation levels of Hungarian citizens and decry the perpetuation of the very meaning of 'civil society' as well as the loss of the 'democratic fever' of the early 1990s (Lomax 1997; Miszlivetz 1997; Osborne and Kaposvari 1997). Touching upon the crucial question of collaboration between state and societal actors, the much-discussed dilemma perturbed by the state-critical tradition of Eastern European civil society remains whether association with state actors undermines non-state organization's autonomy (Kuti 1990; Benedek and Scsaurszki 2008; Szabó 2009). Recent research on Hungary about collaboration and external ties among Hungarian non-state actors (though not strictly non-profit ones) suggests that such associations with state actors do not necessarily undermine the capacity and legitimacy of these organizations, but can even strengthen them under certain conditions (Stark et al. 2006; Bruszt and Vedres 2008; Bruszt and Vedres 2013).

Domestic Developments and External Effects

Domestic state-society relations have undergone significant changes also due to the external influences. Much of the opposition movements in the late 1980s received funding from external donors, including Western state agencies, philanthropists or (German) party foundations. External influence on domestic developments has become particularly obvious when Hungary started to prepare for membership in the European Union in the late 1990s (Szabó 2004a). Triggered by the 'Europeanization' of its public policies (Börzel and Risse 2003), Hungary has undergone deep changes also affecting its state-society relations.

Analysis of the domestic impact of the EU across different policy fields has been brought together with a theoretical synthesis focusing on political opportunity structures, resources and framing in social movement research (Buzogány 2011a). Of course, external influences are to be interpreted in combination with domestic developments which are shaped by national, sometimes local circumstances. In the case of the Hungarian environmental movement, which has already been mentioned to be a frequently analysed case because of its pre-transition prominence, anthropological research on movement activism has shown how framings of conflicts have become more transnational (Harper 2006). This has been the case in the most prominent environmental conflict Hungary witnessed during the last decade. During the country's accession to the EU, local protest broke out around the deployment of a NATO radar locator on Zengő Hill which was located in a natural reserve in southern Hungary (Vay 2005). As the reserve was under EU conservation law, this allowed the activists to link their protest to EU norms (Börzel and Buzogány 2010). As frame-analyses of the conflict show, what initially seemed to be a local conflict largely bypassed its original scope and became one of the rare cases where the otherwise highly polarised political elites joined forces (Kerényi and Szabó 2006).

In addition, other research has shown that Europeanization connected Hungarian civil society organizations with existing sectoral policy networks on the EU level and made the government more accountable by upgrading participatory rights in national legislation and introducing issues into the public sphere which had not received attention before. Connections with influential advocacy coalitions provided societal actors with the opportunity to complain in Brussels and put pressure on their government both via European institutions as well as through mobilizing international public opinion. This window of opportunity has become particularly valuable for activists facing closed domestic opportunity structures and/or having weak resources, such as Roma rights or LGBT activists (Buzogány 2011b; Holzhacker 2011). Paralleling the strategic litigation culture used by the US civil rights movement in the seventies, the Budapest-based European Roma Rights Centre (ERRC) has used the EU's Race Equality Directive, as well as several directives related to EU anti-discrimination law, as its main tool to achieve progress in the field of Roma Rights. For several Roma groups, such as the Romani Civil Rights Foundation and the Legal Defence Bureau for National and Ethnic Minorities which were already using legal action before accession as a tool for enforcing Roma Rights (albeit with limited success), the new legislation increased the possibility of strategic litigations on Roma-related issues (Buzogány 2011b). Similarly, others have argued that gender equality activism has also profited from EU accession (Fábián 2009; Krizsan 2009; Fábián 2010b); however, this effect was restricted while conservative governments strongly opposed EU agendas (Sedelmeier 2009).

New Developments and Future Directions

More recently, Hungarian social movement research is witnessing a renaissance both in terms of increasing interests in theoretical framework of social movement studies and the new issue areas researchers are focusing on. The first development is partly a result of a generational change among researchers working on social movements, which are less influenced by the normative 'backpack' of old debates on civil society or democratization. This younger generation with freshly minted PhDs and considerable international networking capacity has been typically raised with the reality—and the inherent contradictions—of political activism in a democratic state. At the same time, most of the active younger researchers are also (or used to be) activists, many of them being socialised in the alter-globalization movement or different urban politics movements. During the late 2000s, the popularity of the alter-globalization movement increased in Hungary and a new generation of organizations, such as the emblematic Protect the Future (Védegylet), were founded, which combined an intellectual alter-globalization discourse with new style of conflictive environmentalism, that contrasted with the collaborative strategies of mainstream environmental groups. In contrast to the old debates which centred on politically polarised, and ultimately historical, questions stemming from the heritage of regime change, this generation of activists could formulate new debates that went beyond old schisms (Fábián 2010a). The political wing of Protect the Future, the new party called 'Politics Can be Different' (Lehet Más a Politika) was successful in the 2010 elections and became the first green party elected to the Hungarian Parliament.

Much of the newer literature on social movements in Hungary developed as a reflection of everyday activism and theoretical questions related to globalization. This new research seems to be less normative and less institution-focused: it is more political anthropology than political science or political sociology. Methodologically it tends to be located predominantly in the interpretative tradition. Its main research interests include, on the one hand, theoretical and empirical perspectives on the global and Hungarian Alterglob movement (Mikecz 2008; Scheiring 2008; Mikecz 2010; Gagyi 2012; Gagyi 2013). One the other hand, urban politics—questions of the appropriation of the city, for example by the Critical Mass urban bicycle movement or by inner-city squatters—has emerged as a new lens beyond those focusing on political influence and political mobilization (Udvarhelyi 2009; Kerényi 2011).

Most recently, two developments have raised increased attentions. The emergence of the radical right-wing party Jobbik in the parliamentary elections has also been examined by using social movements–related analytical frameworks by authors arguing that the key to understanding the party's sudden success is the subcultural embedding in various networks of the Hungarian right wing, which was facilitated, among other factors, also by the new opportunity structures offered by new media and social networks (Buzogány 2011c, Bakó et al. 2012). Thus, in contrast to the normatively supercharged term 'civil society', these analyses tend to point to the existence of a 'dark side' of political participation on the radical right side.

The same 2010 parliamentary elections that brought the radical right-wing party Jobbik into parliament were also marked by the land-slide electoral victory of the former alternative movement now turned conservative catch-all party FIDESZ. Under of the leadership of Prime Minister Viktor Orbán, FIDESZ, because of the large majority it controls in the parliament, was able to introduce a new constitution, change the electoral law and re-regulate media oversight. Mobilization against such changes has led to the emergence of 'new style' mass mobilization against FIDESZ projects, for example through Milla—One Million for the Freedom of Press in Hungary, a Facebook group that was founded as a spontaneous result of protest against the government's new media law.

Summarizing the state of the art of Hungarian social movement research, this chapter has presented some of the main developments of this research field in Hungary. The emergence of social movement–related research has largely overlapped with Hungary's transition towards democracy, a process that started in the mid-1980s and witnessed different cycles of mobilization. The consolidation of institutional frameworks and demobilization of movements was characteristic for the second part of the 1990s and much of the 2010s, which were additionally marked by external influences, mainly through the EU membership candidacy and, from 2004 onwards, EU membership of the country. The period after 2006 was discernible by increasing political tensions and the collapse of the dominant party system in the 2010 parliamentary elections, which enabled new movements, alternative and radical right-wing ones at the same time, the opportunity to become involved in mainstream politics.

Regarding the state of social movement research in Hungary, this chapter has highlighted that this tradition falls in the minority within Hungarian social science, which is followed by not more than a dozen researchers at a few research centres. Most of the work carried out is oriented towards US and German traditions in social movement research. Addressing theoretical debates beyond Hungary is highly exceptional, but Hungarian case studies have contributed to understanding regional developments when presented in a comparative perspective. While examining questions relevant to social movement research as such, most of these publications mainly address meta-debates on issues like democratization, regional development or European-ization, which are strictly seen beyond the immediate scope of movement research.

Such a cross-fertilization of movement research with other research frame-works also seems to be a promising pathway for the future. One would wish for a better future of Hungarian social movement research; that it should become more explicitly interested in comparative and methodological issues and leave behind its rather inward-looking tradition. Certainly, this is dif-ficult to manage without institutional stability and adequate graduate edu-cation in the relevant fields of expertise, such as political science, sociology and, more recently, anthropology. At least one aspect seems to be sure: it is not the lack of relevant topics ripe for analysis in current Hungary that will prevent Hungarian researchers from presenting innovative work.

Aron Buzogány is a lecturer at the Otto Suhr Institute of Political Science at Freie Universität Berlin. His doctoral dissertation comes from the same university and examined, *inter alia*, the impact of Europeanization on social movements in Eastern Europe. Before returning to Berlin, he held academic positions at Yale University, the German Public Administration Institute and the University of Munich. His publications appeared in *Environmental Poli-tics, Acta Politica, Europe-Asia Studies, Journal of Common Market Studies* and other journals.

References

Bakó, J., Z. Tóth and J. Jeskó. 2012. 'A radikális jobboldal webes hálózatai (Jobbik: Egy network-párt természetrajza)'. *Politikatudományi Szemle* 21(1): 81–101.

Benedek, G., and T. Scsaurszki. 2008. *Mi és ők? A civil szervezetek és az állam kapcsolata Magyarországon.* Budapest: Nonprofit Kutatócsoport Egyesület.

Bocz, J. 2009. *A nonprofit szektor strukturális átalakulása Magyarországon: A magyar non-profit szektor az 1990-es évek elejétől a 2000-es évek közepéig.* Budapest: Corvinus Egyetem.

Börzel, T., and A. Buzogány. 2010. 'Environmental Organisations and the European-isation of Public Policy in Central and Eastern Europe: The Case of Biodiversity Governance'. *Environmental Politics* 19, no. 5: 708–35.

Börzel, T. A., and T. Risse. 2003. 'Conceptualising the Domestic Impact of Europe'. In *The Politics of Europeanisation*, ed. K. Featherstone and C. Radaelli, 55–78. Oxford: Oxford University Press.

Bozóki, A., 1993. 'Hungary's Road to Systemic Change: The Opposition Roundtable'. *East European Politics and Societies* 7, no. 2: 276–308.

———. 2007. 'Die Politik der Opposition im Ungarn der 1980er Jahre'. In *Weltregionen im Wandel: Mittel- und Osteuropa*, ed. A. Buzogány and R. Frankenberger, 261–75. Baden-Baden: NOMOS.

Bozóki, A., and É. Kovács. 1991. 'Politikai pártok megnyilvánulásai a sajtóban a taxis-blokád idején'. *Szociologiai Szemle* 1: 109–26.

Bruszt, L., and B. Vedres. 2008. 'The Politics of Civic Combinations'. *Voluntas: International Journal of Voluntary and Nonprofit Organizations* 19, no. 2: 140–60.

———. 2013. 'Associating, Mobilizing, Politicizing: Local Developmental Agency from Without'. *Theory and Society* 42, no. 1: 1–23.

Buzogány, A. 2011a. 'Stairway to Heaven or Highway to Hell? Ambivalent Europeanization and Civil Society in Central and Eastern Europe'. In *Protest beyond borders*, ed. H. Kouki, H. and E. Romanos, 69–85, New York: Berghahn Books.

———. 2011b. 'Swimming Against the Tide: Contested Norms and Anti-discrimination Advocacy in Central and Eastern Europe'. In *The Europeanisation of Gender Equality Policies: A Discursive-Sociological Approach*, ed. E. Lombardo and M. Forest. Basingstoke: Palgrave.

———. 2011c. 'Soziale Bewegung von rechts: Der Aufstieg der national-radikalen Jobbik-Partei in Ungarn'. *Südosteuropa Mitteilungen* 5–6: 38–51.

Cohen, J. L., and A. Arato. 1992. *Civil Society and Political Theory.* Cambridge and London: MIT Press.

Ekiert, G. and J. Kubik. 1998. 'Contentious Politics in New Democracies'. *World Politics* 50, no. 4: 547–81.

Enyedi, D., and V. Szirmai, 1998. 'Environmental Movements and Civil Society in Hungary'. In *Environment and Society in Eastern Europe*, ed. A. Tickle and I. Welsh. Harlow: Longman, 146–55.

Fábián, K. 2009. *Contemporary Women's Movements in Hungary: Globalization, Democracy, and Gender Equality.* Washington: Woodrow Wilson Center Press.

———. 2010a. 'Can Politics Be Different? The Hungarian Green Party's Entry into Parliament in 2010'. *Environmental Politics* 19, no. 6: 1006–11.

———. 2010b. 'Mores and Gains: The EU's Influence on Domestic Violence Policies among Its New Post-communist Member States'. *Women's Studies International Forum* 33, no. 1: 54–67.

Falk, B. J. 2003. *The Dilemmas of Dissidence in East-Central Europe: Citizen Intellectuals and Philosopher Kings.* Budapest and New York: Central European University Press.

Gagyi, A. 2012. 'Occupy Wall Street? Position-Blindness in the New Leftist Revolution'. *Journal of Critical Globalization Studies* 5: 143–48.

———. 2013. 'Hungarian and Romanian Experiences'. In *Understanding European Movements: New Social Movements, Global Justice Struggles, Anti-austerity Protest*, ed. C. Flesher Fominaya and L. Cox, 143–59. London and New York: Routledge.

Gille, Z. 2002. 'Social and Spatial Inequalities in Hungarian Environmental Politics: A Historical Perspective'. In *Livable Cities? Urban Struggles for Livelihood and Sustainability*, ed. P. B. Evans, 132–62. Los Angeles: University of California Press.

Greskovits, B. 1998. *The Political Economy of Protest and Patience: East European and Latin American Transformations Compared*. New York: Central European University Press.

Hajba, E. 1994. 'The Rise and Fall of the Hungarian Greens'. *The Journal of Communist Studies and Transitional Politics 2* (3): 180–91.

Haraszti, M. 1984. 'Dialógus. Kétéves a független békemozgalom'. *Beszélő* 9.

Harper, K. 2006. *Wild Capitalism: Environmental Activists and Post-socialist Political Ecology in Hungary*. New York: Columbia University Press.

Holzhacker, R. 2011. 'National and Transnational Strategies of LGBT Civil Society Organizations in Different Political Environments: Modes of Interaction in Western and Eastern Europe for Equality'. *Comparative European Politics* 10, no. 1: 23–47.

Kerényi, S. 2011. 'Using Pollution to Frame Collective Action: Urban Grassroots Mobilisations in Budapest'. In *Urban Pollution: Cultural Meanings, Social Practices*, ed. E. Dürr and R. Jaffe, 144–62. Oxford and New York: Berghahn Books.

Kerényi, S., and M. Szabó. 2006. 'Transnational Influences on Patterns of Mobilisation within Environmental Movements in Hungary'. *Environmental Politics* 15, no. 5: 803–20.

Konrád, G. 1989. *Antipolitika: az autonomia kisertese [Antipolitics: The Temptation of Autonomy]*. Budapest: Codex RT.

Konrád, G., and I. Szelényi. 1979. *The Intellectuals on the Road to Class Power*. New York: Harcourt Brace Jovanovich.

Krizsán, A. 2009. 'From Formal Adoption to Enforcement: Post-accession Shifts in EU Impact on Hungary in the Equality Policy Field'. *European Integration online Papers (EIoP)* 13, no. 2.

Kubik, J. 1998. 'Institutionalization of Protest during Democratic Consolidation in Central Europe'. In *The Social Movement Society: Contentious Politics for a New Century*, ed. S. Tarrow, 131–52. Maryland and Oxford: Rowman and Littlefield.

Kuti, E. 1990. 'The Possible Role of the Non-profit Sector in Hungary'. *Voluntas: International Journal of Voluntary and Nonprofit Organizations* 1, no. 1: 26–39.

———. 2010. 'Policy Initiatives towards the Third Sector under the Conditions of Ambiguity: The Case of Hungary'. In *Policy Initiatives towards the Third Sector in International Perspective*, ed. B. Gidron and M. Bar, 127–58. Berlin: Springer.

Lomax, B. 1997. 'The Strange Death of Civil Society in Post-communist Hungary'. *The Journal of Communist Studies and Transition Politics* 13, no. 1: 41–63.

Mikecz, D. 2008. 'A dinnye a héjától: A bal-jobb vita a magyar alternatív mozgalmon belül'. *Politikatudományi Szemle* 16 (2): 71.

———. 2010. 'Az ellenállás kultúrája: kultúra, identitás a mozgalomkutatás irodalmában'. *Politikatudományi Szemle* 18 (2): 110–26.

Miszlivetz, F. 1997. 'Participation and Transition: Can the Civil Society Project Survive in Hungary?' *The Journal of Communist Studies and Transition Politics* 13, no. 1: 27–40.

Offe, C. 1991. 'Das Dilemma der Gleichzeitigkeit: Demokratisierung und Marktwirtschaft in Osteuropa'. *Merkur* 45, no. 4: 279–92.

Osborne, S. P., and A. Kaposvari. 1997. 'Towards a Civil Society? Exploring Its Meanings in the Context of Post-communist Hungary'. *Journal of European Social Policy* 7, no. 3: 209.

Pickvance, K. 1998. *Democracy and Environmental Movements in Eastern Europe: A Comparative Study of Hungary and Russia*. Boulder: Westview Press.

Scheiring, G. 2008. 'Seattle nyomában: A globalizációkritikai mozgalom mint a globális kormányzás új tényezője'. *Politikatudományi Szemle* 16 (3): 87–107.

Schmitter, P. 1995. 'Transitology: The Science or the Art of Democratization?'. In *The Consolidation of Democracy in Latin America*, ed. J. Tulchin, 11–41. Boulder: Lynne Rienner.

Sedelmeier, U. 2009. 'Post-accession Compliance with EU Gender Equality Legislation in Post-communist New Member States'. *European Integration online Papers (EIoP)* 13 (2), Art. 23, http://eiop.or.at/eiop/texte/2009-023a.htm

Stark, D., L. Bruszt and B. Vedres. 2006. 'Rooted Transnational Publics: Integrating Foreign Ties and Civic Activism'. *Theory and Society* 35, no. 3: 323–49.

Szabó, M. 1993. 'A taxisblokád és utóélete: Kihívás a társadalomtudományok számára'. *Szociológiai Szemle* 1, no. 3: 121–40.

———. 1994. 'A társadalmi mozgalmak szerepe a demokratikus politikai rendszer intézményesedésének folyamatában Magyarországon'. *Szociológiai Szemle* 3: 45–63.

———. 1996. 'Repertoires of Contention in Post-communist Protest Cultures: An East Central European Comparative Survey'. *Social Research* 63, no. 4: 1155–82.

———. 1998. *Társadalmi mozgalmak és politikai tiltakozás*. Budapest: Villányi úti Konferenciaközpont.

———. 1999. 'From a Police State to a Demonstration Democracy: Policing Mass Demonstrations in Hungary before, during and after the Regime Change'. In *Success or Failure: Ten Years After*, ed. V. Dvoráková,35-59, Praha: Friedrich-Ebert-Stiftung.

———. 2001. *Társadalmi mozgalmak és politikai tiltakozás: történeti-összehasonlító perspektívában*. Budapest: Rejtjel.

———. 2004a. 'Globalizáció, europaizálódás, civil társadalom Magyarországon'. *Politikatudományi Szemle* 14 (1–2): 159–80.

———. 2004b. 'Intelligence against Dissidents: The Kadar-Regime, Control of Dissenting Intellectuals, and the Emerging Civil Society in Hungary after 1956'. *Journal of Intelligence History* 4, no. 1: 75–105.

———. 2008. 'A szocializmus kritikája a magyar ellenzék irányzatainak gondolkodásában (1968–1988)'. *Politikatudományi Szemle* 18 (1): 7–36.

———. 2009. 'Autonómia és etatizmus a magyar civil társadalomban'. *Politikatudományi Szemle* 19 (3): 157–163.

———. 2010. 'Revisionismus, Liberalismus und Populismus: Die Opposition in Ungarn'. In *Akteure oder Profiteure? Die demokratische Opposition in den ostmitteleuropäischen Regimeumbrüchen*, ed. D. Pollack and J. Wielgohs, 63–81. Wiesbaden: VS Verlag für Sozialwissenschaften.

Szirmai, V. 1993. 'The Structural Mechanisms of the Organization of Ecological-Social Movements in Hungary'. In *Environment and Democratic Transition: Policy and Politics in Central and Eastern Europe*, ed. A. Vari and P. Tamas, 146–56. Berlin: Springer.

———. 1999. *A környezeti érdekek Magyarországon*. Budapest: Pallas Stúdió.

Udvarhelyi, É. T. 2009. 'Reclaiming the Streets—Redefining Democracy: The Politics of the Critical Mass Bicycle Movement in Budapest'. *Hungarian Studies* 23, no. 1: 121–45.

Vári, A., and P. Tamás. 1993. *Environment and Democratic Transition: Policy and Politics in Central and Eastern Europe.* Berlin: Springer.

Vay, M., ed. 2005. *Zengő: Ökológia, politika és társadalmi mozgalmak a Zengő-konfliktus-ban* [*Zengő: Ecology, politics and social movements in the Zengő-conflict*]. Budapest: Védegylet.

Chapter 24

Social Movements in Pre- and Post-December 1989 Romania

Laura Nistor

Scholarly literature concerning social movements in Romania seems to be uneven and divided. Therefore, it is difficult to talk about a certain school of research regarding Romanian social movements. This is due to the fact that a solid tradition neither exists in research of collective behaviour (social action, social movement) nor in the social psychology of this behaviour. This is partly because the communist regime did not allow the development of a clear research area specializing in social movements and also due to the fact that following the regime change, apart from some major movements immediately after December 1989, the Romanian society was characterised by civic apathy rather than activism, a circumstance which lead to a relatively small number of studies concerned with Romanian social movements or dissent. In general, we can claim that the studies approaching protest and civic movements in Romania usually do by two categories. The first, preponderantly historical and political in outlook, concentrates on the investigation of such phenomena as the social movements under communism, the revolution of December 1989 and the various forms of social mobilization during the incipient phases of transition. But these studies rarely connect with theories about Western social movements. A possible explanation of this phenomenon consists of the multiple discrepancies in terms of the academic and practical knowledge among the Western and Romanian intelligentsia, meaning that especially during the socialist regime, the country experienced an informational isolation, and the effects of this situation are present even today. The social movements studies in Romania usually propose descriptive, historic-demographical approaches which essentially touch on the way that the protests come into being and develop, on the relationship between individual agents (for example, dissidents, mineworkers) and the state and its power. Nevertheless, other studies—for example, those concerning the Mineriads—envisage the protest-repertoires even if their manner of approach is still a descriptive one. When the approach is explorative, this refers to making comparisons between the domestic movements and those of other countries, as well as the differences and similarities between the Romanian case and the movement patterns evident in other countries (for example, concerning the revolution of December 1989, Tilly's theses [1993] are scrutinised and confirmed, whereas regarding the Mineriads, certain comparisons are made between the miners' movements of Romania and those of other countries, etc.). But these explorative-speculative approaches are scarce and sporadic and the descriptive-chronological way of tackling the subject of social movements continues to be the general pattern employed by the studies of this category.

The second category encompasses sociological analyses which belong to the quantitative research trend based on comparative surveys. The key issue of these studies is the question why in Romania, two daceds after the regime change we still have the lowest rates of civic and political activism in Europe? On this topic both categories of research interlock analytically and find common ground in the fact that the contemporary low rates of participation are prompted by the debilitating socialist legacy: the totalitarian regime strongly discouraged and gradually dismantled the political and civic participatory culture; consequently 'the effect of this will be felt in both the amount and forms of contemporary and future political participation' (Sislin 1991: 397).

Behind the validity of this causal reasoning, which argues that the lack of today's mobilization is a consequence of the past, there sits the implicit claim that socialist Romania would have fostered a generalised attitude of civic passivity. But such an argument seems to be incondite when confronted with real life under the communist era. Although the communist society did not produce social movements such as huge union protests for the protection of workers' rights, nor authentic forms of volunteerism, stripped of the 'patriotic work' ideology, there were nevertheless public life manifestations and several social actions. That this type of activism did not grow into massive and sweeping movements like the Polish *Solidarnost* might be explained through the way in which regimes can successfully shape their opposition (Hall 2000).

It is also true that a series of social categories have formulated various demands, and in the relatively safe context of the post-1989 democracy they overcome the 'grounded consensus' specific for the homogenous public of socialism. The guarantee of private property and the claim and need to return to private property was such a demand in the early 1990s, and this was followed by demands in terms of ensuring civic freedom in various spheres of individuals' lives. On the ground of such axiological change, ethnic and sexual minorities (various social categories which were discriminated in the course of the communist regime) and those who thought that transition went wrong in terms of real regime change, etc., considered that their public protests and claiming of rights were legitimate and could bring about a real change in their lives. In this way, right after the change of regime, a new climate of opinion formation and formulation occurred wherein the protesting groups represented a factor of pressure on the political actors, and the pluralist democratic conception began to dominate over the dogmatic conception of the majority consensus specific to the earlier regime.

Was There or Wasn't There?[1]
The Romanian Revolution of December 1989

A major theme of the literature on civic mobilization in Romania revolves around the 1989 change of regime. The transformation of the socialist regimes of the East-Central European countries took place in the form of non-violent actions (Siani-Davies 1996). This was not the case of Romania, 'where street protest played a major role in precipitating the collapse of the communist regime *and* where the regime used substantial violence to prevent its downfall' (Hall 2000: 1069, emphasis in original). The Romanian exceptionalism shaped all the subsequent questions debated in the literature dedicated to the political upheaval of December 1989: whether such violent actions can be qualified as revolution and, crucially, how could such violent street protests emerge under so harsh a dictatorship which studiously created and left behind a vacuum of coherently organised opposition movements (e.g. Roper 1994; Siani-Davis 1996).

The Romanian revolution analysts consider that the majority of perspectives which usually explain the outbreak of social movements as well as the classical definitions of revolutions could only partially be applied to the Romanian uprising. Rather, the revolution of December 1989 comes under the category of 'high risk collective action' (Sharman 2003) or under that of the atypical revolution sparked by a socio-political context which profoundly shaped 'the language and the symbols employed in mass mobilization' and which played 'a critical role in fashioning the eventual outcome of the revolution' (Siani-Davies 1996: 456).

In high-risk collective actions, the emphasis is laid upon the participation in collective actions in spite of the imminent risks to participants' liberty and physical integrity. In such dangerous circumstances, individuals commit to action through 'the dynamic of gradual radicalization': as more and more participants take part in the unfolding events, they practically induce each other towards the implicit or explicit cause of the revolt (Sharman 2003). The trajectory of the social and political movements of December 1989 does conform to this mobilization pattern. Ceaușescu's demise started with an isolated incident: the dissent of a group of supporters against the relocation of Hungarian Reformed Church pastor L. Tőkés, who was a dissident that the government of the time sought to evict as punishment for his previous anti-regime declarations, from Timișoara. The spark rapidly led to explosion: the single-task demonstration from 16 and 17 December 1989 promptly radicalised itself by significantly spreading across the country and setting out a growing list of grievances. If on 18 December the workers from Timișoara were still protesting peacefully, from 20 December onwards they had intensified their anti-Ceaușescu and anti-communist protests, attracting an increasing number of participants despite the gunshots fired at demonstrators in attempts to subdue them (Deletant 2006: 96).

On the other hand, viewed as an atypical revolution, the protests of December 1989 still encompass three of the key elements that generically define revolutions: change in the political institutions, use of violence and class uprising. Yet, their contribution to the burgeoning events of those days is rather ambiguous (Roper 1994).

By comparing the pattern of the Romanian events with that of other revolutions and by pointing to several classical definitions of revolutions in general (e.g. Tilly 1993), the authors who explore the dilemma of whether there was or wasn't a revolution tend to favour the idea that the Romanian uprising combines two types of actors and corresponding events: a spontaneous mass revolt and a 'long-planned coup d'état organized by a coalition of disenchanted Party apparatchiks, top Securitate officials, and some army generals' (Tismaneanu 1990: 16). The latter assumption seems to be supported by several episodes of that turbulent December: a case in point is Ceaușescu's decision to convoke a pro-regime rally in Bucharest on 21 December 1989 as a counter-protest to the spreading Timișoara social unrest. The fact that this manifestation ended as an anti-communist revolt and resulted in the escape of the Ceaușescu couple raises the question as to whether 'Ceaușescu had been goaded by cabinet members to make such a catastrophic mistake' (Hall 2000: 1080). There were other several highly controversial outcomes, among which the capture of state power during the revolution by the Front of National Salvation (FNS) led by Ion Iliescu, a former apparatchik (Bond 2006), ranks highest. Thus this disturbing and confusing train of events legitimately casts doubts upon the authenticity and meaning of the protests: was there a revolution or a *coup d'état*? (e.g. Sislin 1991; Siani-Davies 1996; Kumar 2001).

The chain of events clearly suggests the significant contribution of a *coup d'état* to the outbreak of the revolution. A palace revolution from within the Romanian Communist Party against Ceaușescu took place, amplifying, therefore, the ambiguity of the events. An interpretation exclusively in terms of people uprising (Kumar 2001) does not entirely concur with what really happened. The events rather indicate an interface movement between popular revolt and *coup d'état* (e.g. Ratesh 1991; Sislin 1991; Roper 1994). Nevertheless, the peoples' protest seems undisputable, even though it came to unwittingly accomplish the palace revolution (Siani-Davies 1996: 459).

That doubts still hover over the correct definition of the violent movement of 1989 as a 'revolution' is a testament to the so-called shortcomings of the revolutionary outcomes (cf. Tilly 1993): the failure of a genuine transfer of power from the old communist leaders to a new elite, unbound by the former structures; the fiasco of institutional reforms aimed at creating transparent, democratic structures (e.g. Sislin 1991). Some authors criticised the lack of a real regime changeover in Romania (e.g. Ratesh 1991; Rady 1992; Bond 2006)*. Therefore, they argue that, in the absence of an authentic opposition, the shift of power was not even negotiated, thus clearing the way for a part of the old communist establishment to take hold over the country. Consequently, there are opinions (e.g. Sislin 1991) that the revolution was betrayed by the Front of National Salvation led by former apparatchiks. Analysts conclude that the protesters could not have taken into account difficult and complex issues such as the transfer of power, the institutional restructuration, etc. (Sislin 1991; Siani-Davies 1996; Hall 2000), seeing that those various dissident groups which acted in the country or beyond its borders were fragmented and lacked the resources for negotiating with state officials both before and after the revolution.

Social Actions during Communism

Common sense and even the field of Romanian historical inquiry have suffered from treating the time interval between 1947 and 1989 as one unbroken, monolithic period of oppression (Fichter 2011). Evidence against this homogenous and undifferentiated type of approach is the fact that during the half-century-long period of communism there was 'a cautious, though tenacious, counterculture' (Fichter 2011: 580) which nourished certain forms of intellectual dissidence and enabled several workers movements.

Exploratory approaches, albeit less numerous than the descriptive ones, emphasise the insular nature of the movements from that time, identifying the following as their main causes: the lack of a powerful anti-regime social movement; the weak potential of change inherent to opposition-power negotiations; absence of structural coherence and the inability of intellectuals and workers to build a common front for the protection of their social and political rights and interests. This analytical framework reveals an uncomfortable dilemma: should the riots and dissidence during the communist regime be treated as social movements or rather as social, non-emergent actions that failed due to the coercive context of the political system?

Analysts consider that the least visible modality of protest took the form of illegal emigration, the émigrés frequently offering a kind of transnational support for the internal resistance groups, particularly for intellectual dissidents (Petrescu and Petrescu 2005).

A more visible version of counterculture began to spread across student communities in the form of mass culture rooted in the Western hippie movements and student riots. What is notable for the analysts, such as for Fichter (2011), is that while the counterculture of the 1960s occurred in Romania through the same aesthetic repertoires as in the West, it 'was more discreet and less flamboyant than its Western counterpart' (570). Although youngsters were fighting against the image of the standardised, socialist citizens, they only rarely challenged the regime or manifested political activism; therefore, the Romanian youth counterculture remained mainly focused on individual freedom and entertainment.

In connection with these movements we must refer to those ideologies implicit of the formal socialization processes taking place in schools and universities which promoted the idea that the communist society tries to construct a new type of citizen who is obedient and responsible for his country and nation (the state-oriented nationalist discourse was accentuated through an obsessive reference to potential enemies). Such ideology resulted in the auto-isolation of citizens in their country which put them literally far away from the danger of individual protests or social movements. Following this idea, another explanation for the lack of protests, for the fact that such student protests did not generalise throughout the student campuses of the whole country may be the fear of the citizens (youngsters) of being considered by the regime as Western agents—a fact which would imply serious punishments.

Counterculture reached its peak with the intelligentsia's 'resistance through culture', the public act of overt distancing from totalitarian communist ideas (Boldur-Lăţescu 2005; Deletant 2006). According to scholars, culture enabled in totalitarianism a kind of underground spiritual dialogue to flourish in a context where the secret police were ubiquitous (e.g. Manea 1992). However, the Romanian dissidence as a type of resistance was neither very salient in the public sphere nor internally well-structured (Petrescu and Petrescu 2005; Tatar 2006). In the late 1980s, when the crisis and shortages of communism intensified, dissidence took some shape, but still without a powerful opposition nucleus (Boia 2001; Stefan 2009). This unstructured core of the dissidence, its insularity and internally oriented focus constitute, as Fichter (2011) justly remarks, a recurrent theme in the scholarly literature. Notable here is the commotion surrounding one of the very few riskier and more meaningful acts of resistance during the communist regime: the so-called Goma movement (a human rights protest initiated in 1977 by the Romanian writer Paul Goma) which had reached the establishment and provoked a pouring of wrath upon Goma himself[2] and some of his supporters (Petrescu and Petrescu, 2005). The emulation sparked around this particular movement represents a rare occurrence within the intelligentsia, whose members had usually either complied with the authority or engaged themselves separately in differently conceived gripes with the system.[3] The terror exercised by the police and secret services is the major reason for this situation, which is doubled by informational isolation, respectively by acts of manipulation from the part of several communist ideology and anti-Western propaganda networks which deliberately worked on creating suspicion, lack of trust and rupture between the groups of intelligentsia well before such groups succeeded to coagulate themselves for protest actions. Therefore, the affirmation that 'Romanian dissent lives in Paris and his name is Paul Goma' (quoted by Deletant 2006) stands as an instructive and telling example of the insularity and scarcity of intellectual protests during this epoch.

Besides the dissidence of the intelligentsia, working-class protests represented another form of objection. In spite of the fact that almost all Romanian workers were members of trade unions, there were no real unions in Romania[4] because the official ones were strongly ideologised, and their role was supposed to enable 'constructing the new "socialist citizen"' (Keil and Keil 2002: 13). According to scholars, workers' resistance, similarly to the case of the intelligentsia, was 'often expressed on an individual level by absenteeism, drinking on the job, diversion of state goods and materials to the shadow economy, indifference to the quality of goods being produced.' (Keil and Keil 2002: 15). Consequently, only a few genuine workers' movements sprang up during the communist regime (De Nevres 2003), with two salient ones mentioned in the literature: the miners' strike and the Brașov riot. The studies that approach both movements tend to be more descriptive than exploratory, a research preference which produces more information about the chronology of the events than about their theorization.

The Jiu Valley miners' strike took place between 1 and 3 August 1977 and emerged as the result of several new provisions that would have worsened the miners' working conditions. Petrescu and Petrescu (2005) consider that the strike was the best conducted workers' protest in communist Romania in four respects: it had proper strike leadership; was non-violent nature; the list of demands was clear and leaders expressed aim to negotiate solely with Ceaușescu. This last demand of the strikers was, after all, met: Ceaușescu arrived in the Jiu Valley and practically agreed to the miners' demands. As a result, the strike was terminated, but repression actions began: between 1977 and 1978, four thousand miners were forced to move to other mining areas in Romania.[5]

In the context of harsh economic recession, the most rampant work protest was initiated on 15 November 1987 in the city of Braşov. After the workers of the local truck plant received the announcement that their salaries were cut, they started a spontaneous strike which was quickly followed by their march to the city centre. On their way to the party headquarters, workers from other factories along with city residents joined the march. In spite of the poorly organised nature of the riot (unplanned and lacking in leadership), it turned into a mass demonstration of about four thousand people against Ceauşescu and the communist regime. The mass was dispersed after five hours of protest and vandalism, and the secret police arrested many workers (Petrescu and Petrescu 2005).

According to the authors who tackled these movements, while the miners' strike still engenders contrasting opinions, the Braşov riots clearly stand as an anti-Ceauşescu revolt. In this sense, the former workers' protests are viewed either as an anti-regime and anti-Ceauşescu movement, or merely as a strike for workers' demands, whereas the latter riots were rooted not only in workers' wage dissatisfaction but also in the general 'enormous dissatisfaction' of the population with the communist regime (Petrescu and Petrescu 2005: 334). Thus, the Braşov movement conveyed a much stronger anti-regime outlook, expressing 'major loss of confidence in a corrupt communist party apparatus, its leadership, and perhaps, above all in its ideological underpinning as the party of the working class' (Ciobanu 2009: 326).

We can conclude that the social movements before 1989 represent rather latent forms of manifesting discontent and even such latent movements were destroyed in time by the police and secret services. The totalitarian regime did not solely mean isolation from the West, but also the construction of a parallel society which was connected only to party-controlled information, a fact which constituted a major impediment in the coagulation of a coherent opposition against the regime, which could catalyse a serious mass movement of people with visible manifestations and collective actions. Thus, the Romanian social movements of this period were rather atypical and can be—metaphorically—called a series of subterranean seism occurring on various levels and profundities of discontents and extensions, but without the power of a major seism.

Intellectuals versus Miners in Post-communist Romania

The first post-revolutionary movement started in 1990 and became known as the University Square phenomenon. The authors (e.g. Tismaneanu 1992;

Mungiu 1996; Mungiu-Pippidi 1999; Brotea and Béland 2007; Literat 2012) agree that this constitutes not only the first social movement of post-communist Romania but also that it possesses some characteristics which express its unique nature: the vast discursive repertoire of protest, the manipulation of public opinion by the leading elite, especially by former president Ion Iliescu; the repression of the miners' protest which created the premise for further miners' marches in Bucharest. Although the University Square protest did not reach its explicit goal, i.e. lustration, it nevertheless set the ground for the formation of Romanian civil society and the creation of the Civil Alliance which constituted an enduring organised platform for extra-parliamentary opposition (Mungiu-Pippidi 1999).

On 22 April 1990, in the wake of a meeting arranged by opposition parties, demonstrators started to gather in Bucharest's University Square. Protesters had three major demands: lustration; elections to be postponed until each party had sufficient funds to organise an electoral campaign; and equal access to state-controlled mass media for all electoral candidates. These demands reached their peak around a basic issue which became the ultimate goal of the protest: the deterring of the FNS from election (Brotea and Béland 2007). For almost two months, the square became the stage of a 'marathon demonstration' each evening, and although there were 'all sorts of people' among the demonstrators, the protests were referred to as the movement of the anti-communist intellectuals and students (Mungiu-Pippidi 1999; Boia 2001).

The studies mentioned above show that the dominant pattern of the University Square consisted of its discursive repertoires. Demonstrators initiated the protest by using the protest repertoires of the 1989 revolution with small amendments: instead of 'Down with the Communists!' they used 'Down with the Neo-Communists!' (Brotea and Béland 2007). As a response, president Iliescu called the demonstrators 'hooligans' (the same disparaging word used by Ceauşescu for identifying the Timişoara protesters in 1989). Consequently, this word served to create a common identity among demonstrators, and also played a major role in the subsequent repression of the protest, since Iliescu framed the demonstration as a conflict between intellectuals (i.e. hooligans) and decent workers (Brotea and Béland 2007; Literat 2012). Thus, the repression of the protest by the miners, spurred to come to Bucharest by Iliescu himself, reveals the pattern of the 'reactionary populism' (Tismaneanu 1992), according to which decent miners unwittingly became the custodians of order[6] in the face of reluctant intellectuals.

The miners' repression of the University Square protests violently reached its height during those disturbing days and it justified its special designation as Mineriad (in Romanian: *mineriad,* and the plural: *mineriade*).[7] This denomination is appropriately given to the miners' interventions of June 1990 since they are the continuation of several prior miners' actions in Bucharest.[8] Authors (e.g. Vasi 2004) contend that the Mineriads had a double function: to venture demands in terms of salaries and working conditions, and to serve as the instrument of repression in the hands of the ruling elite. Moreover, Mineriads were characterised by two major patterns: all movements were violent and all were organised by the same group of miners from the Jiu Valley coal mine.[9]

Scholars identify several reasons for the successful handling of miners by the neo-communist establishment in order to put a stop to University Square protests and annihilate the political opposition of the time. In this sense, the authors contend that the miners were already brainwashed by the communist ideology according to which they represented the paramount, archetypal workers of the socialist system and the best citizens of the developing socialist state. To hold such a privileged position contributed to the creation of a strong collective identity, which enabled the miners to mobilise themselves as an army for the common good of the country (Brotes and Bélabd 2007; Rus 2007).

The nature of the miners' protest as a countermovement is emphasised, among others, by Vasi (2004: 152), who contends that 'the miners' first three "crusades" in 1990 were aimed to "discipline and punish" the anti-communist demonstrators. Their leaders presented their actions as "cleaning operations"'. However, the special dynamics of the movement are well illustrated by the fact that, while in 1990 the miners were responding to new political opportunities, in the following years the movement developed its own agenda which was focused primarily on workers' demands (cf. Rus 2007).

There are several other interpretations which can partially explain the rise of the miners' movement. For example, the issue of relative deprivation (Vasi 2004) seems to be another reasonable cause for the manifestations; but, because Jiu Valley miners did not endure greater hardships than other miners groups, this argument is not entirely tenable. Another perspective advances the idea of political conspiracy in the sense that miners became 'easily manipulated by neo-communist or nationalist political forces' (Vasi 2004: 137). The mobilization potential shaped by the strength and density of social networks, as well as by the participants' identity, is considered the key element which facilitated the rise of the movement. In the same line of thought we can refer to the group affiliation dynamics during the evolution of the conflict (based on the conceptual frame produced by Simmel in 1955), a theory which can also be validated in the case of the opponent intellectuals (cf. ingroup-outgroup dynamics).

In the same light, Rus (2007) tackles the miners' protests from a criss-cross perspective of political manipulation and workers' solidarity. The latter is enhanced by the local geography (the quite isolated Jiu Valley, centred solely around mining) and by the arsenal of external instruments (e.g. working clothes, mining tools as potential weapons) which all helped in building the common identity of the miners and which rendered their violent actions to resemble paramilitary organizations (Vasi 2004). All in all, in view of the violent nature of the miners' movements and of the negative, significant impact they had on the international image of the country, etc., the many series of Mineriads are considered 'acrid stories' of Romanian civic participation (Cesereanu 2003).

At the end of this section, as an analytic skew, we can make reference to several relevant theories. First, in order to explain these events, we can refer to the theory of rational choice in the case of collective action (Goode 1997): the miners who were publicly encouraged and manipulated by president Ion Iliescu, showcased into presenting homogenous values and catalysed around a charismatic leader (who was extremely able in serving as an interface between the miners and the president) and thus constituted a mass of optimal manoeuvre in order to sustain a regime contested by other actors of society (especially intellectuals and urban citizens). Miners' demands (maintaining the workplace and privileges in terms of salaries) were rational claims from the perspective of this professional category which was hard hit by the harsh economic changes of the transition period. However, beyond the costs of their protests (including penal acts), they were intensively manipulated on the grounds of common interest.

In terms of the emergence of the protests, reference can be made to the social embeddedness theory (Granovetter 1985).[10] Once a critical point of action has occurred, a social movement emerges which shows behaviour in accordance with the interests of that given period of time. In this way, social embeddedness is transformed into the source of a social capital which individuals explicitly assume and help them catalyse their action.

Besides the other explanations (relative deprivation explanation, workers' solidarity based on strong network ties in the miners' case, group affiliation dynamics, ingroup-outgroup perceptions), these two approaches can be considered in terms of a cumulative and complementary causality and help us to better understand the factors which led to the miners' protests in the context of the economic, social and political peculiarities of the transition period. Mineriads are not—as firstly they may appear—simple riots of several primitive individuals, who are blindly manipulated by their leaders and political actors, etc. The inherent choices and the internal resorts of the miners (ingroup-outgroup dynamics and their rational interests) transformed these protests into rational actions which were easily sustained by the internal solidarity of the group and by the contextual embeddedness of the claims.

In the Context of Civic Apathy, Is a New Social Movement Being Born?

As mentioned in the introductory remarks, a quite consistent array of sociological studies have flourished on the theme of civic participation in Romania (e.g. Bădescu and Sum 2005; Bădescu, Sum and Uslaner 2004; Voicu and Voicu 2003). Since they are not directly connected with the core research issues of this chapter, I will not at this time take further heed of them. However, these analyses tackle topics such as volunteerism and membership in non-governmental organizations, the role of social capital and trust in furthering civic participation, etc. They show that civic participation in Romania engages somewhere around 2 per cent of the adult population and is among the lowest in Europe.

Following the University Square protests of 1990 and the subsequent Mineriads, toward the end of the transition period, a few protests broke out in an entirely disconnected manner which complained against certain entrepreneurial, neoliberal policies. Ecologist ideology clearly shaped these public interventions (for example, the campaigns Save Roşia Montană, Save the Danube Delta, Save Vama Veche, etc.). However, being built around few activists, these protests did not gather a significant group of participants and supporters to sustain their cause.

But, the case of Roşia Montană practically enjoyed a surprising reversal within the area of social movements. The project of the gold mine developed by Roşia Montană Gold Corporation[11] brought forth a host of protests, music festivals, petition campaigns, etc., and all successfully mobilised the ecological and civic spirit in Romania to such an extent that the theme itself became synonymous with ecological issues in general and the campaign around it, with environmental activism and even with social activism in general. The case of Roşia Montană comprises certain patterns which highlight both the ingredients from which a new social movement may spring, and the factors that incite and stimulate civic mobilization: the formation of a coalition between the protestant NGOs from Romania and abroad, which encouraged not only a better circulation of information but also more efficient access to resources and the trans-nationalization of the movement. The authors who studied this case (e.g. Chiper 2012; Egresi 2011; Szombati 2005; Velicu 2012) draw attention to the fact that there are certain discursive, iconic and mobilizing patterns which render the movement trans-national and allow the activity of its discursive community to stay focused on the idea of reflexive modernization. The organizations from abroad lending their support to the Roşia Montană movement acted as agents of international amplification of the issue of the gold mine; consequently, the international echo reverberated until it ultimately 'hit' the agents from Romania whose anti-ecological measures were criticised by opponents (cf. the boomerang effect—Keck and Sikkink 1998). Thus, analyses (e.g. Egresi 2011) show that each party involved desires to convince the public and the official decision-makers about the truth of its claims by using a specific discourse,[12] almost continuously refurbished as a function of the discursive repertoire used by the other part.[13]

The traits of the new social movement created by the Save Roşia Montană case are portrayed, among others, by Velicu (2012: 128), according to whom the movement has 'managed to place on the political agenda the importance of critique and ambivalence with regard to the liberal developmental path. The movement that expanded beyond the local has been an opportunity for the post-communist Romania to address and debate its ethical dilemmas and critically examine the spread of the market and foreign capital, the role of the state and the transformation of social interests, ideas and feelings'. The multi-issue character of the ecologist problematics is precisely highlighted by the way in which the incipient, singular actions of protest became both professional in outlook and execution (bureaucratization and advocacy), and attached to other protests hostile to the political class. We may mention here the street protests from the main Romanian cities during the winter of 2012 when, along with complaints against the austerity measures seemingly imposed by the economic crisis, there were demands for the strengthening of the civic opposition against the project of the gold mine in Roşia Montană. The groups that rallied in support of this cause rapidly captured the protesting public space. Therefore, Roşia Montană was the only form of public protest that espoused the traits of a new type of social movement, but it also occupied an excessively large slice of the public space to the detriment of other manifestations. At any rate, the case of Roşia Montană, so vividly present in the Romanian public sphere and so well-endowed with the characteristics of a new a social movement, still finds itself barely studied from a theoretical and comprehensive point of view. Consequently, the researcher should take up this very special case for study precisely because the Roşia Montană movement lends itself to a wealth of approaches conducive to the founding of a true school of research concerning Romanian social movements at the crossroad between a Romanian profile and the Western scholarly tradition.

Later, the consolidation of the civic voice of Romanian society turned to forms of manifestations specific to the (post)modern Western society and resulted in regular forms of smaller-scale protests such as Occupy movements and anti-governmental protests. These events indicate the existence of a nucleus of dissent within the Romanian society which spreads its message mostly through social media (Twitter, Facebook). This facet of the virtual communities as a source of movements can be explained through social embeddedness: the more or less crystallised group of dissent is sustained through common values and interests (youngsters, ecologists, intellectuals, anarchists, etc.) and the actions generate solidarity.

However, the pressures exercised upon the solidarity of these networks are rationally considered when the participants need to choose between group solidarity and individual-level choices like carrier options, professional status, etc. In this way it is explainable why several youngsters who were first among the initiators of social media protests, later leave these types of movements when they become employed or establish a family. Then, their place is occupied by other people, but it is questionable whether such types of online dissents can emerge into a sufficiently big mass of people in order to be considered critical movements and real challenges of the political power or status quo. Without fail, as already mentioned above, there are situations when such movements become potent, overlap with other protests and dissent and are visibly manifest against the political class, economic capital, etc.

Real Social Movements or Just Protesting Riots?

The topic of social movements in Romania has rarely been approached from a zigzag perspective which takes into account both the factual data from Romania and the theoretical research and methods developed abroad, internationally. Apart from a few studies on the revolution of December 1989, wherein the subject is tackled from the point of view of different theories about social, revolutionary movements, the majority of research dedicated to pre- and post-December 1989 mobilizations uses a descriptive, historic-chronological approach, thus shunning a theoretical perspective.

Even when trying to explain how it was possible for the violent Mineriads of the past to emerge and develop to such a great extent, the studies prefer to engage with issues such as the socioeconomic and political context of the time, without paying attention to similar miners' movements or Mineriads in other parts of the world, in the light of social embeddedness, rational choice in collective action, and strong social networks in miners communities.

In turn, the scholarly literature interventions around the campaign Save Roşia Montană, albeit not very numerous, practically constitute the sole analytical body of work wherein the particular status of this social movement as a *new movement* is thoroughly theoretically approached (reflexive modernity, neoliberalism, the paradigm of collective action and of discursive, protest communities).

Consequently, it seems very difficult to put aside the rhetorical note from the question with which I started my analysis—were there and/or weren't there genuine social movements (with variable patterns) in Romania, or were/are they merely collective actions of protest (emergent, potential movements forms)?

On the grounds of the scholarly literature consulted, it seems that—with the exception of Save Roşia Montană and the Mineriads—the majority of the civic events in Romania rather enter the category of emerging collective actions, too short-lived and unstructured to generate coherent social movements with clear agendas. To identify the causes and motives for such particular situations, critical studies should be undertaken to go beyond the tautologies which claim that the lack of social movements is due to the destructive, socialist legacy, to the wearing down of the population's trust and to the limited resources for participation.

A problem which must be observed in connection with such protests is the emergence of a kind of sectarian character of some movements (especially when they have an anarchist pattern and aim at destruction without construction), generating restrictions in individual liberties and external contacts (group isolation). This pattern appears especially when interests show a weak capacity to attract external support (e.g. gay movements, feminism, etc.). Even if such groups and their claims are expressions of democracy, they rarely succeeded to gather the conditions for generating real social movements. I assume that this is an aspect of contemporary Romanian social movements which must be studied in the analysis of these movements.

Solidarity and mobilizing capacity which are inevitable for collective action can thus limit individual aims and the extension of contacts outside the group. Together with external, structural pressures (economic and political) or individual choices (professional status, family, etc.) these restrictions can prohibit the emergence and development of these types of social movements initiatives. As a consequence, in order to generate adhesion, movements need to encounter not only dissent from a large mass of public, but also there is the need that specific forms of dissent to be interconnected.

In conclusion, Romania is not virgin territory when it comes to mobilizations, even if the studies have shown that the country still has numerous shortcomings in civic participation, and that during communism there were not as many sufficiently structured and coherent movements as in other communist countries. A few examples spring to mind such as the revolution of 1989, the Mineriads, the intellectual dissidence and the Save Roşia Montană movement—but they must be tackled further, both theoretically and in explorative fashion, in order to comprehensively seize and explain the nature and possibility of their emergence, their traits, status, causes, etc. Such studies could certainly offer an enriched perspective on the paramount issue of this chapter.

Laura Nistor, PhD, is a sociologist and senior lecturer at the department of social sciences of the Sapientia—Hungarian University of Transylvania, Romania. She specializes in environmental sociology and sociology of consumption. She has published several books, book chapters and papers on the topics of environmental activism, environmental willingness to pay, sustainable consumption, etc., in Romania.

Notes

1. *A fost sau n-a fost?* (*Was There or Wasn't There?* in English) directed by Corneliu Porumboiu, is a film known under the international title *12:08 East of Bucharest,* the time when Ceauşescu fled in the aftermath of the revolution on 22 December 1989. The film satirically explores the obsessive question concerning the Romanian revolution: was there or wasn't there a proper revolution?
2. Goma was among the international intellectuals who signed the Charter 77, also being among the supporters of the attempts to form a Free Trade Union of the Working People in Romania. For his dissident initiatives, Goma was beaten and expelled from Romania in 1979 (Preda 2009).
3. There were some other smaller independent activist groups, like the Democratic Action, Free Romania or Aktionsgruppe Banat (Fichter 2011; Ramet 1995), but they all remained disconnected from each other.
4. In 1979 there was an attempt to create the Free Trade Union of the Working People of Romania (Boldur-Lăţescu, 2005). The Union survived for five months, with their leaders being imprisoned after Radio Free Europe broadcast the founding declaration of the Union. Thus, the union 'did not live long enough to become a movement' (Petrescu and Petrescu 2005: 336).
5. In the aftermath of the Jiu Valley events, in September 1983 a strike emerged in the mines of the Maramures region and there were also various smaller strikes in other cities (e.g. Cluj, Turda and Iasi). Seeing that the workers were demanding food, the emergence of these protests is explainable on the basis of the aggravation of shortages (Deletant 2006).
6. Between 13 and 15 June 1990 miners literally became the safe-keepers in Bucharest: they controlled personal cars, stopped pedestrians, legitimised them, etc. (Rus 2007).

7. The Romanian word for describing the epic disaster of the miners' attacks on Bucharest in June 1990 (Codrescu 2012).
8. The January 1990 episode, when more than five thousand miners, called by Iliescu, descended upon Bucharest, was the first case of Jiu Valley miners' manipulation by the ruling elite which cunningly proceeded to spread rumours that once opposition parties gained access to positions of power, the mines were going to be closed in high numbers.
9. In the aftermath of the June 1990 episode when the trade union requests went unresolved, the miners from the Jiu Valley arrived in Bucharest in September 1991 with the aim of overthrowing the government. They attacked the parliament building and the national TV and radio headquarters, and toppled the government. A subsequent, violent Mineriad occurred in 1999 as well (Vasi 2004).
10. The theory is linked to conflictualist approaches (the development of the proletarian conscience and the transformation of the working class into a distinct social class with specific endeavours and characterised by internal solidarity, as a reaction against capitalist exploitation—cf. K. Marx) and assumes that solidarity turns to become a source of social capital and a generator of social movements in the case of embedded groups when several contextual conditions are fulfilled.
11. The trans-national company Roşia Montană Gold Corporation envisages to carry out a surface gold (and other precious metals) mining project in Roşia Montană by using technologies based on cyanides which entail the relocation of inhabitants. In view of this prospect, the local people quickly started a grass-roots initiative in order to protect their rights and the environment. They found allies in national and international environmental organizations. To the initial protests of 2000, other subsequent civic actions followed.
12. The company uses a technical discourse focused around three paramount issues: job creation and economic return, environment protection and social equity. Consequently, the NGOs are forced, in turn, to adopt a scientific discourse in order to refute the arguments of RMGC.
13. See, for example, the film *The New Eldorado* (Tibor Kocsis), and in contrast, the documentary *Mine Your Own Business* (Phelim McAleer).

References

Bădescu, G., and P. E. Sum. 2005. 'Historical Legacies, Social Capital and Civil Society: Comparing Romania on a Regional Level'. *Europe-Asia Studies* 57, no. 1: 117–33.

Bădescu, G., P. E. Sum and E. M. Uslaner. 2004. 'Civil Society Development and Democratic Values in Romania and Moldova'. *East European Politics and Society* 18, no. 2: 316–41.

Boia, L. 2001. *Romania: Borderland of Europe*. London: Reaktion Books.

Boldur-Lăţescu, G. 2005. *The Communist Genocide in Romania*. Hauppauge: Nova Science Publishers.

Bond, E. 2006. *Endgame in the Balkans: Regime Change, European Style*. Washington: The Brookings Institute.

Brotea, J. and D. Béland. 2007. '"Better Dead than Communist!" Contentious Politics, Identity Formation, and the University Square Phenomenon in Romania'. *Spaceof-identity* 7, no. 2: 77–100.

Cesereanu, R. 2003. *Imaginarul violent al românilor.* București: Humanitas.

Ciobanu, M. 2009. 'Reconstructing the Role of the Working Class in Communist and Postcommunist Romania'. *International Journal of Politics, Culture and Society* 22, no. 3: 315–35.

Codrescu, A. 2012. *The Muse Is Always Half-Dressed in New Orleans and Other Essays.* New Orleans: Garret County Press Digital Edition.

De Nevres, R. 2003. *Comrades No More: The Seeds of Change in Eastern Europe.* Cambridge: Belfer Center for Science and International Affairs.

Deletant, D. 2006. 'Romania, 1945–1989. Resistance, Protest and Dissent'. In *Revolution and Resistance in Eastern Europe: Challenges to Communist Rule,* ed. K. McDermott and M. Stibbe, 81–100. Dorset: Berg Publishers.

Fichter, M. 2011. 'Rock 'n' Roll Nation: Counterculture and Dissent in Romania, 1965–1975'. *Nationalities Paper* 39, no. 4: 567–85.

Goode, W. 1997. 'Rational Choice Theory'. *American Sociologist* 28, no. 2: 22–41.

Granovetter, M. 1985. 'Economic Action and Social Structure: The Problem of Embeddedness'. *American Journal of Sociology* 91, no. 3: 481–510.

Hall, R. A. 2000. 'Theories of Collective Action and Revolution: Evidence from the Romanian Transition of December 1989'. *Europe-Asia Studies* 52, no. 6: 1069–93.

Keck, M., and K. Sikkink. 1998. *Activists beyond Borders: Advocacy Networks in International Politics.* Ithaca: Cornell University Press.

Keil, T. J., and J. M. Keil. 2002. 'The State and Labor Conflict in Postrevolutionary Romania'. *Radical History Review* 82: 9–36.

Kumar, K. 2001. *1989: Revolutionary Ideas and Ideals.* Minneapolis: University of Minnesota Press.

Literat, I. 2012. '"Original democracy": A Rhetorical Analysis of Romanian Post-revolutionary Political Discourse and the University Square Protests of June 1990'. *Central European Journal of Communication* 5, no. 1: 25–39.

Manea, N. 1992. *On Clowns: The Dictator and the Artists. Essays by Norman Manea.* New York: Grove Press.

Mungiu, A. 1996. 'Intellectuals as Political Actors in Eastern Europe. The Romanian Case'. *Eastern European Politics and Society* 60 (2): 33–364.

Mungiu-Pippidi, A. 1999. 'Romanian Political Intellectuals before and after the Revolution'. In *Intellectuals and Politics in Central Europe,* ed. A. Bozóki. Budapest: CEU Press, 73–100.

Petrescu, C., and D. Petrescu. 2005. 'Resistance and Dissent under Communism: The Case of Romania'. *Totalitarismus und Demokratie* 4, no. 2: 323–46.

Preda, C. 2009. *Dictators and Dictatorships: Artistic Expressions of the Political in Romania and Chile (1970–1989). No paso nada… ?* Boca Raton: Dissertation.com.

Rady, M. 1992. *Romania in Turmoil.* London: IB Tauris.

Ramet, S. P. 1995. *Social Currents in Eastern Europe: The Sources and Consequences of the Great Transformation.* Durham: Duke University Press.

Ratesh, N. 1991. *Romania: The Entangled Revolution.* New York: Praeger.

Roper, S. D. 1994. 'The Romanian Revolution from a Theoretical Perspective'. *Communist and Postcommunist Studies* 27, no. 4: 401–10.

Rus, A. 2007. *Mineriadele: Între manipulare politică și solidaritate muncitorească*. București: Curtea Veche.

Sharman, J. C. 2003. 'Culture, Strategy and State-Centered Explanations of Revolution, 1789 and 1989'. *Social Science History* 27, no. 1: 1–24.

Siani-Davies, P. 1996. 'Romanian Revolution or Coup d'état? A Theoretical View of the Events of December 1989'. *Communist and Post-communist Studies* 29, no. 4: 453–65.

Simmel, G. 1955. *Conflict and the Web of Group-Affiliation*. New York: Free Press.

Sislin, J. 1991. 'Revolution Betrayed? Romania and the National Salvation Front'. *Studies in Comparative Communism* 24, no. 4: 395–411.

Stefan, A. M. 2009. *Democratization and Securitization: The Case of Romania*. Leiden: Koninklije Brill.

Szombati, K. 2005. 'The Spell of "Gold": Portrait of an Eastern European Conquista Featuring Knavish Colonists, Clashing Natives and Battle Roar'. MA dissertation. Budapest: Eötvös Lóránd University of Sciences.

Tatar, M. I. 2006. *Importing Democracy from Abroad: International Assistance for Civil Society in Romania*. Oradea: Editura Universitatii din Oradea.

Tilly, C. 1993. *European Revolutions, 1492–1992*. Oxford: Blackwell.

Tismaneanu, V. 1990. Homage to Golania. *The New Republic*, 30 July–6 August: 16–18.

———. 1992. *Reinventing Politics: Eastern Europe from Stalin to Havel*. New York: The Free Press.

Vasi, I. B. 2004. 'The Fist of the Working Class. The Social Movements of Jiu Valley Miners in Post-socialist Romania'. *East European Politics and Societies* 18, no. 1: 132–57.

Velicu, I. 2012. 'The Aesthetic Post-communist Subject and the Differend of Rosia Montana'. *Studies in Social Justice* 6 no. 1: 125–41.

Voicu, M., and B. Voicu. 2003. 'Volunteering in Romania: A Rara Avis'. In *The Values of Volunteering: Cross-Cultural Perspectives*, ed. P. Dekker and L. Halman, 143–60. Kluwer Publishers.

Chapter 25

Social Mobilization and the Strong State from the Soviets to Putin

Social Movements in the Soviet Union and Russia

Alfred Evans and Laura Henry

In 1848 Marx and Engels exhorted the workers of the world to unite. Their call for revolution by the working class provided the impetus for the remaking of political and economic life in a vast area of Eurasia in the twentieth century. Surely that was fertile ground for social movement scholars. Yet the revolutionary society envisioned by Lenin and created by the Soviet communists did not allow for independent social movements. During the Soviet period, the state prohibited autonomous social mobilization, instead channelling public activism into Communist Party–sponsored clubs, associations, trade unions and interest groups, and using selective repression to punish those who challenged the regime. As a result, most grievances were articulated only within close-knit circles of friends and family, the subject of 'kitchen table' talk but not a basis for public action or political participation. In the late Soviet period, a few scholars employed the concepts of interest group politics and political participation to analyse developments (Skilling 1971; Friedgut 1979). In general, however, the study of social movements did not play a significant role in Soviet-era scholarship, either within Russia or in the West.

Following dramatic developments in Russia beginning in the *perestroika* period, social movements received more scholarly attention, often as a means of understanding the trajectory of change in Russia's political regime—toward greater democracy or authoritarianism. In March 1985, Mikhail Gorbachev became the head of the Communist Party of the Soviet Union and by 1986 he initiated reforms that allowed thousands of independent social organizations to appear in the USSR. Scholarly interest in civil society, illustrated by the work of Robert Putnam (1993), emerged at the same time that anti-communist intellectuals in Eastern Europe had begun to advocate citizen activism within spaces that were not controlled by the state. After

1986 the proliferation of groups outside the control of the Communist Party was seen as a sign of the emergence of civil society in the Soviet Union (Starr 1988; Lewin 1991)—a civil society that could facilitate an eventual transition to democracy. Indeed, many Western scholars studying this phenomenon were political scientists who tended to focus on the role of the state in shaping the development of social movements and civil society.

The Study of Social Movements at the Russian Academy

The study of social movements inside Russia has historically been a marginal area of research. In the late nineteenth century and early twentieth century, two ideologies contended for support among the members of the Russian intelligentsia who embraced the goal of revolutionary transformation. The Populists (*Narodniki*) believed that the peasants would be the basis for a revolution that would destroy the existing regime, while the Marxists saw the industrial workers as the only social class with genuine revolutionary potential. Initially both the Populists and the Marxists found support only within the highly educated minority in society, so each was preoccupied with the potential for interaction between a revolutionary elite and its mass of potential supporters among the common people, or the *narod* (Butenko 2002: 234). Thus, when Russian intellectuals devoted attention to social movements, they were fascinated by the relationship between the leaders of movements, or the 'heroes', and their potential or actual followers, the 'crowd' (*tolpa*).[1] That relationship was addressed by the few academics that began to develop the discipline of sociology in Russia during the last years of the tsarist system.

During the 1920s, however, the Soviet Communists began to suppress sociology, which they regarded as a manifestation of bourgeois ideology (Weinberg 1974: 4–9; Novikov 1982: 97; Greenfeld 1988: 100). There were no sociology departments in Soviet universities and no association of sociologists in the USSR from the 1920s until the 1950s. In the post-Stalin period, after 1953, the Communist leadership allowed a gradual revival of sociology (Katz 1971). However, even after an Institute of Sociological Research was established in the Academy of Sciences of the USSR, and when the journal *Sotsiologicheskie issledovaniia* [*Sociological Research*] was published on a regular basis, Soviet sociologists did not write openly about social movements. The Communist Party made it clear that sociology was to serve practical, 'problem-solving' functions, providing information that would assist in performing the tasks that the party had chosen for Soviet society (Weinberg 1974: 109). In any case, the degree of control of society by the political regime ruled out the possibility of independent movements openly striving for change. An extensive review of the work of sociologists in the USSR from 1965 to 1975, written by two men who were responsible for guiding activity in that field (Osipov and Rutkevich 1978), does not mention any research on social movements. In addition, it was unacceptable for Soviet scholars to cite Western theorists in their published works, except when they occasionally criticised the ideas of such 'bourgeois' thinkers, so the open discussion of Western scholarship on social movements was impossible even after the revival of sociology in the Soviet Union.

Elena Zdravomyslova later admitted that for Soviet scholars the phenomenon of social movements had been 'unknown' (Zdravomyslova 1993a: 3). This situation changed after Mikhail Gorbachev unveiled his program of radical reform in the late 1980s. Within a few years, some articles in Soviet sociological journals discussed the ideas of the leading Western theorists of social movements (Zdravomyslova 1990). Active research on environmental movements in the Soviet Union began towards the end of the 1980s (Tsepilova 1999: 104). In the early 1990s a few sociologists in the USSR published books that discussed the major social movement theories that had developed in the West. From the 1990s to the present, Russian sociologists have engaged in the study of social movements in Russia in academic communities such as the European University and the Centre for Independent Sociological Research in Saint Petersburg. This is where Zdravomyslova continues her work on social movements during the *perestroika* period and gender mobilization in contemporary Russia, and Anna Temkina investigates collective action concerning gender and public health (Zdravomyslova and Temkina 2009). This is also the case of the Institute for Sociology of the Russian Academy of Sciences, where Oleg Yanitsky and Irina Khalii explore the environmental movement and civil society more broadly. Their writings have been profoundly influenced by Western theorists.

However, research on social movements has not been very popular among sociologists in Russia. At the first All-Russian Sociological Congress in September 2000, several hundred papers were presented, but only three of them dealt primarily with social movements (Asochakov et al. 2000: 100–101, 118–20). In 2010 Oleg Yanitsky remarked that the subject of social movements was 'rarely discussed by Russian sociologists', adding that only two or three solely authored books and no more than twenty articles in scholarly journals on that subject had been published in his country during the past twenty years (Yanitsky 2010b: 52). In 2013 Yanitsky published an article in *Sotsiologicheskie issledovaniia,* the leading Russian sociological journal, that consisted mainly of a summary of the main schools of thought on social movements (Yanitsky 2013), clearly suggesting that, in his view, most sociologists in Russia were still not familiar with the most important works in the field. From 2000 to 2013, only eight articles primarily dealing with social movements were published in *Sotsiologicheskie issledovaniia,* which has twelve issues per year. During the same period, five articles focused on social movements appeared in *Polis,* or *Politicheskie issledovaniia,* the top political science journal in Russia.

A few exemplary works illustrate how Russian scholars of social movements have started to apply Western sociological concepts since the early 1990s, for example highlighting ways in which the context for movements in Russia differs from that in Europe and the United States in 1993. Zdravomyslova used the concept of resource mobilization to trace the growth of the democratic movement in Leningrad from 1987 to 1990 (Zdravomyslova 1993b: 110). She noted that because of the dominance of the state in the Soviet Union, reform 'from above' in the form of *perestroika* had been crucial for the development of social movements, as the spread of 'informal' groups was facilitated by the support that they received from established institutions such as the Communist Party and labour unions (Zdravomyslova 1993b: 114–15). She added that another distinctive feature of the Soviet Union was a social structure in which most social groups lacked a clear sense of their own identity and interests, making it difficult for movements to appeal to them. On the other hand, she argued that in Soviet society there was a pervasive sense of a division between the masses and the political elite, which made the 'image of the enemy', personified by the political establishment, a valuable resource for the early democratic movement (Zdrsavomyslova 1993b: 121–22). In a book published in 1996, Zdravomyslova again drew on concepts from Western scholarship. She delineated a 'protest cycle' in the Soviet Union from 1985 to 1991, ending with the failed coup in August 1991. During that period, democracy-seeking groups sought to define their identity in symbolic terms even as they addressed specific political issues (Zdravomyslova 1996: 127–28). Movement organizations developed a repertoire of tactics (ibid.: 129–31), combining protests with electoral activity, placing greater emphasis on elections over time. Zdravomyslova affirmed, as others have, that 'the main political orientation' of most supporters of democracy was 'support for and acceleration of the reform from above' (ibid.: 133).

Oleg Yanitsky has fruitfully brought together concepts from social movement theory—including action repertoires, resource mobilization, political opportunity structures and framing—and extensive fieldwork on the Russian environmental movement in a number of books and articles. His work applies insights from European scholars such as Beck, Touraine, Klandermans, Kriesi and Rucht, among others, informing his analysis of the evolution of Russia's 'post-totalitarian state'. In post-totalitarianism, the 'principal social agent is the state', 'national priorities are ... military and industrial policies' and the system is based on 'economic and political monopolists' (Yanitsky 1996, as quoted in Yanitsky 2010a: 129). Over time, Yanitsky has developed an actor-centred approach to analyse differentiation within the Russian environmental movement. Differentiation, he argues, occurs in response to continued state domination of society, environmentalists' search for resources, the loss of the movement's mass base, and the professionalization and bureaucratization of the movement. One of Yanitsky's key findings is how persistent elements of the Soviet system and the state's shift in strategy from co-optation to repression contribute to the division among those activists oriented toward transnational or local issues. Yanitsky's scholarship also pushes beyond the confines of the mainstream social movement literature to consider how alienation and perceptions of danger influence behaviour in a 'risk society' (2010a: 166–69), and what it means for a society to go through a period of 'demodernization' (2010b).

Irina Khalii, another leading Russian scholar of social movements, acknowledged that her analysis would 'rely on theoretical and methodological approaches developed by western sociologists' (Khalii 2007: 6). Yet Khalii's work emphasises the distinctive conditions in which social movements strive to advance their causes in contemporary Russia. She reports that the mass public is not ready to play the role of the 'crowd' that follows the 'heroes' because the majority of Russians have been absorbed in 'the struggle for existence in the period of establishment of a market economy', which has oriented 'the greater part of the population toward independent resolution of their own problems, without interference from outside' (ibid.: 295). Khalii sees strong elements of 'traditionalism', implicitly inherited from the Soviet system, not only in the tendency toward authoritarianism by the Russian state but also in the majority's scepticism toward organised groups that seek change and most people's preference for more informal and private means of solving problems. She concludes that 'in conditions of the absence of support from the political authorities and [local social] communities, the potential for movements to influence social processes is minimal' (ibid.: 296). This conclusion once again emphasises the difficult relationship between movements and their potential supporters, a frequent theme in studies of Russian movements by both Russian and Western scholars.

Russia's Rapidly Changing Political Opportunity Structure

The remarkable political changes in the USSR after 1985 prompted an upsurge in Western scholarship on the emergence of protests and new citizens' associations in Russia as well. Many scholars focused on the role of the state in enabling or constraining autonomous social action. As Jim Butterfield and Judith B. Sedaitis point out, when authorities in many parts of the USSR did not suppress the growing number of independent groups that increased rapidly, it was apparent to social activists that 'the rules of the game for interest articulation had changed' (Sedaitis and Butterfield 1991: 1, 4). They asserted that in the late 1980s, social movements 'wrested policy initiative away' from the political leadership of the Soviet Union (ibid.: 1). Geoffrey A. Hosking notes that independent groups began to engage in public protests in 1986 and that large demonstrations occurred in Moscow by the spring of 1987 (1992: 9–10), shattering a taboo that had persisted in the Soviet Union for nearly seventy years (ibid.: 24). Protest participants were united only by their opposition to domination by the authoritarian political regime of their country (ibid.: 19, 24). As movement organizations began to articulate their goals and formulate their strategy, disagreements immediately led to internal divisions and fragmentation (ibid.: 19, 21, 23).

A major component of a changing political opportunity structure is the degree of competition in a country's political system (Almeida 2003: 349). Mikhail Gorbachev's call for 'socialist pluralism' was supposed to include elections for legislative bodies and, by 1990, even competition among different political parties. Ultimately, Gorbachev's radical reforms unintentionally caused divisions in the political elite, which encouraged the leaders of independent groups to support forces that pressed for further political openness, resulting in a broad and loosely networked pro-democracy movement. M. Steven Fish agrees that liberalization under Gorbachev stimulated an 'explosion' of activity by pro-democracy groups (Fish 1995: 32). But Fish argues that although political competition increased dramatically during Gorbachev's reforms, *access* to institutions of political authority by organised groups remained severely limited during *perestroika* (ibid.: 51, 122). While many groups could demonstrate in the streets, very few of them substantially influenced state policies (ibid.: 58). In addition, the declining authority of the Soviet state further '*inhibited* the development of the institutions of independent society' (ibid.: 75; emphasis in the original), as the state's loss of authority 'presented opposition organizations with difficulties no less challenging than those posed by direct official interference and sabotage' (ibid.: 125). The absence of effective decision-making institutions heightened the public's sense of the futility of taking part in demonstrations and 'discouraged mass membership and participation in—and therefore retarded the growth of—autonomous organizations' (ibid.). Broadly in agreement with Fish, Powell (2002) contends that environmental organizations did little to resolve Russia's environmental problems, partly because the state lacked the capacity to enforce its own regulations and partly because the public was more concerned about the economy.

Scholars in the post-Soviet period would continue to focus on the concept of 'opportunity structures' as a means of understanding the changed landscape for social movements, often adapting the concept to capture the severe economic dislocation and other changes experienced by Russians. For example, in her study of the post-Soviet women's movement in the 1990s, Valerie Sperling builds upon the political process model and proposes several conceptual innovations, including the 'economic opportunity structure' to highlight the extreme resource poverty of the movement, and the 'international opportunity structure' to illustrate the sudden increase in international ideas, funding, and partnerships in Russian society (1999: 49–52). The work of Sperling and others demonstrates that the chaotic political and economic environment of 1990s Russia proved challenging for social movements, even as opportunities for mobilization expanded.

Identity, Political Culture and Norm Diffusion

In the overriding focus on political factors, the subject of identities, beliefs and values received somewhat less attention in studies of Russian movements. Nationalist movements in the Baltic states served as harbingers of the broader wave of identity-based anti-Soviet mobilization. Mark Beissinger notes that in the Soviet Union, nationalism became the 'dominant force within the *glasnost*' mobilizational cycle' (2002: 49). Within a context of deep structural crisis, nationalist contention by one ethnic group prompted similar mobilization in other groups, through what Beissinger refers to as the 'diffusion and normalization of contention' (2002: 79). These nationalist movements largely demobilised in the aftermath of the USSR's disintegration due to the achievement of independent statehood and the rhetoric of international elites that discouraged further efforts at self-determination.

In *Eco-Nationalism*, Jane Dawson (1996) argues that anti-nuclear activism attracted many individuals who saw environmental protest as a vehicle for voicing broader opposition to the Soviet regime. Bringing together the resource mobilization and new social movement schools, Dawson identifies key mobilizational resources that became available due to political reform, such as meeting spaces and the ability to publicly debate state environmental policy, but she also suggests that national identity served as a further resource. Dawson labels the phenomenon of nationalists' participation in anti-nuclear protests as 'movement surrogacy'. After independent statehood, the anti-nuclear movement lost its mass character in many former Soviet republics.

Socialization in the Soviet period may also have shaped identities and political culture. Ken Jowitt argued that post-socialist citizens had come to 'view the political realm as something dangerous, something to avoid' (1992: 287–89). The clash between new global norms, promoted by movements and Russian beliefs and values has informed the study of Russia's human rights and women's movements. For example, feminism has gained little traction within Russia. Lisa McIntosh Sundstrom examines the diffusion of transnational norms to explain the relative success in the case of movements focused on soldiers' rights and domestic violence and less effective in movements focused on gender equality (2006). Sundstrom demonstrates that frames drawing upon universal norms against bodily harm and the ideal of motherhood resonated with most Russians, while foreign support for feminist groups led to isolation from the general public. In a recent article, Janet Johnson and Aino Saarinen suggest that authoritarian retrenchment under Putin has encompassed a 'neomasculinism' that curtails opportunities for all activists who do not espouse traditional gender norms, providing an inhospitable context for the women's movement (Johnson and Saarinen 2013: 550).

The contemporary human rights movement in Russia is rooted in the dissident movement of the Soviet Union (Reddaway 1972). The Soviet human rights movement drew on international norms and agreements, such as the Helsinki Accords, to publicise rights violations by the state (Thomas 2001). In the post-Soviet period, a small but vocal group, consisting of human rights activists from organizations such as Memorial, For Human Rights and the Sakharov Centre, have demanded information on abuses during the Soviet period and have sought the enforcement of legal protection by the post-Soviet state. Human rights activists have continued to focus on political rights and civil liberties, although opinion polls indicate that the public is more concerned about social and economic rights. Soviet-era human rights activists have been joined by groups such as the Committee of Soldiers' Mothers, an organization dedicated to protecting the rights of young men conscripted into the military (Caiazza 2002; Sundstrom 2006). Caiazza emphasises that social movements operate within an 'ideological opportunity structure' that reflects the 'perceived validity of different claims on the state' and shapes the civic obligations of men and women through military service and motherhood, making gender a resource for activists. Russia's hegemonic ideology continues to emphasise centralised state authority in contrast to the human rights movement's demands for transparency and oversight.

In the Soviet period, a network of academics justified their criticism of the state's environmental policies based on their scientific expertise (Weiner 1999). In the 1990s, as Russians became concerned with their own economic survival, the environmental movement lost its mass character. Tynkkynen's analysis of green NGOs in Saint Petersburg suggests that environmentalists need to develop more positive framing strategies to mobilise the general public (2006). In recent years, some environmental movements have focused on local issues that are of greater concern to the public, such as the effort to preserve Khimki Forest from highway construction (Evans 2012), energizing a new generation of activists, although the movement remains small overall.

Social Movements in Civil Society

Scholars who focused on new social activism in the late Soviet and the early post-Soviet period were interested not only in the causes but also in the political effects of social movements in their role as part of a potentially revitalized civil society. In other words, the study of social movements was part of a broader research agenda on transitions to democracy. However, late Soviet and post-Soviet Russian civil society and social movements were almost universally judged to be weak. Marc Howard's 'experiential approach' to explaining the weakness of post-communist civil society argued that individuals' willingness to engage in politics is constrained by their past experiences, including participation in Communist-era social organizations, the persistence of Communist-era friendship networks, and disappointment with post-Communist political and economic developments (2003: 122–45). Other aspects of post-Soviet Russia cited as contributing to the weakness of civil society include centralised political authority in the hands of the executive power (Henderson 2010) and the post-Soviet economic recession (Sperling 1999).

Civil society may be a partner to or a critic of the state. Janet Johnson's work on social activism around domestic violence has identified new patterns of collaboration between the state and society in the construction of crisis centres across Russia in the 1990s and early 2000s, but also highlights the danger of co-optation of a movement by the political authorities (2009). Under Putin, the state has paid greater attention to social groups than during the Yeltsin years. Graeme Robertson states, 'In fact, Putin's second term saw a major redesign of state-society relations as the regime sought to more closely integrate civil society groups and non-governmental organizations (NGOs) into the state. The result is a strengthening of groups with a non-political or pro-state orientation and the isolation of more adversarial groups or organizations' (Robertson 2009: 531).

Under the Soviet regime citizens were largely isolated from social movements in the West, but in the post-Soviet period, scholars have investigated the consequences of increased transnationalism. Transnational ties can provide leverage for less powerful actors, activating international condemnation and exerting a 'boomerang effect' on a resistant domestic government (Keck and Sikkink 1998: 12–13). Although transnational ties have been advantageous in some cases, facilitating flows of information and resources to Russian groups, reliance on funding from external actors also has led to dependency and disconnection from local constituencies (Henderson 2003). As Tarrow argued, transnational movements may be seen as 'alternatives for many activists who come out of the risky world of domestic movements, and see transnational activism as an alternative to mobilization' (1998: 194).

Environmentalists have been among the most vocal critics of the Russian state and its policies, but they have also had difficulty mobilizing the population. In her study of the post-Soviet environmental movement, Laura Henry (2010) adopted an 'organizational approach', in which the range of development strategies of non-governmental organizations illustrate different responses to the political and economic context and result in different strategies for generating environmental change. Henry also concludes that Russian social movement leaders have been strongly influenced by their pre-existing beliefs, networks and resources, many of which are rooted in the Soviet period and others drawn from new transnational relationships.

When Does Protest Occur?

Most scholars suggest that the citizens of Russia were remarkably quiet after the activism of the Gorbachev years faded away. Russian NGOs increasingly were oriented toward transnational donors and partners and struggled to maintain a connection with the general public. However, Graeme Robertson (2011) contends that Russians were not as passive in the 1990s as has generally been assumed. He presents data that demonstrate a relatively high rate of mobilization of Russians in strikes and protests in the late 1990s in response to economic hardships (ibid.: 14, 41). Protests during that period were 'primarily local in nature', and expressed goals that were narrowly focused and 'defensive or conservative' (ibid.: 42), such as the demand for payment of overdue wages. Robertson argues that the strikes and protests in Russia in the 1990s primarily reflected divisions within the political elite (ibid.: 79, 95, 101). He reports that the level of protests in Russia was lower during Vladimir Putin's first term as president, from 2000 to 2004 (ibid.: 148). He asserts that the nature of protests in Russia changed after 2005, leading to 'the development of an increasingly well organised and significant independent opposition' (ibid.: 170).

Alfred Evans (2012; 2013) agrees that events in 2005 in Russia signalled changes in protest activity there. In January 2005 protests broke out in many

Russian cities in response to the cancelling of certain subsidised benefits for large groups in the population, including retired people (Evans 2013: 108–10). Spontaneous demonstrations spread rapidly as hundreds of thousands of people, mostly older people, expressed their indignation and demanded the reinstatement of the previously guaranteed benefits. The government did not attempt massive repression of the protests, but instead partly backed down from the policy changes. The wave of demonstrations subsided within a few weeks, and left no standing organizational structures.

Yet according to Evans, the protests of early 2005 left a lasting imprint as an example in two ways. First, the actions of those who swarmed into the streets provided a model of protest tactics that would be imitated repeatedly in the repertoire of protest in Russia in subsequent years by groups that were discontented with public policies. Second, the demonstrations contributed to a master frame for protests that would be reproduced and adapted in the years that followed. The frame that was articulated by protesters in 2005 decried the violation of an implicit agreement between the state and people, the abuse of authority and the victimization of vulnerable citizens.

Many observers have said that in Russia under the Putin regime, protests that have focused on local issues important to the daily lives of groups of citizens and that have had a defensive orientation, opposing changes introduced by political authorities or corporate interests, have been seen sympathetically by most people in Russia. On the other hand, demonstrations whose participants charged the political regime with violating broad political principles, such as freedom of speech and the right to assemble, have failed to strike a responsive chord among most Russians. For several years, the demonstrations of members of the Other Russia, Strategy 31, and other organizations opposed to the current political regime in Russia attracted only small numbers of participants, and had very little impact on either public opinion or the actions of the state.

A new cycle of political protest by pro-democracy organizations began in December 2011. In that month tens of thousands of people took part in demonstrations in Moscow against perceived fraud in parliamentary elections, while smaller numbers turned out in other cities at the same time. By February 2012 approximately eighty thousand attended a protest rally in Moscow, though the number of participants in similar events in Moscow since then has decreased. What is different about the recent protests is their explicitly political orientation; participants charge that the implicit contract between rulers and citizens has been violated in a deviation from principles of democracy (Evans 2013: 116). One factor that made it possible to draw thousands of Russians together on short notice is the development of communications technology. The number of Russians turning to the Internet for information and away from the state-controlled television networks has been increasing steadily in recent years. These Russians are more likely to be young, highly educated, and residents of large cities. Also, activists use social media to notify people of demonstrations. In Russia, as elsewhere, the nature of the networks that are the basis for recruitment into social movements is changing rapidly.

Questions for Future Research on Social Movements in Russia

In the 1990s, Sidney Tarrow lamented that the concept of political opportunity structure had rarely been applied outside Western democracies (Tarrow 1998: 19). Russia was ruled by an authoritarian regime when it was part of the Soviet Union, then experienced a significant opening of the political opportunity structure in the late 1980s and 1990s, and has seen a trend towards a semi-authoritarian or 'hybrid' political regime since 2000. A familiar generalization in scholarship on social movements is the curvilinear relationship between the frequency of protests and the degree of openness of the political system, where protests are more likely to occur in a political system with a mix of closed and open structures (Almeida 2003: 354). Scholars who specialise in Russia have a unique opportunity to investigate the relationship between changes in the country's political system over time and fluctuation in protest activity.

Academics know relatively little about the effects of repression on social movements. It is generally thought that repression by a state tends to stimulate an increase in protests (Almeida 2003: 353). Yet one scholar has observed that 'the dazzling array of theoretical arguments' on the effects of repression 'is matched by a similarly large array of discordant findings' (Earl 2007: 4478). In the Russian case, the relationship between repression and the level of protest activity seems to be more complicated, as the Putin regime's responses to opposition demonstrations are not limited to punitive measures. Since institutional allies are valuable for social movements (Della Porta 2011: 2435–36), a state that feels threatened by public challenges may attempt to deny its opponents the opportunity to find allies in elite institutions, as Putin has done. The Russian regime has also attempted to discourage public support for opposition movements. Is the state's strategy for dealing with the perceived threat of protest activity intensifying polarization between social groups with differing values? If so, could it be that the strategy's short-term benefits are creating the potential for more serious trouble in the long run?

The semi-authoritarian character of the political regime in Russia also has implications for how people are mobilised in social movements. One of the most firmly established findings about recruitment into social movement organizations is that 'most movements do not arise because isolated individuals choose to join the struggle' (Friedman and McAdam 1992: 163). Rather, people usually are attracted to movements from pre-existing groups and networks (Johnston 2007: 3067). Alberto Melucci insists that 'recruitment networks play a fundamental role in the process of involving individuals' and that 'networks of relationships already present in the social fabric facilitate the processes of involvement' (Melucci 1997: 339). While some demographic information on the participants in large-scale protest in Moscow is available, we have only anecdotal information about their group affiliations and their social networks. Further research could focus on the connections that were most effective in motivating people to join the opposition movement. What role have the Internet and social media played in attracting people to involvement in movements? Can electronic connections be a substitute for traditional forms of interaction in organised groups? Or do social media connections reflect networks involving face-to-face contacts, so that different forms of interaction are part of an integrated whole?

A closely related question is that of the 'abeyance structures' and organizational infrastructure left behind after the decline of Russian social movements. Doug McAdam describes 'long-standing activist subcultures capable of sustaining the ideational traditions needed to revitalise activism following a period of movement dormancy' (McAdam 1994: 43). In Russian movements that arise as a result of the disruption of people's everyday lives, it may be fairly easy to identify abeyance structures that persist beyond protests because the scale of the local community is small enough to make communication simple. With regard to the current movement protesting against the political regime in Russia, however, reality is more complex and more obscure.

If we had information about the social networks that are being created by the current protest movement in Russia and the abeyance structures in which networks of protesters can find refuge, we would know more about the potential for oppositional protest activity in the future. For Francesca Polletta and James M. Jasper, submerged networks, sequestered social sites and abeyance structures refer to 'institutions removed from the physical and ideological control of those in power', each of which represents a 'free space, in which people can develop counter-hegemonic ideas and oppositional identities' (Polletta and Jasper 2001: 288). Where are the 'free spaces' in contemporary Russia in which distinctive collective identities can take shape safely? Will the abeyance structures be found primarily in formal institutions such as universities, unions and certain types of businesses, or will they consist mainly of more informal social networks, in which interaction through social media plays an essential role?

The lack of autonomous social mobilization in the Soviet system largely excluded the Russian case from scholarship on social movements. The sharp rise in social movement activity during the time of *perestroika* inspired a corresponding increase in scholarly attention. In the late Soviet period and the post-Soviet decades, scholars studying Russian social movements have most frequently turned to the political process model—combining the concepts of political opportunity structure, resources and framing—to study social mobilization. Generally, these scholars have been more focused on understanding the Russian case than self-consciously furthering the development of social movement theory. Nevertheless, studying Russian movements yields valuable insights about how a rapidly changing political and economic context and the introduction of new frames into a society may shape the extent of social mobilization. The severe economic slump of the 1990s and the political disorder of the Yeltsin years shaped the resources and political opportunities that sustained social movements and dampened the impact of these movements that endured tenaciously through great difficulties. The return to political stability and economic growth since 2000 has been accompanied by the consolidation of a soft authoritarian regime under Vladimir Putin that has aroused a new burst of anti-regime activism—activism that draws on new tactics and networks and presents new challenges for scholars.

Alfred B. Evans, Jr. is professor emeritus of political science at California State University, Fresno. He is the author of *Soviet Marxism-Leninism: The Decline of an Ideology* (1993), and a co-editor of three books, including *Change and Continuity in Russian Civil Society: A Critical Assessment* (2006). He has published many book chapters and articles in scholarly journals. Most of his current research focuses on civil society in Russia, with particular emphasis on organizations that engage in public protests. He also writes about trends in ideology under the political regime in that country.

Laura A. Henry is the John F. and Dorothy H. Magee Associate Professor of Government at Bowdoin College in Brunswick, Maine. She received her PhD in political science from the University of California, Berkeley. Henry's research examines state-society relations in Russia, with a special focus on the environmental movement, as well as Russia's participation in global governance initiatives. She is the author of *Red to Green: Environmental Activism in Post-Soviet Russia* (Cornell University Press, 2010) and the co-editor (with

Alfred Evans and Lisa McIntosh Sundstrom) of *Russian Civil Society: A Critical Assessment* (M.E. Sharpe, 2006). Her work also has appeared in journals including *Environmental Politics, Global Environmental Politics, Europe-Asia Studies,* and *Post-Soviet Affairs,* among others. Her current research examines how global initiatives on health, the environment, and corporate social responsibility engage civil society actors in the BRICS states.

Notes

1. The terms 'heroes' and 'crowd' come from an essay by Nikolai Mikhailovskii, one of the most influential Populist thinkers in the late nineteenth century, and one of the first Russian sociological theorists (Khalii 2007: 47).

References

Almeida, P. 2003. 'Opportunity Organizations and Threat-Induced Contention: Protest Waves in Authoritarian Settings'. *American Journal of Sociology* 109, no. 2: 345–400.

Asochakov, I. V., et al., eds. 2000. *Sotsiologiia i obshchestvo: Tezisy Pervogo Vserossiiskogo sotsiologicheskogo kongressa 'Obshchestvo i sotsiologiia: novye realii i novye idei'.* Sankt-Peterburg: Izdatel'stvo 'Skifiia'.

Beissinger, M. 2002. *Nationalist Mobilization and the Collapse of the Soviet State.* Cambridge: Cambridge University Press.

Butenko, I. A. 2002. 'The Russian Sociological Association: Actors and Scenery on a Revolving Stage'. *International Sociology* 17, no. 2: 233–51.

Caiazza, A. 2002. *Mothers and Soldiers: Gender, Citizenship, and Civil Society in Contemporary Russia.* New York: Routledge.

Dawson, J. 1996. *Eco-Nationalism: Anti-nuclear Activism and National Identity in Russia, Lithuania, and Ukraine.* Durham: Duke University Press.

Della Porta, D. 2011. 'Social Movements'. In *International Encyclopedia of Political Science,* ed. B. Badie, D. Berg-Schlosser and L. Morlino, 8:2431–43. Los Angeles: Sage Reference.

Earl, J. 2007. 'Social Movements, Repression of'. In *The Blackwell Encyclopedia of Sociology,* ed. G. Ritzer, 9:4475–79. Malden: Blackwell Publishing.

Evans, A. 2012. 'Protests and Civil Society: The Struggle for the Khimki Forest'. *Communist and Post-Communist Studies* 45, nos. 3–4: 233–42.

———. 2013. 'Civil Society and Protest'. In *Return to Putin's Russia: Past Imperfect, Future Uncertain,* ed. S. Wegren, 103–24. 5th ed. Lanham: Rowman and Littlefield.

Fish, M. S. 1995. *Democracy from Scratch: Opposition and Regime in the New Russian Revolution.* Princeton: Princeton University Press.

Friedgut, T. 1979. *Political Participation in the USSR.* Princeton: Princeton University Press.

Friedman, D., and D. McAdam. 1992. 'Collective Identity and Activism: Networks, Choices, and the Life of a Social Movement'. In *Frontiers in Social Movement Theory,* ed. A.D. Morris and C. McClurg Mueller, 156–73. New Haven: Yale University Press.

Greenfeld, L. 1988. 'Soviet Sociology and Sociology in the Soviet Union'. *Annual Review of Sociology* 14: 99–123.

Henderson, S. 2003. *Building Democracy in Contemporary Russia: Western Support for Grassroots Organizations.* Ithaca: Cornell University Press.

———. 2010. 'Shaping Civil Advocacy'. In *Advocacy Organizations and Collective Action* A. Prakash and M. Gugerty, 252–80. Cambridge: Cambridge University Press.

Henry, L. 2010. *Red to Green: Environmental Activism in Post-Soviet Russia.* Ithaca: Cornell University Press.

Hosking, G. 1992. 'The Beginnings of Independent Political Activity'. In *The Road to Post-Communism: Independent Political Movements in the Former Soviet Union, 1985–1991,* ed. G. A. Hosking, J. Aves and P. J. S. Duncan, 1–28. London: Pinter Publishers.

Howard, M. 2003. *The Weakness of Civil Society in Post-Communist Europe.* Cambridge: Cambridge University Press.

Johnston, H. 2007. 'Mobilization'. In *The Blackwell Encyclopedia of Sociology,* ed. G. Ritzer, 6:3065–68. Malden: Blackwell Publishing.

Johnson, J. 2009. *Gender Violence in Russia: The Politics of Feminist Intervention.* Bloomington: Indiana University Press.

Johnson, J., and A Saarinen. 2013. 'Twenty-First-Century Feminisms under Repression: Gender Regime Change and the Women's Crisis Center Movement in Russia'. *Signs: Journal of Women in Culture and Society* 38, no. 3: 543–67.

Jowitt, K. 1992. *New World Disorder: The Leninist Extinction.* Berkeley: University of California Press.

Katz, Z. 1971. 'Sociology in the Soviet Union'. *Problems of Communism* 20, no. 3: 22–40.

Keck M., and K. Sikkink. 1998. *Activists beyond Borders: Advocacy Networks in International Politics.* Ithaca: Cornell University Press.

Khalii, I. A. 2007. *Sovremennye obshchestvennye dvizheniia: innovatsionnyi potentsial rossiiskikh preobrazovanii v traditsionalistskoi srede.* Moscow: Institut sotsiologii RAN.

Lewin, M. 1991. *The Gorbachev Phenomenon: A Historical Interpretation.* Berkeley: University of California Press.

McAdam, D. 1994. 'Culture and Social Movements'. In *New Social Movements: From Ideology to Identity,* ed. E. Laraña, H. Johnston, and J. R. Gusfeld, 36–57. Philadelphia: Temple University Press.

Melucci, A. 1997. 'Getting Involved: Identity and Mobilization in Social Movements'. In *Comparative Politics: Rationality, Culture, and Structure,* ed. M. Lichbach and A. Zuckerman, 329–48. Cambridge: Cambridge University Press.

Novikov, N. 1982. 'The Sociological Movement in the U.S.S.R. (1960–1970) and the Institutionalization of Soviet Sociology'. *Studies in Soviet Thought* 23, no. 2: 95–118.

Osipov, G. V., and M. N. Rutkevich. 1978. 'Sociology in the USSR 1965–1975'. *Current Sociology* 26, no. 2: 1–160.

Polletta, F. and J. Jasper 2001. 'Collective Identity and Social Movements'. *Annual Review of Sociology* 27: 283–305.

Powell, L. 2002. 'Western and Russian Environmental NGOs: A Greener Russia?' In *The Power and Limits of NGOs,* ed. S. Mendelson and J. Glenn, 126–51. New York: Columbia University Press.

Putnam, R. 1993. *Making Democracy Work: Civic Traditions in Modern Italy.* Princeton: Princeton University Press.

Reddaway, P., ed. 1972. *Uncensored Russia: Protest and Dissent in the Soviet Union.* New York: American Heritage Press.

Robertson, G. 2009. 'Managing Society: Protest, Civil Society and Regime in Putin's Russia'. *Slavic Review* 68, no. 3: 528–47.

———. 2011. *The Politics of Protest in Hybrid Regimes: Managing Dissent in Post-Communist Russia.* Cambridge: Cambridge University Press.

Sedaitis, J., and J. Butterfield. 1991. *Perestroika from Below: Social Movements in the Soviet Union.* Boulder: Westview.

Skilling, H., and F. Griffiths. 1971. *Interest Groups in Soviet Politics.* Princeton: Princeton University Press.

Sperling, V. 1999. *Organizing Women in Contemporary Russia: Engendering Transition.* Cambridge: Cambridge University Press.

Starr, S. 1988. 'Soviet Union: A Civil Society'. *Foreign Policy* 70: 26–41.

Sundstrom, L. 2006. *Funding Civil Society: Foreign Assistance and NGO Development in Russia.* Palo Alto: Stanford University Press.

Tarrow, S. 1998. *Power in Movement: Social Movements and Contentious Politics.* 2nd ed. Cambridge: Cambridge University Press.

Thomas, D. 2001. *The Helsinki Effect: International Norms, Human Rights, and the Demise of Communism.* Princeton: Princeton University Press.

Tsepilova, O. D. 1999. 'Ot sotsial'noi problemy k kollektivomu deistviiu: ekologicheskie dvizheniia v raionakh ekologicheskoi opasnostii'. In *Obshchestvennye dvizheniia v sovremennoi Rossi: ot sotsial'noi problemy k kollektivnomu deistviiu,* ed. V. V. Kostiushev, 101–18. Moscow: Izdatel'stvo Instituta sotsiologii RAN.

Tynkkynen, N. 2006. 'Action Frames of Environmental Organisations in Post-Soviet St. Petersburg'. *Environmental Politics* 15, no. 4: 639–49.

Weiner, D. 1999. *A Little Corner of Freedom: Russian Nature Protection from Stalin to Gorbachev.* Berkeley: University of California Press.

Weinberg, E.A. 1974. *The Development of Sociology in the Soviet Union.* London: Routledge and Keegan Paul.

Yanitsky, O. 1993. *Russian Environmentalism: Leading Figures, Faction, Opinions.* Moscow: Mezhdunarodnoye Otnoshenie Publishing House.

———. 1996. *Ekologicheskoe Dvizhenie Rossii: Kriticheskii Analiz.* Moscow: Russian Academy of Sciences, Institute of Sociology.

———. 2010a. *Russian Environmentalism: The Yanitsky Reader.* Moscow: TAUS.

———. 2010b. 'Seti sotsial'nykh dvizhenii v Rossii'. *Obshchestvennye nauki i sovremennost'* 6: 52–62.

———. 2013. 'Sotsial'nye dvizheniia v sovremennom obshchestve: voprosy teorii'. *Sotsiologicheskie issledovaniia* 3: 50–59.

Zdravomyslova, E. A. 1990. 'Sotsiologicheskie podkhody k analizu obshchestvennykh dvizhenii'. *Sotsiologicheskie issledovaniia* 8: 88–94.

———. 1993a. *Paradigmy zapadnoi sotiologii obshchestvennykh dvizhenii.* St. Petersburg: Nauka.

———. 1993b. 'Mobilizatsiia resursov demokraticheskogo dvizheniia v Leningrade (1987–1990 gg.)'. In *Sotsiologiia obshchestvennykh dvizhenii: empiricheskie nabliu-

deniia i issledovaniia, ed. A. N. Alekseev, V. V. Kostiushev and A. A. Temkina, 110–31. Moscow and St. Petersburg: Rossiiskaia Akademiia Nauk, Institut sotsiologii, Sankt-Peterburzhskii filial.

———. 1996. 'Opportunities and Framing in the Transition to Democracy: The Case of Russia'. In *Comparative Perspectives on Social Movements: Political Opportunities, Mobilizing Structures, and Cultural Framings,* ed. D. McAdam, J. McCarthy, and M. Zald. Cambridge: Cambridge University Press, 122–37.

Zdravomyslova, E. A., and A. Temkina. 2009. *Novyi byt v sovremennoi Rossii: gendernye issledovaniia posednevnosti.* St. Petersburg: Izdatel'stvo EUSPb.

Social Movement Studies in Europe
Achievements, Gaps and Challenges[1]

Dieter Rucht

> XXII Thou shalt not be too optimistic about building
> a science of collective behavior but thou shalt try anyway.[2]

Today, in an era marked by accelerated globalization, the question arises whether or not one should assess the state of the art in any field of the social sciences, including social movement studies, with regard to particular countries and continents. After all, social movement scholars from many countries read or even publish in English as the *lingua franca* of many scientific disciplines; they travel to international workshops and conferences, and increasingly cooperate across national borders. Therefore, we might expect that formerly existing specific national and continental profiles of social movement studies have largely disappeared.

However, before proclaiming the existence of a big melting pot of largely globalised social movement studies, it is necessary to take a close look at theories, methods, empirical work and institutional bases that might be characteristic for, or at least dominant in, certain regions. Scholarship is influenced by prevailing paradigms, intellectual debates, research questions, funding opportunities and, last but not least, social movement activities that may be rather context-specific, notwithstanding the existence of a truly internationalised scholarly community. Accordingly, both the similarities and the differences of social movement studies in particular countries and continents need to be inspected before arriving at general conclusions.

Largely based on the set of movement-specific chapters in part II of this collective volume, I will attempt to provide an overview on social movement studies in Europe. First, I will present a brief historical account of the long-term development of social movement studies in both the United States and Europe. The United States has been chosen as a reference point because it has been, and still is, the country with the largest and most sophisticated scholarly output in this field of study. Comparison with respective work in

Europe may help us in recognizing not only persistent specificities of European-based work but also a potential transatlantic convergence.

Second, in the main part of this concluding chapter, I will take a look at social movement studies in a number of European countries, with an eye at both findings on specific movements and nation-bound research profiles. Given the number and sophistication of this volume's chapters, I apply a broad stroke for drawing a comparative picture. In addition to reading these chapters, I also conducted a content analysis of the fifteen country-specific chapters by using the computer program MAXQDA. Moreover, I distributed a two-page questionnaire to all authors of this volume to get additional, and partly quantitative, information on the state of social movement research in their respective countries. Out of thirty-six authors, thirty have completed this questionnaire.

Finally, in the third section of this chapter, I aim to identify some of the remaining gaps and challenges in European social movement studies.

The Evolution of Social Movement Studies in the United States and Europe: A Brief Overview

Around the turn to the twentieth century, social movements as a scientific subject were approached from two quite different viewpoints: mass psychology on the one hand and sociology and history on the other. Mass psychology, as represented by writers such as Gustave Le Bon, Gabriel Tarde, Scipio Sighele and—somewhat later—also Sigmund Freud, interpreted social movements essentially as a form of crowd behaviour along with fads, fashion and panic. Crowd behaviour was seen as driven by emotions, triggered and steered by manipulative leaders, and spreading like a contagious disease. This interpretation was undergirded by a combination of three factors: first, the anxiety about the destructive and possibly revolutionary potential of the lower classes; second, stereotypes and prejudices about the primitive state of mind and irrationality of what was called mob, riffraff, ragtag, etc.; third, the avoidance of a closer and empirically grounded study of the actual mobilizations and events of collective protest. The basic assumptions of this crude form of mass psychology fell on fertile ground especially among the conservative intellectuals, scientists and politicians of their time in Europe and, to a lesser extent, in the United States where the leftist revolutionary zeal was much weaker.

Sociological and historical approaches to social movements, in their majority, opted for another perspective, less prejudiced and more orientated toward empirical facts. In Europe, social movement studies did not become a scientific field in its own right until the 1970s.

Mass psychology gradually lost its influence because of the weight of sociologically informed or trained writers and, probably still more important, the detailed account of the many historians who studied various kinds of social movements and revolutions of the past. In Europe, the study of historical movements was strongly supported and sustained by institutional means, usually coming from left-wing organizations that funded institutes, research centres, libraries, book series and journals specialised on the labour movement.

In the United States, the study of social movements took on a different shape. Various approaches and schools reflected on and, to some extent, empirically studied social movements, among them the Chicago School originally centred around Robert Park and Ernest Burgess, later on structural functionalists (most importantly Neil Smelser) influenced by Talcott Parsons, symbolic interactionists like Herbert Blumer, and eventually those who, though in less crude forms, adhered to ideas of the old school of mass psychology.

Collective behaviour, a term introduced by Park and Burgess (1921), became the convenient denominator for a broader range of phenomena of which social movements gradually moved into the centre of scholarly interest. Accordingly, 'Collective Behavior and Social Movements' became the title of a professional section created in 1980 that currently comprises more than eight hundred sociologists in the United States.

Contrary to the assertions given by proponents of the resource mobilization approach, earlier work on social movements in the United States was fairly diversified and cannot be subsumed under the label of the contagion approach promoted by mass psychology. However, this simplification was certainly instrumental in raising the visibility and plausibility of the resource mobilization approach. Regarding the number of publications, this approach became the most important strand in social movement research for a while (Edwards and McCarthy 1992). It was definitely influenced by the existence of the civil rights movement and the New Left to whom many liberal-minded scholars were sympathetic. Having had experience with these movements, they rejected earlier and partly derogative accounts on social movements of which proponents of resource mobilization—wrongly—took the contagion approaches as *pars pro toto*.

Later on, the resource mobilization strand was complemented, and partly replaced, by other approaches centred around (and accordingly labelled) political process theory, political opportunity structure, framing, collective identity, movement culture and contentious politics. Because this more recent development and co-existence of various middle-range approaches has been described in a number of introductory books, review articles, and the introductory chapter by Olivier Fillieule and Guya Accornero in this volume, there is no need to lay it out here in detail.

Contrary to the rapidly expanding and gradually institutionalizing social movement studies in the United States, the field was almost a void in Europe until the 1970s. Many historians were writing on social movements without using an explicit concept or theory on this subject. Only few social scientists published on social movement phenomena, again hardly reflecting about these in theoretical and conceptual ways. This changed in the wake of the student movement of the late 1960s and the resulting turmoil and, later, reform-mindedness in quite a number of European countries.

The French sociologist Alain Touraine who was initially involved in industrial sociology and labour studies was among the first to systematically theorise the role of social movements in present times. Against the backdrop of what he described as a shift from the industrial society (with the labour movement as the principal movement agent) to the post-industrial society (Touraine 1969), he identified the new social movement as the principal agent challenging the trend toward 'technocracy' (Touraine 1968). Later on, he and his collaborators began to study social movements in a closer empirical perspective by developing and applying a method called 'sociological intervention' (Touraine 1978). He became influential not only in France but also in a number of other European countries and, due to personal contacts and visits, in Latin America. Also a few social movement students in Canada, such as Louis Maheu and Henri Lustiger-Thaler, were close to Touraine's approach. Interestingly, his influence was relatively marginal in the United States where sweeping generalizations à la Touraine were met with much reservation (e.g. Gamson 1983). Touraine attracted quite a number of students and visitors from abroad, most notably the Italian sociologist and psychotherapist Alberto Melucci, for whose PhD thesis Touraine served as the key adviser.

Melucci wrote his first two articles (in Italian) on social movements in 1977 (1981: 1). Soon he developed his own approach (Melucci et al. 1984) focusing on the concept of collective identity but also covering a number of other aspects including the use of symbols (1995b). Similar to Touraine, Melucci took a broad perspective in situating social movements in their societal context (1997), but being critical especially of Touraine's methodology of 'sociological intervention'.[3]

In Germany, various efforts to vivify the study of social movements via the work of Rudolf Heberle (1967), Neil Smelser's principal book on collective behaviour (published in German in 1972) and Heinz and Schöbers' two-volume edition on theories of collective behaviour (1973) made little impact. Moreover, German historians writing on social movements, as probably historians in almost all European countries including Britain, rarely took notice of sociological work on social movements done in the United States.

This changed in the 1970s and the early 1980s when the new social movements moved to the fore of scholarly interest in almost all Western European countries. Apart from studies on specific movements, more general books on social movements were published in countries such as Italy (Alberoni 1977; Melucci 1984a), Britain (Banks 1972; Marsh 1977), Denmark (Gundelach 1980), Sweden (Friberg and Galtung 1983), the Netherlands (Loo et al. 1984) and Switzerland (Kriesi 1985).

In Germany, a first cornerstone was Otthein Rammstedt's book entitled 'Social Movements' (1978), which, regrettably, was never translated into other languages. Rammstedt traced the concept of social movements back to the nineteenth century but was also referring to contemporary social movement literature from the United States. Several books on (new) social movements were published in Germany during the 1980s,[4] most importantly Joachim Raschke's comprehensive study entitled *Social Movements: A Historical and Systematic Outline* (1985). He situated the new social movements in a broader historical context with a comparative look on movements in the pre-industrial and industrial age. He also drew extensively on US literature.

By the mid-eighties, the 'splendid isolation' of movement studies in both Europe and the United States was over. This was not merely an effect of mutual reading. In fact, little work published in Europe was noticed in the United States, while the opposite stream of influence became increasingly strong.

Another factor were personal encounters, hence a matter that would be part and parcel of a sociology of science. In 1983, I incidentally met the Dutch social psychologist Bert Klandermans in front of Charles Tilly's office at the University of Michigan. We were visiting a number of renowned social movement scholars in the United States. About the same time, Hanspeter Kriesi and a few others made contacts with US scholars. These encounters helped to bring together scholars from various countries. Besides an international workshop on social movements that I co-organised in Cologne in 1985, a much more influential initiative came from Bert Klandermans and Sidney Tarrow. This initiative is worth reporting in more detail.

After having held a small workshop hosted by Tarrow at Cornell University in 1985, Klandermans organised a larger international workshop in Amsterdam in 1986 whose outcome is documented in a collective volume (Klandermans, Kriesi and Tarrow 1988). This meeting provided the major impulse for the gradual formation of a fertile cross-Atlantic and cross-European network of social movement scholars that, though without formal structure and with some fluctuation—a few drop-outs and the inclusion of younger scholars—is still in existence. The Amsterdam workshop was followed by subsequent meetings of this network in Berlin in 1990, Washington, D.C., in 1992, Mont Pélerin (Switzerland) in 1995, and a few other places. The most recent gathering took place in Amsterdam in 2011 and bore fruit in another important collective volume (Stekelenburg, Roggeband and Klandermans 2013).

A further factor for mutual awareness of the work done in the United States and in (some parts of) Europe were the large international conferences of sociologists and political scientists. Within the International Sociological Association, a Research Committee on 'Social Classes and Social Movements', established in 1993, was later complemented by the Committee on 'Social Movements, Collective Action and Social Change', created one year later. While the former, at least in its earlier years, attracted more of the politicised scholars, the latter is more orientated towards politically detached and analytically rigorous work. Noteworthy also is the existence of other committees dealing with social movements, most notably 'Women in Society' and 'Labour Movements'.

The early international meetings also stimulated the first comparisons of work done on both sides of the Atlantic, starting with articles by Klandermans (1986) and Tarrow (1986). Soon, they were followed by a number of subsequent publications, including Rucht's edited volume on the state of the art in the United States and Western Europe (1991a).

The basic message of the first cross-continental comparisons was that of significant differences. Because of different prevailing theoretical traditions and research questions, work in the United States and Europe, respectively, had developed in relative isolation from each other. It was said that the European scholars were focusing more on the *why* of mobilization, were more interested in collective identity formation, and were linking social movements closer to the societal context in which they develop and decay. By contrast, scholars in the United States were portrayed as being more interested in the *how* of mobilization, including organizational aspects, and in paying less attention to different societal und historical contexts of movements (Melucci 1980: 212). When Melucci was talking about collective identity as a constitutive element of social movements in the 1986 Amsterdam workshop, Tarrow dryly asked: 'How can you recognise the collective identity of protesters walking down the street?'[5] Melucci, in turn, criticised the US scholars, certainly with a glance at Tarrow, for their 'political overload' (Melucci 1984: 822) and 'political reductionism' (Melucci 1995a: 112; 1989: 44) in their attempts to explain the rise of social movements.

It was also said that the Europeans are preoccupied with the *new* social movements arising the 1960s and 1970s, whereas this concept, at least initially, did not find much resonance in the United States.[6] Not surprisingly, Tarrow (1986/1991), when contrasting social movement studies in Western Europe and the United States, juxtaposed Alain Touraine and Mayer Zald as the respective key representatives.

These observations, at the time they were made, definitely contained some elements of truth. But it was an 'extremely simplistic and American-centric' view (Fillieule and Accornero, in this volume). It was mainly based on looking at the scholars who were present in the international meetings of those days instead of a comprehensive and close reading of the available literature which, especially in Europe, is hard to overview because of the multitude of languages.

Regarding the ten or twelve years after the Amsterdam workshop in 1986, two significant developments should be underlined. First, scholars from the United States and Europe really took notice of each other's work. Cross-continental co-operation broadened and intensified, including, in a few cases, co-authorship of articles (e.g. Klandermans and Tarrow 1988; Della Porta and Tarrow 1986; McAdam and Rucht 1993) and co-editorship of books (Klandermans, Kriesi and Tarrow 1988; Klandermans and Jenkins 1995). This helped to reduce the formerly existing specific profiles of social movement studies on both continents. In addition, cooperation within Europe also intensified. For example, with a specific focus on Europe and a deliberate attempt to integrate colleagues from the former Soviet bloc, Klandermans and I organised the 'First European Conference on Social Movements and Collective Behaviour' at the Social Science Center Berlin in 1992.

Second, and partly as a corollary of this rapid rapprochement, the then small field of social movement studies in Europe expanded very quickly, catching up with the more sophisticated state of research in the United States. This became clear in a conference in Washington, D.C., in 1992 when almost all participants, regardless of their country of origin, valued the coexistence and prevalence of three approaches: resource mobilization, political opportunity structures and framing (McAdam, McCarthy and Mayer N. Zald 1996). Other approaches, be they Marxist or rational choice theory, were neglected. For example, Karl-Dieter Opp, an ardent promoter of rational choice theory who had participated in the Amsterdam meeting in 1986, dropped out of this network for reasons that are unclear to me, and never became re-integrated into this community. While this may appear as a marginal detail, clearly it has consequences for the field of study. Opp's work, in spite of his numerous publications in English and occasional co-authorship with American colleagues, was hardly acknowledged by the core representatives of the international community of movement scholars. Even his recent book on social movement theory, an attempt to integrate several middle-range approaches into his rational choice approach (Opp 2009), remained largely unnoticed, or at least, tacitly circumvented.[7] More generally, as several reviews of the field document, rational choice approaches based on the paradigm of methodological individualism tend to be neglected instead of being seriously discussed (see Turner 1991; Ferree 1992; Rucht 2001).

On the other hand, a more traditional approach represented by authors such as Herbert Blumer and Ralph Turner, having been largely in abeyance from the 1970s to the mid-90s, began to resurge, though with some new accentuations, towards the end of the millennium. This move, directed against the rational and structuralist bias of what was perceived as the mainstream of social movement studies at that time was pre-empted by the Italian sociologist Alberto Melucci (1985) but more forcefully promoted by a handful of US scholars, especially Jeff Goodwin and James Jasper (1999). Later, it was also adopted by a number of European movement scholars (e.g. Flam and King 2005; Cefaï 2006; Baumgarten, Daphi and Ullrich 2014). These developments are part of a more general 'cultural turn' that could be observed in many special fields in social sciences and history.

When overviewing social movement studies in the United States and in Western Europe since the last fifteen years or so, I would contend that significant discrepancies no longer exist in terms of prevailing theories and methods. This, however, does not mean to deny gradual differences. For example, it seems to me that European scholars more often than their colleagues in the United States engage in cross-national comparisons and are more inclined to embed social movements into their broader societal and historical context. Also, the heritage of Marxist thought in social movement studies, at least among the older generations of scholars, remains stronger in Europe when compared to the United States. Partly related to this aspect, it also appears that social movement scholars in Europe, on average, tend to be more politicised than their colleagues in the United States.

However, when considering other criteria of comparison, some striking differences can be observed. Up to date, social movement research is much better institutionalised in the United States than in any European country, as indicated by the number of courses, textbooks, introductory books, professorships and the size of specialised professional sections in sociology and political science. But also in this respect, Europe on the whole is catching up. However, some European countries with relatively small resources compared to the United States and fewer cross-national contacts are still lagging far behind (see the section on 'Institutionalization and Cross-Fertilization' below).

In the following, neither the situation in the United States nor that in other continents will serve as reference points to characterise social movement studies in Europe. Rather, the focus is comparison of social movement studies *within* Europe—an aspect that has been almost completely neglected until the present.

Social Movement Studies in Europe: A Continent of Exceptions?

In taking a comparative perspective on social movement studies across European countries, I will mainly rely on the country-specific reports provided in part II of this volume. Obviously, these fifteen reports do not cover the whole of Europe. Nevertheless, when taken together, they represent the largest available up-to-date collection of this kind. Moreover, they are an instructive variegated sample in terms of population size, political systems and geographic areas, covering—in terms of demographic volume and economic power—the four major Western European countries (Germany, France, Britain and Italy) and three of the smaller ones (Ireland, the Netherlands and Switzerland), one Scandinavian country (Sweden), and the most important Southern European countries (besides Italy also Spain, Portugal and Greece.) As a novelty in a comparison of social movement studies, also Turkey and three of the notoriously neglected countries of the former Soviet bloc (Russia, Hungary and Romania) are included. Among the European countries with a relatively large population, it is noteworthy to mention the absence of the Ukraine and Poland. In addition to the fifteen national reports, very occasionally I will rely on information from the chapters in part I and my own scattered knowledge on some of the missing European countries.

Before engaging in comparison, a methodological caveat should be acknowledged. The very act of identifying characteristics of a unit of analysis, in our case social movement studies in a given country, requires comparison. However, the authors of the national reports neither structured their chapters along the same questions and criteria, nor did (and, given their task, could) they engage, apart from some side remarks, in a truly comparative endeavour. This makes it difficult to put into perspective some of their characterizations, for example 'Ireland as a peculiar case' (Cox in this volume) or Switzerland as having a low degree of institutionalization of social movement studies (Balsiger in this volume).

Moreover, the identification of characteristics is also dependent on the closeness or distance of the observer vis-à-vis the object. Think about the physiognomy of Asian people who, from the viewpoint of an average Western tourist, all look very similar but, from perspective of an Asian, are quite distinct. The closer one moves to the object under study, the more specificities come to the fore. The same applies to characterizations of national movement sectors. US scholars, when looking at European countries, tend to emphasise differences with regard to their home country and neglect differences within Europe so that they may—wrongly—conclude that there is a single European pattern. However, when specialists are writing on their country only, they tend to emphasise what they perceive as distinct and peculiar. In the end, each specialist may be tempted to classify his or her case as exceptional so that almost all European cases appear as unique.

While such a 'historicist' position goes too far, there remains, however, a lesson to be learned. Meaningful and grounded comparison requires the explicit spelling out of the criterion of comparison as well as specification of the methods and standards to make quantitative and/or qualitative assessments. On this basis, we can identify similarities and differences and, in the aggregate, classify a whole country, social movement sector or national social movement scholarship in a certain way. While the rough dimensions of the following comparison can be named and are indicated by the section headlines, we basically lack standardised criteria, let alone measurements, to determine the values that, on a solid empirical basis, can be attributed to movements and contexts in cross-national comparison (for two of the few exceptions, see Kriesi et al. 1995 and Rootes 2003). These limitations clearly hamper my comparative attempt which mainly relies on information provided by a group of authors who have written in isolation from each other (and consequently not agreed on their criteria) and whose reference points for identifying characteristics are not always made explicit.

Paradigms and Theories

For better or worse, political opportunities, mobilizing structures and cultural framings were identified as the 'international (read: US) approaches' (Cox, in this volume) around the mid-nineties. Other work, for example (neo-)Marxist theories, symbolic interactionism and rational choice theory, remained marginal or were completely ignored. In spite of these omissions, the canonical perception established around the mid-nineties seems to be upheld until the present. According to the respondents of my questionnaire, political opportunity, political process and—as a second choice only—framing are considered as the most influential approaches (see table 1). Political identity comes next. When ignoring the category 'other' in which no clusters can be found, resource mobilization ranges at the bottom. In the country reports, hence a source independent from the questionnaire, the marginal position of rational choice theory is confirmed. 'Rational choice' is only mentioned once, while other concepts have significantly higher scores.[8]

Table 1. Most influential approaches to social movements in the last ten years (Frequencies)

	Most influential	Second most influential	Sum
Resource mobilization	1	2	3
Political opportunities	10	1	11
Political process	7	4	11
Framing/Discourse	—	11	11
Collective identity/culture/emotions	5	4	9
Other	3	5	8

As a further relevant reference point, especially when covering Europe, the new social movements are mentioned in almost every country report. Unlike the aforementioned three approaches that are mainly associated with US scholars, the new social movements approach, at least in social movement studies in general, is almost exclusively attributed to European scholars, especially Alain Touraine, Alberto Melucci, Hanspeter Kriesi and, somewhat surprisingly because of their low investment in this field of study, Jürgen Habermas and Claus Offe.[9]

Also, at least in some of the country reports, the more recent cultural turn in social movement studies is reflected by citing, for example, the work of James Jasper (thirteen references) and Francesca Polletta (two references). While one might argue that these authors could be subsumed to the older trilogy as part of the cultural framings component, this would not do justice to them. First, they were critical of resource and political opportunity approaches. Second, these authors highlight aspects of emotion, narratives, cultural symbols and collective identity building that were hardly part and parcel of the framing approach as promoted, most notably, by David Snow, William A. Gamson and Robert Benford. Other influential US-based scholars, among these a number of female scholars as well as the old guard including Anthony Oberschall, John Lofland, Gary T. Marx, Neil Smelser, Ralph Turner, Immanuel Wallerstein and the duo Frances Fox Piven and Richard Cloward are rarely or never cited in either the movement-centred chapters or the country reports of this volume. The same applies to the earlier generation represented by figures such as Herbert Blumer, Lewis Killian and Joseph Gusfield.[10] This, at least in part, is also an effect of the editors' guideline to rely mainly on scholarly work done in Europe.

Apart from approaches focusing on new social movements, theorizing in Europe was, at least in the common perception, largely seen as an adoption, variation and/or extension of approaches developed in the United States. Scholars who did not fit that image and/or did not or rarely publish in English language, were considered to be marginal or flatly ignored, partly also due to language barriers (e.g. the writings of the German political scientists Roland Roth and Joachim Raschke). The same could be said for scholars from a few other European countries who remained largely unnoticed beyond their domestic readership, for example the French François Dubet and the Italian Luigi Manconi.

In sum, with few notable exceptions, European social movement scholars tended to perceive and adopt in a selective and sometimes biased way the theories developed in the United States and, to a lesser extent, in parts of Europe. Moreover, there was hardly an intense theoretical debate among European scholars of whom a few, however, were voicing a critique towards some US approaches. For example, Alain Touraine tended to show little apprehension for social movement studies from the United States. Also, volumes similar to Morris and Muller's *Frontiers of Social Movement Theory* (1992) are lacking in Europe. Instead, we find compilations of existing approaches and theories (e.g. Hellmann and Koopmans 1998; Della Porta and Diani 1999) as well as a few attempts to bring together various theoretical strands focusing on different aspects in a more integrative and comprehensive perspective on social movements (Neidhardt and Rucht 1993/2001; Cefaï 2006; Pettenkofer 2010; Jasper and Duyvendak 2015).

In my view, little creative and innovative theoretical work in social movement studies has been published in Europe during the last two or three decades. To the extent that genuine theoretical efforts have been made, these remained, contrary to the focus on middle-range approaches prevailing in the United States, mostly macro-sociological approaches adopting concepts such as modernization, post-industrialism, fordism/postfordism, neo-liberalism, information society, etc. Only a few concepts were basically developed in Europe. Examples are: the extension of the political opportunity approach by adding discursive and economic opportunities (Koopmans and Statham 1999; Wahlström and Peterson 2006), Eyerman and Jamison's cognitive approach to social movements (1991) and Klandermans' socio-psychological approach to social movements and protest activity (1997).

With remarkable exceptions, in Europe references to social movement theories are often made in a casual way. The already best-known theories and concepts are cited again and again, thereby reinforcing their already existing prominence. Quite often, these references are restricted to a habit of name-dropping with only loose linkages to the specific empirical case under study. Depending on cultural traditions, the degree of professionalization and internationalization and the profile of the respective social movement sector, preferences for distinct approaches differ from country to country. In some places, for example in Britain, left-wing (neo-)Marxist theorists are far from insignificant. Authors like Eric Hobsbawm and Edward P. Thompson are important points of reference. In France, with its tradition of the academic 'mandarins', intellectual figures such as Bourdieu, Foucault and Touraine have inspired social movement studies for quite some time but are gradually losing their importance relative to the middle-range theories imported from abroad.[11] While social movement research in France was to a large degree self-centred, this has changed profoundly with the presence of a highly active and internationally orientated younger generation of which Olivier Fillieule is a primary example.

Other countries that are rather international in their orientation, for example the Netherlands, Germany, Switzerland and Sweden, were early adopters of approaches developed in the United States and have kept and even intensified their transatlantic connections so that they can no longer regarded as laggards when compared to the United States. Already in the 1980s and 1990s, several scholars from these countries travelled to the United States. In turn, US scholars were invited to visits and research stays in Europe.

Especially in countries that were late in joining the circuit of international social movement studies, such as Russia, Romania, Hungary, Turkey and, to a lesser extent, Portugal and Spain, theoretical approaches in general play only a marginal role thus far. Descriptive and historical accounts on specific movements and conflicts prevail. Also, in these countries there seems a greater emphasis on 'engaged scholarship' by taking political stances (especially Greece and Portugal) or, in the case of potential surveillance and political repression, resorting to research topics that, from the perspective of the authorities, are considered to be neutral or non-political.

Methodologies

By and large, what has been stated for theoretical approaches also applies to methodologies for studying social movements. To a considerable extent, methodologies that had been developed in the United States were imported by a number of Europeans. On the other hand, Touraine's method of sociological intervention and Melucci's experiments to study collective identity in small-group settings were isolated enterprises, neither adopted in other European countries nor in the United States. By contrast, standard methods used in the social sciences at large, for example biographical interviews, quantitative surveys, content analysis, participant observation and narrative interviews, were part and parcel of the wider scientific community and could be easily adopted in social movement studies in Europe. A first edited volume on methods to study collective action, based on a preceding workshop of the European Consortium for Political Research, was published by Mario Diani and Ron Eyerman (1992).[12]

To some extent, however, European social scholars were also among those who developed or at least refined innovative methods. Three examples are especially worth mentioning. First, Ruud Koopmans and Paul Statham (1999), at that time both working at the Social Science Center Berlin, introduced claims analysis (as an extension of protest event analysis) into social movement studies. Second, along with other colleagues mostly from Europe, Stefaan Walgrave refined the method of surveying protesters in the framework of mass events (Van Aelst and Walgrave 2001; see also Walgrave and Wagemann 2010). To be fair, this method had already been applied earlier by James Jasper and Bert Klandermans on a smaller scale in the 1980s. Third, again researchers at the Social Science Center Berlin developed a method of studying communication processes in meetings of social movement groups (Haug, Rucht and Teune 2013).

Especially methods requiring many resources were mainly applied in countries with relatively rich funding opportunities, such as France, Germany, Italy, the Netherlands and Switzerland. In these countries, as stated explicitly in this volume's chapter on the Netherlands, 'methodological nationalism' was soon overcome. These countries, for the most part, also took the lead in joint large comparative projects usually funded by the European Commission (see below). These projects contributed to the spread of methodological knowledge in (parts of) Europe and also to a certain degree of standardization of methods. Some countries with fewer domestic resources, such as Spain and Greece, could profit from this cross-national collaboration within Europe, as exemplified by the research activity of the Greek sociologist Maria Kousis. However, most countries in the Eastern and South-Eastern regions of Europe, for various reasons of which lacking in EU membership was only part of the problem, were not involved in these cross-national endeavours. Among the countries covered in this volume, this is true for Russia, Romania, Hungary and Turkey, but also for Portugal as a member of the EU. In these countries, probably to a greater extent than in the Western European countries, research is conducted by semi-detached or fully engaged political activists. Accordingly, sophisticated and inter-subjectively controllable methods are not a priority. Instead, there is rather a proliferation of descriptive empirical work, usually aimed at documenting and legitimizing social movement activities to which the researchers feel sympathetic.

When asked about the most frequently used methods in social movements studies in the last ten years, the respondents to my questionnaire prioritised (first and second option combined) the narrative interview, closely followed by case study and protest event analysis (see table 2). Not surprisingly, also a mixture of methods is perceived to be quite common, whereas structured interviews and standardised questionnaires are very rarely men-

Table 2. Most used methods in social movement studies (Frequencies)

	Last ten years			Last five years		
	Most used	Second most	Sum	Most used	Second most	Sum
Participant observation/ action research	2	2	4	2	5	7
Narrative interview	6	8	14	6	9	15
Structured interview	1	—	1	1	1	2
Standardised questionnaire	1	—	1	3	2	5
Content analysis	1	2	3	1	2	3
Protest event analysis	7	4	11	3	4	7
Case study	5	7	12	6	4	10
Mixture of methods	5	3	8	4	—	4
Other	1	—	1	1	—	1

tioned. When asked the same question for the last five years, the overall picture basically remains the same, with the exception of protest event analysis that has become less important in recent years.

Empirical Foci

In the more marginal countries in terms of social movement research, empirical work hardly covers the domestic social movement sector as whole. Some movements are completely ignored, whereas especially some more recent, more conflictive and, in relative terms, more spectacular conflicts are studied. A telling example for this is the relatively ample coverage of the case of Rosa Montană, an attempt of large-scale industrial gold mining in Romania. This project was and still is met with considerable levels of resistance. By contrast, other movements and conflicts in Romania are probably not unnoticed but, mainly due to a lack of students and resources, tend to be bracketed.

Compared to this set of countries of which Romania is just one example, social movement studies in most of the Western European core countries are less fragmented and selective. Here, not only do we find a host of studies on each major movement but also studies on movements that are smaller and perceived to be more marginal and/or short-lived. Moreover, in some of these countries, such as Germany and Switzerland, there are studies or edited volumes aimed at providing a comprehensive overview of the social movement sector or, in a more modest attempt, of a large segment of such a sector such as new social movements, workers movements, right-wing movements or violent movements. Also, studies have been published on specific forms or aspects of protest, for example demonstrations, organizational alliances, gendered patterns, protest networks, channels of mobilization including the Internet, social background of activists, etc.

Not surprisingly, social movement studies often flourish in the wake of major social movement cycles. In Western Europe, the rise of new social movements was not only followed by a rise of related studies; it also served as the major trigger for a broader view, including theoretical and methodological aspects, on social movements in general. Related to this was also a growing interest in the forerunners of contemporary movements, thereby putting the latter into a historical context by identifying, for example, the first and second wave (and later: a third wave) of the feminist movement, and the 'old' and the 'new' peace movement. Most recently, the movement of precarious groups, the Occupy movement, the revolutions in Arab countries and the emerging mobilization of refugees seem to stimulate an emerging surge of studies.

Relative to other movements, the politically progressive segment of national movement sectors received ample scholarly coverage. This applies not only to the new social movements of the 1970s and 1980s but also to the more recent global justice movements (see Sommier's chapter in this volume), as indicated in table 3. Supposedly, this is also an effect of the political socialization of researchers who have been, and in some cases still are, active in one or more of these movements. By contrast, with the notable exception of France, social movement students have devoted little attention to labour movements and activities of trade unions. Labour studies have been, and still are, mainly a domain of either historians or, as far as contemporary activity is concerned, a matter of social scientists who work in service of the unions and/or left-wing parties. Similar to the labour movement, also populist and extreme right-wing movements tend to be neglected by genuine social movement researchers. In some countries, research on these movements is

Table 3. Movements attracting most scholarly attention (Frequencies)

	Most	Second	Sum
Global Justice Movements	9	3	12
Environmental movement	4	6	10
Labour movement	3	2	5
Women's movement	3	4	7
Movements of precarious/excluded	3	3	6
Right-wing movements	1	2	3
Peace movement	3	3	6

relinquished to police authorities, intelligence services, criminologists, psychologists, journalists, and the like.

Also regarding different analytical aspects and dimensions of social movements, research in most European countries seems to be unbalanced. Easily visible and accessible features, for example large protest events and campaigns and large social movement organizations with offices, press speakers, newsletters, etc., tend to be well-researched. By contrast, small and local groups, informal networks, countercultural activities, routine meetings of social movement organizations and activities beyond the public appearances receive scarce attention. Studies on the policing of protest have been undertaken mainly in liberal-democratic countries but hardly in semi-democratic regimes such as Russia und Turkey.

Regarding knowledge gaps, worth mentioning is a lesson to be learned from the Swedish case. As Abby Peterson convincingly argues, social movements and, more particularly, the feminist movement in Sweden were grossly misrepresented for quite a while. Work in English published by non-Swedish scholars lacking a profound knowledge on the case under study portrayed Sweden as an anomaly: the existence of movement outcomes without (significant) movements. This view was widely adopted by a few other students of social movements reading English and/or engaging in comparative studies that included Sweden. In fact, however, the creators of the distorted pictures have not only overlooked a great deal of the movement activity across the country but also overestimated the willingness and capacity of policy-makers to meet dissenters' claims. This lesson should make us careful in adopting views from scholars who characterise a national movement sector and its outcomes on the basis of short visits, a handful of interviews with activists in only one city (preferably the capital), without speaking the country's language, and/or using their (probably contrasting) own country as the only reference case for classifying the foreign country under study.

Institutionalization and Cross-Fertilization

Starting in Europe from almost zero in the late 1960s and early 1970s, the recognition, internationalization and institutionalization of social movement studies has definitely progressed in quite a number of European countries. Nevertheless, studying social movements and protest groups was, and partly still is, met with some reservation by parts of both the political and academic establishment mainly for two reasons. First, social movement students may be treated not as 'serious' scientists but rather as movement sympathisers who, more or less accidentally, landed or stranded the academia that should not offer a place for subtle agitation in the disguise of science. This could be seen, for example, when an oral proposal to set up a research institute on social movements in Berlin was made in front of a committee. In reaction, a committee member, actually a member of Parliament, angrily raised the question of whether one should really make an effort that ultimately might stimulate terrorism. While this critique is absurd, it is true that many students of social movements have been, or still are, political activists. In countries where social movement studies are more institutionalised and professionalised, the proportion of activist-researchers has supposedly declined, while in other countries, for example Greece, a close link between scholarship and activism can be observed. Of the twenty-nine European authors[13] of this volume who completed my questionnaire, twelve have been political activists in the past; another eight have been and still are activists. Only nine are not, or have not been, activists. When asked whether most of their colleagues in their home country have a background as a movement activist, fourteen respondents answered yes, seven said no, and eight did not know.

Another reason, more to be found among the academics, is to express doubts on the relevance of the subject. This attitude is likely to be found among those who claim to have a 'realistic' view on society and politics as realms in which only power matters. Accordingly, they focus on big and well-organised players such as governments, major political parties, interest groups, corporations, and the like. This view, for example, was for a long time dominant in the subfield of international relations/international politics but also in some segments of sociology. From this perspective, social movements were perceived as marginal; they produce noise, moralise social questions (Luhmann 1996) and are driven, as exemplified by the new social movements, by anxieties and 'wild wishes' (Luhmann 1991: 137). No wonder that the outsider position often occupied by social movements with regard to the system of power was, and mostly still is, reflected by a marginal position of social movement studies within the academia.

A restriction for the growth and recognition of social movement studies in Europe was its initial lack of internationalization largely due to language barriers. Today, these barriers are basically overcome. This applies especially to countries located in Western and Northern Europe where most scholars fluently speak English, and publications in this language are widely read. But language barriers still exist, though gradually shrinking, in a number other countries, especially in Eastern and South-Eastern Europe. Back in the 1970s and 1980s, the diffusion of thoughts and writings was often influenced by routes of language. In Hungary, for example, work published in Germany and the United States was quite influential; in Portugal, work published in Brazil, and in the French-speaking part of Switzerland, work done in France became key references. In this regard, Italy in an interesting case. As Lorenzo Bosi and

Lorenzo Mosca state in chapter 16 of this volume, social movement studies in Italy were marginal in the 1960s and 1970s. Only when Italian researchers successfully moved to the international stage of the scientific community, the recognition they received at this level also bore fruit in their home country.

In international conferences taking place in Europe as well as in large (comparative) projects usually funded by the European Commission (see below), it is out of the question not to communicate in English. Given the informal requirement of the Commission to include also Eastern and Southern European countries in comparative studies, this fosters the inclusion of the already 'internationalised', meaning English-speaking, scholars from these countries. At the same time, this provides an incentive for their colleagues still confined to their domestic language to catch up and become integrated into the international conference and research circuit.

Regarding the institutionalization of social movement studies in Europe, we can consider several indicators that, when taken together, point to an uneven and/or ambivalent picture: the sheer number of books and articles on social movements has risen considerably in many European countries since the 1990s, though figures are not yet available. Regarding introductory books on sociology and political science as well as handbooks and dictionaries, it also appears that social movements are increasingly taken into account. While, to my knowledge, with the exception of labour studies, no journal specialised on social movements existed in any European country in the 1970s, today we have the peer-reviewed British-based journal *Social Movement Studies* with a truly international orientation, a few more journals or newsletters in various other languages (e.g. the *Forschungsjournal Soziale Bewegungen* in Germany, founded in 1988), and, most recently, electronic journals and newsletters such as *Interface: A Journal for and about Social Movements* (founded in 2009). In France, under the editorship of Nonna Mayer the *Contester* book series on social movement studies and related topics was established in 2008. In Germany, a book series with a broader denomination ('civil society and democracy') which includes work on social movements, is in place since 2002. In addition, the series *Moving the Social—Journal of Social History and History of Social Movements* was established in 2012 as an outgrowth of an earlier series of books and research reports in the German language published by the historically oriented Institute on Social Movements in Bochum (Germany).

These developments, of course, also reflect the more general trend of an increasing specialization within all scientific disciplines and cannot be interpreted as an achievement specific to social movement studies.

According to the surveyed authors of this book, in eleven countries (or twelve countries when Germany, not included in the survey, is added) a newsletter or journal exists focusing on social movements. Eleven countries are lacking such a communication tool. Not surprisingly, falling into this last category are not only Greece, Hungary, Portugal, Romania, Turkey and Russia but also Sweden, the Netherlands, Switzerland and Spain. Interestingly, the respondents on France disagree as three say yes and another three say no, probably because there was a group (Groupe d'études et de recherches sur les mutations du militantisme) that started in 1994 but dissolved around 2005.

The additional question in the survey, whether a nationwide section/ study group exists or not on social movements in the respective home country, was positively answered for fourteen countries and denied for another fourteen. A negative answer on the study group was given by respondents from Hungary, Portugal, Russia, Turkey, the Netherlands, Switzerland and Spain, hence countries that also lack a journal or newsletter. Greece and Sweden, both without a newsletter on social movements, do have a study group (and likewise Germany which was not included in the questionnaire).

An indicator for the relatively advanced state of a research area within a national setting is the existence of broader literature reviews and introductions on the field of study. In Germany, for example, several overviews have been provided at different points of time, starting in the early 1990s (see the chapter by Haunss in this volume). The Italians Della Porta and Mario Diani (1999) have written a comprehensive and widely cited introduction to social movements. And in France, to mention other formats, a dictionary and a handbook on social movements have been published more recently (Fillieule, Mathieu and Péchu 2009; Fillieule, Agrikoliansky and Sommier 2010).

Another criterion for assessing a potential trend toward institutionalization is the establishment of professorships or chairs devoted to social movement studies. In this regard, only tiny progress has been made across the whole of Europe. While the number of professors engaged in social movement studies has increased, a closer look would reveal that almost all of them have a broader nomination, for instance in political sociology, sociology of conflict and the like.

More progress has been made in establishing thematic sections within professional associations of sociologists and/or political scientists, and research groups and research centres. Thematic sections on social movements exist, for example, in some European countries (e.g. Germany since the late 1980s) but also at the level of European associations. Two study centres on social movements, the *Laboratoire des Mouvements Sociaux* (later called the *Centre d'Etudes des Mouvement Sociaux*, established in 1970) and the *Centre d'Analyse et d'Intervention Sociologique* (established in 1981) were set up relatively early in Paris thanks to the initiative of Alain Touraine. A long-standing research group on social movements existed from 1987/88 to 2011 at the Berlin Social Science Center. Also the Centre for the Study of Social and Political Movements at the University of Kent was established relatively early and is still in existence, though it does not have great resources. More recently, other formal or more informal groups and institutions have been set up at the European University in Florence, the University of Lausanne in Switzerland, the University of Gothenburg in Sweden and, most recently, in Berlin.

Though having a shorter existence, major research projects in the field of protest and social movement studies are also indicators for institutionalization. Besides national research councils, the research programmes and funds of the European Commission have provided important stimuli for advancing social movement studies. With national funds from the Netherlands, Hanspeter Kriesi and his collaborators conducted a study on protest events from 1975 to 1989 in four European countries (Kriesi at al. 1995). Work on protest events in Germany has been supported by the German Research Council and the Berlin Social Science Center. Among the major cross-national projects funded by the European Commission are: 'Transformation of Environmental Activism' (TEA, co-ordinated by Christopher Rootes); 'Mobilization on Ethnic Relations, Immigration and Citizenship' (MERCI, co-ordinated by Ruud Koopmans and Paul Statham); 'The Contentious Politics of the Unemployed in Europe' (co-ordinated by Marco Giugni et al.); 'Democracy and the Mobilization of Society' (DEMOS, co-ordinated by Donatella Della Porta). A still on-going large project, 'Caught in the Act of Protest: Contextualising Contestation' (CCC, co-ordinated by Bert Klandermans and Stefaan Walgrave), is funded by the European Science Foundation.

A close look at the fifteen country reports in this volume shows the differential weight of various disciplines[14] in contributing to social movement studies. In Switzerland, for example, social movement studies is mostly embedded in political science; in France it is squarely in political sociology; in Portugal and Greece, historians are strongly represented; in Hungary, both political science and anthropology are important. More generally, it is safe to say that most historians tend to neglect social movement concepts, as stated in several of the country reports in this volume. In turn, most social movement scholars focus on more recent phenomena and are oblivious of the rich information provided by historians, for example Edward P. Thompson, Eric J. Hobsbawm, George Rudé, Marcel van der Linden and Jürgen Kocka.

Regrettably, a prominent figure such as Charles Tilly who was aptly bridging the disciplines of history and sociology is missing in Europe. However, in some countries, for example in Germany, such a bridge is in the making. This is indicated by a few conferences bringing together historians and social scientists as well as by the budding collaboration between historians from the Institute on Social Movements in Bochum and a Berlin-based group of social scientists.

Obviously, the reasons for the differential disciplinary embedding of social movements have nothing to do with the nature of the subject. Rather it can be traced back to factors such as path dependency and the contingent role of individual scholars willing to seize opportunities, build networks and set up research groups.[15] Also public interest in social movements, as indicated by journalistic reports, commentaries and parliamentary debates, can be a factor that is conducive to the gradual establishment of social movement studies.

When asked for the number of social scientists doing 'primarily work on social movements/political protest in these times', the surveyed authors' estimates regarding their own country differ widely. Apart from the number of three hundred social scientists given for the United States, the average value for France (with five respondents) was thirty-eight, followed by Italy (five respondents) with twenty-three. At the bottom range the estimates provided for Russia (ten social scientists), Romania (eight), Hungary (five) and Turkey (five).

In sum, the internationalization and, to a lesser extent, the institutionalization of social movement studies in Europe has advanced significantly during the last two decades. However, compared to other fields in the social sciences, for example the study of political parties, electoral behaviour and a number of specific sociologies, institutionalization is still quite limited and, in some European countries, inexistent.

Coming back to the question whether or not social movement studies in Europe, when disaggregated down to the level of individual countries, comprises only exceptional cases, hence exceptions as a rule, the general answer is no. Broadly speaking, one can identify a group of advanced countries with significant similarities in their degree of professionalization, internationalization and, in relative terms, institutionalization of social movements studies. This, however, does not preclude the existence of significant differences in other respects regarding, for example, the major thematic foci (often reflecting the prominence of certain movements) as well as theoretical and methodological preferences in social movement research. In addition, two more groups of countries and probably a few outliers seem to exist. First, countries in Eastern and South-Eastern Europe show similarities that, by and large, stand in stark contrast to the group of the 'advanced' countries. Second, a set of Southern European countries (Greece, Spain and Portugal, but not Italy, which belongs to the advanced group) exhibit a number of similarities and, taken as whole, can be placed in between the aforementioned two quite distinct groups of countries. As outlier cases in the sample represented here I would classify Russia and Turkey where social movement studies are still very marginal and, related to this, seem to be channelled, restricted or even repressed by authoritarian power-holders.

Gaps and Challenges

The preceding sections of this chapter have demonstrated the uneven quantitative expansion and, in terms of quality, professionalization and sophistication of social movement studies in Europe. Generally speaking, but again with some exceptions, European countries that are large and/or tend to have a more international orientation are more advanced than other countries on the continent. This is probably best illustrated by the lag of countries of the former Soviet Union. Also some 'Western' European countries situated on the Southern periphery, for example Greece and Portugal, seem to fit this pattern irrespective of a few outstanding individual scholars who, typically, have spent some time abroad, notably in the United States. At the same time, there may also be contingent factors or probably still unknown structural conditions that account for the relative strengths or weaknesses in social movements studies across European countries. Compare, for example, Switzerland with its well-developed social movement studies to its neighbour Austria (not accidentally absent in the present volume). Relative to Switzerland, Austria is clearly a laggard.

In taking a more general look at social movement studies in Europe, a number of gaps and respective tasks and challenges can be identified:

1. The prevailing trend from macro towards middle-range approaches and theories (and further towards micro-level work) was certainly a fruitful one but, after several decades, has led to some exhaustion and stalemate. While it is true that these approaches are largely tailored to specific aspects of social movements and therefore may complement each other, some of their proponents tend to ignore this complementary function by privileging their own approach as if it was a matter of truth. In order to strengthen their view, they are tempted to provide a simplified if not stereotyped picture of other approaches from which they can easily set themselves apart (for an excessive critique of this habit, see Lofland 1993). On the other hand, there also exists an opposite trend indicated by a laissez-faire or 'let-all-the-flowers-bloom' attitude, thereby ignoring premises of different approaches that may contradict each other. In this regard, a more rigorous explication of someone's own premises and careful look at overlapping or contradicting premises of other approaches would be required. For example, some scholars dodge away

from a clear stance on the crucial question of whether collective action is a mere aggregation of individual actions or whether it represents an emergent phenomenon that cannot be sufficiently deducted from the perspective of individual actors.

A second and related problem is the largely missing effort towards integrating various middle-range approaches into a broader and more encompassing theoretical construction. Admittedly, this is a difficult task. The few scholars trying to tackle it do so on the basis of a clearly pre-selected paradigm (e.g. structural functionalism, exchange theory or rational choice theory) without feeling the need to demonstrate its usefulness in comparison to other paradigms. According to the surveyed authors of this book, they mostly consider structuralist, cultural, constructivist and rational choice theories to be most influential in their respective countries. Rational choice has been named as a first choice for Hungary, Portugal, Spain and Switzerland (but nowhere as a second choice). Marxism as being most influential has been mentioned only for Greece and, as a second choice, for Ireland, Spain, and Turkey.

A third problem is the readiness to adopt and often merely cite seemingly fashionable new concepts without much scrutiny. This could be observed, for example, when framing concepts were imported from the United States to Europe in the 1990s and when the concept of mechanisms promoted by McAdam, Tarrow and Tilly (2001) travelled across the Atlantic. By contrast, these authors' call for a dynamic instead of static analysis of social movements not only neglected that a political process theory has been advocated in the United States since the early 1980s (ironically, last but not least by McAdam 1982) but has also been applied, though in different forms and under different labels, in quite a number of studies in Europe by Della Porta, Giugni, Rucht, and a few others.

2. A further weakness of social movement studies in Europe is the missing theorizing and empirical researching of certain key aspects and substantive subfields. To mention only a few examples: though stated repeatedly in the literature, the factors and processes of demobilization have hardly been studied (see Fillieule 2005; Klandermans 2007, chap. 4). The same can be said for the formation, maintenance and role of collective identity. This concept is often emphasised as a crucial factor but rarely unpacked, specified and empirically studied.

Although there are a number of studies on movement outcomes (Giugni 1998; Kolb), this dimension, after all the *raison d'être* of almost all social movement activity, remains under-researched. This is not by accident. Explaining movement outcomes is probably the greatest challenge in the field. As stated time and again, among the difficulties are the many causal factors that come into play, the problems of measurement, the arbitrary time perspective (short or long), and the sometimes shifting goals during the existence of social movements.

Another research lacuna concerns the neglect of the role of mass media, both traditional and electronic media. The public perception of social movements is largely shaped by mass media. Most of what the population, including the political decision-makers, know about social movements has gone through the filters of selection and description biases. This, for example, leads to an overestimation of both mass protest and violent actions, whereas small and/or unspectacular activities are grossly neglected.

More recently, many observers have emphasised the crucial role of the Internet and social media in fostering the recent mass mobilizations subsumed to labels such as Arabellion, Occupy, and *Indignados*. However, we lack systematic empirical studies comparing the relative weight of traditional and new media as well as different channels of mobilization.

3. An additional shortcoming in studying social movements results from what Abby Peterson (in this volume) has coined 'movement centrism'. It denotes the tendency to isolate the subject from adjacent and/or closely linked phenomena such as political parties, interest groups, trade unions and churches. While, contrary to the position of a few social scientists (e.g. Burstein 1999), the analytical distinction between genuine social movements and interest groups should be maintained, it would impoverish the understanding of empirical movements if their overlaps, alliances and tensions with other forms of collective organizing were disregarded. Just consider hybrid forms such as social movement parties, church groups and unions that may be part of movement networks. Also, movements may gradually become interest groups or political parties and are not easy to classify in such a transition period.

Related to the need of embedding social movement in their wider context of a 'multi-organizational field' (Curtis and Zurcher 1973) and civil society (see Guya Accornero's chapter on Portugal) is the perspective on movements as actors involved in power struggles. Movements challenge, but sometimes also negotiate and cooperate with agents and institutions holding political and/or economic power. If we would look only at organizational structures, processes of resource mobilization and framing, we would miss this strategic and tactical interplay in which, besides allies and opponents, also third parties, and most importantly the general audience, comes into play. Neglecting these elements would be like watching a football match on a manipulated screen that only shows the actions of one team, but leaves invisible and/or inaudible the rest, hence not only the competing team but also the referee and the spectators.

4. The possibilities of various kinds of systematic comparisons should be better exploited (see also Tarrow 1986/1991: 400). Comparison is the key method for becoming aware of both the general traits and the specificities of a subject under study. Only by comparison can we know whether a phenomenon is typical or atypical, whether it results from specific contexts or is rather universal, and whether it is old or new, small or big, rising or declining, etc. Accordingly, it would be instructive to engage more in comparisons across movements, campaigns and single events. Also, it would be worth comparing not only across (Western) countries and cultures but also across major parts of the globe, especially the Global South which, in many ways, is still *terra incognita* for most students of social movements. Also, when looking at Europe more specifically, the lack of research on social movements, past and present, in Eastern and South-Eastern Europe is evident (see Jacobsson and Saxonberg 2013 for Eastern Europe).

Finally, comparison across larger time spans, preferably in cooperation with historians, might exhibit to which extent problems of contemporary social movements, e.g. motivation, justification, organization, strategy and tactics, were also problems of movements of the past. Regrettably, few social scientists focusing on contemporary movements are aware of the work of historians studying past social movements, and vice versa. Many historians, though widely using the term social movements, do not even feel a need to take notice of the theoretical underpinnings of the concept.

5. With regard to more specific methodological tools, many students of social movements remain reluctant to combine what, somewhat misleadingly, is called 'qualitative' and 'quantitative' methods. Promoters of qualitative methods often present quantitative assessments in vague terms (more or less, usual or unusual, etc.) without much effort to need to substantiate their impressions. By the same token, quite a few social movement students claim to apply specific methods, such as participant observation, content analysis, discourse analysis and frame analysis. In fact, however, they are doing little more than being on the spot or reading written material without an attempt towards methodological rigour that, as sophisticated qualitative methods demonstrate, is possible in many instances.

Promoters of quantitative methods, in turn, are sometimes more interested in the availability of any data than validity of the data. This may lead them to equate the strength of social movements with the presence and accessibility of large and formal social movement organizations, to use representative surveys of attitudes ('Would you consider to sign a letter of protest?') as indicators of the volume of collective action, or to use large datasets provided by international organizations while knowing very little about the underlying criteria and potential problems of validity, reliability and representativeness.

The temptation to ignore methodological standards is particularly strong among researchers who are extremely sympathetic or unsympathetic towards their subjects of research. In the first case, they may shy away from speaking out the truth, assuming that this may damage the public image of their 'heroes'. In the second case, the danger is to stay too far away from the movement under study by relying basically on media and intelligence reports, and the actors' propaganda material.

More generally, the caveats, problems and possible ways of combining a political stance with professional—and in certain ways detached—social movement analysis are rarely discussed,[16] although it is clear that quite many students of social movement have a background as sympathisers, if not activists, of social movements. Some of them continue to be 'activist-researchers' without bothering about the implications of such a precarious positioning.

6. Finally, there is a need to better institutionalise the study of social movements. For many, studying social movements is a transitory engagement often related to a step of academic qualification, but with little chances of getting a respective occupation within the academia. And even among those relatively few scholars who managed to stick to the field of social movement studies, some practise it as a business besides their official and, from an external perspective, more appreciated area of expertise.

This call for better institutionalization in terms of courses, textbooks, professorships, research grants and research centres should not be brushed aside as the notorious rhetoric of almost all scholars seeking appraisal, recognition, jobs and money. Rather, social movement scholars can, and actually should, demonstrate that they are analysing phenomena that, for better or worse, involve millions of people across the globe, have made history (Flacks 1988) and potentially will make history in the future.

Dieter Rucht is retired since July 2011. Before, he was co-director of the research group 'Civil Society, Citizenship and Political Mobilization in Europe' at the Social Science Research Center Berlin, and professor of sociology at the Free University of Berlin. His research interests include political participation, social movements, political protest and public discourse. Among his recent books in English are *The World Says No to War: Demonstrations against the War on Iraq* (joint editor, University of Minnesota Press, 2010) and *Meeting Democracy: Power and Deliberation in Global Justice Movements* (joint editor, Cambridge University Press, 2013). Recent publications in German are a handbook on social movements in Germany since 1945 (joint editor, Campus, 2008) and a book on the media strategies and media coverage of the campaign against the G8 meeting in Heiligendamm in 2007 (joint editor, Campus, 2008).

Notes

1. I am grateful to Olivier Fillieule and James Jasper for their comments on an earlier version of this chapter.
2. The final of the 'twenty-two categorical imperatives along the line of the Ten Commandments for those who would study social movements and collective behavior' (Marx and Wood 1975: 415–16).
3. So did I after having spent some time in Touraine's institute in 1984. For my critique on Touraine's theory and method see Rucht (1991b). For example, I am not convinced that every societal stage gives birth only to one 'real' social movement. Nor do I believe in the role of the sociologist in enlightening social actors about the historical meaning of their struggle. With regard to the method of 'sociological intervention', one of the major problems is the lacking consideration of reliability.
4. Early work on new social movements was written by Brand (1982) and Brand, Büsser and Rucht (1983). Brand (1985) also edited a collective volume on social movements in some Western European countries and the United States.
5. Cited according to my personal memory.
6. Klandermans (1986) identified resource mobilization as 'the' American approach and new social movements as 'the' European approach. Though the distinction between old and new movements was widely accepted in most European countries, there are also some European scholars (e.g. Scott 1990) who question this categorization.
7. See Michael DeCesare's recent review by of this and two more books in *Social Movement Studies* 13, no. 4: 519–23.
8. Political opportunities: seventy-five; contentious politics: fifty-three; political process: twenty-nine; resource mobilization: twenty-one.
9. In the country reports of the present volume, in which predominantly younger social movements are represented, the count of references is forty-seven for Kriesi, forty for Touraine and twenty-one for Melucci. Claus Offe (fifteen) and Jürgen Habermas (five) have relatively low scores. The highest scores received Della Porta (eighty-nine), Fillieule (sixty-three), Karl Marx (sixty) and Rucht (fifty-two). Among the US scholars who, of course, have fewer chances in being cited in reports on social movement studies in Europe, among the leading group are Tilly (forty-six), McAdam (twenty-six) and Tarrow (twenty-six).
10. The number of references are: Piven and Cloward seven, Gusfield three, Oberschall two, Smelser two, Wallerstein two, Turner one, Lofland zero, Gary Marx zero, Blumer zero, and Killian zero.
11. In the fifteen country reports, Bourdieu is mentioned fifteen times, while Foucault is completely absent. Touraine, as a genuine movement scholar, is mentioned forty times.
12. Ten years later, Bert Klandermans and Suzanne Staggenborg (2002) edited a more comprehensive and systematic volume on methods to study social movements.
13. James Jasper, the author of the foreword, completed a questionnaire on the United States. This is excluded when the analysis refers to European countries.
14. On the contribution of various disciplines to the study of social movements, see Klandermans and Roggeband 2007.
15. This applies, to mention only two examples, to Maté Szabó from Hungary who has

spent quite some time in Germany and to Nilüfer Göle from Turkey who did her PhD in France.

16. See the recent debate within the journal *Social Movement Studies,* stimulated by the article of Cresswell and Spandler (2012) who, of course, have forerunners from Michael Burawoy back to C. Wright Mills and Antonio Gramsci.

References

Alberoni, F. 1977. *Movimento e istituzione: Teoria generale.* Bologna: il Mulino.

Banks, J. A. 1972. *The Sociology of Social Movements.* London: Macmillan.

Baumgarten, B., and P. Daphi and P. Ullrich, eds. 2014. *Conceptualizing Culture in Social Movement Research.* Basingstoke: Palgrave.

Brand, K. 1982. *Neue soziale Bewegungen: Entstehung, Funktion und Perspektive neuer Protestpotentiale. Eine Zwischenbilanz.* Wiesbaden: Westdeutscher Verlag.

Brand, K., ed. 1985. *Neue soziale Bewegungen in Westeuropa und den USA: Ein internationaler Vergleich.* Frankfurt and New York: Campus.

Brand, K., and D. Büsser and D. Rucht, eds. 1983. *Aufbruch in eine andere Gesellschaft. Neue soziale Bewegungen in der Bundesrepublik.* Frankfurt and New York: Campus.

Burstein, P. 1999. 'Social Movements and Public Policy'. In *How Social Movements Matter,* ed. M. Giugni and D. McAdam, 3–21. Minneapolis: University of Minnesota Press.

Cefaeï, D. 2006. *Pourquoi se mobilise-t-on?* Paris: La Découverte.

Cresswell, M., and H. Spandler. 2012. 'The Engaged Academic: Academic Intellectuals and the Psychiatric Survivor Movement'. *Social Movement Studies* 11, no. 4: 138–54.

Curtis, R. L., and L.A. Zurcher. 1973. 'Stable Resources of Protest Movements: The Multi-Organizational Field'. *Social Forces* 52: 53–61.

Della Porta. D., and M. Diani. 1999. *Social Movements: An Introduction.* Oxford: Blackwell.

Della Porta. D., and S. Tarrow. 1986. 'Unwanted Children: Political Violence and the Cycle of Protest in Italy 1966–1973'. *European Journal of Political Research* 14, nos. 5–6: 607–32.

Diani, M., and R. Eyerman, eds. 1992. *Studying Collective Action.* Beverly Hills etc.: Sage.

Edwards, B., and J. D. McCarthy. 1992. 'Social Movement Schools'. *Sociological Forum* 7, no. 3: 541–50.

Eyerman, R., and A. Jamison. 1991. *Social Movements: A Cognitive Approach.* Cambridge: Polity Press.

Friberg, M. and J. Galtung., eds. 1984. *Rörelsera [Movements].* Stockholm: Akademilitteratur.

Ferree, M. M. 1992. 'The Political Context of Rationality: Rational Choice Theory and Resource Mobilization'. In *Frontiers of Social Movement Theory,* ed. C. Mueller and A. Morris, 29–53. New Haven: Yale University Press.

Fillieule, O., ed. 2005. *Le désengagement militant.* Paris: Belin.

Fillieule, O., L. Mathieu and C. Péchu, eds. 2009. *Dictionnaire des Mouvement Sociaux.* Paris: Presses de Science-Po.

Fillieule, O., E. Agrikoliansky and I. Sommier, eds. 2010. *Penser les mouvements sociaux : Conflits sociaux et contestations dans les sociétés contemporaines.* Paris: La Découverte.

Flacks, R. 1988. *Making History: The American Left and the American Mind.* New York: University of Columbia Press.

Flam, H., and D. King, eds. 2005. *Emotions and Social Movements.* New York: Routledge.

Gamson, W. A. 1983. 'Review of A. Touraine, the Voice and the Eye: An Analysis of Social Movements'. *American Journal of Sociology* 88, no. 4: 812–14.

Goodwin, J. and J. M. Jasper. 1999. 'Caught in a Winding, Snarling Vine: The Structural Bias of Political Process Theory'. *Sociological Forum* 14, no. 1: 27–54.

Giugni, M. G. 1998. 'Was It Worth the Effort? The Outcomes and Consequences of Social Movements'. *Annual Review of Sociology* 98: 371–93.

Gundelach, P. 1980. *Græsrødder er seje! [Grassroots are tough!]* Århus: Politica.

Haug, C., D. Rucht and S. Teune. 2013. 'A Methodology for Studying Democracy and Power in Group Meetings'. In *Meeting Democracy: Power and Deliberation in Global Justice Movements,* ed. D. Della Porta and D. Rucht, 23–46. Cambridge: Cambridge University Press.

Heberle, R. 1967. *Hauptprobleme der Politischen Soziologie.* Stuttgart: Enke.

Heinz, W. K., and P. Schöber, eds. 1973. *Theorien kollektiven Verhaltens: Beiträge zur Analyse sozialer Protestaktionen und Bewegungen.* 2 vols. Darmstadt-Neuwied: Luchterhand.

Hellmann, K. and R. Koopmans, eds. 1998. *Paradigmen der Bewegungsforschung.* Opladen: Westdeutscher Verlag.

Jacobsson, K., and S. Saxonberg. 2013. *Beyond NGO-ization: The Development of Social Movements in Central and Eastern Europe.* Farnham: Ashgate.

Jasper, J. M., and J. W. Duyvendak., eds. 2015. *Players and Arenas: The Interactive Dynamics of Protest.* Amsterdam: Amsterdam University Press.

Klandermans, B. 1986. 'New Social Movements and Resource Mobilization: The European and the American Approach'. *International Journal of Mass Emergencies and Disasters* 4, no. 2: 13–39.

———. 1997. *The Social Psychology of Protest.* Oxford: Blackwell.

Klandermans, B., and C. Jenkins, eds. 1995. *The Politics of Social Protest: Comparative Perspectives on States and Social Movements.* Minneapolis and St. Paul: University of Minnesota Press.

Klandermans, B., H. Kriesi and S. Tarrow, eds. 1988. *From Structure to Action: Comparing Social Movement Research across Cultures.* Greenwich: JAI Press.

Klandermans, B., and C. Roggeband, eds. 2007. *Handbook of Social Movements across Disciplines.* New York: Springer.

Klandermans B., and S. Staggenborg, eds. 2002. *Methods in Social Movement Research.* Minneapolis and London: University of Minnesota Press.

Klandermans, B., and S. Tarrow. 1988. 'Mobilization into Social Movements: Synthesizing European and American Approaches'. In *From Structure to Action: Comparing Social Movement Research Across Cultures,* ed. B. Klandermans, H. Kriesi and S. Tarrow, 1–38. Greenwich: JAI Press.

Kolb, F. 2007. *Protest and Opportunities: The Political Outcomes of Social Movements.* Frankfurt and New York: Campus.

Koopmans, R. 1999. 'Political Claims Analysis: Integration Protest Events and Public Discourse Approaches'. *Mobilization* 4, no. 2: 203–22.

Koopmans R., and P. Statham. 1999. 'Ethnic and Civic Conceptions of Nationhood and the Differential Success of the Extreme Right in Germany and Italy'. In *How Social*

Movements Matter, ed. M. Giugni, D. McAdam and C. Tilly, 225–52. Minneapolis and London: University of Minnesota Press.

Kriesi, H., ed. 1985. *Bewegung in der Schweizer Politik: Fallstudien zu politischen Mobilisierungsprozessen in der Schweiz.* Frankfurt and New York: Campus.

Kriesi, H., et.al, eds. 1995. *New Social Movements in Western Europe: A Comparative Analysis.* Minneapolis: University of Minnesota Press.

Lofland, J. 1993. 'Theory-Bashing and Answer-Improving in the Study of Social Movements'. *American Sociologist* 24: 37–58.

Loo, H. ans van der, E. Snel and B. v. Steenbergen. 1984. *Een wenkend perspektief? Nieuwe sociale bewegingen en culturele veranderingen.* Amersfoort: De Horstink.

Luhmann, N. 1991. *Soziologie des Risikos.* Berlin and New York: de Gruyter.

———. 1996. *Protest: Systemtheorie und soziale Bewegungen,* hrsg. und eingeleitet von Kai-Uwe Hellmann. Frankfurt: Suhrkamp.

Marx, G. T., and J. L. Wood. 1975. 'Strands of Theory and Research in Collective Behavior'. *Annual Review of Sociology* 1: 363–428.

Marsh, A. 1977. *Protest and Political Consciousness.* Beverly Hills and London: Sage.

McAdam, D. 1982. *Political Process and the Development of Black Usurgency, 1930–1970.* Chicago: The University of Chicago Press.

McAdam, D., J. D. McCarthy and M. N. Zald, eds. 1996. *Comparative Perspectives on Social Movements: Political Opportunities, Mobilizing Structures, and Cultural Framing.* Cambridge: Cambridge University Press.

McAdam, D., S. Tarrow and C. Tilly. 2001. *Dynamics of Contention.* Cambridge: Cambridge University Press.

Melucci, A. 1980. 'The New Social Movements: A Theoretical Approach'. *Social Science Information* 19, no. 2: 199–226.

———. 1984b. 'An End to Social Movements? Introductory Paper to the Sessions on "New Movements and Change in Organizational Forms"'. *Social Science Information* 23, no. 4/5: 819–35.

———. 1985. 'The Symbolic Challenge of Contemporary Movements'. *Social Research* 52, no. 4: 789–816.

———. 1989. *Nomads of the Present: Social Movements and Individual Needs in Contemporary Society.* London: Hutchinson Radius.

———. 1995a. 'The New Social Movements Revisited: Reflections on a Sociological Misunderstanding'. In *Social Movements and Social Classes: The Future of Collective Action,* ed. Louis Maheu, 107–19. London: Sage.

———. 1995b. 'The Process of Collective Identity'. In *Social Movements and Culture,* ed. H. Johnston and B. Klandermans, 41–64. Minneapolis: University of Minnesota Press.

———. 1997. *Challenging Codes: Collective Action in the Information Age.* Cambridge: Cambridge University Press.

Melucci, A. et al. 1984. *Altri Codici: Aree Di Movimento Nella Metropoli.* Bologna: il Mulino.

Morris, A. D., and C. M. Mueller, eds. 1992. *Frontiers in Social Movement Theory.* New Haven and London: Yale University Press.

Neidhardt, F., and D. Rucht. 1993. 'Auf dem Weg in die "Bewegungsgesellschaft"? Über die Stabilisierbarkeit sozialer Bewegungen'. *Soziale Welt* 44, no. 3: 305–26. English version by Rucht and Neidhardt. 2002. 'Towards a "Movement Society"? On the Possibilities of Institutionalizing Social Movements'. *Social Movement Studies* 1, no. 1: 7–30.

Opp, K. 2009. *Theories of Political Protest and Social Movements: A Multidisciplinary Introduction, Critique and Synthesis.* London and New York: Routledge.

Park, R. E., and E. W. Burgess. 1921. *Introduction to the Science of Sociology.* Chicago:
University of Chicago Press.

Pettenkofer, A. 2010. *Radikaler Protest: Zur soziologischen Theorie politischer Bewegungen.*
Frankfurt: Campus.

Rammstedt, O. 1978. *Soziale Bewegung.* Frankfurt: Suhrkamp.

Raschke, J. 1985. *Soziale Bewegungen: Ein historisch-systematischer Grundriß.* Frankfurt
and New York: Campus.

Rootes, C., ed. 2003. *Environmental Protest in Western Europe.* New York: Oxford University Press.

Rucht, D. 1991b. 'Sociological Theory as a Theory of Social Movements? A Critique
of Alain Touraine'. In *Research on Social Movements: The State of the Art in Western
Europe and the USA,* ed. D. Rucht, 355–84. Frankfurt and Boulder: Campus and
Westview Press.

———. 2001. 'Zu den Grenzen von Theorien rationaler Wahl—dargestellt am Beispiel
altruistischen Engagements'. In *Gute Gesellschaft? Verhandlungen des 30. Kongresses
der deutschen Gesellschaft für Soziologie in Köln 2000,* ed. Jutta Allmendinger, 962–
83. Teil B. Opladen: Leske and Budrich.

Rucht, D., ed. 1991a. *Research on Social Movements: The State of the Art in Western Europe
and the USA.* Frankfurt and Boulder: Campus and Westview Press.

Scott, A. 1990. *Ideology and the New Social Movements.* London: Unwin Hyman.

Smelser, N. 1972 [1963]. *Theorie des kollektiven Verhaltens.* Köln: Kiepenheuer and Witsch.

Stekelenburg, J. v., C. Roggeband and B. Klandermans, eds. 2013. *The Future of Social
Movement Research: Dynamics, Mechanisms, and Processes.* Minneapolis: University
of Minnesota Press.

Tarrow, S. 1986 [1991]. 'Comparing Social Movement Participation in Western Europe
and the United States: Problems, Uses, and a Proposal for Synthesis'. *International
Journal of Mass Emergencies and Disasters* 4, no. 2: 145–70. Reprinted in D. Rucht,
ed, *Research on Social Movements: The State of the Art in Western Europe and the USA.*
Frankfurt and Boulder: Campus and Westview Press, 392–420.

Touraine, A. 1968. *Le mouvement de Mai ou le communisme utopique.* Paris: Editions du
Seuil.

———. 1969. *La société postindustrielle.* Paris: Denoël.

———. 1978. *La voix et le regard.* Paris: Seuil.

Turner, R. H. 1991. 'The Use and Misuse of Rational Models in Collective Behavior and
Social Psychology'. *Archives Européennes de Sociologie* 32, no. 1: 84–108.

Van Aelst, P., and S. Walgrave. 2001. 'Who Is That (Wo)Man in the Street? From the
Normalisation of Protest to the Normalisation of the Protester'. *European Journal of
Political Research* 39: 461–86.

Wahlström, M., and A. Peterson. 2006. 'Between the State and the Market: Expanding the
Concept of "Political Opportunity Structure"'. *Acta Sociologica* 49, no. 4: 363–77.

Walgrave, S., and C. Wagemann. 2010. 'Appendix A: Methodology of Protest Surveys
in Eight Countries'. In *The World Says No to War: Demonstrations against the War on
Iraq,* ed. S. Walgrave and D. Rucht, 175–284. Minneapolis: University of Minnesota Press.

Index